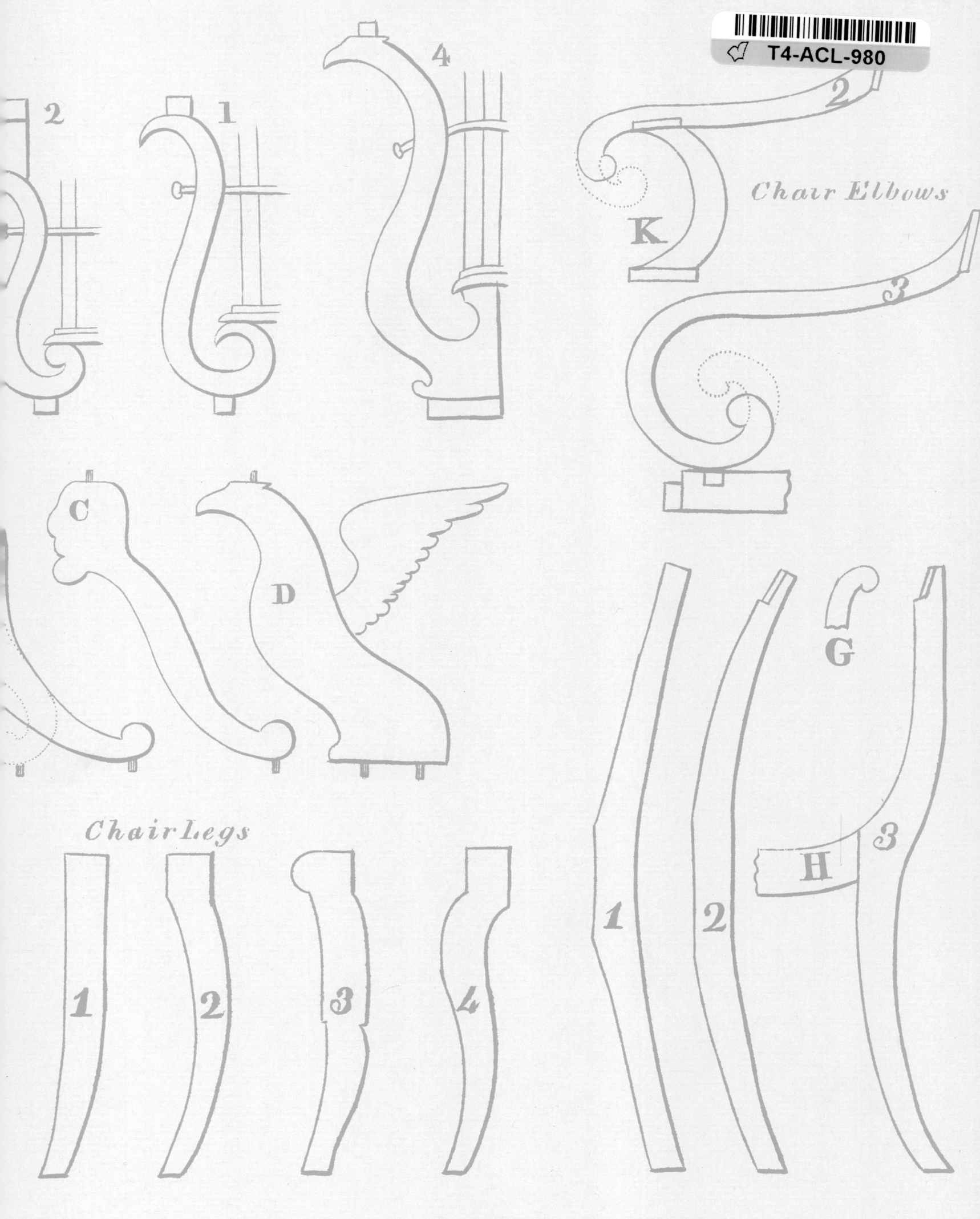

Duncan Phyfe

Duncan Phyfe

Master Cabinetmaker in New York

Peter M. Kenny   Michael K. Brown

Frances F. Bretter and Matthew A. Thurlow

The Metropolitan Museum of Art, New York

Distributed by Yale University Press, New Haven and London

This catalogue is published in conjunction with the exhibition "Duncan Phyfe: Master Cabinetmaker in New York," on view at The Metropolitan Museum of Art, New York, from December 20, 2011, to May 6, 2012, and the Museum of Fine Arts, Houston, from June 20 to September 11, 2012.

The exhibition is made possible by Karen H. Bechtel.

Additional support is provided by The Henry Luce Foundation, Dr. and Mrs. Paul Cushman, the Americana Foundation, Mr. Robert L. Froelich, and Mr. Philip Holzer.

The exhibition was organized by The Metropolitan Museum of Art, New York, and the Museum of Fine Arts, Houston.

The exhibition catalogue is made possible by The William Cullen Bryant Fellows of the American Wing.

Published by The Metropolitan Museum of Art, New York
Mark Polizzotti, Publisher and Editor in Chief
Gwen Roginsky, Associate Publisher and General Manager of Publications
Peter Antony, Chief Production Manager
Michael Sittenfeld, Managing Editor
Robert Weisberg, Assistant Managing Editor

Edited by Emily Radin Walter
Designed by Bruce Campbell
Production by Christopher Zichello, with Bonnie Laessig
Bibliography and notes edited by Jean Wagner

Photography by Bruce Schwarz, The Photograph Studio, The Metropolitan Museum of Art

Typeset in Sabon
Printed on 150 gsm Creator Silk
Separations by Professional Graphics, Inc., Rockford, Illinois
Printed and bound by Graphicom S.r.l., Vicenza, Italy

The following works will be exhibited in New York only: Pls. 6, 9, 12, 13, 14, 16, 21, 22, 23, 25, 26, 27, 29, 30, 31, 36, 37, 38, 39, 42, 45, 46, 47, 50, 51, 56, 66, 67; figs. 18, 115, 161, 164

Frontispiece: Detail of Duncan Phyfe center table, 1825–30 (Pl. 41)

Copyright © 2011 by The Metropolitan Museum of Art, New York
First printing, 2011
All rights reserved. No part of this publication may be reproduced or transmitted in any form or by any means, electronic or mechanical, including photocopying, recording, or any information storage and retrieval system, without permission in writing from the publishers.

The Metropolitan Museum of Art
1000 Fifth Avenue
New York, New York 10028
metmuseum.org

Distributed by
Yale University Press, New Haven and London
yalebooks.com/art
yalebooks.co.uk

Library of Congress Cataloging-in-Publication Data

Kenny, Peter M.
 Duncan Phyfe: Master Cabinetmaker in New York / Peter M. Kenny and Michael K. Brown; with Frances F. Bretter and Matthew A. Thurlow.
   p. cm.
 Published in conjunction with an exhibition held at the Metropolitan Museum of Art, New York, N.Y., Dec. 20, 2011-May 6, 2012 and at the Museum of Fine Arts, Houston, Houston, Tex., June 20- Sept. 11, 2012.
 Includes bibliographical references and index.
 ISBN 978-0-300-15511-2 (hardcover: Yale University Press) -- ISBN 978-1-58839-442-2 (hardcover: Metropolitan Museum of Art) 1. Phyfe, Duncan, 1768-1854--Exhibitions. 2. Furniture--New York (State)--New York--History--19th century--Exhibitions. I. Phyfe, Duncan, 1768-1854. II. Brown, Michael K. (Michael Kevin), 1953- III. Bretter, Frances F. IV. Thurlow, Matthew A. V. Metropolitan Museum of Art (New York, N.Y.) VI. Museum of Fine Arts, Houston. VII. Title. VIII. Title: Master Cabinetmaker in New York.
 NK2439.P5K46 2011
 749.092--dc23

2011036394

Contents

Director's Foreword — vi
Lenders to the Exhibition — vii
Acknowledgments — viii

INTRODUCTION: AMERICAN ICON
Michael K. Brown and Peter M. Kenny — 3

1. LIFE OF A MASTER CABINETMAKER
Michael K. Brown and Matthew A. Thurlow — 23

2. FURNITURE FROM THE WORKSHOP OF DUNCAN PHYFE
Peter M. Kenny and Michael K. Brown — 65

3. PATRONS OF THE CABINET WAREHOUSE
Frances F. Bretter — 115

PLATES — 158

APPENDIX 1: Invoices and Accounts from Duncan Phyfe Relating to Furniture in This Volume — 273

APPENDIX 2: Additional Documented Furniture — 280

Bibliography — 288
Index — 296
Photograph Credits — 302

Director's Foreword

Long renowned for his consistent adherence to the classical design principles of structural coherence, symmetry, and proportion, Duncan Phyfe remains to this day America's most famous cabinetmaker. This enduring fame is owed not only to the exquisite furniture made in his shop but also to the Metropolitan Museum's recognition of Phyfe's achievements as a designer and craftsman at a very early date. In 1909, as part of the landmark Hudson-Fulton Celebration exhibition, an entire section was devoted to his work. The first acquisitions of Phyfe furniture were made just two years later, in 1911, and in 1922 the Museum purchased the iconic watercolor drawing of the cabinetmaker's workshop and warehouse at 68-72 Fulton Street illustrated in this volume. That same year, the first monographic exhibition on the work of an American cabinetmaker, "Furniture from the Workshop of Duncan Phyfe," was mounted in the galleries. Today, ninety years later, and in partnership with the Museum of Fine Arts, Houston, the Museum is proud to present "Duncan Phyfe: Master Cabinetmaker in New York."

The exhibition and accompanying publication cover the full chronological sweep of Phyfe's distinguished career, from his earliest Grecian style furniture, which bears the influence of his British contemporaries Thomas Sheraton and Thomas Hope, to his late simplified designs in the Grecian Plain style. The catalogue is the first major study since Nancy McClelland's *Duncan Phyfe and the English Regency*, published in 1939, and offers a broad reassessment of the craftsman and his world.

Duncan Phyfe's life is the quintessential American success story. Born in 1770 in the Scottish Highlands, Phyfe traveled by ship to the United States, arriving in the mid-1780s. Apprenticed to the cabinetmaking trade probably in New York City, by the early 1790s he was established as an independent cabinetmaker. Fifteen years later, a paragon of style and master cabinetmaker with a brilliant business plan, he had an enviable clientele that included some of the city's wealthiest citizens. And by 1840, his establishment was the largest and most fashionable in the country.

"Duncan Phyfe: Master Cabinetmaker in New York" is the third in a series of monographic exhibitions held in the American Wing that have focused on some of America's preeminent early cabinetmakers. In 1998, "Honoré Lannuier: Parisian Cabinetmaker in Federal New York" explored the sophisticated French-inspired work of one of Phyfe's most able competitors, and in 2005, "John Townsend: Newport Cabinetmaker" centered on one of colonial Newport's finest artisans, whose furniture exemplifies the very best of American design and craft.

We are grateful to Peter M. Kenny and Michael K. Brown, co-curators of the exhibition, as well as to their talented research associates and co-authors, Frances F. Bretter and Matthew A. Thurlow, whose enthusiasm, dedication, and scholarship inform both the exhibition and this publication. The American Wing is fortunate to have a devoted following of enthusiasts and supporters. For this exhibition, we are especially grateful to Karen H. Bechtel for her commitment. We also thank The Henry Luce Foundation, Dr. and Mrs. Paul Cushman, the Americana Foundation, Mr. Robert L. Froelich, and the late Mr. Philip Holzer for their broad support of the department and of this show. The book has been made possible by The William Cullen Bryant Fellows, who remain a critical source of support in bringing a range of Metropolitan Museum publications on American art to the public.

Thomas P. Campbell
Director
The Metropolitan Museum of Art

Lenders to the Exhibition

References are to Plates unless otherwise noted.

Mr. and Mrs. Joseph Allen 31

Carswell Rush Berlin 39

Carswell Rush Berlin, Inc., and Hirschl & Adler Galleries, New York 51

The Brant Foundation, Inc., Greenwich, Connecticut 30

Brooklyn Museum 20, 34, 35; fig. 163

Classical American Homes Preservation Trust figs. 187, 188

Columbia Museum of Art, Columbia, South Carolina 63

Fenimore Art Museum, Cooperstown, New York fig. 47

Susan Paul Firestone 27

James and Laura Freeman 29

Robert L. Froelich 22, 38

Glorianna H. Gibbon 24, 41, 49, 52; figs. 21, 27, 35

Mr. and Mrs. Roland W. Glidden 2

Virginia A. Gould 48

Hagley Museum and Library, Wilmington, Delaware 8

Mr. and Mrs. Robert L. Hammett 44

The Henry Ford, Dearborn, Michigan fig. 75

Elizabeth Feld Herzberg 25

Hirschl & Adler Galleries, New York 33

Richard Hampton Jenrette 36, 58, 60, 62; figs. 161, 164

George M. and Linda H. Kaufman 21, 23

Mr. and Mrs. Richard Kelly 56

Leigh Keno 28

Prof. Maan Z. Madina and Dr. Marilyn Jenkins-Madina 66

The Metropolitan Museum of Art, New York 6, 9, 13, 14, 15, 29, 45, 46, 47, 50, 55, 57, 61; figs. 39, 105, 108, 109, 146

Mulberry Plantation, Camden, South Carolina 64

Museum of Fine Arts, Boston 11

Museum of the City of New York 3, 4, 24, 40

The New-York Historical Society, on loan from the families of Henry Pinkney Phyfe and Churchill B. Phyfe page 22

The Rick Patrick Trust 53, 59

Mrs. H. Pinckney Phyfe and Mr. and Mrs. Henry P. Phyfe Jr. 54

Princeton University Art Museum, Princeton, New Jersey fig. 141

Kelly and Randy Schrimsher 26

Martha Ann Sitterding and Thomas F. Stansfield 43

Thomas Gordon Smith and Marika Wilson Smith 67

The Terian Collection of American Art 12, 42, 65

Billy and Sharon Thompson 7

Mrs. Howard Townsend 5

Descendents of John Wells 16

Winterthur Library, Winterthur, Delaware figs. 44, 149

Winterthur Museum, Winterthur, Delaware 1, 10, 32; 38, fig. 1; fig. 150

Private collections 17, 18, 19, 37; figs. 18, 115

Acknowledgments

Duncan Phyfe: Master Cabinetmaker in New York and the exhibition it accompanies are the result of the combined efforts and distinct talents of many individuals and the generosity of numerous public and private lenders. Our first debt is to the current and former directors of The Metropolitan Museum of Art, Thomas P. Campbell and Philippe de Montebello; the chairman of the American Wing, Morrison H. Heckscher; the interim director at the Museum of Fine Arts, Houston, Gwendolyn H. Goffe, and her predecessor, the late Peter C. Marzio; and the director of Bayou Bend Collection and Gardens, Bonnie Campbell. From the outset of this project and through uncertain economic times their steadfast support has encouraged us and ensured that the story of this important American craftsman and his work would be told.

At the Metropolitan Museum, many individuals helped to make the idea of this book and exhibition a reality. In the Office of the Director, we are indebted to Jennifer Russell and Martha Deese; in the Office of the Vice President for Development and Membership: Nina McN. Diefenbach and Christine S. Begley; in the Office of the Senior Vice President, Secretary, and General Counsel: Sharon H. Cott, Kirstie Howard, and Rebecca L. Murray; in the Office of the Senior Vice President for External Affairs: Harold Holzer and Egle Žygas; in the Office of the Registrar: Aileen Chuk, Nina J. Maruca, Allison Bosch, Willa Cox, Robert Kuszek, and Gerald Lunney; in the Department of Objects Conservation: Linda Borsch, Nancy C. Britton, Helen Esberg, Marijn Manuels, and Pascale Patris; in the Department of Scientific Research: Nobuko Shibayama; in the Department of Paper Conservation: Marjorie Shelley; in the Design Department: for exhibition design, Michael Langley, and for graphic design, Sue Koch; in Buildings: Taylor Miller; in The Photograph Studio: Barbara Bridgers, Joseph Coscia Jr., Einar Brendalen, Thomas Ling, Wilson Santiago, and Karin L. Willis; in Education: Joseph Loh and Alice Schwarz; in Film and Video: Christopher A. Noey; assistance was also graciously provided by Joyce Fung, Chris Paulocik, and Kristen Stewart in The Costume Institute; and by Constance McPhee and Elizabeth Zanis in the Department of Drawings and Prints.

We are particularly grateful to the staff of The American Wing: curators Alice Cooney Frelinghuysen, Elizabeth Kornhauser, Amelia Peck, Thayer Tolles, Beth Wees, and Barbara Weinberg; research associates Medill H. Harvey and Nicholas Vincent; administrative assistants Sally King, Alexandra Klestadt, and Catherine Scandalis; collections manager Leela Outcalt; departmental technicians Sean Farrell, Dennis Kaiser, Nikolai Jacobs, and Chad Lemke; and interns and volunteers Ruthie Dibble, Patti Edmondson, Hannah Freece, Sophia Lufkin, Cynthia Schaffner, and Lori Zabar. In particular, we wish to acknowledge Elaine Bradson and Catherine Mackay, whose enthusiasm and expert assistance on so many aspects of this book and exhibition are deeply appreciated. Special thanks are also owed to Barbara Glauber for her expert research assistance and to Leslie Symington, genealogical researcher extraordinaire, for her indefatigable research into the Phyfe family.

In Houston, we appreciate the forbearance and support of so many at the Museum of Fine Arts and Bayou Bend Collection and Gardens, including: J. Willard Holmes and Marcel J. Fingers, Administration; Caryn Fulda, Jennifer Hammond, Brinn Moore, and Daphne Rozen, Bayou Bend Collection and Gardens; Trevor Boyd, Wynne H. Phelan, and Steven L. Pine, Conservation; Christine Gervais, Emily Ballew Neff, Robin R. Thompson, and Karen Bremer Vetter, Curatorial; Katherine Bate, Amy Purvis, and Dorie Shellenbergar, Development; Margaret A. Mims, George A. Ramirez Jr., and Victoria Ramirez, Education; Jack Eby, Exhibtion Design; Chick L. Bianchi and Phenon G. Finley-Smiley, Graphics; Jon Evans, Beverly Kopp, Sarah Long, and Lynn Wexler, Hirsch Library; Mary E. Haus, Marketing and Communications; Veronica Keyes, Matthew Lawson, and Marcia K. Stein, Photographic and Imaging Services; Margaret Culbertson, Kitty King, Helen Lueders, and Serena Newmark, Powell Library and Study Center; James D. Benson, Preparations; Diane P. Lovejoy, Publications; Julie Bakke, Kathleen B. Crain, and John M. Obsta, Registration.

At Bayou Bend Collection and Gardens, we would like to extend a special thanks to Bayou Bend docents Martha Erwin and especially Carol Jean Moehlman for her enthusiasm and exhaustive research in New York newspapers; curatorial and programs liaison Remi Spriggs Dyll for her skill and for her devotion to so many aspects of this project; and the underwriters of the exhibition at the Museum of Fine Arts, Houston: The Henry Luce Foundation, Mr. and Mrs. John L. Nau III, and Mr. and Mrs. T. R. Reckling III.

We are indebted to our colleagues at numerous museums, libraries, historical societies, and universities for making their collections accessible, assisting with research, providing illustrations, and facilitating loans. Matthew Jarron and the Scottish Society for Art History made a generous grant to further our research and expand our circle of colleagues and contacts in Phyfe's native land. In particular, we offer our thanks to the following institutions and individuals in Scotland: Abernethy Parish Church: the Reverend James A. I. MacEwan and photographer Sandy McCook; Boat of Garten, Kincardine and Duthil Parish: the Reverend David W. Whyte; Grantown Museum: George Dixon; Grantown Society: Molly Duckett; National Library of Scotland, Edinburgh: Brian Hillyard; National Museums of Scotland, Edinburgh: David Forsyth, Stephen Jackson, and Carole Wilson; Scottish National Portrait Gallery, Edinburgh: Sarah Jeffcott; Seafield Estate: Sandy Lewis. Also in the United Kingdom, we thank Dr. Harold Mytum of the University of Liverpool and Frances Collard at the Victoria and Albert Museum, London. We also wish to thank the following individuals and institutions in the United States: Albany Institute of History & Art: Tammis K. Groft, W. Douglas McCombs, and Norman K. Rice; American Jewish Historical Society: former director of library and archives Lyn Slome; The Art Institute of Chicago: Judith A. Barter; Brooklyn Museum: Barry Harwood, Rima Ibrahim, Kenneth Moser, and Kevin J. Stayton; Chipstone Foundation, Fox Point, Wis.: Ethan W. Lasser and Jonathan Prown; Columbia County Historical Society, Kinderhook, N.Y.: Diane Shewchuck; Connecticut Historical Society, Hartford, Conn.: Cynthia Harbeson; Columbia Museum of Art, Columbia, S.C.: Karen Brosius and Brian J. Lang; Classical American Homes Preservation Trust, New York: Louis Hall, Margize Howell, Jeremy Johnson, Bill Thompson, and Jack Smith; The Colonial Williamsburg Foundation: Jay Gaynor; Cooper-Hewitt, National Design Museum, New York: Elizabeth Broman, Sarah D. Coffin, Gregory Herringshaw, and Stephen H. Van Dyk; First Presbyterian Church, Fayetteville, N.C.: Mary Hayslip; Green-Wood Cemetery, Brooklyn, N.Y.: Jeff Richman; Hagley Museum and Library, Wilmington, Del.: Debra Hughes; Hampton-Preston Mansion & Gardens, Columbia, S.C.: John M. Sherrer III; Historic Charleston Foundation: Brandy S. Culp; Historic Huguenot Street, New Paltz, N.Y.: Lelsie Lefevre-Stratton; Louisiana State University Libraries, Baton Rouge: Elaine Smyth; Mount Vernon Estate and Gardens: Mary V. Thompson; Mulberry Plantation, Camden, S.C.: Marty Daniels; Museum of Early Southern Decorative Arts, Winston-Salem, N.C.: Daniel Ackermann and Robert Leath; Museum of Fine Arts, Boston: Elliot Bostwick Davis, Nonie Gadsden, and Gerald W. Ward; Museum of the City of New York: Susan Henshaw Jones, Giacomo Mirabella, James Totis, and former curator Deborah Dependahl Waters; The Girl Scout National Historic Preservation Center, New York: Pamela Cruz and Yevgeniya Gribov; New England Historic Genealogical Society, Boston: Henry B. Hoff; The New York Genealogical and Biographical Society: Catherine M. Ellard; The New York Society Library: Laura O'Keefe; South Plainfield Library, N.J.: Sunnie Randolph; The New-York Historical Society Museum and Library: Margaret K. Hofer, Roberta Olson, and Kimberly Orcutt; Olana State Historic Site, Hudson, N.Y.: Valerie Balint, Linda E. McLean, and Evelyn Trebilcock; Philadelphia Museum of Art: David L. Barquist and Alexandra A. Kirtley; The Rockefeller Archive Center, Sleepy Hollow, N.Y.: Michele Hiltzik; U.S. Department of State Diplomatic Reception Room: former director Gail F. Serfaty; The White House, Washington, D.C.: Wiliam G. Allman, John Courtney, and Hillary Crehan; Winterthur Museum, Garden and Library: Mark Anderson, Stephanie Auffret, Laszlo Bodo, Wendy A. Cooper, Jeff Groff, Emily Guthrie, Charles Hummel, Maggie Lidz, Joyce Longworth, E. Richard McKinstry, Lisa Minardi, Thomas Savage, Jim Schneck, and Jeanne Solensky; Wyck Historic House and Gardens, Philadelphia: Laura C. Keim; University of Notre Dame, Ind.: Deborah M. Webb; Valentine Richmond History Center, Va.: Suzanne Savery; Yale University, New Haven, Conn.: Edward S. Cooke Jr. and Sandra Markham; York County Heritage Trust, York, Pa.: Josh Stahlman. We would also like to acknowledge the following institutions for their support and assistance: William R. Perkins Library, Duke University, Durham, N.C.; Georgia Historical Society, Savannah; Georgia State Archives, Morrow; New York City Department of Records, Municipal Archive; New York Public Library; New York State Historical Association, Cooperstown; New York State Library, Albany; Benjamin S. Rosenthal Library at Queens College, New York; Louis Round Wilson Library at the University of North Carolina, Chapel Hill; South Caroliniana Library at the University of South Carolina, Columbia.

Many other individuals are worthy of mention and deserving of our thanks. In particular, we would like to acknowledge the generosity of Carswell Rush Berlin, Stuart P. Feld, Richard Kelly, Dean and Frank Levy, and Thomas Gordon Smith for sharing with us their extensive knowledge on Phyfe furniture; Gilbert T.

Vincent for his extensive research on the Phyfes in Albany; Richard Hampton Jenrette and Bill Thompson for generously sharing their knowledge on Phyfe's important patrons Robert Donaldson and John L. Manning, for providing us unparalleled access to the documented Phyfe furniture at Millford and Edgewater, and for their tireless support of this project from its inception; Glorianna Gibbon for her extraordinary patience and generosity; and to the other surviving descendants of Duncan Phyfe, especially Ellis Phyfe. Additionally, we owe a debt of gratitude to: Peggy Anderson, Malcolm Archer-Shee, Nina Barker, Susan and William Barker, Gene and Jolie Berry, Mrs. Jerome Blum, Alan Breed, Derin Brey, Andrew Brunk, Douglas Bucher, John Burkhalter, Dick Button, Earl Butts, Meg Caldwell, Donna Cartelli, Brian Crossley, Clarissa deMuzio, Don Didier, Paula Dietz, John Driggers, Eliza Eubank and her late mother Alexandra McPherson Eubank, Nancy Goyne Evans, Dean Failey, Peter A. Feld, Sue Feld, Susan Firestone, John Gibson, Roland and Donna Glidden, Cybele Gontar, Ginger Gould, Erik Gronning, Eleanor Gustafson, Jonathan Hallam, Hilary and Bob Hammett, Ike Hay, Donald Hayes, Sandy and Paul Haygood, John Hays, Judith Hernstadt, Elizabeth Feld Herzberg, Coy Hill, Kathy Hill, Andrew Holter, Melanie and Marshall Hunt, Tony Inson, Thomas Jayne, Manita Johnson, the late Ronald Kane, Linda Kaufman, Leigh Keno, Leslie Keno, Barbara Laux, George Ledes and family, Deanne Levison, Martin Levy, Kathleen Luhrs, Duncan MacPherson, Glenn Marshall, Stewart S. Maxwell, Robert Mussey, Marden Nichols, John Nye, Rick Patrick, Clark Pearce, Harriet and Jim Pratt, Sumpter Priddy III, Pat and Bob Prioleau, John Reinhardt, William Rutledge, the late Albert Sack, Pat Sax, Kelly and Randy Schrimsher, Daniel M. Semel, Egan Seward, Christopher Shelton, Martha Ann Sittending and Thomas F. Stansfield, Bill Stahl, Elizabeth Stillinger, Zane Studenroth, Anthony A. P. Stuempfig, George Subkoff, Gregory Sullivan, Juliana Terian, Sharon and Billy Thompson, Katya Tilton, Zoe H. Tom, Catherine Townsend and her late husband Howard Townsend, Robert Trent, Robert Trump, Tony Walsh, Jack Warner, David B. Warren, Terry Wendell, W. Richard Wheeler, J. Nicholas Wilson, and Philip Zimmerman.

For this handsome volume, we are indebted to Mark Polizzotti and all the members of the superb editorial team responsible for its realization. In particular, we would like to thank Bruce Campbell for his elegant design and for his unabashed passion for great craftsmanship; Peter Antony, Christopher Zichello, Bonnie Laessig, and Robert Weisberg for their dedication to the highest quality production; Jean Wagner for her careful work on the notes and bibliography; and Michael Sittenfeld for his patience and support. Additionally, we offer our thanks to Marcie Muscat, Elizabeth Zechella, and Jane Tai.

Our greatest personal thanks, however, go to two people who have enriched this volume in ways mere curators and historians never could: Bruce Schwarz, Museum photographer, for his energy, good humor, and consummate skill in making Duncan Phyfe's furniture look better than the master cabinetmaker himself could ever have imagined; and Emily Radin Walter, our editor and guide, whose personal grace and editorial genius have endowed this volume with whatever elegance and style it possesses. Lastly, we would like to express our love and gratitude to our families for their encouragement and enduring support.

Peter M. Kenny
Michael K. Brown
Frances F. Bretter
Matthew A. Thurlow

Duncan Phyfe

Cane bottoms —————————— $ 22 —
Cushions ——————————————— 3 —
Stuffed ———————————————— 23 —

Introduction: American Icon

To those with even a passing knowledge of furniture history or American antiques, the name Duncan Phyfe is instantly recognizable. The fires of Phyfe's fame were briefly extinguished after his passing, but rekindled, as if by poetic justice, thirty years later by another cabinetmaker, Ernest F. Hagen, who was apprenticed by his father to the furniture trade in the 1840s but turned to repairing and reproducing antiques for some of New York's prominent old families with the decline of business after the Civil War. As a craftsman, Hagen could not help but be impressed by the quality of some of this old furniture, which on one occasion in the early 1880s was revealed to him by its then owner as the work of Duncan Phyfe (1770–1854). Upon this discovery, Hagen began a lifelong avocation studying Phyfe and his fellow early New York cabinetmakers, whom he romantically linked to a bygone era of craftsmanship and the great eighteenth-century design traditions of George Hepplewhite and Thomas Sheraton. The apotheosis of Duncan Phyfe, described in his own lifetime as the "United States Rage," from a successful furniture maker to an American icon through the early efforts of Hagen and a coterie of influential early twentieth-century scholars, collectors, and connoisseurs provides an essential context and a logical starting point for this reconsideration of the renowned master cabinetmaker and his work.

Discovery and Early Scholarship

By 1815, within the span of a single generation, Duncan Phyfe had achieved a remarkable transformation, from a young immigrant joiner-cabinetmaker to an accomplished master cabinetmaker and businessman, recognized nationally for his superbly designed and crafted furniture in the classical, or Grecian, style. His celebrity seems to have lasted for the equivalent of a second generation, until 1840, when a southern politician and planter, James Henry Hammond, shopping for furniture in New York, leveled this stinging critique in a letter to his wife in Columbia, South Carolina: "[Phyfe] thinks it is still 1836, he is overpriced and out-of-date."[1] Was this the isolated criticism of a single penurious shopper seeking to dissuade his wife from a name-brand purchase? Or had Phyfe grown aloof from the changed economic circumstances following the financial collapse of 1837 and the tastes of customers intrigued by emerging historical revival styles? Perhaps the latter, for by 1844 he publicly advertised the closing of his business and the sale of his remaining stock at auction. Phyfe apparently relented that year, but in 1847 he went through with the sale and shuttered his venerable Fulton Street cabinet warehouse for good.

While purely coincidental, as Duncan Phyfe first contemplated retirement, a few blocks away a fifteen-year-old immigrant destined to become Phyfe's first biographer and to help raise his name to legendary status began his apprenticeship in the field. Ernest Ferdinand Hagen (1830–1913), in many respects like Phyfe himself toward the end of his career, witnessed the transformation of the New York cabinetmaking trade from relatively modest concerns that produced bespoke furniture and ready-made pieces for sale either in their own cabinet warehouses or at others' furniture stores to large-scale manufactories where hundreds of cabinetmakers and other specialists were employed making prodigious quantities of furniture for sale, at the high end in elaborate, well-stocked emporiums along Broadway or for export to the American South and the emerging cities of the Midwest, the Caribbean, and South America. In his later years Hagen, then in the guise of an amateur historian, looked back on the cabinetmaking trade, recognizing the changes that had occurred during the nineteenth century, and drafted a perceptive essay on the period, its personalities, and production: "Personal Experiences of an Old New York Cabinet Maker" (1908). The immense importance of this manuscript has long been recognized by scholars as the only firsthand account to describe the dynamics of the furniture trade in New York City during the second half of the nineteenth century.

Hagen's recollections begin: "Being born in the City of Hamburg in Germany on September 8, 1830, we came to New York June 22, 1844, after a passage of 47 days in a small German sailing vessel."[2] The Hagens were just one family in a mass migration of more than six hundred thousand Germans who ventured to the United States between the 1830s and 1850, drawn by the opportunity to acquire land as well as to escape

Opposite: Detail of a drawing of two chairs attributed to Duncan Phyfe, ca. 1815 (fig. 149)

Figure 1. Ernest F. Hagen (front row center) and other workmen. Undated photograph. Courtesy of Elizabeth Stillinger

religious and political oppression in their homeland. Thousands of these immigrants chose to settle in New York City, and in time many would come to participate in the cabinetmaking trade in workshops on the Lower East Side—an area that became known as Kleindeutschland, or Little Germany—making furniture for the low-end furniture stores along the Bowery and in Chatham Square. Within a year of his arrival, Hagen was indentured by his father as an apprentice to the German immigrant cabinetmakers Ernest Krieg and Augustus L. Dohrmann at 106 Norfolk Street (fig. 1).[3] There, following the completion of his apprenticeship, he stayed on until 1853, when he departed to ply his trade along Broadway, where the city's most extensive and fashionable furniture manufactories and stores were then located. Eventually Hagen went to work at 335 Broadway for Charles A. Baudouine (1808–1895), whom he deemed "the leading cabinetmaker of New York."[4] His tenure, however, would be brief, as a result of Baudouine's decision, in May 1854, to terminate his business in order to oversee his real estate investments.

With the demise of Baudouine's business, Hagen left to explore opportunities in Milwaukee, St. Louis, and New Orleans. He eventually returned to New York, in 1858, and together with his "old friend and shop mate" J. Matthew Meier (1822–1889), a fellow German immigrant, established a partnership at 106 Norfolk Street. In Hagen's words, he and Meier at first "worked mostly for the trade supplying the furniture stores, who paid very poorly; and we had to wait a long time to get it and also lost some pretty large bills altogether by failures."[5] Business continued to deteriorate after the Civil War, with the New York furniture stores retailing the cheaper products of the new furniture factories of the Midwest instead of the smaller New York establishments such as Hagen & Meier. In spite of these setbacks, however, the two partners were able to develop a private trade among some of the old established families of New York, repairing, refinishing, and reproducing antique furniture. Eventually, in response to the Victorian vogue for integrating antiques into the domestic interior and the ever-increasing fascination with the nation's historical past, they expanded their repertoire to include the sale of old furniture and ceramics. And over time they attracted an illustrious clientele that included members of the Roosevelt and Havemeyer families, Louis Comfort Tiffany, and leading furniture and decorating establishments such as Herter Brothers, Leon Marcotte & Company, and Sypher & Company.[6] The partnership of Hagen and Meier persisted for three decades until June 30, 1888, when it was dissolved "by mutual consent."

Hagen continued on his own for another seventeen years, until he turned the business over to his sons Frederick E. (1868–1948) and Henry A. (1877–1927) Hagen in 1905. Hagen's retirement may have allowed him the time to concentrate on the research he had been compiling since the 1880s. In 1907, one year before he recorded his "Personal Experiences," Hagen wrote his famous "Duncan Phyfe Memorandum," which has served as a basis for every Phyfe study since.[7] Here Hagen related that it was not until the early 1880s, when Hagen & Meier was beginning to become known as a source for antiques, that his interest in the master cabinetmaker's furniture was piqued:

> [Miss Louisa Troup] had a lot of Phyfe's furniture presented to her by her father, the Colonel, when she was 18 years old, some of which we reproduced for Mrs. Frederick Bronson, her grandniece, in 1882 [see fig. 7]. This is the first I ever heard of Duncan Phyfe, when Mrs. Bronson sent me to [Miss Troup] to get her consent to copy their dining room chairs. When I came there, I was received very kindly by Miss Troup, who told me all about Phyfe and his work.[8]

Duncan Phyfe

This interest in turn prompted Hagen's study of his renowned predecessor and the reproduction of Phyfe's designs by Hagen & Meier. Eventually, Hagen and his son gained a reputation as the most authoritative experts on the master cabinetmaker and his work.

While Hagen may have lacked professional training as a researcher, he nevertheless did an admirable job investigating Phyfe. He surveyed the price books and directories, located Duncan Phyfe's will, and, perhaps most important, interviewed family members, thus adding a measure of authority to his claims.[9] The research he amassed was published in newspaper and magazine articles as early as 1894, when "Old New York Furniture: Early Cabinetmakers Whose Work Is Prized Highly" appeared in an August edition of *The New York Sun*: "There dwells some blocks northwest of the German quarter a German cabinetmaker who is in love not only with his trade, but also with its traditions."

Unquestionably reporting Hagen's own words, the writer continues: "There never was better furniture made than the best of our day . . . but a few of the early cabinetmakers were wonderfully skillful. Duncan Phyfe was the greatest of them all. . . . He came to New York from Scotland at the age of 13, and probably learned his trade in this city."

The article also makes the claim that at its height the Phyfe shop would "employ fully one hundred of the most skillful journeyman cabinetmakers in New York." And it introduces some of Phyfe's contemporaries, including Michael Allison and the Meeks family of cabinetmakers, whose furniture he describes as "ugly, but durable."[10] Punctuating the text is a series of woodcut illustrations of furniture—all of it "identified" as by Phyfe.

Hagen's "Duncan Phyfe Memorandum" may well have been written in response to the planning then under way at The Metropolitan Museum of Art for an exhibition of early American painting and decorative arts. The show was one of the series of events that made up the Hudson-Fulton Celebration of 1909, a statewide commemoration of the three-hundredth anniversary of Henry Hudson's discovery of the great waterway that came to bear his name and the centennial of Robert Fulton's invention of the steamboat. Spanning seventeen days, the festivities abounded with replicas of Hudson's ship, the *Halve Maen* (*Half Moon*), and Fulton's steamboat, the *Clermont*, navigating upriver to Albany. In New York City the celebratory events included a procession along Broadway and a nine-day regatta, and Wilbur Wright and Glenn Hammond Curtiss piloted the first flights over Manhattan Island. The best-known cabinetmaker of Fulton's day, Duncan Phyfe, would also assume a prominent role.

The Metropolitan Museum observed the occasion by organizing not one but two major exhibitions.[11] In homage to Hudson, it brought together what was then deemed the greatest assemblage of Dutch painting the country had ever witnessed, and Fulton was honored by an installation of early American painting and, for the first time in an American art museum, decorative arts. The reviewer for *The New York Times* heralded the dual exhibitions, commenting on the American paintings that "although they include admirable examples [they] are naturally somewhat eclipsed by the brilliant assembly of Dutch paintings of the first order in the adjoining rooms." As for the industrial arts, however, he described the American section as

> of extraordinary interest and value, including examples of furniture, silverware, and pottery, fine in quality and so discreetly chosen as to illustrate the various developments in forms and styles that took place from the earliest Colonial times to the period of Fulton's death. . . . The value of the present exhibition lies chiefly in the fact that the historical interest has not been allowed to overbalance the aesthetic interest, and the choice of pieces has been made with strict attention to their artistic merit as well as to their representative value.[12]

In his preface to the Hudson-Fulton catalogue, Robert W. de Forest, Metropolitan Museum trustee and chair of the Committee on Art Exhibitions for the Hudson-Fulton Celebration Commission, acknowledged Hagen for contributing his pioneering research "on our earliest New York cabinetmaker, Duncan Phyfe," together with the collector Richard Townes Haines Halsey "for the complete showing of furniture by Duncan Phyfe."[13] In the *Architectural Record*, the third and final gallery was heralded as "the place of honor, the platform at the end of the series of rooms, [which] was reserved for the work of Duncan Phyfe, New York's famous cabinetmaker of the first quarter of the nineteenth century" (fig. 2).[14]

At the time of the exhibition, Halsey owned the most comprehensive collection of Duncan Phyfe furniture in America, which he almost certainly built with the aid of Ernest Hagen. In 1915 it was described by furniture historian Walter A. Dyer in *House Beautiful* as "the largest, and in every way the finest, collection I have seen."[15] Halsey began collecting decorative arts as early as the 1890s, specializing in early American-themed English ceramics, miniatures and engravings by colonial artists, and American Neoclassical furniture, notably the work of Duncan Phyfe—an avocation that over time would come to eclipse his professional interests on Wall Street as a member of the New York Stock Exchange. In 1914, Halsey was elected to the board of trustees of the Metropolitan Museum, where he would later chair the Committee on the American Wing, functioning in essence as the Museum's first curator of American decorative arts.

Halsey's dedication to collecting and studying the furniture of Duncan Phyfe was clearly the driving force behind the

Figure 2. Installation of Duncan Phyfe furniture in the Hudson-Fulton exhibition at The Metropolitan Museum of Art. Photograph, 1909

Museum's serious commitment to acquiring and displaying the work of the master cabinetmaker in the early decades of the twentieth century. And while Halsey's furniture never became part of the Museum's collection—most of it is now in the Mabel Brady Garvan Collection of the Yale University Art Gallery—his keen eye led to the purchase of a number of superb pieces from the collector Louis Guerineau Myers, as well as to the important acquisition of the watercolor of Phyfe's shop and warehouse (see fig. 39), purchased on the eve of the Museum's groundbreaking 1922 exhibition "Furniture from the Workshop of Duncan Phyfe," the first exhibition ever held in an art museum on the work of a single cabinetmaker.[16]

In all likelihood conceived by Halsey, the exhibition, organized by the Museum's young assistant curator of decorative arts, Charles Over Cornelius (fig. 3), brought together more than one hundred pieces of furniture. While Halsey was the principal lender, by this time a cadre of other serious Phyfe collectors—including Allan B. A. Bradley, Francis P. Garvan, Louis Guerineau Myers, and Mrs. Harry Horton Benkard—were available to lend their furniture as well. The exhibition was accompanied by a catalogue by Cornelius titled *Furniture Masterpieces of Duncan Phyfe* (fig. 4). Appropriately, a reproduction of the newly acquired watercolor of Phyfe's shop and

Figure 3. Charles Over Cornelius (1890–1937). Undated photograph, from *Twenty-Fifth Year Record of the Class of 1913, Princeton University* (1938)

warehouse served as the frontispiece. This was followed by halftone illustrations of more than fifty pieces of furniture and a group of detailed line drawings by Stanley J. Rowland (fig. 5) displaying the characteristics of Phyfe's work.[17]

Cornelius seems to have contributed little if any new research on Phyfe, deriving his synopsis of Phyfe's life and career primarily from Hagen's 1907 "Memorandum" and two

6 *Duncan Phyfe*

additional publications by Walter A. Dyer.[18] Instead, he chose to emphasize typical connoisseurship and art-historical concerns—quality and an analysis of the proportion, line, and decoration of Phyfe furniture. He also placed Phyfe's work within the context of the great cabinetmaking traditions of eighteenth-century England and France: "[Phyfe] in America, was the heir of this age and helped to prolong it, in the new land, well into the nineteenth century."[19]

Cornelius goes on to explain that Phyfe's early work shows the influence of Hepplewhite, Sheraton, and the craftsmen of the post-revolutionary French Directoire, which he deems "legitimate" to the history of furniture design.[20] Toward Phyfe's work after 1825, however, Cornelius is less charitable: "As this French influence increased, the heavier forms of the French Empire came into vogue, and in response to the demands of his clients, by this time numerous, Phyfe was forced to enter into a style of work which was much inferior to that of his earlier days." And while he notes that "even this heavier work, with its use of gilt metal, is well made from a craftsman's point of view and possesses a certain character in spite of its over-solidity," he goes on to castigate "the dark ages of black walnut [that] led him into the labyrinth of bad taste from which there was no egress."[21]

In chapter three of *Furniture Masterpieces*, Cornelius explains why Phyfe "is the only early American cabinet-maker to whom may be definitely attributed a large group of pieces."[22] Further elaboration is provided in his 1922 article "The Distinctiveness of Duncan Phyfe (1757–1854?)," published by *The Magazine Antiques* to coincide with the exhibition, in which he states

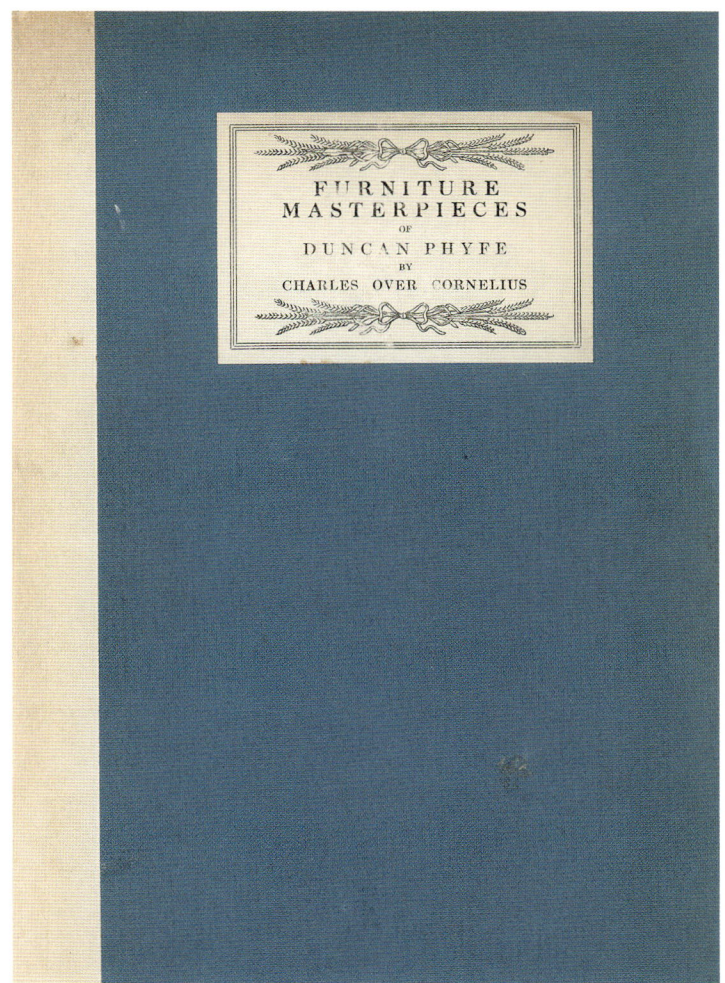

Figure 4. Cover of Charles Over Cornelius. *Furniture Masterpieces of Duncan Phyfe* (1922)

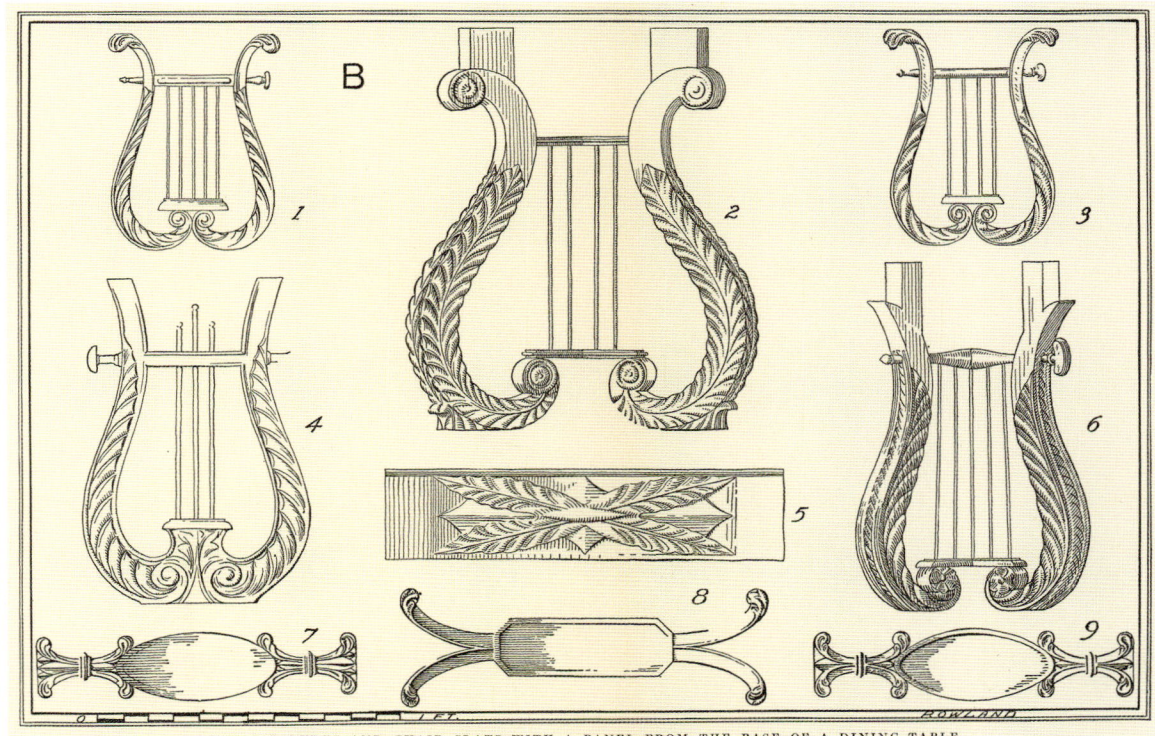

Figure 5. Stanley J. Rowland. Drawing of lyres and other carved details from *Furniture Masterpieces of Duncan Phyfe* (1922), by Charles Over Cornelius

that "for virtually every type of furniture we have an example, known absolutely to have come from his workshop through the possession, in family papers, of bills from Phyfe for the particular article."[23] Cornelius' statement is hardly credible, for even today, nearly ninety years later, only a very limited number of pieces can be linked to bills of sale or other documentation. Cornelius transcribes the only known invoice at the time, one sent to Charles N. Bancker from 1816, but there is no further mention of any other documents or clients. In fact, it is not until 1929 that the existence of a second Phyfe bill is noted in print, suggesting that Cornelius was either exaggerating the number of bills that actually survived at the time or was engaging in circular reasoning: A specific furniture form is listed on a known Phyfe bill; Cornelius is confident he knows what that piece of furniture should look like; he finds an example of the form; and thus can prove his claim.[24] Along these lines, Cornelius points out that in contrast to the work of other craftsmen, Duncan Phyfe's production is "very distinctive and possesses certain personal qualities which render it (in most cases) unmistakable." He observes, for example, that "one of the most distinctive is the ending of the bottom of the leg. Below the reeding occurs a turned, bulbous member, which seems to be, in America, exclusively a Phyfe characteristic."[25] The sentence, however, is flatly contradicted by an editorial comment at the bottom of the page: "It does not necessarily follow that all tables showing this type of foot are by Phyfe, however." This disclaimer was inserted by Homer Eaton Keyes, editor of *The Magazine Antiques*.[26]

Keyes was committed to "substituting facts for traditional or romantic stories," a determination that is evident in the journal's response to Cornelius' book.[27] While Keyes must have supported Cornelius' efforts to further his readers' appreciation and understanding of Duncan Phyfe, his editorial comments question the soundness of some of Cornelius' scholarship. Under a column titled "Cobwebs and Dust," Keyes counsels readers, "It is well to bear in mind that Phyfe was neither the only furniture maker, nor the only excellent furniture maker in the New York of his day."[28] And in a prefatory remark to Cornelius' article, "The Distinctiveness of Duncan Phyfe," he adds: "Perhaps this Phyfe exhibit—the bringing together of a number of representative and indisputable examples—may enable the student of furniture to determine the ear-marks by which even undocumented pieces may be accurately classified. . . . In the following brief article Mr. Cornelius makes an attempt in this direction. It will, no doubt, arouse considerable interest,—possibly some controversy."[29] Keyes' admonition has proved to be providential, as over the years far too many collectors, dealers, and curators have consulted Cornelius' *Furniture Masterpieces* and far too few have considered the editor's reservations.

STOKING PHYFE'S FAME: REPRODUCTIONS AND EARLY COLLECTORS

Halsey and Cornelius were the first art museum curators to organize an exhibition that examined the work of an early American cabinetmaker. A landmark event, the project dovetailed nicely with the planned interpretive thrust of the Museum's new American Wing, which opened on November 10, 1924, to great fanfare. Explaining the purpose and value of the new wing six years later, Museum president Robert W. de Forest wrote:

> It was not merely historical interest which [the] American Wing aroused. Collectors came to view our exhibition, as did women from all states, and students of art, architects from many cities, designers. And finally, manufacturers and merchants came, curious about the source of this spontaneous and intense new public interest.[30]

Front and center on the first floor of the American Wing, in the Gallery of the Early Republic available for close study by all of

Plate XIV. A corner of the GALLERY of the EARLY REPUBLIC. The ARCHED OPENING and OVAL COLUMNS are from a house in BALTIMORE. In the blue damask curtains are large classic designs in silver. The sofa is one of DUNCAN PHYFE's masterpieces

Figure 6. A corner of the Gallery of the Early Republic, the American Wing, The Metropolitan Museum of Art. Plate XIV, *The Homes of Our Ancestors as Shown in The American Wing of The Metropolitan Museum of Art of New York* (1925), by R. T. H. Halsey and Elizabeth Tower

these interested parties, was furniture, including a sofa with lyre ends, attributed to the recently lionized Duncan Phyfe (fig. 6).

Interest in authentic early American furniture and fine reproductions began considerably earlier than the opening of the American Wing. In 1901, *The New York Times* published an article with the unwieldy title "Old Colonial Furniture: Genuine Pieces Are Hard to Find, a Dealer Says. Reproductions Are Really Better Than Originals—Hand Work and Machine Work." The discussion centers on antiques, comments on "Pfiffe" and his cabinetmaking contemporaries, and includes an interview with the now septuagenarian Ernest Hagen, who offers an enthusiastic endorsement of reproductions: "I like a genuine old piece when it is good and has been put in proper condition, but otherwise it is much better to go over on Fourteenth or Twenty-third Street and get good factory made furniture."[31] Reproductions of Phyfe furniture by Hagen and his partner, J. Matthew Meier, run the gamut from unlabeled but relatively easy to recognize as out of period, such as an armchair they probably reproduced for the Bronsons in 1882 (fig. 7), to considerably more difficult, as in a labeled cane scroll-back sofa (fig. 8) that could only be positively identified as made in the late nineteenth century by x-raying the joints, which reveal modern construction methods. Hagen and Meier also produced and labeled some odd-looking pastiches of old parts with added carving, including a pillar-and-claw card table in the collection of the New York State Museum, Albany, and a music stool at the Newark Museum.[32]

Figure 7. Hagen & Meier. Armchair, 1882. Mahogany, 32½ × 21¼ × 24¼ in. Collection of Richard Hampton Jenrette

Figure 8. Ernest F. Hagen. Sofa, ca. 1898. Mahogany and cane, 36 × 59⅝ × 30 in. The Metropolitan Museum of Art, Gift of Lee McCanliss, 1961 61.254

Figure 9. Blueprint drawing of lyre-back side chair No.14199, ca. 1925. The Company of Master Craftsmen, New York. The American Wing, The Metropolitan Museum of Art

A variation on the subject is raised a few years later in an article that appeared in *House Beautiful* titled "The Cost of Furniture a Century Ago," which endorses the concept of modern copies by contrasting the prices Duncan Phyfe charged for his furniture with what the same piece would retail for in 1905. While Hagen is not identified by name, the article is based on Phyfe's 1816 bill to Charles N. Bancker, which was then in Hagen's possession. The author compares Phyfe's charge for a pier table he billed at $265 with an estimate of $300 to reproduce it in 1905. For one of his signature pieces, a lyre-back chair that cost $22 in 1816, it was estimated that the best cabinetmaker working in 1905 would charge $25 or $26. The analysis led the writer to conclude that Phyfe's clients paid handsomely for their furniture; and, taking into consideration the difference in the purchasing power of the dollar between 1816 and 1905, readers were prompted to consider fine reproductions as an alternative to the original.[33]

While Ernest Hagen's sons continued to carry on their father's cabinetmaking and antiques business, by the 1920s they must have faced growing competition, as the market for Duncan Phyfe "style" furniture was rapidly transformed from one of handmade to factory-made reproductions. Walter A. Dyer, writing for *Country Life* in 1921, contrasts a period lyre-back armchair with the Kensington Company's version, promoting the latter as "a modern reproduction based on originals in the Halsey collection and the Metropolitan Museum."[34] While it is unclear if the Kensington interpretation was formally authorized by Halsey, he undoubtedly recognized the lucrative potential as well as the opportunity to fulfill the Metropolitan's stated mission of "encouraging and developing the application of arts to manufacture and practical life" and entered into a partnership with William Sloane Coffin, a fellow museum trustee whose family business was the furniture and decorating firm W. & J. Sloane.[35] Under the names Oneidacraft and The Company of Master Craftsmen, Halsey and Sloane manufactured fine home furnishings and even marketed a line of "registered reproductions," many of them based on furniture in the American Wing, including some in Phyfe's inimitable style then on loan by Halsey (fig. 9). A sofa adapted from an original owned by Halsey then on display in the Gallery of the Early Republic in the American Wing (see fig. 6) was W. & J. Sloane's entry in the Metropolitan Museum's "Ninth Annual Exhibition of American Industrial Art" (March 28–May 23, 1925).[36]

Furniture in the Phyfe aesthetic was not only the subject of publications about antiques; interest extended far beyond their purview to an expanded audience comprising interior designers, furniture manufacturers, housewives, and even amateur craftsmen. By 1918 references to Phyfe began to appear in books and periodicals on home decorating.[37] In 1931, Charles Stuart contributed to *Arts and Decoration* "Duncan Phyfe Furniture Inspires Modern Craftsmen," which illustrated pieces by the Erskine-Danforth Corporation, the Shaw Furniture Company, the Kittinger Company, the Richter Furniture Company, and Cooper-Williams, Inc.[38] For those who aspired not only to live with reproduction Phyfe furniture but to experience the process of actually creating a masterpiece themselves, Ralph Ogden Buck's article in *Popular Mechanics Magazine* supplied the specifications for reproducing a table from the collection of the Metropolitan Museum.[39] And evidently no challenge was too great, as resourceful designers were poised to adapt Phyfe motifs to contemporary furniture forms for those embracing a contemporary lifestyle. The Sonora Phonograph Company offered not only phonograph cases in the Italian Renaissance, Louis XIV, William and Mary, Gothic, Chippendale, Louis XV, Jacobean, Adam, Colonial, and Queen Anne modes, but the "Highest Class Talking Machine in the World" in the Duncan Phyfe style.[40]

Reproductions were not, however, enthusiastically embraced by one and all. Following the close of "Furniture Masterpieces of Duncan Phyfe," Allan B. A. Bradley, one of the lenders to the exhibition, wrote to Henry W. Kent, warning: "I realize that the purpose of the exhibition was largely to encourage the production of modern furniture of a high standard of quality and workmanship, but the repeated reproduction of antique furniture may greatly tend to lessen the interest of the original."[41]

Yet there didn't seem to be any danger of that happening. Indeed, the dynamism that characterized American decorative arts in the 1920s rose to a crescendo in 1929 with the landmark sale and exhibition at the American Art Association of the extraordinary decorative arts collection assembled by the late Howard Reifsnyder, a Philadelphia wool merchant.[42] The historic sale realized $600,000. The high point was reached when Henry Francis du Pont prevailed over William Randolph Hearst to purchase the famed Van Pelt high chest for $44,000—an auction record that would remain unchallenged for decades. Reifsnyder had been attracted by the arts of his native Pennsylvania, perhaps most notably the eighteenth-century school of Philadelphia cabinetmaking, but his collection also included an upholstered Phyfe sofa he purchased a decade earlier at the estate sale of Mrs. F. H. Bosworth, described as "a group of collections that will bring ardent lovers of American furniture to their knees."[43]

The name "Duncan Phyfe" was important enough in the cabinetmaker's lifetime that it was often used to spur interest by including it in auction advertisements, and by March 1909 furniture recorded as "Phyfe" was once again being promoted at auction in the city. Just six months prior to the cabinetmaker's debut at the Hudson-Fulton Celebration, Fifth Avenue Auction Rooms, Inc., conducted a sale highlighting a group of family pieces that had come down to Mrs. Henry Llewellyn Daingerfield Lewis Sr., in addition to consignments from the notable collection formed by the antiques dealer James Curran of Philadelphia. Lot 63 was given the improbable description of a "Beautiful old Colonial card table of the Duncan Phyfe period," and six subsequent lots were catalogued as "Duncan Phyfe," implying the craftsman's actual handwork.[44]

Increasingly, "Phyfe" furniture was making its way to the salesrooms, and, as one could foresee before long, Phyfe's name would eventually headline an auction. Anderson Galleries appears to have initiated this approach, and in a bit of shrewd marketing scheduled the vendue to coincide with the 1922 exhibition at the Metropolitan Museum.[45] In 1927 the American Art Association, the Anderson Galleries' principal competitor,

Figure 10. Display of Phyfe furniture at the 1929 "Girl Scouts Loan Exhibition," American Art Association, New York

offered the collection formed by Alexander M. Hudnut—purportedly the most notable group of Phyfe furniture to come to auction up to that time. The catalogue included a profile of Hudnut that described him as "an intimate friend of Hagen" and noted that over the years he had acquired pieces in consultation with, if not directly from, him. Riding the wave of Phyfe enthusiasm, it was reported that the sale witnessed the rise of Phyfe pieces to "record-breaking figures."[46] Two years later, Anderson Galleries offered "Furniture by Duncan Phyfe & Other Early American Craftsmen."[47]

The marriage of scholarship and collecting was consummated in 1929 by a landmark exhibition to benefit the Girl Scouts of America, an exhibition organized in recognition of the advancements that had been made in the study of American painting and decorative arts, and that had elevated the discipline from the pursuits of the antiquarian to the scholarly realm of connoisseur and curator.[48] The concept for the exhibition is credited to Florence Guerineau Myers, a member of the National Girl Scouts board, though it was her husband who actually assumed responsibility for both the displays and the scholarly catalogue. Like R. T. H. Halsey, Louis Guerineau Myers was an early and passionate collector of American Neoclassical furniture and a lender to the 1922 Duncan Phyfe exhibition. He was also among the first to develop a keen interest in American glass and pewter. Myers' aesthetic intuition and careful attention to authenticity are evident in the extraordinary quality of the works he brought together for the exhibition.

Included among the highlights were some of the Reifsnyder pieces, which, by coincidence, were shown in the same velvet-draped rooms at the American Art Association where only a few months earlier they had been dispersed. The exhibition included paintings, watercolors, lusterware, Chinese export porcelain, and an outstanding assemblage of approximately five hundred glass objects from the collection of George S. McKearin. But pride of place was given to a superb group of more than three hundred pieces of furniture arranged in five sections: "Early American," "American Windsors," "American Queen Anne and Chippendale," "Hepplewhite and Sheraton," and "Duncan Phyfe" (fig. 10). The lenders to the Phyfe section included not only the Benkards, the Bradleys, the Garvans, and of course the Myerses, all of whom had participated in the 1922 exhibition at the Metropolitan Museum, but a new group as well: Mrs. J. Amory Haskell, the Walter B. Jenningses, and Mr. and Mrs. Andrew Varick Stout. Once again, R. T. H. Halsey was a major lender, but this time he chose to do so anonymously.

In what must have been viewed as an advanced approach at the time, Myers attempted to create groupings that reflected the preferences and characteristics of the regional cabinetmaking centers of New England, Philadelphia, and Baltimore. As such, they underscored his observation that "one of the mysteries of furniture lore is the absence of any group in any period, until Phyfe's time, structurally identifiable with New York."[49] Myers then grappled with the challenge of identifying Duncan Phyfe's work. His observations suggest a measured approach:

> The first thing we must recognize when trying to make attributions is that no cabinet-maker with any pretense to popularity can hope to do more than design and supervise the construction of his output. This means that Phyfe worked no more with his own hand than did the famous Chippendale. Then we also know that men trained in the shop of a master to certain proportions, methods and mechanics of construction often separate from him and continue to reproduce the things his hand is accustomed to, albeit more mechanically and less carefully.[50]

And then, either flattering his own skills as a connoisseur or perhaps bowing to pressure exerted by important lenders, Myers proceeds to describe all but one of the forty-nine pieces exhibited, including those from his own collection, as "by Phyfe."[51]

Henry Francis du Pont, the preeminent collector of his day, was the principal lender to the "Girl Scouts Loan Exhibition." He does not, however, seem to have contributed any furniture to the Duncan Phyfe section, possibly because up to this time he had shown little interest in it. In anticipation of the exhibition, Albert J. Collings, an established New York antiques dealer, had confided in du Pont that he understood the show to have been concocted by Myers and others in part to inflate the prices of Phyfe furniture.[52] This was perhaps the case. Nevertheless, the exhibition proved to be responsible for bringing du Pont and Myers together and nurturing in the former an interest in the craftsman and his work. Within the year, du Pont had acquired no fewer than eleven pieces from Myers' collection, including a unique worktable with a marble top distinguished for bearing a Phyfe label (Pl. 10). Shortly after the furniture arrived at Winterthur, du Pont's family estate near Wilmington, Delaware, he wrote to Myers: "Your Phyfe looks beautiful and I must say that for a long while I could not see Phyfe. Its charm, however, does grow on one more and more as time goes on."[53]

In 1929, du Pont successfully negotiated the purchase of a superb set of chairs (Pl. 1), along with the original bill documenting their receipt from Duncan Phyfe by the New York merchant William Bayard in 1807. Years later he would reflect upon the significance of his acquisition. "The Phyfe chairs," he wrote, "pleased me especially because they were not only fine furniture; they were identified."[54] Eventually, the Myers and Bayard furniture would be assembled in the Phyfe Room that du Pont installed at Winterthur—complete with architectural woodwork from the home of Moses Rogers, William Bayard's

Figure 11. Phyfe Room at the Winterthur Museum. Photograph, 1938

next-door neighbor (fig. 11). Du Pont also recognized the great documentary value of Duncan Phyfe's personal copy of *The New-York Revised Prices for Manufacturing Cabinet and Chair Work* (1810; see fig. 44), as well as that of the only known copy of the Halliday & Jenkins auction catalogue, *Peremptory and Extensive Auction Sale of Splendid and Valuable Furniture*, which records the dispersal of the Phyfe shop in 1847. These, too, he brought to Winterthur.[55]

Between the time of Phyfe's debut at the Hudson-Fulton Celebration in 1909 and the "Girl Scouts Loan Exhibition" exactly two decades later, his furniture came to be viewed both by connoisseurs and by the public in general as highly artistic and valuable. The year 1929, with its prominent display at the American Art Association, would prove to be pivotal as well for nurturing an appreciation of Duncan Phyfe furniture, as indicated by fully six more publications on the cabinetmaker and his work.[56] Despite the accolades received by the "Girl Scouts Loan Exhibition," some began to question in print whether the burgeoning enthusiasm for Phyfe had come at the expense of objectivity and fairness.

Reassessment and Scholarly Synthesis

The next true high-water mark in Phyfe studies, after the 1922 exhibition at the Metropolitan Museum and its accompanying catalogue, arrived in 1939 with the publication of *Duncan Phyfe and the English Regency, 1795–1830*, by Nancy Vincent McClelland (1876/77–1959). In the intervening years, however, a number of important articles and essays were written, some of which sought to counterbalance the adulation Phyfe was receiving and to challenge the scholarly approach of Hagen, Halsey, Cornelius, and a growing coterie of collectors and dealers giving easy answers to hard questions about attributions. In his book *Genuine Antique Furniture* (1929), Arthur de Bles concedes that "Phyfe had his moments of genius," but goes on to say, "[W]e fear, from such study as we have been able to make of his work at the exhibition at the Metropolitan Museum some years ago and of the pieces attributed to him in the American Wing, that his worth has been considerably overrated at the expense of better men," including the Newport craftsman John Goddard (1723–1785) and his Philadelphia counterpart, William Savery (1721–1787).[57]

William Macpherson Hornor Jr., writing for *Country Life*, added the name of a third cabinetmaker, Philadelphian Henry Connelly (1770–1826), whom he lauded as another "worthy luminary in the annals of furniture design and artistry," adding, "When the importance of his productions is fully appreciated, it is certain that Connelly—not Phyfe—will be recognized as the outstanding craftsman of the period."[58] Hornor, an inveterate advocate for the Philadelphia school, it seems made it his personal mission to take Phyfe down from his pedestal and to draw Phyfe's devotees into a reasoned debate, with observations such as the following: "General types and periods are ascribed to his hand and eye without reserve, until it would almost appear that he alone is to be studied, praised, and credited with all the fine articles for household use and adornment originating in America during the first half of the nineteenth century."[59]

In 1930, Hornor published an important—and contentious—article on Phyfe in the pages of *The Antiquarian*.[60] He began with a harsh critique of past Phyfe scholarship, dismissing most of it as a "response to the popular demand for knowledge concerning the makers of our antique furniture, coupled with natural romantic instincts" and a "pretty tradition of Duncan Phyfe's initial career [that] has sprung into being and fascinated the public mind." He then went on to debunk some of the multitude of "traditions" that had been printed and reprinted over the years.[61] At the same time, Hornor offered readers new insights about Phyfe's real estate holdings and introduced additional family members who had made their livelihood in the cabinet and related trades. Furthermore, he reminded his readers that there were "numerous other good artisans and worthy proprietors of cabinet shops in New York . . . they all had access to the same pattern books, they served a fashionable clientèle, they could employ the same carvers and journeymen, and were themselves just as capable, as well established and as successful as Phyfe."[62] Even Hornor's illustrations made a key scholarly contribution, as they included the 1807 invoice to William Bayard that had only recently been uncovered and eight pieces of furniture believed to be those listed therein. Aside from some of the Phyfe family furniture pictured in an article by James Collier Marshall in 1915, the Bayard commission was the first of Phyfe's documented work to be published.[63]

To this day, Hornor's edifying revisionist article remains a central contribution to Phyfe scholarship. Perhaps the lone criticism that can be leveled is that he continued to promulgate the general perception that Phyfe's work deteriorated after 1825:

> Even Phyfe's greatest exponents concur that his later productions show a tendency to disregard accepted traditions and adopt the newer, admittedly incorrect forms for which there was a ready market. Any good craftsman could supply such objects, but a true artist would never degrade himself by allowing them to leave his shop, for, if born a genius, he could create a taste for orthodox patterns out of his own imagination.[64]

Taking up Hornor's cry for a more reasoned approach to New York furniture scholarship was the newly minted curator of the American Wing, Joseph P. Downs, who together with assistant curator Ruth Ralston in 1934 mounted "A Loan Exhibition of New York State Furniture." The exhibition was accompanied by a catalogue which included an essay that identified attributes of New York furniture and introduced a number of makers and manufacturers, eighteen of whom were represented by signed or labeled examples. The catalogue

Figure 12. Nancy Vincent McClelland (1876/77–1959). Undated photograph. Nancy McClelland Archive, Cooper-Hewitt, National Design Museum, Smithsonian Institution

recorded more than two hundred pieces of furniture, twenty-seven of which were illustrated, along with detailed entries providing a range of information including primary and secondary woods, provenance, period inscriptions, and, on occasion, a curatorial observation.

Walter Rendell Storey, in his review for *Parnassus*, remarked that the exhibition had clearly established that New York State had enjoyed a much richer cabinetmaking tradition than had previously been thought. He noted that while New York cabinetmaking is closely identified with Duncan Phyfe, Phyfe's actual contribution had been narrowed down by the organizers, as he had been the subject of the Museum's 1922 exhibition. Nevertheless, Storey wrote:

> Phyfe's fame as an outstanding craftsman is not . . . detracted from by the discovery and inclusion in the exhibition of the work of some of his contemporaries, such as George Woodruff and Michael Allison, so well done that it might have been mistaken for his own. What these pieces do suggest is that we should no longer attribute to Phyfe every fine piece of furniture in the Sheraton or Empire style made in his time.[65]

Be that as it may, Downs and Ralston, with the "Loan Exhibition of New York State Furniture," did contribute, albeit minimally, to Phyfe scholarship. They published for the first time the writing table and bookcase said to have been made for Thomas Lattimer Bowie, which bore a Phyfe label dated 1820 (Pl. 25), and they included collector Henry Francis du Pont's previously mentioned labeled worktable dating from 1811–16. In the catalogue, Downs and Ralston cite the existence of Phyfe's own copy of *The New-York Revised Prices for Manufacturing Cabinet and Chair Work* (1810), as well as the Halliday & Jenkins printed catalogue recording the dispersal of "Messrs. Duncan Phyfe and Son" in 1847. Refreshingly, they were for the most part cautious in their attributions, stating that some of the undocumented pieces were "probably made by Duncan Phyfe." In constructing a more expansive picture of New York cabinetmaking, the "Loan Exhibition of New York State Furniture" at last began to identify the attributes of that regional school, and finally crossed the mythical, forbidden 1825 dateline for furniture studies, acknowledging the contributions of the subsequent stylistic periods and generations of craftsmen, including the work of the Meekses, Elijah Galusha, and John Henry Belter.

Hornor's instructive article threw down the gauntlet for future Phyfe scholars, challenging them to be more thorough in their research, more demanding of documentation, and more conscientious about their attributions. When Nancy McClelland (fig. 12) embarked on research for *Duncan Phyfe and the English Regency, 1795–1830*, she clearly understood that Hornor, Downs, and Ralston had significantly raised the bar. Undaunted, she strove to synthesize previous scholarship and produced a grand and elegant study of Phyfe in the context of international style that to this day remains a classic. Published in 1939 in the depths of the Great Depression, the boxed first edition was offered for the hefty prepublication price of $15 per copy. A limited number of deluxe copies, autographed by the author and bound in a reproduction Regency fabric woven under her direction, were also offered to a select group of her "friends, acquaintances, and business associates" (fig. 13). Publisher William R. Scott, in announcing the book's publication, touted it, for the following reasons, as "a genuine contribution to an important field":

> FIRST, the classic Regency period is the coming trend in decoration, and this is the book that covers it completely; SECOND, Duncan Phyfe is the outstanding exponent of the classic style in America, and this book gives the first comprehensive account of the man, his background, and his work, based on the discovery of a large amount of new material; THIRD, much new light is shed on Phyfe's competitors, all of whom derived their inspiration from England but in varying degrees invested their work with American spirit and individual interpretation; FOURTH, by dint of persevering detective work, Miss McClelland has tracked down thirty-seven of Duncan Phyfe's customers, the furniture they bought, the bills they received from Phyfe, and the present location of various pieces.[66]

While there is truth to all these claims, it is the first that best represents the book's principal raison d'être and was most closely aligned with McClelland's professional expertise and interests, and the second and fourth that reflect her regard for the high standards of scholarship practiced by Hornor and Downs. An accomplished, entrepreneurial, and well-respected interior decorator and the proprietor of Nancy McClelland, Inc., in New York City, McClelland recognized an opportunity with this book to place America's best-known cabinetmaker and his furniture in the mainstream of the Regency Revival, a decorating trend started in England just after World War I that remained in full force in the 1930s.

One of the early proponents of the Regency Revival in England was Edward Knoblock, an expatriate American actor who had decorated several homes with authentic period furnishings, including some pieces designed by Thomas Hope that he had acquired in 1917 at the sale of the contents of The Deepdene, Hope's country house near Dorking, Surrey. McClelland drafted Knoblock to write the foreword for *Duncan Phyfe and the English Regency*, and he produced a breezy fifteen pages

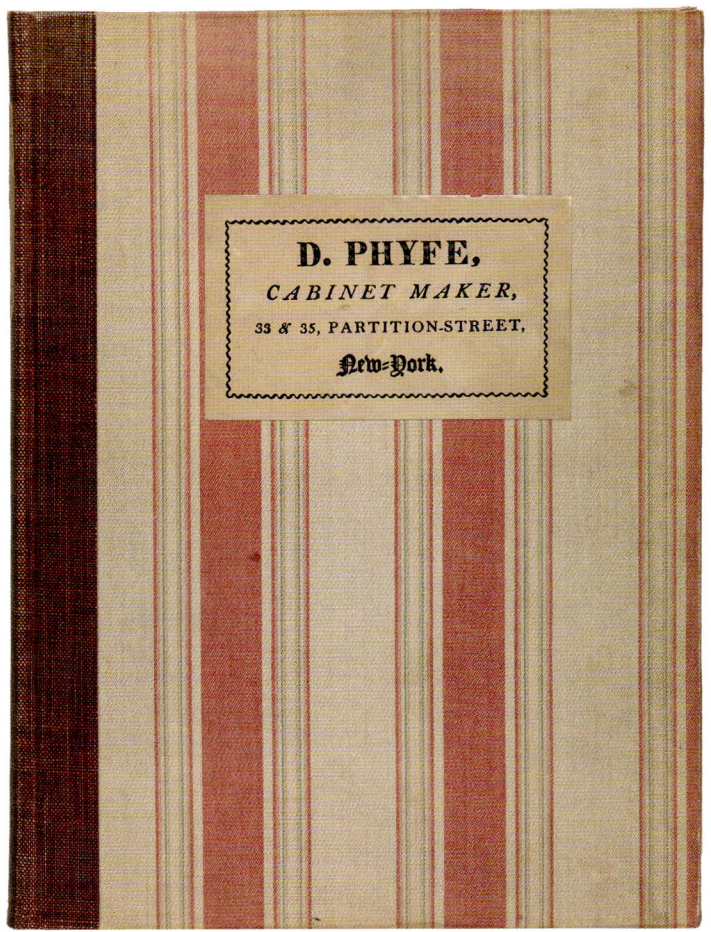

Figure 13. Cover of the limited numbered edition of Nancy Vincent McClelland, *Duncan Phyfe and the English Regency, 1795–1830* (1939)

Introduction: American Icon   15

on the Regency style that ends with a paragraph in praise of Phyfe, who is described as a "keen advocate" in the United States and who "may justly be looked upon as the American 'opposite' to Thomas Hope." Also included in the book is a pictorial supplement on Regency design that depicts period furniture and metalwork from London and New York dealers, interior decorating firms, and private owners, and contemporary photographs of interiors in the Regency Revival style. Among these were a dining room and library with Thomas Hope furniture from Knoblock's London house, the drawing room of the late Charles Over Cornelius, and the dining room in the House of History, the 1816 James Vanderpoel house in Kinderhook, New York.[67]

McClelland was not a furniture expert in the mold of Hornor or Downs, and her essay on Phyfe's "Work and Manner" largely reflects the style and content of Cornelius' 1922 *Furniture Masterpieces of Duncan Phyfe*. This is especially apparent when she illustrates and discusses the full range of Phyfe forms and decorative motifs, going so far as to reprint Stanley J. Rowland's detailed line drawing from the earlier publication as an appendix (see fig. 5). In light of the new standards for documentation and the emerging interest in local schools of cabinetmaking established by Hornor and Downs and Ralston, McClelland, to her credit, did present two previously unpublished Phyfe labels on worktables and a D. Phyfe & Sons trade card on a pier table, as well as images of labeled furniture by some of Phyfe's contemporaries in Boston, Salem, and Philadelphia.

McClelland attempted to add many more examples to Phyfe's documented oeuvre by bringing to light furniture with histories of ownership in families believed to have been original clients. Unfortunately, this attempt is marred by the fact that the author lends as much credence to traditional oral histories as she does to documented evidence. Thirty-seven "original" Phyfe clients are listed in alphabetical order, and the "Phyfe" furniture they inherited is illustrated and discussed. An example of a well-documented history is the pair of John Wells pier tables (Pl. 16), one of which is illustrated, along with the partial transcription of a letter written by Wells in 1815 on his honeymoon trip to Boston asking his sister-in-law in New York to oversee his order from Phyfe.

Furniture without documented proof but only a traditional history of having been made by Phyfe is represented by chairs and a dining table end inherited by the descendants of Charles Gustavus Smedberg, an immigrant Swede who arrived in New York in 1812 as the representative of a British bank. According to family tradition, Smedberg "once did a great favor for Duncan Phyfe who, to show his appreciation, presented him with a sideboard, a dining table and twenty-four chairs." McClelland then relates how the furniture was divided up among later descendants. Two dining table ends wound up in the possession of Mrs. Carl G. Smedberg of Summit, New Jersey (the center part belonged at the time to Mrs. Edward Carnes Weeks, who "cut it down"); twelve of the dining chairs were in the possession of Adolphus Smedberg of New York; and the sideboard was said to have been sold at auction in Saugerties, New York, in 1874 and purchased by a member of the Livingston family.[68]

The story of the Smedberg sideboard underscores one of the problems with traditional histories, for once a piece of furniture leaves the family line and is purchased by another prominent family (in this case the Livingstons, two of whom are also listed as original Phyfe clients by McClelland without any corroborating evidence), what is to keep that piece (here the sideboard) from becoming an "original" family possession in subsequent generations? Another distortion results from the prominence gained by Phyfe as a result of the two exhibitions on the cabinetmaker's work held at the Metropolitan Museum in 1909 and 1922. What New York family with "Phyfe" style furniture would not have wanted earlier generations to have patronized the master cabinetmaker? In essence, once Cornelius' book was published and people—including McClelland—learned the hallmarks of the Phyfe style, the well was poisoned. It could have worked like this: Nancy McClelland is summoned by a prominent New York family to see its "Phyfe" furniture, which they are certain—but lacking in proof—was purchased by their relative from the cabinetmaker himself. McClelland sees the furniture and, based on her knowledge of what Phyfe furniture should look like, proclaims the owner correct and adds said relative to a list of original Phyfe clients. A perfect example of circular reasoning.

When considering traditional histories, it is helpful also to remember that John Wells in the 1815 letter to his sister-in-law in New York instructed her to go to Phyfe for the pier tables, because "tables you will get best at Phyfe's than elsewhere." He did not, however, restrict her choice of cabinetmakers for the chairs and bedroom furniture he also asked her to procure for him. Some, perhaps even a majority, of the testimonials given to McClelland by families with "Phyfe" furniture are accurate, or at least partially so, but traditional histories, for the reasons cited above, are notoriously unreliable.

McClelland's pursuit of Phyfe family documents resulted in at least one disappointing discovery. Among her papers in the archives at the Cooper-Hewitt, National Design Museum in New York are some unpublished notes about important Phyfe artifacts and business records. Two sheets titled "Phyfe Notes" record a conversation between McClelland and a Mr. Harry Bland, who informed her that on December 21, 1921, Samuel Marx held a sale in his auction rooms on Twenty-third Street in Manhattan of furniture from the estate of Duncan Phyfe, not the cabinetmaker but his grandson, the son of James Duncan

Phyfe. According to Bland, included in the sale was the "fitted chest of tools" now on loan from descendants of Duncan Phyfe to the New-York Historical Society (see frontispiece on page 22), as well as a workbench and six or seven lots of tools, all now missing. Lot 44 was reported to be "a box containing old account books and papers of Duncan Phyfe," possibly the business records ominously referred to in another of McClelland's notes, which reads: "Mr. Ormsbee [the furniture historian] tells me that he missed having Duncan Phyfe's account books by three months," and that a Mrs. Lawson Phyfe, of Cold Spring, New York, stated that she "had just cleared out all of Phyfe's papers." Scholars have been searching for these account books and Phyfe's business papers in vain for more than a century. Apparently, Ormsbee and McClelland came tantalizingly close to getting them.

The script of an address delivered to the National Arts Club in November 1940, also among McClelland's papers, includes some charming and informative anecdotes about the pressures of producing a major book while maintaining a busy schedule—McClelland's editor bribed her weekly with boxes of orchids, gardenias, camellias, and "sometimes a big spicy striped carnation made up of half a dozen bunched together"—and dealing with surviving members of the Phyfe clan, some of whom, as a result of the sizable fortune left by Duncan Phyfe "and disputes over it [that] seem to have sown dissension between many branches of the family," were "at swords' points with others." According to McClelland, one descendant, Percy Vail, Duncan Phyfe's eighty-year-old great-grandson, could be quite irascible, responding to her first request for an interview with, "I am weary of it all," and her second with, "I am feeling a little *more* weary now."

With an extensive appendix that includes Hagen's "Duncan Phyfe Memorandum," a genealogy of three generations of the Phyfe family in America, a listing of Duncan Phyfe's real estate holdings and deeds of conveyance, and the inventory of the contents of Phyfe's home at the time of his death, McClelland's magisterial *Duncan Phyfe and the English Regency* was a watershed publication that in its comprehensiveness made it the final word on Phyfe for years to come. Proof of this is the fact that in the more than seventy years since it was published, no scholar has taken Phyfe on in such an all-embracing manner.

Legacy of an American Icon

McClelland's artful elevation of Duncan Phyfe into the mainstream of Regency Revival interior design cemented his status as a world-class interpreter of the classical mode. Not surprisingly, therefore, Phyfe furniture, then more than ever considered the epitome of American high style, became enshrined in some of the nation's elite historic houses and museums. Winterthur's Phyfe Room, which Henry Francis du Pont had installed earlier, became an object lesson in taste when this grand country house was opened as a museum to the public in 1951. At the White House, Jacqueline Kennedy "assumed a new role for a first lady, that of a curator and lady of the manor," and initiated a program in 1961 that continues to this day of collecting and decorating with furniture by America's acknowledged masters of Neoclassical design: Samuel McIntire, John and Thomas Seymour, Charles-Honoré Lannuier, and, of course, Duncan Phyfe.[69] At Boscobel Restoration in Garrison-on-Hudson, New York, American Wing curator Berry B. Tracy was engaged by the project's sponsor, Mrs. Lila Acheson Wallace of the *Reader's Digest* fortune, to reinterpret and redecorate this 1808 Neoclassical house in 1977, making it a virtual showcase of Phyfe furniture. And in 1980 and 1984, the American Wing added two more period rooms filled with Phyfe furniture—the Richmond Room (1810) and the Greek Revival Parlor (ca. 1835)—to its extensive array of historic interiors. Also beginning in the 1970s and continuing to the present, superbly documented furniture from the workshop of Duncan Phyfe made for Robert Donaldson of Fayetteville and New York in 1822 and 1826 and for South Carolinian John Laurence Manning in 1841 has been successfully returned to its historic settings: Edgewater in Barrytown, New York, and Millford Plantation near Pine Woods, South Carolina, by the preservationist and collector Richard Hampton Jenrette.

The aforementioned Berry B. Tracy (1933–1984) and the architect and interior design consultant Edward Vason Jones (1909–1980), who worked for him at the Metropolitan in the 1960s and 1970s and on renovations to the White House during the Nixon, Ford, and Carter administrations (fig. 14), were the pivotal figures in the Phyfe story after McClelland. At the age of twenty-seven, Tracy became assistant curator of the Newark Museum and three years later conceived a brilliant exhibition titled "Classical America, 1815–1845," featuring the fine and decorative arts of this period. The show was supported by Newark Museum trustee Charles Engelhard and his wife, Jane, and through them and its resounding success Tracy achieved national recognition and gained entrée to leading collectors and patrons of the arts. Henry Francis du Pont was said to be "blown away" by the display, which included several pieces of furniture documented and attributed to Duncan Phyfe in his previously neglected late Grecian style.[70]

In 1964, Tracy came to the Metropolitan Museum as assistant curator in the American Wing, where his fervor for later nineteenth-century decorative arts was met with approval by then head of the American Wing, James Biddle. By 1968, Tracy was in charge, and he embarked on an ambitious program of acquiring a cross section of decorative arts from the 1820s to the early 1900s. Tracy was remarkably acquisitive, and his contacts

Introduction: American Icon 17

Figure 14. Green Room, The White House, during the Nixon administration. Photograph, 1971. White House Historical Association, Washington, D.C.

with antiques collectors, "pickers," and dealers legendary; in his dragnet he would catch a pier table which he attributed to Phyfe and had borrowed earlier for the Newark show. That table, along with a suite of mahogany seating furniture in Phyfe's late Grecian Plain style purchased in 1966 from direct descendants of its original owner, Samuel Foot, now stands in the Greek Revival Parlor of the American Wing.

A dynamic visionary, Tracy was intent on pushing the American Wing a hundred years forward, past its traditional collecting terminus date of about 1820. The culmination of his work throughout the 1960s was "19th-Century America," a landmark exhibition mounted in 1970 to celebrate the Museum's one hundredth anniversary. It was here that Tracy, in a series of period room settings depicting the prevailing nineteenth-century Greek, Rococo, Gothic, and Renaissance Revival styles, planned and executed, in consultation with Edward Vason Jones, a dress rehearsal of what he hoped to achieve permanently in a new and expanded American Wing, which opened with his dream at least partially fulfilled in 1980.

As comfortable as Tracy was with the various historical revival styles of the nineteenth century, his first love, and that of Jones as well, was the furniture of Duncan Phyfe in all its stylistic guises, from the early 1800s into the 1840s. Their attributions to Phyfe were many and expressed with extreme

18   *Duncan Phyfe*

confidence. Yet despite their deep experience and knowledge, their record of serious published scholarship on Phyfe is thin, with Tracy's restricted to an essay and catalogue entries on the collection at Boscobel and Jones' to a single article in *The American Art Journal* titled "Two Creative Geniuses of Federal New York" that deals with how to separate the work of Duncan Phyfe from that of Charles-Honoré Lannuier in furniture of very similar design.[71] Tracy had planned to write a book on New York furniture of the Federal period, and under the auspices of the Metropolitan Museum hired grant-funded researchers to comb the New York directories, newspapers, and jury lists in preparation. Phyfe and his work would have formed a large segment of this book had it ever come to fruition. When Tracy left the Museum in 1981, he took this research material with him. But he never produced the book. His estate eventually returned the material to the American Wing, where it has proved helpful to the current authors and for the Museum's 1998 book and exhibition on Lannuier.

With Tracy and Jones in hegemonic roles as impresarios and connoisseurs in all matters Phyfe, scholarship on the cabinetmaker was taking a more serious bent. In 1978 a graduate student in the Winterthur Program in Early American Culture revisited the cabinetmaker and his career in a master's thesis, the stated purpose of which was "[to] reexamine and reevaluate" received knowledge on Phyfe. To that end, new and previously examined primary and secondary materials were consulted to provide a clearer understanding of Phyfe's cabinetmaking business and to assess his importance in the trade as well as his role as a tastemaker. A group of labeled pieces known at the time were also examined and studied, although these, in the author's own words, "did not figure prominently in my study."[72]

More recent articles by Jeanne Vibert Sloane on the furniture Phyfe supplied to James Lefferts Brinckerhoff of New York City in 1816, by Thomas Gordon Smith on a large Phyfe commission for Millford Plantation in South Carolina in 1841, and by Paul M. Haygood and Matthew A. Thurlow on the furniture purchased from Phyfe in 1836 by the planter Lewis Stirling for Wakefield, his home in Saint Francisville, Louisiana, have taken a refreshing turn toward documentation and, in the case of the last two, exploring Phyfe's often neglected later work.[73] A thought-provoking exhibition held at the Museum of the City of New York in 1993, "Is It Phyfe?," and an eponymous follow-up article by its curator, Deborah Dependahl Waters, posed a question that one would have thought had been answered long ago in the hundred-plus years since Ernest Hagen's discovery of the cabinetmaker and through the efforts of Cornelius, McClelland, Tracy, and numerous others to explicate his work.[74] The title and the content of the article in fact serve as a challenge as well to those who would pose an easy answer to such a complex question.

The present study of Phyfe seems long overdue. A broad reassessment of Duncan Phyfe and his world, it attempts to document as complete a picture as possible of the cabinetmaker's work over the course of his long career. In 1997 a number of curators of fine and decorative arts from American museums were asked to select and write about an iconic object from their collection to celebrate the seventy-fifth anniversary of *The Magazine Antiques*. Morrison Heckscher, longtime curator in the American Wing of the Metropolitan Museum, chose the famous watercolor that depicts Phyfe's shop and warehouse (see fig. 39), declaring it to be "[of] supreme antiquarian interest." Phyfe he describes as a man "whose name, more than any other, is synonymous with American craftsmanship." Of Phyfe's previous two biographers, Charles Over Cornelius and Nancy McClelland, he states that neither "ever assembled the master's documentable *oeuvre* in order to codify convincingly the telling characteristics of his work . . . [the] generally accepted benchmarks by which to distinguish Phyfe's work from that of his contemporaries."[75] The authors have undertaken the present work with this specific objective in mind. What more essential purpose, no matter how hard to ever completely fulfill, could there be for the furniture historian.

Michael K. Brown and Peter M. Kenny

1. Letter from James H. Hammond to Catherine E. Hammond, August 25, 1840, James Henry Hammond Letters, #305-z, Southern Historical Collection, The Wilson Library, University of North Carolina at Chapel Hill.
2. Ingerman 1963, p. 577.
3. Ibid.
4. Ibid., p. 578.
5. Ibid., p. 580. Stillinger 1988, pp. 11D–12D; and Stillinger 1980, pp. 52–54. For example, in June 1886, Hagen billed Lenox Smith for "1 Phyfe's Arm Chair (antique) in XVI Century old blue plush & fancy bronze nails 35.00," as well as "1 small chair to match (reproduction) 22.00" (Ernest Hagen order books, June 15, 1886, New-York Historical Society).
6. Stillinger 1988, p. 11D.
7. For a comprehensive discussion of Hagen's manuscripts, see Stillinger 1988. These two manuscripts and later versions of them are in the Winterthur Library.
8. Stillinger 1988, p. 8D. An earlier version of this account appears in "Old New York Furniture: Early Cabinetmakers Whose Work Is Prized Highly," *New York Sun*, August 12, 1894. The writer states that "[t]he part was reproduced in mahogany by the German cabinetmaker [Hagen] at the order of Frederik Bronson. Mr. Bronson, Egerton Winthrop, and Mrs. Horace Hunnewell of Boston now share the original set."
9. The original will, certified November 8, 1854, is housed in the Downs Collection, Winterthur Library. Concerning his father's interviews with Phyfe family descendants, Frederick Hagen relates in a letter, dated February 22, 1915, to Walter Dyer, that "what [information about Phyfe] there is—is absolutely reliable as my father & my self took [a] great deal [of] pain in having this accurate, and we own the old directories. My

father even went over to Jersey City several times to visit the one Phyfe ther [*sic*] and got his information direct, also went to see the New York Phyfes quite often . . . they are the people who have the picture of the Phyfe shop—a Water color" (R. T. Haines Halsey Research Papers, Collection 56, 75x80.38, Downs Collection, Winterthur Library).

10. *New York Sun*, August 12, 1894.
11. "Tell City's History in Hudson Pageant," *New York Times*, September 21, 1909, p. 4.
12. "Art at Home and Abroad," *New York Times*, October 10, 1909, p. SM12.
13. Kent and Levy 1909, pp. ix–x. Ernest Hagen responded to a request from Robert W. de Forest, in anticipation of the Hudson-Fulton exhibition, that he considered it "a compliment" that the Metropolitan wanted to copy his notes on Duncan Phyfe, and went on to offer his assistance "in helping to arrange things for the museum" (Ernest F. Hagen to Robert W. de Forest, July 27, 1909, Hudson-Fulton Celebration, scholarship files, American Wing, Metropolitan Museum). A letter from R. T. Haines Halsey to Florence Levy, again in regard to the exhibition, elucidates his collaboration with Hagen, "my cabinet maker" (Halsey to Levy, June 16, 1909, ibid.).
14. Levy 1909, p. 456.
15. Dyer 1915a, p. 124.
16. Halsey and Cornelius 1922; Heckscher 1997; and Kenny 2000, pp. 188–89, pl. v.
17. Cornelius 1922b. Other publications relating to the exhibition that appeared at this time include Cornelius 1922a and 1922c; and Halsey and Cornelius 1922. Along with Cornelius' article in *The Magazine Antiques* (1922a) is a column titled "Still Shrilling on Phyfe" and an article, "Duncan Phyfe: Artist or Mechanic," by Homer Eaton Keyes, the magazine's editor.
18. Dyer 1915a and 1915b. Cornelius included information that has never been verified. For example, he cites an unidentified gentleman who ordered furniture from Phyfe following his marriage in 1797 and notes that Phyfe received commissions from Philadelphia, New Jersey, and the Hudson Valley as far north as Albany. While the mention of Philadelphia must refer to Charles N. Bancker, whose 1816 invoice is quoted in the text, there was at the time no documentation known for clients residing in the other locations. Cornelius also notes that Phyfe supplied kitchen furniture and that he repaired furniture, facts that have subsequently been corroborated.
19. Cornelius 1922b, p. 36.
20. Ibid., p. 43.
21. Ibid., p. 41.
22. Ibid., p. 48.
23. Cornelius 1922a, p. 205. At the time of Cornelius' writing, the only documented Phyfe furniture published were the pieces that had descended to his great-grandson F. Percy Vail. These were illustrated in Marshall 1915.
24. Hornor 1929, pp. 47–48.
25. Cornelius 1922a, pp. 205, 206.
26. Ibid., p. 206.
27. For a review of the catalogue, see "Current Books and Magazines," *The Magazine Antiques* 3, no. 1 (January 1923), p. 38. For more on Keyes as the first editor of *The Magazine Antiques*, see Stillinger 1980, pp. 197–99.
28. Keyes 1922a, p. 201.
29. Cornelius 1922a, p. 205.
30. Undated manuscript, circa 1930, of a speech or article by Robert W. de Forest (scholarship files, American Wing, Metropolitan Museum), quoted in Peck 2000, p. 181.
31. "Old Colonial Furniture: Genuine Pieces Are Hard to Find, a Dealer Says. Reproductions Are Really Better Than Originals—Hand Work and Machine Work," *New York Times*, January 27, 1901, p. 18. While Ernest F. Hagen is not identified by name, there can be no doubt from the description and commentary that he is indeed the person interviewed.

32. Waters 1996, pp. 66, 78.
33. Hagen 1905.
34. Dyer 1921, p. 72.
35. Halsey's correspondence with E. H. Wileman, instructor of interior decoration at University of California, Los Angeles, on W. & J. Sloane letterhead, expresses his interest in "the thought that American arts and crafts are being taught on the Pacific Coast." He goes on to mention his collaboration with Sloane: "[I]t is possible for Messrs. Sloane to completely furnish houses in Early American style, fine Chippendale, or in the best Sheraton and Phyfe. The project has been a most interesting one, as we have taken a group of the best furniture craftsmen into partnership and their work more than satisfies in quality our fondest expectations" (R. T. H. Halsey to E. H. Wileman, April 18, 1927, R. T. H. Halsey correspondence, scholarship files, American Wing, Metropolitan Museum).
36. The authors would like to thank Cynthia Schaffner for sharing this information from an unpublished manuscript on furniture in the American Wing reproduced by The Company of Master Craftsmen.
37. Hunter 1918; McClure and Eberlein 1918; Eberlein, McClure, and Holloway 1919; and Holloway 1922.
38. C. Stuart 1931.
39. Buck 1935.
40. Advertisement for the Sonora Phonograph Company, Inc., in *McClure's Magazine* 52, no. 3 (March–April 1920), p. 36.
41. Allan B. A. Bradley to Henry W. Kent, November 10, 1922, Loan Exhibitions-Held-1922, Furniture-Duncan Phyfe-Lenders, A-G, 1922–23 (scholarship files, American Wing, Metropolitan Museum).
42. American Art Association, New York, *Colonial Furniture: The Superb Collection of the Late Howard Reifsnyder, Including Signed Pieces by Philadelphia Cabinetmakers Formerly Contained in the Reifsnyder Residence, the Pennsylvania Museum and Mount Pleasant Mansion, Philadelphia . . .*, sale, April 24–27, 1929.
43. "Early American Furniture: Several Collections on View at American Art Galleries," *New York Times*, November 6, 1919, p. 14; and "Phyfe Settee Brings $1,025. Highest Price at Sale of Bosworth Antiques Yielding $36,191," *New York Times*, November 15, 1919, p. 10. For the Phyfe settee, see American Art Association, New York, *Colonial Furniture: The Superb Collection of the Late Howard Reifsnyder . . .*, sale cat., April 24–27, 1929, lot 678, pp. 238–39.
44. Fifth Avenue Auction Rooms, New York, *Catalogue of Rare Antiques*, sale, March 25–27, 1909, lots 63, 258, 283, 488, 500, 526, 565. The auctioneer Henry A. Hartman offered an additional Phyfe piece two years later; see Fifth Avenue Auction Rooms, *Catalogue of a Magnificent Collection of Rare Antiques*, sale cat., March 21–25, 1911, lot 771.
45. Anderson Galleries, New York, *The Wilbur J. Cooke Collection, Philadelphia: Early American & English Furniture, Including Specimens by Duncan Phyfe & Savery*, sale, December 5–8, 1922.
46. Stillinger 1988, p. 14D, fig. 19; and American Art Association, New York, *Duncan Phyfe and Other Fine Early American Furniture and Decorations: The Private Collection of Alexander M. Hudnut, Removed from His Country Residence at Princeton, N.J.*, sale, November 19, 1927. In his professional life as a Wall Street broker and bond dealer, Hudnut was also acquainted with Halsey (R. T. Haines Halsey to Florence Levy, June 16, 1909, Hudson-Fulton Celebration, scholarship files, American Wing, Metropolitan Museum).
47. Anderson Galleries, New York, *Furniture by Duncan Phyfe & Other Early American Craftsmen*, sale, April 20, 1929.
48. For a detailed discussion of this important exhibition, see Cooper 1980, pp. 4–13. See also Stillinger 1980, pp. 202–3, 267–71.
49. Louis Guerineau Myers, "Hepplewhite and Sheraton," in New York 1929, unpaginated.
50. Ibid.

51. Ibid.
52. Stillinger 1980, p. 229.
53. H. F. du Pont to Louis Guerineau Myers, May 1, 1931, Winterthur Archives, Winterthur Library, Box AD45, quoted in Cooper 2002, p. 172.
54. Quoted in C. Montgomery 1966, p. 6.
55. Both publications are in the collection of the Winterthur Library.
56. See the bibliography for the 1929 publications by De Bles, Hornor, Keyes, Ormsbee, C. Stuart, and Valentine.
57. De Bles 1929, p. 341.
58. Hornor 1929, p. 48.
59. Ibid., p. 47.
60. Hornor 1930.
61. Ibid., p. 38.
62. Ibid., p. 39.
63. Marshall 1915.
64. Hornor 1930, p. 96.
65. Storey 1934, p. 39.
66. Letter from Nancy V. McClelland to Mrs. Herman Livingston, Greendale, New York, dated August 10, 1939, with the publisher's announcement of and prospectus for *Duncan Phyfe and the English Regency*, Livingston Family Papers, Beinecke Rare Book and Manuscript Library, Yale University, New Haven. The authors would like to thank Sandra Markham for bringing this letter and the prospectus to their attention.
67. McClelland's precise involvement in the furnishing of the House of History remains uncertain, but she may have been connected through business relationships with New York City dealers Charles Woolsey Lyons and James Graham of Clapp & Graham, who lent furniture and decorations for the installation. E-mail from Diane Shewchuk, Columbia County Historical Society, Kinderhook, New York, to Remi Spriggs Dyll, Bayou Bend Collection, Museum of Fine Arts, Houston, January 22, 2009.
68. McClelland 1939, pp. 296–97.
69. Dietz and Watters 2009, p. 268; and Monkman 2000, pp. 266–71.
70. Abbott 1994, p. 10; and Tracy and Gerdts 1963, especially nos. 41, 59, 67, and 78.
71. Tracy 1981; Jones 1977.
72. Brown 1978, p. vii.
73. Sloane 1987; T. G. Smith 1997; Haygood and Thurlow 2007.
74. Waters 1996.
75. Heckscher 1997, p. 236.

1. Life of a Master Cabinetmaker

"DIED . . . in this city, on Wednesday August 16th, Duncan Phyfe, in the 86th year of his age."[1] Typical in terms of its terseness in a period before the obituary became a staple of newsprint, the *New York Times* notice of Phyfe's death in 1854 may seem an unusual preface to a discussion of the biography and career of the city's most famous cabinetmaker. Yet while marking the conclusion of a long, remarkable life, it also underscores, in its brevity, the myriad questions that Phyfe has left for us to unravel.

In announcing the death of Duncan Phyfe (1770–1854), the *Times* noted that he had attained the venerable age of eighty-six, which concurs with both public and family records. But in the course of retracing the craftsman's steps for this publication, the discovery of his baptismal record reveals that Phyfe was actually eighty-four years old when he died. Typically, the amendment of one's age is an attempt to expunge rather than gain a few years. However, as we came to know Phyfe from the small scattering of documents that illuminate his biography, this discrepancy in date raises the question whether it was a simple error of fact or intentionally altered. The latter explanation would not be out of character for an ambitious personality hoping to accelerate his career.

Highland Origins

The archives of Abernethy and Kincardine parish in northern Scotland record that "Duncan Fife" was born there on April 27, 1770, and baptized two days later (fig. 15).[2] They also document the nuptials of his parents, Isobel Grant (d. 1794) and Donald Fife, on January 8, 1767, as well as the birth and baptism of his older brother, John (1767–1827), on October 1 of that same year.[3]

For Donald Fife, the marriage (his second) appears to have been a propitious one, as signaled by his bride's maiden name, Grant, which identifies her kinship with a large, powerful Scottish clan.[4] As early as 1316, the Grant clan secured title to lands at Strathspey, approximately thirty miles east of Inverness and the legendary Loch Ness, and even four centuries later many members of the clan could be found there. Donald Fife at the time of his marriage to Isobel was employed on the Grant estate. While his occupation has not been identified, it was most likely related to harvesting and processing lumber. Donald and Isobel would have two more sons, James (d. 1817) and Laughlin (ca. 1778–1869), as well as two daughters, Mary and Isabella, whose life dates are unknown.

Following Duncan's birth, the family's whereabouts and movements are sketchy. Archival collections are the only means available to retrace the history of the Fife family, a task made more daunting since few Scottish public records survive from the eighteenth century. Scottish migration coincided with the establishment of the permanent British settlements in North America in the early 1600s. However, it was relatively gradual until 1763, when the conclusion of the French and Indian War prompted a more sizable exodus. Many of the Highland regiments who had fought in America chose to remain rather than to return to Scotland, the majority settling along the New York frontier west of Albany. Highlanders had long been dependent on subsistence agriculture. Improvements made to agricultural practices in the mid-eighteenth century had triggered increases in land rents, and these increases, combined with the region's crippling poverty, mounting overpopulation, and severe climate, would force thousands to leave their homeland and their families in search of more viable opportunities elsewhere. In Britain's North American colonies, Scots saw prospects for a better life.

Early Years in New York

Although family tradition maintains that the Fifes arrived in Albany in the early 1780s, the earliest record to substantiate their presence in New York is the 1790 United States Census.[5] Isobel Phyfe is listed in Albany, a town with a prominent Scottish population, along with two boys under the age of sixteen. Because there is no mention of a father, it is presumed that Donald Fife was by this time deceased.[6] The young boys may well be Duncan's younger brothers James and Laughlin. According to family tradition, the Fifes' daughter Isabella died during the voyage from Scotland and Mary died shortly after their arrival in the United States.[7]

Opposite: Duncan Phyfe's tool chest. The New-York Historical Society, on loan from the families of Henry Pinkney Phyfe and Churchill B. Phyfe

Figure 15. Parish church of Abernethy and Kincardine parish, Scotland. Photograph, 2009

Duncan Phyfe's omission from the 1790 federal census is not surprising, as during this period the compilation specified only the head of household by name. Like most young men his age, Phyfe was most likely no longer living at home. At twenty he would have been completing the final year of his apprenticeship, as a youth's twenty-first birthday marked the legal completion of his indenture. Typically, under the terms of such an agreement, it was understood that "the said Master shall use the utmost of his endeavors to teach, or cause to be taught or instructed the said Apprentice, in the trade or mystery of a Cabinet Maker and procure and provide for him sufficient meat, drink, washing and lodging."[8] Parents were thereby able to transfer the financial burden of rearing their child to a master tradesman, who would then recoup the expenses through the young man's labor.

Once again, while family lore maintains that Phyfe apprenticed in Albany, there is no documentary evidence to place him there. In recognition of his accomplished cabinetmaking skills, it is more likely that he served an apprenticeship in New York City, an urban center with a highly developed furniture-making industry. By the 1780s, New York City was recovering from the devastating years of the American Revolution, when from 1776 to 1783 it was occupied by the British military. The period that followed was characterized by optimism and phenomenal growth (fig. 16). The population increased from 18,000 at the end of the Revolution to 33,000 by 1790. A decade later it had climbed to 60,000, and it stood at 96,000 in 1810. New York was also emerging as the country's leading economic center, attracting financiers active in investment banking and stock trading. In 1790 the city's exports totaled more than $2.5 million, with trade increasing especially to the American South and the West Indies.

Unlike the limited opportunities found in a provincial town such as Albany, New York would have offered great attraction for a young, ambitious craftsman. It is there, in 1792, that we find the earliest mention of "Duncan Fife" in this country, when he was elected to join the General Society of Mechanics & Tradesmen of the City of New York. The General Society had been founded seven years earlier, with its "declared intention . . . to promote mutual fellowship, confidence and good understanding among various descriptions of mechanics; as far as possible to prevent litigation and disputes amongst tradesmen; to promote mechanical knowledge; afford relief to distressed members; and to establish funds to enable the society to carry

24   *Duncan Phyfe*

Figure 16. Charles Balthazar Julien Fevret de Saint-Mémin (1770–1852). [View of the city and harbor of New York, taken from Mount Pitt], 1796. Etching, 12 3/8 × 18 1/4 in. I. N. Phelps Stokes Collection, Miriam and Ira D. Wallach Division of Art, Prints and Photographs, The New York Public Library, Astor, Lenox and Tilden Foundations

their laudable designs into effect."[9] Established business connections were prerequisites for a young cabinetmaker seeking entrée to the organization. Phyfe was nominated by two members in good standing, Isaac Nichols and Seabury Champlin (fig. 17), either of whom may have employed Phyfe as an apprentice.[10]

Diverse in occupation and socioeconomic status, the constituency created broad networking opportunities while supporting the society's benevolent endeavors. By 1805, eighty of the society's members were employed in cabinetmaking trades. Phyfe's business relationship with two members, John J. Post, an upholsterer, and Daniel Turnier, a cabinetmaker, perhaps implies that his membership in the society resulted in new sources for subcontracting.[11] A third, John B. Dash Jr., a tinsmith who later became a prosperous merchant, wrote a recommendation for Phyfe's application for American citizenship in 1803.[12] Phyfe is named as a debtor in Dash's estate records.[13]

The year after he joined the General Society, Duncan Phyfe married Rachel Louzada (ca. 1781–1851), on February 17, 1793. Rachel was descended from Sephardic Jews who had established themselves in New York City by the eighteenth century. Of particular note is Isaac Louzada (ca. 1776–1858), of indeterminate relation to Rachel, who worked there as a cabinetmaker in the first decade of the nineteenth century.[14] The wedding took place at the First Presbyterian Church on Wall Street (fig. 18). Rachel's age at the time of her marriage— if the Manhattan Register of Deaths is correct she would have been either twelve or thirteen—and her marriage to Phyfe given her religious affiliation raise many questions as to societal norms in the 1790s.[15] Rachel was baptized into the Presbyterian church in 1841; the Phyfe children, however, were baptized in the 1790s and early 1800s. Other than the date of Rachel's marriage, baptism, and death, the documentary record reveals nothing about the matriarch of the Phyfe family.

The year of Phyfe's marriage also coincided with his initial appearance in the city directory. Over the next three years, the directories chart the young mechanic's rapid progress. Initially listed as "Duncan Fife," a joiner sharing shop space on Broad Street with the turner and rush-bottom chairmaker Vincent Tillou, he made his debut in New York City's competitive cabinetmaking trade. The following year he dropped the

Life of a Master Cabinetmaker

Figure 17. Membership certificate of Seabury Champlin, designed and engraved by Abraham Godwin (1763–1835). The General Society of Mechanics & Tradesmen of the City of New York, 1791. Engraving with watercolor and wax on laid paper, 8½ × 11⅛ in. Winterthur Museum, Winterthur, Delaware

appellation "joiner" in favor of the term "cabinetmaker," a more fashionable label for mechanics specializing in furniture production, and in 1795 he established his own manufactory at 35 Partition Street (fig. 19). But by far the most intriguing change he made was the revision, in 1794, in the spelling of his family name from "Fife" to "Phyfe," which suggested a more elegant classical derivation without changing the pronunciation. Both the modification of his last name and Phyfe's printed occupation may be interpreted as attempts to promote an image of sophistication; they suggest an ambitious craftsman repositioning himself in an effort to launch a profitable enterprise.

In moving uptown from Broad Street to Partition Street, Phyfe traded the crowded streetscape of traditional Dutch stepped-gable façades and Georgian-style buildings occupied by merchants, craftsmen, and gentlemen for a newly built mixed-use neighborhood west of Broadway. In 1794, François-Alexandre-Frédéric, duc de La Rochefoucauld-Liancourt, a French visitor to New York, admired this "new part of the city built adjoining to Hudson's River," which was "infinitely more handsome, the streets there being straight, broad, and better built."[16] Partition Street led from Broadway to the city's docks along the Hudson, an ideal location that facilitated access to the ships bringing raw materials into the city and departing with furniture and other manufactured goods. There Phyfe would live, work, and add to his real estate holdings for the rest of his life.

Early Career

From his headquarters on Partition Street, Phyfe began to establish himself as a notable cabinetmaker, as well as the patriarch of the Phyfe family. Rachel gave birth to their first child, Michael (1794–1836), in 1794, and when Phyfe's mother died in Albany that same year, it was Duncan and not his older brother John who traveled upstate to settle her affairs.[17] John, however, likely supervised his brother's business dealings in New York. He first appears in the 1794 directory as a cartman, an individual who hauls goods, at 38 Dey Street, which shared a rear property line with Phyfe's house and shop at 35 Partition. Although cartmen were independent operators licensed by the city, John Fife was perhaps regularly engaged by his brother to transport wood as well as finished furniture for the cabinet shop. The early nineteenth century witnessed increased specialization among carters, particularly among those who practiced "fine arts carting," which required a spring cart and "other fixtures suitable for removing pictures, looking glasses, and all other kinds of household furniture with care and dispatch."[18]

Phyfe's Partition Street address became increasingly prominent at this time. Not only was the building catercorner from the venerable St. Paul's Chapel, but in 1800 the city's Common Council announced its intention to build a new City Hall in the wedge-shaped park bounded by Broadway, Chatham Row, and Murray Street (fig. 20). The commission was awarded to the French-born architect Joseph François Mangin and John

26   *Duncan Phyfe*

Figure 18. Johan-Heinrich Jenny (1786–1854). *View of Wall Street, New York, in 1820,* 1820, showing the First Presbyterian Church on the right. Oil on canvas, 34½ × 28 in. Private collection

Figure 19. Cornelius Tiebout (1777–1832) after John McComb Jr. (1763–1853). New York City map from *The New-York Directory and Register for the Year 1789* (1789), showing the location of Phyfe's home and manufactory on Partition Street. Copperplate engraving, 8⅞ × 14⅜ in. The New-York Historical Society

Life of a Master Cabinetmaker

Figure 20. George Hayward (ca. 1800–ca. 1872) after John Evers (1797–1884). *View of City Hall, Park Theatre, Broadway & Chatham St. &c*, 1822. Lithograph, 7⅞ × 14¾ in. Eno Collection, Miriam and Ira D. Wallach Division of Art, Prints and Photographs, The New York Public Library, Astor, Lenox and Tilden Foundations

McComb Jr., whose refined structure would come to be recognized as the signature Neoclassical-style building of Republican New York.

Phyfe's surroundings had improved in accordance with the wealth and social station of his patrons. His earliest documented customer, Thomasin Gordon, a boardinghouse operator on Greenwich Street, is known through a 1796 court case rather than an extant bill.[19] The New York court system would prove to be a noteworthy means of recovering past-due debts from wayward patrons throughout Phyfe's career. Only two other recorded sales are known from the 1790s, both in 1798: the purchases of a coffin by Jane Bruce, widow of John, a tanner on Partition Street, and a pair of tables by John Cruger, a wealthy merchant.[20]

During these early years, Phyfe's clients turned to him for the repair and refinishing of used furniture as well as the purchase of new wares. Between 1804 and 1807, for example, Phyfe billed George and Catherine Brewerton for a variety of services, including varnishing chairs, mending bedsteads, and altering blinds; they also purchased a new dining table.[21] However, the patronage of prominent New York merchant Edmund Morewood in 1802 and Scottish immigrant scholar and financier George P. MacCulloch in 1806 foreshadows Phyfe's ability to fill a substantial commission, such as the one received from the New York merchant William Bayard in 1807.[22]

Bayard, a scion of an old New Jersey family and related by marriage to the Livingstons, the Van Cortlandts, and the Stuyvesants—all members of New York's propertied elite—was the principal partner in one of the city's premier mercantile houses, Le Roy, Bayard & McEvers. In 1806 he moved from Greenwich Street to a far grander town house on State Street, with a sweeping view of the Battery and New York Harbor.[23] In November 1807, Bayard ordered an extensive quantity of furniture in two bills totaling $1,779. He returned to Phyfe for more furniture in 1809 and 1810, and in 1819 he issued a payment for undisclosed goods or services for $1,305.77.

Phyfe was emerging as an established mechanic by the time he became an American citizen in 1803.[24] Unlike his highly regarded competitor Charles-Honoré Lannuier (1779–1819), who immigrated to the city the same year Phyfe gained citizenship and could parlay his Parisian training into greater patronage, Phyfe did not have as much to gain by promoting his Highland roots. Perhaps to distinguish his qualifications from the promotional exoticism of Lannuier, Phyfe embraced his adopted country as he became more prominent in the New York trade.

A silver-lidded cowrie shell snuffbox adorned with a cast thistle, symbol of Scotland, is a rare illustration of Phyfe's appreciation of his Scottish heritage (fig. 21). However, his absence from the roster of the Saint Andrew's Society, a Scottish charitable organization, perhaps implies ambivalence to that birthright not shared with his older brother John (who joined in 1817) and nephews William F. (1834) and Robert (also 1834).[25]

Further exemplifying Phyfe's expanding role in the city's cabinetmaking industry are his first documented forays into the export market, albeit limited to bespoke work rather than speculative manufacturing. Phyfe's wares were found in Savannah, Georgia, as early as 1802, when the wealthy planter William Gibbons Jr. returned from New York having ordered a tea table and a pair of card tables from the cabinetmaker's shop.[26] Charles N. Bancker, a former New Yorker living in Philadelphia, paid Phyfe for a sideboard sent to him in 1804.[27]

Shipments of Phyfe's furniture headed as far afield as the French settlement at Pointe-à-Pitre, in the colony of Guadeloupe, in 1805 through the assistance of the French expatriate Victor Marie du Pont, great-uncle of Henry Francis du Pont, whose commission house was in New York City. According to a letter from R. de Rezeville, du Pont's associate in Guadeloupe, Phyfe's wares met a ready market there: "The 6 mahogany Bedsteads were elegant & they fetch'd the price of 50 [dollars] each. My little beds have sold wonderfully, so much so that I have not been able to keep a single one for myself.... Go to Phyfe in Partition Street and order 12 beds made exactly like mine, only 6 in. and 9 in. wider; also some pretty chests of drawers; but above all no inlay, they don't like it here."[28]

Rezeville's one concern was with the method of packing furniture for export, and he implored du Pont to "supervise the crating, because American furniture always arrives here in poor condition due to carelessness."[29] Phyfe charged an additional fee for furniture that required crating for shipment. Of the $50 charged for a dining table sent to Lady Elizabeth Heylinger of Saint Croix in 1811, $4 went toward the cost of packing.[30] Out-of-town purchasers, or their local agents, then arranged transportation and insurance for the furniture.

Phyfe's nascent efforts to advance his name and reputation beyond New York City were greatly hindered by the passage of the Non-Importation and Embargo Acts of 1806 and 1807, respectively. The resumption of the Napoleonic Wars in 1803 had reignited the struggle between Great Britain and France for European supremacy. After Britain established a blockade of the European continent in 1806, it began subjecting American vessels to search and seizure, and their sailors to forcible impressments. Toward the end of 1807, President Thomas Jefferson, in an effort to protect American sailors from being seized by the British Navy and to avoid war with Britain, instituted the Embargo Act, which prohibited American ships from entering foreign ports and restricted trade along the American coast. Thus, American cabinetmakers were left with limited access to imported hardware and textiles from Europe, lumber from the West Indies, and open markets in the American South and the Caribbean.

Jefferson's Democratic-Republican Party (the forerunner of today's Democratic Party), which supported the Embargo Act, suggested that the legislation would encourage the development of domestic manufactures, thereby making the country less dependent on imported foreign goods. But as its opponent, the Federalist Party, predicted, the embargo proved disastrous for New York, as it did for the entire country. Its impact was observed firsthand by the British traveler John Lambert in November 1807 and April 1808. During his first visit, Lambert remarked: "Everything was in motion. All was life, bustle and activity. The people were scampering in all direction to trade with each other." When he returned, five months later, he was stunned by the contrast: "How shall I describe the melancholy dejection that was painted upon the countenances of the people." The embargo had "completely annihilated foreign commerce" in the nation's primary commercial city.[31] This was the first of many economic storms that Phyfe's cabinetmaking business would weather.

With an understanding of the significance of international trade, Phyfe encouraged the Federalist Party's political platform, which supported commercial interests. His name is included on a roster of the New York City chapter of the Washington Benevolent Society from 1810 to 1812.[32] While founded with the laudable goal of educating underprivileged boys, this pro-British organization served as a vocal supporter of the Federalist attack on Jefferson's pro-French Democratic-Republicans of Tammany Hall in the era leading up to the War

Figure 21. Snuffbox. Possibly New York City, ca. 1810–15. Silver, cowrie shell, 3 × 2⅜ × 1¾ in. Collection of Glorianna H. Gibbon

Life of a Master Cabinetmaker

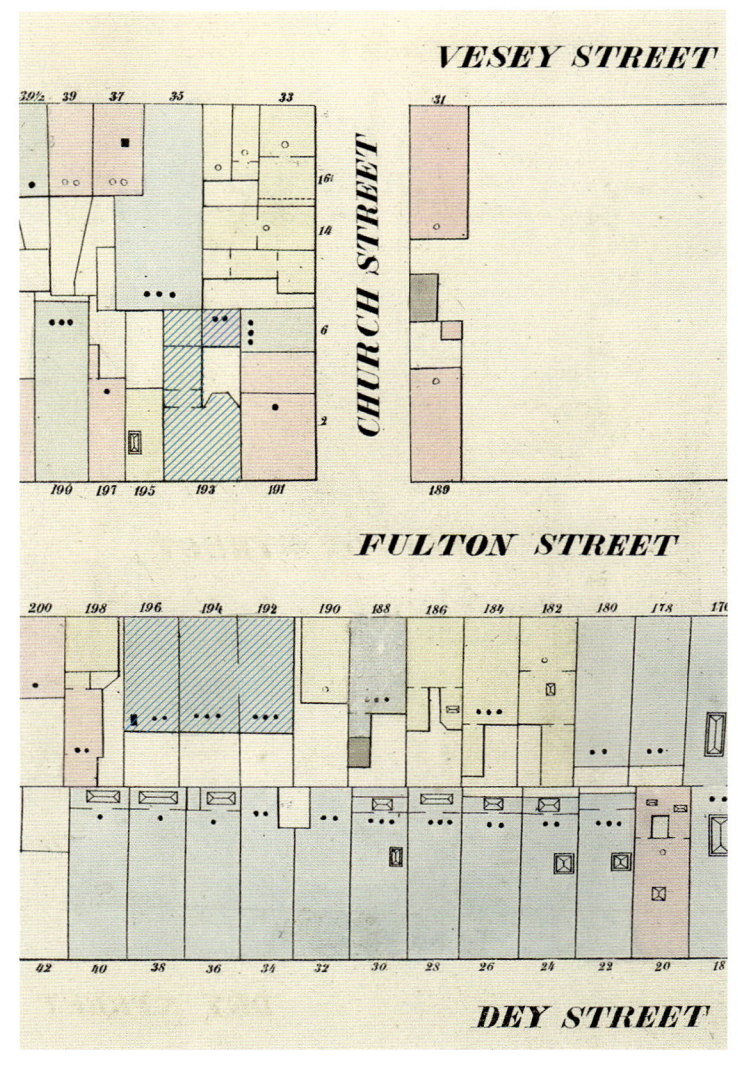

Figure 22. Map showing site of Phyfe's workshops and warehouse and his home across the street (indicated by hatching). William Perris, *Maps of the City of New York* . . . vol. 1 (1852), pls. 7–9. Lithograph, 25 × 34¼ in. The Lionel Pincus and Princess Firyal Map Division, The New York Public Library, Astor, Lenox and Tilden Foundations

of 1812. Phyfe's compatriots in the society included fellow master cabinetmakers William Mandeville and William Dove, as well as prominent New York grandees such as Gulian Crommelin Verplanck. Phyfe's name also appears in 1810 as a commissioner for the mayor's court under DeWitt Clinton, a Democratic-Republican turned avid Federalist, and in 1821 as the Third Ward's representative for the Independent Republican Electors, the successor party to the Federalists.[33]

Phyfe's appointment to the New York City fire department during this period indicates that he had emerged as an artisan of some standing. From 1806 to 1813, he belonged to the Third Ward's Fire Company No. 16. Membership in the fire company also provided Phyfe with social outlets, as such groups were characterized as gentlemen's clubs and populated by upwardly mobile tradesmen. Furthermore, the threat of fire was never far from a mechanic's mind, especially in a trade such as cabinetmaking, which involved highly combustible materials such as seasoned wood, sawdust, and varnish. Phyfe's company helped fight the Great Fire of 1811 in the area surrounding Chatham Street, which destroyed more than one hundred houses.

On Partition Street

Although Phyfe's early financial success is evident through court records and bills of sale, his accumulation of property on Partition Street between 1795 and 1807 also suggests a cabinetmaker on the rise. Phyfe quickly achieved what has been referred to as "proprietary independence," the freedom enjoyed by an artisan who has become a landowner or leaseholder operating as his own master.[34] While he first rented in the Third Ward, he went on to purchase Nos. 29, 31, 33, and 35 Partition Street between 1802 and 1807, for a combined sum of $12,125.[35] No. 35 was the family residence until 1806. By this time the family had expanded to include Michael, Mary (1795–1870), Eliza (1801–1890), and William (1803–1875), leading Duncan and Rachel to move with their children across the street to 34 Partition. Phyfe rented that residence until he purchased the lease rights for $9,250 in 1815, by which time Rachel had given birth to Edward (1808–1887), Isabella (ca. 1814–1841), and James Duncan (1814–1887). Another strong indicator of Phyfe's success is the exponential increase in the assessed value of his personal estate, which rose from $50 in 1795 to $200 in 1802, $800 in 1809, and $3,000 in 1815. The Phyfes' world was not without sadness during these early years. As was common in this time period, they lost two sons in infancy.[36]

Phyfe's holdings at Nos. 31, 33, and 35 Partition became the nexus of his manufacturing complex, which became Nos. 168, 170, and 172 Fulton Street when the thoroughfare was renamed in honor of the inventor and engineer Robert Fulton (1765–1815) in 1817 and then Nos. 192, 194, and 196 Fulton after the street was renumbered in 1827 (fig. 22). As his workshop expanded, Phyfe printed new labels and trade cards and updated his directory listing (figs. 23–26). He also extended his work area southward in 1818 after procuring 38 Dey Street, a house and lot formerly occupied by his brother John that abutted the rear of 172 Fulton. Duncan's eldest son, Michael, is listed as a cabinetmaker at 38 Dey from 1818 to 1823, and an 1832 court case indicates that a shed in the rear yard served as lumber storage for Phyfe's workshop.[37]

It would seem logical to expect that, as Phyfe's manufactory and landholdings expanded, he turned to his siblings and sons to help him manage the cabinetmaking business and oversee his investment properties. Throughout his life, Phyfe endeavored to ensure that his family shared in and benefited from his success. Phyfe's younger brothers James and Laughlin

30 *Duncan Phyfe*

(fig. 27) were affiliated with his cabinet shop in New York, but they remain enigmatic figures throughout their lives. The 1790 census records a James Fife in Baltimore County, Maryland, who also appears without an occupation in the Baltimore city directory of 1796.[38] The Phyfe family had no documented ties to that city, but a post office notice locates Laughlin in Baltimore by 1800, and in 1807 and 1808 the city directories place him at Robert Fisher's fancy chair shop at 37 South Gay Street.[39] Baltimore was an attractive destination for a cabinetmaker in need of work. In the last quarter of the eighteenth century, it emerged as one of the fastest-growing port cities on the Atlantic seaboard. Merchants grew wealthy on the steady profits from domestic and international exchange, and they supported a thriving cabinet trade. To satisfy this growing demand, furniture makers occasionally recruited journeymen from New York City, such as when Baltimorean Henry Purcell advertised in the *New-York Gazette and General Advertiser* on May 21, 1800, that "the highest prices and constant employ, will be given to Two Journeymen Cabinet Makers, who are sober and attentive to business."

Although they struck out on their own initially, both James and Laughlin eventually found employment in Duncan's workshop in New York. James signed two receipts in 1807, the assumption being that Duncan had passed on to James the authority to transact business when he was out of the shop.[40] James eventually moved to Philadelphia, where he died in 1817. Laughlin was in New York by 1812, when as a cabinetmaker on Partition Street, presumably working for his brother, he was appointed to the fire department.[41] The authors have found no additional references to Laughlin's association with Phyfe's shop, but family tradition maintains that he worked there for the remainder of his career, was the most talented cabinetmaker in the shop, and traveled to England to purchase hardware on Duncan's behalf.[42] Perhaps in recognition of his brother's dutiful service, Duncan included in his will a stipend to Laughlin of $420 per year.

As Duncan Phyfe's younger brothers found employment in the cabinet and related trades, so did three of his sons, Michael, William, and James D. Presumably, all three apprenticed in their father's shop. A fourth son, Edward D., never appears in the city directory and was unmarried and living with his parents at the time of the 1850 census.

Michael is listed in the city directories as a cabinetmaker from 1818 to 1827. After vacating his father's property at 38 Dey Street, he spent three years making furniture at 31 Harrison. By 1831 he is a dealer in mahogany and lumber in partnership with John Turnbull at 33 Harrison. Cabinetmakers occasionally abandoned their profession for such mercantile pursuits, as skilled woodworkers were well equipped to judge the quality and value of the wood being imported to New York City. Michael

Figure 23. Label used at 35 Partition Street, Phyfe's business address from 1795 to 1811

Figure 24. Label used at 33 and 35 Partition Street, Phyfe's business address from 1811 to 1816

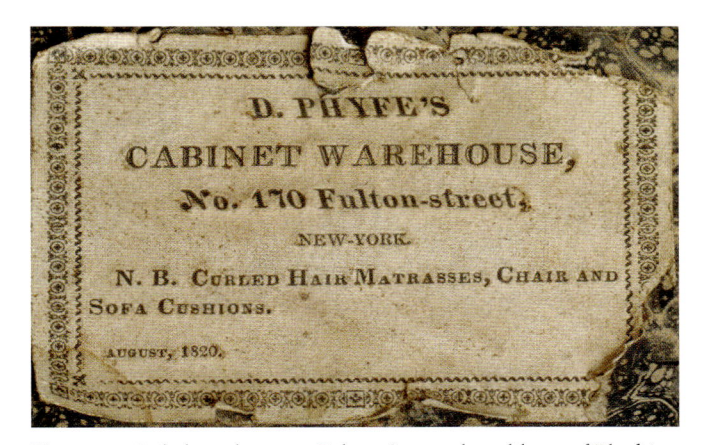

Figure 25. Label used at 170 Fulton Street, the address of Phyfe's cabinet warehouse from 1817 to 1826

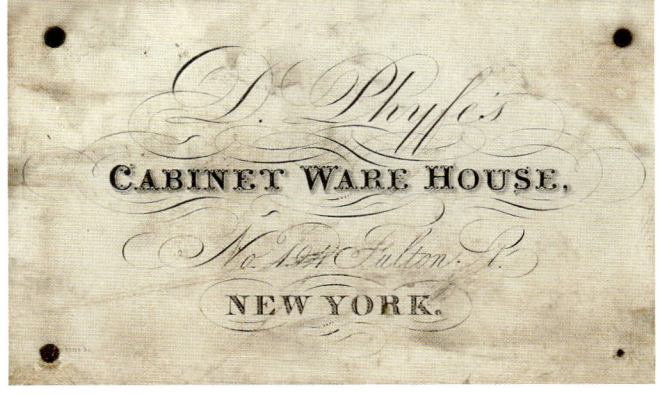

Figure 26. Trade card used by Duncan Phyfe at 194 Fulton Street from 1827 to 1837. The New-York Historical Society

Life of a Master Cabinetmaker 31

eventually moved to Rahway, New Jersey, where he died in 1836. The ever-supportive Phyfe likely provided capital for Michael's endeavors. He also adopted his three orphaned grandchildren after his son's death, and employed Michael's eldest son, Duncan (b. 1818), in the Fulton Street shop.[43] To each grandchild he bequeathed $14,000 in his will.

James D. (fig. 28) and William first appear in the city directories in 1837, when they were taken on as partners in their father's cabinetmaking business, which was then renamed D. Phyfe & Sons (fig. 29). While this is the first documentation of James' involvement in the family trade, William's signature is on a bill dated 1825, which he signed on his father's behalf at the age of twenty-two.[44] Between 1827 and 1836, William operated a large farm in Hudson, New York, purchased with $10,000 provided by his father.[45] Presumably, William returned to the Fulton Street workshop and worked alongside his brother until the partnership with Duncan was formalized. The arrangement was short-lived, as William opened a turpentine store in 1841, a naval supply store the following year, and later relocated to Stamford, Connecticut. The firm became D. Phyfe & Son, and James remained at his father's side until the shop closed in 1847.

In addition to rearing four sons, Duncan and Rachel Phyfe had three daughters. The eldest, Mary (fig. 30), married Capt. Sidney B. Whitlock (1794–1849) in 1818. Sidney followed in the footsteps of his father, a sea captain, and established a shipping company with his brother William Jr., but later became a ship chandler.[46] During their first years of marriage, the young couple lived at 171 Fulton Street, next door to Mary's parents and in a house owned by them. Speculative investments in Brooklyn property turned sour for Sidney and Mary in 1843, and Edward D. Phyfe foreclosed on a mortgage co-signed for them by Duncan.[47] The Whitlocks continued to live in grand style, however, for the elder Phyfe in 1843 had presented them with the Mitchell S. Mitchell estate in Southbury, Connecticut (fig. 31).[48]

The second daughter, Eliza (fig. 32), became the wife of William Vail Jr. (1802–1875), a partner in the dry goods firm of Vail & Reed, in 1825 (see fig. 184). The couple left New York by 1832 and settled in New Market (now

Figure 27. Laughlin Phyfe (ca. 1778–1869). Photograph, ca. 1860. Collection of Glorianna H. Gibbon

Figure 28. Unidentified artist. *James D. Phyfe*, ca. 1845. Oil on canvas, 41½ × 31¾ in. (framed). Collection of Glorianna H. Gibbon

Duncan Phyfe

Figure 29. Trade card used at 194 Fulton Street, 1837–40

Figure 31. "Mitchell's Mansion House, Southbury," from *Connecticut Historical Collections* (1836)

Piscataway), New Jersey, Vail's hometown. Between 1849 and 1851, they built Valmere, a grand Greek Revival house on a thirty-two-acre parcel purchased from William Vail Sr. in 1830 (see fig. 186). A large collection of furniture dating from their marriage in 1825 and the late 1830s remains in the hands of their descendants.

The Phyfes' youngest daughter, Isabella, named for Duncan's mother, is known only through reports of her alleged suicide in 1841, when she disappeared from a steamboat making an overnight passing between Providence, Rhode Island, and New York City. In the article that reported the event, Isabella is described as having been "in a distressed

Figure 30. Mary Phyfe Whitlock (1795–1870). Photograph, ca. 1860. Collection of Glorianna H. Gibbon

Figure 32. Eliza Phyfe Vail (1801–1890). Photograph, ca. 1870. Collection of Glorianna H. Gibbon

Life of a Master Cabinetmaker 33

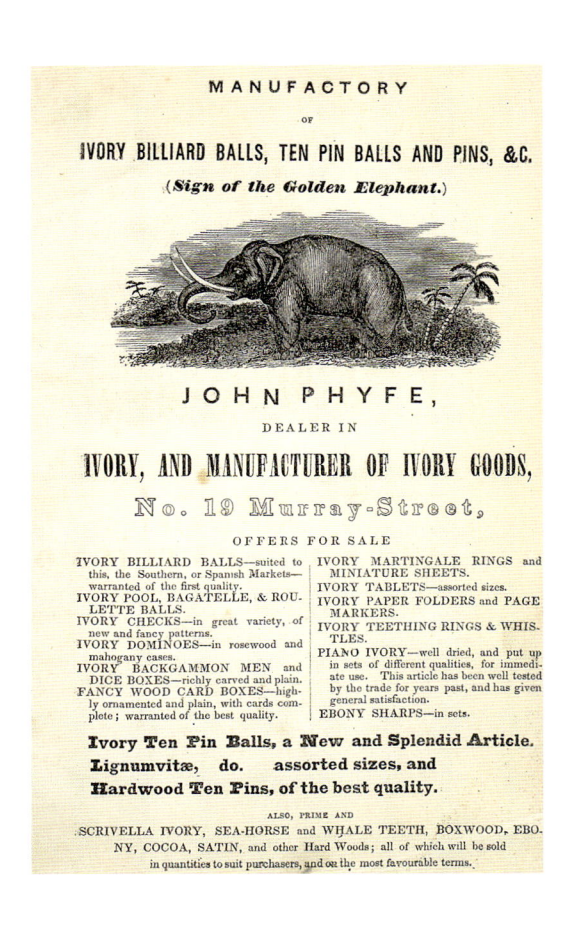

Figure 33. John Phyfe Jr. Advertisement in *Doggett's New-York City Directory for 1843 & 1844* (1843). The New-York Historical Society

Figure 34. View of James Phyfe's shop at 43 Maiden Lane, from *The New York Pictorial Business Directory of Maiden Lane* (1849). Lithograph, 8¼ × 9⅞ in. The New-York Historical Society

state of mind for several weeks past . . . supposed to have escaped from her berth in her night clothes, through the window of the Saloon, and jumped or fallen overboard."[49] Isabella was not baptized until the year of her death, and we surmise that she received this rite in recognition of her declining mental condition. It is testimony to the grief suffered by her parents that they offered the extraordinary reward of $500 for the recovery of her body, although there is no record of its being found.[50]

Although Phyfe's older brother, John, was possibly associated with the cabinet trade in the 1790s as a cartman, six of his seven sons who lived to adulthood worked in furniture-related businesses. Isaac M. Phyfe (1796–1881) found employment as a pianoforte maker, paperhanger, and upholsterer. And John Jr. (1798–1872) was trained as an ivory turner under James Ruthven & Son, heralded as the "great ivory and hardwood turners of their day" (fig. 33).[51] James (1800–1887) worked as a carver from 1821 to 1824, before partnering with his younger brothers William (1803–1842), Robert (1805–1890), and George (1812–1857) to form a series of upholstery shops under the titles J. & W. F. Phyfe (1824–33), R. & W. F. Phyfe (1833–35), Phyfe & Brother (1835–43), James and George Phyfe (1843–47), and James Phyfe (1847–51) (fig. 34).[52] These businesses advertised a variety of products and services—from upholstery trims to hair and feather mattresses and imported paper hangings—but they always operated independently of the older brother Isaac, who worked in the trade. The firm is known to have provided window treatments and bed hangings in 1842 for Millford, the South Carolina plantation residence of John Laurence and Susan Hampton Manning, who also purchased furniture from D. Phyfe & Son.[53]

The Community of Craftsmen

In addition to family members, Phyfe was associated with a network of New York City craftsmen, recognizing the advantages in belonging to such a community, which constituted a dynamic and influential workforce in the city. Considering the large number of mechanics working in the cabinetmaking-related trades, there is a dearth of manuscript documentation about these artisans. During Phyfe's fifty-five-year career, ledgers and account books are known from only seven New York craftsmen in cabinetmaking and allied trades: five furniture makers (Fenwick Lyell, John Hewitt, David Loring, Daniel Turnier, and Elisha Blossom Jr.), a turner (James Ruthven), and a cabinetmaker turned hardware and lumber dealer (Charles Watts Sr.).[54] Considering the scarcity of these primary sources, it is telling that within this limited body of material, three of these individuals conducted business with Duncan Phyfe and the work of a fourth was greatly influenced by him.

The records of Fenwick Lyell (1767–1822), a cabinetmaker working on Beaver Street between 1795 and 1809,

Duncan Phyfe

include occasional transactions with Phyfe, as well as with prominent New York cabinetmakers Elbert Anderson, Jacob Brouwer, Samuel and William Burling, William Dove, and the firm of Abraham Slover and Jacob Taylor.[55] In 1802, Lyell purchased an easy chair frame from Phyfe, applied casters to the legs, and then sold the chair to upholsterer John J. Post, who presumably covered it for a customer.[56] In turn, Phyfe purchased sofa frames from Lyell to be upholstered by a separate subcontractor.[57]

Upholstery was a distinct and specialized craft within the furniture trade. Many cabinet shops did not employ an in-house upholsterer, and this work was delegated to independent craftsmen. The upholsterer Lawrence Ackerman's name is inscribed alongside Phyfe's on a sofa dated 1804 and on an library chair dated 1811, suggesting that he provided Phyfe with such assistance.[58] From the mid-1810s onward, Phyfe likely retained the services of upholsterers willing to work in-house, and in Joshua Shaw's *United States Directory for the Use of Travellers and Merchants*, of 1822, he is listed as a "Cabinet-maker & Upholsterer."

Lyell's reputation as a specialist for manufacturing knife boxes was widely known through his newspaper advertisements, and Duncan Phyfe is recorded as placing an order for them in January 1809.[59] Lyell's account book entry specifies "1 Pair of Knife Cases / Veneers found," suggesting that Phyfe supplied the mahogany veneer applied to the exterior of the boxes. Perhaps he did so to ensure that the veneers were consistent with his preference and that they would match the veneers on an en suite sideboard ordered from Phyfe. The account lists the boxes at £16, a seemingly precious sum compared with the £13.12.0 Lyell charged Phyfe for the sofa frames. As Lyell was someone he contracted with only on occasion, possibly Phyfe's own journeymen typically supplied this form. Producing such specialty items in-house enabled Phyfe to maintain the level of quality he desired, as well as to reduce the expenses incurred by jobbing out the work.

References to extensive purchases of furniture hardware by Duncan Phyfe appear in the account books of Charles Watts Sr. (ca. 1756–1811).[60] Like Phyfe, Watts was a native of Scotland who immigrated to New York by 1789. He quickly relocated to Charleston, but maintained a presence in New York, where he amassed extensive real estate holdings. In Charleston he entered cabinetmaking partnerships with Thomas Wallace (1758–1816) and Robert Walker (1772–1833), both also Scots who moved to Charleston from New York. The success that Watts realized in South Carolina can be inferred from his advertisement, which was published in the *New York Diary* on January 28, 1797, inviting eight to fifteen journeymen cabinet- and chairmakers to leave New York and relocate to Charleston, "where they will receive generous encouragement."

Watts parlayed the profits of his cabinetmaking firms into considerable investments made in British and West Indian venture cargo, notably hardware and exotic hardwoods. His six account books, spanning the years 1802 to 1815, document his travels to England and Scotland, as well as the importation of mahogany from Santo Domingo and hardware from Liverpool.[61] In addition to Duncan Phyfe, Watts' clientele included a number of prominent cabinetmakers, upholsterers, and turners in New York, including Michael Allison, Elbert Anderson, Jacob Brouwer, William Burling, John T. Dolan, and William Mandeville, and artisans in Charleston and Scotland. Phyfe's extensive purchases of hardware from Watts suggest that Watts was among his principal suppliers. Phyfe was also associated with the New York hardware manufacturer Andrew Thorp, whose marked casters appear on a canterbury that descended in the family of Eliza Phyfe Vail (see fig. 128).

Phyfe conducted business with a second New York cabinetmaker, Daniel Turnier, a member of the General Society of Mechanics and Tradesmen who worked at 417 Pearl Street from 1820 to 1826.[62] Turnier recorded the sale to Phyfe of cherry, white wood (or poplar), and pine boards, veneer, hardware, and furniture legs.

Considered as a whole, these accounts indicate that Phyfe turned to other craftsmen on a limited basis but found a reliable source for hardware in Watts. It is also notable that Phyfe looked outside his immediate vicinity for subcontracting. Neither Lyell, Ackerman, nor Turnier worked in close proximity to his manufactory. Phyfe settled his debts in both cash and furniture, but we are unable to say whether the goods he offered as payment were for the recipient's personal use or for resale. Between 1803 and 1811, for instance, Phyfe provided Watts with a bedstead, a tea table, a secretary and bookcase, two stands, a chest of drawers, a chamber table, and a footboard for a bedstead.[63]

Whereas the account books of Lyell and Watts, together with the notations in Turnier's price book, are central to understanding the complexity that characterizes the interactions within the New York cabinet trade, the daybook maintained by their contemporary John Hewitt (1777–1857) is unusual for the detail in which it relates one craftsman's perceptions of his contemporaries' designs and the influence they had on his shop production.[64]

Hewitt's most intriguing entries are his appraisals of the work of Phyfe and Lannuier. Hewitt recognized the salability of Phyfe's furniture and was probably also aware of his reputation and success. In March 1811 he recorded a customer's request for a "French Sideboard like Phyfes" with "2 shelves in center and as many locks as possible," for which he billed $80—a figure consistent with most of his recorded examples of this form. Another entry from that same month specifies his observations and analysis of Phyfe's, as well as Lannuier's, furniture: "Phyfe Collum 23 [28?] Inches with leafe carv'd 2⁸⁄₇ wide / Lanuas Collum 2 ft 3 Long 2½ Wide Bottom," suggesting a desire to compete with the two preeminent shops in New York.⁶⁵

"Mr. Phyfe . . . so much the United States rage"

Phyfe was clearly a respected and highly sought-after craftsman at an early date, and he was described as such from the 1810s through the end of his career. Despite the limitations on international and coastwise shipping experienced during the War of 1812, the New York cabinetmaking trade continued to operate, albeit at a reduced level. The situation appeared dire at the outset of the hostilities. In October 1812, Sarah Huger cautioned her friend Harriott Pinckney Horry in Charleston against ordering furniture from New York, as it would not be prudent "in these disastrous times" to incur "the risk of the seas."⁶⁶ Nevertheless, we can document the patronage of six customers during the first eighteen months of the war, indicating that consumer confidence remained high. The account books of Phyfe's contemporary John Hewitt indicate a steady business during this period as well.⁶⁷ However, the situation may have worsened over the course of the war, as we have yet to document a single business transaction involving Phyfe between December 1813 and March 1815, the longest such stretch from 1801 through 1827.

Thus Phyfe had reason to celebrate the war's end, and his patriotic fervor crescendoed during a grand illumination of the city of New York. In February 1815 he strung a series of transparent lamps, commissioned from the portrait painter John Wesley Jarvis, across Partition Street between his house and warehouse. The presentation included a portrait of George Washington and the names of prominent naval heroes. In his "centre store," Phyfe hung a "transparency with a figure resembling Justice and Liberty standing on a pedestal, the Eagle and Lion drinking out of a bowl [next to] emblems of commerce, and in the foreground, implements of war, destroyed and scattered around. . . . Mr. P[hyfe]'s elegant assortment of furniture was fancifully displayed in the window so as to produce on the whole a fine [effect]."⁶⁸ This installation clearly illustrated Phyfe's hope that American and British relations would quickly refocus on the prosperous trade that previously existed between them. The Federalist Party, to which Phyfe belonged, hosted a grand ball at Washington Hall, which was the "most splendid and brilliant display of beauty and fashion that had ever before been seen in this city."⁶⁹ According to family tradition Phyfe, to mark the cessation of hostilities with Britain, presented Rachel with a tea service by the local silversmith William B. Heyer (fig. 35).⁷⁰

When trade resumed following the war, the resulting economic boom propelled Phyfe's cabinetmaking business to new heights. During this period, customers endured long waits for their orders and paid a premium for his wares. Sarah Elliott Huger deftly describes the aggravation of ordering from the celebrated Phyfe in a January 4, 1816, letter to the friend she had previously cautioned against purchasing furniture in New York:

> Mr. Phyfe is so much the United States rage, that it is with difficulty now, that one can procure an audience even of a few moments; not a week since I waited in company with a dozen others, at least an hour [in] his cold shop and after all, was obliged to return home, without seeing the "great man"; however a few days since "That happy chance which oft decides the fate of Kings" decided mine, for I had the great and good fortune to arrive at his house just at the moment he was entering and consequently extorted from him another promise that the furniture should certainly be finished in three weeks, but like the promises of other important personages, I fear they are little to be relied on; for the last three months he has said every week that in ten days [my sister] should have her Tables &c&c, but never have they made their appearance, and yet they were engaged last June.⁷¹

Thus, not only did Phyfe refuse to provide Huger with a firm date for delivery, he was also unwilling to commit to an estimate of the tables' cost. As Sarah explained to her friend, "he cant tell precisely what will be the price" until the work was finished.

Phyfe often placated anxious customers by explaining that the delays were necessary to ensure the highest quality of craftsmanship. In 1813 he told Victor du Pont's factor, Anthony Girard, that a worktable ordered for the wedding of du Pont's niece and namesake, Victorine du Pont, was not ready because he "wanted it to be made by . . . workmen who best [understand] this kind of work," those workmen presumably being occupied with other projects.⁷² When Jane Bowne Haines wrote to her sister Sarah Minturn in 1819 to inquire about a sofa ordered for Wyck, her husband's home in Germantown, Pennsylvania, the response was similar. Minturn replied that although it "will not be ready by the time thee wishes," Phyfe had assured her that he had taken "great pains to select the handsomest wood—the nicest hair[cloth] etc," and insisted that "he must not be hurried as he wishes to finish it in a manner to do himself credit and give satisfaction to the Lady who sent for it. He seemed much pleased when he heard it was to go to Phila[delphia]. And said he should exert himself to have it surpass any that could be made there."⁷³ Such delays were likely limited to bespoke work, and illustrate Phyfe's concern with satisfying his more prominent patrons, in particular those in export markets where he hoped to gain a foothold. Minturn's letter also implies the theatrical nature of Phyfe's customer relations.

36 *Duncan Phyfe*

Figure 35. William B. Heyer (1776–1828). Silver tea service, ca. 1815. Collection of Glorianna H. Gibbon

Nevertheless, the Haines sofa (see fig. 158) is remarkable more for its unusual length of 96¼ inches than for its mahogany veneer, which cannot be considered exceptional when compared with the figured wood found on other furniture documented to Phyfe's workshop.

Issues with delays extended into the latter part of Phyfe's career as well, and resulted in some hardship for Lewis and Sarah Turnbull Stirling of Wakefield in St. Francisville, Louisiana.[74] Four months after they had placed an order with Phyfe, which included two bespoke pier tables (fig. 36), a sideboard table (see fig. 174), a dining table, and nine high-post bedsteads, the Stirlings were still living with their daughter and son-in-law, as their furniture had not yet arrived. According to Lewis, they could not occupy their new home until the bedsteads from Phyfe were installed.

The buying patterns exhibited by Huger, du Pont, the Haineses, and the Stirlings also reinforce the notion that a limited percentage of Phyfe's customers purchased large quantities of furniture from his warehouse. Most of Phyfe's clientele were juxtaposing the products of his workshop with those of one or two other New York cabinet- and chairmakers, whose interpretation of the current style often differed from his. This contrast is seen when comparing the Stirlings' pier tables from Phyfe with the sofas they ordered from the New York firm Edwards & Baldwin (fig. 37). We are aware of only a handful of instances when patrons purchased one or two rooms' worth of parlor, dining room, or bedroom furniture, but even major patrons such as William Bayard did not purchase exclusively from Phyfe. There is a single occasion when a client, John Laurence Manning, filled an entire house with Phyfe's wares.

In addition to his inability to guarantee delivery dates and cost estimates, Phyfe was seemingly unconcerned with providing prospective customers with precise and attractive renderings of the furniture available in his wareroom. One wonders why a finely tuned workshop responsible for the manufacture of elegant and well-proportioned furniture did not employ someone with such drafting skills, but two contemporary references support this notion. In an 1812 letter, Sarah Huger included "two drawings of furniture, rather uncouthly executed," which had been obtained from her neighbor Maltby Gelston, whose "two communicating rooms" were recently "furnished by Mr. Phyfe with considerable taste."[75] The second is a drawing of two chairs thought to have accompanied an 1816 letter to Charles N. Bancker in Philadelphia (see fig. 149).[76] These charming but poorly wrought sketches of a lyre-back klismos and a forward-facing curule side chair, annotated with prices for their upholstery, lack even a true understanding of perspective. Nonetheless, despite this shortcoming, Bancker proceeded to purchase from Phyfe a set of the lyre-back model (Pl. 20).

Life of a Master Cabinetmaker

Figure 36. Duncan Phyfe. Pier table, 1836. Mahogany veneer, mahogany, marble, looking-glass plate, 37¼ × 60½ × 19⅛ in. Private collection, St. Francisville, Louisiana

Figure 37. Edwards & Baldwin. Sofa, 1836. Mahogany veneer, mahogany, 40 × 84¾ × 29 in. Private collection, St. Francisville, Louisiana

Figure 38. Joseph Louis Fermin Cerveau (ca. 1806–1896). *View of Savannah*, 1837. Tempera on paper, 27½ × 49½ in. (framed). Georgia Historical Society, Savannah

The Export Market

Duncan Phyfe's fame was reinforced by the widespread regard for New York furniture, especially in the American South. In 1817, Susan Wheeler Decatur advised the newly appointed United States attorney general William Wirt upon his arrival in Washington: "You must not get your furniture here. . . . [D]epend upon the furniture you have for this winter, and get what you want from N. York in the Spring."[77]

While skilled cabinetmakers were found in urban centers throughout the South, from Washington and Richmond to Charleston and Savannah, well-to-do householders regularly looked to the North for their furnishing needs. New York makers competed with their counterparts in Boston, Salem, and Philadelphia for this market, but controlled a large share because of their city's stronghold on Southern commerce. Coastal cities maintained direct ties with European ports such as Liverpool, Glasgow, and Le Havre, but a sizable percentage of southern agricultural products, notably cotton, sugar, and tobacco, traveled through New York and were shipped, insured, and traded by New York firms. Thus, while Southern planters often visited Boston and Philadelphia for their genteel society and refreshing climes, they spent a significant amount of time and money in New York meeting with the factors who ensured a steady return on their heavy investments in land and slaves.

With ready access to southward-bound shipping, New York cabinetmakers profited not only from bespoke commissions from the southern grandees but also from opportunities for speculative exporting to Southern warehousemen and retailers.[78] This second type of trade was exploited most efficiently by fancy and Windsor chairmakers, but cabinetmakers also sent tables and case furniture to Southern ports, the Caribbean, and South America. These ventures were not without their pitfalls, however, and the correspondence of New York furniture maker John Hewitt describes in detail the ruinous effect of damp holds and overly saturated markets. After unpacking a shipment in January 1818, William Scott, Hewitt's agent in Savannah, wrote: "I have opened a few of the Boxes today of the most elegant piece[s] of [work] to arouse attention. I am sorry to observe that it is all injured. . . . One End of the Canted Corner Sideboard is very much [damaged,] the rosewood banding and the veneer in the End Door has all started."[79]

Oversupplied markets were also a concern for cabinetmakers engaged in the export market. Hewitt sent a shipment of furniture to New Orleans in 1818, but there were no takers. Hewitt's agent in that city wrote to say that Phyfe had recently lost $2,500 on venture cargo sent to Louisiana and was forced to sell "[extension dining] tables for $30, Sideboards at $40, Bureaus for almost nothing."[80]

The market for Phyfe furniture was quite strong in Savannah (fig. 38). Calvin Baker advertised that he was selling "a large and elegant assortment of Cabinet Furniture just received from New York, and manufactured by the experienced workmen of Mr. D. Phyfe," which included a broad selection of tables, case furniture, and fancy chairs.[81] Commission agents such as Baker, who had sold furniture from John Hewitt's shop in the early 1810s, typically earned 4 to 5 percent of proceeds from such sales.[82] The mercantile firm George Anderson & Son received six boxes of furniture and one bundle of chairs from Phyfe in 1817, and an additional twenty boxes in 1820.[83] Phyfe's reputation in Savannah also benefited from the patronage of that city's elite. In the 1810s Mary Telfair, whose uncle William Gibbon had imported Phyfe tables in 1802, ordered from Phyfe a secretary bookcase (see fig. 155) and a worktable, enlisting the help of her close friend Mary Few, a Savannahian living in New York.[84] Like many wealthy southerners with ties

Life of a Master Cabinetmaker 39

to northern commercial centers, Mary Telfair patronized a variety of furniture makers in New York and Philadelphia, the two cities she visited during her annual pilgrimage north. And like her contemporaries Sarah Huger and Jane Haines, she experienced difficulties with her modest order and was forced to implore Few to "call on Phyfe. You recollect I paid him sixty dollars for my work Table & 1.50 for boxing it. He never sent it on board the Tybee as he promised."[85]

Isaac W. Morrell, who opened a furniture workshop and warehouse in Savannah in the mid-1810s, refers to himself as an "agent for D. Phyfe. New York" in a notice in the May 2, 1821, issue of the *Georgian and Evening Advertiser*. A massive fire in 1820 created a ready demand for furniture as Savannahians rebuilt their homes, and Morrell sold Phyfe chairs, sofas, tables, and mattresses in "all the latest fashions."[86] The following June, Morrell advertised that he was returning to New York for the summer and accepting orders "for furniture of the newest fashions made by D. Phife of New York on accommodating terms."[87] In this manner, Morrell acted as a conduit for Phyfe's foray into the speculative market by handling large shipments of shopwork while offering bespoke work on commission. Customs records indicate that Phyfe sent at least fourteen orders of furniture to Savannah between 1817 and 1823, including forty-four boxes that left New York on January 31, 1821, with Phyfe listed as both shipper and consignor, and possibly destined for Morrell's warehouse.[88]

The partnership between Morrell and Phyfe must have concluded by 1825, for in the ensuing three years Morrell accepted sixty-nine shipments of lumber, hardware, and furniture from New York, none of which originated with Phyfe.[89] In the years following the 1820 fire, the city experienced a pronounced economic recession that likely precipitated Phyfe's abandonment of that market. On only one occasion did Morrell receive furniture other than chairs from New York, which suggests either that he began manufacturing tables and case pieces locally and was supplementing his Savannah-made wares with a steady supply of imported seating furniture or that there simply was not a market for such goods in Savannah at the time.

The Panic of 1819

Phyfe's removal from the export market was likely hastened by the Panic of 1819, when the period of unchecked speculation and easy credit that followed the War of 1812 resulted in widespread financial turmoil, bank closures, and depressed markets for agricultural products and manufactured goods. His involvement in the export trade seems tightly contained between 1815 and 1823. One of Phyfe's deliveries in this time frame was to Charleston, destined for the house of a Scottish immigrant merchant, Dunbar Paul. It included a card table with a label in the well that bears the date "August, 1820" (Pl. 27). This label is found on a writing table and bookcase, three additional card tables, and a worktable (Pls. 25, 26, 28). Three of these objects were sent to customers outside New York, which leads us to conclude that Phyfe was trying to systematically promote his wares outside the local market. Perhaps he borrowed this technique from his long-standing competitor Michael Allison, who printed a series of dated labels in 1817, 1823, 1825, and 1831.[90] By pushing his most *au courant* furniture into export markets with a dated label to clearly denote their maker and novelty, Phyfe may have been attempting to take proactive measures to battle the adverse effects of the Panic. Because cabinetmakers' labels are associated with export furniture, it is telling that the 1820 label is the last one Phyfe printed.

Despite the Panic's devastating impact on the economy, the 1820 Census of Manufactures indicates that the furniture market had begun to slide as early as 1817. Only two surveys of New York cabinetmakers from this census survive, but the sentiments expressed are unequivocal. Stephen and Moses Young, who produced $8,000 in wares the previous year, witnessed a decline of "about one Third in Demand of Wares since 1816."[91] The Youngs' neighbor John Van Boskerck also generated annual sales of $8,000. Van Boskerck noted that while production volume "is not diminished, the number of manufacturing establishments in our line multiplied rapidly over 4 or 5 years; but many have lately failed" as a result of a flood of cheaply manufactured domestic goods, European imports, and competition from auctioneers.[92] For the coachmaker Abraham Quick, a market saturated by "paltry carriages" from New Jersey sold "at any price" had hindered his ability to earn a "fair & honest" wage over the preceding three years.[93] Organizations such as the Friends of National Industry, established in the wake of the "numbers of our merchants and manufacturers . . . reduced to bankruptcy," petitioned Congress for relief of the "great proportion of our mechanics and artists [who] are unemployed."[94]

Manufactory and Warehouse

The often reproduced watercolor of Phyfe's workshop and warehouse complex on Fulton Street (fig. 39) provides not only a sense of the scale of the operation at its heyday during the late 1810s but also the function of the specific buildings.[95] While it has been suggested that the watercolor is a "fanciful depiction of what Phyfe thought a fashionable furniture manufactory and warehouse should look like," certain facts suggest that it may be a fairly accurate representation.[96] The vantage point appears to be from an upstairs window at Phyfe's house across the street. Although the cabinetmaker had separated his family's dwelling space from the side of Fulton Street where business was transacted, this view suggests his ease in maintaining a watchful eye over his large staff of employees.

Of particular note is 170 Fulton, at the center of the frame (see frontispiece on page 114), the awkward design of which led to the above claim of the drawing's fictitious nature. This is the "centre store," where Phyfe's "elegant assortment of furniture was fancifully displayed in the window" following the War of 1812. By illustrating a figure, probably intended to represent Phyfe, engaged in conversation with two well-heeled ladies and his signature wares—including a pillar-and-claw table and a klismos chair with lyre splat—the artist clearly identifies this floor as the main showroom, the public face of the cabinetmaking business. The large bay windows flanking the door were intended to entice pedestrians inside with a view of the elegant stock on display.

Phyfe wears the fashionable businessman's attire of the day—long white pants and a blue tailcoat over a waistcoat and collared dickie—as he presents furniture to two chic young women in bonnets and white Grecian dresses with long sleeves. William Buttre wears similar garb in an advertisement for his chairmaker's shop as he gestures toward his journeymen, whose clothing stands in stark contrast as they toil in his midst (fig. 40).

In a comparable manner, Phyfe attends to matters in the wareroom while his journeymen are seen exiting from 168 Fulton, intentionally isolated from the firm's patrons. The elegant façade suggests a secondary showroom. The auction catalogue for the sale of D. Phyfe & Son's stock in 1847 reveals that the building included a single large room on each floor and an extensive array of ready-made furnishings on all three stories.[97] The commodious windows could, alternatively, have served to light a work space as well, an assumption the presence of the journeyman in the watercolor would tend to reinforce. An 1852 fire insurance map shows that Nos. 192 and 194 Fulton (previously 168 and 170) featured an interior pass-through but does not indicate the floor on which it opened (see fig. 22). With a side entrance at 170 Fulton providing access to two rooms on the second floor, workmen could have moved between the two buildings without descending to street level.[98]

On the right of the watercolor is an elegant three-and-a-half-story brick structure at 172 Fulton, also at least partially devoted to work space. The skylight and side windows in the garret—indicated by the artisan who leans out—provided light for the journeymen and apprentices working there. The building, a typical New York town house of the 1790s, served as both a domestic space and work area until 1806. Phyfe's

Figure 39. Unidentified artist. *Shop and Warehouse of Duncan Phyfe, 168–172 Fulton Street, New York City*, 1817–20. Watercolor, ink, and gouache on white laid paper, 15⅞ × 19⅝ in. The Metropolitan Museum of Art, Rogers Fund, 1922 22.28.1

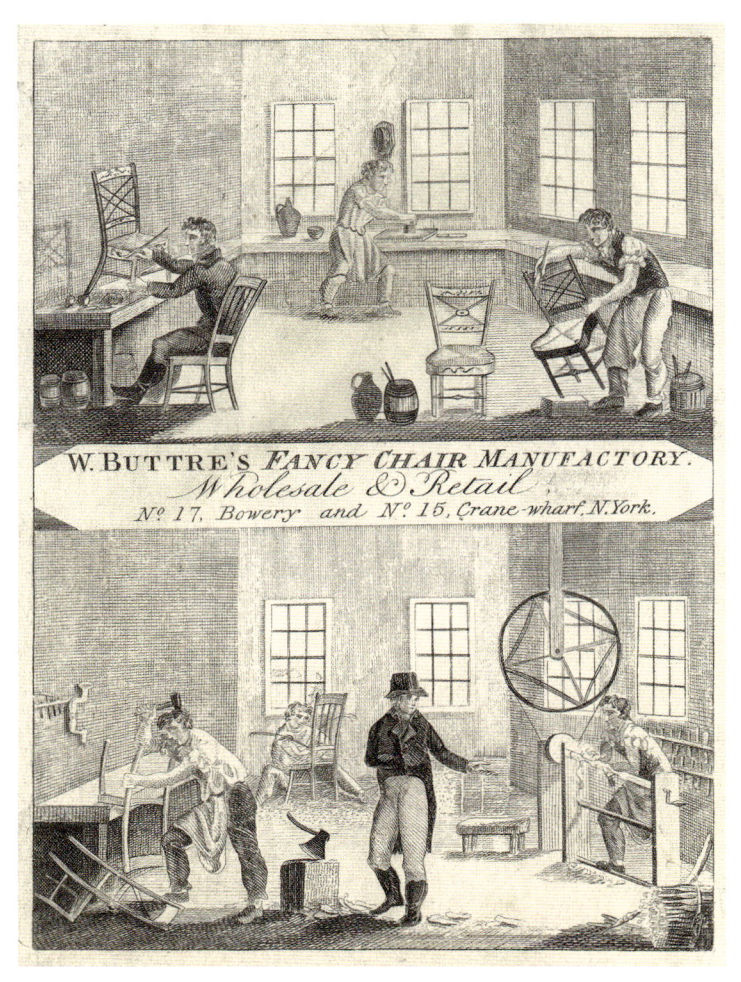

Figure 40. Advertisement of William Buttre, ca. 1815. Wood engraving, 6 3/8 × 4 5/8 in. Winterthur Library, Joseph Downs Collection of Manuscripts and Printed Ephemera

name is painted on the leaded fanlight window over the doorway. In comparison, the anomalous classical buildings at Nos. 168 and 170 Fulton suggest that they may have been built under Phyfe's direction and served to advertise his elegant, similarly inspired classical or Grecian style furniture.

Phyfe also maintained shop space outside of this tightly knit manufactory. According to the estate inventory, he had a shed and a two-story shop behind the family's house at 169 Fulton. The 1852 Perris map (see fig. 22) illustrates this structure as a two-story brick building with a slate roof suitable for a trade using combustible materials, such as cabinet- or chairmaking. The tools, benches, hardware, veneer, and "1 lot Patterns for Cabinet Makers" listed there in Phyfe's estate inventory suggest that this structure was either in active use at the end of his life or held the leftover shop goods brought from across the street when he retired in 1847. Phyfe was also the owner of 38 Dey Street, behind 172 Fulton, where his son Michael worked as a cabinetmaker, and he rented a shop ten blocks uptown on Harrison Street.

Perhaps the most informative description of the internal divisions of an early nineteenth-century warehouse and manufactory is found in testimony from the Manhattan Insurance Company's pursuit of arson charges against New York cabinetmaker Staats M. Mead in 1829.[99] Mead occupied, with Alexander P. Kinnan, his partner since 1811, a five-story building that featured a wareroom on the first and second floors with $24,000 in furniture on display. The plaintiff accused Mead of setting fire to a wardrobe in his second-story wareroom with the hope of collecting an insurance claim. Kinnan testified against his partner and publicly accused him of being a "villain." Apparently, the two men had earlier owned a lumberyard on Bridge Street that burned under suspicious circumstances. Mead was ultimately acquitted of all charges, and both cabinetmakers continued to work in New York, albeit independent of one another.

Kinnan and Mead allocated space for cabinetmakers and varnishers, a "turner's apartment," and a "carver's room" on the third, fourth, and fifth floors, respectively, which housed an additional $20,000 in property. To isolate the workmen from customers, the upper stories were accessed from a staircase in a side alley. If Kinnan and Mead kept upward of $45,000 in merchandise and materials in one five-story building, Phyfe's holdings in 1829 must have approached two or three times that amount.

The watercolor of Phyfe's workshops and wareroom is especially telling when compared with printed illustrations of the stores occupied by his main competitors. Michael Allison (1773–1855), Phyfe's neighbor to the north at Nos. 46 and 48 Vesey Street, included a view of his "Cabinet and Upholstery Furniture Warehouse" in a dated label of May 1817 (fig. 41). Allison owned the adjacent two-and-a-half-story Federal-period brick structures that likely integrated shop and domestic space and closely resemble Phyfe's original building at 35 Partition Street.

Joseph Meeks (1771–1868), who like Phyfe and Lannuier began his career on Broad Street (fig. 42), occupied a small two-story frame structure until 1828, when he acquired the adjacent property and built a six-bay, five-story brick manufactory with large windows on the ground level to display the contents of his wareroom. This expansion parallels Meeks' rise to prominence in the New York furniture trade and the subsequent success of his sons John and Joseph W. Like the manufactory operated by Kinnan and Mead, the Meeks shop emphasized the importance of attic-story work space and the vertical organization of a furniture manufactory.

"EXPERIENCED WORKMEN"

We know surprisingly little about the artisans who worked inside Phyfe's manufactory—the "experienced workmen" mentioned by Calvin Baker, Phyfe's agent in Savannah. Phyfe

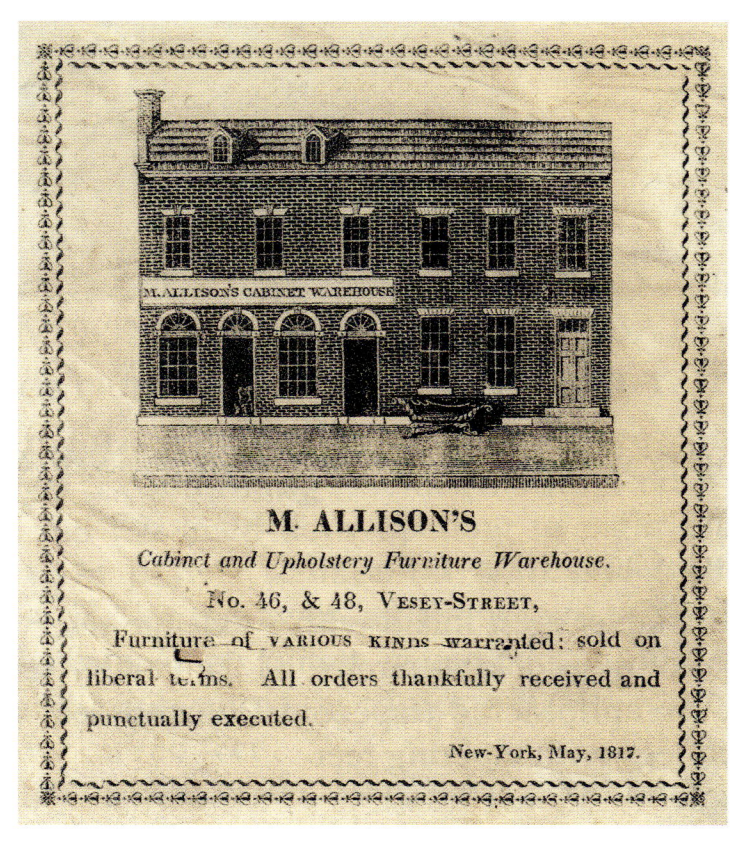

Figure 41. Label from a sideboard made by Michael Allison, 1817

employed a large number of skilled craftsmen to produce his elegant line of furniture, and the competition to hire them must have been fierce. Even cabinetmakers in other cities recruited New York's skilled journeymen, and local pianoforte and organ builders, such as John Geib and his sons Andrew and William, relied on them to produce the decorative cases in which their instruments were housed.[100]

The business records of John Hewitt provide a rare glimpse into the relationship between a master and his journeymen and apprentices.[101] Hewitt noted that the wages earned by journeymen were paid according to the value of the furniture they produced, as set forth in the cabinetmakers' book of prices, or occasionally as an hourly wage that varied according to the skill required for the specific job at hand. While Hewitt's employees made a variety of forms, journeymen such as Thomas Constantine built a greater number of sideboards relative to other cabinetmakers in the shop, as did John Devoe with breakfast and dining tables. These patterns suggest specialties among the journeymen employed. The assistance of anonymous apprentices indentured at Hewitt's Water Street workroom is hinted at in entries for journeyman Abraham S. Egerton, which include a postscript citing work done "by boy."[102]

We suspect that Phyfe himself stopped working alongside the journeymen and apprentices by the 1810s. Hence Sarah Huger's comment in 1816 following her extended wait in his cold workshop "without seeing the *great man*."[103] Information gleaned from receipted bills and family history suggests that Phyfe employed shop foremen to oversee the day-to-day operations once his business was established. The consistently high quality of furniture linked to Phyfe's workshop, especially the attention paid to unseen interior construction, suggests that he or his foremen closely observed the journeymen's work to ensure a level of excellence. Phyfe likely maintained strict control over the design of his furniture line, but his foremen filled the essential role of monitoring shop production, accepting

Figure 42. James Archer (act. 1835–60) after Alexander J. Davis (1803–1892). "Broad Street," from Theodore S. Fay's *Views in New-York and Its Environs* (1831–34). Etching, 3½ × 5¾ in. I. N. Phelps Stokes Collection, Miriam and Ira D. Wallach Division of Art, Prints and Photographs, The New York Public Library, Astor, Lenox and Tilden Foundations

Life of a Master Cabinetmaker 43

Figure 43. Sideboard. New York City, ca. 1810. Mahogany, mahogany veneer, brass, 52¼ × 80⅛ × 26⅛ in. Private collection

payments, and producing receipted bills. The earliest evidence that we have for this practice is two receipts signed in 1807 by Phyfe's younger brother James, with the assumption being that Duncan gave this responsibility to him when he was absent from the shop. According to Phyfe's grandson, who worked in the shop in the late 1830s and 1840s, Robert Shaefer served as foreman at that time, although a cabinetmaker with that name does not appear in the New York directory during this period.[104]

The two other names associated with this responsibility in the Phyfe workshop are Jacob P. and Isaac W. Morrell, who receipted bills in 1813 and from 1812 to 1819, respectively.[105] Jacob is listed in the New York City directories as a cabinetmaker from 1794 to 1809 and as a cartman in the early 1810s. Perhaps Phyfe employed Jacob to deliver shipments of furniture and, in recognition of his expertise in the cabinetmaking trade or his skill in double-entry bookkeeping, assigned him the task of recording financial transactions. As was noted earlier, "fine arts carting" was a specialty within the trade, and only the most assiduous cartmen were trusted with valuable household furnishings. Isaac does not appear in the directory, but, as mentioned, he played a prominent role in Phyfe's pursuit of the southern export market by serving as the cabinetmaker's agent in Savannah.

Foremen had the responsibility of overseeing the broad range of specialists employed in a given shop. A survey of Phyfe's documented furniture suggests that, in addition to cabinetmakers, he employed turners, carvers, gilders, varnishers, caners, upholsterers, and perhaps lumbermen, sawyers, and veneer cutters. Since the late nineteenth century, furniture historians have claimed that Phyfe retained more than one hundred journeymen in his manufactory, but not once has this figure been substantiated with documentary evidence.[106] Even in the 1810s, when Phyfe's operation was at full tilt, such a large workforce might have inhibited the functioning of the dozens of other cabinetmaking shops in New York City. It is known that cabinetmakers John and Joseph W. Meeks employed a staff of 130 in 1850, but that number was partly enabled by the influx of craftsmen from continental Europe beginning in the 1830s.[107]

The only journeyman definitively linked to Phyfe's workshop is Robert Kelly. In an 1814 advertisement, Kelly sought to capitalize on an earlier connection he had with Phyfe, whose "best side-boards" Kelly claimed he had made between 1810 and 1813.[108] Craftsmen capable of manufacturing the elegant and complex sideboards of this period (fig. 43) were highly sought after. An etching of this sideboard type was featured on the title page of the New York price book of 1810 (fig. 44). For the last thirteen years of his career, Kelly operated within five doors of Phyfe at 23 Partition Street (later 164 Fulton). Kelly's decision to remain in close proximity to his former place of employment may be explained as an attempt to draw on the foot traffic generated by Phyfe's wareroom with an offering of furniture "of the best materials, of the best quality, and on the most reasonable terms," or at least more reasonable than Phyfe's.[109] By 1816, Kelly's workshop was of moderate size, with a few journeymen on staff, and his presence on Fulton Street until his death testifies to the success of his

Duncan Phyfe

cabinetmaking business during the economic slump that followed the Panic of 1819.[110]

Other artisans working in furniture-related trades are loosely connected with Phyfe's workshop as tenants in the numerous properties he owned or leased. This group includes cabinetmaker Walter Moffatt, 1810; chairmakers William Stackhouse and Grove B. West, 1810–11; looking-glass maker John Steen, 1817; cabinetmaker Asa Butman, 1820; carver and gilder Peter Clover, 1828–34; upholsterer John Constantine, 1834–41; upholsterer Gabriel P. Gratacap, 1839–43; and upholsterer Peter Wiminel, 1843. Whether these men were business associates of Phyfe's or merely his renters is left to speculation, as they shared these accommodations with a broad range of tradesmen and professionals, including tailors, merchants, dentists, and auctioneers.

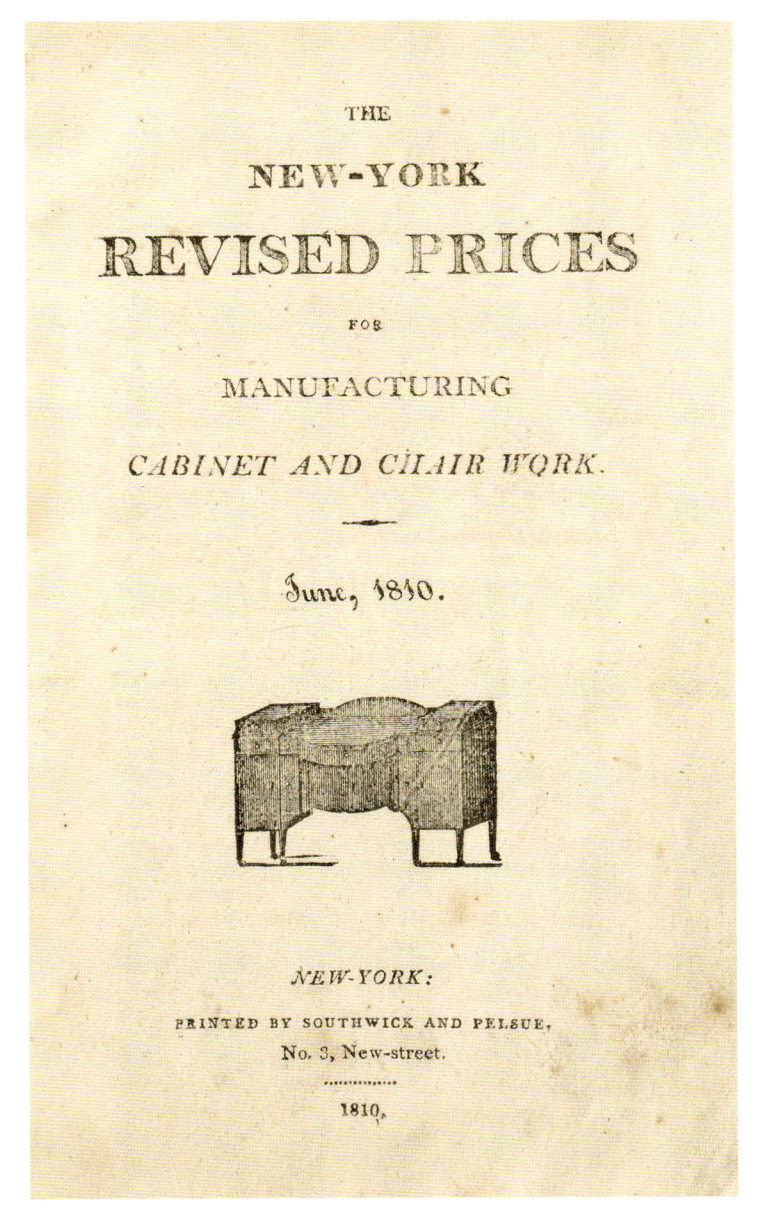

Figure 44. Title page from Duncan Phyfe's copy of *The New-York Revised Prices for Manufacturing Cabinet and Chair Work* (1810). Winterthur Library, Collection of Printed Books and Periodicals

The 1819 Walkout

Phyfe's relationship with his workforce was not without fault. In May 1819 many of his journeymen left the Fulton Street shop to establish an independent cabinet warehouse as part of the Journeymen Cabinet and Chair Makers of New-York. According to a notice published in *The National Advocate* on May 12, their departure was incited by Phyfe's "demand for the reduction of [their] wages." With the experience of working in New York's premier cabinetmaking shop, the journeymen offered wares "executed in a style equal to any on the continent," and at a price that was significantly less than what their former employer charged. With the onset of the Panic of 1819 and its traumatic effects on the American manufacturing sector, both Phyfe and his employees had cause for alarm. Although Phyfe's strong financial standing would keep his business secure during the lean years ahead, he had perhaps deemed a reduction in his employees' salaries essential to weather the economic downturn.

The 1819 walkout was not the first instance of journeymen protesting wage reductions. In 1802 the journeymen cabinetmakers of New York attempted to open a wareroom after publicizing grievances in response to the publication of a revised book of prices "agreed upon by the employers" and printed without the "mutual consent" of the journeymen.[111] Such price books set salaries for the construction of specific pieces of furniture. A group of anonymous master craftsmen responded to assure their fellow New Yorkers that a "very large majority of the Journeymen expressed themselves satisfied with the prices lately established."[112] Phyfe is not specifically cited in this notice, but one suspects that as a "Master Cabinet Maker" of increasing importance, his opinion would have been solicited regarding a change in workmen's wages.

With the hope of avoiding disagreements between employers and laborers, the New-York Society of Cabinet-Makers adopted a constitution and a revised book of prices in 1810, stipulating that its goal was to "maintain good understanding between employers and employed; prevent and adjust disputes; make and establish equitable prices for the various articles manufactured by them."[113] The society included a committee appointed to "inspect and value the work should any disputes arise between the members and employers."[114] The 1819 work stoppage implies, however, that individual masters could adjust their employees' wages as they saw fit.

Our understanding of Phyfe's use of the apprenticeship system is severely limited by the lack of records from early nineteenth-century New York City. While masters continued to teach the "trade or mystery of a Cabinet Maker" and to provide apprentices with "sufficient meat, drink, washing and lodging," the length of indenture was shortened over Phyfe's

Life of a Master Cabinetmaker

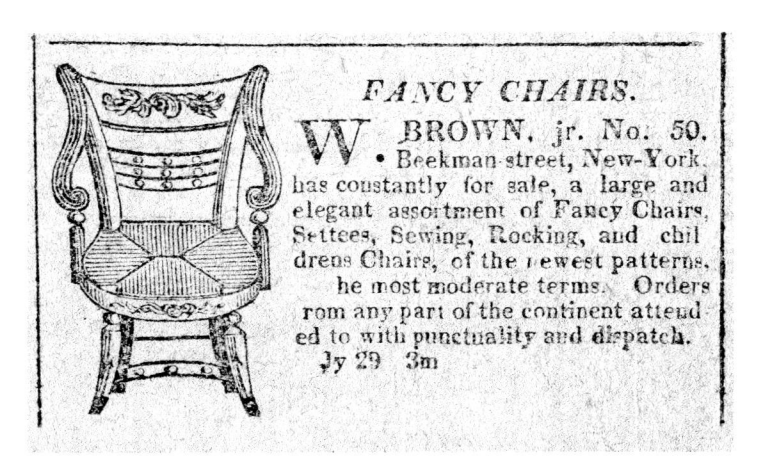

Figure 45. Advertisement from the *Mercantile Advertiser*, January 29, 1816. The New-York Historical Society

career as the average age of the apprentices entering into such bonds increased. The average age of six boys documented as entering into furniture-related apprenticeships in New York between 1792 and 1794 was under thirteen years, whereas that of eleven boys named in contracts signed between 1816 and 1820 was over fifteen years.[115]

Phyfe's prominence in the trade would suggest that dozens of young men apprenticed on Fulton Street over the cabinetmaker's fifty-five-year career. However, we know of only three individuals who served Phyfe in this capacity. A contract with seventeen-year-old William Brown Jr. (1785–1819), a son of William Brown Sr., sexton at St. Paul's Chapel, is the sole indenture that makes reference to Phyfe. Dated July 28, 1802, the document bound William Jr. to Phyfe until his twenty-first birthday in 1807.[116] In the records of the Washington Benevolent Society for 1810, when Brown was likely working as a journeyman, his address is listed as Phyfe's workshop at 35 Partition Street, and he appears in the New York City directories between 1811 and 1819 as a fancy chair painter (fig. 45). Although Phyfe's name is not generally associated with the production of fancy chairs, Brown's specialty suggests that he used the services of such men. In 1822, Phyfe billed Robert Donaldson for a dozen "ornamental" chairs (App. 1.7).

The two other apprentices attached to Phyfe's manufactory, Beverly Marsh and David Van Tassel, are known from runaway notices Phyfe submitted to the *New-York Evening Post* on October 2, 1809, and September 17, 1812. The five-dollar reward Phyfe offered for the twenty-year-old Marsh and the six-cent reward he offered for Van Tassel suggest his pronounced disinterest in the latter's return. Neither Marsh nor Van Tassel appears in the New York City directory following their apprenticeship, but their reasons for deserting could not have compared with the experiences of four young men indentured to cabinetmaker-turned-auctioneer Charles Christian,

who was convicted of beating his apprentices "without cause," failing to provide them with sufficient clothing, and paying "no attention to his business of cabinetmaker."[117]

Marketing the Phyfe Name

A remarkable aspect of Phyfe's commercial success, especially during periods of economic depression, was his ability to draw customers to his manufactory without the assistance of advertising. Even before his emergence as New York's premier cabinetmaker in the 1810s, Phyfe did not place notices in the city papers. Some of his business associates, however, did not hesitate to use his name for their own benefit. George Newberry, an enterprising importer of luxury goods and musical instruments, capitalized on the strength of Phyfe's position in the marketplace by placing pianofortes at the cabinetmaker's warehouse, presumably to be sold on commission, and then advertising their location "at Mr. Phyfe's."[118] In addition to maintaining his own store at 132 Pearl Street from 1817 to 1819, Newberry advertised on numerous occasions that his fine London-made instruments could also be found at Phyfe's on Fulton Street and at cabinetmaker Brazilia Deming's shop as well.[119]

Phyfe suffered from the unsolicited attention offered by the auctioneers of secondhand furniture. From 1814 onward his name appeared regularly in the New York papers as the maker of domestic wares being sold by families "breaking up housekeeping," "removed to the country," or "about to leave the city."[120] Thus, in addition to battling with other New York cabinetmakers for a sizable share of the market, Phyfe also had to compete with auctioneers who were selling used Phyfe furniture at a lower price. Frequently the sale included a solitary item, such as a set of "dining tables (Phyfe's make)," but occasionally an entire household, "consisting of mahogany bedsteads, chairs, sofas, sideboard, dining, tea and card tables, all of Phyfe's make."[121] While other cabinetmakers appear in these auction notices, none did so with the consistency of Phyfe until the ascendancy of Joseph Meeks & Sons in the 1830s.

In a similar vein, entrepreneurs hoping to promote the utility of new products and services occasionally incorporated Phyfe's name into their advertisements. In 1820 the aptly named Safety Magee cited Phyfe as a customer satisfied with Magee's new approach to fireproofing chimneys.[122] Four years later Phyfe was mentioned in William Appleton's advertisement for the "Hindostan sharpening stone," capable of "setting an edge quickly, and sufficiently, smooth" for the purposes of "Carpenters, Cabinet-makers, Cutlers, and Engravers."[123] The New York varnish manufacturers P. B. Smith & Co. also used Phyfe as an endorsement for its superior merchandise.[124]

The Phyfe name was so closely tied to sentiments of craftsmanship and elegant design that when James Monroe furnished the East Room of the President's House with imported French sofas and chairs in 1817, a proponent of American manufacturers felt moved to submit an editorial to the *New-York Evening Post* that assured its readership of the high quality of furniture manufactured in the United States, a claim that could be confirmed "by calling, at any time, at Mr. Phyfe's cabinet warehouse in Fulton-street."[125] The reprinting of this editorial in newspapers such as the *Richmond Enquirer* and the *Frederick Town Herald* suggests its traction with readers in the South as well.[126]

This plea carries a certain degree of irony in that prominent public commissions were not a factor in Phyfe's career. Such opportunities did not necessarily result in significant income for the manufacturer, but the contract to furnish a noteworthy civic building was a form of political patronage that could attract new clientele and endorse the quality of a mechanic's wares. Phyfe's chief opportunity to capitalize on his reputation was the completion of New York's new City Hall in 1812. In democratic fashion Nicholas Fish, chairman of the committee appointed to purchase furniture for the chambers of the Common Council, spread its furniture and upholstery needs among a variety of New York craftsmen, including Lannuier, William Mandeville, and Henry Andrew.[127] Although Phyfe had provided the council with a desk in 1803, his role in furnishing New York's most important public building was limited to a pair of writing tables ordered by Federalist mayor DeWitt Clinton later that year.[128]

Recognition of Phyfe's prestige was given at the celebration of the completion of the Erie Canal in 1825 (fig. 46), but this was the exception to the rule. The canal secured New York's status as the preeminent center for trade on the eastern seaboard, as it served to couple a thriving deepwater port with extensive access to the American interior. This unparalleled contact with both Europe and the American Midwest was a boon to merchants as well as mechanics such as Phyfe. The city commemorated the grand achievement with parades, speeches, and canon salutes. The fête culminated in the dumping of a keg of water from Lake Erie into New York Harbor, thereby commingling the Great Lakes and the Atlantic Ocean. A portion of this water was reserved in American-made bottles and placed in "a box by Mr. D. Phyfe . . . in order to send it to our distinguished friend, and late illustrious visitor, Major General Lafayette," who had recently visited New York during an extensive journey through the United States.[129]

The Corporation of the City also commissioned a commemorative medal to present to various dignitaries associated with the canal celebration. Depending on the individual's importance, the medal he received was in gold, silver, or "semimetal," an alloy with tin and trace amounts of lead. The latter two were placed in a box made from "curious woods, such as birdseye, and curled maple, red cedar, &c. the produce of the western forests" that had been "brought from Erie in the first Canal-boat, the Seneca Chief."[130] The boxes were produced by Phyfe with the assistance of turner Daniel Karr (fig. 47).[131]

From Tenant to Landlord

Throughout his career, Phyfe wisely invested the profits reaped from his cabinetmaking business into property in Manhattan, Brooklyn, and upstate New York. All told, Phyfe owned, rented, or leased eighteen different parcels in the city, with as many as fourteen under his control by 1830. While the majority of this real estate lined Fulton Street, over the years he acquired properties elsewhere in Manhattan: a lease on 40 Vesey Street in 1817 and 38 Vesey in 1823, and the deed to 97 Reade Street in 1819 and 71 Murray Street in 1850. With his son-in-law Sidney B. Whitlock, Phyfe also speculated in housing and land in Brooklyn in the early 1840s.[132]

Although Phyfe may have required loans and mortgages to finance some of these acquisitions, land ownership certainly provided him with an additional source of income. Those properties not incorporated in his cabinetmaking business were let out as domestic, commercial, or mixed-use structures. Rents obviously varied according to location and the condition of the property, the quality of the dwelling or shop, and the strength of the economy, as tenants were difficult to come by during times of economic decline. Nonetheless, in the late 1820s Phyfe's annual income from his leased properties and tenants likely exceeded $3,000.[133]

As the value of New York real estate climbed rapidly upward—it quadrupled between 1795 and 1815—property proved a reliable asset that enabled the raising of additional capital through mortgages and provided a secure means of transferring wealth to younger generations. If Phyfe's approach to investing his profits can be characterized as conservative, this restraint was to his credit. The real estate market in particular could lead to significant wealth. Phyfe operated on a smaller scale than his fabulously wealthy neighbor John Jacob Astor, but he gradually accumulated property in close proximity to his residence and place of business in the hope that it would steadily increase in value and generate income through leases and rents. He also benefited from New York's robust economy, as the city quickly became the nation's principal commercial center. New residents arrived in droves and fueled a rapid rise in population, which stood at 96,000 in 1810 and pushed New York past Philadelphia as the principal metropolis of the United States.

As the financial struggles of his heralded contemporaries Lannuier in New York and Thomas Seymour (1771–1848) in Boston indicate, exceptional nineteenth-century craftsmen were

Life of a Master Cabinetmaker

Figure 46. Anthony Imbert (act. 1825–34) after Archibald Robertson (1765–1835). *Grand Canal Celebration*, from Cadwallader D. Colden, *Memoir*... (1825). Lithograph, 8½ × 40⅛ in. Print Collection, Miriam and Ira D. Wallach Division of Art, Prints and Photographs, The New York Public Library, Astor, Lenox and Tilden Foundations

Figure 47. Grand Canal Celebration medal and original box, 1826. Medal: Silver, diam. 1¾ in. Box: Bird's-eye maple, paper, diam. 2 in. Fenimore Art Museum, Cooperstown, New York

not guaranteed great wealth from the sale of furniture alone. The adverse effects of illness, stiff competition, and the Panic of 1819 led Lannuier to falter at the end of his tragically brief career, and Seymour in his last years survived on the largesse of relatives. Phyfe is extraordinary in that his documented oeuvre warrants the same accolades for aesthetic merit awarded to Lannuier and Seymour, but his workshop achieved an economy of scale and profit margins that resulted in remarkable fiscal security.

Phyfe's equity also provided easier access to credit for the purchase of the raw materials—lumber, veneer, hardware, and upholstery goods—requisite for an active furniture manufactory. According to one of Phyfe's contemporaries, businessmen who were able to prove their "honesty, industry, and integrity" could access "unlimited credit which enabled them to do a large and successful business for many years."[134]

Mahogany was an essential commodity in the cabinetmaking business, and Phyfe had sufficient capital to acquire this expensive, high-quality wood (fig. 48). Family lore claims that the best pieces of mahogany brought from the Caribbean were referred to as "Phyfe logs" and purchased for $1,000 apiece, and that Phyfe occasionally brought his own shipments to New York rather than purchasing from a local lumber merchant.[135] An 1811 letter to the aforementioned Charles Watts Sr. from his son Charles Watts Jr. in New York notes,

> Mr. Phyfe wishes you to procure for him three, four or a half dozen logs of St. Domingo mahogany as he understands it is abundant with you—it must be large size, of the fines[t] quality and I think he calls it crochets or cross grained—will not mind giving a good price if you can get good wood.[136]

48 *Duncan Phyfe*

The implication is that Phyfe would have the logs processed into boards and veneer in the New York City area. In 1811 the younger Watts mentions a mill near Chatham, New Jersey, twenty miles west of New York, used to saw veneers for the Charleston cabinetmaker Robert Walker.[137] John Hewitt is known to have sent logs to Springfield, New Jersey, on the Passaic River near Chatham.[138]

The "St. Domingo" wood that Phyfe sought was a dense, highly desirable, expensive island mahogany used extensively in the best early nineteenth-century New York furniture. As Henry Bradshaw Fearon, an Englishman who toured the United States in 1817 and 1818, wrote in *Sketches of America* (1818), "Veneer is in general demand, and is cut by machinery. Chests of drawers are chiefly made of St. Domingo mahogany . . . shaded veneer and curl maple are also used for this purpose."

Fearon also shared his impressions of New York City's mahogany yards, commenting that they were "generally separate concerns" from cabinetmaking shops.[139] Contrary to Fearon's observations, documentary evidence suggests that Phyfe maintained a supply of hardwood in his own lumberyards. This is revealed first in an 1832 court case prosecuted by Phyfe against the merchants Charles Wardell and Brittain L. Woolley, lesees of 38 Vesey Street. The defendants testified that the plaintiff "reserved to himself the remainder of said lot which he occupied as a Lumber yard for the storing of Lumber and other materials used by him in his business of a Cabinet-Maker."[140] And second, when Duncan and James decided to close the doors of D. Phyfe & Son in 1847, they auctioned "Mahogany, Rosewood, and Ambina Boards, Planks and Veneers" from 194 Fulton Street.[141] Phyfe's estate inventory reveals that he owned $100 worth of mahogany veneer at his death.

As a wealthy and respected businessman, Phyfe held an elevated position in New York society, best reflected in his presence on the first board of directors of the North River Bank, incorporated in 1821 at 186 Greenwich Street, around the corner from his house and warehouse. Leonard Kip, president of the board, was Phyfe's former neighbor on Partition Street and served as the cabinetmaker's legal representative on four occasions between 1827 and 1848. The bank's location was significant, as it was one of a small minority operating above Wall Street. With the intent to serve "the inhabitants of the northern and western parts of the city of New-York," the bank was situated two blocks from the Hudson River, a location that proved fortuitous with the opening of the Erie Canal.[142] Phyfe's decision to support a bank in the Third Ward can also be interpreted as a savvy method of reinforcing, if not augmenting, the value of his extensive land holdings in the neighborhood.

Competition in the New York Furniture Trade

The Erie Canal proved to be a boon for New York commercial interests as a whole, but the late 1820s and early 1830s marked the beginning of a slow decline in Phyfe's market share. Phyfe's retraction from speculative exporting in the early 1820s stands in stark contrast to the thriving business of New York firms such as Deming & Bulkley and Joseph Meeks & Sons. The

Life of a Master Cabinetmaker

Figure 48. "Cutting & Trucking Mahogany in Honduras," from E. Chaloner and W. Fleming, *The Mahogany Tree: Its Botanical Character, Qualities, and Uses* . . . (1850). The New-York Historical Society

wares of Erastus Bulkley (1798–1872) first arrived in Charleston in 1818. After entering into a partnership with his cousin Brazilia Deming (1781–1854) in 1820, Bulkley continued to supply a well-heeled South Carolinian clientele with richly decorated Grecian-style furniture, like the center table made for Governor Stephen Decatur Miller of Camden, South Carolina (fig. 49).[143] Joseph Meeks opened a furniture workshop in New York City in 1797 and almost immediately sought out customers in Savannah.[144] Then in 1820 he shifted his gaze to the burgeoning wealth of the Deep South and established a warehouse in New Orleans, which his sons John (1801–1875) and Joseph W. (1805–1878) maintained until 1839.[145] From this outpost, the Meekses tapped an active market among planters in Louisiana and Mississippi. John Hewitt also received patronage from Gulf Coast customers and in the early 1830s sent furniture to Alabama.[146]

American consumers nevertheless continued to regard Phyfe as a respected and much sought-after manufacturer during this period. Southern planters visited his wareroom to furnish grand houses back home. Those exporting sugar and cotton were more beholden to New York merchant houses and insurance and shipping companies than ever before. Surprisingly, the authors have found documentation for only one customer from the Deep South. When Lewis Stirling of St. Francisville, Louisiana, came to New York in 1836 to procure furnishings for his new dwelling, Wakefield, he divided his expenditures between Phyfe for tables and bedsteads and the firm of Edwards & Baldwin for chairs and sofas. Family tradition maintains that in 1842 Phyfe received another noteworthy visitor, British commodore Lord John Hay, who visited Fulton Street to inquire about cabinet woods. But the cabinetmaker, it was reported, "would not even take the pipe out of his Mouth."[147]

Furthermore, Phyfe remained in the public eye. A posting in the *American Advertising Directory, for Manufacturers and Dealers in American Goods*, of 1832, reminded consumers that he still offered a "splendid selection of the best Manufactured Cabinet Furniture of his own establishment . . . always on sale and sent per order to any part of the Union."[148] Phyfe served as a judge of cabinet wares submitted to the American Institute Fairs of 1832 and 1834 and is mentioned in the *Commercial Advertiser*'s coverage of the latter event as a leading figure in the trade.[149] He also participated in a celebration of the French Revolution on November 25, 1830, with the city's Workingmen's Party. This prolabor organization endeavored to help "the poor and middling classes understand that their oppressions come from the overgrown wealth that exists among them" in the hands of master craftsmen and merchant capitalists.[150] While contrary to Phyfe's position as a wealthy mechanic, the Workingmen's Party admitted a large number of these tormentors into their ranks in order to "render the contemplated celebration more effective, and to divest it of all party feeling."[151] Thus Phyfe and aristocratic New Yorkers such as Gulian Verplanck, Philip Hone, and Jacob Lorillard marched alongside those they allegedly oppressed.

A market crash and the ensuing economic troubles contributed to the wane of D. Phyfe & Sons. The Panic of 1837, the first significant reversal since the Panic of 1819, was especially destructive to the New York cabinetmaking industry and related trades. In a contemporary New York political cartoon titled *Specie Claws* (fig. 50), an unemployed joiner or carpenter, his tools strewn about on the bare floor, is beset by his hungry children and a pair of rent collectors. The title is a play on the Democratic Party's legislation to require specie, or hard currency, for the purchase of public land. The "specie clause" was intended to check rampant speculation by investors using paper money but was blamed by the Republicans as a major accelerant for the country's financial collapse. The prints of Andrew Jackson and Martin Van Buren tacked to the back wall pinpoint the Democratic presidents responsible for the nefarious law and suggest the misguided political leanings of the impoverished artisan.

Between 1841 and 1843, thirteen cabinetmakers, four chairmakers, nine carriagemakers, twenty-one lumbermen, and three pianoforte makers in the Southern District of New York declared bankruptcy under a new federal law.[152] As they had in the wake of falling wages and unemployment after the Panic of 1819, New York journeymen once again struck out on their own. Operating as the Association of Cabinet Makers, their wareroom offered "a stock of every description of Cabinet Furniture, of the best and well seasoned materials manufactured in the most faithful manner, and sold at the lowest prices that can be afforded."[153]

The economic downturn came at a pivotal point in Phyfe's career. In 1840, Phyfe entered his seventy-first year, and the three-year-old partnership with his sons William and James D. as D. Phyfe & Sons was reduced to D. Phyfe & Son when William chose to go into business on his own. Although James would continue to work with his father through the latter's

Figure 49. Deming & Bulkley. Center table, 1828. Rosewood veneer, marble, gilded gesso and *vert antique*, 30½ × 36 in. Private collection

Life of a Master Cabinetmaker 51

Figure 50. Henry Dacre (b. ca. 1820). *Specie Claws*, 1838–39. Lithograph with watercolor on wove paper, 12 × 16¼ in. Library of Congress, Washington, D.C.

retirement in 1847, he does not appear to have had the desire or the wherewithal to shoulder the business as John and Joseph W. Meeks did when their father retired in 1836. Because James' signature does not appear on receipted bills predating 1837, we are at a loss to explain his role in the business prior to that point. Neither brother is listed independently in the city directory, where their elder brother Michael appears as a cabinetmaker and then the owner of a mahogany yard.[154]

The effects of a downtrodden economy that hindered the cabinetmaking trade were coupled with a drastic shift in the popular design of household furnishings, both of which would prove troubling for the Phyfes. After visiting their Fulton Street warerooms in 1840, James Henry Hammond, a planter and politician from Columbia, South Carolina, observed that the Phyfes were "as much behind the times in style as [they were] in price. He thinks it is still 1836."[155] Evidently, D. Phyfe & Son had not reduced their prices in recognition of the ensuing depression nor had they brought their stock in line with the new vogue for parlor and dining room furnishings in the Old French style that revived Rococo designs developed during the reigns of Louis XIV and Louis XV. On that front they faced significant competition from a variety of immigrant and native cabinetmakers who were more intimately versed in the revival styles quickly growing in popularity among New York's fashionable elite.

All, however, was not lost for the Phyfe business. Hammond in fact confirmed that it continued to operate in a high traffic area among "excellent workmen [on] Broadway near the Astor House [which] is the center of business & fashion."[156] Hammond's fellow South Carolinian John Laurence Manning visited D. Phyfe & Son the following year and purchased enough furniture to fill seven rooms at Millford, his country estate in Clarendon County, South Carolina. Another prominent South Carolinian, William Aiken of Charleston, acquired furnishings in New York, some likely from Phyfe, in 1838, after expanding a house inherited from his father.[157] However, other than an extensive suite of avante-garde rosewood seating furniture for Manning's double parlor, most of his furnishings resembled the elegant but plain Grecian-style furniture Phyfe had sold since the early 1830s. The latest extant bill of sale known for D. Phyfe & Son is dated October 1841, which leaves a great deal of uncertainty in the interpretation of their final years.

The inability of D. Phyfe & Son to compete is most clearly illustrated by a series of newspaper advertisements in 1843 and 1844 that announced a wholesale reduction in the firm's stock (fig. 51). In April 1843, Phyfe offered "for sale at greatly reduced prices, their large and fashionable assortment of Mahogany and Rosewood Cabinet Furniture."[158] While Duncan and James believed their reputation "at home and abroad is too well appreciated by the public to need any commendation," this was the first newspaper advertisement placed by Phyfe in his fifty-one years of cabinetmaking. At the same moment, in an adjacent announcement, his seasoned competitor Michael Allison, whose store was situated a block north on Vesey Street, offered "a large quantity of Furniture, manufactured in the best manner . . . in the most fashionable style, in rosewood, mahogany, &c., which he offers at very reduced prices."[159] After a half century in the business, New York's two longest-standing

Duncan Phyfe

furniture manufacturers were suddenly breaking up shop. The relocation of J. & J. W. Meeks' highly successful firm to 14 Vesey Street after the Great Fire of 1835 destroyed their building on Broad Street provided a source of competition as well as a constant reminder of the evolution of taste in household furnishings.

Customer traffic continued to decline, and in 1844 the New York auction company Halliday & Jenkins advertised that it would assist "Messrs. Duncan Phyfe & Son, who are closing their business." The sale included "the most extensive and valuable assortment of highly finished furniture of the best quality and of their well known manufacture, ever offered in this market, comprising every variety of fashionable and seasonable furniture."[160]

Because D. Phyfe & Son continued to operate until 1847, this may have been a ploy to liquidate outmoded stock. Shortly after the 1844 sale, the *New Mirror of Literature, Amusement and Instruction* reported that "the oldest and most wealthy of the cabinet warehouse-men in this city has completely abandoned the making of English furniture. He sold out an immense stock of high-priced articles last week at auction." The unnamed cabinetmaker, presumably Phyfe, had "sent to France for models and workmen to start new with the popular taste [for] the fashion of French furniture has come in lately with a rush, and the nabobs are selling out, from sideboard to broom, and furnishing anew, *à la Française*, from skylight to basement."[161]

Charles A. Baudouine (1808–1896), an American of French extraction, and Alexander Roux (1813–1886), an immigrant from France, were leading this trend with a steady supply of imported and locally made furniture in the latest continental taste. Furthermore, in the early 1840s Parisian *ébéniste* Auguste-Émile Ringuet-Leprince (1801–1886) sent large quantities of household furnishings to wealthy New York clients such as Matthew Morgan and James Colles (see fig. 132).[162] Business was strong enough to convince Ringuet-Leprince to relocate to New York in 1848. And as fashionable New Yorkers continued to move uptown, this new crop of cabinetmakers followed suit. While D. Phyfe & Son and J. & J. W. Meeks remained in the Third Ward off lower Broadway, Baudouine, Roux, and Ringuet-Leprince all set up shop farther north, in the Eighth Ward, on Broadway between Canal and Bleeker Streets.[163] As suggested by the six-story warehouse opened by Baudouine in 1849 at 335 Broadway, the city's furniture trade was literally expanding to new heights at the close of Phyfe's career (fig. 52). Such structures were in dramatic contrast to those occupied by cabinetmakers thirty years earlier and stood witness to the development of large-scale manufacturing facilities capable of housing upward of two hundred employees.

Closing Shop

D. Phyfe & Son survived for another three years before officially closing shop in 1847. When we examine the inventory listed by Halliday & Jenkins for the firm's true closeout auction on April 16 and 17 of that year, we are left to wonder what affect the 1843 and 1844 sales had had on thinning their stock, and whether they ever employed French craftsmen or embraced the new taste for French furnishings. The twenty-page catalogue covers an astounding 430 lots of furniture, a significant percentage of which cite the plain Grecian style that Phyfe adopted in the early 1830s, such as lot 208, a mahogany dressing table with "scroll standards, marble top, round corner, plate glass."[164] The sale also included a variety of French bedsteads with scrolled head- and footboards that James H. Hammond had claimed were "decidedly going out [of fashion]" in 1840.[165] While there is a rosewood sofa and chairs "style of Louis XIV" and a pair of "magnificent rosewood French Couches" with *Voltaires* to match, we find limited evidence of the Old French style, as the Rococo Revival was known.[166] However, D. Phyfe & Son placed these *en mode* items in a prominent position—the same first-floor showroom at 194 Fulton where Phyfe is depicted with two customers in the watercolor from thirty years earlier.

Despite D. Phyfe & Son's limited revenue in the last years, between his retirement in 1847 at the ripe age of seventy-seven and his death seven years later, Phyfe continued to profit through his rental properties. A series of lawsuits filed by Phyfe and his children between 1849 and 1857 help illuminate the annual proceeds garnered from these buildings.[167] Those on Fulton

Figure 51. Advertisements from the *New-York Commercial Advertiser*, April 28, 1843. The New-York Historical Society

Life of a Master Cabinetmaker

Figure 52. Label from a lady's writing desk made by Charles A. Baudouine, 1849–54. Museum of Fine Arts, Boston

Street were particularly lucrative, with leases ranging from $1,600 per year for Phyfe's house at 193 Fulton to $4,350 and $1,550 for Nos. 190 and 192, respectively. When these figures are multiplied over the numerous residential and commercial spaces let by Phyfe, it is clear that they maintained a reliable source of income once the cabinetmaking business closed.

Phyfe's real estate investments placed his affluence on a par with the city's most notable patrician landholders and merchants. Nevertheless, other than through his participation in benevolent and political associations, Phyfe made no attempt to interact with the upper echelons of New York society. He either did not aspire to or chose not to pursue the limelight of the fashionable upper class. In this he avoided criticism as a parvenu and maintained his role as a dedicated craftsman-mechanic. During his own lifetime, Phyfe was recognized and publicly lauded for his work ethic and financial success. Moses Beach's *Wealth and Biography of the Wealthy Citizens of New York* (1845) describes how Phyfe, whose wealth was assessed at $300,000, "commenced on Fulton Street . . . a poor cabinet-maker, and has now the largest and most fashionable establishment in the country."[168] The only other cabinetmaker mentioned in this volume was Phyfe's then-retired competitor Joseph Meeks Sr., also worth $300,000, who "by assiduous care and attention amassed the above fortune" through careful

Figure 53. Architectural drawing of Phyfe's house at 193 Fulton Street, early 20th century. Watercolor, gouache, gum arabic, and graphite on off-white wove paper, 15 5/8 × 11 3/8 in. The Metropolitan Museum of Art, Rogers Fund, 1922 22.28.2

investment in real estate. In a telling omission, however, both Phyfe and Meeks are absent from William Armstrong's *The Aristocracy of New York: Who They Are and What They Were* (1848), despite the inclusion of gentrified neighbors worth one-third as much as they. Although wealthy, they remained outside the city's network of prominent citizens.

This is not to imply that Phyfe was reticent about his success, for it was prominently displayed in an elegantly appointed home at 193 Fulton Street (fig. 53). Likely built in 1816–17, shortly after Phyfe purchased the lease rights to the property and when he was flush with the profits of a cabinetmaking business at its peak, the two-and-a-half-story dwelling was a frame structure with a brick façade.[169] It is notable for its stone lintels and decorative door surround and was as stylistically advanced as his workshops and warehouses across the street.[170] An unusually wide lot allowed Phyfe a four-bay house that included an office on the first floor across the hall from a formal parlor and dining room.

In addition to the detailed inventory of Phyfe's estate, the auction notice for the sale of Duncan and Rachel Phyfe's furnishings shortly after Duncan's death provides additional insight into the appearance of 193 Fulton, particularly with reference to upholstery fabrics.[171] The parlor, with a pair of windows hung with "Satin Damask Curtains" overlooking Fulton Street, was

Life of a Master Cabinetmaker

Figure 54. Phyfe family mausoleum at Green-Wood Cemetery, Brooklyn, New York. Photograph, 2010

clearly the finest room and was furnished with rich furniture, decorative vases, gilt clocks and lighting devices, and numerous mirrors, which the advertisement describes as "superb French-plate." While the preponderance of mahogany furniture throughout the house implies that Phyfe did not bring home the cream of his stock-in-trade, some rosewood furnishings were prominently featured in the parlor.[172] A pair of "carved rosewood chairs in velvet" was placed next to an "elegant carved mahogany suite . . . in hair cloth," along with two rosewood center tables, a rosewood worktable, and a marble-topped mahogany sideboard and cellaret that are a tour de force of the pedestal-end sideboard form popular in the city in the late 1810s and early 1820s (see Pl. 24). The inventory lists eight "mahogany French chairs" in addition to the eight en suite with the sofa.

Regrettably, nearly all of the couple's furnishings were auctioned shortly after Phyfe's death in 1854. Their children quickly emptied the house so that it could be converted into a rental property. Other than the aforementioned sideboard and

Figure 55. Edward D. Phyfe (1808–1887). Photograph, ca. 1880. Collection of Glorianna H. Gibbon

Duncan Phyfe

Figure 56. Wedding of Duncan P. Whitlock (b. 1821) and Margaret P. Ronaldson. Photograph, 1860. Winterthur Library, Joseph Downs Collection of Manuscripts and Printed Ephemera

cellaret, the family's silver, including a ewer made by Phyfe's nephew William M. Phyfe (1810–1893) and his partner Garrett Eoff, and some of Duncan's personal affects, the remainder was sold to the public.[173] But if the furniture owned by William and Eliza Phyfe Vail and James and Julia Phyfe is representative of their parents' personal taste in home furnishings, we can surmise that 193 Fulton included household goods in a broad range of styles and of a consistently high level of quality. The two constants among extant Phyfe family furnishings are their impeccable construction and the superb quality of the veneers.

The inventory and auction notice of the Phyfes' household furnishings also provide a rare, albeit restricted, view into the family's lifestyle. Worktables, writing desks, checker stands, and an extensive library, including "superbly bound illustrated books," characterize their recreational pursuits, while a plaster bust in the front hall and twenty-five inexpensive "pictures," which the auction notice refers to as "oil paintings and engravings," added a layer of artistic appreciation to their surroundings.[174] Furthermore, while Phyfe is commonly remembered as a teetotaler, bottle racks, a gin case, and the cellaret in his parlor imply only a partial rejection of tippling, and the spittoons in the dining room and porch suggest a taste for chewing tobacco common among Americans during this period.

When Duncan Phyfe died on August 16, 1854, from "Old Age," he left behind a grand legacy, both as a legend in the cabinetmaking trade and in his attainment of significant affluence.[175] He was buried beside Rachel, who died in 1851 from "paralysis" at the age of seventy, in the nonsectarian Marble Cemetery on Second Street, where other notable and wealthy figures of his day, such as James Monroe, Stephen Allen, and Luman Reed, were laid to rest.[176] The Phyfes' stay was brief, however, for sixteen months later their children reinterred them at Green-Wood Cemetery in Brooklyn (fig. 54). Green-Wood had been established in 1838 as a rural, landscaped burial ground in the mode of Laurel Hill in Philadelphia and Mount Auburn in Cambridge, Massachusetts, and would remain a fashionable final destination for members of the New York gentry. Although his contemporaries Robert Troup

Life of a Master Cabinetmaker

and DeWitt Clinton, among others, may not have considered him of equal stature, Phyfe has remained by their side at Green-Wood ever since.

At the time of his death Phyfe held $25,000 in stocks, bonds, and outside promissory notes, but the great majority of his net worth remained in real estate.[177] Estate papers reveal that he had transferred nearly $265,000, or 85 percent of his wealth, to his children in the form of promissory notes and gifts of property. Through bonds dated May 2, 1853, and August 14, 1854, he gave his five surviving children his holdings on Fulton, Reade, and Dey Streets, and, in the case of Mary Whitlock, title to the Mitchell Mansion in Southbury, Connecticut, that he had presented to her in 1843.

While Phyfe's children shared in a comfortable lifestyle provided by a successful career and wise investments, none of them shared his drive to work well into old age. Remarkably, Edward (fig. 55) and James were still living with their parents in 1850, despite being forty-two and thirty-six, respectively, the latter with his wife, Julia, and an infant son, Duncan (1848–1919), in tow. As we have no indication that Edward was ever employed in the family business or elsewhere, he must have been completely reliant on his father for financial support.[178] In the 1860 federal census, James and William are listed as "Gentlemen" retirees living a life of leisure, the former in Bethlehem, Pennsylvania, and the latter in New York City; William and Eliza Vail, four children, and four Irish servants are listed as living in New Market, New Jersey. Not surprisingly, four of Phyfe's children named sons in his honor. Phyfe's grandchildren also benefited from inherited wealth. James' family traveled to Europe in the 1850s, and he sent at least one son, William H. P. Phyfe (1855–1915), to Columbia College. William Phyfe used a portion of his inheritance to underwrite his son Duncan's venture into the lumber trade.[179] And the widowed Mary Whitlock, matriarch of a large family, could proudly oversee the nuptials of her son Duncan in a grand Connecticut house (fig. 56) with a table from her father's workshop (Pl. 53) to support the wedding cake.

Michael K. Brown and Matthew A. Thurlow

1. According to New York public records, Phyfe died of "Old Age" (Manhattan Register of Deaths, 1795–1865, Liber 19, New York Genealogical and Biographical Society).
2. Abernethy and Kincardine parish records, Family History Center of the Church of Jesus Christ of Latter Day Saints. Phyfe's 1770 baptismal record states that it was witnessed by Peter Grant and Duncan Grant, the latter perhaps his grandfather. This record differs from the previously published date of 1768, which appears in McClelland 1939; conversely, it does concur with the age implied by the 1850 United States Census.
3. Some of the confusion regarding Phyfe's origins stems from an early biography which states that his mother's last name was McGregor ("Phyfe, Duncan," in *National Cyclopedia of American Biography* [New York, 1926], p. 422). The McGregor clan's name was banned by the Privy Council in 1603 after it lost a feud to the Campbells. Its members subsequently adopted other names, such as Grant.
4. The Abernethy and Kincardine parish manuscripts cite Donald Fife's marriage to Elizabeth Fraser on July 15, 1751. The principal history and genealogy on the Clan Grant are found in Fraser 1883.
5. The only extant cache of eighteenth-century Scottish immigration papers spans the months between January 1774 and September 1775 (Cameron 1965, pp. 57–58). Coincidentally, among them is a citation which records that twenty-seven-year-old "Isobell Fife & a Child," formerly of Paisley, left the Lowland port of Greenock between April 7 and 14, 1775, for New York and explains that she was "Going to her husband." In the Phyfe genealogy published in McClelland (1939, pp. 318–19), which presumably was assembled from information provided by the family, Duncan Phyfe's younger brother Laughlin's life dates are given as 1773–1869. Census returns for 1850, however, state that he was born in Scotland and suggest a birth date of circa 1778 (see note 42). If the earlier date of birth is accurate, then it is possible that this woman was their mother.
6. Initially this research was published in Ormsbee 1929. Ormsbee had access to the original manuscript of the census at the National Archives and notes: "An alteration, by erasure seems to indicate a recent tragedy. The Christian name of the head of the family has been changed to read Isabel," suggesting that Donald Fife had only recently died.
7. McClelland 1939, pp. 99, 318; and Research Notes for William MacBean's Biography of Members of the St. Andrew's Society, Manuscript Collection, New-York Historical Society.
8. Quotation taken from an apprenticeship contract between Duncan Phyfe and William Brown Jr. reproduced in Bassett 1976, p. 61. If it was at this time that Phyfe claimed 1768 as his date of birth rather than the actual date of 1770, his circumstances in 1790, at the age of twenty-two, would have been markedly different. Having satisfied the requirements for his apprenticeship, he would then have been engaged as a journeyman in the shop of a master craftsman. An early start on an apprenticeship may have been a financial necessity, for the widowed Isobel Fife's estate inventory in 1794 indicates that she was not a prosperous woman ("Inventory of the Goods Chattel and Credits of Isabella Phyfe," August 11, 1794, New York State Archives, Albany).
9. General Society of Mechanics and Tradesmen of the City of New-York, *List of Members of the Society from Its Institution in 1785 to December 31, 1916* (New York, 1917), p. 4.
10. General Membership Meeting Minutes of the General Society of Mechanics and Tradesmen of the City of New York, vol. 1, 1785–1802, p. 172.
11. John J. Post is cited as the upholsterer of an easy chair frame manufactured by Phyfe in the Fenwick Lyell Ledger, 1800–1813, Monmouth County Historical Association Library and Archive, Freehold, New Jersey (copy available in the Downs Collection, Winterthur Library, Microfilm 2436.3). For Turnier, see note 62.
12. Scott 1981, p. 15.
13. Estate inventory of John B. Dash Jr., March 13, 1805, 54x37.40, Downs Collection, Winterthur Library.
14. Isaac Louzada appears in the New York directories as a cabinetmaker from 1803 to 1806 and later as a grocer, tavern keeper, and milkman. Phyfe purchased 97 Reade Street from Louzada in 1819 (New York County Register of Deeds, Liber 141, pp. 26–29). Louzada was living in Brooklyn at the time of his death in 1853 ("The Last Will and Testament of Isaac Lowzada," May 15, 1853, Kings County Surrogate Court Records, New York Genealogical and Biographical Society).
15. Manhattan Register of Deaths, Liber 18, New York Genealogical and

Biographical Society. Rachel is listed as seventy years of age at her death on July 17, 1851; her date of birth is not known.
16. François-Alexandre-Frédéric, duc de La Rochefoucauld-Liancourt, *Travels through the United States of North America, the Country of the Iroquois, and Upper Canada, in the Years 1795, 1796, and 1797* (London, 1799), quoted in Still 1956, p. 67.
17. Albany County Probate Records, Letters of Administration, vol. 1, p. 3.
18. Hodges 1986, p. 108; Lyon 1872, pp. vii, 2–4.
19. *Duncan Phyfe v. Thomasin Gordon*, September 26, 1796, 1796–442, New York City Court of Common Pleas.
20. John Bruce Papers, Estate Executors' Accounts, May 18, 1798, 65x086, Downs Collection, Winterthur Library; and John Cruger receipt book, May 21, 1798, 68.5282, Decorative Arts Photographic Collection, Downs Collection, Winterthur Library.
21. For receipted bill, see Appendix 1.1.
22. For receipted invoice, see Appendix 1.2; receipted invoice and bank draft, Duncan Phyfe to George P. MacCulloch, October 8, 1806, 54.37.33, Downs Collection, Winterthur Library.
23. See pages 115–18.
24. Scott 1981, p. 15. In contrast, Phyfe's younger brother Laughlin did not gain citizenship until 1839 (ibid., p. 138). The authors have been unable to locate naturalization papers for the other Phyfe siblings.
25. MacBean 1922–25, vol. 2, pp. 58–59, 162–63. Note that MacBean misstates the generational relationship of the Phyfe family. We do not believe that Duncan's father lived in New York City. The John Phyfe who joined the Saint Andrew's Society in 1817 was Duncan's brother. Two other individuals associated with the Phyfe family, the turner James Ruthven (1826) and the lumber merchant John Turnbull (1827), belonged to the society as well (ibid., pp. 111, 125).
26. William Gibbons account book, January 12, 1802–April 4, 1804, MS 304, Telfair Family Papers, Georgia Historical Society, Savannah.
27. Bound inventory of furniture, n. d. [1804]: "Inventory of Furniture and of whom it was purchased . . . " Charles Nicall Bancker Papers, American Philosophical Society, Philadelphia (copy available in the Downs Collection, Winterthur Library, Microfilm 101.3).
28. Letter from R. de Rezeville to Victor du Pont, August 20, 1805, Winterthur MS, Group 3, Victor du Pont Papers, no. 2594, Hagley Museum and Library, Wilmington, Delaware. The authors thank Joyce Longworth for translating the correspondence of Victor du Pont.
29. Ibid.
30. Bank draft, January 1811, 69x62.3, Downs Collection, Winterthur Library.
31. Quoted in Rock 1984, p. 79.
32. Washington Benevolent Society in the City of New York, Membership List, 1810, Manuscript Collection, New-York Historical Society.
33. [New York] *American Citizen*, February 23, 1810; and *New-York Evening Post*, June 1, 1821.
34. Blackmar 1989, pp. 2, 9–10.
35. Phyfe initially rented 35 Partition Street from Isaac Vanderbeck. Phyfe's property ownership is difficult to establish, for there are frequent discrepancies between New York City directory listings, tax rolls, and deed books. For example, Phyfe is first listed at 35 Partition in the 1795 directory and appears at that address in the 1796 tax assessment, but he does not purchase the property until 1802. For a complete directory listing, see C. Montgomery 1996, p. 481.
36. The first William (1799–ca. 1802) died in infancy, and the first James was presumably dead by James D.'s birth in 1814.
37. *Duncan Phyfe v. Charles Wardell and Brittain L. Woolley*, October 31, 1832, BM-831-P, New York City Chancery Court.
38. If this is indeed Phyfe's younger brother, then James, like Duncan, was also claiming an earlier birth date.
39. Laughlin's signature is found on an 1807 petition to Baltimore's mayor and city council requesting that a person familiar with the cabinetmaking trade be appointed as an inspector of the foreign woods imported for use in furniture production (Hill 1967, p. 144).
40. Receipted bill from James Phyfe to Mr. Talbot, April 11, 1807, Box 9, Folder 1, Papers, 1807, Silas Talbot Collection, G. W. Blunt White Library, Mystic Seaport, Mystic, Connecticut; receipted bill from James Phyfe to Elizabeth Rose, George Clinton Quackenbos Papers, Rare Book, Manuscript, and Special Collections Library, Duke University, Durham, North Carolina.
41. Minutes of the Common Council of the City of New York, 1784–1831, vol. 7, p. 302.
42. Laughlin was in New York City as late as 1839, when he applied for United States citizenship (Scott 1981, p. 138). He is absent from the city directories, the tax records, and the census returns until 1850, when he is recorded as "Lockland Phife" at the farm of James Cole in Westfield, Essex County, New Jersey. Laughlin's relationship to the Cole family is unclear, but it is intriguing that the Westfield return also records a James Fife, a weaver aged sixty and a native of Ireland, and his wife, Catharine, living nearby. Laughlin is not recorded in the 1860 United States census. Whereas the Phyfe family recorded his date of birth as 1773, the census suggests a date of circa 1778.
43. McClelland 1939, p. 315. Ernest Hagen mistakenly referred to this Duncan as a nephew rather than a grandson, which led to inaccuracies in McClelland's Phyfe family tree. For more information on Duncan, see the *New York Herald*, May 27, 1911, p. 9.
44. This receipt is one of a group of three that cite George Newbold and date between September 11, 1823, and December 11, 1826 (73x1–73x3, Downs Collection, Winterthur Library). The bill signed by William Phyfe spans June 14, 1825, through December 11, 1826, and is catalogued as 73x3. William Phyfe's signature also appears on a deed dated June 11, 1825, for his father's purchase of 164 Fulton Street from Isaac Vanderbeck (New York County Register of Deeds, Liber 193, pp. 162–65).
45. *New-York Gazette and General Advertiser*, March 12, 1831.
46. Barrett 1863–70, vol. 1, pp. 423–32.
47. *Edward Phyfe v. Sidney Whitlock and Duncan Phyfe*, December 12, 1843, D CH 261-P, New York City Chancery Court.
48. The purchase on September 30, 1843, is noted in the Southbury, Connecticut, Register of Deeds, vol. 11, p. 480; the transfer of title on May 2, 1853, vol. 14, p. 78.
49. "Melancholy Occurrence," [New York] *Commercial Advertiser*, December 13, 1841, p. 2.
50. Based on Carol Jean Moelhman's exhaustive reading of the *Commercial Advertiser*, it would appear that most rewards offered for the recovery of bodies from the water ranged between $50 and $100, with a few as high as $200.
51. James Ruthven daybook, 1792–1804, and Ruthven cash book, 1843–1849, Manuscript Collection, New-York Historical Society. The Ruthven shop is discussed in Barrett 1863–70, vol. 3, pp. 444–45.
52. James later went into business with his son John G. (1829–1907) and James Jackson as Phyfe & Company (act. 1851–58). John G. and Jackson then established Phyfe & Jackson, which operated from 1858 to 1861. See Amelia Peck, "The Products of Empire: Shopping for Home Decorations in New York City," in Voorsanger and Howat 2000, pp. 283–84.
53. T. G. Smith 1997, pp. 737–38.
54. For Loring, see Sikes 1976, pp. 147–49. Photocopies of five pages from Loring's account book, now missing, are in the scholarship files, the American Wing, The Metropolitan Museum of Art. For Blossom, see Elisha Blossom Jr., account book, 1811–1818, New-York Historical Society; and Kenny 2003.
55. Frelinghuysen 1970.
56. Fenwick Lyell Ledger, 1800–1813, p. 3, Monmouth County Historical Association Library and Archive, Freehold, New Jersey (copy

57. Ibid., p. 104.
58. See Appendix 2.21. The names of Phyfe and Ackerman appear also on a pair of window seats in the White House collection.
59. In the *New-York Gazette and General Advertiser* of June 19, 1802, Lyell advertised: "Any persons wishing to be furnished with knife cases, of a superior quality made after any fashion, to contain any number of knives, forks, and spoons, or any other furniture in the cabinet line will please to call at above." Thomas Sheraton confirms that they were a specialty practice: "As these cases are not made in regular cabinet shops, it may be of service to mention where they are executed in the best taste, by one who makes it his main business" (*The Cabinet-Maker and Upholsterer's Drawing-Book* [London, 1794], p. 392).
60. The most detailed biographical portrait of Charles Watts appears in Rauschenberg and Bivins 2003, vol. 2, pp. 583, 601–2, 747, vol. 3, pp. 1290–96.
61. Charles Watts Accounts, 1802–1815, 69x212 and 81x15, Downs Collection, Winterthur Library; and Charles Watts Letter Book, New-York Historical Society.
62. Turnier recorded transactions on two back pages of his bound copies of the 1796 and 1810 New York price books, which are owned by the Powell Library, Bayou Bend Collection and Gardens, Museum of Fine Arts, Houston.
63. Charles Watts Accounts, 69x212.2, pp. 10, 16–17, 36, 40, 58–59, 61, 74; 69x212.4, pp. 13–14; and 69x212.5, p. 31, Downs Collection, Winterthur Library.
64. John Hewitt Cabinetmaker Records, 1800–1814, Manuscript Group 84, New Jersey Historical Society, Newark. Hewitt's career and account book are analyzed extensively in M. Johnson 1968.
65. M. Johnson 1968, pp. 196–99. For a slightly different reading of this quotation, see Kenny, Bretter, and Leben 1998, p. 44 and p. 99 n. 37.
66. Letter from Sarah Elliott Huger, New York, to Harriott Pinckney Horry, Charleston, October 15, 1812, Harriott Horry Ravenel Family Papers, 1694–1935 (1086.00), South Carolina Historical Society, Charleston.
67. Phyfe's clients between June 1812 and November 1813 include Francis Sexton, Montgomery Livingston, the Corporation of the City of New York, James Kelso, Oliver Wolcott Jr., and Victor Marie du Pont. Regarding the pace of the cabinetmaking trade during this period, Hewitt paid journeyman cabinetmaker Thomas Constantine more than $1,100 between February 1812 and April 1814 (Thurlow 2006, p. 186).
68. *New-York Evening Post*, February 28, 1815. A transparency is a picture made with water-based paints on fabric or oiled paper and lit from behind in the manner of a stained-glass window. They were common at public celebrations in Britain and the United States in the late eighteenth and early nineteenth centuries.
69. Hubbard 1875, pp. 71–73.
70. McClelland 1939, p. 129, pl. 107.
71. Letter from Sarah Elliott Huger, New York, to Harriott Pinckney Horry, Charleston, January 4, 1816, Harriott Horry Ravenel Family Papers, 1694–1935 (1086.00), South Carolina Historical Society, Charleston.
72. Letter from Anthony Girard to Victor du Pont, November 21, 1813, Winterthur MS, Group 3, Victor Marie du Pont Papers, no. 2790, Hagley Museum and Library, Wilmington, Delaware. Additional letters that discuss this commission are nos. 2781 (October 14, 1813), 2782 (October 16, 1813), and 2795 (December 13, 1813).
73. Letter from Sarah Minturn to Jane Bowne Haines, April 4, 1819, II/22/324, Wyck Association Collection, American Philosophical Society, Philadelphia.
74. Haygood and Thurlow 2007, p. 133.
75. Letter from Sarah Elliott Huger, New York, to Harriott Pinckney Horry, Charleston, March 17, 1812, Harriott Horry Ravenel Family Papers, 1694–1935 (1086.00), South Carolina Historical Society, Charleston.
76. Because the bill and the drawing are on separate pieces of paper, we cannot be certain that they belong together. Ernest Hagen referred to them, however, as companion pieces as early as 1905, when they are first cited in "Cost of Furniture a Century Ago" (Hagen 1905, pp. 47–48).
77. Letter from William Wirt to Elizabeth Wirt, December 3, 1817, William Wirt Papers, Virginia Historical Society, Richmond.
78. Alexander 1989; and Gross 1967, pp. 1–14.
79. M. Johnson 1968, p. 190.
80. Allan Nevins, *Abram S. Hewitt, With Some Account of Peter Cooper* (New York, 1935), p. 12, quoted in M. Johnson 1968, p. 192.
81. *Savannah Daily Republican*, December 2, 1820.
82. M. Johnson 1968, pp. 187, 191, 194.
83. Manifest of the schooner *Ariadne*, October 13, 1817, Ph1081, Downs Collection, Winterthur Library; and Manifest of the ship *Thorn*, November 17, 1820, Collection 36, Box 14, Coastwise Manifests, National Archives and Records Administration, Washington, D.C.
84. Letter from Mary Telfair to Mary Few, postmarked December 8, [no year], and letter from Mary Telfair to Mary Few, October 28, [1816], William Few Collection, Georgia Division of Archives and History (Manuscripts Section), Atlanta.
85. Letter from Mary Telfair to Mary Few, postmarked December 8, [no year], William Few Collection, Georgia Division of Archives and History (Manuscripts Section), Atlanta.
86. Morrell's first advertisement in Savannah appeared in the *Republican and Savannah Evening Ledger*, May 2, 1815. He refers to his warehouse as "Just opened from New York," and includes a long list of articles that are "elegant" and "of the latest fashion," suggesting that most of these wares were imported from the North. However, Morrell's claim that he "will be happy to execute any order for Furniture that he may be favored with" indicates that he had the capability of manufacturing cabinetwork on-site or regular access to New York–made goods.
87. *Savannah Museum*, June 12, 1822.
88. Manifest of the ship *Comet*, January 31, 1821, Collection 36, Box 15, Coastwise Manifests, National Archives and Records Administration, Washington, D.C. Morrell also received four boxes via the ship *Augusta*, which left New York on May 11, 1822, Collection 36, Box 17, Coastwise Manifests.
89. Morrell's major suppliers were the mahogany merchant John L. Brouwer (31 shipments) and the fancy-chair maker John K. Cowperthwaite (12 shipments). Between 1825 and 1828 Cowperthwaite shipped more than 700 bundles of chairs to Morrell, and the chairmaking firm of Wheaton & Davis sent an additional 99 (Ship Manifests, January 10, 1825–September 24, 1827, Boxes 168–172, Coastwise Manifests, National Archives and Records Administration, Washington, D.C.).
90. Scherer 1984, pp. 43, 56, 73.
91. United States Census of Manufactures, 1820, Survey #1232, First Ward, New York City, New York Public Library.
92. Ibid., Survey #1250, First Ward, New York City.
93. Ibid., Survey #1259, First Ward, New York City. Mechanics in other trades were feeling a similar pinch. Silversmith John W. Forbes (Survey #1249) found his business "40 pr ct worse than two years since" on account of "the Non-Circulation of Money."
94. Convention of the Friends of National Industry, *Extract from Minutes of a Convention of the Friends of National Industry, Assembled in the City of New York* (Boston, 1819), pp. 1–2.
95. The drawing was acquired by the Metropolitan Museum in 1922 from Robert Fridenberg and, presumably, was the same watercolor that Duncan Phyfe's grandsons Duncan and Harry showed Ernest Hagen in 1907 as a "water colour picture of the Shop made by an apprinteze" (McClelland

1939, p. 316). While it was formerly attributed to the London-trained painter and art instructor John Reubens Smith, authorship by an unnamed apprentice seems more likely. Although executed without a true grasp of the techniques of perspective drawing, the overwhelmingly detailed presentation suggests a draftsman with an intimate understanding of the shop's structure. The Smith attribution was offered in Carson 1979; and refuted in Avery 2002, pp. 112–13.

96. Heckscher 1997, p. 238.
97. Halliday & Jenkins 1847. The only known copy of this publication is in the Downs Collection, Winterthur Library. The sale included 430 lots of furniture, of which 178 were split between the three floors of 192 Fulton and the remaining 252 between the two floors of 194 Fulton.
98. The 1847 auction catalogue distinguishes between the "Large Room on First Floor of 194 Fulton-St." and "No. 194, 1st Door on Entrance," which suggests that the first door led to a room inaccessible from the main wareroom. The second floor at 194 Fulton was divided between "Second story, Large Room" and "Room in Second Story . . . Connecting with the preceding Room" (Halliday & Jenkins 1847, pp. 12, 16, 18).
99. "Trial of Mead," *Commercial Advertiser*, October 16, 1829.
100. [New York] *Mercantile Advertiser*, September 24, 1810; and *New-York American*, May 31, 1826. In the former, John Geib & Son requested six journeymen cabinetmakers or joiners who "must be the best workmen; likewise, ingenious, sober and industrious." The relationship between Phyfe and the Geib family as referenced in Singleton 1900, p. 526, has yet to be proven. See Brown 1978, p. 55 n. 61.
101. M. Johnson 1968, pp. 200–201.
102. John Hewitt Cabinetmaker Records, 1800–1814, p. 46, Manuscript Group 84, New Jersey Historical Society, Newark.
103. See note 71 above.
104. Hagen [1907], R. T. Haines Halsey Research Papers, Box 2, no. 36, Downs Collection, Winterthur Library.
105. While the authors assume that Jacob and Isaac were related, documentary evidence to support this claim has not surfaced. In 1818, Duncan Phyfe became associated with the Morrell family of Newtown, New York, through his daughter Mary's marriage to Sidney B. Whitlock, the son of William and Sarah Morrell Whitlock. In 1819, George Morrell and Isaac W. Morrell witnessed the sale of 97 Reade Street from Isaac Louzada to Phyfe (New York County Register of Deeds, Liber 141, pp. 28–29). Furthermore, Sidney B. Whitlock's brother William Whitlock Jr. operated a shipping line between New York and Savannah from 1824 onward, which was eventually taken over by the mercantile firm Scott & Morrell and then Scott, Shapter & Morrell (Barrett 1863–70, vol. 1, pp. 423–24).
106. "Old New York Furniture: Early Cabinetmakers Whose Work Is Prized Highly," *New York Sun*, 1894.
107. Seventh Census of the United States, Fifth Series, Productions of Industry Census, 1850, p. 363. According to the census survey, the Meeks brothers employed 125 men and six women, had $150,000 of capital invested in the business plus $70,000 in wood and upholstery, and were producing furniture worth $200,000 annually.
108. *New-York Evening Post*, February 18, 1814.
109. Ibid., June 9, 1814.
110. The 1816 New York City jury list references eight males in Kelly's household, some of whom were likely journeymen and apprentices.
111. [New York] *American Citizen*, December 8, 1802. The publication was *The New-York Book of Prices for Cabinet and Chair Work, Agreed Upon by the Employers* (New York, 1802).
112. [New York] *American Citizen*, December 31, 1802, cited in Gottesman 1965, pp. 146–47.
113. New-York Society of Cabinet-Makers, *Revised Constitution and Rules of Order of the New-York Society of Cabinet-Makers of the City of New-York* (New York, 1810), p. 3.
114. Ibid., p. 5.
115. New York City Apprenticeship Papers, New-York Historical Society.
116. Bassett 1976, p. 61. Phyfe's close proximity to St. Paul's Chapel facilitated his introduction to William Brown Sr. at an early date, and both are listed in the estate papers of John Bruce, who was buried in a Phyfe-made coffin in the St. Paul's churchyard in 1798 (Estate Papers of John Bruce, Downs Collection, Winterthur Library). William Jr. should not be confused with two other artisans by that name working in New York at the same time. A cabinetmaker, William Brown, appeared in the New York directory from 1810 to 1823 and occupied 23 Partition Street for the two years prior to Robert Kelly's move there in 1813. A chairmaker, William Brown, is in the New York directory from 1812 to 1823, and is listed at 53 Broad with William Brown Jr. between 1812 and 1814. Perhaps William Sr., the sexton at St. Paul's, joined his son in the chairmaking trade at this time.
117. Kenny, Bretter, and Leben 1998, p. 63.
118. *New-York Evening Post*, November 11, 1817. While it is unclear whether Phyfe continued to retail pianos throughout his career, when the stock of D. Phyfe & Son was dispersed in 1844, the auctioneer announced the availability of four "elegant Rosewood Piano Fortes of the richest quality and tone" ([New York] *Commercial Advertiser*, March 25, 1844).
119. *New-York Evening Post*, January 14, 1819. Newberry also advertised pianos for sale at Phyfe's warehouse in the *Post* on August 31, 1818; November 4, 1818; January 4, 1819; and February 8, 1819.
120. *New-York Evening Post*, March, 20, 1820; June 3, 1830; and February 20, 1817, respectively.
121. [New York] *Commercial Advertiser*, May 5, 1831; and *New-York Evening Post*, March 30, 1820, respectively. Because the documentary record reveals that few customers placed extensive orders with Phyfe, the authors doubt the veracity of many such advertisements.
122. *New-York Evening Post*, March 18, 1820.
123. *Baltimore Patriot*, September 20, 1824; and [Philadelphia] *Saturday Evening Post*, August 6, 1825.
124. *Alexandria Gazette and Virginia Advertiser*, October 19, 1840.
125. *New-York Evening Post*, November 11, 1817.
126. Brown 1978, p. 65.
127. Kenny, Bretter, and Leben 1998, pp. 139–40.
128. Phyfe's workshop also mended chairs on the council's behalf in 1817. See Account of Repairs at Federal Hall, Nicholas Carmers for payment to Phyfe, May 26, 1803, Ph1106.2, Downs Collection, Winterthur Library; Request of warrant for payment to Duncan Phyfe and others, September 7, 1812, Minutes of the Common Council of the City of New York, 1784–1831, vol. 7, p. 248; and Request of warrant for payment to Duncan Phyfe and others, May 18, 1817, Minutes of the Common Council of the City of New York, 1784–1831, vol. 9, p. 163.
129. Stone 1825, p. 373.
130. Ibid., p. 374.
131. Although the report does not explain Phyfe's role in the production of the boxes, Phyfe was likely responsible for their design. The lids relate closely to the applied bosses found at the top and bottom of scrolls on his furniture in the Grecian Plain style (see fig. 114). The report of the Department of Fine Arts, by Archibald Robertson, that is part of Colden's 1825 *Memoir* states that Duncan's shop is on Murray Street, where his nephew, John Phyfe Jr., an ivory and hardwood turner, worked from 1825 onward and thus may have assisted with the project along with Daniel Karr.
132. Kings County Register of Deeds, Liber 177, p. 24; and *Edward Phyfe v. Sidney Whitlock and Duncan Phyfe*, December 12, 1843, D CH 261-P, New York City Chancery Court.
133. Blackmar (1989, pp. 87–88) estimates that in the first two decades of the 1800s the average rent for a two-story brick-front house on Murray Street, four blocks north of Fulton, was $450 a year. Annual rent may be calculated as 10 percent of a property's assessed value.

Life of a Master Cabinetmaker

134. Hubbard 1875, p. 48.
135. Dyer 1915b, p. 57. These claims have not been confirmed by primary sources.
136. Letter from Charles Watts Jr. to Charles Watts Sr., January 17, 1811, Box 1, Folder 4, Watts-Jones Family Papers, New-York Historical Society.
137. Letter from Charles Watts Jr. to Mr. E. Barnell, December 14, 1811, Charles Watts Jr. Letter Book, 1811–1820, New-York Historical Society. Charles Jr. maintained the family business after his father's death in 1811.
138. M. Johnson 1968, p. 201.
139. Fearon 1818, p. 23.
140. *Duncan Phyfe v. Charles Wardell and Brittain L. Woolley*, October 31, 1832, BM-831-P, New York City Chancery Court.
141. *New-York Evening Post*, April 14, 1847. The sale consisted of "the entire stock of unmanufactured materials of Duncan Phyfe & Son."
142. Hanyan 1996, pp. 30–31.
143. McInnis and Leath 1996, pp. 150–53.
144. Pollack 1998, pp. 6–7. Remarkably, despite Joseph Meeks' start in 1797, the earliest labeled piece of furniture connected to his shop dates to 1828.
145. Ibid., pp. 8–9.
146. M. Johnson 1968, p. 193.
147. Hagen [1970], R. T. Haines Halsey Research Papers, Downs Collection, Winterthur Library; and McClelland 1939, p. 317. Lord Hay and British foreign minister Alexander Baring, 1st Baron Ashburton, were in New York in September 1842 following the negotiation of the Webster-Ashburton Treaty in Washington, which resolved several border issues between the United States and Britain's North American colonies ("Dinner to Lord Ashburton," *The Albion: A Journal of News, Politics and Literature* 1, no. 36 [September 3, 1842], pp. 1, 36).
148. *The American Advertising Directory, for Manufacturers and Dealers in American Goods* (New York, 1832), p. 143.
149. Judges' Reports for 1832 and 1834, Records of the American Institute of the City of New York, New-York Historical Society; and [New York] *Commercial Advertiser*, October 10, 1834. The *Commercial Advertiser* questioned Phyfe's ability to distinguish between real mahogany and the highly realistic paint-grained mahogany submitted to the fair by a decorative painter named Degroot.
150. Thomas Skidmore, *The Rights of Man to Property!* (New York, 1829), p. 388. The Workingmen's Party was established in 1829 in New York City by, among others, the radical publisher George H. Evans and the educator Thomas Skidmore in support of the working class. The movement was defined in part by Skidmore's 1829 treatise.
151. Moses 1830, pp. 7–8.
152. Clerk's Office, United States District Court, *An Alphabetical List of Applicants for the Benefit of the Bankrupt Act, (Passed August 19, 1841) within the Southern District of New-York* (New York, 1843).
153. [New York] *Commercial Advertiser*, May 16, 1838.
154. William Phyfe witnessed the deed for his father's purchase of 164 Fulton Street in 1825 and the lease for part of John Turnbull and Michael Phyfe's lumberyard on Washington Street in 1837 (New York County Register of Deeds, Liber 193, pp. 162–65; and Liber 372, pp. 244–46).
155. Letter from James H. Hammond to Catherine E. Hammond, August 25, 1840, James Henry Hammond Letters, #305-z, Southern Historical Collection, The Wilson Library, University of North Carolina at Chapel Hill.
156. Ibid., September 4, 1840.
157. Although bills or correspondence do not survive to prove William Aiken's patronage of D. Phyfe & Sons, furniture he purchased in New York in the late 1830s is closely related to pieces documented to Phyfe's workshop (Garrett 2005, pp. 119, 138, 141, 161).
158. [New York] *Commercial Advertiser*, April 24, 1843.
159. D. Phyfe & Son's advertisement ran on three occasions, and Allison's notice appeared with it on the second and third printings ([New York] *Commercial Advertiser*, April 24, 26, and 28, 1843). In the April 28 issue, Allison appears to have altered his advertisement to more closely resemble that of D. Phyfe & Son, and the two were placed one above the other.
160. [New York] *Commercial Advertiser*, April 6, 1844.
161. *New Mirror of Literature, Amusement and Instruction* 3, no. 6 (May 11, 1844), p. 90.
162. See Catherine H. Voorsanger, "'Gorgeous Articles of Furniture': Cabinetmaking in the Empire City," in Voorsanger and Howat 2000, pp. 309–12.
163. Catherine H. Voorsanger, "From the Bowery to Broadway: The Herter Brothers and the New York Furniture Trade," in Howe et al. 1994, pp. 60–61.
164. Halliday & Jenkins 1847, p. 9.
165. Letter from James H. Hammond to Catherine E. Hammond, August 25, 1840, James Henry Hammond Letters, #305-z, Southern Historical Collection, The Wilson Library, University of North Carolina at Chapel Hill.
166. Halliday & Jenkins 1847, pp. 16–17.
167. See *Duncan Phyfe v. Joseph T. Bell*, New York City Court of Common Pleas, 1851–1069; *Duncan Phyfe v. John Stevenson*, New York State Supreme Court, 1849 S-57; *Duncan Phyfe v. John T. Auchinloss and Henry T. Croxon*, New York State Supreme Court, 1852 A-88; *James D. Phyfe et al. v. Curtis G. Gardiner and Sylvanus Lyon*, New York City Superior Court, 1858–1345; *James D. Phyfe et al. v. George T. Green*, New York City Superior Court, 1858–1381; and *William Phyfe et al. v. Patrick Mulligan*, New York City Superior Court, 1857–1574.
168. Beach 1845, p. 26.
169. The date is inferred from a significant jump in the assessed value of the house and lot at 169 Fulton Street in the New York City tax rolls between 1816 and 1817. Although the value of Phyfe's other properties remained steady, that of his house doubled from $5,000 to $10,000.
170. The authors thank architectural historian Andrew S. Dolkhart for sharing with us his analysis of Phyfe's house.
171. On September 19, 1854, William Irving & Co. auctioned the contents of 193 Fulton Street with "Household Furniture Made by Duncan Phyfe" (*New York Times*, September 18, 1854, p. 7).
172. Another concentration of rosewood furniture was found in the front bedroom on the second floor, presumably the one shared by Duncan and Rachel ("Inventory of the Contents of Duncan Phyfe's House at 193 Fulton Street Made after His Death," September 14, 1854, Duncan Phyfe Papers, 54 x 37.34, Downs Collection, Winterthur Library).
173. Phyfe's will stipulates that his daughters Mary and Eliza divide equally between them his "Silver Ware, china & glass ware, Curtains both Bed and Window, All Beds, Bed Linen and Bedding of every Kind, Table Linen, Sett of Knives & Forks and Box containing therein, which Box was made by me" ("Last Will & Testament of Duncan Phyfe," January 7, 1854, Thomas J. Watson Library, Metropolitan Museum).
174. *New York Times*, September 18, 1854, p. 7.
175. Manhattan Register of Deaths, Liber 19, New York Genealogical and Biographical Society.
176. Ibid., Liber 18.
177. At his death, Phyfe held promissory notes from two neighbors for money recently lent. Stephen Burkhalter, a grocer and Phyfe's tenant at 191 Fulton Street, owed $562.50. Burkhalter's signature on Phyfe's will and estate inventory implies a close relationship. A Pembroke table of about 1815–20, similar to the Brinckerhoff example (Pl. 19), descended in Burkhalter's family, perhaps purchased by him at the auction of the contents of 193 Fulton in 1854. Because Burkhalter did not arrive in New York until 1822, when he was only sixteen, he could not have been the original owner. The lumber merchant John L. Brouwer, who was also a business associate of Phyfe's former agent in

Savannah, Isaac W. Morrell, owed Phyfe's estate the more substantial sum of $5,600.

178. Edward Phyfe was first married in 1852 to Ann Eliza Voorhis (Register of Marriages in the Parish of Trinity Church, New York, vol. 2, Trinity Church Archives). He may have suffered from physical or mental shortcomings, as he never worked and was not, like his brothers and brother-in-law, selected to be an executor of his father's estate ("Last Will & Testament of Duncan Phyfe," January 7, 1854, Thomas J. Watson Library, Metropolitan Museum). Furthermore, despite his extensive wealth, in 1880, then seventy-one, he was living with his son, Harry, in the house of his deceased second wife's parents, John D. and Permilla Matlake, who were younger than Phyfe (United States Population Census, 1880, Westchester County, New York). Before his death in 1887, Edward wrote his son out of his will and "was unfit to take care of the child, having suffered during the closing years of his life with softening of the brain" ("Ignoring His Son: A Father Wills His Money to His Nephew," *New York Times*, December 6, 1888).

179. "The Courts," *Brooklyn Eagle*, July 8, 1856; and July 9, 1856.

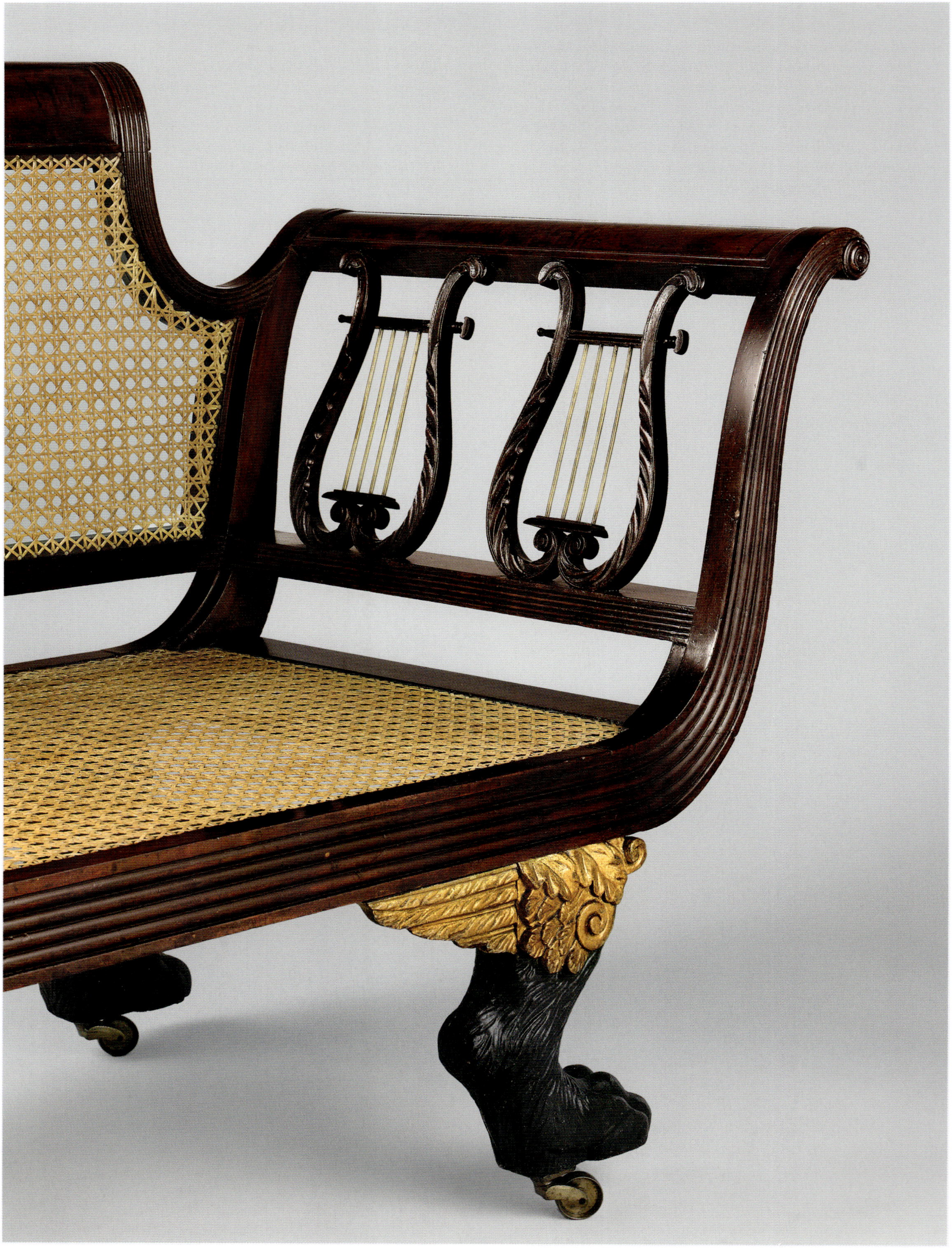

2. Furniture from the Workshop of Duncan Phyfe

Duncan Phyfe's chief merrit lies in the carrying out and Especially improving of the "Sheriton" style of Settees, Chairs and tables in his best period the work about 1820 although the workmanship was perfect gradually degenerated in style at first to the questionable "American Empire" and after 1830 to the abominable heavy Nondescrip veneered style of the time when the Cholera first appeared in New York 1833 to 1840–1845 when the overdecorated and Carved rosewood style set in which Phyfe himself called the "Butcher" furniture.

Ernest F. Hagen, "Duncan Phyfe Memorandum," 1907[1]

Although more than a century has passed since Ernest Hagen drafted his now-famous "Memorandum" on the life and work of Duncan Phyfe, the colorful language and strong negative opinions expressed by this early biographer of the master cabinetmaker on some of the later furniture produced in his workshop continues to resonate in certain circles to this day. One might quibble with Hagen's perception of Phyfe's furniture design over time, but he is dead-on about one thing: the workmanship is nearly always "perfect." As with so many areas of artistic endeavor, knowledge and understanding help one to acquire a taste, or at least an appreciation, for them. Such is the case with Phyfe furniture in all its stylistic guises.

Duncan Phyfe was a demanding master, a stickler for quality, and an aesthetically intelligent interpreter of British and French Neoclassical furniture design, which arrived in New York in a steady stream of printed sources, imported furniture, and immigrant craftsmen from the 1790s to the 1840s. As a creative designer and an astute businessman, he had an uncanny knack for grasping and absorbing fashion trends through the precise development of stylistically coherent lines of furniture that, once established, were produced in his workshop with only minor incremental changes, often over a period of a decade or more. This process had the salutary effect of making Phyfe's furniture and many of his decorative motifs veritable trademarks for his enterprise. Singularly recognizable, the work of Duncan Phyfe consistently adheres to the classical design principles of structural coherence, balance, and proportion. For purposes of this essay it has been divided into four broad style categories: early Neoclassical, based on the eighteenth-century designs of George Hepplewhite and Thomas Sheraton; the Classical or Grecian style, which encompasses Hagen's late "Sheriton" and "questionable 'American Empire'"; an architecturally derived, veneered plain style, in which richly ornamented Grecian-style forms were stripped to their essentials; and the emerging Gothic and Rococo revivals of the 1840s at the end of Phyfe's career. Despite historical gaps resulting from the scattershot survival of documented Phyfe furniture, major examples from every decade of his production except the 1790s make it possible to explicate in fair detail the stylistic development of this celebrated American cabinetmaker.

Early Neoclassical Style

It is ironic that so little early Neoclassical furniture is known from a craftsman whose name is virtually synonymous with the style's succeeding phase in New York and whose formative years as a cabinetmaker align so perfectly with the publication of the two principal pattern books of the period, George Hepplewhite's *Cabinet-Maker and Upholsterer's Guide* (London, 1788) and Thomas Sheraton's *Cabinet-Maker and Upholsterer's Drawing-Book* (London, 1793). Phyfe was familiar with these style guides, and in at least one instance, it would seem, furniture made in his shop was copied directly from a plate in Sheraton's *Drawing-Book*. Documented furniture in the early Neoclassical style is known from the workshops of Thomas Burling, Robert Carter, Elbert Anderson, and William Whitehead, to name a few of the leaders in the cabinetmaking trade in New York in the 1790s and early 1800s, but where is the well-known master's early furniture in this style today?

This question has long frustrated students of Phyfe's work. In 1929, for example, the intrepid early collector and connoisseur Louis Guerineau Myers teamed up with the editor of *The Magazine Antiques*, Homer Eaton Keyes, in an attempt to sort out Phyfe's early Neoclassical furniture from that of his contemporaries by linking the carving on a type of New York vase-back chair of about 1795 with a Phyfe-attributed klismos

Opposite: Detail of Duncan Phyfe Grecian sofa, 1816 (Pl. 18)

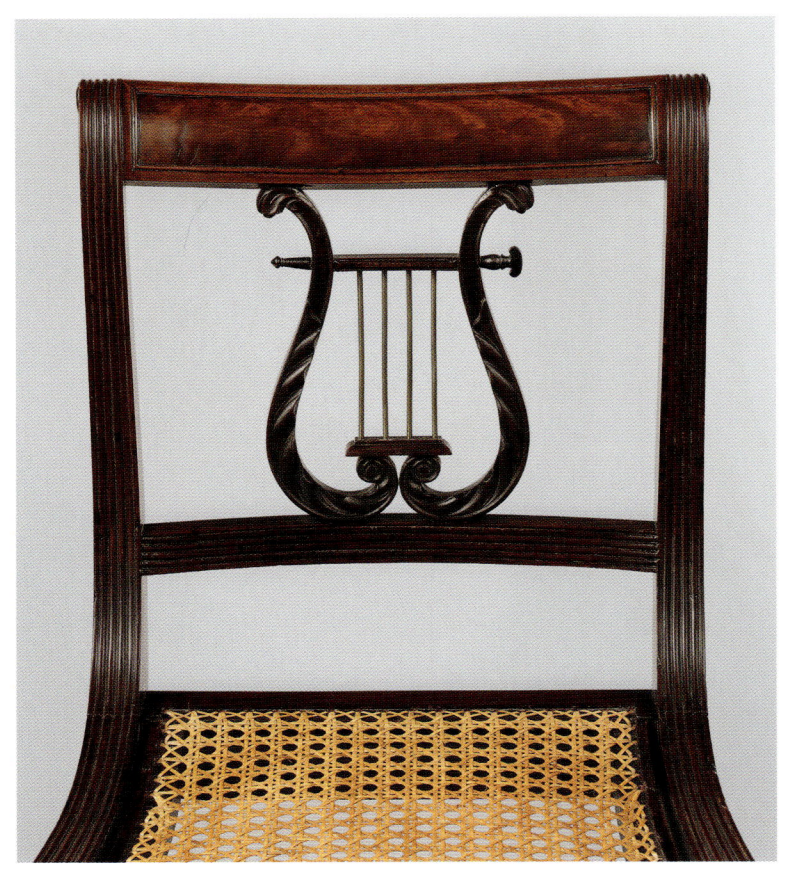

Figure 57. Detail of lyre banister on the Duncan Phyfe side chair in Plate 17

Figure 58. Detail of banister of a New York side chair, 1790–1800. The Metropolitan Museum of Art, Gift of H. D. Perine, 1925 25.157

chair with a lyre banister made nearly twenty years later. Detailed photographs of the backs were used to demonstrate the similarities in the carved ribbed patterns and scrolled leaves on the banister and lyre (figs. 57, 58). Myers and Keyes believed that these similarities offered evidence that the carving on both chairs was by the same hand and hence that both were made in Phyfe's shop.[2] Their attribution is questionable, however, because it assigns an earlier chair to Phyfe based on the attribution of a later one, which in turn had no basis in Phyfe's documented work and was selected on a stylistic basis alone. Nonetheless, their theory is thought provoking because it suggests continuity in the motifs and techniques employed by New York carvers over time from one phase of the Neoclassical style to the next.[3]

The number of pieces of early Neoclassical furniture that can be assigned to the Phyfe shop even tentatively is extremely limited. It includes two square-back chairs of classic New York design that descended in the family of the cabinetmaker's son James and a square-back sofa with an inscription on an unseen framing member that reads: "For Duncan Phyfe, L. Ackerman, his stuffing, July 1804, A.D." (fig. 59).[4] L. Ackerman is most likely Lawrence Ackerman, an upholsterer who also inscribed a rare library chair he upholstered for Phyfe in 1811 (App. 2.2). Square-back chairs and sofas of this type, with carved sunflower demilunes in raised rectangular crest tablets, are traditionally attributed to the New York cabinetmaking partnership of Abraham Slover and Jacob Taylor (act. 1802–5), based on a partial set of chairs with fragmentary labels discovered in 1923.[5] One of the two square-back armchairs passed down in the Phyfe family is of this so-called Slover & Taylor type, but with a carved drapery swag instead of a demilune sunflower in the crest tablet.[6] The other, also a popular New York pattern, with a tall, drapery-swagged pierced vase and three Prince of Wales feathers in the back, was copied directly from plate 36, no. 1, in Sheraton's *Drawing-Book*.

The intersection of Slover & Taylor and Phyfe is further highlighted by the appearance of debit charges in both their names in the account book of the cabinetmaker Fenwick Lyell (1767–1822), who worked on Beekman and Beaver Streets in New York between 1795 and 1809. On March 23, 1805, Lyell recorded a charge to Slover & Taylor of £27.12.0 for "12 Mahogany Chair frames," and less than two months later, on May 3, £13.12.0 for "2 Sopha frames" to Phyfe. Later the same year, a debit charge appeared in the account book to the upholsterer John J. Post for "putting castors to an easy chair frame of Mr. Phyfe's make," and in January 1809, Phyfe returned to Lyell again for "1 Pair Knife Cases Veneers found."[7]

While the limited descriptions given for these chair and sofa frames make it impossible to identify their specific designs, the possibility exists that Lyell was making Slover & Taylor–type seating forms for both Slover & Taylor and Phyfe. The documented practice of New York cabinetmakers selling each others' work naturally wreaks havoc with attributions based on style alone, and makes ascribing any of this early Neoclassical furniture to Phyfe highly problematic.

That Phyfe produced more than chairs and sofas in the early Neoclassical style is indicated by a bill dated July 26, 1800, that lists a total debit charge of £309.18.00 to a Mr. Brewerton for forty-five pieces of furniture (App. 1.1). In addition to tables, chairs, and case pieces, Phyfe also sold Brewerton window blinds, a bracket, and a safe, and provided him with other typical cabinetmakers' services, including "mending and varnishing" and "putting handles" on several pieces of furniture, and "seating chairs."[8] None of the entries are descriptive enough to provide a precise image of what this furniture looked like, but we can be fairly certain, given their date of manufacture, that they were in the general style of Hepplewhite and Sheraton. The most expensive item on the Brewerton bill of sale was a "Sideboard" priced at £26.

Concerning the retail price of furniture in America about 1800, furniture scholar Charles Montgomery has asserted that "[i]n addition to labor, the masters paid for materials, rent, heat, candles and other overhead. These costs with profit increased the retail price to an average of three and one half the times the labor cost."[9] According to this formula, Phyfe's approximate labor cost for the sideboard would have been £7.8.0. Seven cellaret sideboards are listed in the 1796 price book. The four with the most complex façades have starting labor charges exclusive of any structural or ornamental extras that range from £8.2.0 to £9.13.10, all higher than Brewerton's. Three are lower and include "A Strait front Celleret Sideboard" (£3), "A Round Front Celleret Side-board" (£6), and "A Serpentine Front Celleret Sideboard" (£7). This would seem to suggest that the sideboard Phyfe manufactured for Brewerton was likely one of these lower-cost models. In 1802, Phyfe probably made an even simpler sideboard priced at £16.0.0 for a Mr. Morewood (App. 1.2). And we can be fairly certain that at least in one instance before 1804, he made a very elaborate sideboard with a complex façade and extensive inlay in the early Neoclassical style based on a sideboard valued at $130, or about £50, described in an 1804 inventory of the contents of the Philadelphia house of Charles N. Bancker.[10]

Unfortunately, constructing scenarios such as these does little to illuminate the character of Phyfe's Neoclassical work of the 1790s and early 1800s. Phyfe's use of subcontractors within the New York cabinetmaking community also makes it difficult to determine his personal style in this early period. Curiously, a similar conundrum exists for furniture made in the last several years of Phyfe's career in the emerging Gothic and Rococo Revival styles. As the second stage of the Neoclassical style unfolds in New York, however, and surviving

Figure 59. Attributed to Duncan Phyfe. Sofa, 1804, originally upholstered by Lawrence Ackerman. Mahogany, 39¼ × 72 × 25 in. Private collection

Furniture from the Workshop of Duncan Phyfe

Figure 60. Pierre de La Mésangère. Two plates, 1797 and 1798, from M. Paul Cornu, *Meubles et objets de goût, 1796–1830: 678 documents tirés des journeaux de modes . . .* (1914)

examples of Phyfe's documented work become more abundant, his identity as a master interpreter of the Grecian style more clearly emerges.

Grecian Style

During the first quarter of the nineteenth century, New York was a beehive of commercial activity and civic improvement. Some of the fruits of this remarkable period were increased opportunities for entrepreneurs and a rapid accumulation of wealth, the invention of the steamboat, the completion of the Erie Canal, a handsome new City Hall, and the founding of a National Academy of Design. Such achievements, in the words of Charles Over Cornelius, curator of the first Phyfe exhibition, held at The Metropolitan Museum of Art in 1922, are the "necessary background against which to judge [Phyfe's] utilitarian art which served its purpose of contributing largely to the creation of worthy standards of taste in the public of the time."[11] As early as 1815, the midpoint of his career, Phyfe was the pride of New York and a nationally recognized figure.

The cabinetmaker's renown was based on his superbly proportioned and exquisitely made furniture in the fashionable Antique or Grecian style, an idiom currently referred to as the Classical style.[12] In *The Cabinet Dictionary* (London, 1803), Thomas Sheraton states that the word "antique" "is generally applied to such painting and sculpture, or architecture, as were executed at the period, when these arts arrived to their utmost perfection amongst the Greek and Romans."[13] Phyfe seemed to be aiming to match this perfection with a new line of Grecian-style furniture he probably began experimenting with as early as 1805, established by 1807, and then augmented and refined until about 1815, when he merged it with the richer, more archaeologically correct designs of Thomas Hope and Napoleon's architects Charles Percier and Pierre-François-Léonard Fontaine. By the early 1830s, this later phase of the Grecian style was supplanted in turn by an elegantly simple plain style stripped of the ornamental excess of the preceding decade, which lent this furniture a dignity and repose that suited the fashionable new Greek Revival interiors of the time. It is for his early work in the Grecian style before 1820, however, that Phyfe is best known today—the timeless classics that Nancy McClelland linked so closely to early nineteenth-century English Regency furniture design and Charles Over Cornelius praised for the "exquisite balance" between their component parts and for their "strong sense of structural integrity and economy in construction."[14] But Cornelius' further contention, that this furniture represents the only contribution by Phyfe that may be considered "a legitimate part of the history of furniture design," is surely a narrow assessment colored by the collecting world of the 1920s, one that can no longer be sustained.[15]

Phyfe's earliest documented furniture in the Grecian style was made in 1807 for the wealthy New York City merchant William Bayard. Like his counterparts in Regency England, Bayard was a man of taste and means. In the early 1800s, he completely refurbished a comfortable town house for himself and his family, furnishing it with mahogany furniture in the latest Regency-based Grecian style. Refined elegance, convenience, compactness, and mobility were the hallmarks of late eighteenth- and early nineteenth-century Regency furniture

68 *Duncan Phyfe*

design, as was an emerging interest in the forms and ornament of *le goût antique* of Directoire (1795–99) and Consulat (1799–1804) France (fig. 60). This French taste, transformed and made their own by English Regency designers and cabinetmakers, was the foundation for Phyfe's new line of furniture in the Grecian style, which in the past has been characterized inaccurately as being directly influenced by French design.[16]

Scroll-Back, Klismos, and Curule Chairs
The surviving scroll-back chairs made for William Bayard demonstrate Phyfe's early mastery of the Regency-based Grecian style (Pls. 1–3). The finest and most expensive of the three sets of chairs Phyfe made for this wealthy and influential client were highly advanced for New York in 1807. They feature saber-shaped legs based on ancient Greek chair design, double-cross banisters in the back, and relief-carved crests that depict a cluster of thunderbolts bound by a bowknot, an attribute of the Greek god Zeus, whose vaunted eagle messenger is frequently depicted clutching them in his talons (fig. 61). The Bayard chairs also reveal Phyfe's intimate knowledge of English Regency chair design as he attempted to create the equivalent of London high style for his well-heeled clients. In overall form, Phyfe's scroll-back chairs of 1807 can be traced directly to patterns shown in the 1802 and 1807 editions of *The London Chair-Makers' and Carvers' Book of Prices for Workmanship* (figs. 62, 63).[17] No English Regency scroll-back chairs have been discovered to suggest that in establishing his design Phyfe directly copied an imported model. Rather, the known relationship between English Regency scroll backs and their New York cousins indicates that they are cognates.

Two other essential early Regency Grecian-style chair designs, the klismos and the curule, were subsequently illustrated and described in the 1808 *Supplement to the London Chair-Makers' and Carvers' Book of Prices for Workmanship* (figs. 64, 65), and Phyfe wasted little time interpreting these as well. Delicately scaled and exquisitely crafted, Phyfe's new triad of Grecian-style chairs were probably all in production by the early 1810s and served to advance the Phyfe brand both locally and nationally. It is thus hardly surprising that these chairs are the very items the well-dressed salesman—perhaps Phyfe himself—is shown offering to his elegant lady customers through the open wareroom door in the well-known watercolor of his shop (see frontispiece on page 114).

One of Phyfe's earlier customers, Charles N. Bancker, was attracted to these Grecian-style chairs in 1815, when the cabinetmaker sent sketches and pricing options for a klismos and a curule chair to his attention in Philadelphia (see fig. 149). The klismos chair shown in Plate 20 is reputed to be one of the set Bancker eventually ordered from Phyfe and represents a sleek, locally made version of the English Regency form. In London, and probably in New York as well, inward-curved and crossed legs were the shapes most closely associated with ancient Greek furniture design, as indicated by the language used to describe these elements in the 1808 *Supplement to the London Chair-Makers' and Carvers' Book of Prices for Workmanship*. Here, the inward-curved front and back legs pointing in opposite directions and the sweeping inward-curved rear stiles that characterize the ancient Greek klismos (fig. 66) were all designated "Grecian," but the chairs on which they were featured were called "Trafalgar" chairs, a name believed to derive from their association with the London firm of Morgan & Saunders, suppliers of furniture to Lord Nelson, who, after Nelson's heroic death at the Battle of Trafalgar in 1805, renamed their business Trafalgar House and sold numerous chairs of this type.[18] Ogee-crossed legs on curule chairs and stools were designated "Grecian Cross Fronts" (see fig. 65).

New York curule chairs with Grecian cross fronts, like those depicted in the London price book supplement and in the Phyfe sketch, are exceedingly rare. More common, though far from ordinary, are those with side-mounted Grecian crosses. The placement of the cross under the side seat rail is thought to be a New York innovation, possibly Phyfe's, that imparts a long serpentine line to the chair extending from the tip of the front leg through the center and up into the scrolled rear stile.[19] Firm, elegantly drawn serpentine and elliptical curves that animate a form and give it dynamic tension were said to be Phyfe trademarks by Cornelius, who likened the shape of the rear stile on a Phyfe scroll-back chair to that of "a bent steel rod."[20] New York curule chairs with side-mounted Grecian crosses, such as the example shown in Plate 13, have been called "surely the noblest of all early nineteenth-century chairs," a fitting tribute to a form descended from the *sella curulis*, the

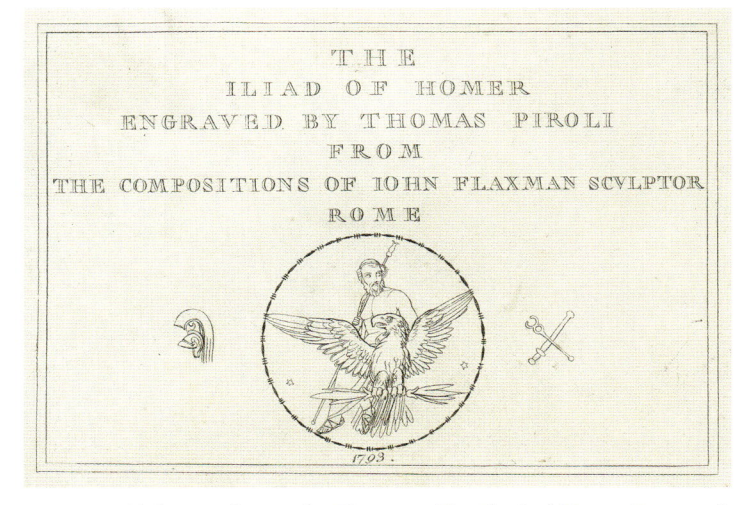

Figure 61. Title page from John Flaxman, *The Iliad of Homer Engraved by Thomas Piroli from the Compositions of John Flaxman Sculptor . . .* (1793). The Metropolitan Museum of Art, Gift of Harvey Smith, 1977 1977.595.50

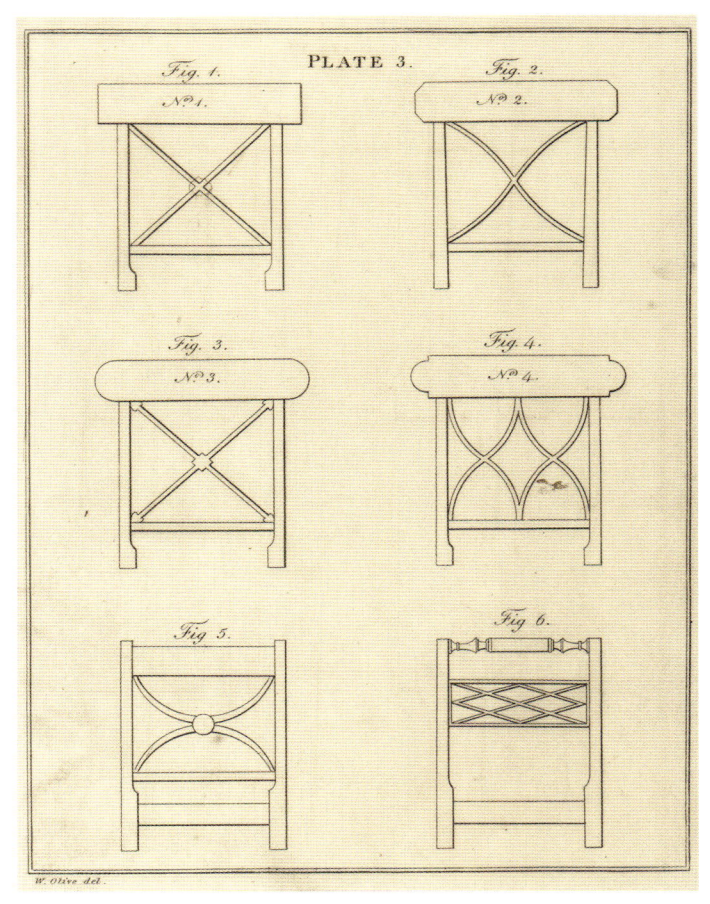

Figure 62. Plate 3, *The London Chair-Makers' and Carvers' Book of Prices for Workmanship* (1807). The Metropolitan Museum of Art, Harris Brisbane Dick Fund, 1940 40.76.6

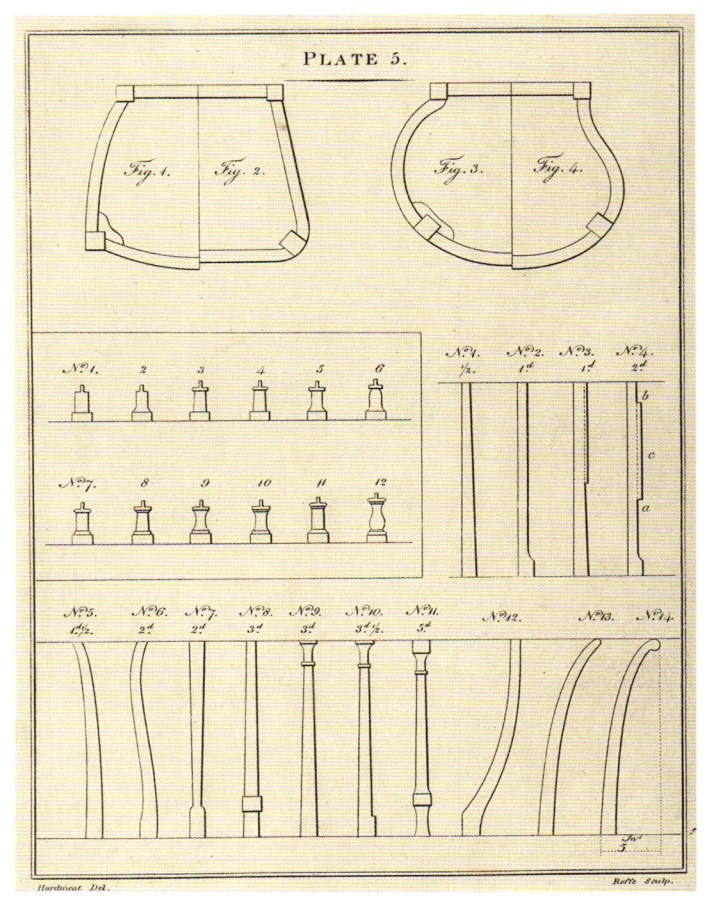

Figure 63. Plate 5, *The London Chair-Makers' and Carvers' Book of Prices for Workmanship* (1807). The Metropolitan Museum of Art, Harris Brisbane Dick Fund, 1940 40.76.6

seat of honor accorded to Roman magistrates with even earlier origins in ancient Etruria and Greece.[21]

Regency-based Grecian-style chair design moved into the mainstream of the New York furniture-making industry within a few years of Phyfe's commission from Bayard, as exemplified by the inclusion of "A Scroll Back Chair" in the revised New York price book of 1810.[22] Klismos chairs were probably still being refined by that date and did not appear in the price book until 1817, where they are described under the generic heading "A Square Back Chair"; their component parts are depicted graphically in a plate at the back of the book (fig. 67).[23] Curiously, no reference to curule chairs appears in the New York price books. Front curule bases are listed and illustrated as options, however, for "A Grecian Sofa" and "A Window Seat" in the 1817 edition.[24]

Phyfe, more likely than not, was a driving force behind the appearance of scroll-back and klismos chairs in the price books and their widespread manufacture in New York. That others made scroll-back chairs like his is a matter of record at least in one instance and a fairly safe supposition otherwise. Copyists, however, probably were not too much of a concern for Phyfe and may actually have helped his sales.

Much like today, intellectual property laws in the early nineteenth century were weak in the area of original furniture designs, and copyists fulfilled an important role by keeping new designs in the public eye while at the same time spurring the top designers to stay ahead of them with fresh ideas.[25] These factors may be behind Phyfe's sometimes subtle but continued development of his line of Regency-based Grecian-style chairs; the curule and the klismos after the scroll back was established; the permutations we see in the carved ornaments and fancy veneers on crest panels; and the waterleaf carving, diminishing bead molding, and fancy panels of veneers on the front face of saber-shaped Grecian legs.

One of Phyfe's most tenacious competitors in New York at the time he was developing his line of Grecian-style chairs was the immigrant French cabinetmaker Charles-Honoré Lannuier (1779–1819). About 1810 or slightly earlier, Lannuier flattered the master by making a nearly exact copy of one of his scroll-back armchairs (fig. 68). If we compare this armchair with one made for William Bayard in 1807 (Pl. 1), however, the Frenchman is shown not to have been Phyfe's equal in this type of furniture. The seat on the Lannuier armchair is overly wide, and the bowknot-and-thunderbolt ornament is carved

70   *Duncan Phyfe*

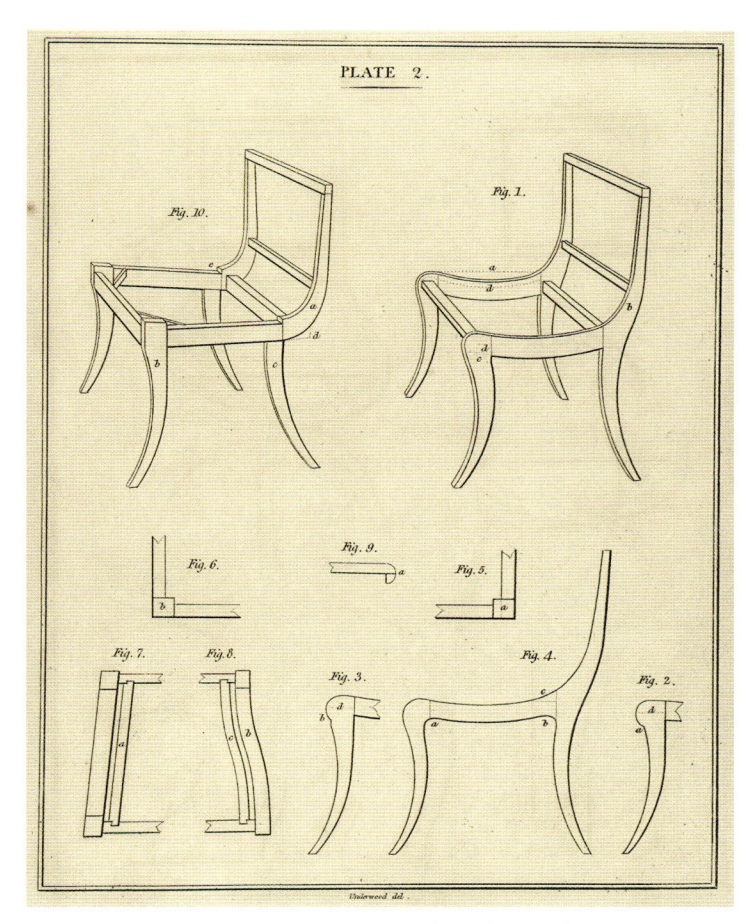

Figure 64. Plate 2, *Supplement to the London Chair-Makers' and Carvers' Book of Prices for Workmanship* (1808). The Metropolitan Museum of Art, Harris Brisbane Dick Fund, 1940 40.76.6

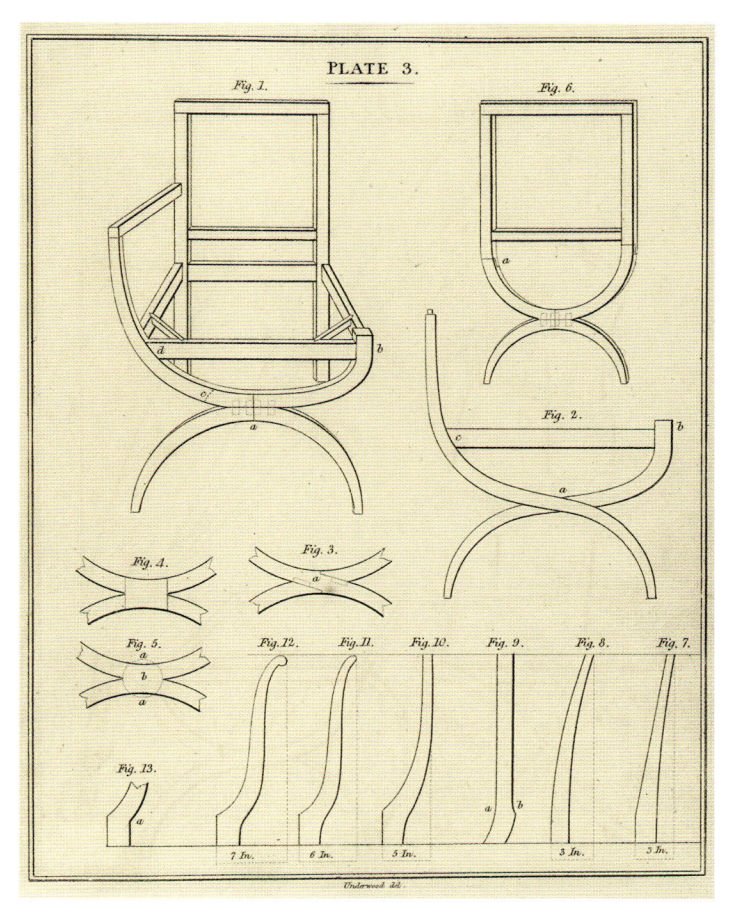

Figure 65. Plate 3, *Supplement to the London Chair-Makers' and Carvers' Book of Prices for Workmanship* (1808). The Metropolitan Museum of Art, Harris Brisbane Dick Fund, 1940 40.76.6

with tiny crinkles and folds like a French eighteenth-century Neoclassical bowknot. Underscaled, it is set in the center of the crest rail like a small applied appliqué, as opposed to the larger, more languid version of the bowknot on the Phyfe chair.[26] Later it will be shown that Phyfe similarly struggled in his attempt to reproduce one of Lannuier's signature furniture designs.

Sofas, Couches, and Upholstered Armchairs

Paired en suite with Phyfe's scroll-back chairs were handsome scroll-back sofas, both upholstered and caned. These sofas, which can be traced directly to *The London Chair-Makers' and Carvers' Book of Prices for Workmanship* and the 1808 *Supplement*, were built on the chassis of earlier square-back models updated by the addition of a scrolled, paneled crest and optional serpentine arms with scrolled handholds and bell-shaped seats (Pl. 6). Three sofas are recorded in Phyfe's 1807 bills to William Bayard, all priced at $65. The only known example of the three is a caned scroll-back model of fine quality but with straight arms with scrolled handholds and straight side seat rails (Pl. 4), cheaper alternatives to bell-shaped seats with S-curved arms to match. The equal prices on the bill might suggest that all three sofas were of the same design. However, because one of the three sets of scroll-back chairs is upholstered, it is possible that at least one of the sofas also had an upholstered back and seat.[27]

The Bayard scroll-back sofa is the only one that can be assigned with confidence to the Phyfe shop, although three other similar sofas marked by New York makers other than Phyfe exist. One is by his lifelong competitor and frequent imitator Michael Allison (1773–1855; fig. 69), the other two are by William Mandeville (act. 1800–35) and J. S. Taylor.[28] The Allison sofa has the more expensive and elaborate bell-shaped seat and serpentine arms and is half-upholstered over the seat rails. If it did not bear Allison's ink-stamped mark, the sofa's superior design and elegant lines could surely qualify it as a Phyfe shop production. There is, however, a perceptible difference in the quality of the bowknot-and-thunderbolt carving in the crest rail compared with that on the documented Bayard sofa, which is more precise and lively in the way the thunderbolts flex where they are bound together in the bowknot (compare figs. 70 and 71).

But does the relative quality of the carving on a piece of furniture allow us always to make a Phyfe attribution? Within

Furniture from the Workshop of Duncan Phyfe

Figure 66. Pierre d'Hancarville. Plate from *Collection of Etruscan, Greek, and Roman Antiquities from the Cabinet of the Honorable William Hamilton* (1767). The Metropolitan Museum of Art, Thomas J. Watson Library

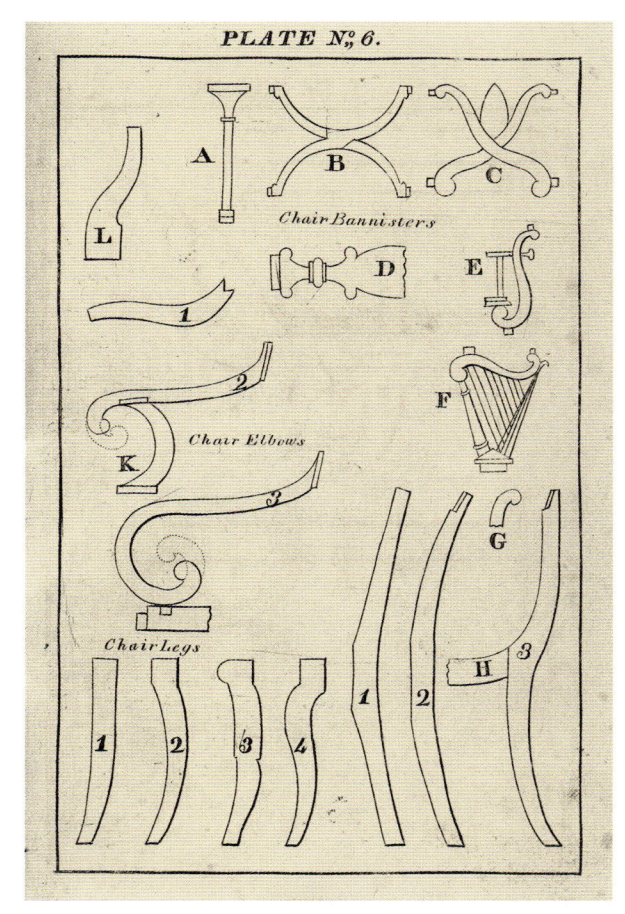

Figure 67. Plate 6, *The New-York Book of Prices for Manufacturing Cabinet and Chair Work* (1817). The Metropolitan Museum of Art, Harris Brisbane Dick Fund, 1939 39.32.1

Figure 68. Charles-Honoré Lannuier. Armchair, ca. 1810. Mahogany, 33 1/8 × 22 3/4 × 24 1/8 in. The Metropolitan Museum of Art, The Sylmaris Collection, Gift of George Coe Graves, 1931 31.44.2

72   *Duncan Phyfe*

Figure 69. Michael Allison. Sofa, 1814–17. Mahogany, 36 × 79¾ × 32 in. The Art Institute of Chicago, Restricted gift of the Antiquarian Society in honor of Milo M. Naeve

the three sets of scroll-back chairs William Bayard bought from Phyfe in 1807, the work of two distinctly different carvers can be discerned. The bowknot on one of them (see detail, Pl. 2) clearly is more loosely rendered than that on the other (see detail, Pl. 3). So the answer to this question is probably no. However, it will be shown that Allison copied Phyfe again in some later Grecian-style furniture. That his carvers still did not measure up to Phyfe's on this furniture is noteworthy and may suggest a certain aesthetic "handwriting" on Allison's part.

Two other Grecian-style seating forms, "Grecian" sofas and couches, probably were made in the Phyfe shop by 1810, although the earliest documented examples date to 1816 and 1826, respectively (Pls. 18, 35). The Grecian couch has deep roots in classical antiquity. Its defining feature, a scrolled, fulcrum-like end that echoes the serpentine curve of the rear stiles on klismos chairs, derives from the couches and lounges on which ancient Romans reclined while taking their meals (fig. 72). The principal difference between Grecian sofas and couches is that on the former the scrolled ends are of equal height, while on the latter, one end is higher than the other. Either one could be used for reclining, although the couch clearly is the more inviting of the two for this purpose. Both forms were also listed for the first time in the 1810 New York price book and described in greater variety and detail in the 1817 edition.

The documented 1816 Grecian sofa by Phyfe (Pl. 18) has large gilded and *vert antique* lion's-paw feet that bespeak the bolder and more archaeologically correct second phase of the Grecian style that was emerging at the time. The continuous line of the reeded front rail and scrolled ends and the paneled crest, however, appear to derive from an earlier design for a Grecian sofa published in Sheraton's *Cabinet Dictionary* of 1803. Two other Grecian sofas, possibly made in the Phyfe shop, are more delicate in scale and relate perfectly in form to curule and klismos chairs. One has a curule base (Pl. 15) and is part of the suite of parlor seating furniture made for Thomas Cornell Pearsall about 1810–15. The other (Pl. 23), without provenance, was probably made only slightly later and has carved lion's-paw feet with hairy shanks like those on Phyfe klismos chairs and similarly compact and upright scrolled fulcrum ends that relate to rear stiles on the chair. This particular Grecian sofa cannot be linked to any of the several klismos chairs known with lyre backs and carved fasces or cornucopias in the crests, though chairs of this type (see, for example, Pl. 22) would seem to be its logical suite mates.

A rare library chair inscribed on the outside of the back frame, "Stuffed by . . . L. Ackerman Oct 18, 1811 upholsterer / This frame made by D. Phyfe / For Mr. Van Ransellaer Albany" (App. 2.21), reveals once again Phyfe's reliance on *The London Chair-Makers' and Carvers' Book of Prices for Workmanship* for the general form of his early Grecian-style seating furniture. Practically a line-for-line copy of an example illustrated in the 1807 London price book (fig. 73), the Van Rensselaer library chair has the same deep seat and ogee-shaped back legs, but is missing the built-in footrest that slides out from inside the seat frame. Phyfe added his own touch to the London design with scrolls on the front of the arms and his signature reeded front legs ending in balloon-shaped inverted balusters and casters. No specific heading for a library chair appears in the 1810 or 1817 New York price books, but there are entries in both for the old-fashioned easy chair, with an option in the

Furniture from the Workshop of Duncan Phyfe 73

Figure 70. Detail of bowknot-and-thunderbolt carving on the Michael Allison sofa in figure 69

Figure 71. Detail of bowknot-and-thunderbolt carving on the Duncan Phyfe sofa made for William Bayard in Plate 4

later edition for "making the back legs ogee."[29] An identical library chair almost certainly from the Phyfe shop (fig. 74) has recently been upholstered in tufted morocco leather, a popular period covering for library chairs.

Pillar-and-Claw and Other Table Forms

Nearly as iconic as Phyfe's scroll-back and klismos chairs in the Grecian style are the double and treble elliptic pillar-and-claw tables attributed to his shop. These include card, Pembroke, sofa, dining, and pier tables with double and treble elliptic tops, which also were made with the typical Hepplewhite- and Sheraton–based New York tapered, turned, and reeded legs. Despite the attributions to Phyfe of so many of these iconic table forms, at present only a double elliptic mahogany card table with straight reeded legs, probably one of the pair listed on Phyfe's 1807 bill to William Bayard priced at $75, can be linked by documentation to his shop (Pl. 5). Labeled double and treble elliptic card and Pembroke tables with either straight reeded legs or pillar-and-claw bases (fig. 75) are known by John Dolan, George Woodruff, Stephen and Moses Young, and Michael Allison, and these constitute a larger and more diverse group of tables in this typical Grecian style than the work of Phyfe.[30]

With the furniture form considered by many to be one of Phyfe's most quintessential missing from the documented oeuvre—the so-called trick-leg double elliptic pillar-and-claw card table—a fine satinwood example has been chosen to stand in here (Pl. 11). The very best of its kind, it has precisely carved waterleaves on its vase-shaped pillar and claws.[31] The minimum starting labor charge for a table like this in the 1810 New York price book was a substantial £5.8.0, or just over double the starting charge for the Bayard card table with one fly and four fixed legs (Pl. 5).[32] The trick legs point to the sides when the table is closed; when it is open, they turn 45 degrees to the rear to provide a stable tripod base, a transformation accomplished by a mechanical system hidden within the upper frame and its turned and carved pillar (fig. 76). A clever mechanical feature like the trick leg was right in step with the Regency vogue for the "most novel" or "technologically impressive furniture that could be devised," and was aimed to appeal to upscale patrons eager to keep abreast of the latest London trends in furniture design.[33]

The precise origin of the trick-leg design so distinctive to New York remains uncertain.[34] The pillar with three incurved, saber-shaped legs may have conjured up associations with ancient bronze tripod stands, but the truth is that the design was impractical, dangerous, and doomed to failure because the tables, when the tops are closed, are so poorly balanced that they are perpetually in danger of tipping backward. Sometime between 1810 and 1815, a considerably more stable design featuring a swivel top was adapted to the pillar-and-claw base. This design also provided an opportunity for a new array of structural supports below, including clusters of columns, lyres, griffins, and siren-like caryatids, all of which play a major role during the richer, more archaeologically correct second phase of the Grecian style. A double elliptic pillar-and-claw mahogany card table with a Bayard family history (see fig. 144) is a good example of this type, with a cluster of four turned and carved columns on the plinth and a top that pivots 90 degrees on the apron in order for it to be laid open for card playing. It is identical in design to a pair of tables that descended in the family of Thomas Cornell Pearsall (Pl. 12), who is believed to have purchased them from Phyfe about 1810–15 along with the previously discussed curule sofa and chairs.

Worktables in the early Grecian style were also made with straight legs and pillar-and-claw bases. The earliest documented Phyfe example (Pl. 7) has turned and reeded legs and bears the label used by the cabinetmaker prior to 1812, when he maintained his shop at 35 Partition Street. Noteworthy features include the gently swelled reeded legs with peg-shaped feet and the thin cock bead along the bottom edge of the

74 Duncan Phyfe

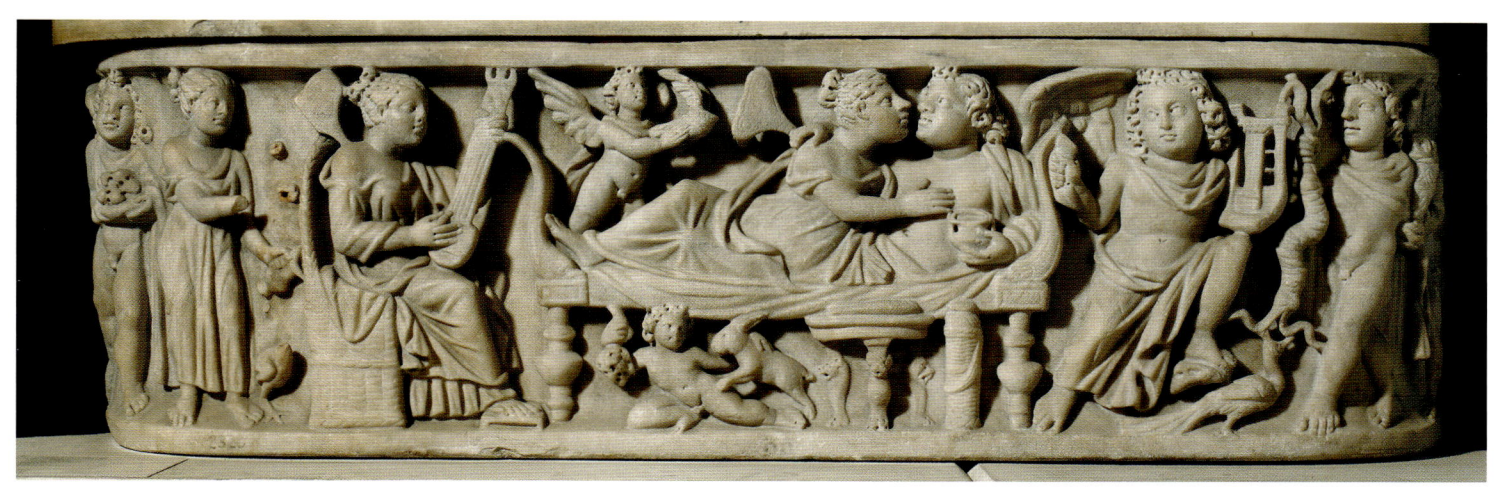

Figure 72. Detail of a Roman sarcophagus depicting Cupid and Psyche. Marble, 3rd century A.D. The Trustees of the British Museum, London

reeded compartment, which imparts a delicacy and lightness akin to the pleated fabric bags on many Federal-era worktables.

Another documented worktable made of satinwood with a pillar-and-claw base and a compartment section with astragal ends was purchased from Phyfe in 1813 as a wedding gift for Victorine du Pont by her uncle Victor Marie du Pont and his wife for $40 (Pl. 8). This price represents a very good value considering the expensive exotic wood used and the amount of labor required to make the reeded compartment with sliding tambour shutter and all the delicate interior fitments. The microscale dovetail joints on the sliding trays reveal the high level of craftsmanship that Phyfe demanded from his workmen. In the case of this particular worktable, we are fortunate to have written evidence of how Phyfe assigned its manufacture to one of his most talented journeyman, apparently a specialist, "whom he knows best does this sort of work." Comparison of the dovetails on the du Pont worktable with those on another, superior satinwood example long attributed to the Phyfe shop (Pl. 9) reveals no discernible difference in the quality of workmanship. These tables also share the same precise construction and superfine inlaid stringing of cross-grained kingwood used to border the bottom edge of the veneered apron and form panels on the faux drawer front and flanking dies.

Two additional pillar-and-claw worktables documented to the Phyfe shop have a cluster of four pillars on a compact

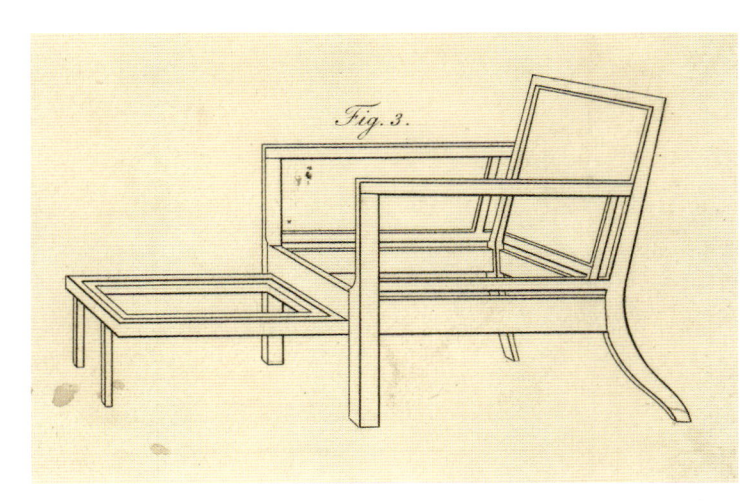

Figure 73. Plate 8, *The London Chair-Makers' and Carvers' Book of Prices* (1807). The Metropolitan Museum of Art, Harris Brisbane Dick Fund, 1940 40.76.6

Figure 74. Attributed to Duncan Phyfe. Library chair, 1810–15. Mahogany, 40½ × 28⅝ × 36 in. The Metropolitan Museum of Art, Gift of Mrs. J. Insley Blair, 1950 50.20.1

Furniture from the Workshop of Duncan Phyfe

Figure 75. Michael Allison. Card table, 1808–15. Mahogany, mahogany veneer, 30 × 20 × 18 in. From the Collections of the Henry Ford, Dearborn, Michigan

Figure 76. Detail of the trick-leg mechanism on a New York card table, ca. 1810. The Metropolitan Museum of Art, The Sylmaris Collection, Gift of George Coe Graves, 1930 30.120.16

plinth like those seen on the previously mentioned Bayard and Pearsall card tables. The remarkable discovery of a bill of sale to James Kelso of New York City under a lift-out tray in the compartment section of one of these tables allows it to be dated precisely to 1813 (see fig. 153 and App. 1.4).[35] With its fashionable canted corners, this worktable presents an entirely different aesthetic from that of the examples with astragal ends (Pls. 8, 9). In place of a tambour shutter in the upper compartment, it has a deep drawer with a reeded applied facing. The rectilinear compartment section with canted corners and the use of a French-style brass baguette molding on the lid foreshadow the coming changes in the Grecian style, which privileged flat planar surfaces over the earlier elliptical and astragal end shapes. The fluted ellipsoid and baluster-shaped pillars are more robust than the small twist-reeded orbs and waterleaf-carved vases and columns seen on the Bayard and Pearsall card tables, which may be of a slightly earlier date.

The other worktable with a cluster of four pillars is labeled and was made between 1811 and 1816 (fig. 77). The sarcophagus-shaped midsection is separated from the apron

76 *Duncan Phyfe*

by a silver-plated filet, and although it has the same combination of pillar turnings as the Kelso worktable, the tapering form and faceted, planar surfaces veneered with iridescent cuts of crotch mahogany render it the more brilliant and successful of the two designs. The diminishing bead molding and the carved lion's-paw feet with cuffs are so close in design and execution to those on the du Pont worktable (Pl. 8) that one senses they were carved by the same skilled craftsman. The tapering sarcophagus shape has deep roots in ancient funerary traditions and marks the table as a piece of furniture in the vanguard of the next, more archaeologically correct phase of the Grecian style, as opposed to the du Pont worktable, which already by 1813 looks a little old-fashioned with its reeded, vase-shaped pillar and astragal ends, a Neoclassical shape in use in American furniture beginning as early as the 1790s. Phyfe continued to exploit the sarcophagus shape into the 1840s, using it on a cellaret with Grecian scrolls made for the dining room at Millford, the home of John Laurence and Susan Hampton Manning in Clarendon (now Sumter) County, South Carolina (Pl. 60). Sheraton illustrates a wine cistern, which he calls a sarcophagus, in *The Cabinet Dictionary*, stating that "as a piece of furniture, [it] is in some faint degree, an imitation of the figure of these ancient stone coffins."[36]

Case Furniture

Documented case furniture from the Phyfe shop in the early Grecian style is remarkably rare. A pedestal-end sideboard, whose location is now unknown, was published in March 1930 in *The Antiquarian* as the one purchased by William Bayard from Duncan Phyfe in 1807 for $125 (fig. 78). Pedestal-end sideboards were the flagship pieces of case furniture made by New York cabinetmakers in 1810, when the form was used to grace the title page of the newly issued price book that year (see fig. 44). The design is a more compact, simplified reworking of one by John Shearer published in the 1788 and 1793 editions of *The Cabinet-Makers' London Book of Prices, and*

Figure 77. Duncan Phyfe worktable, 1811–16, in Plate 10, with front open

Figure 78. Duncan Phyfe sideboard, 1807, published in *The Antiquarian,* March 1930

Figure 79. John Shearer. Design for a sideboard. Plate 6, *The Cabinet-Makers' London Book of Prices, and Designs of Cabinet Work,* 2nd ed. (1793). The Metropolitan Museum of Art, Harris Brisbane Dick Fund, 1924   24.42.2

Designs of Cabinet Work (fig. 79). Also included in the 1810 New York price book was a new model called a French sideboard, which was more rectilinear in form, with a straight front and four tall cupboard doors. Early versions of the French sideboard more closely matched the scale and proportions of the pedestal-end models, but by 1815 they had grown massive, foursquare, and architectural, with Ionic columns or pilasters supporting a projecting frieze of drawers and resting on a stout plinth with lion's-paw feet (Pl. 24).

A delicately scaled secretary bookcase believed to have been ordered from Phyfe in 1816 by Mary Telfair of Savannah, Georgia (see fig. 155), has typical New York tapered and reeded legs ending in balloon-shaped inverted baluster turnings like those on the 1807 Bayard card table (Pl. 5), but substantial

78   *Duncan Phyfe*

carved lion's-paw feet and gilded composition rosettes in the cornice soffit are more indicative of its date of manufacture. Mary Telfair had earlier patronized Phyfe for a worktable and, like some of his other customers, was dismayed by how long she had to wait to receive it. But the powers of exclusivity and fashion and knowing that she would be getting excellent value for the money apparently outweighed her concerns, so she returned once again to Phyfe for her secretary bookcase.[37]

A cylinder desk and bookcase (fig. 80) represents a grander version of a similar form and may have been made in the Phyfe shop about the same time or just slightly later. Like the Telfair secretary bookcase, it has a flat projecting cornice soffit. The fluted ellipsoids that surmount the tapering faceted front legs are like those on the previously discussed worktables with canted corners documented to the Phyfe shop (Pl. 10 and see fig. 153).

Ornamented Grecian Style

The second phase of Phyfe's work in the Grecian style is a bold synthesis of late English Regency and French Empire furniture design characterized by the use of opulent materials and sculptural and architectural elements derived from classical antiquity. The overall effect is one of brilliance, monumentality, and archaeological correctness, especially when compared to the suave, almost delicate character of his earlier work in the style. The transition was gradual and probably occurred sometime between 1810 and 1815 under the general influence of several important English and French design publications, including Thomas Hope's *Household Furniture and Interior Decoration* (London, 1807), George Smith's *Collection of Designs for Household Furniture and Interior Decoration* (London, 1808), Percier and Fontaine's *Recueil de décorations intérieures* (Paris, 1812), and two important fashion magazines, Pierre de La Mésangère's *Collection de meubles et objets de goût* (Paris, 1802–35) and Rudolph Ackermann's *Repository of Arts, Literature, Commerce & C.* (London, 1809–29).[38] This transition was also likely spurred by Phyfe's most able competitor in New York, the Parisian-trained *ébéniste* Charles-Honoré Lannuier, who organized his manufactory to take advantage of these international trends by staffing it with *ébénistes* and other specialists who, like himself, had once worked in Paris, the epicenter of the opulent Greco-Roman revival under way in Europe. By 1815–20 the Grecian style as formulated by Lannuier and Phyfe was a rich mélange of French Empire and late English Regency design trends. Lannuier was in some ways more avant-garde and successful at this visually complex and technically challenging furniture, but his untimely death in 1819 cleared the field for Phyfe, who continued to refine his ornamented Grecian-style furniture. By the 1820s it was the finest available in New York.

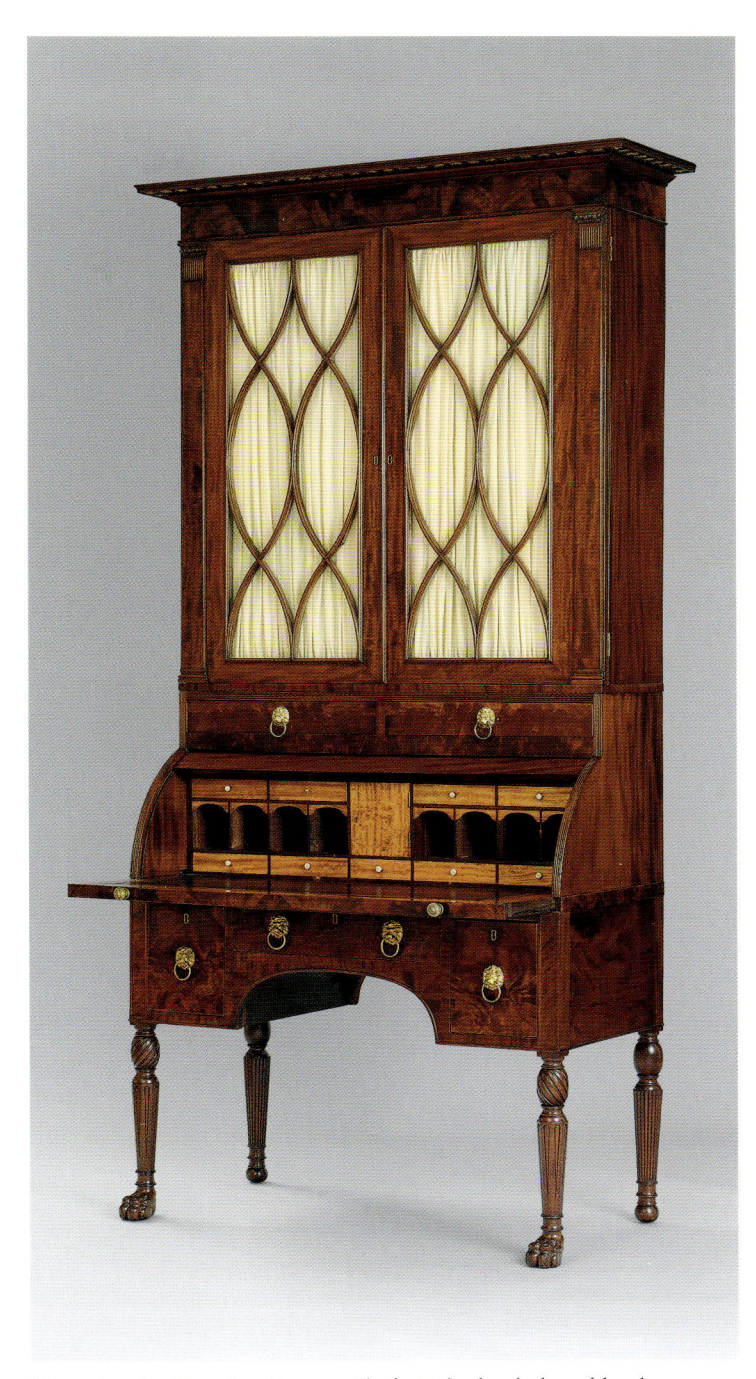

Figure 80. Attributed to Duncan Phyfe. Cylinder desk and bookcase, 1815–20. Mahogany, mahogany and satinwood veneers, gilded composition ornaments, 95 3/8 × 48 1/8 × 24 in. The Metropolitan Museum of Art, Purchase, The Horace W. Goldsmith Foundation Gift, in memory of Berry B. Tracy, 1985 1985.236a, b

Two tables from a set of parlor furniture made for James Brinckerhoff in 1815 are highly expressive of the changes wrought in the Grecian style by this time. The pillar-and-claw card table with canted corners from this set (fig. 81), when compared with a pair probably made in the Phyfe shop for Thomas Cornell Pearsall several years earlier (Pl. 12), has a broader stance, heftier pillars, massive lions' paws gilded and painted *vert antique* in imitation of excavated ancient bronzes, and a gilded brass French Empire ornament applied to the

Furniture from the Workshop of Duncan Phyfe

Figure 81. Duncan Phyfe. Card table, 1816. Mahogany, mahogany veneer, gilded gesso, and *vert antique*, gilded brass, 30 × 36 × 18 in. Private collection

Figure 82. Michael Allison. Pembroke table, 1817–19. Mahogany, mahogany veneer, gilded gesso and *vert antique*, 28¾ × 45¾ × 37⅞ in. The Metropolitan Museum of Art, Rogers Fund, 1948 48.100

Figure 83. Duncan Phyfe. Pembroke table in Plate 19 with leaves up

80 *Duncan Phyfe*

Figure 84. Detail of foot of the Duncan Phyfe Grecian sofa, 1816, in Plate 18

Figure 85. George Smith. Detail of foot of a *chaise longue*. Plate 65, *Collection of Designs for Household Furniture and Interior Decoration . . .* (1808). The Metropolitan Museum of Art, Harris Brisbane Dick Fund, 1930 30.48.2

Figure 86. Detail of foot of a Grecian sofa attributed to Duncan Phyfe, ca. 1815–20. Collection of Mr. And Mrs. Stuart P. Feld

Figure 87. Detail of foot of the Duncan Phyfe Grecian sofa, 1819, in figure 158

front apron identical to the type Lannuier used on some of his card tables and chairs.[39] The Pembroke or "tea table," as it was called on Phyfe's bill, is similarly foursquare and massive with analogous turned pillars, lion's-paw feet, and canted corners on the falling leaves (Pl. 19). Michael Allison, ever ready to mimic the style setter Phyfe, produced his own version of the Brinckerhoff table between about 1817 and 1819, with closely related but less precise turnings, a similar shelf-like, veneered plinth, and idiosyncratic carved lion's-paw feet (compare figs. 82 and 83). His table leaves are cut double elliptic, an earlier shape slightly out of sync with the rest of the design.[40]

The klismos chairs and Grecian sofa from the Brinckerhoff parlor set (Pls. 17, 18) also have the latest gilded and *vert antique* carved lion's-paw feet. The winged paws on the sofa, distinguished by their prominent Ionic volutes of unequal size and draped oak leaves (fig. 84), relate to a more animated version of the design illustrated in George Smith's *Collection of Designs for Household Furniture and Interior Decoration* and to another undocumented example (figs. 85, 86). On another Grecian sofa, made in the Phyfe shop for Reuben and Jane Bowne Haines in

Furniture from the Workshop of Duncan Phyfe   81

Figure 88. Pierre de La Mésangère. Plate 494, *Collection de meubles et objets de goût* (1820). Colored engraving. The Metropolitan Museum of Art, Harris Brisbane Dick Fund, 1930 30.80.2

Figure 89. Attributed to Duncan Phyfe. Box sofa. New York, ca. 1820. Rosewood, rosewood veneer, gilded gesso, gilded brass, die-stamped brass border, 33¾ × 82 × 27¼ in. The Art Institute of Chicago, Restricted gift of the Antiquarian Society and Mrs. Herbert A. Vance

1819, the winged lion's paws are of nearly identical design but made of solid mahogany versus painted and gilded carved ash and pine (fig. 87). This sofa also differs from the Brinckerhoff example in the way the scrolled ends are set on top of the veneered seat platform rather than forming a continuous line with the front seat rail (compare Pl. 18 and fig. 158).

Both construction methods are outlined in plate 7 of the 1817 New York price book and are suggestive of later Grecian-style design trends. The clarity of the structural elements in the method used to construct the Haines sofa would have been admired by early nineteenth-century devotees of ancient Greek design but apparently was less pleasing to some early twentieth-century connoisseurs of Phyfe furniture, who considered later Grecian-style furniture like the Haines sofa, with its mixture of solid mahogany reeded scrolled ends atop a rectilinear veneered seat platform, ponderous and disjointed.[41] A mahogany Grecian sofa, which according to family tradition was made for Phyfe's daughter Eliza Phyfe Vail (App. 2.15), appears even more massive than the one made for the Haineses. Nonetheless, it is a coherent design, with veneered scrolled ends, seat rails, and a cylindrical crest rail with downward carved volutes large enough to counterbalance the mass of the carved lion's-paw feet. The upright scrolled ends are nearly identical in profile to those on the Phyfe-attributed Grecian sofa, of about 1815 to 1820, with a rosewood-veneered seat platform and gilded and *vert antique* winged lion's-paw feet very close in design to those on the Brinckerhoff and Haines sofas, one of which is shown in detail in figure 86.

The veneered cylinder that forms the crest rail on the Eliza Phyfe Vail Grecian sofa is a key structural component of another new model developed about 1820, the box sofa, which employed this element for the side and sometimes the back top rails. New York box sofas appear to relate to both French Restauration and late English Regency design (1815–30). A plate from Pierre de La Mésangère's *Collection de meubles et objets de goût*, for example (fig. 88), may have influenced the development of the form in New York.[42] A number of high-quality New York box sofas with cylindrical, scrolled, or flat back rails, veneered front columns, and turned-and-carved feet are known (fig. 89), and some of these undoubtedly were made in the Phyfe shop.[43] The earliest documented Phyfe box sofas, however, are a pair made in 1834 as a wedding gift for Maria Franklin Clark and George Fox (Pl. 43). It is interesting to note that even at this late date, Phyfe still retained the scrolled crest rail used on a scroll-back sofa he made for William Bayard twenty-seven years earlier (Pl. 4).

Sculptural and Architectonic Table Forms

A documented pair of marble-top mahogany pier tables with canted corners and lion's-head consoles made in 1815–16 for the New York lawyer John Wells (Pl. 16) and a more richly ornamented example of identical design attributed to Phyfe (fig. 90) may represent some of the cabinetmaker's earliest known attempts to incorporate into his work the kind of three-dimensional sculptural elements seen in the design publications of Thomas Hope and Percier and Fontaine. They also provide an interesting counterpoint to the sculptural pier tables then being made with great success by Lannuier, which for all intents and purposes could be called French Empire in terms of their ornamental program.[44]

The Wells pier tables by comparison are plainer and a little ungainly and give one pause to wonder, quite frankly, what the

82 *Duncan Phyfe*

Figure 90. Attributed to Duncan Phyfe. Pier table, ca. 1815. Mahogany, mahogany veneer, gilded gesso and *vert antique*, gilded brass, marble, looking-glass plate, 36 × 43 × 13 in. Bernard & S. Dean Levy, New York

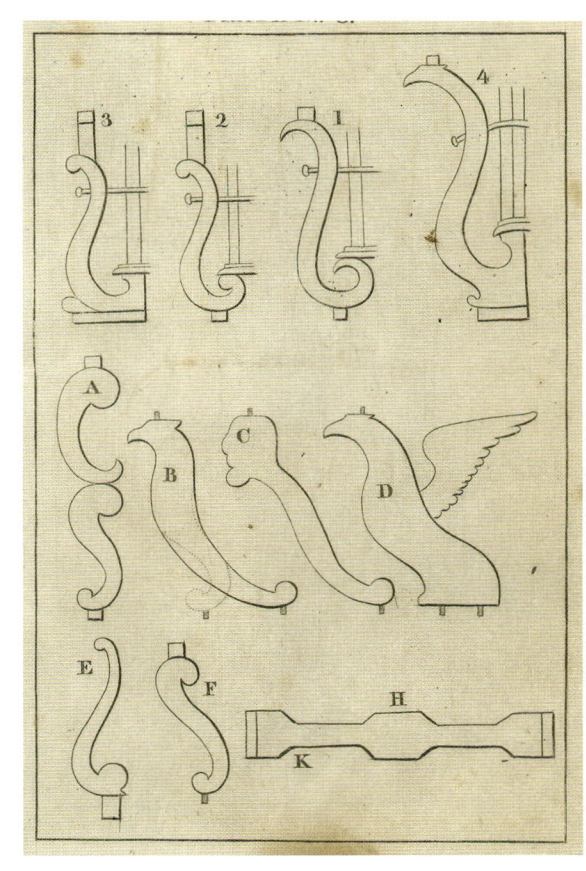

Figure 91. Plate 5, *The New-York Book of Prices for Manufacturing Cabinet and Chair Work* (1817). The Metropolitan Museum of Art, Harris Brisbane Dick Fund, 1939 39.32.1

Figure 92. Detail of the card table attributed to Duncan Phyfe in Plate 29

Figure 93. Attributed to Duncan Phyfe. Card table, 1815–20. Mahogany, mahogany veneer, gilded gesso and *vert antique*, brass, ebony, 30½ × 36 × 18 in. Collection of Carswell Rush Berlin

Figure 94. Detail of interior of the card table in figure 93

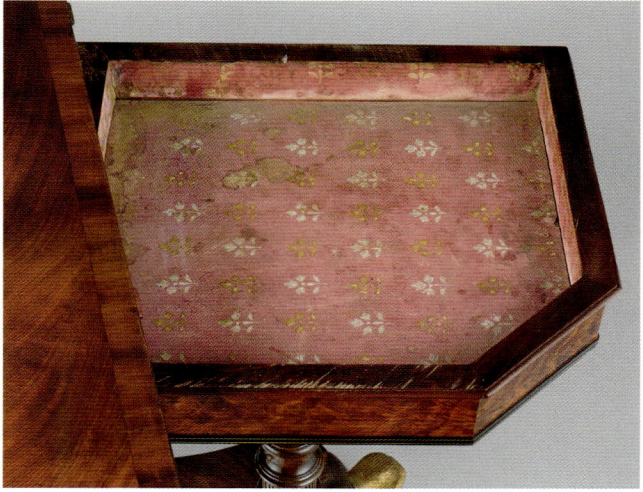

man who ordered them had in mind when he instructed his sister-in-law, who was acting as his agent: "The tables you will get best at Phyfe's than elsewhere, & I wish you therefore to give him the preference."[45] Perhaps Wells was convinced that whatever he got from Phyfe would necessarily be of the best quality and highest style. We can never know what Wells thought of the work of Lannuier at the time, but its strong French character, according to at least one contemporary observer, did not appeal to all New Yorkers, some of whom preferred the English taste to the French or a blending of the two.[46] Phyfe's choice of a lion's head atop carved, scrolled supports on the Wells tables is an intriguing one and may suggest that, in contradistinction to Lannuier and French Empire design, he intentionally chose to follow English Regency fashion, which favored lion and panther sculptural supports in the manner of Thomas Hope.[47]

Lannuier was not the only local competitor to prompt Phyfe to create his own distinctive line of richly ornamented Grecian-style furniture. In the aftermath of the War of 1812, New York became the main entrepôt in America for imported English manufactured goods, as well as a place for immigrant English cabinetmakers seeking their fortunes to sell furniture in their own late Regency style. In 1818 Gillespie & Walker, "Lately From London," offered for sale in the city "rosewood card tables, richly ornamented with high polished brass," and A. M. Haywood advertised a "grand sideboard, inlaid with high polished ornamental brass-work, and rosewood, card tables to match . . . of the newest European fashions."[48] Phyfe and Lannuier both took advantage of this propitious moment to expand their businesses and compete directly with European imports and craftsmen by developing enticing new furniture forms with sculptural and architectural elements derived from the antique that set the stage for the opulent era of the 1820s and early 1830s.

Around the time of the completion of the Wells commission, Phyfe may also have been developing additional table forms with structural supports derived from classical mythology. A number of these supports, including scrolled standards with lions' and eagles' heads and full-bodied griffins, found their way into the 1817 New York price book (fig. 91). To link Phyfe with this development would be logical given his prominence in the industry, but he can also be linked specifically to at least one griffin card table (Pl. 29 and fig. 92) through careful comparison of distinctive design elements that it shares with other documented and undocumented examples. Made of rosewood, it has carved feet in the form of tiny dolphins with bulbous heads, pronounced lips, and scales formed of delicate cross-hatching. The canted-corner top swivels to reveal a well lined with patterned pink wallpaper. A mahogany example of similar form has the same feet and identically patterned wallpaper in the well, but turned pillars instead of griffins (figs. 93, 94). The pillars are identical in design and in the precision with which they are turned to those on the documented 1815 Brinckerhoff card table (fig. 81). Thus, in a roundabout way, we are able to say with some degree of confidence that both the griffin and the columnar canted-corner card tables were made in the Phyfe shop.[49]

84   *Duncan Phyfe*

Figure 95. Attributed to Duncan Phyfe. Card table, 1815–20. Mahogany, mahogany veneer, gilded gesso and *vert antique*, brass, ebony, 30 × 36 × 18 in. Westervelt-Warner Museum of American Art, Tuscaloosa, Alabama

Figure 96. Charles-Honoré Lannuier. Card table, 1817. Mahogany veneer, gilded gesso and *vert antique*, gilded brass, die-stamped brass borders, 31 1/8 × 36 × 17 3/4 in. The Metropolitan Museum of Art, Gift of Justine VR Milliken, 1995 1995.377.1

The distinct possibilities that Phyfe made this griffin table and masterminded the introduction of the mythological beast as a sculptural support for tables are important because they reveal him as the master of an entire class of sculptural table forms, just as Lannuier was with his signature winged-caryatid card and pier table. Phyfe's griffins are a strange, even preternatural, presence and effective in their mythic role as guardians of ancient treasures. It is ironic that they appear on card tables, where many a fortune was lost. Trying to capitalize on Lannuier's success, Phyfe may even have tried his hand at winged caryatid card tables of his own. One, probably from his shop, is very similar in form to typical Lannuier examples (compare figs. 95 and 96). The other (Pl. 31) has back columns identical to those on the documented Brinckerhoff card table. Turnabout is fair play, however, and just as Lannuier was less than successful at making a Phyfe scroll-back armchair around 1810 (compare fig. 68 and Pl. 1), Phyfe it seems, was unable to find modelers and carvers capable of matching the French master's highly sophisticated sculptural work.

Pier tables with square corners, veneered wood columns, and applied ormolu appliqués and mounts were first made in New York under Lannuier's influence probably as early as 1805. Within ten years, however, when the French Empire–influenced later phase of the Grecian style had taken hold, examples by Lannuier, Phyfe, and others grew increasingly lavish, with rosewood and light-colored veneers, marble columns, massive carved lion's-paw feet, and more inlaid and applied ornaments than ever before. Not surprisingly, Phyfe's and other makers'

"square pier tables," as they were called in the New York price books, look a great deal like Lannuier's. Two distinctive features that seem to set Phyfe's work apart from that of his competitors beginning about 1815 and continuing into the 1820s are the style of his carved lion's-paw feet, which feature lively gilded acanthus that appears pinched at the base between the ankles and toes, and slightly thicker-than-average brass stringing on the plinth (fig. 97). Michael Allison, Phyfe's perennial imitator, made a labeled square pier table that is very similar overall to one attributed to Phyfe. Its carved feet (fig. 98), however, are less cooly abstracted and have exaggerated well-defined claws, much like those on his labeled Pembroke table (see fig. 82), which may have been carved by the same hand.

About 1820, or just slightly earlier, rounded corners entered Phyfe's design repertoire, as evidenced by five card tables with this feature that bear the cabinetmaker's August 1820 label. All of fairly minimalist design, one appears almost stick-built, with a faceted, rosewood-grained turned maple trestle base (Pl. 26). Another (Pl. 27) has a busy, almost mechanical-looking, turned mahogany plinth and shaft with a large crotch-mahogany veneered central drum, a slightly larger version of the ones used on the footposts of a bedstead made in the Phyfe shop, possibly for his own home (Pl. 42). A third, also made of mahogany, has veneered columns with ormolu caps and bases and a veneered cylindrical stretcher (App. 2.22).

The corners of the tables are formed of thin laminated boards, kerf-sawn and bent round in cauls. Dovetailed on their ends to the front and side apron boards, they are overlaid with plaques

Furniture from the Workshop of Duncan Phyfe 85

Figure 97. Detail of foot on the pier table attributed to Duncan Phyfe in Plate 38

Figure 98. Detail of foot on the Michael Allison pier table, 1817–19, in Plates 38–39, figure 1

of mahogany or rosewood that are placed slightly proud of the flanking veneered surfaces (fig. 99). Use of these corner elements, which could be prepared in advance and used as stock parts, undoubtedly speeded production and ensured that the joined substrate did not crack or read through thin veneers. The spare design of the August 1820 labeled card tables and their efficient system of corner construction may be indicators of Phyfe's desire to keep his "Cabinet Warehouse," as it is described on the label, stocked with ready-made furniture that was not too expensive to produce. It may also have helped Phyfe cope with the pressure of increased competition in the late 1810s and the downturn in the economy after the Panic of 1819.[50] Two other noteworthy examples of August 1820 furniture include a simple worktable (Pl. 28) and a mahogany writing table and bookcase of elegant design (Pl. 25), with a minimal amount of carving restricted to the finial in its spirited, almost playful scrolled pediment.

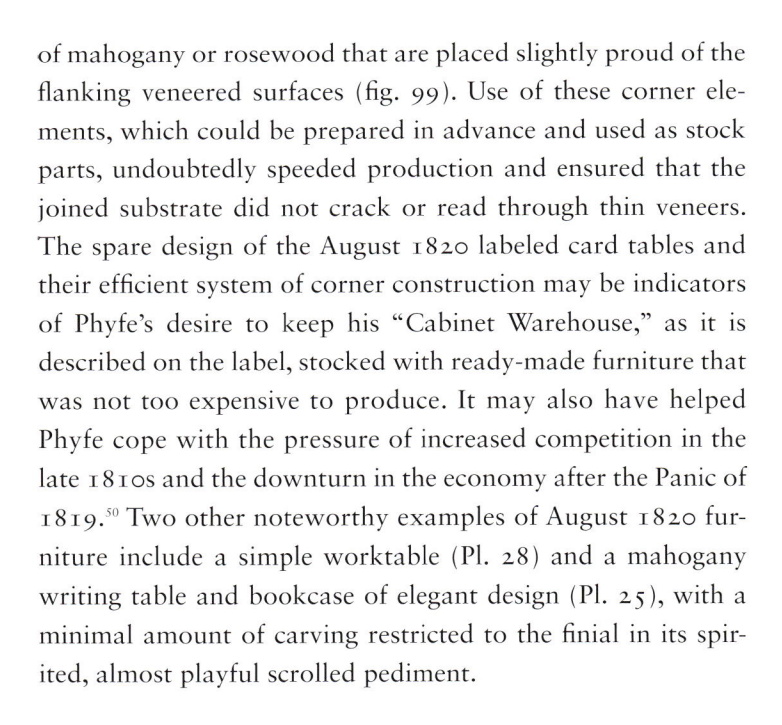

Key Works of the 1820s

The main source of documented Phyfe furniture in the ornamented Grecian style is a surviving group of richly gilded rosewood and mahogany examples made for Robert Donaldson of Fayetteville, North Carolina, and New York City between 1822 and 1826. Some pieces are recorded in an account of furniture purchased from Phyfe in 1822, when Donaldson was living in Fayetteville, that includes a center table, a pair of card tables, a pier table, a rosewood sofa, and fourteen "ornamental chairs" (App. 1.7). Others were purchased in 1826, around the time of Donaldson's move to New York City. A unique rosewood Grecian couch or daybed (Pl. 35) with gilded and *vert antique* melon-shaped feet identical to those on a pair of window seats (Pl. 34 and fig. 100), one of which bears the name "D Phyfe" in ink on the original underupholstery (fig. 101) and the date July 4, 1826, on the linen cover of the original hair cushion, unquestionably were made later for the New York house. Three additional pieces of furniture that descended in the Donaldson family and were also likely made in the Phyfe shop include a small rolling canterbury with gilded faux-brass inlaid decoration meant to hold Mrs. Donaldson's sheet music (Pl. 36), a rosewood ladies' secretary bookcase (Pl. 33), and a mahogany worktable with rounded corners and columnar supports with cast and chased ring-like

86 *Duncan Phyfe*

Figure 99. Detail of corner construction of the Duncan Phyfe card table in Plate 26

ormolu caps (see fig. 168) similar in design to those on a rosewood pier table attributed to the Phyfe shop made in the 1820s (Pl. 39).

The Donaldson furniture substantially augments our view of Phyfe's ornamented Grecian style and one of its premier new forms, the center table. The example Phyfe made for the North Carolinian (Pl. 32) has a reeded marble top, a central shaft rising out of a gilded foliate collar, thicker than usual brass stringing on the plinth, and gilded and bronzed lion's-paw feet with lively scrolled acanthus brackets that link it stylistically to an even grander example probably made in the Phyfe shop for the Whitney family of New York City (Pl. 40). Singularly spectacular, the Whitney table is distinguished by its painted top depicting an ancient Roman allegory, a bronzed and gilded reeded shaft, beautifully carved rolling acanthus and volutes on the feet, and stenciled and freehand gilded decoration on the apron identical in almost every way, save the central element, to that on the front rail of the Donaldson window seat (compare figs. 102 and 103). A recently discovered center table depicted in a circa 1833 interior view of the home of Mr. and Mrs. John Q. Aymar on Greenwich Street in New York City (figs. 104, 105) reveals how another, unidentified New York

Figure 100. Detil of foot on the Duncan Phyfe window seat in Plate 34

Figure 101. "D Phyfe" signature on linen underupholstery of the window seat in Plate 34

Furniture from the Workshop of Duncan Phyfe   87

Figure 102. Detail of apron of the center table attributed to Duncan Phyfe in Plate 40

Figure 103. Detail of front rail of the Duncan Phyfe window seat in Plate 34

cabinetmaker working in a loose vernacular style riffed on Phyfe's opulent model. This table, with its coarsely carved legs and shaft, is the very embodiment of the "questionable 'American Empire'" style to which Ernest Hagen felt Phyfe had stooped in the 1820s (see introductory quotation on page 65). Had Hagen been aware of the Donaldson and Whitney center tables (Pls. 32, 40) and compared them objectively with the Aymar example, he would perhaps have reconsidered.

One of the most interesting aspects of the Donaldson furniture is the way Phyfe mixes several sophisticated decorative techniques on a single piece of furniture and within the parlor set. The Grecian couch, for example (Pl. 35), has applied cast brass ornaments on the front rail centered by a panel of inlaid brass and ebony, while the window seats (Pl. 34), presumably used nearby, have extensive gilded decoration and die-stamped brass banding. This seeming disjuncture may have been intentional, however, meant to playfully trick the eye. The amount of work lavished on the gilded decoration of both the Donaldson window seats and the Whitney center table suggests that this was a form of embellishment deemed exquisite in its own right, not, as is frequently claimed, just a less expensive alternative to cast-brass ornamentation. Phyfe's gilder, or at least the individual he employed for these pieces, executed this decoration with an artistry that arguably surpasses that of most of his contemporaries in the 1820s, including some of the gilders

Figure 104. Center table. New York, 1825–30. Ebonized mahogany veneer, gilded gesso, stenciled ornament, faux die-stamped brass border, marble, height 37⅞ in.; diam. of top 34⅛ in. The Metropolitan Museum of Art, Gift of A. Grima Johnson, 2008 2008.640.1a–c

Duncan Phyfe

Figure 105. Attributed to George T. Twibill Jr. (1806–1836). *The Family of John Q. Aymar*, ca. 1833. Oil on canvas, 34¾ × 42 in. The Metropolitan Museum of Art, Gift of A. Grima Johnson, 2008 2008.573

employed by the Meeks cabinetmaking firm and the partnerships of Deming and Bulkley and Holmes and Haines, who frequently used a type of coarse faux die-stamped brass banding applied with a stamp or roller and theorem-like stenciled compositions of fruit and foliage in bronze powders like those on the apron of the Aymar family center table (fig. 104).[51]

A square pier table with fine gilded decoration on the apron and die-stamped brass banding on the plinth (Pl. 39) has no known provenance but may well be a product of the Phyfe shop. The apron decoration depicts two faux brass curtain pins supporting scrolling acanthus that emerges from the tails of two swans in a paneled reserve (fig. 106). That this table was meant to stand against a pier between two windows with sumptuous curtain treatments held open or draped in swags on gilded brass curtain pins was not lost on the clever gilder, who executed the work with the utmost finesse, first applying gold size through a stencil, laying on gold leaf, and then precisely shading the gold with india ink or cutting through the gilding with a stylus to lend it the appearance of three-dimensionality. The superior quality of the gilding and shading technique accords perfectly with that seen on the Donaldson window seats (Pl. 34) and the Whitney center table (Pl. 40) and suggests that all these decorations were executed by the same hand.

Figure 106. Detail of gilded ornament on the pier table in Plate 39

Furniture from the Workshop of Duncan Phyfe   89

Figure 107. Side chair. New York, ca. 1815. Cherry paint-grained to imitate rosewood, gilded decoration, cane, 32 5/8 × 18 1/4 × 19 5/8 in. The Metropolitan Museum of Art, Gift of Mrs. Bayard Verplanck, in memory of Dr. James Sykes Rumsey, 1940 40.159.2

Scroll-back and curule chairs gradually fell out of favor by the 1820s, but klismos chairs, because of their more durable construction and their affinity with the most recognizable of ancient Greek furniture forms, continued to be made throughout the decade and into the 1830s. Numerous mahogany, rosewood-grained and gilded, and ebonized and gilded New York klismos chairs survive from the 1820s, most with a single carved or decorated cross splat in the back. None, however, have been associated definitively with the Phyfe shop. Some of the "14 ornamental chairs" made in 1822 for Robert Donaldson may be visible in an early twentieth-century photograph of a Donaldson descendant's parlor in Summit, New Jersey (see fig. 167). A pair of rosewood-grained and freehand-gilded klismos chairs with cane seats donated to the Metropolitan Museum in 1940 by a direct descendant of their original owner, Robert Gill, were said at the time to have been purchased from Phyfe and are of the same general type but with paw feet on saber-shaped legs (fig. 107).[52]

Also visible in the Summit, New Jersey, photograph is a rosewood secretary bookcase attributed to Phyfe (Pl. 33). Relatively small in scale, it is nonetheless monumental in appearance as a result of its strong architectural character and the use of opulent materials. The same can be said of a *secrétaire à abbatant* attributed to Phyfe that stands a mere sixty inches tall (Pl. 37). The carving on both is meticulously executed, and the moldings and turned elements are crisp and precise. This is the kind of superior design and workmanship that has always been ascribed to Phyfe, although now we can see them in his later Grecian-style work, disparaged first by Hagen as the "questionable 'American Empire'" and then by legions of other collectors and scholars who conflated Phyfe's work with that of less talented makers who created their own versions of Phyfe's high-end designs. Indeed, looking back to Phyfe's earliest documented scroll-back chairs of 1807 (Pls. 1–3) or the labeled worktable of 1811–16 (Pl. 10) and then forward to the Donaldson secretary bookcase and window seats (Pls. 33, 34), we can recognize, on the continuum of Neoclassical style, a consistency in precision, clarity, and economy of mass, no matter when the piece was made.

Grecian Plain Style

About 1830 the Neoclassical idiom evolved into its final phase—an arresting contrast to the richly ornamented later Grecian style, with its archaeologically inspired designs. This final incarnation was a vastly subdued aesthetic, and in recent times it has been aptly referred to as the "Grecian Plain style," an admixture of the period phrases "Grecian" and "present plain style."[53] By this date the idiom had been refined to a simplicity that relies solely on line and subtle detail. Gone are the painted and gilded sculptural elements, the complex brass inlays, gilded cast-brass appliqués, and stenciled decoration. The scale, however, remains unchanged, and the richly veined rosewood and brilliant crotch-mahogany veneers, which were central to defining the previous phase, persist as the preferred cabinet woods. The mode that evolved is defined by broad planar wood surfaces, often accentuated with artfully placed veneers and delineated by carefully executed architectural moldings and applied turned roundels as the terminus for the graceful scrolled supports. In many respects this aesthetic has antecedents in seventeenth-century Baroque furniture design. And yet it is as consistent as in our own era with a minimalist approach to design.

Hagen's claim that the arrival of the Grecian Plain style occurred in 1833 and coincided with the cholera epidemic (see introductory quotation on page 65) was not far off the mark. Among the earliest datable American expressions of this new

Figure 108. Broadside for Joseph Meeks & Sons, 1833. Lithograph with hand coloring. The Metropolitan Museum of Art, Gift of Mrs. R. W. Hyde, transferred from the Library, 1943 43.15.8

Furniture from the Workshop of Duncan Phyfe

Figure 109. Joseph Meeks & Sons. Pier table, ca. 1835. Mahogany veneer, marble, looking-glass plate, 37 × 43 × 20⅛ in. The Metropolitan Museum of Art, Gift of Emil and Dolores Pascarelli in honor of Catherine Hoover Voorsanger, 2001 2001.640a, b

Figure 110. Duncan Phyfe. Pier table, 1834. Mahogany veneer, marble, looking-glass plate, 35½ × 42¾ × 18⅛ in. The White House, Washington, D.C., White House Acquisition Fund, 1961

aesthetic is the well-known Joseph Meeks & Sons 1833 broadside (fig. 108). In addition to depicting the Meeks manufactory in New York City, the sheet illustrates designs for three window treatments and forty-one pieces of furniture, seventeen of which can be identified as being taken directly from George Smith's *Cabinet-Maker and Upholsterer's Guide* (London, 1826). Together these figures span the diverging expressions of the ornamented Grecian and Grecian Plain styles, and while not quite equally divided, they suggest the continued popularity of the former in 1833.[54] The complexity and detail of each image, as well as the coded price list for the various items at the bottom, indicate that the lithograph was conceived as an advertisement, though it seems unlikely that some of the more fantastic designs were ever realized at the Meeks shop.[55] Duncan Phyfe's approach to the new aesthetic clearly is different. Compared with a labeled Grecian Plain style pier table by the Meekses, with wildly profuse scrolled supports, a bowed plinth, and a deeply creased apron, the same form by Phyfe appears strikingly spare and restrained (compare figs. 109 and 110). And with Phyfe, less was more. In 1834 he charged Benjamin Clark of New York $130 for this very pier table, a price that was more than 40 percent higher than the $90 the Meekses asked for a mahogany pier table with a white marble top illustrated in their 1833 advertising broadside that is very similar in design to the labeled example mentioned above.

Phyfe's Grecian Plain style work of the 1830s and 1840s has also been called his architectural furniture because, as one scholar has explained, "architecture and architectural elements dictated" its form.[56] At its best, Phyfe's Grecian Plain style furniture captures the strength, simplicity, and noble repose that characterize the best Greek Revival architecture. Phyfe achieved this effect by using the classical orders, often in abstracted form, and a quiet yet radiant palette of warm-toned rosewood and mahogany veneers meticulously selected and precisely applied in an architectural manner. The architectural character of this furniture is vividly expressed in a wardrobe made in the Phyfe shop in 1841 for Millford, the South Carolina home of John Laurence and Susan Hampton Manning (App. 2.8). The entablature (fig. 111) is dominated by two major components, a bold cyma recta cornice and an attenuated cavetto frieze, each enriched by crotch-mahogany veneers applied at right angles to one another and edged along their tops with contrasting crossbanding. A fine band of fiddleback mahogany forms a narrow architrave below. The sturdy square piers that support the entablature are veneered with yet another cut of mahogany featuring cross-grain flashes of contrasting light and dark tones, a kind known by cabinetmakers as mottled wood. The cavetto-shaped capitals share the same profile as the frieze but are scaled to match the proportion of the piers. The figure of the crotch-mahogany veneer applied to their face is also smaller

Figure 111. Detail of cornice of the D. Phyfe & Son wardrobe, 1841, in Appendix 2.8

in scale than that in the frieze and inverted to provide definition and contrast. Such sensitivity in the selection, placement, and scale of the figure in the veneers is a hallmark of Phyfe's late work in the Grecian Plain style.

Influence of the French Restauration Style

Phyfe's design aesthetic in the 1830s and 1840s was driven largely by fashion trends in Paris after the fall of Napoleon, when French furniture was no longer defined by the grandiose majesty of the Empire but assumed a more restrained appearance. The furniture associated with the reigns of Louis XVIII (r. 1814–24) and his successors Charles X (r. 1824–30) and Louis-Philippe (r. 1830–48) has come to be referred to as the Restauration style. The qualities that characterize Phyfe's Grecian Plain style—the simplicity of line and reliance on brilliantly figured mahogany and rosewood veneers—were inspired by this aesthetic. The French *ébénistes* in their designs

Furniture from the Workshop of Duncan Phyfe

Figure 112. *Secrétaire à abattant*. French, 1830–40. Rosewood veneer with lightwood inlay, marble, 58⅞ × 38 × 17¼ in. Olana State Historic Site, New York State Office of Parks, Recreation, and Historic Preservation

also incorporated dark wood inlays in light-colored woods, or *bois clairs*.

Published collections of furniture designs offered an easily accessible means of communicating the Restauration style. Among the best known and most widely circulated was La Mésangère's voluminous *Collection de meubles et objets de goût*. From 1802 until 1835, this series of hand-colored engravings, eventually totaling 755 sheets, was distributed annually.[57] In 1839 the furniture designer and publisher Désiré Guilmard initiated a similar periodical, *Le Garde-meuble, ancien et moderne*, in which appeared the late classical furniture designs made under Louis-Philippe and the revived Gothic and Old French styles of Louis XIV and Louis XV during the Second Empire (1852–70) of Napoleon III.[58] A superbly carved and inlaid *secrétaire à abattant* (fig. 112) made in France but inscribed "G. Ponsot"—probably the New York cabinetmaker and import merchant George Ponsot (act. 1830–54)—is highly expressive of the Gothic or *cathédral* aesthetic in French Restauration furniture and indicative of the market forces that drove Phyfe and some of his contemporaries strongly toward Gallic design in the 1830s and 1840s.[59]

Merchant-cabinetmakers such as Ponsot played an important role in the dissemination of French taste, keeping both their customers and their local competitors focused on France as the fountainhead of the latest fashions. Charles A. Baudouine (1808–1896) was one such competitor. An American of Huguenot descent, Baudouine opened a business that would benefit from his French surname, not to mention his fluency in the language. His own production was enhanced by the imported furniture, upholstery materials, hardware, and trimmings that he purchased during his annual shopping sprees in France. In his shop at 335 Broadway, he is said to have employed seventy cabinetmakers and no fewer than 130 carvers, upholsterers, and varnishers.[60] Alexander Roux (1813–1886), a French national who immigrated to New York in 1835, initially established himself as an upholsterer on Broadway. By 1843 he was proclaiming himself a "French cabinetmaker" and announcing that he would also commission furniture abroad. Andrew Jackson Downing, at the time the country's foremost landscape architect and unofficial spokesman for American taste, wrote admiringly of Roux's furniture as "the most tasteful designs of Louis Quatorze, Renaissance, Gothic, etc., to be found in the country."[61] Also by 1843, Auguste-Émile Ringuet-Leprince (1801–1886), a Parisian *ébéniste* and interior designer, had begun to develop an American clientele (see fig. 132). Drawn to the potential of this promising market abroad and spurred by the political uprisings of 1848, Ringuet-Leprince resolved to establish a branch of his firm in New York City, placing his brother-in-law Leon Marcotte in charge. Ringuet-Leprince & L. Marcotte would manufacture and import a range of home furnishings, providing a comprehensive decorating service otherwise unknown in the United States.[62]

Exactly what influence these waves of French *ébéniste*-manufacturers had on D. Phyfe & Son is not recorded, but an article that appeared in the May 11, 1844, edition of *The New Mirror* suggests that it may have been profound:

> So marked is this change of taste, and the new school of furnishing, that the oldest and most wealthy of the cabinet warehouse-men in this city has completely abandoned the making of English furniture. . . . He sold out an immense stock of high-priced articles last week at auction, and has sent to France for models and workmen to start new with the popular taste.

Although the author does not refer to the cabinetmaker by name, it has been assumed that it must be Phyfe. An advertisement published by the auction house of Edward C. Halliday and Edgar Jenkins a month earlier in the *New-York Commercial Advertiser*—announcing the "Positive Sale of the entire stock of Messrs. Duncan Phyfe & Son, who are closing their business"—may be the auction cited. As it turns out, the firm did not go out of business, though presumably the vendue was held.

French Restauration furniture emerged in response to the

ornamental excesses of the Empire. Its unpretentious elegance, comfort, and harmonious scale and proportions make it among the finest furniture ever made in France. Phyfe's refined sensibilities melded perfectly with this aesthetic, and his surviving work of the 1830s and 1840s reveals a good knowledge of published design sources and imported French Restauration furniture. The creative ways in which Phyfe reinterpreted this furniture in form, scale, and proportion lend credence to the maxim that "originality is a new way of expressing things that have already been said."[63] The S-shaped console supports, ubiquitous in La Mésangère's *Collection de meubles et objets de goût* in the 1820s (fig. 113), for example, also became a Phyfe mainstay. Phyfe used these consoles most often as table standards (see fig. 110 and Pl. 58) but also incorporated them into other forms, such as box sofas and cellarets (Pls. 43, 60).

Consoles are used on furniture made by Phyfe as early as 1834 and are still recognizable in 1847 in the descriptions of furniture included in the sales catalogue of the contents of the D. Phyfe & Son warerooms, which suggests that he still maintained his earlier habit of establishing a trademark form or motif and then sustaining it over a period of a decade or more. In the sales catalogue, there are references to "1 pier table, Grecian scroll standard," "1 mahogany double washstand, Grecian scroll, marble top," and "1 mahogany French Secretaire, cylinder fall, 12 drawers and pigeon holes of amboyna wood, with book case, Plate glass panels, and OG cornice, drawers and scroll standards," all of which have analogues in surviving Phyfe or Phyfe-attributed furniture.[64]

Phyfe's Grecian scrolls are well proportioned and precisely drawn, with slightly convex discs of figured wood affixed to their circular ends (fig. 114). On pier tables and sideboards, these meticulously turned discs also serve to cover horizontal slots cut into the sides of the consoles where nuts were inserted to receive the connecting bolts that hold them together (fig. 115). Phyfe used these distinctive rimmed discs on other parts of Grecian Plain style furniture as well, such as the scrolled ends of Grecian couches, where they are among the few raised elements on a sleek, streamlined design (see fig. 185), at the crossing of the ogee-shaped legs on taborets (Pl. 47), or in tiny scale on the scrolled supports and trestle feet of a delicate drop-leaf table (Pl. 53) and the fly rails on a sofa table (fig. 116).

These discs, as well as the deep cavetto aprons on the pier tables and sideboards, have a strong Egyptianizing character ultimately derived from the winged discs so frequently used in Egyptian symbolism and the powerful, coved cornices on Egyptian temples. Cavetto aprons are fairly common on French Restauration pier tables, and these probably provided the direct inspiration for Phyfe's design. Reflecting this exotic style on a grand public scale was John Haviland's 1835 Egyptian Revival Halls of Justice and House of Detention, also known

Figure 113. Pierre de La Mésangère. Plate 631, *Collection de meubles et objets de goût* (1827). Colored engraving. The Metropolitan Museum of Art, Harris Brisbane Dick Fund, 1930 30.80.3

Figure 114. Detail of Grecian scroll and apron of the Duncan Phyfe pier table in figure 110

Furniture from the Workshop of Duncan Phyfe

Figure 115. Deconstructed pier table, ca. 1835, attributed to Duncan Phyfe. Private collection

Figure 116. Detail of fly rail on the sofa table attributed to D. Phyfe & Son in Plate 51

as the Tombs, which once stood on Centre Street in Lower Manhattan and featured massive cavetto cornices above its porticoes and forbidding battered walls.[65]

The French Chair

During the 1830s and 1840s Phyfe, like the Meekses and his other competitors, made compact, elegant French Restauration–style chairs with rounded backs and rear stiles that curve forward and rest on the side seat rails. Chairs of this type were called *chaises gondoles* in France and were made there beginning in the Consulat period (1799–1804) and for the next forty years into the reign of Louis-Philippe (r. 1830–48).[66] In New York the form was simply called a French chair because of its fidelity to its foreign counterpart. French chairs may

96 *Duncan Phyfe*

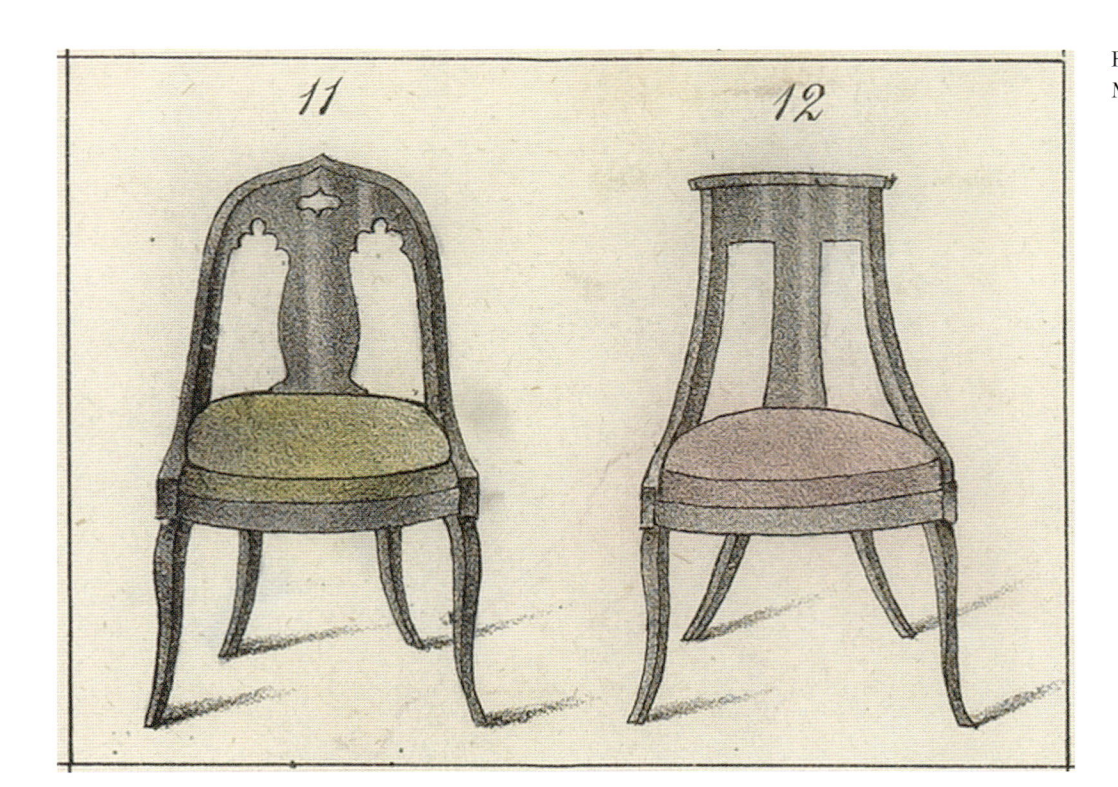

Figure 117. French chairs from the Joseph Meeks & Sons' broadside in figure 108

have been made in New York as early as 1825 to 1830, but the form's earliest manifestation there does not occur in print until 1833, on the Meeks broadside, where a mahogany example with a haircloth seat is priced at $12 (fig. 117 right).[67] By 1834 the French chair had become popular enough to be included in the cabinetmakers' price book of that year. In 1835, Phyfe made sixteen mahogany French chairs for Stephen Van Rensselaer IV of Albany priced at $12 each (see fig. 181). The chairs are of the simplest type, without any carving on the knees or on the curved rear stiles, where they terminate on the tops of the seat rails. A nearly identical set of French chairs believed to have been made by Phyfe for the New York lawyer Samuel Foot about 1837 (Pl. 46) have the same severe, straight-sided banisters veneered with the finest crotch mahogany both front and back. In the 1847 D. Phyfe & Son sales catalogue, "12 mahogany French chairs, doric pattern" are recorded. Much like columns in the Greek Doric order, simple and austere and without a base, the straight-sided banisters in the backs of the Van Rensselaer and Foot French chairs rise directly out of the seat frame to connect to the frieze-like crest tablet. Were these perhaps the "Doric pattern" French chairs referred to in the sales catalogue?

Another version of the French Restauration form made by Phyfe in the 1830s has a stuffed back and open scrolled arms ending in volutes; it was known in France as a *fauteuil gondole*. Two models of these upholstered French armchairs, or "drawing room French chairs, stuffed backs," as they are referred to in the 1847 Phyfe auction sales catalogue, were made in the Phyfe shop for Millford in 1841. One (fig. 118) has pointed Gothic crests and is made of mahogany grain-painted to imitate rosewood so that it could be used with the rest of the rosewood-veneered and rosewood-grained furniture in the drawing room. The other (see fig. 200), made of fine dense mahogany for use in the dining room, has a rounded top and lacks any carving on the arms or legs. The carving on the knees and the lower half of the arm supports on the drawing room chairs is modeled directly after a popular type of scrolled lotus-leaf carving known in France as *cuisses de grenouille*, or "frog thighs," a type commonly found on the knees and arm supports of a variety of Restauration upholstered armchairs, including a new model of the late 1820s known as the *fauteuil Voltaire*.

An upholstered armchair that once belonged to John Jacob Astor, said by Phyfe's descendants to be one of the cabinetmaker's best customers, is of this *Voltaire* type, with a scrolled back and a prominent bulge just above the seat intended to support the small of the back.[68] The *Voltaire* was designed for the long-term comfort of sitters, especially readers, and frequently was used in private libraries. The only documented *Voltaire* from the Phyfe shop has rockers and was purchased by Josiah Hasbrouck of New Paltz, New York, in 1841 (fig. 119).[69] This rocking chair, with old but likely not original tufted black horsehair upholstery in the back, is a remarkable essay in ergonomic minimalism, with springs in the seat for additional comfort. Frequent references to this French Restauration seating form appear in New York newspaper auction ads of the late 1830s and 1840s, indicating that it was made by a number of New York cabinetmakers and also imported from France. Although the number that can be linked to the Phyfe shop is small, the *Voltaire* clearly was one of his specialties; nine separate examples in mahogany or rosewood with seating surfaces of horsehair, silk, plush, or tufted morocco leather in purple or light green are included in

Furniture from the Workshop of Duncan Phyfe

Figure 118. D. Phyfe & Son. Armchair, 1841. Mahogany, originally grain-painted in imitation of rosewood, 33 × 21¼ × 23¾ in. Collection of Richard Hampton Jenrette

the D. Phyfe & Son auction catalogue of 1847. An armchair probably made by Phyfe for the New York art patron Luman Reed (fig. 120), who paid the cabinetmaker $910 for unspecified goods or services in 1833, has a curved back and rounded top like the French armchairs made for the dining room at Millford, but its closed sides serve to house a down or hair-stuffed cushion.[70] The scrolled mahogany arms terminate in volutes much like those on the Millford armchairs, but are supported on a different type of plinth with superb lotus-leaf carving that again relates closely to French Restauration examples.

One of the most appealing aspects of French Restauration seating furniture, ladies' writing desks, and tables is their diminutive scale and portability, which allowed them to be arranged in comfortable groupings for conversation, reading, or any number of genteel pursuits in the drawing rooms, parlors, and private boudoirs of wealthier citizens. A number of Phyfe's documented screens and game, work, writing, and occasional tables in his Grecian Plain style have these virtues as well and thus bespeak a French influence. A checker stand on a simple tapered and chamfered post that descended in the family of James Phyfe (Pl. 54), partner with his father in the 1830s and 1840s, relates, for instance, to plates in La Mésangère's *Collection de meubles et objets de goût*, where various small table forms with delicate scrolled legs and trestle feet are shown. Typical of the diminutive scale that marks French Restauration design is a mahogany ladies' worktable (fig. 121), one of two

98   *Duncan Phyfe*

Figure 119. D. Phyfe & Son. Rocking chair, 1841. Mahogany, mahogany veneer, 43 × 26½ × 36¾ in. Locust Grove Historic Site, Poughkeepsie, New York

with a Phyfe family history, made about 1844 for Emily Walls, who married Peter Lewis Van Deverter, a relative through marriage of Phyfe's daughter Eliza. The other, veneered in rosewood, descended directly in the family of James Phyfe. The so-called wedding cake table, used in the Connecticut home of Phyfe's daughter Mary Phyfe Whitlock (Pl. 53), and a ladies' writing fire screen made in the Phyfe shop in 1841 for Susan Manning's mother, for use in her bedroom at Millford (Pl. 59), are other portable forms that share in this French aesthetic.

Influence of Late Regency Design

While the genesis of much of Duncan Phyfe's documented work in the Grecian Plain style can be found in French Restauration design, it can also be seen in British pattern books and late Regency furniture. In the 1820s, Phyfe likely consulted plate 52 in George Smith's *Collection of Designs for Household Furniture and Interior Decoration* (London, 1808) for the pair of rosewood window seats he supplied to Robert Donaldson in 1826 (Pl. 34), the correspondence between them being most evident in the corner posts, with their distinctive quartered spherical caps inspired by classical acroteria.[71] The same year these were made, Smith issued *The Cabinet-Maker and Upholsterer's Guide* (London, 1826), noting that his earlier publication had now "become wholly obsolete and inapplicable to its intended purpose, by the change of taste and rapid improvement which a period of twenty years has

are characteristic of both late English Regency and French Louis-Philippe furniture in the revived Old French style of Louis XIV and Louis XV.

Thomas King (active ca. 1790–ca. 1842) is another of the more influential British designers active during the first half of the nineteenth century, and certainly the most prolific. He is credited with having published no fewer than twenty-eight titles between 1822 and 1848. King is best known for his *Modern Style of Cabinet Work Exemplified*, which remained in publication from 1829 to 1862.[74] While his pattern books were intended for the English middle class, in America they were widely consulted by the wealthy, as evidenced by the furniture they purchased. An upholstered armchair that descended in the family of Eliza Phyfe Vail can be related to a plate in King's *Cabinet Maker's Sketch Book of Plain and Useful Designs* (London, 1835–36), the principal difference being that the sides of the Vail armchair are not upholstered but left open (compare figs. 125 and 126).

Figure 120. Attributed to Duncan Phyfe. Upholstered armchair, ca. 1833. Mahogany, mahogany veneer. 39 × 25 × 20⅞ in. Westervelt-Warner Museum of American Art, Tuscaloosa, Alabama

introduced."[72] In spite of this claim, the majority of Smith's designs remain in the ornamented Grecian style, though some are described as Gothic and in the revived Old French style of Louis XIV. Included among these are three for "occasional or sofa tables," which he explains are "intended as meubles for the drawing room; in which case they may be executed wholly in fine rosewood, or they may have a portion of the ornamental work in gilding or *Or molu*" (fig. 122).[73]

Smith's drawing is reminiscent of a table that is thought to be a part of the Manning commission for the drawing room at Millford in 1841 (Pl. 64). As adapted by Phyfe, the design embodies the aesthetics of the Grecian Plain style and late French Restauration taste. The graceful scrolls that form the lyre-shaped ends (fig. 123), now broadened and more prominent, are boldly carved, with a stylized lotus-leaf overlay that conforms to and emphasizes the curvilinear scroll. Further simplifying the overall form, the tapered columnar uprights at either end of the Smith design are here omitted. The bracket feet under the lyres are outlined with flat fillets like those on the scrolled arms, front rails, and feet of the Millford drawing room sofa and couches (fig. 124). Such paneling and outlining

Figure 121. Attributed to D. Phyfe & Son. Worktable, 1841–47. Mahogany veneer, mahogany. 28⅝ × 21 × 15½ in. Private collection

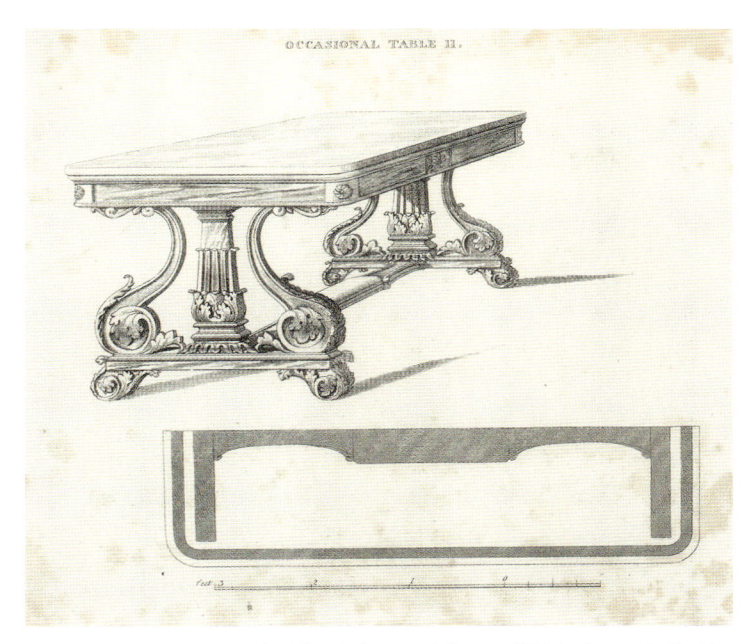

Figure 122. George Smith. *The Cabinet-Maker and Upholsterer's Guide* (1826). Plate CXVIII, from the 1828 edition. The Metropolitan Museum of Art, The Elisha Whittelsey Collection, The Elisha Whittelsey Fund, 1953 53.514.5

By the 1830s an entirely different type of publication made its debut with John Claudius Loudon's *Encyclopaedia of Cottage, Farm, and Villa Architecture and Furniture*, first published in 1833. In contrast to earlier volumes, such as those by Hope, Smith, and Ackermann, it was intended as an informative guide for every level of society. "One of the grand objects of our work," Loudon proclaimed, "[is to enlighten] the minds of the public in general on the subject of taste."[75] Included among the more than 150 designs for furniture is one for a canterbury: "Its use," Loudon explains, "is to hold music-books; and, as may be seen in the figure, the feet have castors for moving it about at pleasure." The Loudon canterbury (fig. 127), "of an elegant but rather expensive construction," is directly related to a canterbury that was owned by Eliza Phyfe Vail (fig. 128). Loudon's canterbury is ornamented with a prominent, classically inspired wreath. When Phyfe reinterpreted the stand, a large wooden ring was substituted for the wreath, perhaps because it was more in keeping with the Grecian Plain style aesthetic, or because it was less expensive to execute. Eliza Vail's upholstered armchair and canterbury represent the rare examples of Phyfe's furniture being related to specific published designs, in this instance Thomas King's *Cabinet Maker's Sketch Book* and Loudon's *Encyclopaedia*, copies of which may have been among the "1 lot Cabinet Makers Books & Drawings" that the appraisers of Phyfe's estate located in the "Open Garrett."[76]

Phyfe seems to have maintained his earlier habit of co-opting English Regency chair design in the 1830s with a model that, after the French chair, seems to have been one of his more distinctive and popular. The best known of these chairs are the set he made for his daughter Eliza (Pl. 49), with the characteristic curved back, dipped crest, and pinched waist that foreshadow the general outline of the backs of Rococo Revival side chairs of the late 1840s and 1850s. But the overall aspect of the Vail chairs is very different from that later fussy and frequently overwrought mode, as reflected in the sleek silhouetted outline of the banister and stay rail, ornamented only with a richly figured mahogany veneer, a clear nod to the Grecian Plain style (fig. 129). More commonly such chairs are made of rosewood, with carved banisters and stay rails (fig. 130). Some of these more typical examples descended in the Clark/Fox family, purchasers of a large group of Grecian Plain style furniture from Phyfe in 1834. Another fine example is in the collection of the Metropolitan Museum (Pl. 50). The Egyptian-inspired carved banisters on these chairs are crowned by a lotus blossom, emblem of Upper Egypt and symbol of the continuity of birth and rebirth, as each morning the flower emerges from the water, then blossoms, and at the end of the day again closes. All of the aforementioned chairs relate closely to an English rosewood chair probably made by Gillows of Lancaster or another quality English manufacture in the mid-1820s (fig. 131). A related back design also appears in Loudon's

Figure 123. Alternate view of the D. Phyfe & Son occasional table in Plate 64

Furniture from the Workshop of Duncan Phyfe 101

Figure 124. Detail of scrolled end of the D. Phyfe & Son couch in figure 197

Figure 125. D. Phyfe & Sons or D. Phyfe & Son. Upholstered armchair, 1837–47. Mahogany, mahogany veneer, 35¼ × 27¼ × 28¾ in. Collection of Glorianna H. Gibbon

Figure 126. Thomas King. Plate 7, *Cabinet Maker's Sketch Book of Plain and Useful Designs* (1836). University of Notre Dame, Architecture Library, South Bend, Indiana

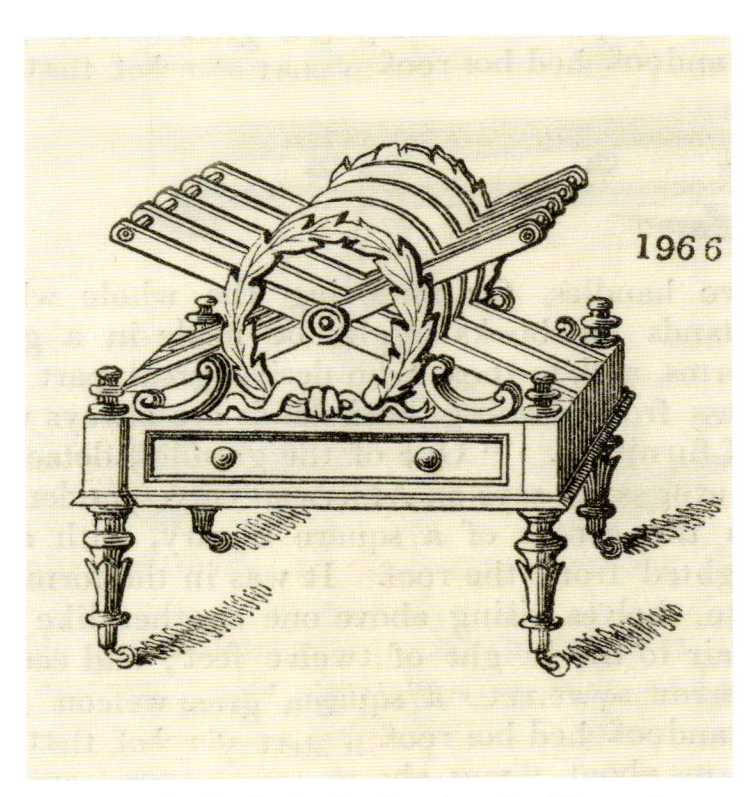

Figure 127. John Claudius Loudon. *Encyclopaedia of Cottage, Farm and Villa Architecture and Furniture* (1839), fig. 1966. The Metropolitan Museum of Art, Harris Brisbane Dick Fund, 1924 24.66.110

Figure 128. D. Phyfe & Sons or D. Phyfe & Son. Canterbury, ca. 1840. Mahogany, mahogany veneer, 20½ × 18¾ × 13¾ in. Collection of Glorianna H. Gibbon

Furniture from the Workshop of Duncan Phyfe   103

Figure 129. Detail of chair back of the D. Phyfe & Sons side chair in Plate 49

Figure 130. Detail of chair back of the side chair attributed to Duncan Phyfe or D. Phyfe & Sons in Plate 50

104 *Duncan Phyfe*

Encyclopaedia, which suggests that Phyfe, despite his apparent fascination with French Restauration furniture design, kept a weather eye out for new models and trends in late Regency furniture as well (see Pl. 50, fig. 1).[77]

Revival Styles of the 1840s

The 1840s were a time of change and transition in the decorative arts, from the Neoclassical style of the preceding fifty-plus years to a new era of eclecticism. During this period a dizzying new array of furniture, both imported and locally made, in the Gothic, Renaissance, and Rococo Revival styles, began arriving in the furniture warerooms of New York merchant cabinetmakers like Charles A. Baudouine, Alexander Roux, and Auguste-Émile Ringuet-Leprince (fig. 132), as well as lesser-known figures such as P. Chatereau, whose entire stock of furniture in the "styles of Louis XIV, Louis XV, and Elizabeth" were offered for sale at auction in April 1847.[78] Nonetheless, the Grecian Plain style persisted, sometimes overlaid with Gothic or Old French style motifs. Andrew Jackson Downing touches on this subject in 1850, in *The Architecture of Country Houses*:

> The furniture most generally used in private houses is some modification of the classical style, and usually in what is called Grecian or French taste—the former being characterized by lines and forms found in the antique classical compositions, and the latter being variations of the same, with the addition of some modern embellishment of detail and decoration.[79]

Based on the admittedly slim body of documented furniture from the Phyfe shop in the 1840s, it would seem that Phyfe's work during this period was less adventurous stylistically than that of some of his new, younger competitors and may have fit

Figure 131. Side chair. English, 1825–30. Rosewood, rosewood veneer, 34 × 18 × 19¼ in. Collection of Dr. Kenneth N. Giedd and Gary R. Conroy, Esq.

Figure 132. Auguste-Émile Ringuet-Leprince. Armchair. Paris or New York, ca. 1845. Ebonized applewood or pearwood, gilded brass, 38½ × 23¼ × 26⅛ in. The Metropolitan Museum of Art, Gift of Mrs. Douglass Williams, 1969 69.262.3

Furniture from the Workshop of Duncan Phyfe

Figure 133. Thomas King. *The Modern Style of Cabinet Work Exemplified* (1829). Plate 8, from the 1832 edition. The Metropolitan Museum of Art, Museum Accession, transferred from the Library, 1972 1972.638.3

Figure 134. Frame of an upholstered armchair. New York, 1840–47. Mahogany, mahogany veneer, 40½ × 25½ × 30¼ in. The Metropolitan Museum of Art, Gift of Carswell Rush Berlin, 1996 1996.459

Downing's description of a modified classical style. That is not to say that this characterization could not be reconsidered should some documented Phyfe furniture in a full-blown revival style be discovered. What survives from this late period, however—both furniture that is documented and furniture possibly made in the Phyfe shop—is an intriguing mix of Grecian Plain style forms with Old French and Gothic Revival overtones, suggesting that Phyfe, by this time nearly a half century in the business, while he was willing to modify his classically derived compositions to keep his furniture current, remained a conservative classicist at heart.

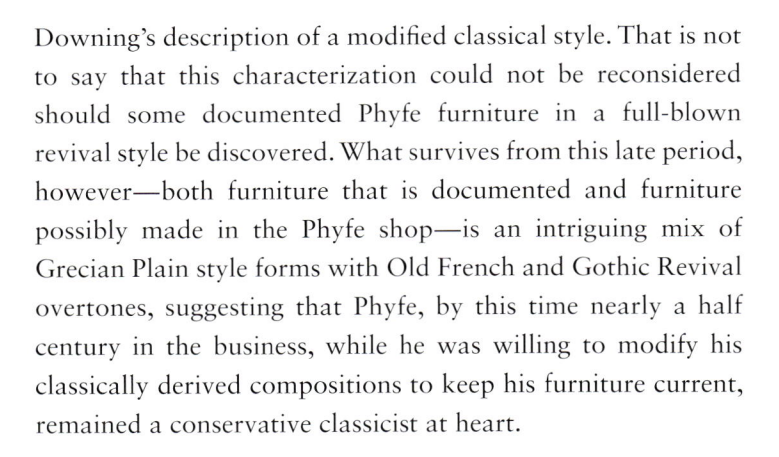

Rococo Revival or Old French Style

The origins of the revived French styles of Louis XIV and Louis XV are rooted in the magnificence of the eighteenth-century French court. Paradoxically, the roots of their revival originate across the Channel, at the Court of St. James. George IV (r. 1820–30) was one of the earliest champions of this aesthetic, as he had been for the resurgence of the Gothic in England.

Enamored of the life and legacy of Louis XIV (r. 1643–1715), he strove in his own reign to emulate the Sun King. Eventually these styles merged into one style that embodied the aesthetics associated with Louis XIV's great-grandson and heir, Louis XV (r. 1715–74). Known also as the Rococo, and probably derived from a blending of the terms *barocco* and *rocaille*, the latter denoting rock- and shellwork for grottoes, it came to be synonymous with the fantastic flights of fancy that define the idiom. The first recorded use of the term "Rococo" in New York seems to have occurred in 1844, in an article that appeared in *The New Mirror* titled, "Chit-Chat of New-York":

> Those . . . who have been lately in France will be familiar with the word. The etymology of *rococo* has been a matter of no little fruitless inquiry. It came into use about four or five years ago, when it was the rage to look up costly and old-fashioned articles of jewelry and furniture. . . . A chair, or a table, of carved wood, costly once but unfashionable for many a day, was rococo . . . things intrinsically beautiful and valuable, in short, but unmeritedly obsolete, were rococo.[80]

Duncan Phyfe

Figure 135. Désiré Guilmard. *Le Garde-meuble, ancien et moderne* (1842), livraison 25, plate 134. Lithograph with hand coloring. Smithsonian Institution Libraries, Cooper-Hewitt, National Design Museum

In England George Smith, who enjoyed the patronage of the king, published a somewhat apathetic endorsement of the style, observing that despite its "bad taste," the Old French style had never been surpassed for its richness and splendor.[81] By the 1830s, however, the detractors of the Louis XIV style had been turned around.[82] Of these, Thomas King was the most successful in popularizing the Old French style, among both the English middle class and the growing American upper class, beginning with his best-known work, *The Modern Style of Cabinet Work Exemplified* (London, 1829). King's designs in the Old French style have resonance in some of Phyfe's furniture for the drawing room at Millford, the finest and most important room in the mansion.

The best way to understand Phyfe's approach to the modification of his classically derived forms to give them an Old French style character is by comparing one of the Millford drawing room couches, dating from 1841, with a Grecian Plain style interpretation that descended in the family of Eliza Phyfe Vail (see figs. 197 and 185). The Vail couch fully embraces the Grecian Plain style aesthetic, as its design principally relies on line and the selection of choice, figured mahogany veneers for the planar surfaces, which are punctuated by applied, turned roundels that function as terminals for the contoured supports. The Manning drawing room couch, on the other hand, fashioned of more expensive rosewood veneers, transforms the Grecian Plain style that defines the Vail couch by the addition of sprightly scrolled brackets outlined in flat strapwork crossbanding that is integral to the rounded feet (fig. 124). The strapwork, characteristic of the interlaced and bordering strapwork found in the work of André-Charles Boulle (1642–1732) and on other paneled and carved Louis XIV forms, is used over the entire couch to outline and ornament its various structural components and contours, including the scrolled end, where, instead of his trademark rimmed disc, Phyfe uses a strapwork volute.

Similar strapwork, especially in the form of C-scrolls like those on the Millford drawing room couch, seems to be a defining feature of Old French style forms in Thomas King's *Modern Style of Cabinet Work Exemplified*. A prime example is the fire screen in plate 8, described by King as in the "old French style" (fig. 133). The strapwork on the Millford drawing room sofa (Pl. 63) is identical to that on the couch but is even more profoundly Old French style, tracing the line of the cupid's bow–shaped back that follows in outline, if not in carved and molded detail, the backs of some Louis XV sofas. A rosewood occasional table from the Millford drawing room has Old French style trestle feet outlined with strapwork (see fig. 133), but its lotus-carved end scrolls and flat veneered stretcher with paired Ionic volutes in profile are stronger classicizing elements.

Granted they are few in number, but the Millford sofas, couches, and occasional tables may represent the principal means through which Phyfe chose to engage the Old French style in the 1840s. It is noteworthy that of the nearly six hundred pieces of furniture listed in the sale catalogue of the contents of the Phyfe warerooms in 1847, only "1 rosewood Sofa, style of Louis XIV, serpentine front, covered with rich fig'd crimson plush," and "8 rosewood Chairs to match" can be positively identified with this style. An upholstered mahogany armchair with a serpentine front rail and Phyfe's trademark rimmed discs on the arm terminals (fig. 134) presents an intriguing possibility as an analogue to the suite of Louis XIV seating furniture described in the catalogue, and relates to a design published in Désiré Guilmard's *Le Garde-meuble, ancien et moderne* (fig. 135). If Phyfe in fact made this armchair and an identical pair in the Aiken-Rhett House in Charleston, South Carolina, then our vision of the extent to which he engaged the Old French styles of Louis XIV and Louis XV must be expanded.[83] In this vein, two additional side chairs should be considered, one (fig. 136) representing a whimsical, almost Rococo take on a well-established Phyfe

Furniture from the Workshop of Duncan Phyfe

Figure 136. Attributed to D. Phyfe & Son. Side chair, 1840–47. Rosewood, rosewood veneer, 32¾ × 17½ × 18 in. Collection of Carswell Rush Berlin

Figure 137. Side chair. New York, ca. 1845. Mahogany, mahogany veneer, 33½ × 18¾ × 20⅝ in. Hirschl & Adler Galleries, New York

design of the 1830s (Pl. 50), the other because it is of very fine quality, was made in New York, and has an even stronger Louis XV character (fig. 137). A large documented set of New York chairs in the Old French style made for the White House by Charles A. Baudouine in 1845 (fig. 138), however, cautions against reaching hasty conclusions as to who might have made the latter chair.

Gothic Revival Style

Gothic motifs were being incorporated into American domestic furnishings as early as the 1760s. Initially these were introduced through the British furniture designs published by Thomas Chippendale, William Ince, and John Mayhew, and subsequently by Thomas Shearer, George Hepplewhite, and Thomas Sheraton. In 1808 George Smith, in *A Collection of Designs for Household Furniture and Interior Decoration*, illustrated a comprehensive range of Gothic patterns. Rudolph Ackermann's monthly *Repository of Arts, Literature, Commerce, & C.* followed suit the next year, and toward the end of its more than twenty-year run introduced twenty-seven plates by the architect, designer, and medievalist Augustus Welby Northmore Pugin (1812–1852), whose name would come to be synonymous with the proliferation of Gothic taste in Britain. As the Gothic aesthetic continued to be explored by Pugin and his contemporaries, including the father of the Gothic Revival in America, Alexander Jackson Davis (1803–1892), they looked increasingly to ecclesiastical architecture for their inspiration. During the Restauration, French designers also focused on medieval ecclesiastical architecture, which resulted in the development of the delicate, highly refined *cathédral* style established in the late 1820s and 1830s (see fig. 112). In New York, Phyfe clearly was exposed to both English and French Gothic Revival furniture design through published sources and imported examples. How he embraced the mode is difficult to know, however, because of the dearth of documented Gothic Revival or Gothicized furniture from his shop.

108   *Duncan Phyfe*

Figure 138. Charles A. Baudouine. Side chair, 1845. Rosewood, rosewood veneer, 35 1/8 × 18 × 21 1/4 in. The White House, Washington, D.C.

The 1847 auction catalogue of the Phyfe warerooms records sixteen lots in the Gothic idiom, far fewer than in the Grecian Plain style. Interestingly, two of these, lots 352 and 353, describe "1 mahogany Grecian Sofa, spring and tufted seat, and back covered with dark purple plush" and "12 mahogany chairs to match, Gothic pattern." These catalogue descriptions affirm that it was perfectly acceptable to combine the two genres and again focus attention on the drawing room at Millford, where a good deal of style mixing was going on as well. Here, the Mannings chose rosewood Grecian couches and sofas overlaid with Old French style detailing (see fig. 197 and Pl. 63) to go with upholstered French armchairs given a Gothic air by the addition of ogee pointed crest rails (see fig. 118). When D. Phyfe & Son was awarded the contract for Millford in 1841, possibly the largest the firm had ever received, Alexander Jackson Davis was at the same moment avidly promoting his own vision of the Gothic. For Knoll, a Gothic villa he designed in 1838 for William and Philip R. Paulding in Tarrytown, New York, Davis also designed the furniture. Studies by Davis dated 1841 for several Gothic Revival pieces bearing the notation that they were intended for use in the Pauldings' "saloon" include a wheel-back chair based on studies of rose windows in medieval cathedrals (fig. 139). By comparison, D. Phyfe & Son's interpretation of the fashion in their French armchair with a pointed crest for Millford is only a timid allusion to the Gothic Revival, testament to the difference between a seasoned furniture manufacturer's pragmatic approach to incorporating elements of a new style and a brilliant architect's striving to create something unique for his client.

The set of rosewood side chairs for the Millford drawing room (Pl. 62) are another story, however, and reveal a far more

Figure 139. Andrew Jackson Davis. Study of furniture for Knoll, 1841. Graphite on paper, 4 1/4 × 6 5/8 in. Drawings & Archives, Avery Architectural and Fine Arts Library, Columbia University

Furniture from the Workshop of Duncan Phyfe 109

Figure 140. Detail of crest rail on the box sofa in Plate 66

creative approach to the Gothic Revival. To achieve this, Phyfe transformed the borrowed late Regency hoop-back design that was the basis of his daughter Eliza's chairs (Pl. 49), entirely reinterpreting the form by sculpting the back frame into a taut, angular shape with a pointed crest rail and a pierced splat with pointed Gothic shapes in both positive and negative spaces. While the Millford chairs do not proclaim their Gothic roots as forthrightly as do the Davis chairs for Knoll, they are nonetheless sleek abstract expressions of the Gothic Revival mode.

Phyfe's use of the Gothic is subtle and often within the context of his dominant Grecian Plain style. An example of this mode is the inward-curving hexagonal pillar on a dining table purchased from Phyfe by Lewis Stirling for his Louisiana plantation, Wakefield, in 1836.[84] Relying solely on its tapering, paneled shape and crotch-mahogany veneers for effect, the shaft on the Wakefield table lacks the delicate Gothic tracery delineated on that of the circular center table shown in the Davis study (fig. 139), but it clearly mimics the shape, something one might expect from a stealth Gothicizer like Phyfe. Another way Phyfe added Gothic detailing to his furniture was by arching the tops of cupboard doors. A pedestal-end sideboard of superb quality probably made in the workshop of D. Phyfe & Son in the 1840s (Pl. 67) has plate glass Gothic cupboard doors and may be of the exact type described in lot 278 in the 1847 auction catalogue as "1 splendid rosewood Sideboard, with marble top and back, gothic door and plate glass panels, mirror back, lined with white silk." A rare and stylish box sofa also incorporates pointed Gothic arches (Pl. 66 and fig. 140). Possibly from the Phyfe shop, this sofa again reveals the cabinetmaker's tendency to modify established Grecian Plain style forms to meet new style demands. Here, however, the modification is more overt, with applied tracery arches along the length of the scrolled crest rail, blind lancet arches on the front seat rail and chamfered plinths, and blocks at the tops of the tapering arm supports.

By the mid-1840s, five decades into Duncan Phyfe's storied career and on the verge of his retirement, the historical revival styles that would come to define a new generation of furniture design and interior decoration began to take root in New York. Phyfe may have looked back nostalgically upon the return of the Rococo style, one he had probably first encountered while working as an apprentice in the 1780s as well as in the pages of Thomas Chippendale's *The Gentleman and Cabinet-Maker's Director* (London, 1754, 1755, 1762), the most widely owned furniture design book in eighteenth-century America. Many of the chair designs in the *Director* displayed luxuriant, asymmetrical French-style Rococo ornament, sometimes in combination with pierced and carved Gothic and Chinese details. Knowing that his chair designs would be used by provincial makers, Chippendale emphasized that the amount of carved ornament could "be lessened by an ingenious workman without detriment to the Chair." He also stressed the importance of scale, regulating the sizes of chairs to "suit the Chairs to the Rooms." Phyfe seemed to have grasped these design principles intuitively and clung to them throughout his career, making ornamental restraint and exquisite scale and proportion the watchwords of his cabinetmaking enterprise, regardless of the methods of production or the various styles he employed over time. And while it may never be possible to know whether Phyfe, as reported by his first biographer, Ernest F. Hagen, actually muttered the now infamous epithet "Butcher furniture" to describe the overdecorated and carved Rococo Revival furniture of some of his competitors, this master cabinetmaker's long record of achievement certainly earned him the right to be critical. Today, with the fullness of time and a more perfect knowledge of his furniture legacy, Duncan Phyfe's reputation as a virtuoso of the Neoclassical style who directed the course of furniture design history in New York for nearly half a century seems more secure than ever.

Peter M. Kenny and Michael K. Brown

1. Hagen [1907], reproduced in McClelland 1939, pp. 315–17.
2. Keyes in Ormsbee 1929, pp. 498–99.
3. Hornor 1930, pp. 40, 96, takes issue with Keyes' justification of Myers' attributions.
4. The location of the chairs is unknown, but a picture of one with a carved urn and Prince of Wales feather in the back, when in the possession of family descendant Churchill B. Phyfe in the mid-1990s, was shown to Peter M. Kenny. Other examples of early Neoclassical furniture possibly made in the Phyfe workshop include a pair of knife boxes that descended in the family of Phyfe's daughter Eliza Phyfe Vail and a Pembroke table and corner basin stand with tapered legs that descended in the family of William Bayard and were claimed by W. M. Hornor Jr. to be the "Tea table" and "Bason Stand" on Phyfe's 1807 bill to Bayard (App. 1.3a). For these tables, see Hornor 1930, pp. 39–40. The Ackerman inscription on the sofa frame is shown in *The Magazine Antiques* 72, no. 4 (October 1982), p. 609. If the Ackerman inscription is authentic, it makes this sofa the only known documented example of Phyfe furniture in the early Neoclassical style.
5. P. Warren 1961.
6. Ormsbee 1930, pl. XXXI.
7. Fenwick Lyell Ledger, 1800–1813, Monmouth County Historical Association Library and Archive, Freehold, New Jersey (copy available in the Downs Collection, Winterthur Library, microfilm 2436.3).
8. In the 1800 edition of *Longworth's Directory*, a Henry Brewerton, attorney-at-law, is listed at 36 Church Street, near Phyfe's establishment, then at 35 Partition Street, and a James Brewerton, merchant, is listed on Duane Street. The authors would like to thank Carswell Rush Berlin for these references.
9. C. Montgomery 1966, p. 23.
10. Bound inventory of furniture, n.d. [1804]: "Inventory of Furniture and of whom it was purchased...." Charles Nicoll Bancker Papers, American Philosophical Society, Philadelphia (copy available in the Downs Collection, Winterthur Library, microfilm 101.3). The authors are most grateful to Charles F. Hummel for providing this information.
11. Cornelius 1922b, p. 3.
12. "Classical" is currently the accepted term used to describe all later American Neoclassical furniture made between roughly 1810 and 1845. For the purposes of this essay, it has been subdivided into the Grecian mode and the later Grecian Plain style, the former covering Phyfe's work from his so-called best period, circa 1805 to 1820, and his lesser-known richly ornamented work of the period 1815 to the early 1830's.
13. Sheraton (1803) 1970, p. 9.
14. Cornelius 1922b, p. 49.
15. Ibid., p. 43.
16. Ibid., pp. 51–52. Cornelius thought that he recognized direct French influence in Phyfe's work, stating, for instance, that "[a]mong the chairs executed by Jacob Frères, 78 rue Meslée, Paris, between 1797 and 1803, are several which contain the germ both of Phyfe's chair design and of his decorative methods. Although it is unlikely that Phyfe actually ever saw a Jacob chair (though some of this furniture may well have been brought to New York), he certainly shared with them the models and published designs from which each developed his style." For more on the role of direct French influence on New York furniture design, see Kenny, Bretter, and Leben 1998, pp. 37, 42, 43, 57.
17. R. Smith 1958. Robert Smith was the first to suggest a possible link between Phyfe's seating furniture and *The London Chair-Makers' and Carvers' Book of Prices for Workmanship*, of 1802, 1807, and 1808. Charles Montgomery agreed with Smith's hypothesis and cited the London price books in several of his entries on New York chairs in his catalogue of the Federal furniture collection at Winterthur; see C. Montgomery 1966, pp. 120–21, 124. Searching for a British design source for Phyfe's scroll-back, klismos, and curule chairs, Charles Over Cornelius (1922b, p. 51) overlooked the London price books, stating in the publication relating to the 1922 Phyfe exhibition at the Metropolitan Museum: "We search in vain the 'Guide' of Hepplewhite and the 'Drawing Book' of Sheraton for a suggestion of the characteristic line which is found in practically every chair back of Phyfe's best periods.... For this treatment we turn to France, and in the chairs executed during the Directory and early Consulate we have not only this treatment of the back posts and legs but also the methods suggested for many details of decoration." Cornelius' assessment is clearly a case of confusing direct and indirect French influence in New York. Smith and Montgomery would appear to have it right: New York chairs of the period 1805–20 were influenced by French Directoire and Consulat chair design, but design that had been filtered through London.
18. See Gloag 1991, p. 674; and http://collections.vam.ac.uk/item/052959/chair-trafalgar/.
19. C. Montgomery 1966, p. 124. An English chair with side-mounted Grecian crosses is shown in McClelland 1939, pl. 70. On this chair the rear stiles are based on the klismos chair, whereas on all known New York curule chairs they are curved like scroll-back chairs.
20. Cornelius 1922b, p. 51.
21. C. Montgomery 1966, p. 124; Barquist and Lasser 2003, p. 10 and n. 6.
22. *The New-York Revised Prices for Manufacturing Cabinet and Chair Work* (New York, 1810), p. 56.
23. *The New-York Book of Prices for Manufacturing Cabinet and Chair Work* (New York, 1817), pp. 106–9 and pl. 6.
24. Ibid., pp. 102, 110. Here they are called "cross legs" and "ogee cross legs."
25. Surowiecki 2007.
26. For a discussion of the discovery of the label on this chair, see Kenny 2000.
27. *New-York Revised Prices* (1810), p. 57. Here the base labor charge for "A Scroll Back Cane Sofa" is £6.12.0, and for sofa "No. 2" with a "scroll, top and scrolls in front of the arms" and a "Bell seat for stuffing over," £3.12.13. Adding in the cost of upholstery foundations and show covers, depending on the quality of the material used, could make the retail price of a cane and upholstered scroll-back sofa equal.
28. Mandeville made field bedsteads and a high-post bedstead for William Bayard in 1811 and the next year supplied tables and desks for the Common Council Chamber of New York's new City Hall; see Kenny, Bretter, and Leben 1998, pp. 109–10, 140. The Mandeville sofa is illustrated in Christie's, New York, sale cat., June 18, 1998, lot 358. The third scroll-back sofa has the initials and surname "J. S. Taylor" chip-carved into the secondary wood below the top rail. A Jacob Taylor, cabinetmaker, is listed in the New York City directories from 1804 to 1812. A detail of the sofa's right arm and crest rail and the initials are illustrated in an advertisement by Benjamin Ginsburg, "Antiquary," in *The Magazine Antiques* 112, no. 5 (November 1977), p. 815.
29. *New-York Revised Prices* (1810), p. 58; *New-York Book of Prices* (1817), p. 109.
30. For a treble elliptic card table with five turned and reeded legs labeled by the cabinetmaker John Dolan (act. 1805–15), see Waters 1996, p. 71. For a Pembroke table with double elliptic leaves and turned and reeded legs bearing the label of George Woodruff (act. 1808–16), see C. Montgomery 1966, p. 330. For a pillar-and-claw Pembroke table with double elliptic leaves labeled by Stephen and Moses Young (in partnership 1804–24), see Rollins 1991, p. 235.
31. Drawings for pillar-and-claw tables with saber-shaped legs appear as early as 1795 in the Estimate Book of the Gillows firm of Lancaster and London. For examples, see Boynton 1995, nos. 27, 68, 69.
32. *New-York Revised Prices* (1810), pp. 25, 26.
33. Collard 1985, pp. 20–24.
34. Zimmerman 2005b, pp. 127–28 and 143 n. 14. Zimmerman states that the early generation of the mechanical-leg New York card table was produced in New York and to a lesser degree in Philadelphia, which

suggests either that Philadelphia cabinetmakers borrowed what was essentially a New York method or that both New York and Philadelphia makers adopted it from English sources. A pair of English pillar-and-claw card tables that may have trick legs is illustrated in Apicella 2007, p. 129.

35. Blum 1948.
36. Sheraton (1803) 1970, vol. 2, p. 301.
37. Letter from Mary Telfair to Mary Few, October 28, 1816, William Few Collection, Georgia Division of Archives and History (Manuscripts Section), Atlanta. See Talbott 1995, pp. 129, 165 n. 8.
38. Copies of Thomas Hope's *Household Furniture and Interior Decoration* were offered for sale in the *New-York Daily Advertiser*, January 1, 1819, and the *New-York Columbian*, January 18, 1819, as cited in Frances Collard and David Watkin, "The Afterlife of Thomas Hope: Designers, Collectors, Historians," in Watkin and Hewat-Jaboor 2008, p. 26 n. 4. Rudolph Ackermann's serial publication *The Repository of Arts, Literature, Commerce, Manufactures, Fashion and Politics* was offered for sale in the *New-York Daily Advertiser*, January 26 and December 3, 1819, and the *New-York Evening Post*, May 14, 1823, as cited in Waxman 1958, pp. 52, 53. The use of Percier and Fontaine's *Recueil de décorations intérieures* by New York cabinetmakers is known from the comments of Jacques Milbert ([1828–29] 1968, p. xxiv), who stated: "French workmen started this business [furnishings] . . . and it is they who are developing it most successfully. They use the best models and books on furniture and interior decoration by Messieurs Percier and Fontaine."
39. Kenny, Bretter, and Leben 1998. For a discussion of the introduction and use of canted corners on English Regency and American card tables, see pp. 96 and 100 n. 111. For card tables and chairs with the same applied gilded ornament as on the Brinckerhoff card table, see pp. 117, 134.
40. Allison applied dated trade labels to his furniture roughly every two years beginning in 1817 and continuing to 1831, perhaps intending to provide a kind of "freshness dating" for style. For several examples of dated furniture and the Allison label, see Scherer 1984, pp. 43, 52, 72.
41. Early admirers of Phyfe put a cutoff date of 1825 on what they considered his best work. Of the four Grecian sofas illustrated by Charles Over Cornelius, none has scrolled ends set on top of a platform base; see Cornelius 1922b, pls. xxv–xxviii.
42. A design for a box-shaped sofa with front and back posts in the shape of bound fasces also appears in G. Smith 1808, pl. 60.
43. Tracy and Gerdts 1963, p. 63, cat. no. 57, illustrates a mahogany box sofa of classic New York form with a scrolled top rail. Tracy (p. 30) claims that "[b]y 1810 the rectangular pillared sofa had been published in France," though he cites no definitive printed source.
44. See, for example, plates 52 and 56 in Kenny, Bretter, and Leben 1998.
45. Letter from John Wells to Sarah Elliott Huger, July 25, 1815, in *South Carolina Historical and Genealogical Magazine* 43, no. 1 (January 1942), p. 53.
46. For contemporary comments on English versus French taste in fashion in New York during the early nineteenth century, see Kenny, Bretter, and Leben 1998, pp. 66–67.
47. Hope 1807, pl. 19, no. 5.
48. *New-York Daily Advertiser*, May 14, 1818; *New-York Evening Post*, May 30, 1818.
49. A Phyfe attribution for some of the griffin card tables was first suggested by Stuart P. Feld. See Feld and Feld 2001, pp. 16–17.
50. In 1817 Henry Bradshaw Fearon, an Englishman traveling in the United States, noted that he had conversed with several New York City cabinetmakers: "They state their business to have been at one time good, but that there is now too much competition." Fearon 1818, as cited in Kenny, Bretter, and Leben 1998, p. 45.
51. For a Joseph Meeks & Sons (1829–35) pier table with freehand gilded decoration and faux die-stamped brass banding, see Hawley 1982, pp. 327, 329. For work by Deming & Bulkley, see McInnis and Leath 1996. For work by Holmes and Haines, see Rini 2005.
52. Downs 1941.
53. For the use of the phrase first advanced by Thomas Gordon Smith, see T. G. Smith 1996, p. v. The Grecian Plain style is referred to as "Modern Grecian" by Andrew Jackson Downing (1850, p. 413) when he states: "Modern Grecian furniture has the merit of being simple, easily made, and very moderate in cost. Its universality is partly owing to the latter circumstance, and partly to the fact that by far the largest number of dwellings are built in the same style, and therefore are most appropriately furnished with it."
54. The plates at the back of the 1834 New York price book include designs that first appeared in the 1817 edition, including griffin, eagle, and lyre standards for card and pier tables, supporting the notion that late Grecian-style forms continued to be made into the 1830s.
55. Pollack 1998, pp. 103, 106–7. At the bottom of the sheet is a detailed index that describes the materials and embellishments, as well as specifying the retail price, for each of the items. This article is illustrated by a number of labeled pieces that can be dated between 1829 and 1835, thereby affirming that Meeks had embraced the style by then. The broadside is also discussed in Voorsanger 2000, pp. 296, 516–17, pl. 225.
56. Zimmerman 2005a, p. 14.
57. See Woodside 1986.
58. Schaffner 2010. See also Voorsanger and Howat 2000, pp. 304, 306–7.
59. In the 1850 census Ponsot, aged forty-five, is listed as a cabinetmaker in the Fifth Ward of New York City and his place of birth given as France. He is recorded in the 1850s and 1860s in *The New York Daily Times* and *The New York Times* listings of ship passengers sailing to and from Le Havre and Brest. In 1857, Ponsot brought action against the collector of the Port of New York to recover an excess of duties on imported rosewood, mahogany, and oak furniture that he paid in 1851; Samuel Blatchford, *Reports of Cases Argued and Determined in the Circuit Court of the United States for the Second Circuit Court* (New York, 1868), vol. 4, pp. 43–45. The authors would like to thank Barbara Glauber for this reference.
60. Voorsanger and Howat 2000, pp. 289–90, 312–15; Ingerman 1963; and Franco 1973.
61. Downing 1850, p. 432; see pp. 440 and 451 for additional accolades. See also Hauserman 1968 and Voorsanger and Howat 2000, pp. 305, 318, and 317 n. 203.
62. Voorsanger and Howat 2000, pp. 93, 309–12, and Gray 1994.
63. Chadenet 2001, p. 146.
64. Halliday & Jenkins 1847, p. 2, lot 39, p. 1, lot 16, and p. 12, lot 271.
65. For a bird's-eye view of the Tombs by Haviland, see Voorsanger and Howat 2000, p. 429, fig. 81.
66. Cooper 1993, pp. 32–33. Illustrated in Cooper is a *chaise gondole* (fig. 5), one from a set brought back to New York by Robert Livingston in 1805 at the conclusion of his tenure as Thomas Jefferson's minister to France. These chairs may have played some role in popularizing the form in New York in the 1830s, but more likely it was the French furniture imports to New York during the Restauration that exerted the most influence.
67. Pollack 1998, pp. 103, 106–7, pl. iv.
68. McClelland 1939, p. 251, pl. 238.
69. Receipt from D. Phyfe & Son to Mr. [Josiah] Hasbrouck, October 17, 1841. Huguenot Historical Society, New Paltz, New York.
70. A receipted bill signed by Duncan Phyfe and dated March 12, 1833, indicates that he was paid in full by Luman Reed for charges totaling $910. A photograph of this receipted bill (location of the original unknown) is in the Decorative Arts Photographic Collection (DAPC) at the Winterthur Museum. The upholstered armchair referred to here, along with several other pieces of furniture with a history of descent from Luman Reed to his granddaughter Mary Mulford, sold at Christie's,

New York, on January 22, 1994, *The Collection of Ronald S. Kane: Important American Furniture And Decorative Arts,* sale 7822, lots 357–362.

71. Smith simply lists p. 11, pl. 52, and fails to comment on the image, one of only two out of 158 reproduced for which there is no explanatory text. Smith is the subject of an insightful essay by Constance V. Hershey in G. Smith (1808) 1970.
72. G. Smith 1826, p. vi.
73. Ibid., pls. 24, 118, p. 195.
74. For an excellent biographical sketch of King and an analysis of his publications and their impact, by Thomas Gordon Smith, see King (1829) 1995.
75. Loudon 1839, p. 1041.
76. "Inventory of the Contents of Duncan Phyfe's House at 193 Fulton Street Made after His Death," September 14, 1854, Duncan Phyfe Papers, 54x37.34, Downs Collection, Winterthur Library, reproduced in McClelland 1939, pp. 332–39.
77. Reproduced in *Pictorial Dictionary* 1977, p. 217.
78. *New-York Commercial Advertiser*, April 3, 1847.
79. Downing 1850, pp. 412–13.
80. "Chit-Chat of New-York [The Rococo]," *The New Mirror*, February 17, 1844, p. 318, quoted in Voorsanger and Howat 2000, pp. 303, 304 n. 111.
81. G. Smith 1826, p. 173.
82. Whitaker 1825. For more extensive discussions on the British reaction to the style and its dissemination, see Joy 1977, pp. 144–53; and Morley 1993, pp. 407–8, 410.
83. The pair of armchairs at the Aiken-Rhett House are illustrated in McInnis and Leath 1996, p. 167.
84. Haygood and Thurlow 2007, p. 132

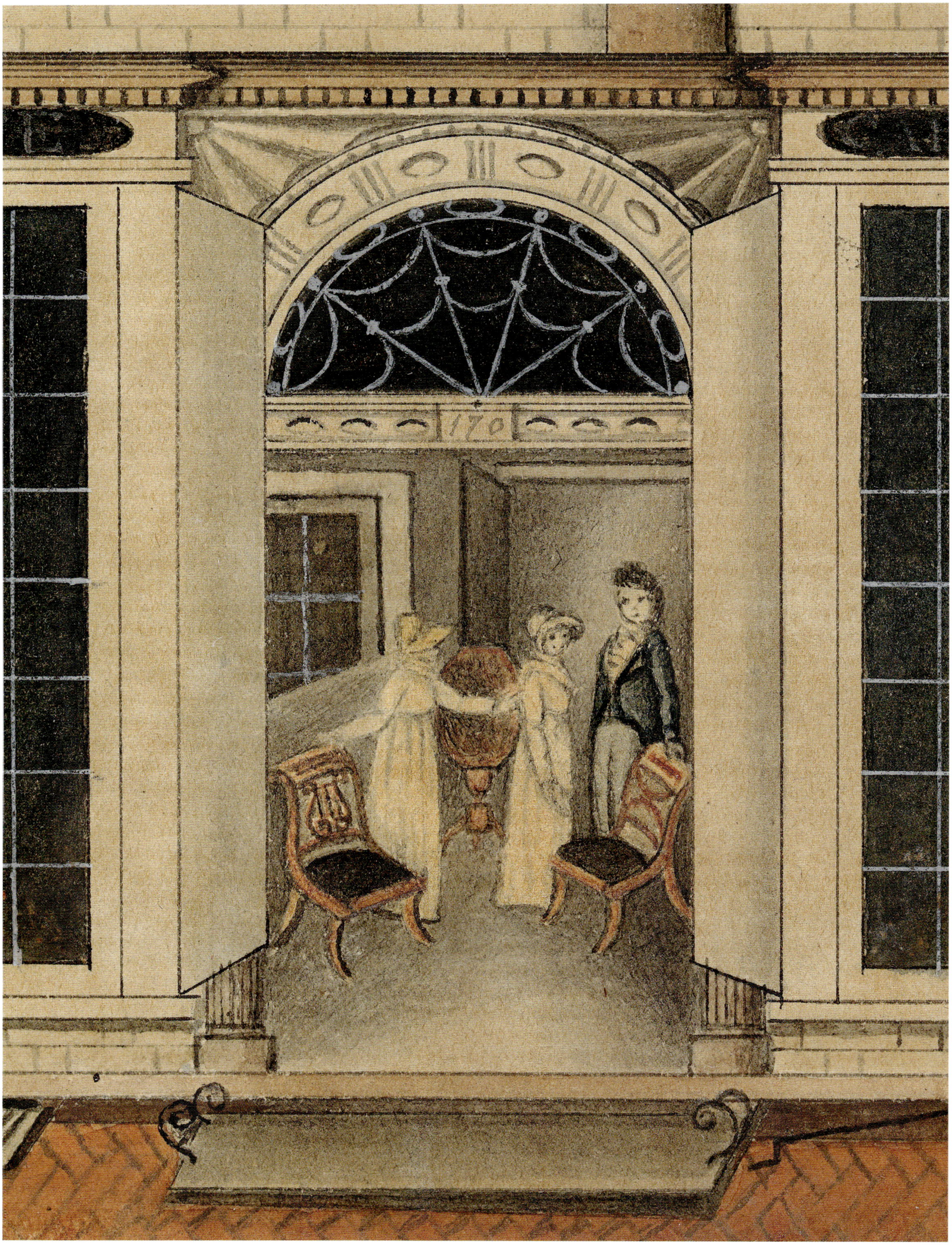
170

3. Patrons of the Cabinet Warehouse

The tables you will get best at Phyfe's than elsewhere, & I wish you therefore to give him the preference.

John Wells, letter to Sarah Elliott Huger, 1815[1]

The instructions were from the lawyer John Wells to his sister-in-law Sarah Huger asking her to select furniture for his new home while he and his bride were on their wedding trip. Wells' directive implied that Phyfe's tables excelled in style and workmanship. For these qualities the customer had to pay a premium. Delighted with the results of the pier tables that Phyfe had earlier made for Wells, Sarah, for the sake of economy, nevertheless obtained tables for another relative from a different New York maker and was dismayed that they "neither accorded with my Fancy or Directions."[2]

Phyfe's clients—some, wealthy New York merchants or lawyers and others, Southern planters and businessmen or gentlewomen working through their agents in New York—went to him for well-made furniture in modern classical styles. Phyfe suited their taste and understood their ambitions. In her 1939 monograph on the cabinetmaker, Nancy McClelland included a chapter on his customers, citing thirty-seven clients with surviving furniture from documents or family histories. Recently discovered material has identified new clients and given additional support to some of her findings. The selection of fifteen customers included here represents an illustrative cross section of clientele over time and, with only two exceptions, are those who can be linked to a document from which at least some furniture is known today. This chapter tells their stories. Certainly knowing the working relationship between Phyfe and his clients and the personal choices they made provides a broader framework to his output, enriching the narrative of his career.

Men of Taste

William Bayard

In 1807 the New Yorker William Bayard (1761–1826) placed a large order with Duncan Phyfe for fifty-six pieces of furniture for his new house on State Street. Although by then Phyfe had been in the cabinetmaking business for fifteen years, Bayard is the earliest client whose bills of sale can be linked to identifiable furniture. In 1786 he founded the commercial house of LeRoy and Bayard, later LeRoy, Bayard & McEvers, with Herman LeRoy, a brother-in-law of his wife, Elizabeth Cornell Bayard (1763–1854). Elizabeth, one of the five Cornell sisters of New Berne, North Carolina, and Bayard married in 1783. The firm capitalized on the opportunities of post-Revolutionary America, profiting handsomely from trade with Europe, the East and West Indies, and later coastal South America. Bayard became the firm's principal partner and one of the city's wealthiest merchants. During the War of 1812 the partners owned several successful privateers, and for the duration of the trade embargo played a role in land speculation in northern New York State. In 1793–94, Bayard sat for Gilbert Stuart, who captured the kind and dignified countenance for which Bayard was known (fig. 141). He also presented him as a figure of fashion, in a bright green coat and dotted silk waistcoat.

In 1806, Bayard purchased and remodeled part of the late eighteenth-century red-brick James Watson mansion at 6 State Street, in the city's most elegant quarter looking out over the greensward of the Battery to panoramic views of New York Harbor. His designer-builder was the master carpenter John E. West, who had earlier worked with the architect John McComb Jr. on the new City Hall. West retained the old red-brick front elevation but added a classical doorway with architrave and columns above a high basement. At the rear, facing Pearl Street, he erected a curved three-story garden façade with elliptical room ends, arched stone-framed windows, and a large stable.[3] An illustration in Valentine's *Manual* (fig. 142) shows Bayard's house at the right before it was converted into a rooming house for immigrants in the 1850s and then demolished. To its left, 7 State Street, is the house of Moses Rogers, who divided the Watson mansion, selling the eastern part to Bayard and retaining the two western bays for his own home. Remodeling at the same time as Bayard, Rogers built the graceful bowed double-colonnaded addition to the west, which follows the bend in State Street. Often attributed to McComb, but lacking tangible evidence, the façade of the Rogers house stands today,

Opposite: Detail of *Shop and Warehouse of Duncan Phyfe*, 1817–20 (fig. 39)

Figure 141. Gilbert Stuart (1755–1828). *William Bayard*, 1793–94. Oil on canvas, 36 × 28 in. Princeton University Art Museum, Gift of Viscountess Eccles

the sole survivor of the elegant Federal town houses that once lined the Battery.

The interiors of Bayard's house are known only from the numerous craftsmen's invoices preserved among his papers. A bill from the London-trained carver and gilder John Dixey documents that he executed classical-style architectural ornament for the principal rooms: large Ionic capitals with carved leaves on the necks for two columns and for matching pilasters, four rich composite capitals for pilasters, twenty paterae for cornices, and two rich trusses for the stairs.[4] Dixey, best known as the sculptor of the figure of Justice that stood atop the dome of City Hall, arrived in New York in 1801 and carved architectural elements for more than two decades. Bayard for his most important rooms ordered four expensive marble mantelpieces from Livorno, Italy. The most elegant one is described by Bayard's daughter Maria, in a diary she kept while traveling in England and France. It had two marble caryatid figures that supported the mantel shelf, which she compared with the grand pair of caryatid mantels in the main gallery at Corsham Court near Bath.[5] Although she confessed that the State Street mantel was smaller and less opulent, it nevertheless represented the height of modern classical taste in New York.

Bayard's cabinetmaker of choice was Duncan Phyfe, who provided furniture in a new version of the Neoclassical style, only just becoming available in New York. Three invoices survive. The most extensive one, from November 1807 (App. 1.3a), lists twelve entries for parlor, dining room, and bedroom furniture and gives a glimpse of the furnishings of Bayard's rooms. The bill includes forty-two chairs, three sofas, two pairs of card tables, a tea table, a set of dining tables, and a sideboard. A set of chairs in the latest Grecian style (Pl. 1 and fig. 143), acquired from a Bayard descendant together with one of the original Phyfe invoices, is today in the collection of the Winterthur Museum. Twelve in number—two armchairs and ten side chairs—from an original group of fourteen, at $15 each they are the more expensive chairs recorded on the invoice. At Winterthur they are displayed in the Phyfe Room (see fig. 11), a period room setting with woodwork removed from an upstairs parlor in the Moses Rogers house. The scroll-back chairs have banisters with double lattice-like crosses with carved rosettes at the center, bell-shaped seats upholstered over the seat rail, and reeded swept front legs in a new style first described in *The London Chair-Makers' and Carvers' Book of Prices for Workmanship*, of 1802. While the origins of this style derive from French adaptations of ancient Greek and Roman forms, the scroll-back chair arrived in New York by way of London. Phyfe made this shape his own (though it was also made by other New York cabinetmakers), constructing a neat, smaller scale chair with tight proportions and, on the crest rail, carved motifs that would become his hallmark: five thunderbolts bound at the center with a bowknot. The thunderbolt, an attribute of the Greek god Zeus, may well have been chosen by Bayard, Phyfe, or a New York carver as a symbol of the power and energy of the rapidly expanding city and its entrepreneurial merchants—such as the client himself.

Some of the twenty-eight chairs billed on the invoice at $12.50 apiece are also known today. Both groups include side chairs and armchairs, but the invoice does not distinguish between the more expensive armchairs and side chairs, which suggests that Phyfe may have extended a special rate for a set. Also with scroll backs, these chairs have a single cross in the banister, cane seats, and the more common turned and reeded front legs. The twenty-three chairs of this type with a Bayard provenance known today are from two sets that have been combined: nine side chairs are owned by a direct descendant (Pl. 2), ten side chairs and two armchairs (Pl. 3) are in the collection of the Museum of the City of New York, and two side chairs are at Winterthur. Although the sets are very similar, there are small differences in the urn and column turnings on the rear stiles just above the seat, and the carved thunderbolts on the crest rails of one group appear to be the work of a different hand. This may be explained by a second bill to William Bayard

116   *Duncan Phyfe*

Figure 142. A. Weingartner. *View of State Street*. Lithograph, from D. T. Valentine, *Manual of the Corporation of the City of New-York for 1859*. The Metropolitan Museum of Art, Bequest of Charles Allen Munn, 1924 24.90.1852

from Duncan Phyfe of the same November 1807 date that lists fourteen chairs at $12.50 each (App. 1.3b). This bill for a parlor set is perhaps for wedding furniture, a gift from Bayard to his eldest daughter, Susan, who married Benjamin Woolsey Rogers, the boy who lived next door at 7 State Street, on December 10, 1807. A cane sofa (Pl. 4) owned by the Museum of the City of New York and having the same Bayard provenance has carving which matches that on one set of the single cross-back chairs. The sofas on both invoices were billed at $65. It is possible that one or perhaps two sofas had upholstered seats and backs en suite with the more expensive upholstered chairs. A third Phyfe bill for furniture spanning the period March 1809 to May 1810 (App. 1.3c) lists four additional mahogany chairs at $50, or $12.50 each; these must have had cane seats and single crosses. In 1819, Bayard issued a check to Phyfe for $1,305.77 for unspecified services.

Of the eleven furniture forms listed on the three invoices, only the seating furniture discussed above and one card table from the three pairs of card tables listed on the bills can be identified today. The card table (Pl. 5), which has five turned reeded legs and a double elliptic top, is a frequently found New York form. With the exception of figured mahogany veneers and crossbanding on the top and apron, the table has no ornament and must therefore be one of the less expensive $75 pairs. Phyfe charged an additional $5 for the third pair, which probably looked much like this table but had added extras— either a carved tablet at the center of the apron or a center panel of contrasting veneer on the façade. A card table made a few years later and owned by the same Bayard descendant

Figure 143. Duncan Phyfe. Scroll-back chair, 1807. Mahogany, 33 × 19⅞ × 21 in. Winterthur Museum, Bequest of Henry Francis du Pont, 1957 57.719.8

Patrons of the Cabinet Warehouse

Figure 144. Attributed to Duncan Phyfe. Card table, 1810–15. Mahogany, mahogany veneer, 29⅜ × 36 × 18½ in. Collection of Mr. and Mrs. Roland W. Glidden

as the nine single cross-back chairs (fig. 144) has a double elliptic top that swivels, a reeded plinth with four carved columns, and carved and reeded legs. It is a near duplicate of a pair of tables owned by Thomas Cornell Pearsall (Pl. 12) and, because the families intermarried, could be either a Bayard or a Van Rensselaer table. The Pearsall card tables are nearly always attributed to Phyfe, although there is no known documentation.

Bayard patronized a number of New York furniture makers.[6] In an article that appeared in the magazine *The Antiquarian* in 1930, W. M. Hornor Jr., writing about Bayard's Phyfe furniture, illustrated a pedestal-end sideboard (see fig. 78) that he believed to be the sideboard listed on the November 1807 invoice at $125. Unknown to Hornor, who knew only the Phyfe invoice, a year earlier Bayard had purchased a pedestal-end sideboard from the New York cabinetmaker Jacob Brouwer for £36 (about $90).[7] Is the Bayard sideboard by Phyfe or by Brouwer? Circumstances such as this make a Phyfe attribution tenuous at best. In 1805, Bayard purchased a mahogany bedstead from Charles-Honoré Lannuier, the French-trained cabinetmaker and Phyfe's chief rival in New York for superior cabinetwork. No bed is listed on the Phyfe invoices, but there are other bedroom pieces: an expensive wardrobe, a dressing table, and a basin stand.

Bayard's personal preference for English Regency design is apparent in his Phyfe furniture choices. Of expensive mahogany, superbly proportioned and skillfully carved, the pieces lack the gilding and decorative gilded brass mounts associated with the French Empire style. To furnish the homes of two of his daughters, Maria, a passionate Francophile, traveler, and independent spirit who wed Duncan Pearsall Campbell, and Harriet, the youngest child and a captivating New York belle who married the sophisticated "Grand Tourist" Stephen Van Rensselaer IV, Bayard became an important client of Lannuier's in 1817. Both couples married in that year, and for each he bought a pair of gilded figural card tables (see fig. 96) and a pier table in the late French Empire style from Lannuier and a suite of seating furniture imported directly from France. There is no evidence, however, that Bayard bought gilded French-style furniture for himself. Now past middle age, his tastes had been set years earlier.

Thomas Cornell Pearsall

About 1810 New Yorker Thomas Cornell Pearsall (1768–1820) purchased a superb suite of seating furniture in the English Regency interpretation of the ancient Roman curule form and a pair of pillar-and-claw card tables. The furniture cannot be documented either by a maker's signature or by a bill of sale, but it is attributed to Phyfe on the basis of its supreme quality and its relationship to a design drawing of a curule chair produced by the Phyfe shop. The seating pieces descended directly in the Pearsall family until 1946, when they were sold at auction in New York and then placed on loan to the Metropolitan Museum.[8]

Duncan Phyfe

Figure 145. Attributed to John Opie (1761–1807). *Thomas Cornell Pearsall*, ca. 1795. Watercolor on ivory, 3⅞ × 2⅞ (framed). Collection of Richard T. Button

Pearsall was wed to Frances Buchanan (1779–1863) in 1799. After their marriage the Pearsalls resided at 43 Wall Street, the address as well of the eponymous family firm. About 1810, if not a few years earlier and following the death of Pearsall's mother, Phoebe Cornell Pearsall, the young couple moved to Belmont, the family country estate inherited from his father, Thomas Pearsall. The elder Pearsall had acquired the farm of about twenty acres in 1797 and built the house probably shortly thereafter.[9] The curule furniture is thought to have been purchased for the couple's move to Belmont. The house, which no longer stands, had sweeping views of the East River from the foot of what is now Fifty-eighth Street on land that ran from below Fifty-seventh Street, north past Fifty-ninth Street, and from the East River to what is now Third Avenue.

The little that is known about Pearsall comes from the commentary of his contemporaries. He had traveled in Europe, to England where John Opie painted his portrait (fig. 145), and to Rome. At the time of Pearsall's death at the age of fifty-two, his fellow New Yorker John Pintard described him as "a bon vivant, who gave the best dinners & best wines, but never performed a single act of benevolent duty . . . and fell a sacrifice to high living."[10] Nearly twenty years later, in 1839, the diarist George Templeton Strong, lamenting the sale of Pearsall property, wrote: "A queer rigmarole my abstract will be. It has gone from father to son since . . . 1685, and now the dissipation of that worthless scamp Tom Pearsall sends it under the hammer—to pay debts that he has (*de facto*) contracted for tippling expenses."[11]

At the pinnacle of fashion in New York in the 1810s, suites of curule furniture epitomized the increasingly cosmopolitan tastes of the city's merchant elite and displayed Phyfe's full mastery of the ogee-cross form. The suite purchased by Pearsall comprises a sofa with Grecian crosses at both front and rear, a pair of armchairs and twelve side chairs with Grecian-cross legs at the sides, and two footstools with canted corners and tapered reeded legs (Pl. 13, fig. 146, and Pl. 14). The ogee cross is repeated in the chair splats. Tablets with gracefully carved laurel branches ornament both the crest rails of the chairs and the center tablet of the sofa, which has flanking tablets of cornucopias; carved laurel branches are repeated on the sofa arms. All have cane seats; the sofa, caning on the back as well. The curule form—the prototype of which is the folding stool (*sella curulis*) used by Roman magistrates—came to the attention of the public following the rediscovery of Herculaneum (1738) and Pompeii (1748) and was popularized by French and English designers. In 1808 it was illustrated in the London cabinetmakers' book of prices paid to journeymen, which is the probable source for the design of the Pearsall furniture. The pillar-and-claw card tables (Pl. 12), each with a cluster of four carved and fluted columns, also follow English adaptations of antique forms. Pearsall owned as well a columnar pier table in the pure French antique style, made in New York between 1805 and 1810 by Charles-Honoré Lannuier.[12] English- and

Figure 146. Attributed to Duncan Phyfe. Curule side chair, 1810–15. Mahogany, cane, 32⅝ × 17⅞ × 21⅞ in. The Metropolitan Museum of Art, Gift of C. Ruxton Love Jr., 1960 60.4.9

Patrons of the Cabinet Warehouse

Figure 147. Interior view of the home of Mrs. Henry Wilmerding Payne, 14 West 36th Street, New York City. Photograph, early 20th century. Museum of the City of New York, Gift of Mrs. Samuel S. Walker 43.155.1

French-style goods of excellent quality were available to meet the discerning tastes of wealthy New Yorkers.

A recently discovered inventory of the Pearsall furnishings, undated but probably from around the second quarter of the twentieth century, records "the Duncan Phyfe furniture": the set of seating furniture, the footstools, and the pair of pillar-and-claw card tables.[13] A photograph of the parlor of a Pearsall great-granddaughter, Mrs. Henry Wilmerding Payne, shows part of the curule suite and damask window curtains in a pattern of baskets with flowers purported to be the original (fig. 147).[14] A version of this damask is on the furniture today, fabricated when the suite was installed in the Richmond Room of the American Wing of the Metropolitan Museum in 1979.

Other Pearsall pieces illustrated by Nancy McClelland in the Phyfe monograph that descended to Mrs. Payne and are possibly by Phyfe are a card table with five legs similar to the pair owned by William Bayard (Pl. 5) and a French sideboard with four Egyptian term figures at the front.[15] A high-post bedstead of about 1810 (private collection), with richly carved posts and upholstered panels on the head- and footboards, and an English glass and gilded brass chandelier of about 1800 with opalescent arms and amethyst drops with a matching pair of candelabra (Metropolitan Museum) were also owned by Pearsall.[16]

Charles Nicoll Bancker

In 1816, Phyfe completed a large parlor suite for Charles Nicoll Bancker of Philadelphia (1777–1869; fig. 148). Descended from a loyalist New York family, Bancker moved to Philadelphia about 1804, the year of his marriage to Sarah Upshur Teackle (1783–1843), of Accomack on the Eastern Shore of Virginia. The couple resided first on Mulberry Street, where an inventory taken on the last day of December 1804 indicates that they had purchased a sideboard (whereabouts unknown) from Duncan Phyfe, which Bancker valued at $130.[17]

By 1816, when they bought the furniture, the Banckers were residing on Chestnut Street. Three pieces of correspondence—a letter, a drawing, and an invoice (App. 1.6)—indicate their continued patronage of the Phyfe workshop and provide the most detailed record of his work for a client known to survive. In September of the preceding year, Phyfe had written:

> I acknowledge the Receit of your third letter and Should have answered it before this time but could Not Inform you wether i could have Card & Pear Table To Show you, when you come to New York. I will Endeavour to have Card & Pear Tables Dun by the 1 of October and Should Mrs. Bancker not like Them I will Except of your offer. I Have Put the Chairs & Sofa in hand and will have them Dun As Soon as Possible.[18]

Work had already begun on the seating pieces, so it must have been earlier in the year that Phyfe provided the Banckers with a sketch of two chairs whose forms have become so closely identified with him that they are almost synonymous with his shop (fig. 149). This often published sketch, presumed to be Phyfe's only known drawing, depicts a klismos chair with lyre back and an uncommon variant of a curule chair with crossed legs at the front. Included are prices for stuffed seats and cane

120   Duncan Phyfe

Figure 148. Thomas Sully (1783–1872). *Charles Nicoll Bancker*, 1830. Oil on canvas, 30 × 25 in. Philadelphia Museum of Art

seats with cushions. Sometimes viewed pejoratively for Phyfe's lack of drawing skills, the sketch actually depicts very clearly the shape and carved motifs of each chair to aid Bancker in his choice. The lyre especially is precisely drawn; less visible is a pair of lightly sketched cornucopias on the crest rail, a detail that rarely appears in combination with lyre splats and animal-paw feet. Ten side chairs, which today are in the collection of the Brooklyn Museum, are thought to be Bancker's only identifiable Phyfe furniture. Klismos chairs with lyre splats, veneered crest rails, and "stuffed" seats (Pl. 20), they were billed at $22 each, indicating that Phyfe had charged one dollar less than the $23 indicated on the drawing, perhaps because they lacked cornucopias in the crest rails. The January bill remained unpaid, and Bancker failed to take advantage of an offered 3 percent discount for cash. The bill was sent again in August, at which time Bancker ordered two additional chairs and a pair of footstools. Consistent with their purchase eight months later, two chairs from the surviving group of ten exhibit minor variations in detail.[19]

The Phyfe parlor set—a mahogany sofa, fourteen mahogany chairs, a pair of footstools, a pier table with marble top, and a pair of card tables (App. 1.6)—stood in the back parlor of the Bancker house at 320 Chestnut Street, according to an inventory made in 1819. The Phyfe sideboard from 1804 was in the front parlor with a dozen chairs and a tea table, both by unknown makers, together with a piano and piano stool.[20]

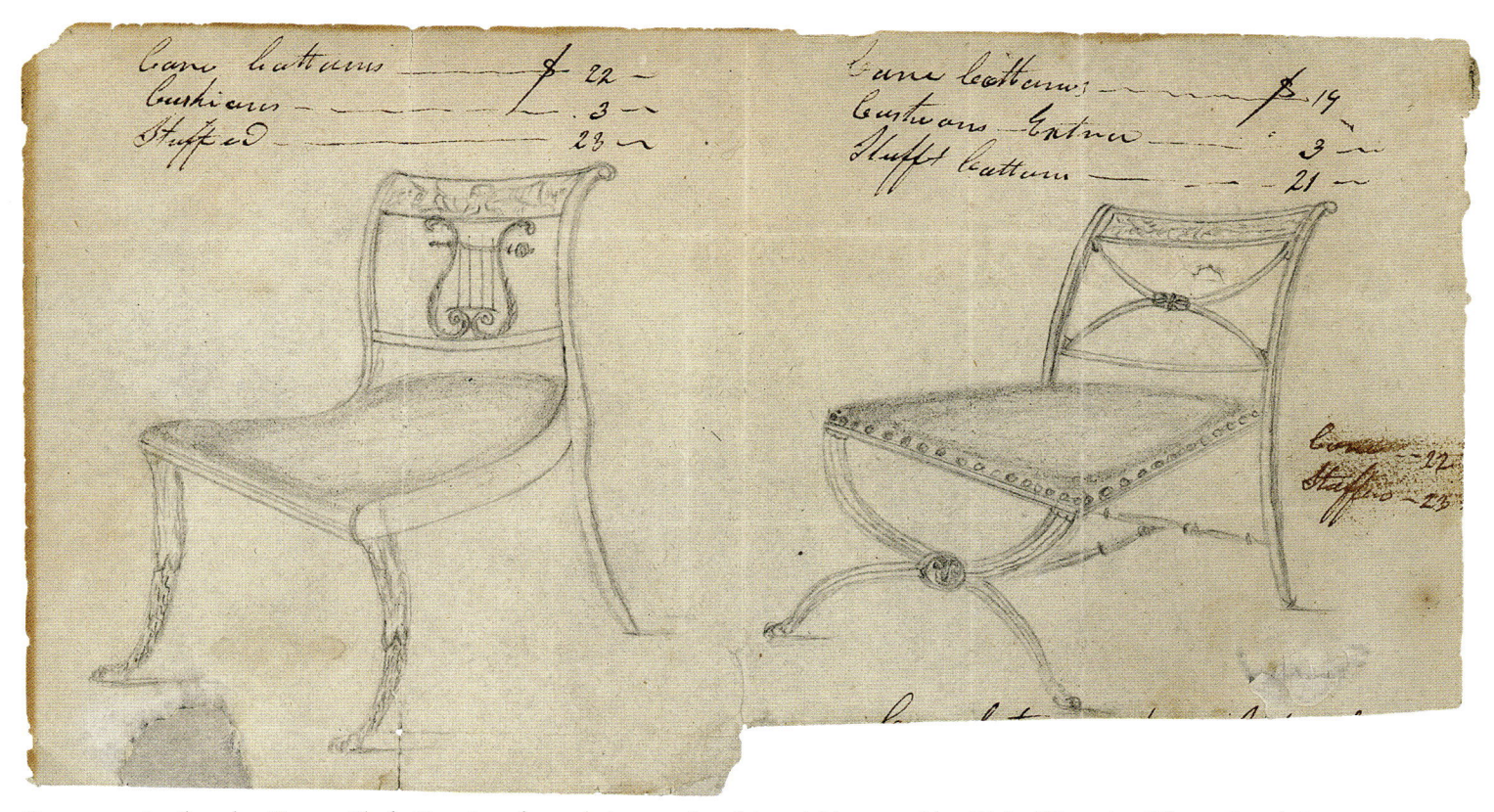

Figure 149. Attributed to Duncan Phyfe. Drawing of two chairs, ca. 1815. Ink on laid paper, 4 3/8 × 8 1/8 in. Winterthur Library, Joseph Downs Collection of Manuscripts and Printed Ephemera

Patrons of the Cabinet Warehouse

From 1837 until his death thirty-two years later, Bancker served as president of the Franklin Fire Insurance Company. After his wife died in 1843, he began to amass a large private library and a collection of scientific instruments that were sold, following his death in 1869, at a public auction in Philadelphia that ran for several days.[21]

Ladies and Worktables

Victorine du Pont Bauduy

In celebration of her marriage on November 9, 1813, to Ferdinand Bauduy (1791–1814), Victorine du Pont (1792–1861; fig. 150) received a satinwood worktable (fig. 151) from her uncle Victor Marie du Pont and his wife, Gabrielle Josephine de Pelleport. Victorine was born in Paris during the darkest days of the French Revolution, the eldest child of Eleuthère Irénée du Pont, chemist, printer, and later the founder of E. I. du Pont de Nemours and Company in America, and Sophie Madeleine Dalmas. At the instigation of her grandfather Pierre Samuel du Pont, the entire family immigrated to New Jersey and then moved to Delaware, to the banks of the Brandywine River. Pierre Samuel, rising from humble beginnings as an apprentice to his watchmaker father and always of a highly romantic and quixotic nature, wrote as a young man to the great Voltaire,

Figure 151. Alternate view of Duncan Phyfe worktable, 1813, in Plate 8

who advised that he was possessed of two natures, one with a gift for finance, the other for poetry. Choosing finance over verse, Pierre Samuel later wrote several pamphlets on economic and agricultural reform and eventually rose to become inspector general of commerce under Louis XVI.[22] A friend of both Benjamin Franklin and Thomas Jefferson and twice imprisoned in Paris by the revolutionaries, Pierre Samuel, forever the optimist, looked to America as an Edenic land of liberty.[23]

Following a harrowing three-month voyage at sea, the family disembarked at Newport, Rhode Island, in January 1800, more than a hundred and fifty miles off course from their intended arrival in New York Harbor. Victorine was seven years old and would become the first in her family to speak English. Unlike her wildly unrealistic grandfather, her father's character was one of sober determination, and he established the gunpowder works that lay the foundation for what would become the family fortune. Victorine's fiancé's family were also émigrés, having fled the slave uprisings in Santo Domingo. Ferdinand's father, Peter, for a time became Irénée's partner in

Figure 150. Rembrandt Peale (1778–1860). *Victorine du Pont Bauduy*, 1813. Oil on canvas, 28½ × 23 in. Winterthur Museum, Bequest of Henry Francis du Pont

122 *Duncan Phyfe*

Figure 152. Baroness Hyde de Neuville (ca. 1749–1849). *Eleutherian Mills Residence*, ca. 1817. Sepia on paper, 7¼ × 9¼ in. Hagley Museum and Library, Wilmington, Delaware

the gunpowder works, and is thought to have directed the design of both the du Pont family home, Eleutherian Mills, and the powder works located on the opposite riverbank. The house (fig. 152), perhaps inspired by architecture of the West Indies, features on the rear façade a two-story piazza with columns facing the Brandywine.

The purchase of Victorine's worktable was arranged by Catharine Cruger, who placed the order through Anthony Girard, an agent of the du Pont powder works. It cost $40, a price both parties agreed was acceptable. What followed would become a pattern of mounting frustration, not only for Girard but for Phyfe clients in general: Phyfe was usually late in filling his orders. Girard, writing to Victorine's uncle Victor Marie du Pont in late November, provided encouragement, "I think that the little work table should be finished by now. Phyfe wished it to be made by one of his workers whom he knows best does this sort of work."[24] Aunt Josephine's feathers, for one, were not so easily smoothed. Her displeasure is evident in a December 19, 1813, letter to an old friend:

> We had been led to order from New York a very pretty sewing and writing table, made in satinwood and in very good taste.... Well! First, this wretched table, ordered a full six weeks before her marriage... has still not arrived. And to finish me, on going to see [Victorine] yesterday, I noticed in a corner of the room a little piece of furniture designed for the same purpose—mahogany, fortunately, that she had brought back with her. Isn't that annoying! Such frivolities lose almost all their merit when they do not come at the right moment, and seem completely stupid when they can no longer please.[25]

These diminutive tables were intended for ladies, especially for the storage of their needlework. Most New York examples with astral ends, like this one, served also as writing tables; the adjustable writing flap was exposed when the hinged top was lifted. Removable trays at the sides with extra space below and two small drawers concealed behind the sliding tambour door provided extra room for storage. Victorine's small red leather sewing case remains in one compartment.

Tragically, less than three months after his marriage to Victorine, Ferdinand Bauduy died of pneumonia. Victorine lived in her father's house after her husband's death, and became superintendent of the Brandywine Manufacturers' Sunday School, where lessons in reading, writing, arithmetic, and Bible study were given to workers of the local manufactories and their children.

Leah Henry Kelso

Phyfe charged $52 for a mahogany worktable (fig. 153) that he made for the New York merchant James Kelso (1781–1842) and his wife, Leah Helen Henry Kelso (b. 1786), who married on Christmas day in 1810. In 1813, when the worktable was billed, the couple lived at 84 Leonard Street, but within two

Patrons of the Cabinet Warehouse

Figure 153. Duncan Phyfe. Worktable, 1813. Mahogany, mahogany veneer, ebony, gilded brass 30⅜ × 23⅝ × 15¾ in. Collection of Mr. and Mrs. Jerome W. Blum

years they had moved to 49 Stone Street, where they remained until 1819. Leah Kelso's table, a square worktable with canted corners, features the added expense of a brass baguette molding on the top edge and a base with four spiral fluted columns resting on a fluted plinth. It also functioned as a sewing and writing table. Unlike Victorine's worktable (fig. 151), which has a single false drawer front above a sliding tambour shutter, Leah Kelso's table has two working drawers on the front, the lower one faced with tambour reeding. Neither worktable has a pull-up dressing glass behind the writing flap like the satinwood worktable in the Metropolitan Museum (Pl. 9), an option that would have added to their cost. Two Phyfe invoices (App. 1.4) rendered to James Kelso were discovered among a packet of bills in the space below one of the side trays; the worktable was the third most costly item on the Phyfe invoices.

Mary Telfair

Mary Telfair (1791–1875; fig. 154), of Savannah, Georgia, ordered a worktable and a secretary bookcase from Duncan Phyfe about 1816 through her friend Mary Few, who was living in New York. Mary Telfair attended schools in New York and New Jersey, was a great fan of the novels of Sir Walter Scott, and an enthusiastic reader of poetry. She looked down on the isolation of plantation life and in her later years voiced an interest in national affairs and politics. On trips to Philadelphia and New York, she may have seen and admired Phyfe's furniture. In a letter of October 28, 1816, to Mary Few she asked, "Have you paid Phyfe a visit & what does he say about the Secretary?" adding a postscript, "Keep the change of the hundred after you settle with Phyfe . . . as I may trouble you soon if you have no objection to being my Banker."[26] A secretary bookcase of a design associated with Phyfe but with an unusual, perhaps unique, tympanum that copies the glazing pattern of the doors, has a Mary Telfair provenance (fig. 155). The soffit under the cornice is enriched with carved and gilded rosettes. One can imagine the empty voids of the pediment festooned with swags, jabots at the sides, and fabric gathered behind the doors. The effect was meant to heighten the secretary's feminine appeal. A second letter, postmarked December 8, perhaps of the same year, to the same correspondent, notes, "I must trouble you dear Mary to call on Phyfe you recollect I paid him sixty dollars for my work Table & 1d 50 cts for boxing it, he never sent it on board the Tybee as he promised and probably if any accident happened to the Table he will be honest enough to return you the money."[27] This table is unknown.

Figure 154. Enrichetta Narducci (1806–1892). *Mary Telfair*, 1842. Gouache on ivory, 3⅛ × 2¾ in. Telfair Museum of Art, Savannah, Georgia, Bequest of Mary Telfair, 1875

124   *Duncan Phyfe*

Figure 155. Duncan Phyfe. Secretary bookcase, ca. 1816. Mahogany veneer, mahogany, glass, 81¾ × 36 × 22¼ in. Private collection

Mary Telfair never married and directed that at her death her estate be used to establish a library and an academy of arts and sciences bearing her family name that would be open to the public. Her bequest became the progenitor of the South's first public art museum, the Telfair Museum of Art, which opened eleven years after Mary Telfair's death in 1875.

SISTERS AND SOFAS

Jane Bowne Haines

In 1819, Phyfe made a sofa in the Grecian style for Reuben Haines III (1786–1831) and his wife, Jane Bowne Haines (1790–1843; fig. 156), shortly before their move that spring from their Philadelphia town house on Chestnut Street to Wyck, the family summer home in Germantown, a distance of seven miles from the city. The working farm had been enlarged and the house remodeled into a fashionable countryseat at the end of the preceding century by Reuben's father, Caspar Wistar Haines, but Reuben chose to have the interiors remodeled again in a Greek Revival scheme in 1824 by his friend the Philadelphia architect William Strickland (1788–1854). A pencil sketch of Jane, baby Hannah in her lap, seated with family and friends in the new conservatory, looks out to her beloved rose garden with roses trained to trellises on the façade (fig. 157).

Both Reuben and Jane Haines were Quakers. Jane was descended from the Bownes, one of New York's earliest and most important Quaker families, who had settled in Flushing in the seventeenth century. The move to Wyck, seven years after their marriage in 1812, enabled Haines to pursue his interests in agriculture and natural science and to build a substantial library on farm husbandry. Their city house was furnished largely with pieces from Philadelphia cabinetmakers: Jacob Super supplied a mahogany dining table, maple-grained beds, and two elliptical bureaus; Haydon & Stewart, twenty-four satinwood-grained fancy chairs (two can be seen in the drawing and others remain today at Wyck).[28] The purchase of the Phyfe sofa (fig. 158) may have been intended to buoy Jane's spirits for their anticipated move to the country, as Jane, the daughter

Figure 156. Possibly Nathaniel Rogers (1787–1844). *Jane Bowne Haines*, 1835. Watercolor on ivory, 2¾ × 2½ in. Private collection

Patrons of the Cabinet Warehouse

of a prominent New York stationer and printer, grew up on Pearl Street and was more accustomed to city life. Her sister Sarah Minturn, who supervised the order from New York, wrote to Jane that although several sofas had been examined, the commission was not yet executed. "The price of such as thee would like," she wrote, "are from 115 to $120 & Mother would be glad to know whether thee would object to the single row of brass nails which confine the hair."[29] Sarah herself owned chairs that have been attributed to Phyfe. One, a scroll-back armchair with a single cross at the back, bears many of the hallmarks of Phyfe's work and, additionally, has a bowknot and thunderbolts carved on the front seat rail, a placement that is rarely seen; the thunderbolt motif is repeated on the crest rail.[30] Sarah wrote to her sister:

> The sopha we fear will not be ready by the time thee wishes—there has been great pains to select the handsomest wood—the nicest hair etc. and Phyfe says he must not be hurried as he wishes to finish it in a manner to do himself credit and give satisfaction to the lady who sent for it. He seemed much pleased when he heard it was to go to Phila. and said he should exert himself to have it surpass any that could be made there—in doing so Aunt Lydia says he will waste enough [time] to make three or four pieces of furniture & perhaps then not succeed. but I have no doubt it will please us all—he promises to pack it & put it on board the vessels for $120.[31]

The sofa, now covered in black horsehair fastened with a single row of brass nails, as described in the letter, is consistent with Quaker aesthetics; it is stylish and of fine quality but not ostentatious. The crest and front seat rail are veneered in finely grained mahogany and the winged animal-paw feet carved in the modern classical fashion, but the covering is haircloth, not silk, and there is no gilding. The sofa's broad front seat rail anticipates the bolder forms of the 1820s and 1830s.

"The tables . . . best at Phyfe's"

John and Sabina Wells

That obtaining furniture from Phyfe in a timely manner was frequently a problem is borne out in several pieces of surviving correspondence. When John Wells (1770–1823; fig. 159), the distinguished New York lawyer, married his second wife, Sabina Elliott Huger (1781–1845) of Charleston, South Carolina, in 1815, they moved to their new home at 292 Broadway. Wells wanted the house readied for Sabina to receive her friends when they returned from their wedding trip. In anticipation of their homecoming, he wrote from Boston in July to his new sister-in-law, Sarah Elliott Huger (b. 1775), who was living in New York. Asking her to oversee the order of certain furniture and decorations, he requested that she

> select a carpet for our two lower rooms with proper tables for the front room and a tea table for the back room. Chairs will also be wanting. . . . I wish you also to direct them. I leave the whole to your selection & taste promising most faithfully to thank you for whatever you do and to approve and confirm all your acts. . . . The tables you will get best at Phyfe's than elsewhere, & I wish you therefore to give him the preference.[32]

Sarah acted as Wells' agent, a role she also assumed for Southern friends and relatives. A few days into the New Year she wrote to her cousin Harriott Pinckney Horry regarding the order of tables from Phyfe and a second order in which her cousin had participated for a Charleston friend. The Wells tables, though ordered six months earlier, still were not ready.

> Poor Sabina was terribly chagrined on new year's Day to find her rooms still exhibiting its ancient appearance. . . . [T]he first of January is a very important day with the ladies of this country; from 10 in the morning until 4 they are receiving gentlemen, and therefore like their houses to be in the nicest order, and besides this, my sister had a large company to dinner, which was quadrupled in the evening. . . . [I]t would have been a relief to Sabina to exhibit something which should incur criticism although the occupation [cardplaying] was procured, probably at the expense of her taste.[33]

It is not known when the new tables arrived, but a pair of pier tables from the Phyfe shop with carved lion's-head consoles in the latest Grecian mode (Pl. 16 and fig. 160) has descended in two branches of the Wells family. Their flamboyance must have provoked the comments that Sarah so wished for her sister.[34]

Letters exchanged between the two Charleston ladies, Sarah Huger and Harriott Pinckney Horry, illustrate the process and frustrations of obtaining furniture for out-of-town clients. Four years earlier, in 1812, Sarah had included in a letter to her cousin two sketches of furniture by Duncan Phyfe, "rather uncouthly executed, but yet I think some idea of the originals is conveyed."[35] As cost was always a consideration, she included descriptions of what could be purchased at what price from New York makers: "a dozen chairs with two settees of the latest fashion will cost $144, made of cane, if rush, $120, the shape is quite plain and nothing like the mahogany; in fact there is a great difference in the appearance as there is in price; two Sofas and twelve chairs of Mahogany of the best taste will be $500."[36] Receiving no response for seven months, Sarah wrote, "I was quite mortified not to have heard from you about the furniture; I fear the drawings I enclosed were not as tasty as you wished; as yet we have had nothing newer."[37]

The order was put aside because of the risks involved in shipping during the War of 1812, and the two ladies' correspondence about furniture does not resume until 1815. In September Mrs. Horry's daughter wrote to her mother in Philadelphia

Figure 157. Charles A. LeSueur (1778–1846). *The Hall at Wyck*, 1824. Graphite on wove paper, 6 × 9 in. The Wyck Association, Philadelphia, Pennsylvania

Figure 158. Duncan Phyfe. Grecian sofa, 1819. Mahogany, mahogany veneer, 34 × 96¼ × 24½ in. The Wyck Association, Philadelphia, Pennsylvania, Gift of John Carey, 1988

Patrons of the Cabinet Warehouse 127

Figure 159. John Frazee (1790–1852). *Bust of John Wells*, 1824. Marble. St. Paul's Chapel, New York City

Figure 160. Detail of Duncan Phyfe pier table, 1815–16, in Plate 16

that Mrs. Lowndes (Sarah I'on Lowndes) desired furniture for her daughter Mary, who was to be married in the spring:

> She wishes you to get a set of drawing room chairs for her at least 18 in number to have cain seats and cushions covered with chintz not of a very large pattern, and not to require washing very often, with Sophas to your taste and Curtains with fringe to the draperies. . . . I think she said it would not be necessary to have fringe to the sides and ends of the curtains [as] she says she limits $700 seven hundred doll[ars] for these things.[38]

Mrs. Horry again turned to her friend Sarah Huger to select the furniture, relying on her taste to please Mrs. Lowndes. Mrs. Lowndes' budget would not cover the cost of mahogany chairs and settees from Phyfe's shop, since tables and curtains were required as well. She chose instead the New York chair-makers Jesse Ellis and Stephen Wheaton, who specialized in maple painted fancy furniture and whose final bill was $316.[39] Not pleased with the result, Miss Huger asked her friend to explain to Mrs. Lowndes that her furniture

> is by no means as handsome as I wished it, or, as The nature of The wood could admit of; The Chairs for example should certainly have been scrolled backed, to Correspond with Their attendant Lounges, and I think an insertion of gilt moulding in place of The black line would prove more appropriate to Drawing Room display.[40]

Although the chairmakers had agreed to these changes at an added cost of $4 for each chair, Miss Huger decided it would exceed the approved amount.

For tables Sarah continued to rely on the advice of her brother-in-law John Wells that it was best to purchase them from Duncan Phyfe. In January, after visiting the Phyfe shop, she wrote to Mrs. Horry:

> What shall I say to you about Mrs. Lowndes's Furniture? . . . It is impossible for me to prophesize when the good lady will receive the card and pier tables. Mr. Phyfe is so much the United States rage, that it is with difficulty now, that one can procure an audience even of a few moments.[41]

Miss Huger had to concede that, alas, the Wells tables were not ready either. By March, however, Mrs. Lowndes' tables were finished and placed aboard a schooner bound for Charleston. Miss Huger was very pleased with the pier table: "I think you will admire [it] as a remarkably chaste and tasteful ornament," although the card tables, made in maple to match the grain-painted seating furniture, "neither accorded with my *Fancy* or *Directions*." Nevertheless,

> Phyfe assured me that curled maple could not be worked in the shape I ordered but at an immense price; so high, that Mrs. L. he was sure could never be reconciled to give it for,

what is generally so roughly used as Card Tables; Articles by the way that are now become obsolete in drawing rooms, which should only exhibit marble Tables in every pier, and a round centre one, corresponding in marble and finish with the side ornaments.[42]

A pier table similar to the pair made for John and Sabina Wells was recently found in England (see fig. 90). Unlike the Wells tables, which rely solely on carved mahogany for embellishment, it has a large brass mount at the center of the apron, brass stringing, and gilded gesso and *vert antique* legs. While an attempt to trace the provenance of this table was unsuccessful, one wonders whether Sarah Huger was so pleased with the Wells tables that she ordered a similar pier table for Mrs. Lowndes. Was this perhaps the "remarkably chaste and tasteful ornament" of which she wrote?

"Arbiter Elegantiarum"

Robert Donaldson

The furniture Duncan Phyfe made for the North Carolinian Robert Donaldson (1800–1872) is among the most elegant produced in the classical style in New York during the decade of the 1820s. Donaldson was also a patron and friend of two of the most talented designers of his day, the architect Alexander Jackson Davis (1803–1892) and the horticulturalist and landscape designer Andrew Jackson Downing (1815–1852).

Figure 161. Charles R. Leslie (1794–1859). *Robert Donaldson*, 1820. Oil on canvas, 30½ × 25½ in. Collection of Richard Hampton Jenrette

Figure 162. Edgewater. Built ca. 1825, with additions and alterations by Alexander Jackson Davis, 1854

Downing's dedication of his book *Cottage Residences* (1842) is to "Robert Donaldson, Esq. of Blithewood, on the Hudson, Arbiter elegantiarum," ultimate judge in matters of taste. While Downing was referring to Donaldson's taste in architecture and gardening, the same could be applied as well to his taste in bespoke Phyfe furniture.

Robert Donaldson was born and grew up in Fayetteville, North Carolina, a large trading center on the Cape Fear River, where his Scottish-born father, also named Robert, had consolidated his shipping business. The eldest son of six children and orphaned when he was eight years old, Donaldson was sent with his younger siblings to live with nearby family members. His parents' house on Union Street, to which he later returned, would for many years be entangled in business partnerships and debt. Following his graduation from the University of North Carolina at Chapel Hill in 1818, he embarked on a five-month journey through the mid-Atlantic, the northern states, and Canada during which he kept a diary of the sights and places he visited. His observations informed his future interests in art and architecture, which became a passion for him and would assume a central role later in his life.[43]

In the spring of 1820, Donaldson traveled to England, Scotland, and France. In London he received a bequest from the estate of his late bachelor uncle Samuel Donaldson, owner of a successful commission house, and sat for Charles R. Leslie, the resident American portrait painter (fig. 161). Now a man of means—a beneficiary of both his uncle's bequest and the final settlement of his father's estate—Donaldson moved with his younger siblings back to the family house on Union Street. A young friend visiting in September 1822 remarked, "They lived splendidly in Fayetteville beyond any other family in the place."[44] Dated a month earlier, an invoice from Duncan Phyfe records a suite of seating furniture and tables (App. 1.7), perhaps now installed in the parlor of Donaldson's Fayetteville house.[45] Isabel Bronson (1846–1931), a Donaldson daughter, noted in her family history an often repeated tale of her father's that the Phyfe furniture, placed onboard a boat for the voyage to North Carolina, sank to the bottom of the Cape Fear River after the vessel sprang a leak. When the cargo was raised the furniture was intact, "wonderful proof of the excellence of Phyfe's work, nothing came apart, nor was loosened."[46] Only the red damask upholstery, it was said, had to be replaced.

Much of the Donaldson furniture that is known today at the Brooklyn Museum and at Edgewater, his last home on the Hudson (fig. 162), is ornamented with gold leaf, highly figured wood veneers, and gilded brass mounts. The finest examples are the extraordinary window seats with elaborate gilded decoration of scrolled foliate designs (Pl. 34). The recent discovery of the date July 4, 1826, on the linen filler cover of one seat cushion establishes that the pair were ordered in anticipation of the family's move to New York. In 1827, Donaldson purchased 15 State Street, a fashionable ten-room brick house with marble mantelpieces and mahogany doors built in 1812 by the merchant Archibald Gracie.[47] The following year he married Susan Jane Gaston (1808–1866), of New Bern, North Carolina, a daughter of the eminent William Gaston, a North Carolina legislator, state supreme court justice, and two-term member of the United States Congress.

Susan was painted by the American artist George Cooke in 1832 (fig. 163), the year after Cooke's return from Europe, where he had spent time in Florence and Rome sketching ancient works of art. Cooke's recent study of the still-fashionable antique would have especially appealed to Donaldson, who was establishing his place among the city's cultural and artistic elite. The year before, Donaldson had employed the talented young architect Alexander Jackson Davis to update and make renovations to the exterior of his State Street home. Davis' firm provided a new doorway and an iron railing, which Davis described as honeysuckle (Greek) ironwork.[48] Cooke's portrait depicts Susan in the State Street house, standing behind a classical balustrade of the artist's invention with her harp (fig. 164) and, most important here, one of the Duncan Phyfe window seats.

A Grecian couch (Pl. 35) and the pair of window seats descended to the same Donaldson daughter, with the portraits and other attributed Phyfe furniture. They share similar boldly reeded and gilded leaf-carved legs. Neither form is included on the 1822 bill. A sofa at Edgewater (fig. 165), acquired by its present owner at auction with no known provenance, has ornament exactly matching that on the couch: identically carved and gilded legs, identical brass inlay at the center of the front rail and brass mounts, even the same configuration of brass stringing.[49] The two pieces, of unique design, are clearly en suite and relate closely to the window seats. A rosewood canterbury (Pl. 36), called a music stand by the family, has feet with similar gilded wide reeds. Photographs dating from the early twentieth century show interiors of Isabel Bronson's home in Summit, New Jersey, with some of the Phyfe furniture: a marble-top center table in the entrance hall (fig. 166 and Pl. 32); two footstools (whereabouts unknown) and the portraits of Robert and Susan Donaldson in the dining room; a sofa table, two ornamental side chairs (all whereabouts unknown), and a secretary bookcase in the parlor (fig. 167 and Pl. 33). A second pair of window seats with upholstered scrolled ends, rosewood graining, and gilded decoration have a Donaldson history and were sold at auction in 1944 with the two footstools.[50] They look to be earlier, and perhaps they and the ornamental side chairs—conceivably those listed at $12 apiece on the 1822 invoice and glimpsed in several rooms in the photographs—were among the legendary furniture that went to the river bottom.

Figure 163. George Cooke (1793–1849). *Susan Gaston Donaldson*, 1832. Oil on canvas, 50 × 40¼ in. Brooklyn Museum, Gift of Mrs. Henry M. Post (Mary R. Haskell), on long-term loan to Edgewater

Figure 164. Susan Donaldson's harp. Alexander Barry, London, first quarter 19th century. Height 66 in. Collection of Richard Hampton Jenrette

Figure 165. Attributed to Duncan Phyfe. Grecian sofa, ca. 1826. Rosewood veneer, gilded brass, gilded gesso and *vert antique*, 34 × 95 × 27¾ in. Collection of Richard Hampton Jenrette

Patrons of the Cabinet Warehouse

Figure 166. Hallway with center table, home of Isabel Bronson, Summit, New Jersey. Photograph, early 20th century. Collection of Richard Hampton Jenrette

Figure 167. Parlor with sofa table, secretary bookcase, and ornamental side chairs, home of Isabel Bronson, Summit, New Jersey. Photograph, early 20th century. Collection of Richard Hampton Jenrette

Figure 168. Attributed to Duncan Phyfe. Worktable, 1822–26. Mahogany veneer, gilded brass, gilded gesso and *vert antique*, 29¾ × 24½ × 18 in. Collection of Richard Hampton Jenrette.

At Edgewater, Richard H. Jenrette, the architectural connoisseur and collector who purchased the house in 1969 from the writer Gore Vidal, has gathered more Donaldson pieces thought to be by Phyfe. Among the gifts from a Donaldson great-granddaughter are the rosewood canterbury and a mahogany worktable with carved and gilded feet (fig. 168).[51]

In 1835, eight years after the purchase of the State Street house, Donaldson acquired Annandale, a ninety-five-acre estate on the Hudson, in Dutchess County, New York, enabling him to pursue his rural interests in farming and scientific agriculture. Delighted with their new life in the country, Susan renamed the property Blithewood (fig. 169). Here Donaldson was able to continue his fruitful collaboration with Alexander Jackson Davis. Ardent patron and innovative architect together transformed the existing house according to the former's ideas and the latter's expertise.[52] By 1841, when Downing chose to use the house as the frontispiece for his first book, the roof extended from a wide low-pitched gable with eave brackets to an ornamental veranda that wrapped the house on three sides.

Among Davis' numerous sketches of outlying structures for Blithewood are an Egyptian Revival toolhouse, a grapery (greenhouse), a rustic temple, an ornamental springhouse, and two well-known gatehouses.[53] The earlier gatehouse (1836), with high-peaked central gables, would become the prototype for Gothic-style cottage architecture in the United States. The second gatehouse (1841), a hexagon in the bracketed style, is the only building from Donaldson's ambitious building scheme to survive today, though in much altered form.[54] Downing transformed Donaldson's ideas on landscape design into terraced gardens and walks made to look "wild and natural," with rustic seats terminating in long vistas that were integrated in harmonious union with fields and farm buildings.[55]

Preferring a countryseat to city life, in 1842 Donaldson sold his State Street residence. The decision to live at Blithewood year-round called for a family wing on the river side in 1842. A picture gallery with a half-octagonal end, also facing the river, was built in 1845 to exhibit Donaldson's most prized possessions: Leslie's *Gypsying Party;* Samuel F. B. Morse's copy of Raphael's fresco *The School of Athens,* made for him in 1831; several Dutch landscapes; and some portraits and Italian paintings.

In 1852, Donaldson sold Blithewood and purchased Edgewater (formerly Sylvania), one of the Livingston estates that lie on a twenty-mile stretch of the Hudson River near Barrytown on a tract of 250 acres. The Neoclassical house (see fig. 162), was built about 1825 in a Greek temple form with a two-story piazza framed by Doric columns that rise to an impressive triangular pediment. As its name implies, the house stands at the water's edge, on a small peninsula with the river on three sides. Donaldson abandoned his plan to build a villa on the heights and instead asked Davis to assist him in the design of an octagonal picture gallery and library, "books to alternate with pictures" on the north end of the house, and a greenhouse, "elegant & commodious . . . an octagonal or circular form will be best," at the south.[56] Only the picture gallery was built; a bay window was substituted for the greenhouse. Although Donaldson maintained that he did not wish to duplicate Blithewood, he could not contain his passion for building and improvements. The brick exterior of the house was covered with tinted stucco and scored in imitation of stone, and several outbuildings were designed and constructed: the greenhouse at a considerable distance behind the house, two facing octagonal gatehouses—one in the bracketed style, the other Italianate—a boathouse, a summerhouse, and a school, among others. The gatehouses, much altered, remain at Edgewater today.

The Phyfe furniture in the State Street town house was moved to Blithewood and then to Edgewater, where it remained

Figure 169. Alexander Jackson Davis (1803–1892). *Blithewood*, ca. 1841. Original watercolor for engraved frontispiece of Andrew Jackson Downing, *A Treatise on the Theory and Practice of Landscape Gardening* . . . (1841), 4⅛ × 6⅜ in. The Metropolitan Museum of Art, Harris Brisbane Dick Fund, 1924 24.66.361

until Edgewater was sold in 1902. It descended to Donaldson's daughter Isabel Bronson and, with the exception of the pieces she sent to dealers, went in turn to her daughter, Pauline Bronson Cromwell, and then to her granddaughter Mary Cromwell Allison, Donaldson's last direct descendant. Mary Allison donated the family portraits and furniture to Edgewater, where they remain today among other Donaldson possessions.

Grecian Plain Style

George and Maria Clark Fox

The carved and gilded Grecian style of the 1820s, stripped of most of its ornament, gave way to the Grecian Plain style in the 1830s. Closely allied to the French Restauration style after the second Bourbon Restoration, it relied for decorative effect on highly figured mahogany or rosewood veneers. The style's robust forms, Grecian in inspiration rather than in archaeological accuracy, suited the large-scale interior spaces of Greek Revival architecture. Phyfe made furniture in this new mode for Maria Franklin Clark (1812–1836) and her husband, George Fox (b. 1809), who married in 1833. The furniture, a wedding gift from her father, Benjamin Clark, a Quaker judge, and her mother, Deborah Morris Franklin, is described in an invoice dated the following year (App. 1.8) that totaled $1,154.50 but was adjusted to $990. The young couple lived in the city at 71 Madison Street, between Catherine and Market Streets, in an area that had been a part of the old Harmanus Rutgers Farm. George Fox was a merchant. His business address coincided with that of his father, William W. Fox, who was president of the New York Gas Company.

In 1940 Mary Zeigler, a grandniece of Maria Fox, wrote to Nancy McClelland, author of the 1939 Phyfe monograph, including a copy of the original bill of sale and six snapshots of furniture with her letter.[57] She recalled that the three sofas listed on the invoice were similar in style and that all three were covered in black horsehair. One sofa, itemized separately, she remembered as having hard square hair pillows about five inches thick. The pier tables are described as having tall gold-framed mirrors that either hung above them or rested on the marble tops. Two dressing bureaus were missing their mirrors and carved arms and so were discarded. A pier table with marble top (see fig. 110), its mate sold earlier, was acquired by the White House in 1961, at the time of Jacqueline Kennedy's refurbishing campaign. It relates closely to a French model, plate 631 in Pierre de La Mésangère's *Collection de meubles et objets de goût* (Paris, 1827; see fig. 113), but lacks a lower shelf

Figures 170–172. Center table, worktable, and dining table made in 1834 by Duncan Phyfe for George and Maria Clark Fox, seen at Fanewood, the Clark family country house. Photographs, ca. 1925. Nancy McClelland Archive, Cooper-Hewitt, National Design Museum, Smithsonian Institution

Patrons of the Cabinet Warehouse 135

and has frontal scroll supports rather than canted ones, and is nearly identical to a pair of pier tables that Phyfe made for his daughter Eliza (Pl. 48).

Some of Maria Fox's Phyfe furniture, together with the original bill of sale, was discovered during the course of research for this exhibition. Two sofas (Pl. 43) remained with family descendants until 2005. Other pieces associated with the invoice that were identified are a center table, a worktable, a set of dining tables (figs. 170–172), and ten of what were originally twelve mahogany chairs (Pl. 44). The center table and worktable derive from English Regency design, with bases in the simplified geometry of a Grecian cross; a card table with a cruciform base and carved animal-paw feet is illustrated in plate 35 of *The Cabinet-Maker and Upholsterer's Guide* (London, 1826), by the English Regency furniture designer George Smith. The dining table is an extension table with a trestle base and a top that pivots 90 degrees; two hinged legs concealed in the sliding frame drop down at one end to support extra leaves.[58] The chairs have bold concave crest rails based on ancient Greek examples and the newly fashionable "French" cabriole legs. Their minimalist form recalls the simplified Biedermeier furniture made for the new urban middle class in Europe.

In 1836, following the death of his second child and his wife two months later, George Fox moved from the Madison Street house and, according to family tradition, returned the Phyfe furniture to his father-in-law, Benjamin Clark. The furniture descended to Maria's younger sister Anna (1819–1914), who married William J. Roe (1811–1875). Roe is listed in the New York City directories at 1 Bridge Street from 1837 until 1843. At some point the furniture was moved to Fanewood, Benjamin Clark's country home at New Windsor-on-Hudson near Newburgh, New York, where it remained for many years. In 1922 Mary Zeigler, a Roe granddaughter and the later McClelland correspondent, offered to lend some of the furniture to the Duncan Phyfe exhibition held that year at the Metropolitan Museum, but the loan was turned down as the choices were already set.[59] The exhibition generated widespread interest in Phyfe, and in 1925 Mary Zeigler's brother William J. Roe III sold the dining table, ten chairs, and the original bill of sale to Alfred Cowles II, publisher of the *Chicago Tribune*. Cowles installed the furniture in his Chicago home and had at least four armchairs made to match the side chairs. Two years after his death in 1939, the dining table was examined by furniture historians who, failing to recognize it as an example of Phyfe's extension dining table, concluded erroneously that the table had been made over from a console or pier table and its top reduced in size. Also advising on the offer of sale of one of the sofas, the curator echoed the prevailing opinion that "the luster of Phyfe's name" could not offset "the commonplace design [of the 1830s] in which all the grace of his earlier period is lost."[60] The Cowleses' heir who inherited the table later chose to have a new double pillar-and-claw base in Phyfe's early style made for the original dining table top and a new top made for the original trestle base.

Lewis and Sarah Stirling

The pier tables that Phyfe made for the Louisiana cotton planter Lewis Stirling (1786–1858) and his wife, Sarah Turnbull Stirling (1789–1875) (fig. 173), are similar to those he made for Maria and George Fox, except that they are much longer (compare figs. 36 and 110). In 1836 the Stirlings made a five-month trip to the East Coast and Canada, stopping for nearly three months in New York to shop for furnishings for their newly completed plantation home, Wakefield, and in Connecticut to enroll a son at Yale University. Stirling carried with him a sketch of the interior, and the tables were customized to fit between the windows.[61]

Built of wood in the vernacular Greek Revival style, with twelve monumental plastered brick columns on high plinths supporting a front and rear two-story portico and gable roof, Wakefield is situated in the fertile and lushly landscaped Feliciana region of Louisiana a few miles north of St. Francisville. As Lewis and Sarah had wed in 1807 and several children were living elsewhere, Wakefield was built for entertaining and for the extended visits that were a part of plantation life.

Although no invoices or bills of lading survive, Stirling's payment of $1,900 to Phyfe is indicated in the accounts of his New Orleans factor. The pair of pier tables was split between the parlor and the dining room, which were located to one side of the wide central hallway and could be divided by paneled sliding doors. One pier table (see fig. 36), a dining table, and a sideboard table remain in the house. The sideboard table (fig. 174) has three drawers in the apron for the storage of linens and flatware and lacks a mirror at the back; otherwise it looks much like the pier tables, with marble top, scrolled console supports, and convex front feet. A marble backsplash originally attached to the back at the two short marble columns on top is missing. It was customary for a cellaret to be stored under a sideboard table, but none in this case is known. The extension dining table features a bold octagonal pedestal base. Like Phyfe's best work in the Grecian Plain style, the tables are veneered in superbly figured crotch mahogany.

In addition, Phyfe's workshop supplied at least nine maple high-post bedsteads, of which five remain at the house. Lewis and Sarah Stirling's choice of this style rather than the more fashionable Grecian or French bedsteads with scrolled ends, provided by the firm for several other clients, may have reflected a local preference.

The seating furniture at Wakefield was procured from the New York chairmakers Oliver Edwards and Cyrus Baldwin

Figure 173. Attributed to P. R. Vallée (act. 1803–15). *Lewis and Sarah Stirling*, ca. 1810. Watercolor on ivory, height 2⅝ in. Private collection

for $534.38. The order included a pair of mahogany sofas (see fig. 37), three dozen maple side chairs, and assorted chairs in maple or mahogany. The sofas, with their beefy scrolls and exaggerated moldings, more closely resemble a sofa illustrated in the Meeks broadside (see fig. 108) than the refined pair that Phyfe made for the Foxes (Pl. 43). As noted earlier, several of Phyfe's customers would purchase tables from the Phyfe workshop and less costly seating furniture from other cabinetmakers.

Samuel Alfred Foot
There is no surviving documentation for the Grecian Plain style seating furniture that Phyfe is presumed to have made for the eminent New York lawyer Samuel Alfred Foot (1790–1878; fig. 175), but the couches so closely replicate features of the pair that Phyfe made for his daughter Eliza Vail and for John L. Manning that their manufacture by the cabinetmaker is virtually guaranteed. Furthermore, family tradition has always main-

Figure 174. Duncan Phyfe. Sideboard table, 1836. Mahogany veneer, marble, 38¾ × 66¾ × 24⅜ in. Private collection

Patrons of the Cabinet Warehouse   137

tained that Foot purchased his furniture from Phyfe in 1837, when the family moved into their new home at 678 Broadway.

In his "plain and truthful autobiography," compiled late in life from his extended diary and addressed to his fourteen children, Foot wrote modestly of his distinguished career: "My life has been mainly that of a laborious, persevering, earnest lawyer, and my studies have been principally directed to obtaining success in my profession."[62] Foot's beginnings were on a farm in Watertown, Connecticut, where his father's early dementia forced him at age twelve to take over the farm's management. The life of virtuous industry and self-denial that Foot acquired early on, he professed throughout his life. When he was fifteen he traveled on foot to Troy, New York, to join his older brother Ebenezer, a lawyer, whose support enabled him to attend the grammar school at Union College in Schenectady and to graduate from there in 1811. After nine months reading law, he became a clerk at his brother's Albany office and was admitted to the bar in 1813. In 1818 he married Mariam Fowler (d. 1832); the couple resided in Albany.

To further his career Foot decided to relocate to New York City, and in 1829 he and his wife leased a handsome three-story brick house at 88 Greenwich Street. Foot noted in his autobiography, "Mrs. Foot, with some assistance from me, purchased the furniture we needed."[63] The 1829 date is thought to be too early for the Phyfe seating furniture that he owned. In 1832 Mariam died suddenly, and two years later Foot married Jane Campbell (1809–1867). Family tradition is probably correct in saying that the Phyfe furniture was acquired for the new house Foot began constructing in 1836 at 678 Broadway that, he wrote, "has occupied too many of my thoughts, and too large a portion of my time. A wise man will never build a house."[64]

The following year the family moved in and at that time probably acquired the furniture attributed to Phyfe, though Foot merely noted, "[F]urnishing our new house, arrangements to move and moving into it necessarily took portions of my time."[65] The twelve-piece parlor set that came to the Metropolitan Museum from his descendants includes a pair of couches with scrolled ends of unequal height, two pairs of taborets, two window seats, and four side chairs from a much larger set. Like the Fox pieces, the set lacks ornamentation; rather, its simplicity is relieved by handsome figured mahogany veneers with circular discs applied to the ends of the scrolls. The pair of asymmetrical couches in the French Restauration style, one the mirror image of the other (figs. 176, 177), have broad front seat rails, stout legs with elliptical feet, and tightly scrolled arms. Their flowing top rails bring a more graceful curvilinear line into the classical idiom. The four French chairs (Pl. 46) have deep concave backs with straight splats and curved stiles that extend to the front seat rail. The suite's show covers imitate the original crimson wool and cotton rep with pale yellow

Figure 175. Photograph of a painting attributed to Ezra Ames (1768–1836). *Samuel A. Foot*, ca. 1815. Whereabouts unknown. Nancy McClelland Archive, Cooper-Hewitt, National Design Museum, Smithsonian Institution

woven medallions and trim. Initially the backs and seats of the couches were embellished with a woven classical wreath and acanthus leaf scrolls. This large-scale design was not reproduced, but it can be seen in a photograph from the 1930s, when the original fabric remained on the couch backs but not on the seats (fig. 177). A mahogany card table, one of a pair, with rounded corners and a trestle base and with the same provenance as the seating furniture, is illustrated in the McClelland monograph.[66] Their form suggests that they may have been part of the 1829 furnishings. A sofa with a Foot history, en suite with the couches, appeared at auction in 2005.[67]

Seeking respite from the stress of his professional life and a different environment for his children, Foot sold his Broadway house in 1847 and moved his family to Geneva, New York, on Seneca Lake in the Finger Lakes district. There he purchased Mullrose, a house on Delancey Drive, and made additions and improvements to it for his growing family. Foot's most significant career achievements lay ahead. He was appointed judge of the New York State Court of Appeals in 1851, and during the two terms he served in the state legislature (1856 and 1857) he introduced resolutions condemning the court verdict against the former slave Dred Scott. A painting by his son-in-law, the Hudson River School artist Worthington Whittredge, married

138   *Duncan Phyfe*

Figure 176. Attributed to Duncan Phyfe. Couch, ca. 1837 Mahogany veneer, mahogany, 38½ × 74 × 24½ in. The Metropolitan Museum of Art, Purchase L. E. Katzenbach Fund Gift, 1966 66.221.1

Figure 177. Attributed to Duncan Phyfe. Couch, ca. 1837, in partial original fabric. Photograph, ca. 1939. Nancy McClelland Archive, Cooper-Hewitt, National Design Museum, Smithsonian Institution

Patrons of the Cabinet Warehouse

Figure 178. Worthington Whittredge (1820–1910). *Geneva House*, 1877. Oil on canvas, 23 × 17 in. Private collection

to his eldest daughter, Euphemia, shows Foot at eighty-seven seated on the porch of his Geneva house with two Whittredge grandchildren playing in the garden (fig. 178).

Stephen and Harriet Van Rensselaer

Two generations of Van Rensselaers were customers of Duncan Phyfe. In 1811, Stephen Van Rensselaer III patronized the cabinetmaker for a library chair (App. 2.21), and two decades later Stephen IV (1789–1868) and his wife, Harriet (1799–1875) (fig. 179), purchased a set of sixteen French chairs. These were made for their Albany town house, built in 1816–18 by the architect Philip Hooker (1766–1836), and later were used in the venerable eighteenth-century Van Rensselaer Manor House (fig. 180). As noted earlier Harriet's father, William Bayard, had presented the couple with wedding furniture in 1817, tables in the French late Empire style by Charles-Honoré Lannuier and a suite of parlor seating furniture from France. The chairs (fig. 181), which closely resemble the Foot parlor chairs (Pl. 46), reflect the couple's continuing infatuation with French styles. Several remnants of invoices from Duncan Phyfe are among the few Van Rensselaer family papers to survive the 1911 fire at the New York State Library in Albany. An undated invoice from 1834, totaling $276 for nine items, includes an

Figure 179. Artotypes by E. Bierstadt of a portrait of Stephen Van Rensselaer IV, ca. 1810, and a miniature of Harriet Bayard Van Rensselaer, ca. 1820. From May King Van Rensselaer, *The Van Rensselaers of the Manor of Rensselaerwyck* (1888)

expensive wardrobe, a pair of basin stands, and a fire screen. None of this furniture has been located. A partially burned bill dated June 20, 1835, indicates that Phyfe supplied twelve mahogany chairs at $12 each. The following month he billed for "[4] chairs" and "Packing [for] 4 chairs."[68]

Following the death of Stephen Van Rensselaer III in 1839, Harriet and Stephen IV engaged the New York City architect Richard Upjohn (1802–1878) to make extensive alterations to the family's 1765 Manor House, from which three generations of Van Rensselaers had acted almost as feudal proprietors, administering enormous tracts of land in Rensselaer and Albany counties. Upjohn covered the exterior walls in sanded mastic, replaced the stonework with brown New Jersey sandstone decorated with classical motifs, added a porch to the front

Figure 180. Thomas Cole (1801–1848). *The Van Rensselaer Manor House*, 1841. Oil on canvas, 24 × 35 in. Albany Institute of History & Art, Bequest of Miss Katherine E. Turnbull, granddaughter of Stephen Van Rensselaer III

Figure 181. Duncan Phyfe. French chair, 1835. Mahogany, mahogany veneer, 31 × 18⅞ × 20 in. Hirschl & Adler Galleries, New York

Figure 182. Attributed to Duncan Phyfe. Upholstered armchair, ca. 1835. Mahogany, mahogany veneer, 38 × 24 × 32 in. Westervelt Collection, Westervelt Warner Museum of American Art, Tuscaloosa, Alabama

Patrons of the Cabinet Warehouse 141

Figure 183. Dining room, William Bayard Van Rensselaer residence, 385 State Street, Albany. Photograph, ca. 1900, Gustave Lorey Studios, Albany. Albany Institute of History & Art Library, Gift of Mrs. F. Carrington Weeds

façade, and enlarged and remodeled the wings from Philip Hooker's 1818–19 renovations.[69] Upjohn completed his work in 1843. In a late nineteenth-century photograph of the interior of the house, some of the Phyfe French chairs can be seen in the dining room with a late classical armchair and taboret possibly by Phyfe.[70] The chairs may have remained at that location until 1893, when William Bayard Van Rensselaer (1856–1909), a grandson of Stephen and Harriet, had the Manor House razed. Five French chairs and a pair of upholstered armchairs of closely related design also probably by Phyfe (fig. 182) are visible in a circa 1900 photograph of the dining room of William Bayard Van Rensselaer's newly completed Albany town house at 385 State Street (fig. 183), which incorporated some of the eighteenth-century interior woodwork from the Manor House. Reflected in the overmantel mirror is the large archway with Rococo foliate carving in the spandrels and flanking Ionic pilasters originally from the stair hall opening of the Manor House and now installed in the Van Rensselaer Hall at the Metropolitan Museum. Designed by the architect Marcus T. Reynolds (1869–1937), a Van Rensselaer cousin, the Albany town house was one of three residences built behind a grand Italian Renaissance palazzo façade ornamented with Van Rensselaer heraldic devices, giving the appearance of a single palace.[71] The chairs are listed in a 1937 inventory of the estate of Van Rensselaer's wife, Louisa, as "Manor House Side Chairs 16/Manor House Arm Chairs, 2."[72] All were sold at auction in 1999 by a Van Rensselaer descendant.[73]

William and Eliza Phyfe Vail

Phyfe also made furniture in the Grecian Plain style for his second daughter, Eliza (1803–1890), who in 1825 became the wife of William Vail Jr. (1802–1875), a partner in the dry goods firm of Vail & Reed (fig. 184). The furniture can be dated by a trade card of D. Phyfe & Sons, the name used by the firm from 1837 to 1840, tacked inside the back apron of a pier table (Pl. 48). In 1830 the couple purchased an estate of thirty-two acres from William Vail Sr. in New Market (now Piscataway), New Jersey, relocating there from New York City soon after. They lived in an old house on the property before building Valmere, a handsome Greek Revival home constructed between 1849 and 1851, after the Phyfe cabinetmaking enterprise had closed, leading one to believe that the Vails acquired the Grecian Plain style furniture for the earlier house. A pair of couches that Phyfe made for his daughter and son-in-law

Figure 184. William and Eliza Phyfe Vail. Photographs, ca. 1870. Collection of Glorianna H. Gibbon

Figure 185. D. Phyfe & Sons. Couch, 1837–40. Mahogany veneer, mahogany, 33¾ × 72 × 24⅛ in. Collection of Virginia Anne Gould

Patrons of the Cabinet Warehouse 143

Figure 186. Valmere, New Market, New Jersey. Photograph, July 1868. Collection of Glorianna H. Gibbon

(fig. 185) is similar to the pair made for Samuel Foot (see fig. 176) and to the couches he made for John L. Manning at Millford (see fig. 193). Eliza's couches have a gently inclined back, less pronounced than the curve of the Foot and Manning examples, terminating in a large disc. Striking visual effects are created by figured mahogany veneers, which are book-matched on the front seat rail. A set of side chairs (Pl. 49) presumably made en suite with the couches were at the forefront of the new French styles then being adopted by New York cabinetmakers. The couches, chairs, a taboret, and a pair of pier tables with scrolled supports (Pl. 48) remain with Eliza's descendants along with furniture dating from the time of her marriage and other Phyfe memorabilia. A photograph of Valmere (fig. 186) shows Eliza and her brother Edward seated at the center of the porch, her husband standing to her right, and three generations of the family.

Millford

John Laurence and Susan Hampton Manning

The agricultural prosperity of the pre–Civil War South enabled wealthy planters to travel to New York and other East Coast cities to shop for furnishings for their plantation homes. Among these affluent Southerners was Princeton-educated John Laurence Manning (1816–1889; fig. 187). Scion of a politically prominent family Manning, like others of his social class, pursued agriculture and politics and would serve as governor of South Carolina from 1852 to 1854. In 1838 he married Susan Frances Hampton (1816–1845; fig. 188), a daughter of the legendary Wade Hampton I, whose large fortune lay behind the building of Millford, in the sand hills of Clarendon (now Sumter) County, central South Carolina.[74] The house, which Manning built between 1839 and 1841 on more than four thousand acres that were a gift from his maternal grandparents, is one of the finest extant examples of Greek Revival residential architecture in America (fig. 189). Manning filled it, appropriately, with the very finest furniture made in New York. The quantity of Phyfe pieces that survive there, produced in the last years of the cabinetmaker's career, is truly remarkable.

Plans for the house were drawn up in 1839 by a Providence, Rhode Island, builder, Nathaniel Potter (ca. 1807–1874). Potter charged $34,000 for constructing the house, with the stipulation that Manning also supply the building materials. The actual designer of Millford, however, may have been the German architect Charles Friedrich Reichardt (1803–after 1852), whose influence is clearly visible in its design. Immigrating to New York City in 1832, Reichardt moved four years later to Charleston, where he designed several buildings, including the Charleston Hotel, which served as the prototype for Millford.[75] The principal façade of Millford, dominated by a monumental portico with six stop-fluted columns of stuccoed brick and wood-carved Corinthian capitals, once overlooked formal gardens and rice fields, with a view to the swamplands of the

Duncan Phyfe

Figure 187. James DeVeaux (1812–1844). *John Laurence Manning*, 1838. Oil on canvas, 30½ × 25½ in. Classical American Homes Preservation Trust

Figure 188. Attributed to James DeVeaux (1812–1844). *Susan Hampton Manning*, 1839. Oil on canvas, 30½ × 25¾ in. Classical American Homes Preservation Trust

Figure 189. Millford Plantation, built 1839–41. Sumter County, South Carolina. Photograph, 2008

Patrons of the Cabinet Warehouse

Figure 190. Attributed to Viviano Codazzi (1603–1672); figures by an unidentified, possibly Northern European, painter. *Roman Ruins*. Oil on canvas, 23½ × 28¾ in. Collection of Richard Hampton Jenrette

Figure 191. Unidentified artist. *Jupiter*. Roman head, 1st–3rd century; body, 18th century. Marble, height 28½ in. Columbia Museum of Art, Columbia, South Carolina, Gift of Admiral Cato D. and Ellen Manning Glover

Wateree River. Following Potter's specifications, the brick house was stuccoed and painted a straw color with white trim. The main stairway is located not in the central hallway but, recalling English Regency design, within a cylinder joined to the rear façade that rises three stories to a shallow-ribbed dome with a stained-glass oculus. To each side covered walkways lead to two small dependencies, the kitchen and a laundry.

From the moment that he began to build Millford, Manning wanted to acquire fine art for his new home. In 1838 or 1839 he met with the Italian-born Count Joseph Binda, his neighbor in South Carolina and the owner of an art gallery in New York. A seductive and charismatic man with contacts among Europe's titled aristocracy, Binda had married a granddaughter of the Revolutionary War general Thomas Sumter in Paris and followed the family to Stateburg, South Carolina. Manning perhaps felt unsure of his own judgment in fine art as he sought the opinion of several artists, among them Henry Inman and the miniaturist Thomas S. Cummings. Both men advised Manning in his choices from Binda's gallery.[76] A painting that today hangs at Millford of a fashionable couple visiting the site of an ancient ruin (fig. 190) is recorded by Manning in his fine arts inventory as "Roman Ruins," by Giovanni Paolo Panini—a grand but inaccurate attribution.[77] The picture was probably painted nearly a century earlier by the Italian painter Viviano Codazzi, with figures executed by another hand.[78] Most of the art that Manning acquired from Binda had highly questionable provenances: a trade with Napoleon's brother Joseph Bonaparte, then residing on his estate in Bordentown, New Jersey, for three paintings that "once hung" in the royal palace in Madrid, where Bonaparte briefly resided; "ancient" sculptures purchased from the Roman gallery of "the renowned" Cardinal Buonvisi. A bust of Jupiter (fig. 191), an antique Roman head married to an eighteenth-century body, is one of eight life-sized busts that Manning installed. Perhaps Binda was himself naïve in his purchases, though more likely he was taking advantage of his Southern client.[79] Nevertheless, through his art collection Manning was able to realize his personal vision for Millford as the embodiment of classical taste in America.

In October 1840 Manning was in New York, where he stopped at the Astor House, the city's first luxury hotel, which had been completed two years earlier. On this visit, or perhaps a previous one, he may have called at the D. Phyfe & Son warerooms to select furniture in the sophisticated French-inspired Grecian Plain style that Phyfe was known for and that was so well suited to Millford's architecture. Could Manning have sought advice on his choice of a cabinetmaker as well? From Inman, or James DeVeaux, Inman's assistant, who had just completed Manning's portrait (fig. 187), or even from Binda himself? Or was Phyfe's reputation so widespread that his work was known to Manning, who chose to rely on his own taste? There is no evidence one way or another, but in June of the following year D. Phyfe & Son shipped forty-seven boxes of furniture to Manning's agent in Charleston; the contents of each box is recorded on a bill of lading (App. 1.9).[80] Twelve boxes of furniture

146 *Duncan Phyfe*

had arrived earlier, and a letter dated September 11, 1841, states that the balance of the furniture, an additional thirty-nine boxes, had been shipped from New York.[81] Unfortunately, no further documentation for either shipment survives and the contents of the boxes are unknown. Complementing these records are two letters dated, respectively, January 5 and 7, 1842, and an invoice dated January 5, 1842, in the amount of $2,047.14, for work completed between January 1841 and January 1842, from Phyfe & Brother, the upholstery firm of James and Robert Phyfe, the sons of Duncan's brother John.[82]

A photograph of the first-floor center hallway (fig. 192), taken about 1900, shows what is likely the original placement of some of the furniture. Two pairs of Grecian couches are seen on opposite walls of the sixteen-foot-wide hall. The couches flank two massive sideboard tables with marble tops, and several armchairs stand about. The 1841 bill of lading identifies the four couches as made of walnut and records eight walnut armchairs, though it does not specify the wood of the two sideboard tables. Three of the walnut couches (fig. 193) and the two walnut sideboard tables (fig. 194) are at Millford today. The selection of this less expensive wood, which had mostly gone out of fashion since its wide use in the mid-eighteenth century, at first seems unusual. But in the 1840s, walnut returned to style as a less costly alternative to mahogany. Two of the three known walnut armchairs, today housed at the Hampton-Preston Mansion, Columbia, South Carolina (fig. 195), are of the klismos type, with wide vase- or baluster-shaped splats. The chairs' original faux-leather red upholstery survives beneath two layers of modern fabric. In the hallway photograph, the couches have tufted seats and appear to be in the same simulated leather covering.

Manning's second wife, Sally Bland Clarke (1829–1885), recorded the impressions of her first sight of Millford following their marriage: "Millford far surpassed my expectations in every respect.... The hall was the first thing which struck me as I entered. It is enormously large with sofas & chairs of leather on either side and tables with marbles [sic] slabs on which are placed old busts which were dug from the earth in Italy."[83]

The most elegant of Millford's interiors, the drawing room (fig. 196), is distinguished by richly carved Corinthian columns and embellished with Grecian ornaments cast in plaster that were copied from Minard Lafever's popular pattern book *The Beauties of Modern Architecture* (New York, 1835). The folding mirrored doors, visible on either side behind the pair of ottomans, are based directly on plate 7 in that publication. When pulled shut, they divide the room into a double parlor. The pair of white statuary marble mantels were procured from John Struthers & Son in Philadelphia, which also provided mantels of black and gold Egyptian marble for the dining room and library.[84] The original large gilt-framed mirrors shipped from New York hang on the piers and above the mantels and add brightness with their reflected light from floor-to-ceiling windows. Much of the original Grecian-style parlor furniture is at Millford today, and more pieces are

Figure 192. Center hallway, Millford Plantation. Photograph, ca. 1900. Collection of Richard Hampton Jenrette

Figure 193. D. Phyfe & Son. Couch, 1841. Walnut veneer, walnut, rosewood banding, 32¾ × 76½ × 23¾ in. Collection of Richard Hampton Jenrette

known in private and public collections. As almost none of these pieces appear on the surviving bill of lading, they must have been part either of the earlier or the later shipment. All the parlor furniture is veneered with richly hued Brazilian rosewood, except for several upholstered armchairs with peaked crest rails and elements of the couches and occasional tables, which are painted in imitation of the exotic hardwood. A pair of sofas and two couches (Pl. 63 and fig. 197) show the influence of a new fashion: the revival of the Old French styles of Louis XIV and Louis XV then becoming popular in Europe and America. Phyfe sought ways to embrace these forward-looking styles even in the last years of his firm's production. Bands of flat molding, fresh to his vocabulary, form volutes and C-scrolls that define the contours and legs of both the sofa and the couches.

A new furniture arrangement was then coming into fashion. Sofas and couches were pulled away from the walls to the middle of the room facing a center table. This modern, more

Figure 194. D. Phyfe & Son. Sideboard table, 1841. Walnut veneer, walnut 38¼ × 78⅛ × 25⅝ in. Collection of Richard Hampton Jenrette

Duncan Phyfe

casual layout indicated a growing informality in lifestyle. At Millford, each parlor was likely furnished with a sofa, a couch, and an occasional table (Pl. 64), all equipped with casters so that they could be moved to the center of the room in a formal arrangement or placed by the windows or fireplace for reading or casual conversation.[85] A pair of ottomans, a shape adapted from a Western perception of Eastern luxury and ease, were always placed against the wall. A pair at Millford (fig. 198), a form not seen earlier in Phyfe's work, have low upholstered seats with spring supports and straight backs meant to be piled with loose pillows. The openwork fan ornament is inspired by an ornament in George Smith's *Collection of Designs for Household Furniture and Interior Decoration* (London, 1826), the honeysuckle fan, though Phyfe's interpretation is more akin to one half of a Gothic rose window. This motif is repeated at the center of the bottom rails of the four window seats.

One window seat now in the Metropolitan Museum (Pl. 61; three of the original four remain in the parlor at Millford)

Figure 195. D. Phyfe & Son. Armchair, 1841. Walnut, walnut veneer, 34⅜ × 22 × 22⅜ in. Historic Columbia Foundation, Hampton-Preston Mansion, Columbia, South Carolina

Figure 196. Drawing room, Millford Plantation. Photograph, 2008

Patrons of the Cabinet Warehouse 149

Figure 197. D. Phyfe & Son. Couch, 1841. Rosewood veneer, rosewood-grained in imitation of mahogany, 35⅜ × 73¼ × 22⅞ in. Collection of Richard Hampton Jenrette

Figure 198. D. Phyfe & Son. Ottoman, 1841. Rosewood veneer, 34¾ × 70⅜ × 26¼ in. Collection of Richard Hampton Jenrette

Duncan Phyfe

retains its original upholstery and silk damask covering in a meandering floral pattern that recalls Louis XV textile designs. The fabric, thought to have covered all the upholstered drawing room furniture, has been replicated for the exhibition.

The concordance of furniture and fabric styles was proposed by the English furniture designer Thomas King. In *The Modern Style of Cabinet Work Exemplified* (London, 1829), King illustrates a fire screen that he describes as in the "old French style," with flat banded molding and a screen covered in a fabric of serpentine flowering vine (see fig. 133). The visual impact of the parlor furniture at Millford relied largely on its fabric, freely adapted from Rococo designs that, together with the exotic rosewood veneers, enrich the Grecian Plain style.

The elegant and refined side chairs, part of a set (Pl. 62), have peaks at the center of the crest rails and openwork splats, hinting at the new Gothic style. Additionally, two pairs of rosewood-veneered taborets (Millford and private collections; App. 2.5) illustrate the enduring fashion of this classical form. The taborets and a set of six nesting tables (Pl. 65) are portable and versatile and could be placed about the room as needed. Four rosewood corner tables with scrolled supports and marble tops (two remain at Millford) also survive (App. 2.6), along with two marble-top rectangular occasional tables (Pl. 64).

Manning purchased directly from the Charleston retailers Hayden & Gregg four impressive seven-arm lacquered-brass candelabra for the parlor and two bronze hanging lanterns for the hallways. All are at Millford today.[86] The candelabra stand on circular pedestals that have been cut down from their original height, which was nearly twice what it is today (see fig. 196).

For the parlors, dining room, and bedchambers, the upholsterers Phyfe & Brother fabricated curtains and supplied hardware to hang them. The most costly items on the invoice were eight large gilded cornices for the parlor curtains at $40 each. These were perhaps gilded gesso on wood and not metal, as the letter included with the invoice twice emphasizes that the box be handled with great care and kept from dampness. The firm did not supply the fabric but furnished silk cords and slides for tassels, silk cables (twisted roping), rosettes (curtain pins), and other trimmings, and charged for sewing the curtains, which brought their bill for the parlor draperies to more than $500. The letter further indicates that the curtains were made of satin fabric. There is no evidence, however, that Phyfe & Brother were the upholsterers of the furniture. Interestingly, Manning purchased two antique chairs ("2 Carvd Chairs [antique]") for $220 from Phyfe & Brother.[87] Such chairs were usually used in libraries, but a photograph probably dating to the early twentieth century (Pl. 61, fig. 1) shows that two Elizabethan-style armchairs in needlework upholstery had been moved to the parlor. The final item on the invoice, silk and gimp for the backs of library chairs, gives evidence of the chairs' planned-for location and suggests that they were in old fabric. Only the backs were to be recovered, perhaps to coordinate with the room's décor.

The furniture for the dining room, all recorded in the 1841 bill of lading, is in mahogany. The large extension dining table (fig. 199) features a richly veneered faceted central pedestal and is designed to accommodate five leaves when fully extended. Two turned legs stored in the frame at each end could be pulled down for added support. The French upholstered armchairs (fig. 200) are a simplified version of the four rosewood examples with peaked crest rails and elegantly carved lotus arm supports that stood in the parlor (see fig. 118). The dining table, a dozen armchairs, and the original cellaret (Pl. 60) are today in the dining room at Millford. The mahogany sideboard table is unknown, but it probably looked much like the Stirling sideboard table (see fig. 174). The sarcophagus-shaped cellaret would have been stored beneath the open sideboard and rolled out to the dining table for use at dinner parties. Phyfe also supplied two corner cupboards, two knife boxes, and three dinner wagons, pieces not at Millford today.[88] Phyfe & Brother fabricated curtains in merino wool with silk tassels.[89]

For the bedchambers, D. Phyfe & Son indicated that they had shipped one French and two Grecian bedsteads, two wardrobes, two swing or cheval glasses, four washstands, and two nightstands. A fourth bed must have arrived in a separate shipment, because Phyfe & Brother billed the following January for four canopies at $40 each: two octagonal, one round, and one oval, with four sets of bed curtains (one set in blue and white), in addition to pillows, bolsters, and bedding, and eighteen pairs of lined and interlined window curtains. Instructions were included for installing the canopies with an iron bolt passed through the floor above. The Grecian bedstead and a nightstand (Pls. 55, 57), both now in the Metropolitan Museum, are part of what was originally a much larger rosewood bedroom suite. A wardrobe in the Grecian Plain style with two glass-paneled doors that were originally mirror plate (Hampton-Preston Mansion; App. 2.9) and a basin stand with four scrolled supports, a marble top, and brass railings (Pl. 58), both also in this exotic wood, were part of the same suite, which may have included a rosewood "swing glass" like the mahogany example shown in Plate 56.

Susan Manning died in 1845, at the birth of her third child, and three years later Manning married Sally Bland Clarke. Following the expiration of his governorship in 1854, he continued to play a role in state politics. A Unionist opposed to secession of any kind, Manning at first urged a moderate course, but finding no means to preserve the state's plantation system, he abandoned this position and joined the radical faction. South Carolina became the first state to secede from the Union.

Patrons of the Cabinet Warehouse 151

Figure 199. D. Phyfe & Son. Dining table, 1841. Mahogany, mahogany veneer, 28¾ × 65⅞ × 65½ in. closed; 187 in. extended with five leaves. Collection of Richard Hampton Jenrette

Manning was by far the wealthiest delegate to the South Carolina Secession Convention of 1860, with real property appraised at $1,256,000 and personal property at $890,000. He owned 648 slaves, all but 32 of whom worked on his Louisiana sugar plantation.[90] During the Civil War, Manning served as a colonel in the Confederate Army. Millford narrowly escaped destruction by Union troops at the end of the war, and during the Reconstruction, in spite of the great privations suffered in the South, the family managed to hold on to it. Manning was, however, forced to sell his Louisiana holdings for lack of funds to pay taxes or to assemble an adequate labor force. In 1902 Millford was sold to Mary Clark Thompson of New York, who bequeathed it to her Clark nephew, who then passed it on to his son. Ninety years later Millford was purchased by Richard H. Jenrette, who restored the house and its outbuildings, re-created formal gardens against a backdrop of longleaf pines, magnolia, and moss-trailing live oak, and successfully reassembled much of the original Manning furniture.[91] In 2008 Millford Plantation became part of the Classical American Homes Preservation Trust, established by Jenrette in 1994.

Frances F. Bretter

Figure 200. D. Phyfe & Son. Armchair, 1841. Mahogany, mahogany veneer, 34¼ × 21¼ × 25 in. Collection of Richard Hampton Jenrette

1. Letter from John Wells, Boston, to Sarah Elliott Huger, New York, July 25, 1815, in *South Carolina Historical and Genealogical Magazine* 43, no. 1 (January 1942), pp. 52–53.
2. Letter from Sarah Elliott Huger, New York, to Harriott Pinckney Horry, Charleston, March 5, 1816, Harriott Horry Ravenel Family Papers, 1694–1935 (1086.00), South Carolina Historical Society, Charleston.
3. For the purchase and building of 6 State Street, see "Lannuier's Clients in America: A Taste for French Style," in Kenny, Bretter, and Leben 1998, pp. 104–10.
4. Ibid., pp. 107–8.
5. Ibid., p. 108.
6. In addition to buying a pedestal-end sideboard from Jacob Brouwer and a bed from Charles-Honoré Lannuier, between 1805 and 1812 Bayard purchased furniture from William Palmer, William Mandeville, John Ball, and Joseph W. Meeks Jr.

7. Hornor 1930 and Kenny, Bretter, and Leben 1998, p. 109. Hornor also illustrated the card table shown in figure 144, which he believed was on the 1807 Phyfe bill.
8. Parke-Bernet Galleries, New York, *Fine English and American Furniture and Decorations*, sale 805, November 9, 1946, lots 139–143.
9. Stokes 1915–28, vol. 6, pp. 78–79, 126–28. In 1809, Thomas Cornell Pearsall acquired the adjacent four acres to the north on the East River, property that had formerly belonged to Stephen and Abigail Adams Smith, although Pearsall never lived at Mount Vernon, the mansion begun by Smith.
10. Pintard 1940–41, vol. 1, Nov. 7, 1820, p. 343. Two Madeira wine bottles with "T. C. Pearsall" impressed in a circle on the body and a printed label reading, "Madeira Wine. / Imported by T. C. P. / From Murdock, Masterton & Co. / 1800" are in the Metropolitan Museum. The Museum of the City of New York has two identically labeled Madeira bottles, but with the date 1806.
11. Strong 1952, entry for April 13, 1839, p. 101.
12. Kenny, Bretter, and Leben 1998, p. 68, pl. 28, no. 94.
13. The inventory, a copy of which is in the scholarship files of the American Wing of the Metropolitan Museum, was brought to the author's attention by Richard Kelly. It also records a large set of "Sheraton" dining room furniture that was a wedding present from the bride's parents, Thomas and Almy Townsend Buchanan. It includes a sofa, two armchairs, and thirteen side chairs. This set probably was in the square-back style of the 1790s and originally intended for the parlor, but later used in a dining room setting.
14. For the Pearsall furniture fabric, see Little 1931, fig. 59a, and pp. 246–47.
15. McClelland 1939, pp. 290–91, pls. 277, 279.
16. For the high-post bed, see Caldwell 1988, pp. 106–11. The Metropolitan chandelier is acc. no. 68.177.1–3. One girandole is illustrated in McClelland 1939, pl. 278.
17. Bound inventory of furniture, n.d. [1804]: "Inventory of Furniture and of whom it was purchased . . . ," Charles Nicoll Bancker Papers, American Philosophical Society, Philadelphia (copy available in the Downs Collection, Winterthur Library, microfilm 101.3). Bancker had also purchased a convenience ($6) from Phyfe. I am grateful to Charles F. Hummel for this information and for making available to me the Winterthur microfilm.
18. Letter from Duncan Phyfe, New York, to Charles N. Bancker, Philadelphia, September 5, 1815, Downs Collection, Winterthur Library.
19. Brooklyn Museum, acc. nos. 67.19.1 and 67.19.10. Unlike those of the other eight chairs, which have legs with recessed panels at the top, the tops of the front legs are framed with a contrasting veneer and the back inside edges of the front legs are not chamfered.
20. "Rough Draft of Inventory," by location, 1819, Charles Nicoll Bancker Papers, American Philosophical Society, Philadelphia (copy available in the Downs Collection, Winterthur Library, microfilm 101.18). A set of dining tables was placed in the entryway.
21. W. B. Selheimmer, Philadelphia, *A Collection of Rare and Valuable Books . . . Catalogue of the Entire Private Library of C. N. Bancker . . .* , sale, December 8, 1869, and following days.
22. See Wall 1990, pp. 11–16. The French economist Turgot, as godfather, chose the name of du Pont's second son, Eleuthère Irénée, meaning "freedom and peace."
23. Pierre Samuel du Pont's plans for a utopian colony in Virginia were a failure, but he is credited with originating an idea that led to the Louisiana Purchase, which offered equal shipping rights to French and American vessels to the ports of New Orleans and the Floridas and free navigation for American ships on the Mississippi, thus avoiding certain confrontation with France asserting its former colonial power. Ibid., pp. 30, 46–49.
24. Letter from Anthony Girard, New York, to Victor Marie du Pont, Wilmington, November 21, 1813, translated from the French by Joyce Longworth, MS W3-2790, Eleutherian Mills Historical Library, Greenville, Delaware.
25. Letter from Mrs. [Josephine] du Pont, Philadelphia, December 19, 1813, to Mrs. [Margaret] Manigault, Louviers, as quoted in Low 1976, p. 198.
26. Letter from Mary Telfair, Savannah, to Mary Few, New York, October 28, [1816], Item 10, William Few Collection, Georgia Division of Archives and History (Manuscripts Section), Atlanta.
27. Letter from Mary Telfair, Savannah, to Mary Few, New York, December 8, [no year], Item 139, William Few Collection, Georgia Division of Archives and History (Manuscripts Section), Atlanta.
28. Reuben Haines III, bills of sale and receipts, IV/146/208-218, Wyck Association Collection, American Philosophical Society, Philadelphia, as in Groff 2003, p. 97 n. 27.
29. Letter from [Sarah Minturn], New York, to Jane B. Haines, February 12, 1819. Wyck Association Collection, American Philosophical Society, Philadelphia.
30. An armchair and a side chair from two sets that were, according to family tradition, made by Phyfe are in the collection of the Museum of the City of New York. See McClelland 1939, pp. 286–87 and pls. 271, 272.
31. Letter from Sarah Minturn, New York, to Jane Haines [Germantown], 4 day 4 mo 1819, II/22/324, Wyck Association Collection, American Philosophical Society, Philadelphia, as quoted in Groff 2003, p. 104. The actual cost was $121, freight from New York an additional $7.60. Reuben Haines Accounts, Germantown, May 19. Reuben also noted Jane's move to Germantown on May 10. IV/126/19, Wyck Association Collection, American Philosophical Society, Philadelphia.
32. Letter from John Wells, Boston, to Sarah Elliott Huger, New York, July 25, 1815, in *South Carolina Historical and Genealogical Magazine* 43, no. 1 (January 1942), p. 53. Wells also requested that she order a dressing table for the bedroom. See also McClelland 1939, pp. 304–7 and pl. 291.
33. Letter from Sarah Elliott Huger, New York, to Harriott Pinckney Horry, Charleston, January 4, 1816, Harriott Horry Ravenel Family Papers, 1694–1935 (1086.00), South Carolina Historical Society, Charleston. Harriott Pinckney Horry (1748–1830) was the widow of Daniel Huger Horry. Her receipt book, which she began in 1770, was published as *A Colonial Plantation Cookbook: The Receipt Book of Harriott Pinckney Horry, 1770*, edited by Richard J. Hooker (Columbia, S.C., 1984).
34. Other Wells furniture described in McClelland 1939—a dressing table, card tables, and a set of twelve chairs that McClelland believed were by Phyfe—has not been located.
35. Letter from Sarah Elliott Huger, New York, to Harriott Pinckney Horry, Charleston, March 17, 1812, Harriott Horry Ravenel Family Papers, 1694–1935 (1086.00), South Carolina Historical Society, Charleston, as quoted in McInnis and Leath 1996, p. 146.
36. Ibid., pp. 146–47.
37. Letter from Sarah Elliott Huger, New York, to Harriott Pinckney Horry, Charleston, October 15, 1812, 11/332/2A, Harriott Horry Ravenel Family Papers, 1694–1935 (1086.00), South Carolina Historical Society, Charleston.
38. Letter from Harriott Pinckney Rutledge, Charleston, to Harriott Pinckney Horry, Charleston, September 20, 1815, Harriott Horry Ravenel Family Papers, 1694–1935 (1086.00), South Carolina Historical Society, Charleston. Mary I'on Lowndes (1800–1865), the daughter of Sarah I'on Lowndes (1778–1840), married Frederick Kinloch (ca. 1791–1856) in 1816.
39. Letter from Sarah Elliott Huger, New York, to Harriott Pinckney Horry, Charleston, March 5, 1816, Harriott Horry Ravenel Family Papers, 1694–1935 (1086.00), South Carolina Historical Society, Charleston.
40. Ibid.
41. Ibid., January 4, 1816.
42. Ibid., March 5, 1816.
43. "A Tour of Recreation: Journal of Robert Donaldson, 1818," an edited

transcript by John L. Sanders, the owner of the manuscript. See also Anderson 1996, p. 54.

44. Letter from Rachael Lazarus to Ellen Mordecai, September 29, 1822, Mordecai Family Papers, University of North Carolina, Chapel Hill, as quoted in Anderson 1996, p. 75 n. 24.

45. All the earlier furnishings from the Union Street residence were sold following the death of the Donaldson children's mother in 1808. See Anderson 1996, p. 36.

46. Isabel Bronson, "Reminiscences," August 1928, Donaldson Family Papers, collection of Richard H. Jenrette.

47. When the house was for sale or let in 1823, it was described in the *New-York Evening Post*, April 25, 1823. Isabel Bronson affirmed that her father acquired more furniture from Phyfe in 1828 (no bill survives), a tall desk writing table, a maple chair, and a "whole set of mahogany [furniture] and brass trimmings in N.W. Bedroom upstairs," although she believed the gilded furniture to date to 1822. Isabel Bronson, "Reminiscences," August 1928, Donaldson Family Papers, collection of Richard H. Jenrette.

48. Daybook, vol. 1, p. 113, Alexander Jackson Davis Papers, New York Public Library. See also Anderson 1996, p. 296 n. 17.

49. The sofa was acquired at Sotheby Parke Bernet Inc., New York, sale 4338, February 2, 1980, lot 1644. Isabel Bronson in her "Reminiscences" notes that circumstances forced her to sell a sofa and two card tables.

50. The window seats are recorded in a bedroom in an 1872 inventory of Donaldson's estate. See Parke-Bernet Galleries, *The Collection of Mrs. J. Amory Haskell*, sale, December 9, 1944, lot 837. See also McClelland 1939, p. 175 and pl. 168.

51. For a description of Edgewater, see Jenrette 2000, pp. 78–105.

52. See Anderson 1996, p. 169. A year earlier, Davis had executed a plan for a Gothic villa in the English Collegiate style for Donaldson at Fishkill Landing that was never built. The villa is illustrated in Alexander Jackson Davis, *Rural Residences, etc. . . .* (1837). See also Peck 1992, colorpl. 43.

53. See Anderson 1996, pp. 158, 169, 170, and Peck 1992, pp. 16, 109, colorpl. 46. Sketches of some of these structures are in Avery Library, Columbia University, New York. Donaldson frequently recommended Davis for commissions in his native state, especially at the University of North Carolina at Chapel Hill, and was indirectly responsible for many of Davis' southern buildings, most of them in the Greek Revival style.

54. The second gatehouse is today part of Bard College, Annandale-on-Hudson, New York.

55. See Anderson 1996, pp. 176, 179. The author maintains that Downing advised Donaldson, although he was not the landscape architect of Blithewood.

56. Letter from Robert Donaldson to Alexander Jackson Davis, January 18, 1854, Alexander Jackson Davis Collection, Avery Library, Columbia University, New York, as quoted in Anderson 1996, p. 239.

57. Letter from Mary Roe Zeigler, Newburgh, New York, to Nancy McClelland, March 17, 1940, Nancy McClelland Archive, Cooper-Hewitt, National Design Museum, Smithsonian Institution, New York.

58. The center table is in the possession of a Fox family descendant. The worktable is privately owned in Maryland. The dining table is also privately owned. I am grateful to architect and furniture historian Thomas Gordon Smith for the comparison of the center table and worktable in George Smith's pattern book.

59. Letter from Mrs. Lee Woodward [Mary Roe] Zeigler to Edward Robinson, received September 29, 1922, Archives, The Metropolitan Museum of Art.

60. Letter from Meyric R. Rogers, Art Institute of Chicago, to Mr. Alfred Cowles, Chicago, February 24, 1949. A copy is in the scholarship files of the American Wing, The Metropolitan Museum of Art.

61. For the building and furnishing of Wakefield and the Phyfe furniture ordered by the Stirlings, see Haygood and Thurlow 2007.

62. Foot 1873, vol. 1, pp. iv, v. Volume 2 contains Foot's legal arguments and writings.

63. Ibid., vol. 1, p. 109.

64. Ibid., p. 176.

65. Ibid., p. 180.

66. McClelland 1939, p. 272, pl. 259.

67. Northeast Auctions, Manchester, New Hampshire, "Important New York Furniture and Decorative Arts: The Richard and Beverly Kelly Collection," sale, April 3, 2005, lot 1222. The sofa was acquired from Foot's house in Geneva, New York.

68. The bills are to Van Rensselaer Jr., or Stephen IV, as his father Stephen III (1764–1839) was still living. The June 20, 1835, bill also lists a sofa table, fourteen covers for chairs at $3 each, and a sofa cover. The July bill includes a nightstand and packing. Van Rensselaer Family Papers, Albany Institute of History & Art, as transcribed by Mary Alice Mackay from a photocopy of the originals at the New York State Library, Albany. The authors gratefully acknowledge Gilbert T. Vincent's research on the Van Rensselaers and Duncan Phyfe.

69. See Reynolds 1911, vol. 1, p. 21, and Bucher and Wheeler 1993, p. 188.

70. The photograph is in the collection of the Albany Institute of History & Art.

71. See E. Johnson 1993, pp. 43–44.

72. Inventory of Louisa Greenough Lane Van Rensselaer (Mrs. William Bayard Van Rensselaer), October/November, 1937, Surrogate's Court, Albany, New York.

73. Christie's, New York, *Important American Furniture, Folk Art and Chinese Export Porcelain*, sale, October 14, 1999, lots 229, 230. The William Bayard Van Rensselaers had no children. After Louisa's death in 1937, the chairs descended to the Barber line, from which they were sold by John F. Barber, Stephen IV's great-great grandson.

74. At his death in 1835, Wade Hampton was known as the wealthiest planter in the United States. He bequeathed his entire fortune to his son, Wade Hampton II, who contested the will and shared the estate equally with his two sisters. Susan received a one-half share in Houmas Plantation, in Ascension Parish, Louisiana, whose numerous slaves and sugarcane production constituted a large part of her wealth.

75. For the design and building of Millford, see T. G. Smith 1997. The Charleston Hotel burned down soon after it was completed in 1838. Nathaniel Potter supervised its reconstruction, based on Reichardt's original design, which was completed in 1839. Reichardt, who trained in Berlin, worked in the studio of the architect Karl Friedrich Schinkel (1781–1841) before coming to New York.

76. Copy of a letter from John L. Manning describing his relationship with Count Joseph Binda, circa 1880, which accompanies a statement from Manning's granddaughter Mrs. Walter A. Metts, April 1, 1963, Columbia Museum of Art, South Carolina. I would like to thank Brian J. Lang at the Columbia Museum for providing this information.

77. Inventory of art compiled by John L. Manning, circa 1885, Williams-Chesnut-Manning Family Papers, South Caroliniana Library, University of South Carolina, Columbia.

78. I am grateful to Keith Christiansen and Walter Liedtke in the Department of European Paintings at the Metropolitan Museum for their attribution of this painting.

79. The career of the peripatetic Count Giuseppe Agamemnon Binda was a remarkable one. He first met the Sumter family in Brazil, where Thomas Sumter Jr. served as minister to the exiled Portuguese court beginning in 1810. He reestablished his friendship with the family in Paris, where Sumter's French wife, Natalie Delage Sumter, had gone to visit her mother and find husbands for two daughters. Binda married Stephanie ("Fanie") Sumter in 1825 in Paris. Both Binda and Sumter (land rich but cash poor) were financially squeezed. Binda's situation improved when he obtained an appointment as United States consul to Livorno, Italy, in 1840. Binda, however, chose to remain in

New York, managing his art business until 1845, when he was ordered by Congress to assume his duties in Italy. On Count Binda, see Blumberg 1966.

80. Bill of lading, D. Phyfe & Son, New York, to James L. Manning Esq., care of J. Kirkpatrick, Charleston, South Carolina, June 2, 1841, Williams-Chesnut-Manning Family Papers, microfilm, South Caroliniana Library, University of South Carolina, Columbia.

81. Letter from John Kirkpatrick, Charleston, to John L. Manning, Columbia, June 4, 1841, and letter from D. Phyfe & Son, New York, to James L. Manning Esq., care of J. Kirkpatrick, Charleston, September 11, 1841, Williams-Chesnut-Manning Family Papers, microfilm, South Caroliniana Library, University of South Carolina, Columbia.

82. Invoice and letter from Phyfe & Brother, New York, to John L. Manning Esq., Fulton, South Carolina, January 5, 1842; letter from Phyfe & Brother, New York, to John L. Manning Esq., Fulton, South Carolina, January 7, 1842. The firm urged Manning to insure the shipment, which it valued at between $6,300 and $6,500, more than three times the amount rendered on their bill. Although the bill did not include the cost of curtain fabrics, such a large difference cannot be accounted for. Williams-Chesnut-Manning Family Papers, microfilm, South Caroliniana Library, University of South Carolina, Columbia.

83. Letter from Sally Bland Clarke Manning, Millford, South Carolina, to Mary Goode Lyle Clarke, Warner Hall, Gloucester Co., Virginia, May 11, 1848, Williams-Chesnut-Manning Papers, South Caroliniana Library, University of South Carolina, Columbia.

84. Letter of John Struthers & Son, Philadelphia, to John L. Manning Esq., Charleston, March 19, 1840, Williams-Chesnut-Manning Family Papers, South Caroliniana Library, University of South Carolina, Columbia. The firm also provided four mantels for the bed chambers, two in black and gold marble and two in veined and white Italian marble.

85. See "A Selection of Nineteenth Century Drawings of Room Settings by Gillow & Co. of Oxford Street, London, 1813–1830," in S. Stuart 2008, vol. 2, pp. 347–58.

86. See invoice from Hayden Gregg & Co. (Nathaniel and Sidney Hayden and William Gregg), Charleston, to Col. J. L. Manning, March 11, 1840–December 9, 1841, Williams-Chesnut-Manning Family Papers, South Caroliniana Library, University of South Carolina, Columbia. The four candelabra cost $1,020 and the pair of lanterns $500. Included on the invoice was a silver flatware service for thirty-six in the King pattern, specialized flatware pieces, and several sets of mantel and astral lamps.

87. Invoice from Phyfe & Brother, January 5, 1842, Williams-Chesnut-Manning Family Papers, microfilm, South Caroliniana Library, University of South Carolina, Columbia.

88. One dinner wagon is with a family descendant but was not seen by the authors.

89. McClelland notes that the border trim on the Millford curtains, which she saw at the home of a Manning granddaughter, was exactly like the mohair borders on the front seat rail of the Foot couches (see McClelland 1939, p. 282, and fig. 177 in this volume). The Foot suite was then owned by Olive Whittredge, a Foot granddaughter, who had moved the furniture to Camden, South Carolina, where she was then living. The Manning heir gave a roll of the Millford curtain border to Miss Whittredge, who was replacing some of the worn original upholstery on the Foot pieces. The mohair trim would have been on the wool dining room curtains at Millford, not the satin parlor curtains.

90. Ralph Wooster, "Membership of the South Carolina Secession Convention," *South Carolina Historical Magazine* 55, no. 4 (October 1954), pp. 185–97.

91. For a loving description of Millford, which he calls "My Taj Mahal," see Jenrette 2000, pp. 176–209.

PLATES

The Bayard Furniture (Plates 1–5)

Plate 1

Scroll-Back Armchair, 1807

Duncan Phyfe

Mahogany; secondary woods: ash, cherry
33 x 21¼ x 21 in. (83.8 x 54 x 53.3 cm)
Winterthur Museum, Bequest of Henry Francis du Pont

Provenance: William Bayard (1761–1826); his daughter Maria (Mrs. Duncan Pearsall Campbell; 1789–1875); her daughter Maria Louisa Campbell (1831–1911); her niece Justine Van Rensselaer Townsend (Mrs. Howard Townsend; 1828–1912); her son Howard Van Rensselaer Townsend (1858–1935); [Loudonville Exchange, Loudonville, New York, 1929]; Henry Francis du Pont (1880–1969); Winterthur Museum, Winterthur, Delaware.

References: Hornor 1929, pp. 47–48; Hornor 1930, pp. 38–39, 96; McClelland 1939, pp. 245, 258–61; C. Montgomery 1966, pp. 6, 117–21; Cooper 2002, pp. 172–74. See also Chapter 3, "William Bayard," pp. 115–18.

The earliest documented commission from Duncan Phyfe for which furniture survives includes three sets of seating furniture (Pls. 1–3) made for William Bayard's brick residence at 6 State Street, situated at the tip of Manhattan Island. Duncan Phyfe's three invoices for this commission, two from November 1807 and another from 1809 (App. 1.3a–1.3c) list the extraordinary number of no fewer than sixty mahogany chairs in three separate sets. Two sets of fourteen chairs were charged at $12.50 apiece, the remaining set at $15 each. It seems most likely that the more expensive chairs were those with saber legs and upholstered seats (Pl. 1), while those with caned seats (Pls. 2, 3) were the less expensive ones. Any one of the three sets could have been destined for the principal parlor on the first floor, an upstairs drawing room or boudoir, or perhaps the dining room—along with the set of dining tables and a pedestal-end sideboard that also appear on one of the invoices. As suggested in Chapter 3, one of the caned sets may also have been a gift for Bayard's eldest daughter, Susan, who married on December 10, 1807.

The graceful armchair in Plate 1 and its surviving mate and ten matching side chairs (see fig. 143) are in the collection of the Winterthur Museum, while the location of the remaining two is currently unknown. The $2.50 price differential per chair between those with upholstered seats and those with cane can be accounted for by additional charges for "Each extra cross banister," "Each rose in the center of the cross," "Stuffed seats," and "Springing the front legs one way."[1] The last noted, an elegant incurvate contour of the front legs, is less commonly seen than straight reeded legs. Sprung legs first appear in the New York price book of 1810. Their use on chairs manufactured in 1807 signaled a dramatic development in the metamorphosis of the Neoclassical idiom toward a more archaeologically correct interpretation, in imitation of the inward curve of the legs on the ancient Greek klismos form.

The significance of these chairs in New York, and even in a national context, cannot be overstated. Documented to 1807, the Bayard chairs with incurvate Grecian-style front legs are contemporary with the publication of Thomas Hope's *Household Furniture and Interior Decoration*, which was one of the earliest, if not the first, exposure New Yorkers had to archaeologically correct Grecian-style furniture and interior decoration. The set was also made at precisely the moment when the celebrated immigrant English architect Benjamin Henry Latrobe (1764–1820) was overseeing the manufacture of an extensive suite of painted Grecian furniture, including side chairs with similar sprung legs, for the residence he designed for William and Mary Waln of Philadelphia. With the production of the Waln suite, the Antique, or Grecian, style was firmly established in this country. Its popularity and duration would surpass that of any other aesthetic in nineteenth-century American furniture design.[2]

Surviving caned chairs from the other two sets are now scattered between the Museum of the City of New York, the Winterthur Museum, and a direct Bayard family descendant. While a cursory examination might suggest that all twenty-three surviving chairs are identical, on closer inspection differences in the turning of the rear stiles and in the articulation of the carving in the cross banisters and the crest rails clearly distinguish them as two distinct sets (compare these features on page 160). Six side chairs that have come down in the family (Pl. 2), seven in the Museum of the City of New York, and two at Winterthur, represent one group; a pair of armchairs (Pl. 3) and six side chairs, the former in the Museum of the City of New York and the latter divided equally between that institution and the Bayard descendant, constitute the other.[3] The inverted cup-and-column turning on the rear stiles of the armchair in Plate 3 are identical to those on the one surviving Bayard sofa (Pl. 4), indicating that they were probably originally used en suite. The surviving chairs with urn-and-column turning on the rear stiles (Pl. 2) number fifteen, which may suggest that the set was added to bet-ween March 1809 and May 1810, when four additional mahogany chairs were sold by Phyfe for a total of $50.

Comparative prices for caned and upholstered seating furniture can also be gleaned from a drawing of a curule chair with a Grecian cross front and a klismos chair with a lyre banister, attributed to

158

1

Plate 2

Scroll-Back Side Chair, 1807

DUNCAN PHYFE

Mahogany; secondary wood: cherry or red gum
33 x 18¾ x 21⅜ in. (83.8 x 47.6 x 54.3 cm)
Collection of Mr. and Mrs. Roland W. Glidden

Provenance: See Plate 1 through 1912; her granddaughter Margaret Schuyler Townsend (Mrs. Arthur Boynton Glidden; 1890–1934); her son Stephen Van Rensselaer Glidden (1920–1996); his nephew Roland W. Glidden; the present owners.

References: Hornor 1930, pp. 36–40, 96.

Detail, Plate 2

Plate 3

Scroll-Back Armchair, 1807

DUNCAN PHYFE

Mahogany; secondary wood: cherry or red gum
33 x 22⅜ x 23⅞ in. (83.8 x 56.9 x 60.6 cm)
Museum of the City of New York, Gift of Mrs. Screven Lorillard 53.263.12A–B

Provenance: See Plate 1 through 1911; her nephew Eugene Van Rensselaer (1840–1925); his daughter Elizabeth (Mrs. James Carroll Frazer; b. 1866), who owned the sofa in 1930; Natalie K. Knowlton (Mrs. J. Insley Blair; 1887–1952); her daughter Joan (Mrs. J. Woodhull Overton; 1915–1998); Museum of the City of New York.

Detail, Plate 3

2

3

Duncan Phyfe (see fig. 149) and understood to refer to Charles N. Bancker's 1816 commission, which indicates that for the cane-seated renditions he charged $19 and $22, respectively, with an optional outlay of $3 for a cushion. By comparison, the same chairs with "stuffed" seats are priced at $21 and $23. It should be remembered, however, that the cost of silk damask as opposed to wool or horsehair could significantly increase the cost of an upholstered armchair, and the Bancker estimate may refer only to the cost of upholstery foundations and linen covers on the chairs. In the long term, the combination of caning and a loose cushion had the advantage that the latter could be cleaned or recovered more simply and economically than an upholstered one.

In New York the popularity of chairs with cross banisters was widespread, yet of the numbers that have survived, only the Bayard sets and an armchair labeled by Charles-Honoré Lannuier (see fig. 68) are documented to a specific shop. The city's rush-seat chairmakers responded quickly to the market demand, and, in addition to its interpretation in mahogany, the design was crafted of maple and other less expensive indigenous woods, which could simply be given a coat of clear varnish or painted, such as the "Cross Back Green & Gold Fancy Chairs" ordered by Elizabeth Corne Dyckman from the New York fancy chairmaker Henry Dean within a year of Bayard's purchase from Phyfe.[4]   MKB

1. *The New-York Revised Prices for Manufacturing Cabinet and Chair Work* (New York, 1810), p. 56.
2. Lindsey 1991, pp. 208–19; Priddy 2004, pp. 57–61; Kirtley 2006, pp. 137–40.
3. C. Montgomery 1966, pp. 121–22, no. 68. The two side chairs at Winterthur identical to the chair in Plate 2 were acquired from Howard Townsend, along with the ten scroll-back side chairs and two armchairs with Grecian-style legs discussed above.
4. Tracy 1981, pp. 18, 30, 46.

Plates 161

Plate 4

Scroll-Back Sofa, 1807

Duncan Phyfe

Mahogany, cane; secondary woods: ash, maple

35⅝ x 75½ x 24⅛ in. (90.5 x 191.8 x 61.3 cm)

Museum of the City of New York, Gift of Mrs. J. Woodhull Overton, in memory of Mrs. J. Insley Blair 77.21

Provenance: See Plate 3.

Reference: Miller 1956, p. 63.

This scroll-back caned sofa is believed to be one of the four listed on two separate invoices from Duncan Phyfe to William Bayard in November 1807, each specified at a cost of $65. Of the four, it is the only one currently known.

A British dictionary dating from the 1730s defines the sofa more in architectural terms, as a form that had only recently been introduced, "A sort of Alcove much used in Asia. . . . An apartment of State, raised about two Foot higher than the Floor, and furnished with rich Carpets and Cushions, where honorable Personages are entertained."[1] Throughout the eighteenth century sofas as we know them today remained relatively uncommon, more because of the high cost of upholstery materials and labor than because of the wooden frame. With the advent of Neoclassicism in the 1780s, the form was updated by the introduction of the cabriole and square-back versions with tapered or thermed legs, which evoke a classically inspired aesthetic.

By 1810 the scroll-back caned sofa was the epitome of fashion and the most costly piece of seating available to New Yorkers. The design of the Bayard sofa corresponds to a descriptive entry published in the 1802 edition of *The London Chair-Makers' and Carvers' Book of Prices for Workmanship*, and its use of cane rather than upholstery for the seat and the side and back panels is a British Regency feature that would have added to its appeal for an elite patron such as Bayard.[2]

In *The Cabinet Dictionary* (1803), Thomas Sheraton comments on the application of cane in Britain thirty years earlier and explains that more recently, with the revival of japanned furniture, it has once again come into fashion. Citing more practical considerations, he endorses its use on "any thing where lightness, elasticity, cleanness, and durability, ought to be combined."[3] There is little to explain the complexities of caning in the 1810 New York price book, where a scroll-back cane sofa appears for the first time. The journeyman who made the sofa probably bored the holes in the seat and the side and back panels, but specialists working either in the Phyfe shop or who functioned as subcontractors most likely wove the cane, which in the period was graded in quality according to how many skeins or strands were passed through the bored holes. Double and triple skeins provided the finest and firmest seating surfaces. The caning currently on the Bayard sofa is formed of two skeins passed through each hole and is probably fairly close in appearance to the original when it arrived at Bayard's home, along with separate cushions of silk, wool, or even cotton chintz.   MKB

1. N. Bailey et al., *Dictionarium Britannicum; or, A More Compleat Universal Etymological Dictionary Than Any Extant . . .* , 2nd ed. (London, 1736).
2. *The New-York Revised Prices for Manufacturing Cabinet and Chair Work* (New York, 1810), pp. 56–57; and Committee of Master Chair-Manufacturers and Journeymen, *The London Chair-Makers' and Carvers' Book of Prices for Workmanship* (London, 1802), pp. 46–47. An entry for "A Scroll Back Sofa For Caning" subsequently appears in New-York Society of Journeyman Cabinetmakers, *The New-York Book of Prices for Manufacturing Cabinet and Chair Work* (New York, 1817), pp. 105–6.
3. Wilford P. Cole and Charles Montgomery, introduction to Sheraton (1803) 1970, vol. 1, pp. 29, 126–27.

4

Plate 5

Card Table, 1807

DUNCAN PHYFE

Mahogany veneer, mahogany, kingwood; secondary woods: white pine, cherry
29 x 36 x 17¾ in. (73.7 x 91.4 x 45.1 cm)
Collection of Mrs. Howard Townsend

Provenance: See Plate 1 through 1935; his son Dr. Howard Van Rensselaer II (1900–1959); his son Howard Van Rensselaer Townsend III (1930–2009); the present owner.

Reference: McClelland 1939, pp. 259–61, pl. 246.

Card tables, intended for a variety of games, were introduced in New York City by the second quarter of the eighteenth century. Like so much of the furniture made during the colonial period, when no longer required for a specific function they would be repositioned in the room and used for another purpose—in this case placed against a wall as a side table. Made in either the Rococo and Neoclassical idioms, New York card tables are readily distinguished from their regional counterparts by the addition of a fifth leg. Referred to in the period as a "fly leg," it was hinged to pivot and provide support for the folding top when the table was in use. Although the fly leg added stability, it did so while compromising aesthetics and comfort and, most important, increasing expense.[1]

This card table is believed to be from one of the two pairs charged at $75 on two separate invoices in November 1807 from Duncan Phyfe to William Bayard (App. 1.3a–1.3c).[2] A handsome, restrained interpretation, the table and its mate (whereabouts unknown) were probably en suite with the cane sofas (Pl. 4) and chairs with single cross backs and straight reeded legs in the Bayard commission (Pls. 2, 3). By the Federal period, card tables were generally produced in pairs. They were often placed in the principal parlor, where they would contribute toward the visual symmetry that the period dictated and to which their owners aspired.

Signature elements of the New York aesthetic include a contoured double elliptic top and reeded legs with distinctive capitals and inverted baluster-shaped feet. On this example the legs are extremely tall and slender, providing an attractive counterpoint to the feet on the sets of Bayard caned chairs. At one time feet of this design were presumed to be a signature of Phyfe's hand, but their presence on furniture labeled by his contemporaries, including Charles-Honoré Lannuier, John T. Dolan, Michael Allison, and George Woodruff, distinguish this component as characteristic of a school of cabinetmaking rather than specific to a single shop. The daybook maintained from 1792 to 1804 by James Ruthven, whose family were heralded as "the great ivory and hardwood turners of their day," affirms this interpretation, recording among its transactions charges for furniture legs to Lannuier and William Dove, as well as to an unspecified member of the Burling family.[3]

The Bayard table closely corresponds to the description of the "Elliptical Veneered Card Table" initially described in the 1810 price book.[4] Double-elliptic tabletops, which are distinctively American in their contour, are closely identified with New York, although on rare occasions the shape was produced in Philadelphia as well; the treble elliptic version is unique to New York.   MKB

1. On card playing and card tables in early America, see Hewitt, Kane, and Ward 1982 and Zimmerman 2005b.
2. A second surviving card table with a Bayard provenance is illustrated in figure 144.
3. Barrett 1863–70, vol. 1, pp. 444–45; and James Ruthven daybook, 1792–1804, New-York Historical Society.
4. *The New-York Revised Prices for Manufacturing Cabinet and Chair Work* (New York, 1810), pp. 25–27; and Hewitt, Kane, and Ward 1982, pp. 46–47, 63–65, 67–68.

5

Plate 6

Scroll-Back Sofa, 1805–15

NEW YORK

Mahogany; secondary woods: maple, white pine
37 x 80¼ x 31⅞ in.(94 x 203.8 x 81 cm)
The Metropolitan Museum of Art, Gift of Mrs. Harry H. Benkard, 1942 42.16

Provenance: Mrs. Harry Horton Benkard (Bertha King Bartlett; ca. 1882–1945); The Metropolitan Museum of Art.

References: McClelland 1939, p. 177, pl. 145; Downs 1942, pp. 136–38; Rogers 1947, fig. 88.

Long considered a classic of its type, this graceful scroll-back sofa has been described as the "perfect collectors' piece" and said to "epitomize a style which a vast number of contemporary pieces express feebly or at best incompletely."[1] Simply put, it is the best of its kind, and if indeed it was produced in the Phyfe workshop, then it is apparent that Phyfe had in his employ some of the finest specialty chairmakers and carvers working in the United States at the time.

Within fine furniture-making establishments in London and Paris at the turn of the nineteenth century, chairmaking, which also included sofa making, was a distinct branch of the trade. As Sheraton recounts in his *Cabinet Dictionary* (1803), however, "in the country manufactories it is otherwise; yet even these pay some regard to keeping their workmen constantly at the chair, or to the cabinet work."[2] Such was the likely scenario in many early nineteenth-century New York City workshops, which the British traveler Henry Bradshaw Fearon described in 1817 as "generally small concerns, apparently owned by journeymen who had just commenced on their own account."[3] A sofa like the present example and the documented scroll-back sofa and chairs made by Duncan Phyfe for William Bayard in 1807 (Pls. 1–4) are of extraordinary quality and clearly made by proficients in their craft, which would seem to suggest that a strict division of labor existed within the Phyfe workshop. For as Sheraton points out, and Phyfe obviously knew, chairs require "a particular turn in the handling of shapes, to make them agreeable and easy," as well as no "want of taste concerning the beauty of an outline, of which we judge by the eye, more than the rigid rules of geometry."[4]

The gently scrolled back and inward curved serpentine arms of this sofa, snugly padded for comfort, fairly welcome a sitter to settle into one of its ends for an afternoon of reading or restful repose. Fine reeding accentuates the lines of the arms and the seat rails and diffuses the sharp reflections of the light, an effect amplified by the softly burnished old finish, which provides a fine, matte background for the delicate carving in the crest, polished rubescent from years of human touch. The modern black horsehair fabric, affixed with gilded tacks, tightly covers firm, well-modeled foundations that hold close to the lines of the frame to accentuate the overall effect of the form. Such upholstery treatment was recently discovered to be the original and confirms the popularity of this material in the period, as represented by the black fabric seats on the klismos chairs Phyfe offers to his customers in the watercolor of his Fulton Street furniture warehouse (see frontispiece on page 114).[5]

The sofa is notably one of only a handful of pieces of New York furniture to have brass cup casters impressed with the name "Thorp" with a crown centered above the name. Another is a chiffonier, or occasional table (App. 2.17), with brass casters impressed with the name "A. Thorp," which descended directly in the family of Eliza Phyfe Vail, daughter of the cabinetmaker. An Andrew Thorp, possibly the hardware merchant who supplied the casters and may have imported them from England and impressed them with his mark, is listed in the New York City directory starting in 1822.[6] The casters on this sofa appear to be original. Remnants of the old gilded lacquer finish can still be seen on the casters, an original treatment that would have harmonized with the gilded upholstery tacks.

PMK

1. Downs 1942, p. 136.
2. Sheraton (1803) 1970, vol. 1, p. 145. In London a separate price book for carvers and chairmakers existed beginning in 1802. In this and subsequent volumes, and in the supplements of 1807 and 1808, sofas, stools, and other seating forms were described and illustrated, which indicates that these were the province of chairmakers as well.
3. Fearon 1818, p. 24.
4. Sheraton (1803) 1970, vol. 1, pp. 145–46.
5. Notes by conservator Nancy Britton (December 4, 2008), in accession file 42.16, the American Wing, The Metropolitan Museum of Art.
6. Karen M. Jones, "Collectors' Notes: Andrew Thorp, Furniture Hardware," *The Magazine Antiques* 111, no. 4 (April 1977), p. 698.

6

Plate 7

Worktable, 1806–11

DUNCAN PHYFE

Mahogany, mahogany veneer; secondary woods: yellow poplar, white pine
30½ x 23¼ x 12¾ in. (77.5 x 59.1 x 32.4 cm)
Collection of Billy and Sharon Thompson

Labeled: "D. PHYFE'S / CABINET WAREHOUSE / No. 35 Partition-street, / NEW-YORK" (see fig. 23)

Provenance: A 1984 Christie's catalogue traces the ownership to Henry MacFarlan (1772–1830), New York; his son Francis Blanchard MacFarlan; his son Francis MacFarlan; his daughter Caroline Nichols MacFarlan Bunker;[1] Dr. C. Ray Franklin (ca. 1939–1984); private collector, 1984; (Christie's, New York, sale 5736, October 13, 1984, lot 457); the present owner.

References: *American Collector* 8, no. 4 (May 1939), p. 4; McClelland 1939, pp. 142–43, 165, pls. 121, 122; Christie's, New York, *Highly Important American Furniture from the Collection of Mr. C. Ray Franklin*, sale cat., October 13, 1984, lot 457, pp. 106–7.

Bearing the earliest known Phyfe label, this compact worktable could date as early as 1806, the year Phyfe moved his family across the street to 34 Partition Street and transformed his former residence into a cabinet warehouse, a major step for an urban cabinetmaker that signaled an entrepreneurial spirit and a sense of confidence that his business would flourish. Cabinet warehousing was an increasing trend in Federal America, as master cabinetmakers seeking to expand their businesses produced stocks of ready-made furniture, or "wares," to be available at all times for customers who patronized their warehouses. Was this simple yet stylish worktable a piece of ready-made furniture? This question is difficult to answer with certainty. The four turned legs rather than the more complicated and expensive pillar-and-claw base, and the hinged cupboard door instead of a sliding tambour shutter in the lower case as seen on the du Pont worktable (Pl. 8), may be economies that allowed Phyfe to manufacture the table without fear of investing too much in a more speculative piece.

Worktables like this example, with astragal-shaped compartments on the ends, were the most popular type in early nineteenth-century New York until their popularity began to wane around 1812, when a boxier canted-corner model came into fashion (see fig. 153). In architectural usage, an astragal is a convex, half-round molding with a flat fillet or break on either side. Such terminology was common among early nineteenth-century furniture makers who used the names of other molding profiles as well, such as the ogee, to describe the two overlapping S-shaped bars in the backs of chairs (Pl. 13). Typical of all New York astragal-end worktables, this one has smooth, figured mahogany veneer on its upper apron section that visually unifies the table part of the design and separates it from the profusely reeded central cupboard and tall lidded storage compartments on the ends. Overall the form is delicate, light, and well suited to its use by a lady. The legs are swelled slightly at the top, which adds unexpected but welcome mass above the peg-shaped feet and casters. Reeded legs swelled at the top also appear on a set of armchairs made by Charles-Honoré Lannuier for the Common Council Chamber of New York's recently completed City Hall in 1812.[2]

PMK

1. This worktable was said to have been discovered in Yonkers, New York. It was published in the *American Collector* in 1939. No history connecting it to Henry MacFarlan of New York was mentioned when it was published again that year by Nancy McClelland in *Duncan Phyfe and the English Regency* (p. 142, pl. 121).
2. Kenny, Bretter, and Leben 1998, p. 138, pl. 62.

7

Plate 8

Worktable, 1813

Duncan Phyfe

Satinwood, satinwood veneer, mahogany; secondary woods: yellow poplar, mahogany, white pine
30⅞ × 25⅝ × 13 in. (78.4 × 65.1 × 33 cm)
Hagley Museum and Library, Wilmington, Delaware

Provenance: Victorine du Pont Bauduy (1792–1861); probably her brother Henry du Pont (1812–1889) and his wife, Louisa Gerhard du Pont (1816–1900); their son Henry A. du Pont (1838–1926); his daughter Louise Evelina du Pont Crowninshield (1877–1958); Eleutherian Mills-Hagley Foundation; Hagley Museum and Library.

Reference: Quimby 1973, p. 555.

The documentary record on Phyfe's career offers numerous instances of sewing tables purchased by women or for their domestic activities. As discussed in Chapter 3, Victor du Pont and his wife, Gabrielle Josephine de Pelleport, ordered this table from Phyfe as a wedding gift for their niece Victorine, who married Ferdinand Bauduy on November 9, 1813.

The du Pont table is especially noteworthy for the artifacts that descended with it, a sewing bird and a morocco leather–covered *nécessaire*, which reinforce its function as a luxury item of feminine utility. Referred to as an "Astragal End Work Table" in the 1810 price book,[1] the present example includes a false drawer front, now with replaced pulls, and a hinged writing flap covered in wool baise and accessed by lifting the lid (see fig. 151). Segmented trays that conform to the shape of the astragal ends flank the hinged writing surface and lift out to reveal storage compartments below. The tambour door slides open to reveal two mahogany sliding shelves within the center section.

Early nineteenth-century furniture in light-toned solid satinwood is rare, and this example, now slightly reddish in color, is one of a small handful of worktables in that medium.[2] Satinwood was originally harvested in the West Indies, after which a variant species was obtained from India and Sri Lanka. Although satinwood was a more precious commodity than mahogany,[3] at $40 the du Pont table was significantly less expensive than a mahogany example made only months prior at $52 for James Kelso as a gift for his wife (see fig. 153).[4] The upper cabinet of the Kelso worktable is a square with canted corners that rests on four columnettes with spiral-turned ellipsoids and saber legs. The additional costs associated with turning and fluting four legs and framing the plinth below, as well as the increased complexity of canting the corners of the box, likely resulted in the Kelso table's higher price tag. Although the pillar-and-claw form is thought to have preceded the columnette style, the written evidence that dates the Kelso and du Pont tables establishes that they were made at the same time.

Among the large group of New York City worktables with unidentified makers is a subset that closely relates to the du Pont table yet illustrates a variety of leg profiles, urns, and patterns of inlay.[5] Both the du Pont table and a mahogany example formerly in the collection of Berry B. Tracy have single faux drawer fronts above tambour cases and reeded urns on legs with a diminishing bead molding.[6] While the former has carved paw feet and splayed legs, the latter has a more attenuated pillar-and-claw base and brass paw feet. A satinwood worktable owned by the Metropolitan Museum and attributed to Phyfe (Pl. 9) has saber legs with waterleaf carving but is otherwise consistent in design and construction with the du Pont table.[7]

MAT

1. *New-York Revised Prices for Manufacturing Cabinet and Chair Work* (New York, 1810), p. 30.
2. Satinwood furniture from this period is hard to identify as occasionally it is stained in mahogany color.
3. There are few early nineteenth-century references to the cost of satinwood as a commodity, but according to the Philadelphia price book of 1811, furniture made in satinwood "either solid or veneered" was 13 percent more expensive than if made out of mahogany (*The Journeymen Cabinet and Chairmakers' Pennsylvania Book of Prices* [Philadelphia, 1811], p. 81). The authors thank Alexandra Kirtley and Clark Pearce for bringing this document to their attention.
4. Bill of sale, Duncan Phyfe to James Kelso, May 10, 1813, collection of Mrs. Jerome W. Blum.
5. Few New York worktables are connected with a particular cabinetmaking shop. Other than the example at hand, only two pillar-and-claw worktables have an established maker: a table with hollow corners now at Boscobel labeled by Joel Curtis (act. 1817–20) (Tracy 1981, pp. 102, 106; and I. Sack 1969–92, vol. 5 [1974], p. 1379), and an astragal-end table labeled by John T. Dolan (act. 1808–13) (Northeast Auctions, Portsmouth, N.H., *August Americana Auction*, sale, August 4–6, 2006, lot 1864).
6. Sotheby's, New York, *Important American Furniture: The Collection of the Late Berry B. Tracy*, sale cat., February 1, 1985, lot 770. The Tracy table is nearly identical to one from the W. Starbuck Macy collection sold at Anderson Galleries, New York, *A Small Choice Collection of English, American, and French Furniture*, sale cat., January 18, 1936, p. 28, lot 124.
7. The pillar on a saber-leg astragal-end worktable in mahogany with a history in the Charlton family of Savannah features a compressed ball between two reels instead of the reeded urn, although the molding profile on the legs is consistent (Bivins 1989, p. 77).

8

Plates 171

Plate 9

Worktable, 1810–15

ATTRIBUTED TO DUNCAN PHYFE

Satinwood veneer, satinwood, kingwood; secondary woods: mahogany, yellow poplar
29 3/8 x 25 1/4 x 17 5/8 in. (74.6 x 64.1 x 44.8 cm)
The Metropolitan Museum of Art, Gift in loving memory of Gardner D. Stout, from his wife and children, 1986 1986.84.2

Provenance: Andrew Varick Stout (1872–1953) and his wife, Ethel Dominick Stout (1875–1965); their son Gardner D. Stout (1904–1984) and his wife, Clara Kellogg Stout; The Metropolitan Museum of Art.

References: New York 1963, p. 47; Oswaldo Rodriguez Roque in The Metropolitan Museum of Art, *Recent Acquisitions: A Selection 1986–1987* (New York, 1987), p. 66.

Associated with ladies' needlework, when they are often called sewing tables and have silk workbags hanging beneath, worktables were usually designed for multiple functions, especially in New York. On this exquisitely constructed example, the hinged top lifts to expose an adjustable baize-covered writing panel directly behind the false drawer front and removable semicircular trays with dividers in the astragal ends. Stored behind the writing panel, a looking glass can be pulled up by a small leather tab, transforming the table into a dressing table. Contrast to the light-colored satinwood is provided by mahogany crossbanding on the framing of the looking glass, the writing surface, and the two side trays. The reeded tambour case, made of narrow strips of wood glued to a linen canvas backing, has a sliding door giving access to two small mahogany drawers. A few satinwood pillar-and-claw worktables with astragal ends of New York make have fabric-covered midsections, the fabric gathered or pleated sometimes with added swags, as indicated by English pattern books, in place of tambour reeding.[1] The legs of all these tables appear to terminate in wooden paw feet instead of the more customary imported brass feet.

Choice veneers and delicacy of scale add to the worktables' feminine connotations. This table is made almost entirely of satinwood, a wood nearly as hard as ebony, imported from both the East and West Indies, and here inlaid with dark kingwood stringing. It is considerably more expensive than mahogany. The extra charge for work executed in satinwood is noted in *The New-York Revised Prices for Manufacturing Cabinet and Chair Work* for 1810. One-third more was added for veneering in this wood, and half again as much for the veneer when it was paneled with bands or stringing.[2] Like nearly all of its New York counterparts, this worktable has a false drawer front in the veneered apron. The two ivory drawer pulls are backed with brass escutcheons surrounded with the ghost of larger rings in the wood, indicating that the table had different escutcheons in the past.

Of the small number of satinwood worktables that were made in New York and Philadelphia, most that survive are of exceptional quality. This worktable is attributed to Duncan Phyfe on the basis of its superb proportions and craftsmanship and its close relationship in overall design and construction to the documented worktable made in the Phyfe shop for Victorine du Pont Bauduy in 1813 (Pl. 8).   FFB

1. See Cornelius 1922b, pl. XXX, opp. p. 47.
2. *The New-York Revised Prices for Manufacturing Cabinet and Chair Work* (New York, 1810), p. 7. See also Cooper 1980, p. 262.

Alternate view, Plate 9

9

Plate 10

Worktable, 1811–16

DUNCAN PHYFE

Mahogany, mahogany veneer, brass, silver-plated copper, marble; secondary woods: mahogany, yellow poplar, white pine
30⅞ x 22⅛ x 15⅝ in. (78.4 x 56.2 x 39.7 cm)
Winterthur Museum, Bequest of Henry Francis du Pont

Labeled inside drawer: "D. PHYFE, / CABINET MAKER, / 33 & 35, PARTITION-STREET, / NEW=YORK." (see fig. 24)

Provenance: William Dearing (d. 1852); . . . ; [Israel Sack, Inc., New York]; Louis Guerineau Myers (1874–1932); Henry Francis du Pont (1880–1969), 1930 until 1957; Winterthur Museum.

References: McClelland 1939, pls. 117, 118, pp. 138–39, 159; C. Montgomery 1966, no. 409.

Possibly the best-known piece of labeled Phyfe furniture, this worktable was one of Henry Francis du Pont's most important acquisitions as he began to assemble a Phyfe collection beginning in the late 1920s. Du Pont purchased the table in 1930 from the noted American furniture collector Louis G. Myers for the substantial sum of $4,535, obviously drawn to its superb documentation, rich mahogany veneers, elegant proportions, and brilliant display of craftsmanship.[1] Accordingly, the table has since remained a mainstay of du Pont's Phyfe Room at Winterthur.

Although referred to as a worktable, the presence of an inset marble top and the absence of a hinged writing flap or subdivided compartments behind the upper sham drawer suggest that it may have been used as a mixing table or kettle stand as well (see fig. 77). In 1815 Isaac W. Morrell, who operated a furniture warehouse in Savannah where he sold imported New York wares, advertised "Lady's elegant work Tables, with marble tops."[2] The applied waist banding is silver-plated copper, and it is possible that the marble top had banding, or even a now-lost raised, pierced gallery of this material as well. The drawer pulls are also replaced, and Phyfe would likely have incorporated silver-plated models to coordinate them accordingly. These precious details would indeed have elevated the table to a remarkable level of resplendency.

Unlike the more common astragal-end worktable model ordered by Victor and Gabrielle du Pont (Pl. 8), the truncated sarcophagus shape of the Winterthur table is rare outside of the cellarets made by New York City cabinetmakers between 1810 and 1840, such as the example that John L. Manning purchased for Millford (Pl. 60). Like other classical furniture of this period, the source of the shape derived from ancient forms and was disseminated through design books published by Thomas Sheraton, Thomas Hope, and George Smith.[3]

The table's base offers a noteworthy comparison to the du Pont and Kelso worktables (see fig. 153), both dating to 1813. The three share the same diminishing bead molding extending down the saber legs. The Winterthur and Kelso tables also have canted corners and columnettes with spiral fluted ellipsoids. The diminishing bead molding appears on the fronts of saber legs on a number of New York klismos chairs—some undoubtedly from the Phyfe shop—as well as on the legs of a pillar-and-claw pembroke table of about 1825 descended in the family of Duncan Phyfe's daughter Eliza Phyfe Vail (App. 2.13).

According to correspondence in the Winterthur archives, Louis G. Myers purchased the table from Israel Sack, who had acquired it from a member of the Dearing family of Athens, Georgia. The original owners were likely William Dearing, a cotton planter, railroad and real estate investor, and mill owner, and his wife, Eliza Pasteur Dearing.[4] The Dearings moved to Athens in the 1820s from Charleston, where they likely would have purchased the table.[5] Of the nine labeled pieces of Phyfe furniture, three have a Charleston provenance, which suggests that Phyfe took particular interest in promoting his work there.[6]   MAT

1. Louis G. Meyers to Henry Francis du Pont, October 27, 1930, Winterthur Museum archives. Myers wrote an enlightening introduction to the Phyfe section of the "Girl Scouts Loan Exhibition" (New York, 1929).
2. *The Republican and Savannah Evening Ledger*, May 2, 1815, p. 3.
3. See Sheraton 1803, pl. 41; Hope 1807, pl. 26; and G. Smith 1808, pl. 98.
4. "Remarks made by Mr. Sack, Aug. 14, 1941," typescript, p. 8, Winterthur Museum archives; and Jack Evans, "Sewing Table by Duncan Phyfe," typescript, 1966, Winterthur Museum object files, 57.725. For information on Dearing and his descendants, see Thomas 1999, pp. 20–22, and Hull 1906, p. 449.
5. [Sylvanus Morris], *History of Athens and Clarke County* (Athens, Ga., 1923), p. 31.
6. See Plates 27 and 28.

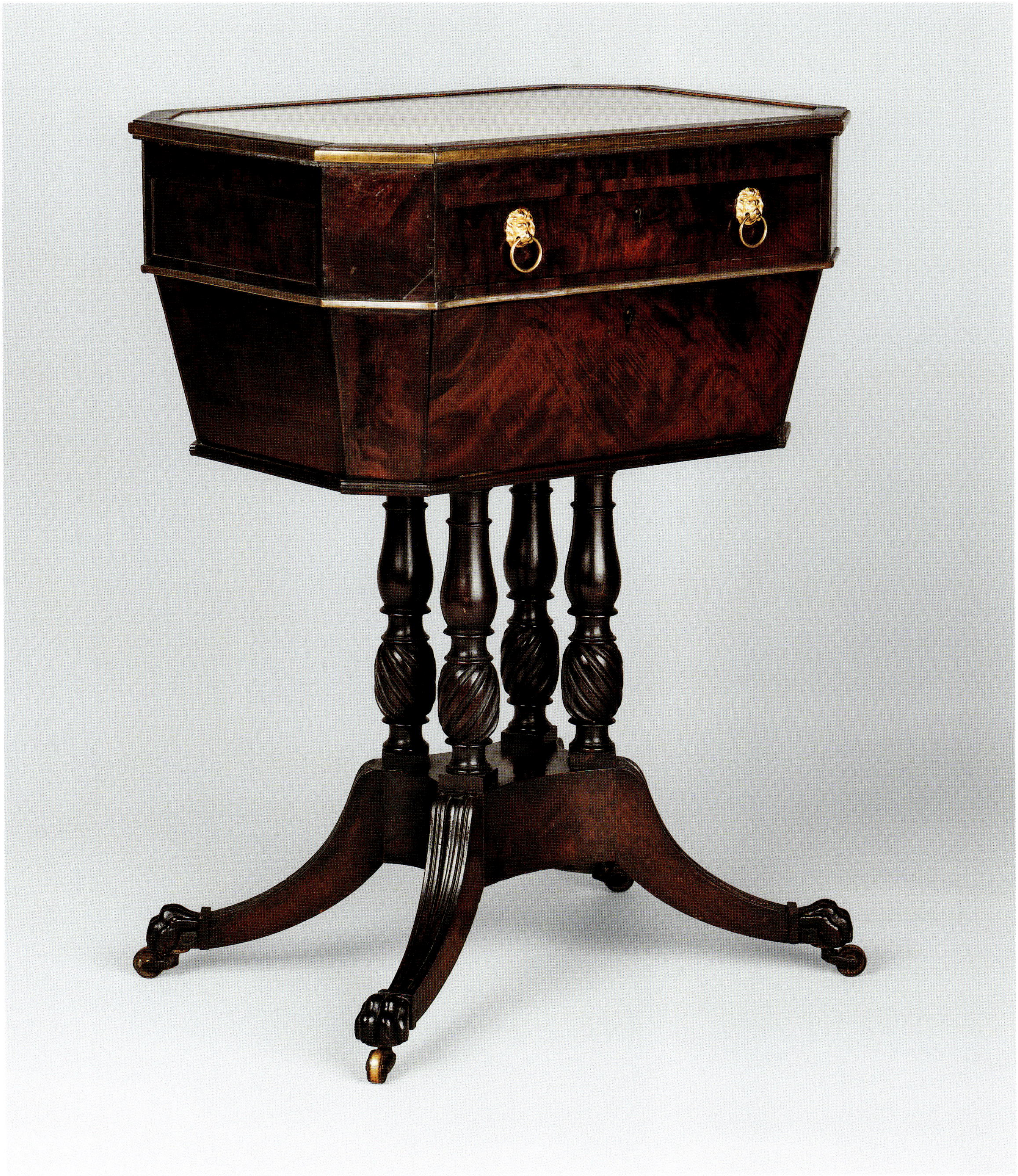
10

Plate 11

Card Table,
1805–15

NEW YORK

Satinwood, satinwood veneer: secondary woods: mahogany, white pine, yellow poplar
28¾ x 35⅞ x 17¾ in. (73 x 91.1 x 45.1 cm)
Museum of Fine Arts, Boston. The M. and M. Karolik Collection of Eighteenth-Century American Arts

Provenance: By 1928, [Ginsburg & Levy, Inc., New York]; Maxim Karolik (1893–1963), Boston, until 1938; Museum of Fine Arts, Boston.

References: *American Collector* 6, no. 7 (August 1937), p. 2; Hipkiss 1941, p. 122, no. 65.

Plate 12

Card Table,
1810–15

ATTRIBUTED TO DUNCAN PHYFE

Mahogany, mahogany veneer; secondary woods: mahogany, white pine, yellow poplar
29⅝ x 36 x 18½ in. (75.2 x 91.4 x 47 cm)
The Terian Collection of American Art

Provenance: By tradition made for Thomas Cornell Pearsall (1768–1820) and his wife, Frances Buchanan Pearsall (1779–1863). A 1946 Parke-Bernet catalogue (sale 805, November 9, 1946, lots 139–143) traces the ownership to the Pearsalls' daughter Phoebe (1813–1895); her niece Frances Pearsall Bradhurst (Mrs. Augustus Field; 1834–1907); her daughter Mary Field (Mrs. Henry Wilmerding Payne; 1860–1942); her brother Augustus Field (1866–1948); his son Malcolm Graham Field, Sloatsburg, New York; [Richard Kelly]; (Sotheby's, New York, sale 5473, June 26, 1986, lot 149); Peter G. Terian (1937–2002); The Terian Collection of American Art.

These superb pillar-and-claw card tables with double-elliptic tops represent the most stylistically advanced versions of the card table form available from cabinetmakers such as Duncan Phyfe and Michael Allison in early nineteenth-century New York (for the Allison table, see fig. 75). One (Pl. 11) of lustrous satinwood, lost its history long ago when it entered the antiques trade and was soon after declared to be "as clearly his [Phyfe's] work as if it bore his label," a plausible claim yet difficult to prove.[1] The other (Pl. 12) is veneered in rich crotch mahogany and has a traditional history of being made in the Phyfe shop for Thomas Cornell Pearsall of New York City.

Though closely related stylistically, the tables are quite different in the way the hinged leaves are supported when they are opened for use. The two mechanically activated side legs of the tripod base of the satinwood table are the more technically complex, their action tersely described in the 1810 New York cabinetmakers' price book as "three claws [legs], two of ditto to turn out with the joint rail," the latter being a hinged bracket on the back rail connected by a system of metal rods running through the pillar to the two side legs (see fig. 76).[2] Compared to this complicated mechanism, the swivel top system on the mahogany table is simplicity itself; the folded leaves turn 90 degrees on an iron pivot mounted off-center on the frame so that when the top is opened it rests squarely over the support pillars. Swivel tops postdate the mechanically activated pivot leg system and were probably made for the first time in the early 1810s. In the 1811 *London Cabinet-Makers' Union Book of Prices*, card table tops are described that are "made to turn on an iron center, fix'd to a cross rail." A nearly identical description appears in an undated twelve-page list of *Additional Revised Prices*, tipped into journeyman cabinetmaker Daniel Turnier's 1810 New York price book, issued several years later.[3]

The softly swelled double-elliptic tops and conforming aprons of these two tables offer an elegant counterpoint to their inward-curved Grecian legs. Calling these tables double elliptic is, however, somewhat deceptive, as only partial segments of ellipses are actually visible when the tops are closed. One of these segments is the bowed center section, which is superimposed on the larger second segment visible only in the curved corners at the ends. Making card tables double and treble elliptic substantially increased their cost of production, driving up the price as much as 20 percent and more.[4] Highly desired objects in their own time, such tables held great appeal for early collectors of Phyfe furniture as well, some of whom were so taken by them that they chose to display their tables with the top leaves tipped up 90 degrees to show off their double- and even rarer treble-elliptic trophies in profile.[5]

While a mahogany-veneered double elliptic card table with mechanical legs was already among the most technically challenging pieces of furniture a New York cabinetmaker could produce, if it were crafted in satinwood, a lustrous blond-colored wood imported to New York from the West Indies, it became even more expensive, hence its rarity. (Nancy McClelland acknowledged this fact, referring to the present satinwood example as a "rare example of Phyfe's work . . . an albino among his mahogany masterpieces.")[6] Satinwood was admired by Sheraton for its "fine straw colour cast," which gave furniture "a cool, light, and pleasing effect," and described by him as an extremely hard wood subject to becoming "foxy, or red coloured" if it was cut at the wrong season, when the sap was rising, or when exposed to dampness or excessive sunlight, an effect, he said, that "may be helped, after the work is finished, by rubbing the surface over with lemon juice and salt, a little aqua-fortis, and oil of vitriol."[7] New York master cabinetmakers and their journeymen were well aware of satinwood's inherent problems and thus agreed to a premium of "three shillings in the pound" for all work made of solid satinwood and a third extra over the standard charge when it was used as a veneer.[8]

An intriguing parallel exists between the Pearsall card table and a table that descended in the family of William Bayard, a well-documented patron of Duncan Phyfe (see fig. 144). So alike are these

176   Duncan Phyfe

11

12

Plates 177

References: Cornelius 1922b, pl. XXXVii (this table is Plate 12 or its mate, which is also in The Terian Collection of American Art); McClelland 1939, p. 290, pl. 278; *The Magazine Antiques* 43, no. 3 (March 1943), p. 135; Cooper 1993, pp. 163, 294, no. 119.

tables in design and workmanship that they are virtually interchangeable, the only recognizable difference being the use of thirteen versus eleven flutes on the wide sides of the plinths. Bayard's several documented dealings with Phyfe add to the possibility that the Bayard table came from his shop. That the Pearsall table is nearly a precise match adds to the probability of its having been made by Phyfe as well. PMK

1. *American Collector* 6, no. 7 (August 1937), p. 2.
2. *New-York Revised Prices for Manufacturing Cabinet and Chair Work* (New York, 1810), p. 25. For further discussion on this type, see page 74 in this volume and Zimmerman 2005b, pp. 127–31.
3. Kenny, Bretter, and Leben 1998, pp. 178 and 101 n. 90, and Zimmerman 2005b, p. 130.
4. *New-York Revised Prices for Manufacturing Cabinet and Chair Work* (New York, 1810), p. 26. Applying brass-covered moldings to a double-elliptic apron incurred an extra charge of 3 shillings and on a treble-elliptic apron 4 shillings.
5. In a half-dozen instances McClelland illustrates card tables displayed this way, including one with a treble-elliptic top in the home of collectors Mr. and Mrs. Andrew Varick Stout (1939, p. 140, pl. 119).
6. Ibid., p. 93, pl. 83.
7. Sheraton (1803) 1970, vol. 2, pp. 314–15.
8. *New-York Revised Prices for Manufacturing Cabinet and Chair Work* (New York, 1810), p. 7.

Plate 13

Curule Armchair, 1810–15

ATTRIBUTED TO DUNCAN PHYFE

Mahogany, cane; secondary woods: cherry, ash
32⅞ x 21⅛ x 24¾ in. (83.5 x 53.7 x 62.9 cm)
The Metropolitan Museum of Art, Gift of C. Ruxton Love Jr., 1960 60.4.2

Provenance: See Plate 12 through 1942; her nieces Frances Field Walker (Mrs. Samuel S. Walker; d. 1964) and Mary Field Hoving (Mrs. Osgood F. Hoving; d. 1954), until 1946; (Parke-Bernet Galleries Inc., New York, sale 805, November 9, 1946, lots 139–43 [the set]); C. Ruxton Love Jr. (1903/4–1971); The Metropolitan Museum of Art.

References: Cornelius 1922b, pl. IX (armchair and footstool), pl. XVIII (sofa); McClelland 1939, pl. 276 (armchair and footstool), pl. 280 (sofa), pp. 288–93; *The Magazine Antiques* 43, no. 3 (March 1943), p. 135; Parke-Bernet Galleries, New York, *Fine English and American Furniture and Decorations*, sale cat., November 9, 1946, lots 139–143 (the suite); Otto 1965, no. 119 (armchair); New York 1970, no. 17 (armchair); Bishop 1972, no. 342 (armchair).

This armchair, footstool, and sofa (Pls. 13–15) are part of a large suite of seating furniture with curule or Grecian-cross legs numbering seventeen pieces that includes a pair of armchairs, twelve side chairs (see fig. 146), and two footstools with short cabriole legs made for the New York merchant Thomas Cornell Pearsall. All but two side chairs are in the collection of the Metropolitan Museum.[1] Wealthy, stylish, and cosmopolitan, Pearsall would have sought the most fashionable furniture obtainable in New York, and this suite in the Regency interpretation of a new, more archaeologically accurate style copied from antique forms must have well matched his tastes. No documentation survives confirming that Duncan Phyfe was the maker of this furniture, but its superior workmanship and the mastery and execution of its design, as well as the long-held family belief that it was made by Phyfe, make it highly likely that the suite was indeed produced in his workshop.

The ultimate source for curule seating furniture is the Roman *sella curulis*, which was restricted to ceremonial use by magistrates who represented the central authority of Rome during the Republic. Two such ancient stools in bronze from the first century A.D. were unearthed in the excavations at Herculaneum in the 1750s and published by the English architect Charles Heathcote Tatham in 1799. The form was adapted by both the French (the fashion journalist Pierre de La Mésangère illustrated two stools with cross bases in 1806) and the English (stools with crosses appeared in the publications of Thomas Sheraton [1803], Thomas Hope [1807], and George Smith [1808]). But the more likely source for curule furniture in New York is the 1808 *Supplement to the London Chair-Makers' and Carvers' Book of Prices for Workmanship*.[2]

Plate 3 of the 1808 edition of the London *Supplement* illustrates curule chairs with and without arms (see fig. 65), described as "Chairs with Grecian Cross Fronts," the placement followed by most English furniture designers. With the exception of the Kaufman side chair (Pl. 21) and a few others, New York chairs have curules placed at the sides. This placement creates the appearance of a

178 *Duncan Phyfe*

13

Plate 14

Footstool, 1810–15

ATTRIBUTED TO DUNCAN PHYFE

Mahogany, cane
7 x 13¾ x 8⅞ in. (17.8 x 34.9 x 22.5 cm)
The Metropolitan Museum of Art, Gift of C. Ruxton Love Jr., 1960 60.4.14

Provenance: See Plate 13.

References: See Plate 13.

Plate 15

Grecian Sofa, 1810–15

ATTRIBUTED TO DUNCAN PHYFE

Mahogany, cane; secondary woods: cherry, ash
34 x 84¾ x 26¾ in. (86.4 x 215.3 x 67.9 cm)
The Metropolitan Museum of Art, Gift of C. Ruxton Love Jr., 1959 59.197

Provenance: See Plate 13.

References: See Plate 13.

14

continuous curve from the leg to the chair back; the ogee-cross shape is repeated once again in the banister. The side curules are connected under the seat by a turned stretcher with bilaterally opposed balusters. Centering each Grecian cross is a turned boss that, unlike the discs on the ancient Roman *sella curulis*, is purely decorative. The cane seats originally had cushions covered in a blue silk damask basket pattern, which can be seen in a photograph of the parlor of a Pearsall descendant (see fig. 147).

The two caned footstools from the Pearsall set, one shown in Plate 14, would have had the same top cushions of blue damask silk. Their canted corners and bandy-legged stance at first seem at odds with the rest of the set, but the horizontal reeds that wrap the rails are the same as on the curule chairs and serve as the unifying design element.

Phyfe and possibly other New York cabinetmakers inventively adapted the curule base to the Grecian sofa form by placing a front-facing pair below the seat rail; a second pair is at the rear. The ogee curve of the base is echoed in the elegant, outward-scrolled arms. Borrowed from antiquity, the carved crossed laurel branches on the center tablet of the crest rail are flanked by tablets with carved cornucopias, symbols of good fortune and plenty; the crossed laurel branches are repeated on the arm terminals. In the manner of the best New York cabinetwork, the frame is fully reeded on the front surfaces with gilded brass lion's-head masks applied to the center of the crossed bases. The brass paw feet, imported from England, were originally made bright gold by dipping in acid, burnishing the metal for highlights, and then coating with tinted lacquers to imitate the look of French mercury gilding.

Rarely do sets of curule furniture survive intact. One set, attributed to Phyfe and closest to the Pearsall suite in its completeness, was originally owned by the New York merchant Nathaniel Prime and is presumed to have been made for his

180   *Duncan Phyfe*

The Metropolitan Museum of Art Bulletin, Winter 1975/1976, no. 40 (sofa); Davidson and Stillinger 1985, pp. 70–72; Peck 1996, pp. 219–23; Barquist and Lasser 2003, no. 9 (side chair), pp. 34–39. See also Chapter 3, "Thomas Cornell Pearsall," pp. 118–20.

Palladian-style mansion at 1 Broadway. As displayed today at Boscobel Restoration, Garrison-on-Hudson, the suite consists of a sofa, twelve of the original twenty-four side chairs, and two curule stools or taborets.[3] The crest tablets display identical motifs of crossed laurel branches and cornucopias, but the carving was clearly executed by a different hand. A curule sofa, virtually identical to the Pearsall sofa, was owned by Bronson Winthrop Griscom and his wife, Sophie Gay Griscom.[4]

FFB

1. Three matching side chairs, the gift of C. Ruxton Love Jr., the donor of the Pearsall suite to the Metropolitan Museum, are at the Museum of the City of New York (59.279.1–3). Love purchased twelve side chairs at auction from Pearsall descendants, so he must have added a thirteenth to the set. Three chairs in the American Wing (60.4.6,10,13) and one chair at the Museum of the City of New York are impressed "H. Dorr," probably for Henry Dorr, a chairmaker active in New York from 1842/43 to 1862/63. Close examination has revealed no discernible differences among these chairs. Dorr possibly made repairs to the chairs that bear his stamp.
2. On Phyfe's curule furniture, see pages 69–71.
3. Tracy 1981, pp. 28, 29, and figs. 10–12.
4. The sofa was acquired from the Griscoms in 1977 by the Philadelphia antiques dealer Anthony A. P. Stuempfig. See *Antiques and the Arts Weekly*, May 20, 1994, p. 59.

Plate 16

Pier Table, 1815–16

DUNCAN PHYFE

Mahogany, mahogany veneer, marble, looking-glass plate; secondary woods: white pine, yellow poplar
36¼ × 42 × 18 in. (92.1 × 106.7 × 45.7 cm)
Descendants of John Wells

Provenance: John Wells (1770–1823) and his wife, Sabina Huger Wells (1781–1845); their son Thomas L. Wells (1799–1886) and his wife, Julia Beach Wells (1811–1870); their son Edward L. Wells (1839–1917) and his wife, Anna Mason Smith Wells (1849–1924); their daughter Sabina Elliot Wells (1876–1943); her niece Anna Wells Rutledge (1907–1996); her niece Alexandra MacPherson Eubank (1948–2007); the present owners.

References: McClelland 1939, pp. 302, 304–7. See also Chapter 3, "John and Sabina Wells," pp. 126–29.

A seminal expression of Phyfe's richer and more archaeologically accurate Grecian style of the late 1810s and 1820s, this table and its mate were ordered for John and Sabina Huger Wells by her older sister, Sarah Elliott Huger, when the couple were visiting Boston after their wedding.[1] As Sarah mentioned in a series of letters to her friend and distant relative Harriott Pinckney Horry in Charleston, she had a hard time getting the tables out of Phyfe's workshop.[2] Sarah was concurrently handling an order with Phyfe on Harriott's behalf for a pier table and card tables for the Lowndes family of Charleston, and it is tempting to speculate that the pier table was similar to this one.

A closely related example was advertised in 1996 by Bernard & S. Dean Levy as the mate to the Wells table (see fig. 90), but it features some noteworthy differences: a large central gilded ornament and inlaid brass stringing on the apron, a gilded cavetto on the plinth, and gilded and *vert antique* paw feet. Although we might expect to find similar ornamentation on the Wells table, there is no evidence to suggest that it was originally present. While there is little doubt that both tables were made in the Phyfe shop, the lions' heads and paw feet appear to be the work of different carvers.[3] Additionally, the rear columns of the Wells table are more slender and attenuated. Such differences may suggest that Phyfe employed several carvers and was actively seeking to improve on the proportions of an experimental new form in subsequent iterations.

The rear posts of the Wells and Levy tables are nearly identical otherwise and feature motifs considered hallmarks of Phyfe furniture design of the 1810s: the waterleaf-carved baluster, the reeded drum, and the finely tapered Doric column.[4] The posts potentially link Phyfe with a group of tables with griffin supports, which, as was suggested in Chapter 2, were Phyfe's response to Lannuier's sculptural carved work.[5] Of particular note is a pier table with griffin standards, analogous rear posts, and other related features such as paw feet with acanthus-carved legs, a sharp Grecian molding below the top, and an apron with canted corners and brass stringing (fig. 1, at left).   MAT

Figure 1. Attributed to Duncan Phyfe. Pier table, 1815–20. Mahogany, mahogany veneer, gilded gesso and *vert antique*, gilded brass, marble, 36½ × 44 × 20. Courtesy Bernard & S. Dean Levy, New York

1. Photostat copy of letter from John Wells to Sarah Elliott Huger, July 25, 1815, Wells Family Correspondence, 1802–86, South Carolina Historical Society, Charleston. The mate to this table is owned by another Wells family descendant.
2. Letters from Sarah Elliott Huger to Harriott Pinckney Horry, specifically January 4, 1816, Harriott Horry Ravenel Family Papers, 1694–1935 (1086.00), South Carolina Historical Society, Charleston. Sarah was at the time living with her sister Ann Barnett Elliott Huger and brother-in-law Edward W. Laight.
3. A third variation of the carved lion can be seen on the masks affixed to the plinth of a Pembroke table of approximately the same date; see Bernard & S. Dean Levy advertisement, *The Magazine Antiques* 149, no. 6 (June 1996), p. 1.
4. Harp-standard card tables with this post were accompanied by a trestle-base sofa table (Christie's, *Fine American Furniture, Silver, Folk Art, and Decorative Arts*, sale, October 1, 1988, lots 377, 378). A modification of this column substitutes a ball between two reels for the baluster,

16

as seen on the Brinckerhoff card tables (see fig. 81), as well as a pair of card tables with harp supports and carved eagles' heads (Pl. 29, fig. 1) and a card table with similar columns but a forward-facing lyre support (Pl. 30).

5. Both the scrolled standard with lion's mask and the griffin appear in plate 5 of the New York price book of 1817 (see fig. 91), suggesting that several cabinetmaking shops were familiar with these designs.

The Brinckerhoff Furniture (Plates 17-19)

Plate 17

Klismos Side Chair, 1816

Duncan Phyfe

Mahogany veneer, mahogany gilded and painted *vert antique*; secondary wood: ash
32⅛ x 18⅛ x 19½ in. (81.6 x 46 x 49.5 cm)
Private collection

Provenance: James Lefferts Brinckerhoff (1791–1846) and his wife, Charlotte Troup Brinckerhoff (d. 1873); her sister Louisa Troup (d. 1886); her niece and the granddaughter of James and Charlotte Brinckerhoff, Louisa Bronson Hunnewell (Mrs. Hollis Hunnewell; 1843–1890); her son Hollis Hunnewell II (1868–1922); his son Hollis Hunnewell III (1905–1982); the present owner.

References, Plates 17–19: McClelland 1939, pp. 295–99; Sloane 1987, pp. 1106–13.

Boldly carved, gilded, and painted *vert antique* in the more archaeologically correct Grecian style, this side chair, sofa, and Pembroke table (Pls. 17–19) were part of an extensive order of furniture and related services provided by Duncan Phyfe to New York City dry goods merchant James Lefferts Brinckerhoff that totaled more than two thousand dollars and was recorded in a running bill between September 29, 1815, and July 18, 1816 (App. 1.5). This order, stretched out over ten months, coupled with the comments of Sarah Elliott Huger in January 1816 on the difficulty she encountered in getting from Phyfe the furniture she had ordered for a friend in the late summer or fall the year before—"it is impossible to prophesize when the good lady will receive the card and pier tables"—indicates that the cabinetmaker was inundated with custom work at this time.[1] The occasion for this substantial purchase was the marriage, in January 1815, of James Lefferts Brinckerhoff to Charlotte Troup, daughter of Robert Troup, a prominent New York judge and successful real estate investor,

Plate 18

Grecian Sofa, 1816

DUNCAN PHYFE

Mahogany, mahogany veneer, ash and pine gilded and painted *vert antique*
34 3/8 x 86 1/4 x 25 1/16 in. (87.3 x 219.1 x 63.5 cm)
Private collection

Provenance: See Plate 17.

and their desire to furnish their new home at 12 Pine Street in Lower Manhattan with the best furniture money could buy.[2] The young couple's patience in dealing with the celebrated cabinetmaker was eventually rewarded with a house filled with his furniture in the most up-to-date fashion.

The Brinckerhoffs, both in their mid-twenties at the time, represented new blood, a second generation of customers for Phyfe, who earlier had attracted customers of their parents' generation with Hepplewhite-, Sheraton-, and early Regency-based designs. The Brinckerhoff furniture was decidedly different. More massive and monumental in scale than the earlier Bayard suite (see Pls. 1–5), it bespoke both Phyfe's and his clients' interest in the later, more archaeologically correct version of the Grecian style. The Brinckerhoffs' fascination with this mode, especially with *le goût antique* of Napoleonic France, led them to patronize Charles-Honoré Lannuier, New York's resident *ébéniste de Paris*, as well, acquiring from

him the same year a French-style bedstead with a "Large Eagle & dart" canopy and "Fancy Bed curtains" supplied by the upholsterer Peter Turcot, a tall screen dressing glass, or psyche, and a baby's crib.[3]

The parlor suite, which included the three pieces under discussion here, is recorded on the Brinckerhoff invoice as a "Sofa" ($140), "8 Mahogany Chairs Cained" ($22 apiece), a "Tea Table" ($60), and a "Pair Card Tables" ($135), one of which is illustrated in figure 81. Design harmony is achieved throughout the suite by the caned seating surfaces and scrolled ends and backs on the Grecian sofa and lyre-back chairs; the crisp canted corners and broad, curved, veneered socles on the tables; and the lion's-paw feet, gilded and painted *vert antique* in imitation of ancient excavated bronze. The original gilding and *vert antique* on the carved forelegs of the lyre-back chair (Pl. 17) is an extremely rare survival that leads one to wonder just how many of the numerous refinished

Plate 19

Pembroke Table, 1816

DUNCAN PHYFE

Mahogany, mahogany veneer, ebonized cherry, ash, poplar gilded and painted *vert antique*; secondary woods: white pine, yellow poplar, ash
29 x 24 (with leaves dropped) x 35⅜ in. (73.7 x 61 x 89.9 cm)
Private collection

Provenance: See Plate 17 through 1890; her daughter Charlotte Bronson Winthrop Hunnewell (Mrs. Walton Martin, 1871–1961); probably Hollis Hunnewell III (1905–1982); the present owner.

mahogany chairs of this type that are known may originally have had a similar treatment.[4]

This 1816 parlor suite marks a transition for Phyfe away from the more compact and delicate sets he masterfully designed for the likes of William Bayard and Thomas Cornell Pearsall. By the early 1820s he would take the Grecian style to an entirely new and opulent realm embodied in furniture like the brass inlaid rosewood and painted and gilded parlor suite he made for Robert Donaldson (Pls. 32–36) and other New Yorkers, such as Stephen C. Whitney (Pl. 40), who were wealthy and patient enough to deal with the celebrated cabinetmaker.   PMK

1. Letter from Sarah Elliott Huger to Harriott Pinckney Horry, January 4, 1816, Harriott Horry Ravenel Family Papers, 1694–1935 (1086.00), South Carolina Historical Society, Charleston.
2. Sloane 1987, p. 1107.
3. Kenny, Bretter, and Leben 1998, pp. 121–24 and 230–31.
4. This chair and its mate underwent conservation treatment at Robert Mussey Associates in Boston, Massachusetts, which was completed in December 2005. In the course of the treatment, overpaint and gilding were carefully removed from the carved forelegs to reveal the original gilding and *vert antique* decoration. I would like to thank Robert Mussey, John Driggers, and Chris Shelton for providing this information and for giving me unparalleled access to the Brinckerhoff parlor furniture throughout the conservation effort.

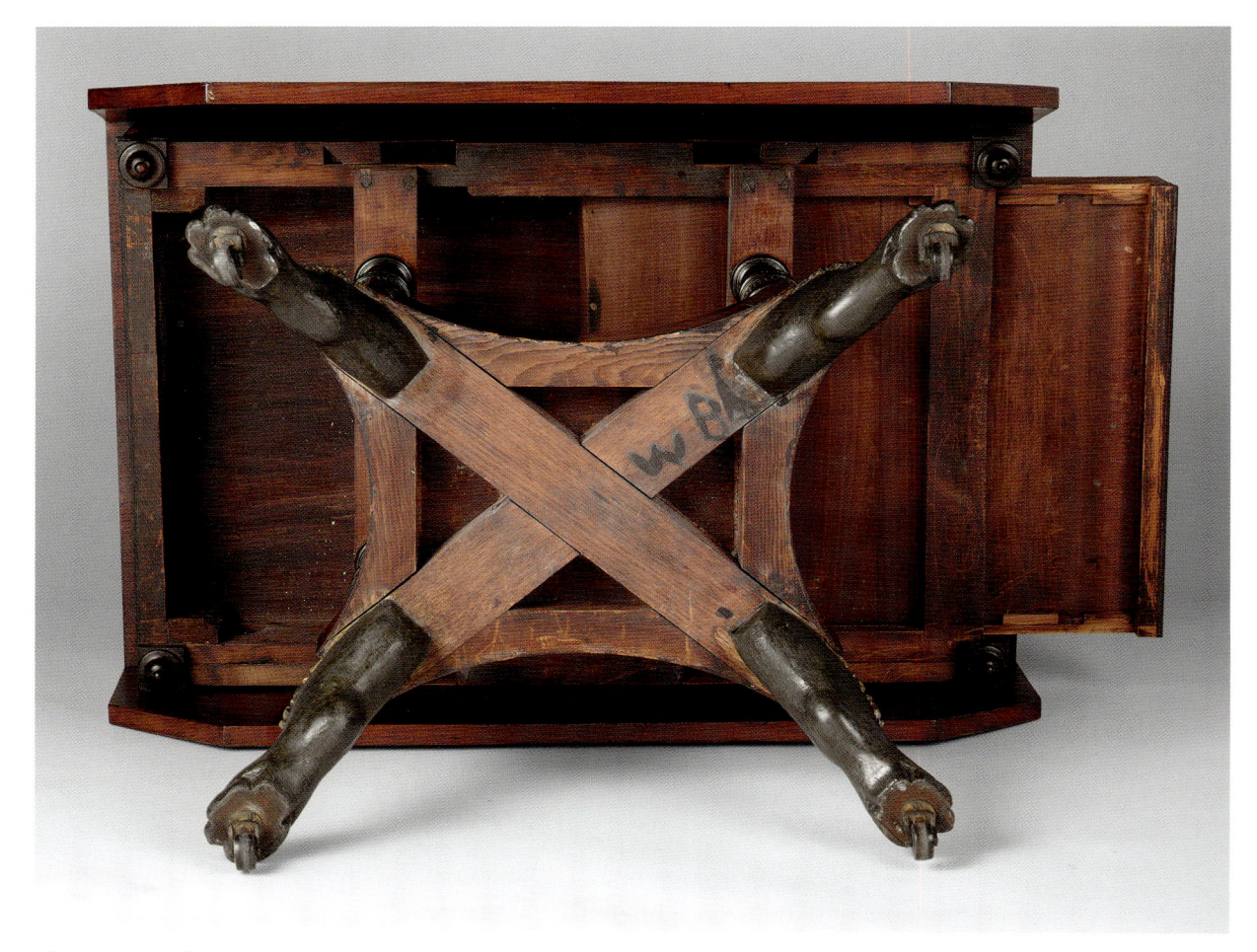

Alternate view, Plate 19

19

Plate 20

Klismos Side Chair, 1816

DUNCAN PHYFE

Mahogany, mahogany veneer, ebony (keys); secondary wood: ash
32 ¼ x 18 ½ x 19 ½ in. (81.9 x 47 x 49.5 cm)
Brooklyn Museum, H. Randolph Lever Fund 67.19.5

Incised on the top surface of the front seat rail: Roman numeral II.

Provenance: The 1950 Parke-Bernet catalogue traces the ownership in 1816 to Charles Nicoll Bancker (1777–1869), New York and Philadelphia; James Bancker, New York (d. 1897); descended through the Rowland-Younger family of Philadelphia; (Parke-Bernet Galleries, Inc., New York, sale 1115, January 12, 1950, lot 388); [Ginsburg & Levy, Inc., New York, until 1967]; Brooklyn Museum, 1967.

References: Parke-Bernet Galleries, New York, *Early American Furniture and Paintings,* sale cat., January 12, 1950, lot 388; Feld and Garrett 1991, p. 25; see also Chapter 3, "Charles Nicoll Bancker, pp. 120–22.

Buoyed by the renewed optimism and improved economic conditions following the ratification of the Treaty of Ghent in February 1815, which brought to an end the War of 1812, a number of custom commissions, a few well documented, were secured by Duncan Phyfe. One of the most interesting, not for the amount of furniture that survives from it but for the variety and quality of its documentation, is the one he was given in 1815 by Philadelphia businessman and former New Yorker Charles Nicoll Bancker. Documenting this order is a letter from Phyfe to Bancker in which he discusses details of the purchase, a signed and dated invoice (App. 1.6), and two unique design drawings with pricing options for chairs which graphically reveal the design process that cabinetmaker and client engaged in for the order (see fig. 149).

The chair in Plate 20 is believed to be part of this commission for a large parlor suite of furniture that originally included a set of a dozen mahogany chairs, a sofa, a pair of card tables, a pier table, two additional chairs, and two pairs of footstools. Ten of the fourteen original chairs are now in the collection of the Brooklyn Museum and are the sole known surviving examples from this suite. The decidedly different-looking chair with a lyre banister in Plate 21 lacks specific documentation linking it to the Phyfe shop, but curiously it too has a Philadelphia history of ownership in the Brown, Glover, and Norris families.[1] In design, this chair bears a close relationship to the one with the front curule base offered by Phyfe to Bancker in the design drawings, and it is conceivable that it was made in the Phyfe shop at roughly the same time. We know that Bancker, offered the choice between Phyfe's version of the ancient Greek klismos and his adaptation of the *sella curulis,* a type of folding stool with an ogee-crossed base used in ancient Rome, chose the former. Was this simply a matter of taste? Perhaps. But Bancker may have shied away from the curule design for another reason. Descended from a loyalist New York family, Bancker, a man undoubtedly educated in the classical past, may have thought it impolitic to have in his home a seating form associated with the autocratic, hierarchical political system of imperial Rome, especially in the aftermath of the War of 1812, when patriotic feelings ran high.[2]

Comparing Bancker's lyre-back chair with one from Phyfe made for James Lefferts Brinckerhoff in 1816 (Pl. 17) makes it clear that they were produced in the cabinetmaker's shop the very same year. Their design, workmanship, and proportions are identical down to the number of tapering reeds that flow in a continuous line from the side seat rails into the rear stiles and the virtually indistinguishable carved lyres in their backs. The only differences between these chairs are their seating surfaces—a slip seat versus a caned bottom—and the use of painted *vert antique* and gilded decoration on the hairy shanks and paws on the Brinckerhoff chairs. Despite these differences, chairs from both sets sold for $22 apiece.

The side chair in Plate 21 is a rare and unusual version of the curule form in New York. The more typical and arguably more elegant version (Pl. 13) has ogee cross banisters and curules on the sides that flow in a continuous line from the tip of the front feet into the scrolled rear stiles. The Bancker example, however, with its single front curule, lyre banister, and standard rear legs, is a hybrid—half curule stool and half scroll-back chair.[3] As David Barquist and Ethan Lasser point out in their study of the curule in American Federal furniture, positioning the curule base in the front was a mode frequently presented in the printed design sources available to American cabinetmakers in the early nineteenth century, so experimentation like this is hardly surprising.[4]

Compare to those found in Phyfe Klismos chairs, the lyre banister is unusually large, making it nearly as prominent a design element as the chair's front-facing curule. Its attenuated proportions and scale in fact seem more closely related to the paired lyres at the ends of the Brinckerhoff sofa (see frontispiece on page 64). This may have been intended to give it a more monumental appearance similar to larger sculptural lyres and other supports popular in card and pier tables of around 1815. In this respect, this unusual curule-base chair is like another rare New York model with a boldly scaled harp in the back which generally has been ascribed to Phyfe (fig. 1, on page 190). These two sets, if they were made by Phyfe, may be indicative of the

20

Plate 21

Curule Side Chair, 1815–20

NEW YORK

Mahogany, ebony; secondary woods: mahogany, ash
32 x 20 x 19¾ in. (81.3 x 50.7 x 50.1 cm)
Collection of George M.* and Linda H. Kaufman   *deceased

Provenance: Lent to the Philadelphia Museum of Art in 1920 by Mrs. Samuel Glover (Dorothea Hamilton Brown), Fairfield, Connecticut; Deborah A. Glover, 1922; her nieces Mrs. Allen A. Johnson and Deborah Norris Glover, Fairfield, Connecticut; on loan to the Philadelphia Museum of Art, 1932–55; returned to a Mrs. Van Kirk; [Bernard and S. Dean Levy, Inc., ca. 1977]; the present owner.

cabinetmaker's desire to amplify certain design elements of his well-known but more delicately scaled chair designs to keep pace with the richer and more monumental late Grecian style of the 1810s and 1820s.   PMK

1. Three chairs from this set are known, the present example and two others in a private collection. All three were once on loan to the Philadelphia Museum of Art and still retain their 1932 loan numbers in red paint. I would like to thank Clark Pearce for providing this information. The provenance in the Brown, Glover, and Norris families is given in Barquist and Lasser 2003, p. 36.

2. Ibid., pp. 10–25, for Ethan Lasser's concise history of the Roman *sella curulis* and his interesting theory on why some wealthy New Yorkers with aristocratic pretensions chose the curule form.
3. Cornelius 1922b, pl. VIII.
4. Barquist and Lasser 2003, pp. 17–18. Sheraton illustrated three different chairs with a front-facing curule base in *The Cabinet Dictionary* (1803); Thomas Hope showed five interiors with similarly designed curule bases in his *Household Furniture and Interior Decoration* (1807); and the same orientation was illustrated as well in the 1808 *Supplement to the London Chair-Makers' and Carvers' Book of Prices for Workmanship* (see fig. 65).

Figure 1. Side chair. New York, 1815–20. The Metropolitan Museum of Art, John Stewart Kennedy Fund, by exchange, 1972 1972.136

21

Plate 22

Klismos Side Chair, 1810–20

NEW YORK

Mahogany
32¾ x 18½ x 22¼ in. (83.2 x 47 x 56.5 cm)
Collection of Robert L. Froelich

Provenance: Berry B. Tracy (1933–1984); (Sotheby's, New York, sale 5285, February 1, 1985, lot 778); [Carswell Rush Berlin, Inc.]; the present owner.

Reference: Sotheby's, New York, *Important American Furniture: The Collection of the Late Berry B. Tracy*, sale cat., February 1, 1985, lot 778.

Although probably not made en suite, these two superbly matched pieces of seating furniture (Pls. 22, 23) nonetheless may represent a fourth and highly successful version of the caned Grecian sofa and chair sets manufactured by Phyfe in the 1810s. The others include the documented sets made for William Bayard and James Lefferts Brinckerhoff in 1807 and 1816 (Pls. 2–4 and 17, 18), and the Thomas Cornell Pearsall set of curule seating furniture (Pls. 13–15), also probably manufactured in the Phyfe shop. Each of these sets displays consummate design unity and an admirable economy of mass in their trim, well-proportioned frames, which combine the qualities of elegance and strength.

That such chairs and sofas belong together is strongly suggested by two partial matched sets recorded in auction sales catalogues and now dispersed among private and public collections. One of these sets, formerly in the possession of the noted American furniture collector Mrs. J. Amory Haskell, sold at Parke-Bernet Galleries, New York, in 1944 and comprised of four side chairs identical in design to the present example and a matching

192   *Duncan Phyfe*

Plate 23

Grecian Sofa, 1810–20

NEW YORK

Mahogany, mahogany veneer; secondary woods: cherry, maple
36 x 72 x 23 in. (91.4 x 183 x 58.4 cm)
Kaufman Americana Foundation

Provenance: Winslow Ames (1907–1990) and his wife, Anna Gerhard Ames (1907–1997); (Christie's, New York, sale 8696, June 17, 1997, lot 429); Kaufman Americana Foundation.

Reference: Christie's, New York, *Important American Furniture, Silver, Folk Art and Decorative Arts*, sale cat., June 17, 1997, lot 429.

The side chair shown in Plate 22 relates in overall form to those made for James Lefferts Brinckerhoff (Pl. 17) and shares the same distinctive reeded front seat rail, shaped like a cylinder for an antique scroll. In the back is an ogee banister, the most frequent alternative to the lyre banister in New York chairs of this type. The term *ogee* stems from architectural usage and describes the reverse or serpentine curve of the bars that extend from one corner of the back to the other and overlap at the center to form the banister. One other notable difference between this chair and the Brinckerhoff examples is the extra set of interior rails used for the caning in the latter, which sweep upward in a gentle curve from front to back. By comparison, the seat of this chair is completely flat. The reason for this difference is uncertain, although flat caned seats may have been preferable if the original seat cushion was firm and substantial, with squared French edges.

In addition to the Grecian sofa shown in Plate 23, only four others of this design are known.[2] One, in the collection of the U.S. Department of State in Washington, D.C., has carved fasces flanking the cornucopias in the crest rail, virtually identical to the present example. Fasces are an uncommon decorative motif in New York furniture of this period. In ancient Rome these tied bundles of rods with a rigged battle-ax at the center were symbols of authority and power, and carried in the presence of consuls and other high officials. They were also symbols of strength through unity, a bundle of rods bound together alluding to the strength that a single rod lacks. The use of the carved fasces in New York at about the time of the War of 1812 or

caned Grecian sofa with carved swags in the crest rail instead of fasces. This partial set also provides a possible link to the Phyfe shop. According to the sale catalogue, the set was purchased in 1818 from Duncan Phyfe by Henry McFarlan of New York City, who had purchased a worktable from the cabinetmaker several years earlier (Pl. 7).[1]

Plates   193

its immediate aftermath, when patriotic feelings ran high, is hardly surprising. An upholstered scroll-back sofa with a traditional history of being made by Phyfe for New York City mayor (and later state governor) De Witt Clinton has fasces flanking cornucopias in the crest rail, but the ax heads are pointed in the opposite direction of those on the present example. The ancient Roman symbol appears as well in the crests of a set of upholstered armchairs and sofas made by Charles Christian in 1814 for the Governor's Room at City Hall.[3]

The woven caning on both the chair and the Grecian sofa was most likely originally covered with cushions formed of tightly packed horsehair with squared French edges. Today, caned sofas owned by museums and private collectors are generally equipped with a long cushion or mattress on the seating surface only, though originally most would have had back cushions as well. Recently, a rare original set of these cushions with French edges was discovered under later show covers on a Grecian sofa with carved wooden banisters in the ends in the collection of the Cooper-Hewitt, National Design Museum, providing evidence that this was indeed the period treatment for sofas with loose cushions.[4] The Cooper-Hewitt sofa originally had a sacking seat bottom and back support. Such sofas had back cushions that abutted one another, but on sofas with three caned panels in the back, the cushions may only have been as wide as these panels and the vertical, reeded stiles between them left exposed. Light cords or ribbons affixed to the backs of the cushions could have been pulled through the caning or frame and tied to keep them in place. PMK

1. For the Haskell furniture with the McFarlan provenance, see Parke-Bernet Galleries, Inc., New York, *The Americana Collection of the Late Mrs. J. Amory Haskell*, part 2, May 17–20, 1944, sale 570, lots 761, 762. The Grecian sofa from this set is now in the collection of the Art Institute of Chicago (acc. no. 1978.301). The four side chairs were sold at Christie's, New York, *Important Americana, American Furniture and Folk Art*, January 18, 1998, sale 7085, lot 1558. The provenance listed in the catalogue indicates that they were purchased by Israel Sack, Inc., New York and then sold to Mitchell Taradash, Ardsley-on-Hudson, New York, before being consigned to this auction. The second partial set is described in an advertisement for Wise Auction Galleries, New York, that illustrates a Grecian sofa (lot 525) and one of the matching side chairs (lot 526) to be sold in the *Auction Sale for the Estates of Emma Thorne, Removed from the Hotel St. Regis, and Bertha Wise*, October 10–12, with no year given; internal evidence in the advertisement, however, suggests a date in the 1930s. A copy of the advertisement is in the scholarship files of the American Wing at the Metropolitan Museum. Six chairs sold at auction in 1997 from the collection of Mr. and Mrs. Winslow Ames were purported to be the four McFarlan/Haskell chairs with two added examples. It seems more likely that the Ameses' chairs were the six without provenance sold at Wise Auction Galleries in the 1930s. For these six side chairs, see Christie's, New York, *Important American Furniture, Silver, Folk Art and Decorative Arts*, June 17, 1997, sale cat., lot 430. A pair of these side chairs is illustrated in I. Sack 1969–92, vol. 1 (1988), p. 213, no. 545.

2. One of the sofas is in the collection of the Art Institute of Chicago; see Barter et al. 1998, pp. 131–34, no. 54. A second sofa is at the U.S. Department of State; see Conger and Itsell 1991, pp. 230–31, no. 128. A third Grecian sofa, which may be the one from the Wise Auction Galleries sale, referred to in note 1 above, was sold at Christie's, New York, *Highly Important Furniture from the Collection of Dr. C. Ray Franklin*, October 13, 1984, sale 5736, lot 458, and then at Sotheby's, New York, *Important Americana*, January 17–19, 1997, sale 6957, lot 951. The fourth sofa is illustrated in Lockwood 1921, vol. 2, p. 161, fig. 664. This last example has paired lyres instead of caned panels in the ends. This may be the sofa that was offered at Bonham's, New York, *American Furniture and Decorative Arts*, January 22, 2009.

3. For the De Witt Clinton sofa, see Miller 1956, pp. 70–71, no. 114. For the Charles Christian furniture at City Hall, see Kenny, Bretter, and Leben 1998, p. 142.

4. Cooper-Hewitt, National Design Museum, acc. no. 1920.19.85.

Plate 24

Sideboard and Cellaret, 1815–25

DUNCAN PHYFE

Sideboard: Mahogany, mahogany veneer, gilded gesso, looking-glass plate; secondary woods: ash, mahogany, white pine, yellow poplar
51⅞ × 76⅜ × 25¼ in. (131.8 × 194 × 64.1 cm)
Museum of the City of New York, Gift of Mrs. J. Bertram Howell

Cellaret: Mahogany, mahogany veneer, gilded gesso; secondary woods: yellow poplar, white pine, ash
26⅜ × 20 × 20 in. (67 × 50.8 × 50.8 cm)
Museum of the City of New York, on long-term loan from Glorianna H. Gibbon

In the period immediately following the American Revolution, the establishment of the dining room gave rise to the development of a new genre of furniture and accoutrements befitting a variety of occasions, from the simple repast to formal entertaining. The sideboard, certainly the most prominent of these, prompted George Hepplewhite to write, "THE great utility of this piece of furniture has procured it a very general reception; and the conveniences it affords render a dining-room incomplete without [one]."[1]

The instant popularity of this form is clearly asserted by the New York price book, which in 1796, its initial edition, specifies no fewer than seven variations. By 1810 the options had been narrowed down to four: "A Straight Front Sideboard Table," "A Straight Front Celleret Sideboard," "A French Sideboard," and "A Pedestal End Sideboard." The last mentioned, its matching ends designed either for a pair of knife cases or for lamps, was the most popular model in New York. So popular, in fact, that between about 1805 and 1815, a woodcut of the form was employed as the frontispiece to that volume (see fig. 44). It also embellished the label of New York cabinetmaker George Woodruff (act. 1808–16).[2]

Provenance. Sideboard: Duncan Phyfe (1770–1854) and his wife, Rachel Louzada Phyfe (1781–1851); their daughter Eliza Phyfe Vail (1801–1890) and her husband, William Vail (1802–1875); their son Duncan Vail (1829–1894); his son Frederick Vail (1861–1948); his daughter Virginia Vail (Mrs. J. Bertram Howell; 1897–1973); Museum of the City of New York. Cellaret: Same as above through 1973; her daughter the present owner.

References: Ormsbee 1930, pl. 33; McClelland 1939, pp. 179–80, pl. 107.

The French sideboard, which succeeded the iconic pedestal-end model, was massive, four-square, and highly architectural, with veneered classical columns, a frieze composed of three drawers, and four lower cupboard doors. Based on the French Consulat and Empire *desserte*, the New York version of the form is of nearly identical conformation, hence its period name. The Phyfe family sideboard is a modified version of the French sideboard, with its two central cupboard doors removed to create two pedestal ends and a large recess for a matching cellaret. The cellaret, as its name clearly implies, was a small case to store bottles of wine and spirits brought up from the cellar so they were close at hand in the dining room.

The sideboard was one of the more expensive case pieces detailed in the price books, and the 1817 edition clearly identifies "A Pedestal End Sideboard" and "A French Sideboard" as sumptuous expressions of the form. Robert Kelly, who was employed as a journeyman in the Phyfe shop between 1810 and 1813, claimed responsibility in an advertisement for making the "best side-boards" at the Phyfe establishment during those years. Whether of this journeyman's manufacture or another's, the quality of these pieces was widely admired; they received no greater complement than that of the cabinetmaker John Hewitt (1777–1857), who supplied a "French Sideboard like Phyfe's" to a client in 1811.[3]

According to the furniture historian Thomas Hamilton Ormsbee, this sideboard and cellaret were made for Phyfe's Fulton Street residence. Presumably it is the "mahogany sideboard and cellaret" that the estate appraisers inventoried in the front parlor and that is specified in the auctioneer's advertisement as the "carved mahogany sideboard marble-tops, with celleret to match."[4]

Although the sideboard has undergone certain alterations, essentially the piece is otherwise little changed. With its dramatic crossbanded and book-matched contrasting mahogany veneers, it continues to command attention and is a noble expression of the Grecian idiom. Defining the tripartite façade is a quartet of freestanding Ionic columns that span the front and frame the pedestal doors and mirrored niche, while carved lion's-paw feet serve to elevate the form and to relieve its massiveness. The draped carved acanthus of the feet relate in overall character to the hocked paw feet on tables from the documented Brinckerhoff suite made in the Phyfe shop in 1816 (Pl. 19 and fig. 83) and to the feet on the 1815–16 pier tables made for John Wells of New York City (Pl. 16), thus suggesting a similar date of manufacture, or just slightly later.

The sideboard was originally fitted with a softly polished marble top, which had the benefit of being impervious to the spills of an upended decanter or the heat of a serving dish. More important, it added an element of luxury to this expensive piece of furniture. As Robert Roberts, a butler, advised in *The House Servant's Directory*: "In setting out your sideboard... you must think that ladies and gentlemen that have splendid and costly articles, wish to have them seen and set out to the best advantage."[5] Such displays could become extravagant and ostentatious. James Fennimore Cooper described one New Yorker's sideboard as "groaning under the piles of silver."[6] From this conspicuous, prominent stage, cut glass, porcelain, and silver would accent the dining room interior, a subtle expression of the host's aesthetic refinement and elevated standing.

Fashioned en suite with the sideboard, the cellaret perhaps counters the notion that Duncan Phyfe was a teetotaler, since it was made for Phyfe's own residence. Historians have chronicled the marked increase in alcohol consumption in the United States between its founding and the Jacksonian era. Among the laboring class, cheap corn whiskey and rum were the alcoholic beverages of choice, but among the wealthy fine wines were favored. "Winebibbing" typically commenced in earnest at dinner parties no sooner than the ladies had risen from the table and lasted, as one English observer has noted, until the gentlemen had "made the complete tour of the cellar."[7]

The cellarets introduced a more satisfying option to the late eighteenth-century liquor case, a simple, fitted, wooden box usually found stowed directly beneath the sideboard. Not only was it more appealing visually but, being fitted with casters, it was more portable. The form had developed on the Continent during the late eighteenth century, and in this country its immediate and general popularity is substantiated by the 1796 New York price book, which published no fewer than three entries: "A Celleret," "An Octagon Celleret," and "An Oval Celleret." What's more, the volume cites at least seven varieties of "celleret sideboards," a rendition fitted out with drawers for bottles. The 1810 price book introduced an important yet subtle difference: the cellaret entries were replaced to immediately follow those of the sideboard, thus

Alternate view, Plate 24

reinforcing the pairing of these key dining room forms. In 1817 a new edition of the price book heralded an expanded range of shapes, with the addition of "Eliptic" and "Ogee" cellarets.[8] The former describes the shape of this Phyfe family example, the convex curve of the side representing a segment of an ellipse. The feet on the cellaret, like those on the sideboards, are of mahogany and were regilded at a later date.

Typically, the cellaret was ordered with divisions to accommodate either four—like the present example—or six glass bottles or possibly cut-glass decanters for wine or liquor; in the most elaborate examples, four concave horizontal channels are present around the perimeter of the partitioned section "for bottles to lie on."[9]

Closely related to the cellaret is the wine cooler, which as its name implies was intended not only to store but also to chill bottles of wine. While similar in appearance to the cellaret, the interior of the cooler was lined with copper, zinc, or lead. The scarcity of this form is underscored by its absence from the succession of New York price books. A lone citation appears among the Phyfe invoices. Oliver Wolcott Jr. was charged $78.25 for a "wine cooler &c" on December 31, 1812, just in time to usher in the New Year.[10]

MKB

1. Hepplewhite (1794) 1969, p. 6.
2. For an illustration of a Woodruff label, see C. Montgomery 1966, p. 478, no. 331.
3. Kenny, Bretter, and Leben 1998, p. 59, and M. Johnson 1968, p. 196.
4. Ormsbee 1930; McClelland 1939, p. 332; and "Executor's Sale of Household Furniture, William Irving & Co., Auctioneers," *New-York Daily Times*, September 18, 1854, p. 7.
5. Roberts (1827) 1977, pp. 48–49.
6. James Fenimore Cooper, *The Pioneers; or, The Sources of the Susquehanna: A Descriptive Tale*, vol. 4 of *The Leatherstocking Tales* (Boston, 1898), p. 54.
7. Hamilton 1833, vol. 1, p. 121, as cited in Coleman 1992, p. 55.
8. *The New-York Book of Prices for Manufacturing Cabinet and Chair Work* (New York, 1817), pp. 74–78.
9. Ibid., pp. 74–75.
10. Receipt book, 1803–14, Oliver Wolcott Jr. Papers, Connecticut Historical Society, Hartford.

Furniture Labeled August 1820 (Plates 25–28)

Plate 25

Writing Table and Bookcase, 1820

Duncan Phyfe

Mahogany, mahogany veneer, ebonized mahogany; secondary woods: white pine, yellow poplar, mahogany
96½ x 36½ x 21⅜ in. (245.1 x 92.7 x 54.3 cm)
Collection of Elizabeth Feld Herzberg

Labeled: "D. Phyfe's / Cabinet Warehouse, / No. 170 Fulton-street, / New-York / N. B. Curled Hair Matrasses, Chair and / Sofa Cushions. / August, 1820."
(see fig. 25)

Provenance: Probably purchased by Thomas Latimer (1765–1833)[1] and his wife, Susan David Latimer; their nephew Thomas L. Bowie (1808–1838) and his wife, Catherine H. Ashhurst Bowie (1814–1910); their son Richard A. Bowie (1836–1887) and his wife, Louisa Bayard Bowie (d. 1887); their son R. H. Bayard Bowie (b. 1868) and his wife, Amy Potter Bowie; their son R. H. Bayard Bowie Jr. (ca. 1899–1961) and his wife, Nancy Crouch Bowie; Mr. and Mrs. Stuart P. Feld; the present owner.

References: Downs and Ralston 1934, p. 23; McClelland 1939, pp. 247, 264–66, pls. 234, 251; Cooper 1980, p. 21, fig. 14.

A noteworthy exception to the general dearth of labeled Phyfe furniture is a group consisting of a writing table and bookcase, five card tables, two of which are described below, and a worktable (Pls. 25–28), all with identical printed labels dated 1820 (see fig. 25). Formal, structural, and ornamental consistencies within the group strongly suggest that the furniture was manufactured within a fairly short period of time. Phyfe may have turned to the use of these labels to promote his wares, especially in export markets, in response to the downtrodden economy following the Panic of 1819, and competition from his neighbor Michael Allison, who first introduced dated labels in 1817 and continued to print updates nearly every two years until 1831.

Some of Phyfe's labeled furniture is highly anomalous relative to his documented and attributed oeuvre. This writing table and bookcase clearly fits in this category, particularly in light of the unique scrolled pediment that sits atop a Phyfesque structure more typical of the 1810s but that lends the bookcase an architectonic presence seemingly associated with late colonial and early Federal case furniture. This sense of unease perhaps reinforces the notion that Phyfe was striving to reinvent his style in 1820 by combining familiar elements in an innovative manner.

The scrolled pediment, for example, incorporates several isolated chords of the Phyfe style, including the generous use of the finest crotch-mahogany veneer on the tympanum and central plinth and crossbanding to outline the paired scrolls. The stacked discs at both ends of the scrolled pediment are identical in design to those on the lobed standards of an 1820 trestle-base worktable (Pl. 28).[2] The spurs and volutes on the ends, however, are distinctive, although such spurs are found on clock cases manufactured by Gillows of Lancaster in the late eighteenth century.[3] The ornamented turned stretchers that extend from front to back on the top of the bookcase resemble those used for curule chairs in the 1810s (Pl. 13).

Elegant and whimsical, this writing table and bookcase could have been intended for use in a parlor or a lady's boudoir. The unusual pediment atop the secretary owned by Mary Telfair (see fig. 155) is equally fanciful and reminiscent in general outline, if not in carved detail, of the delicate constructs that Thomas Chippendale suggested for bookcases and cabinets in his *Director*.[4]

Documented case furniture from the Phyfe shop is exceedingly rare. In addition to this example, two other desk with bookcases above are known: the secretary bookcase linked to Phyfe by a letter from Mary Telfair (fig. 155) and a secretary bookcase that was part of an extensive suite of furniture owned by Robert Donaldson (Pl. 33). Furthermore, relative to other types of case furniture, writing table and bookcases and secretary bookcases appear infrequently on receipted bills.[5] Numerous desk forms with bookcases above have been attributed to Phyfe on stylistic evidence, including a group of cylinder desk and bookcases, such as one in the collection of the Metropolitan Museum (see fig. 80).[6] Whether built with a cylinder mechanism, a writing flap, or a secretary drawer, these typically feature an arched kneehole in the center with drawers to the side and above. The arch on both this and the Telfair examples terminates in decorative brackets like those seen on a Gothic rib-vault.

When illustrated in McClelland, this writing table and bookcase had Chippendale-style escutcheons and back plates with bale handles, which have now been replaced by pulls more typical for the date of the piece.[7] The brass ferrules at the base of the legs appear to be original. Occasionally during this period they are seen on case furniture and in smaller scale on tables and chairs by New York cabinetmakers.[8] The three lancet arches formed by the muntins in the bookcase doors relate to a pattern that appears in the 1817 price book, which may have been modeled after plate 40 in Hepplewhite's *Guide*.[9]

MAT

25

1. Although Nancy McClelland (1939) wrote that this writing table and bookcase was originally owned by Thomas L. Bowie, he would have been only twelve at the time of its construction if the piece is contemporaneous with the printing of the dated 1820 label in two of its drawers. Because Bowie's father, Ralph Bowie (1756–1816), an immigrant from Paisley, Scotland, died prior to that date, it is more likely that his uncle Thomas Latimer (1765–1833), a flour merchant, was the original owner. Following the death of his father, Thomas L. Bowie, his mother, Deborah M. David Bowie (ca. 1778–1845), and his three siblings lived with Latimer and Deborah's sister, Susan, in Philadelphia. The Latimers passed without issue, and Bowie presumably inherited their estate. On the Bowie and Latimer families, see Bowie 1971, pp. 342–46, and Small 1905, pp. 150, 157.
2. The finial's lobed center section with waterleaf carving above closely relates to the feet on the window seats and Grecian couch owned by Robert Donaldson (Pls. 34, 35).
3. S. Stuart 2008, pls. 485, 489, 497, 504.
4. Chippendale 1762, pls. 101, 124.
5. Only four desks appear on Phyfe invoices: a counting-house desk purchased by Thomas Morewood in 1802 for £24; a desk bought by the corporation of the City of New York in 1803 for £5.4.16; a secretary acquired by George Brewerton 1809 for £15; and a writing desk purchased by Thomas Masters in 1810 for $18.
6. For other examples, see Monkman 2000, pp. 267, 310; and Christie's, New York, *Important American Furniture, Silver, Folk Art, and Decorative Arts*, sale cat., June 22, 1994, p. 149, lot 250.
7. McClelland 1939, p. 264, pl. 251.
8. A wardrobe with ferrule feet is illustrated in Sotheby's, New York, *Important American Furniture: The Collection of the Late Berry B. Tracy*, sale cat., February 1, 1985, lot 776.
9. *The New-York Book of Prices for Manufacturing Cabinet and Chair Work* (New York, 1817), pl. 1, no. 26; Hepplewhite 1788, pl. 40.

Plate 26

Card Table, 1820

DUNCAN PHYFE

Rosewood and amboyna veneers, rosewood-grained maple, ebony, gilded gesso, gilded brass; secondary woods: white pine, yellow poplar, maple
29½ x 36 x 18 in. (74.9 x 91.4 x 45.7 cm)
Collection of Kelly and Randy Schrimsher

Labeled: "D. PHYFE'S / CABINET WAREHOUSE, / No. 170 Fulton-street, / NEW-YORK / N. B. CURLED HAIR MATRASSES, CHAIR AND / SOFA CUSHIONS. / AUGUST, 1820."
(see fig. 25)

Provenance: (Sotheby's, New York, sale 5680, January 28–30, 1988, lot 1820); [Israel Sack, Inc., New York]; (Christie's, New York, sale 1617, January 20–21, 2006, lot 867); the present owner.

Plates 26 and 27 are two of the five card tables bearing the dated August, 1820, label. This group includes several variations of the swivel-top form, a type of card table of continental and English derivation that became popular in New York during the 1810s.[1] Certain attributes of these labeled card tables, such as acanthus carved legs and paw feet, recall design features established in the previous decade, while others—with veneered columns and turret feet—reveal the emerging French Restauration style of the 1820s (App. 2.22). The continuing popularity of card tables in the 1820s and beyond refutes the claim of one of Phyfe's customers in 1816 that such pieces "now become obsolete in drawing rooms, which should only exhibit marble Tables in every pier, and a round centre one, corresponding in marble and finish."[2] In fact, the later partnership of D. Phyfe & Son (1840–47) had twelve card tables in stock when the entire inventory of the Phyfe establishment was auctioned in 1847.[3]

In New York about 1820, card tables with rounded corners succeeded those with canted corners. The austere skeletal trestle base of the card table in Plate 26 stands in sharp contrast to that on the table in Plate 27, which has a single robust support pillar and an unusual circular plinth turned with a complex series of architectural moldings stacked on top that appear as if they had been thrown on a potter's wheel. Another labeled August 1820 card table with a single thick turned support post is shown in Appendix 2.23. The tapered hexagonal shape of the posts and stretcher appears both on a small group of card tables attributed to the Phyfe workshop and on the labeled August 1820 writing table and bookcase

26

References: Sotheby's, New York, *Important Americana*, sale cat., January 28–30, 1988, lot 1820; I. Sack 1969–92, vol. 9 (1989), p. 2442, pl. P6037; Zimmerman 2005b, p. 141, fig. 39; Christie's, New York, *Important American Furniture, Folk Art, Silver and Prints*, sale cat., January 20–21, 2006, lot 867.

in Plate 25.[4] A unique feature of the present table is that the feet are of gilded wood carved to imitate the cast brass caps more typically used on tables of this period.

The trestle-base card table form was widely consistent as produced by both Phyfe and his contemporaries. One example sold by the firm of Edward Holmes and Simeon Haines (act. 1825–30) of nearly identical design to the labeled August 1820 example by Phyfe shown in Appendix 2.22 effectively illustrates this point, as it was recently advertised as a Phyfe-made table despite the presence of a Holmes & Haines label.[5]

MAT

1. Zimmerman 2005b, pp. 119–42.
2. Letter from Sarah Elliott Huger to Harriott Pinckney Horry, March 5, 1816. Harriott Horry Ravenel Family Papers, 1694–1935 (1086.00), South Carolina Historical Society, Charleston.
3. Halliday & Jenkins 1847, pp. 1, 9–18.
4. There are at least eight other known tables with hexagonal legs and stretchers attributed to Phyfe. Within the group the saber-shaped legs vary in the type of carving on the

Plates 201

Plate 27

Card Table, 1820

DUNCAN PHYFE

Mahogany, mahogany veneer; secondary woods: white pine, yellow poplar, ash
29 x 35¼ x 17¾ in. (73.7 x 89.5 x 45.1 cm)
Collection of Susan Paul Firestone

Labeled: "D. PHYFE'S / CABINET WAREHOUSE, / No. 170 Fulton-street, / NEW-YORK / N. B. CURLED HAIR MATRASSES, CHAIR AND / SOFA CUSHIONS. / AUGUST, 1820."
(see fig. 25)

Provenance: One of a pair originally owned by immigrant Scottish merchant Dunbar Paul, of Charleston, South Carolina; by direct descent to his great-great-granddaughter; the present owner.

Reference: Kenny, Bretter, and Leben 1998, p. 184.

27

upper portion, as well as in the use of fluting and reeding in the lower section. This group includes an example that descended in the family of John Jacob Astor (McClelland 1939, pp. 252–53, pl. 239) and another that allegedly descended from the Bowie family along with the secretary (I. Sack 1969–92, vol. 4 [1974], p. 1055, fig. P3893). The other examples are illustrated in Christie's, New York, *Important American Furniture, Silver, Folk Art and Decorative Arts*, sale cat., June 4, 1988, p. 111, lot 213; Christie's, New York, *American Furniture, Silver, Folk Art and Decorative Arts*, sale cat., June 25, 1991, p. 96, lot 152; Christie's, New York, *Important American Furniture, Folk Art, and Decorative Arts*, sale cat., October 8, 1998, pp. 73–74, lot 82; and Christie's, New York, *Important American Furniture, Folk Arts and Prints*, sale cat., October 8, 2004, p. 66, lot 125.

5. Rini 2005, p. 126, fig. 1; and Didier, Inc. advertisement, *The Magazine Antiques* 164, no. 1 (January 2005), p. 65.

Plate 28

Worktable, 1820

DUNCAN PHYFE

Mahogany, mahogany veneer; secondary woods: mahogany, white pine, yellow poplar
28½ x 27⅝ x 17⅛ in. (72.4 x 70.2 x 43.5 cm)
Leigh Keno

Labeled: "D. PHYFE'S / CABINET WAREHOUSE, / No. 170 Fulton-street, / NEW-YORK / N. B. CURLED HAIR MATRASSES, CHAIR AND / SOFA CUSHIONS. / AUGUST, 1820." (see fig. 25)

Provenance: [Probably Dixie Antique Shop, Charleston, South Carolina, 1955]; recorded in the Henry Francis du Pont Winterthur Museum Decorative Arts Reference Library (old DARL #L-26); Mariam Cannon Hayes (1916–2007), Concord, North Carolina; (Leland Little Auction & Estate Sales, Ltd., sale, March 1, 2008, lot 382); the present owner.

Reference: Leland Little Auction & Estate Sales, Ltd., Hillsborough, N.C., *Mariam Cannon Hayes Public Auction*, March 1, 2008, lot 382.

28

Formally, the trestle base and broad stance of this worktable seem to have more in common with period designs for a sofa tables (see Pl. 51, fig. 1) than with the compact pillar-and-claw worktables made by Duncan Phyfe (Pls. 8, 9). Its form-follows-function design, with a kneehole between two drum-like storage compartments and a commodious top, makes it extremely comfortable to use either as a writing or as a sewing table. Under its hinged lid, however, it has the same features as its smaller counterparts, including an adjustable-height baize-covered writing flap that could be set at the desired angle flanked by lidded wells where sewing equipment, fabric, or needlework could be stored.

Charles-Honoré Lannuier made trestle-base worktables with lyre ends in the late 1810s, but this example, with its elliptical reeded storage compartments and unusual vertical end supports cut in an odd lobed profile, are without precedent in classical furniture design of this period and are thus far removed from the Lannuier examples.[1] A worktable labeled and dated 1823 by Michael Allison in the collection of the Metropolitan Museum references Lannuier's worktables in its use of lyre end supports and Phyfe's in its kneehole design with flanking elliptical storage compartments.[2] Another worktable, undocumented but nearly identical to this labeled example by Phyfe in the collection of the New-York Historical Society, has more elaborate paired, rope-turned stretchers and legs terminating in carved scrolls.[3]

The comparative simplicity of the labeled Phyfe worktable coupled with a possible Charleston history of ownership (see Provenance, above), may indicate that it was a less costly model made on spec in the Phyfe shop and destined to be sold by an auctioneer or a factor warehousing Northern furniture in Charleston or Savannah.   PMK

1. Kenny, Bretter, and Leben 1998, pp. 155, 157.
2. The Metropolitan Museum of Art, acc. no. 33.160. Illustrated in Downs and Ralston 1934, no. 217.
3. The New-York Historical Society acc. no. 1957.204.

Plate 29

Card Table, 1815–20

ATTRIBUTED TO DUNCAN PHYFE

Rosewood and satinwood veneers, gilded gesso and *vert antique*, gilded brass, die-stamped brass borders; secondary woods: white pine, yellow poplar, ash, cherry. 30 x 36 x 18 in. (76.2 x 91.4 x 45.7 cm) The Metropolitan Museum of Art, Partial and Promised Gift of James and Laura Freeman, 2004 2004.538

For far too long Duncan Phyfe's furniture with carved sculptural supports based on the antique (Pls. 29–31) has stood in the shadow of that of his talented and celebrated competitor, Charles-Honoré Lannuier. Discovering Phyfe's contributions in this opulent, sophisticated realm of furniture making is frustrated by the fact that the only documented pieces from his workshop with carved elements of this type are the pair of pier tables made for John Wells in 1815–16 (Pl. 16). But careful comparison of the legs and back pillars on the Wells tables with other documented tables and with the three under discussion here suggests that Phyfe was a far more adventurous designer of furniture with antique sculptural elements than previously thought, incorporating into his work mythic griffins and eagles, gilded lyres—Apollo's instrument of cosmic harmony—and siren-like winged caryatids.

Griffin tables survive in considerable number and great variety. Among the known examples are card, Pembroke, center, sofa, and marble-topped pier and sideboard tables.[1] The griffins that emanated from Phyfe's shop are full-bodied, with bulging rib cages and powerful hindquarters (Pl. 29); the eagle tables, one of his alternate designs (fig. 1, at left), are, by contrast, slimmer and more delicate, with scrolled tails and, occasionally, harps on their backs. Phyfe's griffins are awesome in aspect: fierce-beaked creatures standing proud and strong in their legendary role as guardians and protectors. Filling a parlor with a suite of these tables was a bold choice by a client and certainly not for the faint of heart.

Carving the griffins was no mean feat. In *Household Furniture and Interior Decoration* (1807), Thomas Hope was concerned about the dearth of craftsmen in London capable of executing the three-dimensional figures that he required for the refined Grecian-style furniture he wanted made for his Duchess Street house, leading him to lament,

Figure 1. Attributed to Duncan Phyfe. Card table, 1815–20. Rosewood and maple veneers, gilded gesso and *vert antique*, gilded brass, 29¼ × 36¼ × 18 in. Collection of Mr. and Mrs. Stuart P. Feld

29

Provenance: Nelson Grimaldi Seabra; (Christie's, New York, sale 1387, October 8, 2004, lot 104); James and Laura Freeman; The Metropolitan Museum of Art.

Reference: Christie's, New York, *Important American Furniture, Folk Art and Prints*, sale cat., October 8, 2004, lot 104.

"Throughout this vast metropolis, teeming as it does with artificers and tradesmen of every description, I have, after a most laborious search, only been able to find two men, to whose industry and talent I could in some measure confide the execution of the more complicate[d] and more enriched portion of my designs."[2] Undoubtedly, such carvers were equally hard to find in early nineteenth-century New York.

Included among Ernest Hagen's handwritten notes from an interview with one of Phyfe's by-then elderly grandsons and namesake in Jersey City are the names of some of Phyfe's workmen, including one "Sloat—Welshman the Carver." Just under Sloat's name is written the word "outside," possibly indicating his status as an outside contractor.[3] A little-known carver and gilder by the name of Alexander Slott (also Slote), who, according to city directories, had a long career in New York spanning the years 1794 to 1834, just may be the man responsible for Phyfe's bronzed and gilded griffins and other sculptural supports.

The 1817 New York price book shows line drawings of a number of table standards, including several types of lyres, the lion's-head consoles seen on the Wells pier tables, a winged griffin, and the body of an eagle. Journeymen cabinetmakers were paid extra according to time "when paw feet, eagle heads, & c. for carving" were filed up (made roughly three-dimensional). In the price book, plate 5 (see fig. 91) specifies the "standards marked B and D [the eagle and the griffin] to be made of pine, and not filed up," indicating their

Plates 205

30

Plate 30

Card Table, ca. 1820

ATTRIBUTED TO DUNCAN PHYFE

Rosewood and satinwood veneers, mahogany gilded gesso and *vert antique*, gilded brass; secondary woods: yellow poplar, white pine
29 x 36 x 17⅞ in. (73.7 x 91.4 x 45.4 cm)
The Brant Foundation, Inc., Greenwich, Connecticut

Provenance: [Hirschl & Adler Galleries, New York]; The Brant Foundation, Inc.

Reference: Kenny, Bretter, and Leben 1998, pl. 45.

complexity and the fact that a specialist carver created them.[4]

The lyre card table shown in Plate 30 is a conspicuous, superbly balanced and well-proportioned essay in the enriched Grecian style. The lyre is sheathed in gilded acanthus and terminates in swans' heads linked by a faceted rosewood bridge. The hocked lion's-paw feet pay homage to the dynamic equipoise of those on Lannuier's signature pier and card tables (see fig. 96), but are unique in the way the gilded acanthus leaves billow upward from the crease and engage the rounded plinth, terminating in a sprightly outward flip. The hocked feet on a card table bearing Phyfe's August 1820 label (Pl. 27) similarly have billowing acanthus and claws and knuckles delineated in an identical manner, adding to the likelihood that this table was produced contemporaneously in the Phyfe shop.

While Phyfe co-opted Lannuier's spread-winged caryatid for one type of winged caryatid card table (compare figs. 95 and 96), for another he created a version with harps on their backs that relates closely to his card tables with eagle and harp supports (Pl. 31). Perhaps meant as a visual pun for another mythic Greek figure, the harpy, a hideous, rapacious, winged monster with the head and body of a woman and the tail, legs, and talons of a bird. The overall design is also strikingly similar to the symbol used on the seal of the Society of United Irishmen, whose mottoes were "Equality" and "It Is New Strung And Shall Be Heard."[5] Inspired by the underlying principles of both the American and French Revolutions, the society was formed with the objective of securing "reform of the Irish Parliament . . . by uniting Protestant, Catholic, and Dissenter in Ireland into a single movement."[6] It is perhaps not too far-fetched to think that this

31

Plate 31

Card Table, 1815–20

ATTRIBUTED TO DUNCAN PHYFE

Rosewood and amboyna veneers, rosewood-grained maple, gilded gesso and *vert antique*, gilded brass; secondary woods: white pine, yellow poplar
29½ x 36 x 18 in. (74.9 x 91.4 x 45.7 cm)
Collection of Mr. and Mrs. Joseph Allen

Provenance: Originally a pair. One table, Clara Vivian Denmead (Mrs. Hiram Walter Basil Williams; 1883–1966); its mate, her sister, Jessie Dresser Denmead (Mrs. Frank Simpson Diuguid; 1886–1981); by family descent, one table, Wisner M. Washam, 1998; the pair [Hirschl & Adler Galleries, New York]; the present owners.

table may have been designed for a patron with similar leanings. The back pillars, here enriched with gilding and painted *vert antique* in imitation of excavated bronzes, are virtually identical to those on the documented 1816 Brinckerhoff card table (fig. 81).   PMK

1. A partial suite of parlor tables with griffin supports, including card, tea, and center tables, all believed to have been owned originally by Robert Smith (1757–1842) of Baltimore, is illustrated and discussed in Weidman 1984, pp. 188–89. A griffin sofa table in the collection of the Museum of Fine Arts, Boston, is illustrated in "Museum Accessions," *The Magazine Antiques* 94, no. 1 (July 1968), p. 58. A rosewood sideboard table, one of two known, now in the collection of the Los Angeles County Museum of Art (acc. M.85.121a, b), with a history of ownership in the Livingston family of New York, is illustrated in *The Magazine Antiques* 122, no. 3 (September 1982), p. 362. The other sideboard table, also veneered with rosewood, is in the collection of the Stanford University Museum of Art (acc. no. 1982.197). A Stanford family possession, it bears the label of Sypher & Company, late nineteenth-century New York City dealers in American and European antiques. More than thirty tables with griffin and eagle supports have been recorded by the author, with more than half of them card tables. What may be the mate to the table in Plate 29, which descended in the Livingston, Lewis, and Hoyt families, is in the collection of the Mills Mansion in Staatsburg, New York.
2. Hope 1807, p. 10.
3. "Duncan Phyfe Notes," undated, 88x207.2, Downs Collection, Winterthur Library.
4. New-York Society of Journeyman Cabinetmakers, *The New-York Book of Prices for Manufacturing Cabinet and Chair Work* (New York, 1817), pp. 6, 146.
5. For an image of the seal containing the harp and caryatid symbol and the society's mottoes, see http://askaboutireland.ie/reading-room/arts-literature/irish-traditional-music/turlough-ocarolan/the-harp-a-symbol-of-irel/.
6. Thomas Bartlett, "The 1798 Irish Rebellion," February 17, 2011, BBC History, www.bbc.co.uk/history/british/empire_seapower/irish_reb_01.shtml.

The Donaldson Furniture (Plates 32-36)

Plate 32

Center Table, 1822

Duncan Phyfe
Rosewood veneer, mahogany, gilded gesso and *vert antique* gilded brass, die-stamped brass borders, marble; secondary woods: white pine, mahogany, yellow poplar
Height 30¾ in. (78.1 cm); diam. 32 in. (81.3 cm)
Winterthur Museum, Bequest of Henry Francis du Pont

Provenance: Robert Donaldson (1800–1872); his daughter, Isabel Donaldson (Mrs. Robert Donaldson Bronson; 1846–1931); her daughter Pauline Bronson Cromwell (Mrs. James W. Cromwell; 1881–1961); [W. S. Holmes Antiques, Freehold, New Jersey]; Henry Frances du Pont, 1934; Winterthur Museum.

Reference: See Chapter 3, "Robert Donaldson," pp. 129–34.

Plate 33

Secretary Bookcase, probably 1822

Attributed to Duncan Phyfe
Rosewood veneer, mahogany, gilded gesso and *vert antique* gilded brass, die-stamped borders, marble, looking-glass plate; secondary woods: yellow poplar, white pine, mahogany, maple
67¾ x 38 x 22⅞ in. (172.1 x 96.5 x 58.1 cm)
Hirschl & Adler Galleries, New York

Provenance: See Plate 32, probably through 1961; Dr. Saul Jaiven, Stamford, Connecticut; his estate, until 2001; [Hirschl & Adler Galleries, New York].

Reference: Feld and Feld 2007, p. 12, no. 25.

32

On at least two occasions during the 1820s, Duncan Phyfe supplied Robert Donaldson with richly ornamented rosewood furniture for his homes in Fayetteville, North Carolina, and New York. This furniture, five pieces of which are represented here (Pls. 32–36), provide a unique window into the cabinetmaker's mature Grecian style. The continued patronage of this sophisticated, affluent young man clearly was important to Phyfe, who personally signed one of a pair of window seats he made for him in 1826 (Pl. 34 and see fig. 101). The distinctive character of these window seats, as well as that of the matching Grecian couch or daybed (Pl. 35), indicates that Phyfe was striving to create something truly unique for a special client.

The center table in Plate 32 almost certainly is the one listed on an August 1822 invoice from Phyfe to Donaldson for the handsome price of $100, less a 3 percent discount for cash (App. 1.7). It has the added distinction of being one of only four documented New York center tables made before 1825; the other three are the work of the immigrant Parisian *ébéniste* Charles-Honoré Lannuier, who advertised upon his arrival in New York in 1803 that he had brought with him "new patterns" of "all kinds of furniture in the latest French fashion," including, no doubt, engraved designs of stylish

33

Consulat *guéridons* with round marble tops.[1] Soon after the Donaldson center table was made, the form became a mainstay of stylish American parlors, its very name denoting its placement away from the wall toward the center of the room. Mobile despite their considerable weight, center tables generally had casters under their feet, which enabled them to be moved closer to a window during the day to take advantage of the light and back into the center of the room after dark, where reading and other intellectual pursuits might continue into the evening under the glow of an Argand lamp or chandelier.

Although a secretary bookcase does not appear on the 1822 Phyfe bill, one that descended in the Donaldson family (Pl. 33) harmonizes so exquisitely with the documented center table in its carved lion's-paw feet and in the pattern and placement of the brass inlay of the plinth that it is hard to imagine it was not made en suite. In 1928, Robert Donaldson's daughter Isabel wrote an account of the furniture she had inherited from her father.[2] Included among a group of pieces she claimed to be "all Duncan Phyfes" was this secretary bookcase, which she called "the cabinet, pier table in parlor," a matter-of-fact description that precisely enumerates its two component parts: a pier table base and a bookcase with two doors on top.[3]

While Robert Donaldson may have ordered this secretary bookcase for his own use, it is a form traditionally associated with women. Hence the possibility that it was intended for his two younger sisters, with whom he lived in the Fayetteville house. In France a secretary bookcase of this type was known as a *bonheur du jour*, an eighteenth-century term for a type of lady's desk with a fitted writing drawer and a low superstructure or cabinet on top. About 1800, under the influence of *le style antique*, the *bonheur du jour* grew heavier and more architectonic, with a columnar pier table base and an upper cabinet with a classical entablature supported by flanking columns. Phyfe added this decidedly French form to his repertoire about 1820 or just slightly earlier and, based on some fine surviving examples in the Grecian Plain style, seems to have kept it in production until the 1840s. About a dozen secretary bookcases like the Donaldson example are known, some, perhaps even the majority, made in the Phyfe shop. One that descended in the Livingston family has beautifully figured mahogany veneers and retains its original looking-glass plates in the doors and white marble top, which provided the precedents for the replacements on the Donaldson example.[4]

Richly ornamented and highly architectural in character, the Donaldson window seats, one of which is shown in Plate 34, are Phyfe's purest expressions of the Grecian style as codified by Thomas Hope and George Smith. The clean lines and solidity lend them an aspect of nobility that reflects the moralizing design philosophy of Hope, who implored wealthy patrons and craftsmen alike to make furniture that served as "instruments of universal and of durable gratification, as well as of solid and permanent grandeur."[5] Both Hope and Smith published images of substantial four-square settees in their design books, which may have inspired Phyfe and his patron. In the Smith design (fig. 1, opposite), as well as on the Phyfe window seats, the blunt, spade-shaped acroteria on the corners are design features taken directly from ancient Greek architecture that Hope also used on cabinets and presses, whose tops, he wrote, "present the shape of ancient Greek house roofs."[6]

One of the Phyfe window seats is depicted in an 1832 portrait by George Cooke of Susan Gaston Donaldson (see fig. 163). There the window seat is shown upholstered in crimson silk damask, some of which, including the original tape borders, still survives on both window seats under the current reproduction upholstery. Inexplicably, the borders were left out of the picture by the artist who otherwise was precise in his rendering of the upholstery and the gilded decoration on the corner post. The original cushions for both window seats also survive, and on one is inscribed the date July 4, 1826. The cushions are densely packed with horsehair and expertly sewn with a firm, square edge. One would expect that by this time there was a separate upholstery shop within the Phyfe establishment where these cushions were made—or even earlier, as suggested by Phyfe's August 1820 label, where the availability of "curled hair matrasses, chair and sofa cushions" is distinctly noted.

The Grecian couch or daybed Phyfe made for Donaldson (Pl. 35) is of a type now often referred to as a recamier, as it is based on Jacques-Louis David's famous portrait *Madame Récamier* (1800; Musée du Louvre, Paris), in which the eponymous subject is shown reclining on her antique-style *lit de repos* gazing back over her shoulder at the viewer. Far removed from the literary and political salons of Paris, the lady who reclined on this daybed, Susan Gaston Donaldson, was nonetheless a highly accomplished woman in her own right, noted for

Plate 34

Window Seat, 1826

DUNCAN PHYFE

Rosewood veneer, rosewood-grained cherry, stenciled and free-hand gilding, gilded gesso and *vert antique,* die-stamped brass borders; secondary woods: ash, cherry or gumwood
19¼ x 42½ x 17 in. (48.8 x 107.9 cm x 43.2 cm)
Brooklyn Museum, Anonymous gift
42.118.12

Signed in ink on underupholstery: "D Phyfe"

Provenance: See Plate 32 through 1931; Mrs. J. Amory Haskell until 1942; Brooklyn Museum.

References: Ormsbee 1942, p. 5; Downs 1943, no. 48; Boicourt 1951, p. 475; Tracy and Gerdts 1963, pp. 63, 79; Banks 1972, pp. 448, 450; Peirce 1976, p. 1297; Peirce 1979, p. 1002; Voorsanger 2000, pp. 292, 294, fig. 238.

her exceptional talents as a singer and musician. After her marriage to Robert Donaldson in 1828, she moved from her native New Bern, North Carolina, into the couple's recently acquired State Street home. There, in her well-appointed drawing room overlooking New York Harbor, she played her imported London harp given to her by her father, surrounded by a suite of highly ornamented rosewood furniture from America's most renowned cabinetmaker. Against this backdrop she and her husband, through their talents, intellects, and social graces, entered the highest echelons of New York society.

Figure 1. George Smith. *A Collection of Designs for Household Furniture and Interior Decoration . . .* (1808). Colored etching and aquatint. The Metropolitan Museum of Art, Harris Brisbane Dick Fund, 1930 30.48.2

Plates 211

Plate 35

Grecian Couch or Daybed, 1826

ATTRIBUTED TO DUNCAN PHYFE

Rosewood veneer, gilded gesso and *vert antique*, gilded brass; secondary wood: ash
30⅜ x 86½ x 25½ in. (77.2 x 219.7 x 64.8 cm)
Brooklyn Museum, Anonymous gift
42.1118.11

Provenance: See Plate 34.

A unifying feature of this Donaldson seating furniture is the shape of its distinctive stacked feet that in general outline recalls the rather eccentric turned feet on ancient Roman couches. A more immediate source, however, are the heavy carved and gilded feet on Regency sofas of the 1820s, like those published in Rudolph Ackermann's monthly *Repository of Arts, Literature, and Commerce, & C.* (1809–28) and other British pattern books of the period. Another Regency feature is the buhl-work panel in the center of the front rail. Regency buhl work, a brass and rosewood version of the elaborate brass and tortoiseshell marquetry by the celebrated seventeenth-century French *ébéniste* André-Charles Boulle (1642–1732),[7] typically featured bands and panels of scrolled leafage, arabesques, and palmettes and became increasingly popular on furniture of the mid- to late 1810s. The most notable London cabinetmaker specializing in this type of decoration was George Bullock (1738–1818), who used buhl work to such an extent in his furniture that "the whole surface" was said to present "a brazen front."[8] It would not be surprising if Robert Donaldson, while on his trip to London in 1820 to settle his uncle's estate and claim his fortune, saw this type of elaborate Regency buhl work and later decided to ask Phyfe to incorporate some of it into the furniture that he commissioned. Buhl-work panels are rare in New York furniture, so it is noteworthy that the same style of buhl-work panel used on the Donaldson couch appears at the center of the front rail on a rosewood sofa that also has identical carved and gilded feet but no provenance to connect it to the Donaldson family (see fig. 165).

The melon-reeded feet on the Donaldson canterbury (Pl. 36) would seem to link it to the 1826 window seats, but it is also possible that it was purchased earlier for use in the Fayetteville house.

Plate 36

Canterbury, 1822–26

ATTRIBUTED TO DUNCAN PHYFE

Rosewood veneer, mahogany; rosewood grain paintings, gilded gesso and *vert antique*, gilded brass, die-stamped brass borders, secondary wood: white pine
22 x 20¼ x 16 in. (55.9 x 51.4 x 40.6 cm)
Collection of Richard Hampton Jenrette

Provenance: See Plate 32 through 1961; her daughter Mary Stuart Cromwell Allison (Mrs. Ivor Allison; 1908–1976); the present owner.

In *The Cabinet Dictionary* (1803), Sheraton defines "Canterbury" as "the name of the metropolis of Kent; but has of late years been applied to some pieces of cabinet work, because, as the story goes, the bishop of that see first gave orders for these pieces."[9] These pieces are described as either a two-tiered portable "supper tray," with a lower shelf partitioned into four sections to hold forks, knives, and plates, or a "small music stand," with two or three partitioned slots for "holding music books" and equipped with casters that allowed it to be "run in under a piano-forte" when not in use. In this sense, the canterbury and pianoforte were the complementary Apollonian counterparts to the cellaret and sideboard, the former "run in" under the latter (Pl. 24) after an evening of bacchanalian feasting and wine consumption.   PMK

1. *New-York Evening Post*, July 15, 1803.
2. A tag attached to the key that opens the drawer on the secretary bookcase bears the inscription, "Drawer / Duncan / Phyfe / Cabinet." Applied to the inside of the upper left door is a paper label that reads: "Belongs to / Isabel D. Bronson / [ES]TATE." And inside the lower back apron another label reads: "Isabel D. Bronson Estate."
3. Account dated August 1928 and signed by Isabel Donaldson Bronson in the collection of Richard H. Jenrette.
4. The Livingston family secretary bookcase is illustrated in Feld and Feld 2001, p. 46.
5. Hope 1807, p. 6.
6. Ibid., p. 40.
7. "Buhl" is the German spelling of *Boulle*.
8. R. Brown 1822–35, as cited in Collard 1985, p. 143.
9. Sheraton (1803) 1970, vol. 1, p. 127.

Plate 37

Secrétaire à abattant, 1820–25

ATTRIBUTED TO DUNCAN PHYFE

Rosewood and kingwood veneers, ebonized mahogany, gilded gesso and *vert antique*, gilded brass, looking-glass plate, marble; secondary woods: mahogany, white pine, yellow poplar
60 x 40 x 19 in. (152.4 x 101.6 x 48.3 cm)
Private collection

Provenance: According to a brass plaque inscribed "Belonged to John Wheeler Leavitt, made to order for him by a French Cabinet Maker, New York, 1830," this *secrétaire à abattant* originally belonged to John Wheeler Leavitt (1790–1852) and his wife, Cecilia Kent Leavitt (1798–1892); their granddaughter Cecilia Beaux (1855–1942); her nephew Dr. Cecil K. Drinker (1887–1956); Decatur House, National Trust for Historic Preservation; (Sotheby's, New York, sale 5551, January 28–31, 1987, lot 1352); [Peter Hill, Inc., New Hampshire]; the present owner.

References: Cooper 1980, pp. 248, 264–65, pl. 52; Sotheby's, New York, *Important Americana: Including Furniture, Folk Art and Folk Paintings, Prints, Silver, and Carpets,* sale cat., January 28–31, 1987, lot 1352.

This fall-front desk represents Duncan Phyfe's exquisite reinterpretation of the French Empire *secrétaire à abattant*. As suggested by Wendy Cooper, the popularity of this Gallic form in New York may have been disseminated through Pierre de La Mésangère's *Collection de meubles et objets de goût*, which features different versions in plates published in the 1803, 1804, 1805, 1823, and 1826 editions.[1] Mésangère's plates emphasize the large swaths of book-matched veneer for the ornamentation of both the fall front and the cupboard doors, and indicate the use of ormolu appliqués on the frieze and ormolu capitals and bases on the columns.

Although no *secrétaires à abattant* by Phyfe's Parisian-trained competitor Charles-Honoré Lannuier are known, the incorporation of veneered columns parallels Lannuier's work in the late 1810s. This *secrétaire* was first published as having been made in Philadelphia, but it clearly exhibits the hallmarks of Phyfe's work in the ornamented Grecian style.[2] A very rare form, only a few other New York City examples dating to before 1830 are known. This dearth suggests their relatively limited appeal, a notion reinforced by the fact that the form was not described in the city's price book for cabinetwork of 1817, although it does appear in the 1834 edition, where it is referred to as a French secretary.[3]

These exquisite compact *secrétaires* were most likely used in a parlor or drawing room setting, where they served not only as writing desks but as stylish cabinets of curiosity, with sculptural busts, French clocks, or Argand lamps displayed on their marble tops or within the mirrored central reserve on the interior.[4] While the desk's small scale belies its otherwise imposing architectonic presence, its functional storage space for books is greatly reduced relative to other cabinet top desk forms. In recognition of the height of the single fixed shelf within the lower cabinet, a *secrétaire* of this type could not have accommodated the large ledger books used for transacting business and thus perhaps appealed less to men than to women.[5] George Smith suggested that the type belonged "chiefly to the Ladies' dressing room, or boudoir."[6]

In contrast to the highly decorative façade, the sides of the case are simply constructed as two framed mahogany panels now coated with a glossy ebonized finish that is not original. Instead, these may have been paint-grained in imitation of rosewood, as they are on a nearly identical secretary in the Westervelt Collection and on a secretary from the late 1820s in a private collection in New York.[7]

The brass ornament affixed around the escutcheon of the fall front speaks to the importation of fancy hardware during this period. Cast into the verso are the letters "CA," which have also been found on mounts used by Lannuier and illustrated in a trade catalogue published by R. Smith & Co. of Birmingham, England.[8] Although the mark has not been associated with a particular brass founder, New York cabinetmakers were clearly accessing common sources of decorative hardware.

MAT

1. Earlier versions are illustrated in Venable 1998, p. 67, and Kenny, Bretter, and Leben 1998, p. 175. New York cabinetmakers do not seem to have adopted the form until the late 1810s at the earliest.
2. R. Smith 1974, p. 180. New York–made French *secrétaires* differ significantly from the standard Philadelphia model, which features a paneled fall front and cabinet doors and often includes an elaborate tabernacle pediment typical of German cabinetwork; see Flanigan 1986, pp. 222–23.
3. *New-York Book of Prices for Manufacturing Cabinet and Chair Work* (New York, 1834), pp. 30–31; *The Philadelphia Cabinet and Chairmakers' Union Book of Prices of Manufacturing Cabinet Ware* (Philadelphia, 1828), pp. 38–39.
4. Agius 1984, p. 138.
5. One of the few period illustrations of a secretary in use shows the Swedish crown princess Josefina writing letters in her private quarters; see Thornton 1993, p. 231.
6. G. Smith 1808, p. 23.
7. Armstrong 2001, p. 205.
8. Kenny, Bretter, and Leben 1998, pp. 168–71.

37

Plate 38

Pier Table, 1815–25

ATTRIBUTED TO DUNCAN PHYFE

Rosewood veneer, gilded gesso and *vert antique*, gilded brass, die-stamped brass borders, marble, looking-glass plate; secondary woods: white pine, yellow poplar
37 x 42½ x 20¼ in. (94 x 108 x 51.4 cm)
Collection of Robert L. Froelich

Provenance: [Hirschl & Adler Galleries, New York, until 2002]; the present owner.

Reference: Feld and Feld 2001, pp. 48–49.

Like the lavish rosewood parlor furniture that Duncan Phyfe made for Robert Donaldson in the early to mid-1820s (Pls. 32–36), these handsome architectonic pier tables (Pls. 38, 39) represent the zenith of the cabinetmaker's work in his mature ornamented Grecian style. Hundreds if not thousands of these tables, of varying quality, were produced by New York cabinetmakers between about 1805 and 1830, with the earliest known labeled examples coming from the shop of the French-born *ébéniste* Charles-Honoré Lannuier, and later ones by Michael Allison (fig. 1, below), Holmes & Haines, and Joseph Meeks & Sons. To date, however, none that is labeled or otherwise documented to Phyfe is known.

Both these pier tables are charged with ornament and employ the finest and most costly materials available at the time—exotic Brazilian rosewood veneers, imported Italian white statuary and black-and-gold Egyptian marble, ormolu appliqués and mounts, brass stringing and die-stamped brass borders, gilded and painted decoration, and large, opulent looking-glass plates at the back. When such tables were deployed in a room ideally, these plates would serve as visual extensions of taller plates mounted above them on architectural piers between two windows (fig. 2, on page 218).[1] Such an extravagant use of looking-glass plate was rare in America, although the newlyweds Maria Bayard and Duncan Pearsall Campbell

Figure 1. Michael Allison. Pier table, 1817–19. Rosewood veneer, gilded gesso and *vert antique*, gilded brass, die-stamped brass inlays, marble, looking-glass plate, 37⅛ x 40 x 19¾ in. Winterthur Museum, Museum Purchase, 1974.2

38

Plate 39

Pier Table, 1820–30

ATTRIBUTED TO DUNCAN PHYFE

Rosewood veneer, stenciled and freehand gilding, gilded gesso and *vert antique*, gilded brass, die-stamped brass borders, marble, looking-glass plate; secondary woods: white pine, yellow poplar
37 x 42 x 18 in. (94 x 106.7 x 45.7 cm)
Collection of Carswell Rush Berlin

Provenance: Unknown.

were treated by the bride's wealthy father, William Bayard, to two extremely large plates each measuring 71 by 34 inches, which he imported from France together with enough gilded molding to frame them when mounted on the wall.[2]

The table with square corners and lion's-paw feet (Pl. 38) follows the earlier format and could have been made as early as 1815, while the one with the rounded front corners and ribbed melon-shaped feet (Pl. 39) is stylistically later. The rounded corners, though tighter in radius, relate to those on the labeled and dated August 1820 card tables by Phyfe (Pls. 26, 27). The spectacular stenciled and freehand gilded decoration on this table is another feature that has yet to be documented as predating 1820 in New York furniture. The painter-gilder who executed this decoration was without peer. His artistry also appears to be in evidence on the front rails and acroterion corners of the 1826 Donaldson window seats (Pl. 34), and the apron and surrounding border of the painted scagliola top on the Whitney family center table (Pl. 40).

In 1998 the American furniture dealer and scholar Stuart P. Feld attributed the pier table in Plate 38 to Duncan Phyfe along with a group of other aesthetically kindred pieces, including *secrétaires à abattant*, center tables, card tables, pier table–form sideboards, and Grecian sofas and couches.[3] Since that time two key pieces of Phyfe furniture that additionally support Feld's attributions—a center table and a secretary bookcase that descended in the family of Phyfe's documented patron of the 1820s, Robert Donaldson—have come to light (Pls. 32, 33). This discovery reaffirms the Phyfe aesthetic as defined by Feld and reveals the cabinetmaker as a masterful exponent of the richly ornamented Grecian style with a stylistic identity all his own.

PMK

1. The probable mate to the pier table shown in Plate 39 is in the collection of the High Museum of Art, Atlanta (acc. 1981.1000.76A–B). The disjuncture of a black-and-gold Egyptian marble top—which is old and perfectly fitted to the frame—and the white statuary marble columns and pilasters on the pier table (Pl. 38) is unusual.
2. Kenny, Bretter, and Leben 1998, pp. 113–14.
3. Feld and Feld 2001, p. 48.

Figure 2. Rudolph Ackermann. Plate 19, *The Repository of Arts, Literature . . . Fashions & C.*, vol. 1 (1809). The Metropolitan Museum of Art, Harris Brisbane Dick Fund, 1942 42.74.2

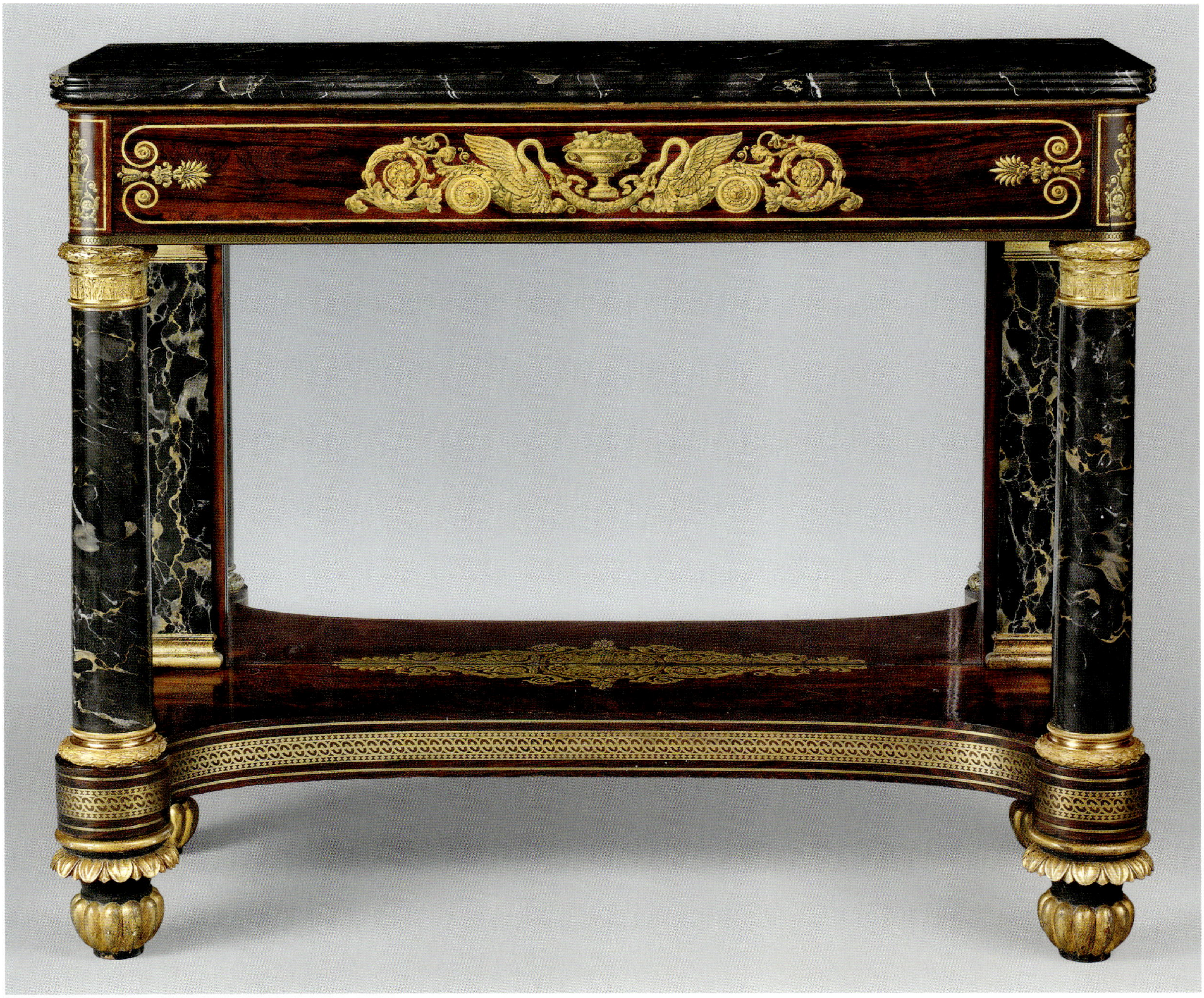

39

Plate 40

Center Table, 1825–30

ATTRIBUTED TO DUNCAN PHYFE

Rosewood veneer, stenciled and freehand gilding, gilded gesso and *vert antique*, die-stamped brass border; secondary woods: mahogany, white pine, painted scagliola
Height 29 in. (73.7 cm); diam. 36 in. (91.4 cm)
Museum of the City of New York, Gift of Mrs. Egerton L. Winthrop 36.160

Provenance: By tradition, Stephen C. Whitney (1776–1830), New York; by descent to Mrs. Egerton L. Winthrop until 1936; Museum of the City of New York.

References: *The Magazine Antiques* 48, no. 4 (October 1945), p. 209; Cooper 1993, pp. 128, 292.

The opulence of this center table bespeaks the spectacular wealth of its likely original owner, the cotton speculator, shipowner, and real estate investor Stephen C. Whitney, whose fortune, second only to that of John Jacob Astor, was said to be between five and ten million dollars at its height. In 1827, with William Backhouse Astor, John Jacob Astor's son, Whitney commissioned the first New York Merchants Exchange Building, designed by the architect Martin Euclid Thompson. That same year he moved to 7 Bowling Green, a handsome three-story town house on the corner of State Street. By tradition, the center table was part of the original drawing-room furniture. The Whitney house was demolished in the early 1900s. Fortunately, some of the woodwork from the drawing room was preserved and donated to the Museum of the City of New York in 1936, where it was installed and is today still part of the museum's permanent display. There the Whitney center table takes pride of place alongside a partial surviving set of ebonized and gilded chairs of outstanding quality with upholstered backs, also said to come from the Whitney house drawing room and possibly by Phyfe as well.

Bold and exuberant, the Whitney center table is a tour de force of Grecian styling in America. The overall form has its origins in the bronze tripod lamp standards of classical antiquity and, in the words of Thomas Hope, is given a look of "solid and permanent grandeur" by its stout tapering column, powerful lion's-paw feet, and a full panoply of ornament ranging from burnished gold and bronzed effects to die-stamped brass inlay and brass stringing, stenciled and freehand gilded decoration, and painted scagliola (an imitation marble made of plaster).[1] The acanthus-leaf carving is lively and distinctive and rendered in a manner identical to that on the documented Donaldson tripod center table (Pl. 32), thus providing a firm basis for the attribution to Phyfe. Additional proof that the Phyfe shop produced elaborately decorated tables like these comes from an auction advertisement that appeared in the *New-York Commercial Advertiser* of April 15, 1844, where, among a number of pieces of furniture offered for sale, there is a "handsome rosewood centre table, inlaid with brass, fine scagliola top, very costly, made by Phyfe."

The painted top on this table is perhaps its most extraordinary feature. A tondo in a gilded trompe l'oeil frame, it depicts a legend concerning the origins of the Lacus Curtius, an ancient site in the center of the Roman Forum. According to Livy (*History of Rome*, book 7, sec. 6), in 362 B.C. a gaping chasm opened in the middle of the Forum. The people tried to fill it with votive offerings, but the chasm remained. The oracles were consulted, and the people were told that the chasm would close only if the "most precious thing of all" were put inside. A young warrior named Marcus Curtius came forward and, declaring that Rome's most precious possession was the courage and strength of its soldiers, mounted his charger and leapt into the chasm, which immediately closed over him. This heroic act was honored by naming the site of the young horseman's self-sacrifice the Lacus Curtius, or Curtius Lake. The integration of a history

Detail, Plate 40

220   Duncan Phyfe

painting depicting a classical legend into the design of this table suggests a patron with a desire to raise a functional, albeit lavish, household object to the status of a work of art.   PMK

1. Hope 1807, p. 6. Already highly ornamented, this table may originally also have had die-stamped banding in the empty channeled recesses around the outer edge of the top and the lower edge of the apron.

Plate 41

Center Table, 1825–30

DUNCAN PHYFE

Mahogany, rosewood, light burlwood veneers, die-stamped brass border; secondary woods: mahogany, white pine
Height 28⅝ in. (72.7 cm); diam. 36 in. (91.4 cm)
Collection of Glorianna H. Gibbon

Provenance: Eliza Phyfe Vail (1801–1890) and her husband, William Vail Jr. (1802–1875); their son Duncan P. Vail (1829–1894) and his wife, Mary F. Onderdonk Vail (1839–1924); their son Frederick P. Vail (1861–1948) and his wife, Ida M. McLaurie Vail (1867–1952); their daughter Virginia Vail (Mrs. Bertram Howell; 1897–1973); her daughter, the present owner.

Aside from being made by Duncan Phyfe, practically the only things this center table has in common with the preceding one are its tripod pillar-and-claw base and the diameter of its top. Lighter and more mobile, the table has a top that tips up, allowing it to be tucked into the corner of a room, where, thanks to its optically brilliant veneers, it could remain very much on display. Tables like these provided an alternative to card tables, which by the late 1820s had been produced in America for nearly a century and were falling out of fashion in some circles. In Great Britain they were often called loo tables, after the popular card game of the same name. Another tilt-top center table documented to Phyfe is the one he made in 1834 for George and Maria Fox Clark of New York City, which has a single, ball-turned pillar and three saber-shaped legs with lion's-paw feet (see fig. 170).

This table's resplendent circular top is composed of a rayed pattern of book-matched, flame-grained veneers that appear to have been sawn from a single crotch of a mahogany tree. Centering the composition is a star-shaped disk of light-colored burlwood. The overall visual effect is remarkable, as if the pattern were created by a kaleidoscope—an optical device, incidentally, that had been patented relatively recently, in 1817, by the Scottish physicist, astronomer, and inventor Sir David Brewster. Brewster's invention was pirated almost immediately and produced widely for sale throughout Europe and the United States, leading to an international craze for the device. Whether Phyfe was directly inspired by the optical effects of the kaleidoscope is difficult to ascertain. Nonetheless, given the interest of artisans and designers in the device and the public's fascination with seeing commonplace materials

Alternate view, Plate 41

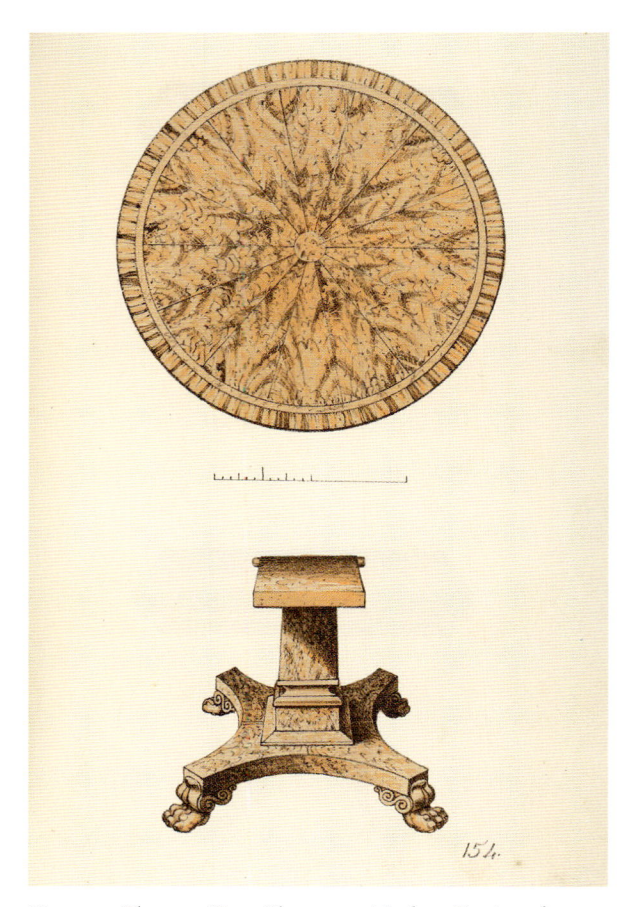

Figure 1. Thomas King. Plate 154, *Modern Designs for Household Furniture* (1827–28). Winterthur Library, Collection of Printed Books and Periodicals

41

transformed into fantastical patterns through its lens, it remains a distinct possibility.[1]

Thomas King published a design for a tilt-top center table with a similarly veneered top in his pattern book *Modern Designs for Household Furniture* (fig. 1, on page 222). The legs on the Phyfe table share the same high-arched, hooked profile as those on a labeled August 1820 card table by Phyfe (Pl. 26), while the die-stamped banding inserted along the outer edge of the top is identical to that on the dated 1826 window seats he made for Robert Donaldson (Pl. 34). Given these similar design features, a suggested date of manufacture around the time of Eliza Phyfe's marriage to William Vail Jr. in 1825, or a couple of years later, would seem likely. — PMK

1. For more on the kaleidoscope craze and its application to the decorative arts, see Priddy 2004, pp. 81–97.

Plate 42

High-Post Bedstead, 1815–25

DUNCAN PHYFE

Mahogany, mahogany veneer, *vert antique*, gilded cast brass
84 × 63 × 80 in. (213.4 × 160 × 203.2 cm)
The Terian Collection of American Art

Provenance: Eliza Phyfe Vail (1801–1890) and her husband, William Vail Jr. (1802–1875), but probably made for Duncan Phyfe (1770–1854) and his wife, Rachel Phyfe (1781–1851); see Plate 24 from 1890 through 1973; her daughter Glorianna Howell (Mrs. John Gibbon); [R. T. Trump and Company, Flowertown, Pennsylvania]; Mr. and Mrs. Edward Stone; [Israel Sack, Inc., New York]; Mr. and Mrs. Peter G. Terian; The Terian Collection of American Art.

References: Marshall 1915, p. 50; McClelland 1939, pp. 133, 184–85; Cooper 1980, pp. 20–21.

This imposing high-post bedstead was recorded by Nancy McClelland as belonging originally to Duncan Phyfe's daughter Eliza Phyfe Vail. However, based on the style of its ornament, as well as some tangential documentation, it seems just as likely that it was originally made for her parents. Perhaps the bed was still at 193 Fulton Street in September 1854, when the appraisers of her father's estate recorded a "Mahogany High Post Bedstead" valued at $2 alongside an "Old Pier Table Rosewood and Gilt" in the "Open Garrett," implying that both were outmoded pieces relegated to storage. Following the deaths of Rachel and Duncan Phyfe, many of their furnishings came into Eliza's possession, this bed perhaps among them.

It may be noteworthy that Duncan Phyfe's own bedstead was of a relatively old-fashioned English form, with four posts and a head- and footboard and tester (now missing), as opposed to the then highly fashionable French bedstead, which stood sideways to the wall with a circular or demilune canopy suspended above. French bedsteads may have been considered *de rigueur* by a new generation of sophisticated travelers to France and continental Europe, such as Stephen and Harriet Van Rensselaer IV, who in 1817 purchased the most elaborate example known from New York's resident *ébéniste* Charles-Honoré Lannuier, but for a sober, industrious tradesman like Phyfe, who, according to family tradition, insisted that his family retire every evening by 9 P.M., the more conservative form seems the better fit.

The assortment of four-post bedsteads enumerated on the invoices from the Phyfe shop reveal much about their production. A bill from July 1800 to George Brewerton denotes charges for "Press," "Field," "High Posted," and, conversely, "Low post" bedsteads with values ranging from £1.16.0 to £12.10.0. Two years later Phyfe submitted another statement to Brewerton, which included charges for "Putting upe 4 beads"—a reminder of the scope of related activities a cabinet shop could be called upon to perform.[1] The low-post bed was routinely fashioned of maple or another indigenous wood, its modest embellishment being limited to the simple turning of the head- and footposts. By comparison, high-post bedsteads encompassed two groups: the field, or camp, bed with its shorter posts and rounded or serpentine tester, and the more imposing form with posts rising six feet or higher and spanned by a narrow horizontal frame to support the bed curtains, which persisted through the first half of the century. The Phyfe bedstead, when fully outfitted "with its heaped-up feather mattresses and down pillows, its fine linen, fragrant with lavender, and its gorgeous or delicate bed-trappings," was the chief feature in the bedchamber.[2]

A small number of bedsteads can be firmly documented to the Phyfe shop. Of these, the only other high-post examples are those commissioned

42

Detail, Plate 42

by Lewis and Sarah Stirling in 1836 for Wakefield, their house near St. Francisville, Louisiana.[3] Originally nine in number, these beds present a decided contrast to the Phyfe family example. They are fashioned of curled or tiger maple, a wood prized for its striking grain but exceedingly chaste in design, with tall tapering columns on molded square plinths.

By comparison, the mahogany frame of the Phyfe family bedstead is distinguished by its lavish rope twist and waterleaf carving and high-quality figured wood. Here, the richest veneers were reserved for the footboard, which presents the broadest expanse to showcase the book-matched grain. Flanking the panel are miniature Doric columns with gilded cast brass capitals and bases. The footposts are firmly grounded by a pair of massive, sculpted paw feet, their legs carved to resemble acanthus leaves. Panels of contrasting veneers with pointed ogival arches into the square sections of the posts assume a verticality aligned to the placement of the footboard and columns. Above these, in ascending order, are reeded then veneered cylindrical components (see detail at left), not unlike those integrated into the turned support pillars on the card and Pembroke tables that Phyfe supplied for James L. Brinckerhoff in 1816 (fig. 81 and Pl. 19) and Dunbar Paul about 1820 (Pl. 27). This feature is also assimilated into the configuration of the headposts, which are a mirrored interpretation of those at the foot of the bedstead.

The articulation of the headposts is yet another indication of the lavishness of the Phyfe bed. Carving and specialized turning were usually reserved for the footposts; the headposts were typically left unadorned so that additional costs were not incurred, for when the bed was fully draped, the headposts were concealed by voluminous textile hangings. For his family's bed, an intimate form associated with the most significant of life's passages—birth, marriage, and death—Duncan Phyfe appears to have spared little expense.

MKB

1. Receipted invoices, Duncan Phyfe to George Brewerton, July [?] 26, 1800 (App. 1.1), and his estate, July 8, 1809, collection of Carswell Rush Berlin.
2. C. King 1937, p. 185.
3. Haygood and Thurlow 2007, pp. 131, 135.

Plate 43

Box Sofa, 1834

DUNCAN PHYFE

Mahogany veneer; secondary woods: ash, white pine
32½ x 81 x 27 in. (82.6 x 205.7 x 68.6 cm)
Collection of Martha Ann Sitterding and Thomas F. Stansfield

Provenance: Maria Franklin Clark Fox (1812–1836) and her husband, George William Fox (b. 1809); her sister Anna L. Clark (Mrs. William J. Roe; 1819–1914); her son William J. Roe, 2nd (1843–1924); his daughter Mary Stuart Roe (Mrs. Lee Woodward Zeigler; 1880–1963); her

The box sofa and klismos side chair made for George and Maria Fox in 1834 represent Duncan Phyfe's earliest documented furniture in the Grecian Plain style. The terms "Grecian" and "present plain style" were used by the English immigrant John Hall to describe furniture in the simplified style of the 1830s in the first of three books he published in Baltimore in 1840 on the household arts.[1] Hall was referring to designs for consoles or scroll supports for pier tables, which he noted could be adapted to other furniture forms. The English designer George Smith in 1826 praised console supports, which he called trusses, whether on sideboards, commodes, or other pieces of furniture, as "admitting of great enrichment."[2] Smith's remarks could also apply to the gorgeous veneers used on the trusses of this sofa, which were called "Grecian scrolls" in the 1847 Phyfe auction sales catalogue.

Phyfe made three sofas for the Foxes, who married in 1833. Part of the wedding furniture, they were a gift from the bride's father, Benjamin Clark, recorded on an 1834 invoice (App. 1.8) as "Sofa and Pillows" and "2 Sofas." Each cost $110,

Plates 227

daughter Audrey W. Ziegler (Mrs. Richard M. Archer-Shee; 1916–1999); her son Malcolm Archer-Shee; [Hudson House Gallery, Funkstown, Maryland]; the present owners.

See also Chapter 3, "George and Maria Clark Fox," pp. 134–36.

and two identical sofas are known today, both in the collection of the owner of this example. The sides and back are of equal height, placing the form under the rubric "square sofa," as described in *The New-York Book of Prices for Manufacturing Cabinet and Chair Work* for 1834. Referred to today as a box sofa because of its foursquare rectilinear shape, the form was produced as early as 1820 (see fig. 89) and remained especially popular in New York until about 1840.

Detail, Plate 43

The Fox sofa exemplifies the reductive geometry of the Grecian Plain style, in which cylinders (arms), cubes (arm terminals), rectangles (legs), squares (feet), and circles (scrolled top rail and applied discs) constitute disparate component parts of a severe form. Here, they are united by the elegance of mahogany veneers in handsomely figured patterns that cover all the exposed wood surfaces. The mahogany is finished to a high luster by numerous coats of transparent varnish in the recently invented technique called French polishing. Metal casters mounted to the bottom of the legs are invisible behind the flat fascia boards that form the feet and provide mobility.

The three sofas were originally covered in black horsehair edged with gilded brass nails. One sofa is described as having loose square hair pillows, or squabs, about five inches thick.[3] This sofa has been handsomely reupholstered in black horsehair for the exhibition and provides a close approximation of the way it looked when it arrived at the Foxes' home on Madison Street, fresh from the Phyfe warehouse, in 1834.

The mahogany klismos side chair (Pl. 44) is one of ten known from the original set of twelve chairs that Phyfe made for Maria Clark Fox, recorded at $10 apiece on the 1834 invoice. The relatively low price of the chair clearly stems from its spare design, one that is both strikingly modern and archaeologically accurate. It's signal feature, the broad deeply curved back, is similar in scale and form to those found on the ancient Greek klismos as depicted in Greek sculpture and vase paintings (see fig. 66). The softly rounded shape of the front edges of the rear stiles, cyma-curved front legs, and bowed front seat rail are nearly identical to those on the French chairs owned by Samuel Foot (Pl. 46) and Stephen Van Rensselaer IV (see fig. 181). The wide crest rail in this example is executed in a fine mahogany veneer to show the beauty of the French polish. The chair is upholstered in black hair cloth, duplicating its first cover.

In its unpretentious elegance and simplified forms, late classical New York furniture bears a resemblance to the "honest" bourgeois German and Austrian Biedermeier styles becoming popular in Europe in the 1820s and 1830s, although the influence on Phyfe furniture by immigrant German craftsmen, whose numbers swelled in New York during the following decade, remains uncertain.

FFB

Plate 44

Klismos Side Chair, 1834

Duncan Phyfe

Mahogany veneer, mahogany; secondary woods: ash, cherry or maple
32½ x 18 x 22 in. (82.6 x 45.7 x 55.9 cm)
Collection of Mr. and Mrs. Robert L. Hammett

Provenance: See Plate 43 through 1914; her grandson William J. Roe 3rd (1875–1945) until 1925; [Half Moon, Cornwall-on-Hudson, New York]; Alfred Cowles (1876–1939), Chicago; his son Alfred Cowles Jr. (1891–1945); his son Richard L. Cowles; the present owners.

44

1. See Hall 1840, pl. XII, p. 25; reprinted in T. G. Smith 1996, pp. v, xxxvii, n. 2.
2. G. Smith 1826, pp. 132–33.
3. Letter from Mary Roe Zeigler to Nancy McClelland, March 17, 1940, Nancy McClelland Papers, Cooper-Hewitt, National Design Museum, New York. The sharp profiles of the upholstery were achieved by the wooden edges produced by the maker of the frame rather than by the stitched edges made by the upholsterer. This approach allowed a greater surface for tacking and created a highly uniform edge while reducing the labor required and the cost of hand stitching. Eight linen twine loops inserted in the rear seat rail and side rails may have been fastened to buttons on the squabs to secure them in place.

Plate 45

Secrétaire à abattant, 1835–47

ATTRIBUTED TO DUNCAN
PHYFE, D. PHYFE & SONS,
OR D. PHYFE & SON

Mahogany veneer, mahogany, gilded brass, looking-glass plate, marble, ivory; secondary woods: white pine, yellow poplar, mahogany
62 x 39¼ x 18⅞ in. (157.5 x 99.7 x 47.9 cm)
The Metropolitan Museum of Art, Purchase, The Manney Collection Gift, 1983 1983.225

Inscribed in center interior drawer: "[B]ought Dec 11 1861/E. P. Chamberlain"; inscribed in right interior drawer: "Purchased of Dauchy & Johnson / Sept. 3, 1873. / C. C. Lee."

Provenance: E. P. Chamberlain, by 1861; [Dauchy & Johnson]; C. C. Lee, by 1873; [M. Finkel, Inc., Philadelphia]; Ramon Ossuna, Washington, D.C.; (Christie's, New York, sale 5370, June 2, 1983, lot 174); The Metropolitan Museum of Art, New York.

References: Christie's, New York, *Important American Furniture, Silver and Decorative Arts*, sale cat., June 2, 1983, lot 174; Peter Hill, "III. Empire Furniture," *Maine Antique Digest*, August 1983, p. 27A; Oswaldo Rodriguez Roque in *Notable Acquisitions, 1983/1984* (New York: The Metropolitan Museum of Art, 1984), pp. 88–89; Davidson and Stillinger 1985, fig. 101; Heckscher et al. 2001, p. 73.

This *secrétaire à abattant*, or French secretary, as it was described in the 1834 New York cabinetmakers' price book, represents the final stylistic iteration of the form as made in the Phyfe workshop beginning around 1815 to 1820 and then produced sporadically until the close of the business in 1847. During this period, the form devolved in terms of its surface decoration from the rich, sumptuously ornamented examples of the 1820s to the chaste beauty of the late Grecian Plain style. Among the earliest versions is a rosewood example (Pl. 37) with gilded and *vert antique* lion's-paw feet, gilded appliqués, and die-stamped brass banding. A *secrétaire à abattant* owned by the Virginia Museum of Fine Arts, Richmond (fig. 1, on page 232), with brass Corinthian capitals and bases and die-stamped inlaid brass banding, might be thought to suggest a link to the earlier style, but its square piers, block feet, and interior arrangement may just as likely indicate a date of manufacture closer to 1830 and link it to the design of the Metropolitan's masterpiece.[1]

The square columnar supports on this example reflect the architectonic massing typical of Phyfe's furniture of the 1830s. With a clearly defined plinth, base, column, and capital, they represent a well-proportioned, abstracted interpretation of the Corinthian order. The partitioning of these components is brought about through an architectural

Alternate view, Plate 45

45

vocabulary—including flat, cavetto, and ovolo moldings, veneered and crossbanded—in a manner consistent with other documented objects from Phyfe's late period (see fig. 111).

The *secrétaire à abattant* is one of several early nineteenth-century case pieces that disguise their desk function within a drawer or behind cylinder or flat-paneled falls. The interior is generally framed by veneered columns with brass capitals and bases that create a broad proscenium ideal for the display of a prized imported porcelain figurine or a silver-gilt inkstand. The flattened arch that spans the area between the columns on the exterior of the example in Plate 37 is brought within on later examples, such as this one, so as not to break the line of the deep cavetto frieze. Here, the interior's mirrored back creates the illusion of a second pair of columns and amplifies the *secrétaire*'s theatrical aspect. Extravagant collectors' cabinets built on the Continent in the late seventeenth century often included columnar stage sets where jewels, medals, documents, and curiosities would be stored and then displayed when the fall front was open.[2] The spring-locked drawers below the mirrored interior of the Metropolitan's exquisitely made *secrétaire* reinforce their intended use for the storage of valuables.

An innovative technical feature distinguishes the later version of the form, known by the 1830s as the French secretary, from those made a decade earlier. Rather than employing an exposed hinge to support the fall front, cabinetmakers used a weighted iron balance hinge cleverly hidden in a cavity between the side of the desk and the interior reserve.[3] With this mechanism and the spring-lock drawers, the Metropolitan's desk features the most sophisticated hardware available in the Phyfe shop, although the balance hinge had been in use in Europe since the late eighteenth century. This type of hinge is illustrated in Thomas Sheraton's design for a "Gentleman's Secretary" in *The Cabinet-Maker and Upholsterer's Drawing Book* (1793),[4] and it is found in desks manufactured by Parisian cabinetmakers such as Jean-Henri Reisner in the 1780s.[5]

The 1834 New York cabinetmakers' book of prices was the first to refer to the "French secretary"; the basic model is specified as having a solid mahogany top.[6] Marble, however, was the preference. The top on the Metropolitan's desk is a replacement modeled after the original on a privately owned example,[7] and the 1847 auction catalogue refers to "1 rosewood French Escritoire . . . marble top."[8] Marble tops were commonly used in this period on pier tables as well as on case furniture. White marble with gray veining, as shown here, was more prevalent than pure white—and more expensive—Italian statuary marble.

MAT

Figure 1. Attributed to Duncan Phyfe. *Secrétaire à abattant*, ca. 1830. Rosewood veneer, gilded gesso, gilded brass, die-stamped brass borders, marble, 63⅞ × 36 × 18½ in. Virginia Museum of Fine Arts, Richmond, Museum Purchase, The Adolph D. and Wilkins C. Williams Fund

1. The Metropolitan Museum and the Virginia Museum of Fine Arts *secrétaires à abattant* are part of a larger group of four related desks, all with square columns at the corners, which exhibit consistencies in construction, proportion, and overall design to support an attribution to a single cabinetmaking shop. The other two examples are owned, respectively, by the Museum of the City of New York and a private collector in New York.
2. Kisluk-Grosheide, Koeppe, and Rieder 2006, pl. 11.
3. This mechanism saw continued use in the Phyfe workshop through the 1840s. The 1847 auction catalogue for the contents of the D. Phyfe & Sons warerooms includes a "splendid French Secretaire with . . . balance hinges." Halliday & Jenkins 1847, p. 10.
4. Sheraton 1793, pp. 409–11, pl. 52.
5. Kisluk-Grosheide, Koeppe, and Rieder 2006, pl. 83.
6. *New-York Book of Prices for Manufacturing Cabinet and Chair Work* (New York, 1834), pp. 30–31.
7. At the time of purchase, the Metropolitan's desk had a replacement mahogany top. Recesses cut for hinges along the back rail suggest that it had been hinged to the upper case to allow the open area behind the frieze to be used as storage space.
8. Halliday & Jenkins 1847, p. 10.

Plate 46

French Chair,
ca. 1837

ATTRIBUTED TO DUNCAN PHYFE

Mahogany veneer, mahogany; secondary woods: mahogany, ash, cherry
31 x 19⅛ x 17 in. (78.7 x 48.6 x 43.2 cm)
The Metropolitan Museum of Art, Purchase, L. E. Katzenbach Fund Gift, 1966 66.221.5

Provenance: Samuel Alfred Foot (1790–1878) and his wife, Jane Campbell Foot (1809–1867); their daughter Euphemia Foot Whittredge (Mrs. Worthington Whittredge; 1837–1920); her daughters Olive W. Whittredge (b. 1875) and Mary Whittredge (Mrs. L. Emery Katzenbach; b. 1879); her sons L. Emery Katzenbach II (1915/16–1999) and William E. Katzenbach (1904–1975); The Metropolitan Museum of Art.

References: McClelland 1939, pp. 272–74, pls. 260, 261; Otto 1965, pp. 102–3, nos. 226, 227, 229; New York 1970, no. 79; Davidson and Stillinger 1985, pp. 78–81; Peck 1996, pp. 238–43; See also Chapter 3, "Samuel Alfred Foot," pp. 137–40.

46

The French chair and taboret in Plates 46 and 47 are from a set of parlor seating furniture made for the New York lawyer Samuel Alfred Foot that family tradition has always attributed to Phyfe. As it exists today at the Metropolitan Museum, the partial suite consists of two Grecian couches (see figs. 176, 177), one the mirror image of the other, two long window seats with scroll standards, four taborets, and four French chairs from a set of at least one dozen, all upholstered in a reproduction of the furniture's original covers.[1] A turn-of-the-century photograph (fig. 1, on page 234) shows one of the couches in its original fabric in the parlor of Hillcrest, the Summit, New Jersey, home of Foot's daughter Euphemia and her husband, Worthington Whittredge (1820–1910), the Hudson River School painter associated with the second generation of these artists. In this image, which also shows a window seat on the stair landing, the pattern of the original upholstery fabric is faintly visible on the couch back but clearer on the seat. Nancy McClelland illustrates the second couch, two of the French chairs, and one of the taborets in her 1939 monograph on Phyfe. That couch also shows, this time more clearly, the large-scale woven design of anthemia and scrolled acanthus

Plates 233

Figure 1. Interior view of the home of Worthington and Euphemia Foot Whittredge. Photograph, ca. 1900. Scholarship files, the American Wing, The Metropolitan Museum of Art

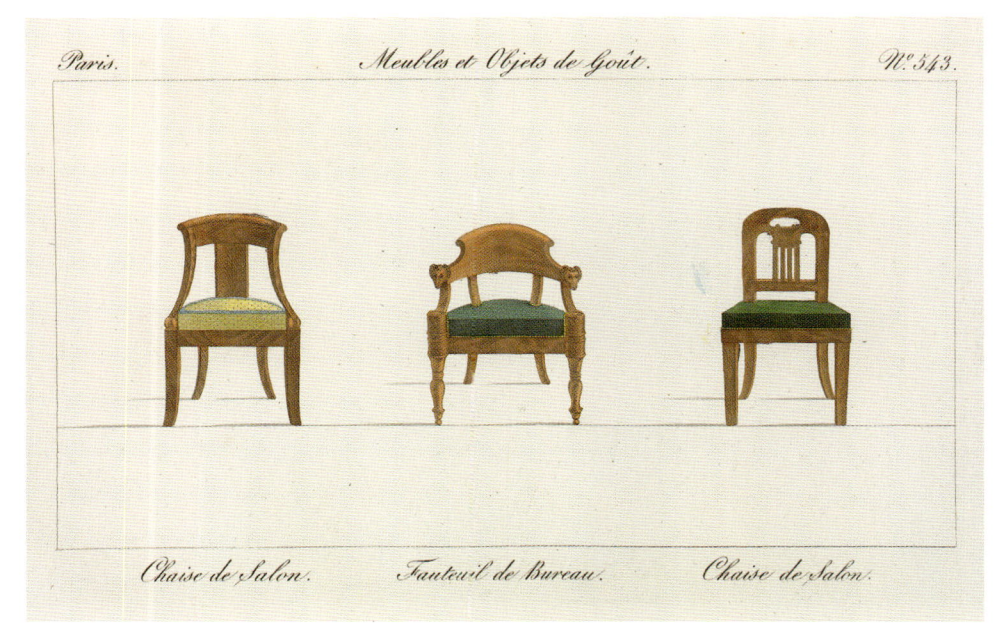

Figure 2. Pierre de La Mésangère. Plate 543, *Collection de meubles et objets de goût* (1822). Colored engraving. The Metropolitan Museum of Art, Harris Brisbane Dick Fund, 1930 30.80.3

leaves on the back, and the original wide borders (see fig. 177). McClelland describes the fabric as crimson mohair with white woven designs, but all remnants of the original had been removed before the furniture came to the Museum and was upholstered with its current reproduction fabric.[2] Recent research points to an original French source for the pattern, which was pirated to England by Morel & Seddon and given the name "English tapestry."[3] This firm may have provided the fabric on the Foot furniture, although the pattern could have been copied by other manufacturers as well.[4]

The chair is of a type known in France as a *chaise gondole*, but called a French chair in New York because it was a derivative of the Gallic form. Characterized by a deep concave back and in-swept stiles that extend forward to the front seat rail, this example also displays the newly revived cabriole or cyma-curved leg often seen in chairs designed during the second Bourbon Restoration of Charles X. With the exception of the front legs, the Foot chairs relate closely to a *chaise de salon* from an 1822 plate in the *Collection de meubles et objets de goût*, by Pierre de La Mésangère (fig. 2, at left), whose hand-colored engravings provided inspiration to the new middle classes on varying aspects of French design, especially furniture and curtains. The New York cabinetmaker Joseph Meeks illustrated a French chair on his 1833 broadside (see fig. 117), proposing to make it either in mahogany with a hair cloth seat for $12—the same price Phyfe charged for the Van Rensselaer chairs in 1835 (see fig. 181)—or in more expensive rosewood with a silk seat for $15.

Taborets like the set of four made for Samuel Foot were an integral part of fashionable American parlors of the 1830s and 1840s. Designs for taborets with curule bases are illustrated in La Mésangère and in Ackermann's *Repository of Arts*, a London fashion journal, before 1810, but New York examples made before 1820 are extremely rare.[5] Five can be documented to the Phyfe shop; one in mahogany for Phyfe's daughter Eliza Phyfe Vail (App. 2.19), and four rosewood and veneered faux-grained rosewood examples from the double parlor at Millford, John L. Manning's South Carolina mansion, completed in 1841 (App. 2.5). The Foot taboret is virtually identical in design and construction to the Vail and Manning examples.

Taborets had a highly specialized meaning and function at the French court of the *ancien régime*, where certain ladies had the *droit de taboret*, or the right to sit on one of these stools in the presence

234   Duncan Phyfe

Plate 47

Taboret, ca. 1837

ATTRIBUTED TO DUNCAN PHYFE

Mahogany veneer, mahogany; secondary wood: ash
15¼ x 20¾ x 15¼ in. (38.7 x 52.7 x 38.7 cm)
The Metropolitan Museum of Art, Purchase, L. E. Katzenbach Fund Gift, 1966 66.221.7

Provenance: See Plate 46.

References: See Plate 46.

of the queen. This honor initially was bestowed only on royalty, but eventually it was extended to all the ladies of the queen's household and then to the wives of other nobles and government officials.[6] By the time the taboret was revived in nineteenth-century American parlors, however, it had become a convenient, yet elegant, form of occasional seating. References to taborets occur with increasing frequency in New York household auction advertisements in the late 1830s and 1840s, such as the one that appeared in the *New-York Commercial Advertiser* of April 22, 1838, for, among other things, an "assortment of elegant furniture consisting of fashionable rosewood French chairs, sofas, divans, and tabarets with ornamental crimson covers, the whole en suite."[7] A set like this could easily have included a dozen or more chairs, pairs of sofas and divans, and four or more taborets, as suggested by the four surviving examples from the Foot and Millford parlor suites.

FFB PMK

1. A fifth taboret stool remains with a direct descendant. The chairs have the incised Roman numerals V, IX, X, XI on the inside back seat rails.
2. See McClelland 1939, pp. 273, 274, pls. 260, 261.
3. See H. Roberts 2001, pp. 34–35, figs. 29, 30. The design is attributed to the Paris weaver Henry Aîné. Four motifs—the central design, round medallion, and two of the border patterns—appear on a chair by Jacob-Desmalter et Cie.
4. For the central anthemion on the couch seat and back, the circular medallion on the arm, and the border on the front seat rail, see F. Montgomery 1984, p. 103. We are grateful to Thomas Gordon Smith for sharing with us his research on this fabric and for providing the references in the preceding note.
5. La Mésangère 1802–31, pl. 201 (1806). The Ackermann plate is shown in Agius 1984, p. 42, pl. 5.
6. Ebenezer Cobham Brewer, *Dictionary of Phrase and Fable* (Philadelphia, 1898), online edition published May 2000 by Bartleby.com.
7. Another reference in the March 26, 1840, edition of the *New-York Commercial Advertiser* refers to the contents of a house at 25 Mercer Street, offering for sale household furniture "made by Ponsot & Shipman consisting of a parlor set of fashionable rosewood chairs with cushion backs; couches with large square pillows; taborets, and music seat—the whole en suite, covered with fine drab cloth, with border, and silk twisted cord edge."

Plate 48

Pier Table, 1837–40

D. Phyfe & Sons

Mahogany veneer, mahogany, looking-glass plate; secondary woods: maple, yellow poplar, white pine
35½ x 41⅜ x 16⅛ in. (90.2 x 105.1 x 41 cm), without marble top
Collection of Virginia A. Gould

Attached to the inside of the rear rail is the trade card for D. Phyfe & Sons (see fig. 29).

Provenance: See Plate 24 through 1973; her granddaughter Virginia A. Gould.

Reference: McClelland 1939, p. 160, pls. 111, 112.

Designated for the pier wall, the expanse between two windows, the pier table was conceived as an integral component of the interior architecture. The form evolved on the Continent and was transmitted to Britain during the final quarter of the seventeenth century. In America, while it was largely unknown prior to the mid-1700s, it persisted well into the nineteenth century.[1]

During the eighteenth century, a distinct variant of the pier table, the sideboard table, emerged. Intended for the display of silver, porcelains, and glass, it was used as well for the service of food and drink. Over time, with the addition of drawers and cupboards, it evolved into the sideboard. Tables of this type were often termed a slab table in the eighteenth century, a reference to its stone top. Functionally, the earliest slab tables were more closely aligned to the nineteenth-century pier table.

The pier table is first cited in the New York cabinetmakers' price book in 1796 and continued to be listed through the final edition of 1834. By the late 1810s the form had become synonymous with the ornamented Grecian style, with a marble top deemed requisite and the finest examples accented by matching columnar supports. An innovation dating from this period was the addition of a rear panel that housed an imported looking-glass plate. The latter was intended as a complement to the large looking glass customarily attached to the architectural pier above the table. When viewed as a whole the ensemble gave the impression that the entire wall was mirrored, which, in turn, enlivened the room by creating the impression of a lighter and more spacious interior.

Invoices from the Phyfe shop indicate that pier tables were commissioned both singly and in pairs. They also provide comparative values for pier tables and related forms. For instance, in 1822, Robert Donaldson paid Duncan Phyfe $100 each for a center table (Pl. 32) and a pair of card tables. Donaldson's bill also lists a pier table priced at $120, which it is reasonable to assume was made en suite with the other tables and probably was close in appearance to the table in Plate 38.

In general, pier tables in the Grecian style of the late teens were more expensive than center, card, and even dining tables, in part because of the added expense of the marble top and columns, the mirror plate, and gilded or lacquered cast-brass ornaments. A similar price relationship extends into the mid-1830s, when Phyfe charged Benjamin Clark $130 apiece for a pair of pier tables (see fig. 110) and $110 for a flip-top center, or loo, table (see fig. 170).

This pier table, originally one of a pair, which descended from William and Eliza Phyfe Vail, espouses the final expression of Neoclassical furniture from the Phyfe shop, now referred to as the Grecian Plain style.[2] The aesthetic is defined by an overall simplicity, with brilliant planar surfaces and elegant scroll supports. By contrast with the earlier expression, the bottom plinth is substantially reduced, essentially corresponding to the configuration of the scroll supports and back panel, and thereby creating the impression of an architectural console.

While the specific date of manufacture for the Vail tables is not recorded, they are closely related to the pier and sideboard tables from the Clark, Stirling, and Manning commissions of 1834, 1836, and 1841 (see figs. 110, 174, and 194). The description of a "mahogany pier Table, white marble top, French plate glass, scroll standards" in the Halliday & Jenkins auction catalogue confirms that the aesthetic persisted in the Phyfe repertoire through 1847, when the surplus stock of the Fulton Street shop was vended. Unfortunately, the original tops on this table and its mate, also presumably white marble, have been replaced with mahogany boards (removed for this photograph to show the interior).

MKB

1. On the pier table, see Barquist 1992, p. 80, and Vincent 2008.
2. While this pair of tables descended in the Vail family, it is not inconceivable that they could have belonged to Duncan and Rachel Phyfe and are perhaps the "2 Pier Tables" listed in 1854 by the estate appraisers in the second-floor "Large Front Room" of 193 Fulton Street; McClelland 1939, p. 335.

48

Plate 49

Lotus-Back Side Chair, 1837–40

D. Phyfe & Sons

Mahogany, mahogany veneer; secondary woods: ash, yellow poplar
32¾ x 17½ x 21¾ in. (83.2 x 44.5 x 55.2 cm)
Collection of Glorianna H. Gibbon

Provenance: See Plate 41.

Reference: McClelland 1939, pp. 119–21, 126, pl. 109.

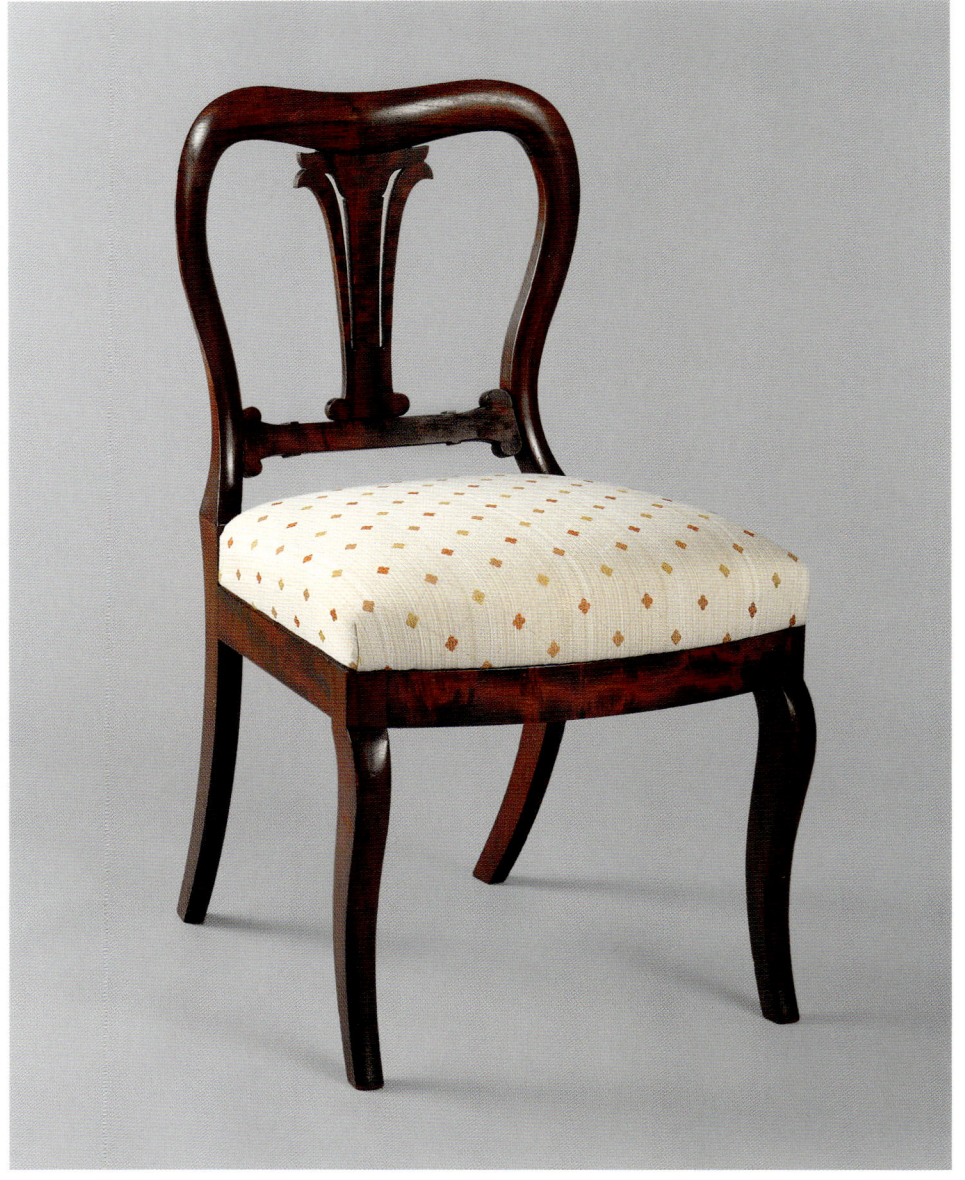

49

Lotus-back side chairs like those shown in Plates 49 and 50 are among Phyfe's most characteristic designs of the 1830s and 1840s. Nancy McClelland was the first Phyfe historian to illustrate the set of sixteen lotus-back chairs that descended in the family of Eliza Phyfe Vail and featured a veneered banister with the shape of a lotus blossom silhouetted at the top.[1] The chair in Plate 49 is from this set. Its sculpted stiles and yoked crest rail recall the serpentine curved backs of mid-eighteenth-century chairs in the Queen Anne style. This sculptural effect is heightened by the large voids on either side of the banister and the transition of the squared edges of the back legs into a crisply modeled profile that sinuously loops around the entire back. Devoid of carving, the Vail chairs have been relied on nonetheless in the attribution to the Phyfe workshop of comparable chairs with carved splats, including the example from the Metropolitan Museum shown in Plate 50.[2] While both models have similar yoke-shaped crests, cabriole front legs, and a curved front rail, the banister of the Vail chair is significantly attenuated and pushes the connecting stay rail much closer to the seat.

The lotus is one of a limited selection of motifs derived from Egyptian architecture and decorative arts to be used in early nineteenth-century New York furniture.[3] It was incorporated into banister designs in a number of English design books, most notably for drawing-room chairs in Thomas King's *Cabinet-Maker's Sketch Book* and J. C. Loudon's *Encyclopaedia* (fig. 1, opposite). The Loudon drawing in particular expresses the vitality of the carved lotus blossom, as seen in the Metropolitan chair, in which the various elements

238 Duncan Phyfe

Plate 50

Lotus-Back Side Chair, 1835–40

Attributed to Duncan Phyfe or D. Phyfe & Sons

Rosewood, rosewood veneer; secondary woods: ash, yellow poplar
32¾ x 17⅜ x 18¼ in. (83.2 x 44.1 x 46.4 cm)
The Metropolitan Museum of Art, Purchase, The Edgar J. Kaufmann Foundation Gift, 1968 68.202.1

Provenance: Descended in the Bloomfield family of New Jersey; [George Scheiner and Son, Newark, New Jersey]; The Metropolitan Museum of Art.

Reference: New York 1970, pl. 77.

50

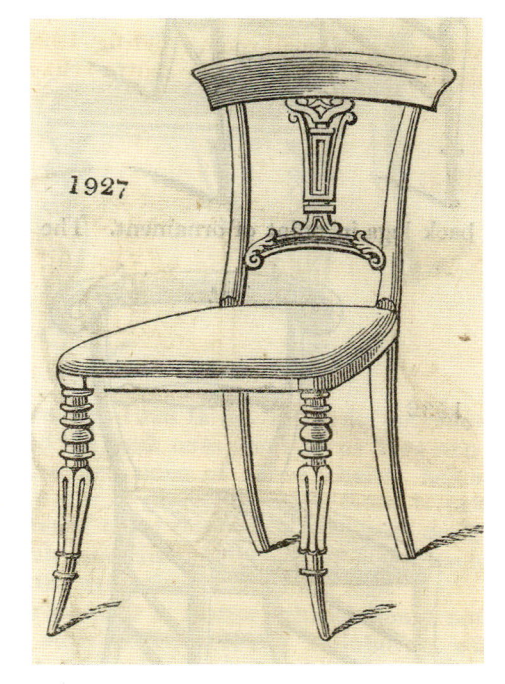

Figure 1. John Claudius Loudon. Illustration from *An Encyclopaedia of Cottage, Farm and Villa Architecture and Furniture* (1835). The Metropolitan Museum of Art, Harris Brisbane Dick Fund, 1924 24.66.110

are unified through the repetition of the carved scrolls on the banister and stay rail, and the flat applied molding that outlines the seat rail and back.

Regarding the evolution of this form, the veneered type owned by Eliza Phyfe Vail was likely contemporaneous with the carved version. The Vail chairs were part of a larger suite of parlor furniture that included a pair of couches (see fig. 185) and a pair of pier tables (Pl. 48), one of which has a D. Phyfe & Sons trade card attached to its frame that dates the group to between 1837 and 1840. Veneered banisters appear in Phyfe's late work, including a set of side chairs with Gothic details ordered by John L. Manning for the drawing rooms at Millford in 1841 (Pl. 62). A later variation of the lotus-banister chair, probably from the Phyfe shop, with a balloon-shaped seat and delicate cabriole legs (see fig. 136), also suggests

Plates   239

the influence of the Old French styles of Louis XIV and Louis XV on New York furniture of the late 1830s and early 1840s.   MAT

1. The chair in Plate 49 is marked "XV" on the inside of the rear seat rail.
2. The chair is marked "II" on the top of the rear seat rail and inscribed in black ink on the underside of the back seat rail: "Property of / Joseph Bloomfield / 1820." Bloomfield (1753–1823) was an officer in the Revolutionary War and the War of 1812 and served as governor of New Jersey and as a member of the U.S. House of Representatives, but died too early to be the original owner of this chair (Lucius Q. C. Elmer, *The Constitution and Government of the Province and State of New Jersey, with Biographical Sketches of the Governors from 1776 to 1845* [Newark. 1872], pp. 114–37). A closely related set of carved-back chairs descended in the family of Benjamin Clark, who presented his daughter, Maria, with a suite of Phyfe parlor furniture following her marriage to George W. Fox in 1834 (Pls. 43, 44).
3. Fennimore 1990, pp. 1190–1201.

Plate 51

Sofa Table, 1837–47

ATTRIBUTED TO D. PHYFE & SONS OR D. PHYFE & SON

Mahogany veneer, mahogany; secondary woods: mahogany, white pine, yellow poplar
30 × 40 × 26 in. (leaves down) (76.2 × 101.6 × 66 cm)
Carswell Rush Berlin, Inc., and Hirschl & Adler Galleries, New York

Reference: Feld and Feld 2001, pp. 64–65 (illustrates and discusses an example that is nearly identical except for the shape of the feet).

By the time this sleek, very modern-looking sofa table was made, the Phyfe shop had been producing this form, an English Regency innovation of the 1790s, for more than a quarter of a century. The earliest known reference to a sofa table is an order, dated July 18, 1801, in the Gillows & Co. *Estimate Sketch Book*, which is accompanied by a drawing of one example with pillar-and-claw standards and drop leaves with rounded corners supported by hinged brackets.[1] Thomas Sheraton had included an image of a sofa table in his *Cabinet Dictionary* of 1803, where it is shown positioned squarely in front of a sofa (fig. 1, below), writing that "the ladies chiefly occupy them to draw, write, or read upon."[2]

Sofa tables appear for the first time in the New York cabinetmakers' price book in 1810, where they are described as having "two turned or square pillars, straight stretcher and four claws," with additional charges if two drawers were added or the cross stretcher was curved. A spare, elegant example of this earliest type, attributed to Phyfe by both the early Phyfe collector Louis Guerineau Myers and the Phyfe historian Nancy McClelland, is in the collection of the Metropolitan Museum. Discussing that very table in the 1929 "Girl Scouts Loan Exhibition" catalogue, Myers reminds us just how anachronistic sofa tables had become: "Sheraton designed them

Figure 1. Thomas Sheraton. Plate 74, *The Cabinet Dictionary* (1803). The Metropolitan Museum of Art, Rogers Fund, 1952 52.519.26

51

to stand in front of a sofa rather than at the back as now used."³ The form remained popular and had become richly ornamented by the late 1810s, as indicated by the survival of four ambitious sofa tables with canted corners and either sculptural griffin or winged-caryatid supports, some or all of which were likely made in the Phyfe shop.⁴ Also probably by Phyfe, and dating to the early to mid-1820s, is the sofa table (whereabouts unknown) that appears in a photograph of the parlor in the Summit, New Jersey, home of Isabel Bronson, daughter of Robert Donaldson (see fig. 167).

The last known New York cabinetmakers' price book, published in 1834, continues to include a heading for a sofa table. Some of the refinements that appear on the present table appear under this heading as "extras," including veneering the top and "making the flies as rule joints to show as brackets in front of the table." On this table the brackets have precisely matched cuts of mahogany veneer and Phyfe's typical rimmed convex discs (see fig. 116). The quality of the crotch-mahogany veneers applied to the top is also truly extraordinary and lends credence to the Phyfe family's long-standing claim that the finest-quality mahogany logs and crotches imported to New York from the Caribbean were referred to as "Phyfe logs."

PMK

1. Zimmerman 1999, pp. 745–46.
2. Sheraton 1803, pl. 74, and 1970 reprint, pp. 305–6.
3. Myers in New York 1929, no. 754. The table is illustrated and discussed in McClelland 1939, p. 153.
4. For the griffin sofa tables, see Christie's, New York, *Fine American Furniture, Silver, Folk Art, and Decorative Arts*, sale cat., October 1, 1988, lot 377, and *The Magazine Antiques* 94, no. 1 (July 1968), p. 58, where an example in the collection of the Museum of Fine Arts, Boston, misattributed to Charles-Honoré Lannuier is shown. Winged-caryatid tables, one in the Bayou Bend Collection, Museum of Fine Arts, Houston, the other in the White House, Washington, D.C., are shown in Zimmerman 1999, p. 744, and Monkman 2000, p. 246.

Plate 52

Dressing Glass or Toy Bureau, 1840–54

D. PHYFE & SON OR
DUNCAN PHYFE

Rosewood, rosewood veneer, looking-glass plate; secondary woods: cherry, mahogany, white pine, yellow poplar
21 x 12½ x 10½ in. (53.3 x 31.8 x 26.7 cm)
Collection of Glorianna H. Gibbon

Inscribed in bottom of top drawer:
"F. PERCY VAIL / APRIL 12 – 1948 / ON THE HOME STRETCH."

Provenance: Possibly Isabella Phyfe Vail Runyon (1834–1901), Sarah Whitlock Vail Mitchell (1836–1899), or Elizabeth Garretson Vail (1839–1871), daughters of Eliza Phyfe Vail (1801–1890) and her husband, William Vail Jr. (1802–1875); their nephew Frederick Percy Vail (1861–1948); his daughter Virginia Vail (Mrs. J. Bertram Howell; 1897–1973); her daughter the present owner.

Reference: McClelland 1939, p. 125, pl. 108.

Duncan Phyfe supplied his affluent clientele with tall screen dressing glasses or dressing bureaus with "swing" glasses as adjuncts to suites of rosewood or mahogany bedroom furniture; for most other types of looking glasses, they would patronize the emporium of a specialist manufacturer or retailer.

As early as 1729, James Foddy, "Looking Glass-Maker, late from London," publicized dressing glasses "of sundry sorts, in Glass-Frames, Glass and Gold Frames, Gold Frames Jappan'd, Wallnutt and Olive Wood Frames" in *The New-York Gazette*. In the 1760s, Sidney Breese advertised that he imported from London "Dressing Glasses" and, curiously, "Undressing Glasses." Fashioned as an adjustable mirror or, alternatively, as a miniature chest with the glass firmly secured between two uprights, the dressing glass was designed for use on a chest of drawers or dressing table and served as a convenient receptacle for jewelry and personal items such as cosmetics and patches, fragrant essences, razors and shaving brushes, powders, combs, and ornaments for the hair. By the time Duncan Phyfe made this example, the form was on the wane, as Eliza Leslie observed in 1840: "The small movable looking-glasses, standing on feet, are much out of favour for dressing tables, as they scarcely show more than your head, and are easily upset."[1]

The present dressing glass descended in the family of Duncan Phyfe's daughter Eliza Phyfe Vail, with a traditional history that it was made for his grandchildren in the years immediately following his retirement.[2] A related example was recorded in another branch of the family by Phyfe's earliest biographer, Ernest F. Hagen. Following the death of Phyfe's eldest son, Michael, in 1836, his three orphaned children went to live with their grandparents on Fulton Street. In his "Memorandum" Hagen recalls his visit to the home of Michael Phyfe's son, Duncan, and granddaughter Emma: "Mrs. [Emma] Purdy showed me a toy bureau with glass which he made for her when a little girl."[3] As Hagen notes in his account, the form may have been intended as a toy made for a child. However, it had the advantage that once the child reached adulthood it could then be used as a dressing glass.

The Vail dressing glass is probably similar to the "toy bureau" that Hagen noted. With its turned feet and rounded corners, it has unadorned simplicity and uncomplicated lines that define bedroom case furniture produced in the mid-nineteenth century. But Phyfe, with his eye for refinement, enriched the façade, with the rosewood veneers that became increasingly popular in the 1840s. MKB

1. Gottesman 1938, p. 133; and Leslie 1840, p. 300. For the evolution of the dressing glass, see Barquist 1992, p. 354.
2. McClelland (1939, p. 125) illustrates a mahogany dressing glass of nearly identical form, which she refers to as a shaving stand, noting that "Duncan Phyfe himself made this stand for his grandchildren after retiring from business." She also states that the dressing glass in Plate 52 belonged to F. Percy Vail. The current whereabouts of the mahogany dressing glass in not known.
3. Hagen [1907], reprinted in McClelland 1939, p. 317. Emma Purdy's memory may have been faulty, or Hagen may have incorrectly stated that the dressing glass was a gift to her, as she was not born until a year after her great-grandfather's death. The present location of the Purdy dressing glass is not known. The mirror is backed by period wallpaper, which appears to be original. A second rosewood dressing glass of nearly identical design but with an extra tier of drawers has descended in the family of James Phyfe, son and one-time business partner of his father, Duncan.

52

Plate 53

Drop-Leaf Table, ca. 1840–47

D. PHYFE & SON

Mahogany veneer; mahogany, secondary woods: white pine, mahogany, yellow poplar
28⅜ x 20 x 18⅞ in. (30⅞ in. with flaps open) (72.1 x 50.8 x 47.9 cm)
The Rick Patrick Trust

Provenance: Mary Phyfe Whitlock (b. 1795) and her husband, Sidney B. Whitlock (1794–1849); their son Duncan P. Whitlock (b. ca. 1826) and his wife, Margaret P. Ronaldson Whitlock (b. ca. 1827); their son James P. Whitlock (b. ca. 1871) and his wife, Mary H. Whitlock (b. ca. 1872); their daughter Helen W. York (b. ca. 1903);[1] (Sotheby's, sale 7756, January 17, 2002, lot 408); The Rick Patrick Trust.

References: McClelland 1939, pp. 118–19, pl. 102; Sotheby's, New York, *Important Americana*, sale cat., January 17, 2002, lot 408.

This table is forever linked to the Phyfe family through a photograph of the wedding of Duncan Phyfe Whitlock to Margaret P. Ronaldson in 1860 (see fig. 56) set in the parlor of the Mitchell Mansion in Southbury, Connecticut, a grand Greek Revival house built in 1827–29 (see fig. 31), which Phyfe presented to his daughter Mary Phyfe Whitlock in 1843.[2]

The defining feature of this small elegant drop-leaf table is the trestle base with paired scroll supports. Intended to resemble attenuated lyres, the form is a remarkably abstract and perhaps the closest in design to Austrian Biedermeier as any piece documented to D. Phyfe & Son.[3] The delicate nature of the lyre supports is attested by the table's inherent instability and the fact that the proper left support is broken at the top. Disc-shaped applied bosses, a trademark of Phyfe furniture in the Grecian Plain style, appear in profusion, on the scrolls and at the out-turned ends of the rectangular stretcher and the scrolled trestle feet, which correlate quite closely with those on the Millford nesting tables (Pl. 65).

As exemplified here, D. Phyfe & Son was lavish in the use of beautifully figured mahogany veneer, a characteristic of most furniture owned by the Phyfe children. Of particular note are the sunburst panels on the rectangular plaque below the lyres. The prominent tiger-stripe crossbanding on the lower edge of the drawer and the small-scale crotch veneer that surrounds it also appear on a crib that descended in the family of James D. Phyfe (App. 2.20).

The Whitlock table represents a form otherwise unknown in Phyfe's documented oeuvre. Although the table never had casters, its lightweight construction permitted easy relocation as entertainment required. Its diminutive scale and shallow drop leaves distinguish it from Pembroke and breakfast tables. As suggested by its function in the wedding photograph, perhaps it is best described as a type of serving or tea table. There are eight "tea tables" cited in the inventory of D. Phyfe and Son's wareroom in 1847.[4] Rather than the fly rails usually found on New York drop-leaf tables, a mahogany loper can be drawn out from a box built under the top through an opening in each side apron to support the leaves. This type of loper support system maintains the pristine cubic geometry of the upper frame unbroken even when the table leaves are raised.

MAT

1. Provenance from James P. Whitlock to Helen W. York is suggested by a letter dated April 15, 1950, written by Whitlock to his daughter Helen, which accompanied a linen press that was sold at auction in 2003 (James D. Julia, Fairfield, Maine, *Winter Antiques & Fine Arts Auction*, January 11, 2003, lot 90). That the table came from the York family is also mentioned in the provenance offered by Sotheby's (*Important Americana*, sale cat., January 17, 2002, p. 167).
2. Prior to moving to Southbury, the Whitlocks lived in Brooklyn; Mary's husband, Sidney, maintained a ship chandler store on South Street in New York City (*New York City Directory*, 1842, p. 343).
3. Ottomeyer, Schröder, and Winters 2006, pls. 1.16, 1.17.
4. Halliday & Jenkins 1847, pp. 3–6.

53

Plate 54

Checker Stand, 1840–47

D. Phyfe & Son

Rosewood, rosewood and satinwood veneers; secondary wood: mahogany
29½ x 20¾ x 16¾ in. (74.9 x 52.7 x 42.6 cm)
Collection of Mrs. H. Pinckney Phyfe and Mr. and Mrs. Henry P. Phyfe Jr.

Provenance: James D. Phyfe (1797–1878); his son, William Henry Pinckney Phyfe (b. 1853); his son Henry Pinckney Phyfe (1911–2003); the present owners.

With a removable top that flips over to reveal a checkerboard with alternating squares of rosewood and satinwood veneer, this small stand is one of several heirlooms that descended in the family of Duncan Phyfe's son James. Among these family treasures are also Phyfe's tool chest (see frontispiece on page 22) and a child's crib (App. 2.20), whose clean, minimalist lines suggest that it too was made between 1840 and 1847, when James D. Phyfe was in partnership with his father. The tool chest and these two pieces of furniture had histories of intimate personal use by Duncan Phyfe himself and by members of his immediate family that make them particularly compelling.

While James Phyfe may originally have owned this checker stand, it seems that his father enjoyed playing checkers or chess as a pastime as well. Listed in the inventory of the contents of Duncan Phyfe's Fulton Street house, compiled after his death in 1854, was "1 checker board" in the front office on the first floor, while in a small front room on the second floor stood a "Mahogany checker stand" valued at one dollar—half the worth assigned to the mahogany dressing bureau in that same room. Eight mahogany "French Chairs" in the front parlor, a standard Grecian Plain style model still highly fashionable in the 1840s, were valued at $12, or $1.50 each, so it is not inconceivable that Duncan Phyfe's checker stand, at only fifty cents less, was also in this mode and was similar in appearance to the present example.

Straightforward and utilitarian in overall design, this checker stand fits well within D. Phyfe & Son's late Grecian Plain style, which is characterized by the use of highly figured and strategically placed rosewood or mahogany veneers and a clean, simple structural clarity. The shallow satinwood well beneath the removable top is flanked by two partitioned channels that hold the opposing players' checkers. Chess pieces could have been stored in the center well or in the single drawer that pulls out from one end. The top has a raised lip around the perimeter to keep the game pieces from sliding off the checkerboard or, perhaps, to hold a tea service or writing implements on the plain rosewood veneered side. The stout tapering pillar that supports the upper frame is nicely veneered with rosewood, even along its chamfered edges. The scrolled feet terminate in turned bosses that are identical to those applied to the scrolled ends of the Phyfe family crib. The delicacy of these classically inspired feet seems somewhat at odds with the support pillar and the chunky faceted cap on the plinth below, which are more elemental—even Gothic—in character. This overlaying or mixing of Gothic Revival details with classical elements was fairly typical of New York furniture from the late 1830s and 1840s. Phyfe, according to his surviving documented furniture, also engaged in this practice.   PMK

Alternate view, Plate 54

54

Millford (Plates 55–65)

John L. Manning's extensive patronage of D. Phyfe & Son to furnish Millford, his Greek Revival mansion in Pine Woods, South Carolina, resulted in the largest body of documented Phyfe furniture known today. In 1841–42, Manning placed an extensive order with Phyfe that includes the examples discussed below. For more on the furnishings at Millford, see Chapter 3, "Millford," pages 144–52.

Plate 55

Grecian Bedstead, 1841

D. Phyfe & Sons

Rosewood veneer; secondary woods: ash, white pine
42 x 95½ x 61¼ in. (without casters)
(106.7 x 242.6 x 155.6 cm)
The Metropolitan Museum of Art, Purchase, Leo and Frances Bretter Gift, 2006 2006.399a–r

Provenance: John L. Manning (1816–1889) and his first wife, Susan Hampton Manning (1816–1845), then his second wife, Sally Blande Clarke Manning (ca. 1829–1885); their daughter Ellen Clarke Manning Williams (Mrs. David Rogerson Williams III; 1857–1930); her daughter Sally Bland Williams Metts (Mrs. Walter A. Metts Jr.; 1894–1981); her daughter Sally Bland Metts Wilson (Mrs. William B. Wilson; 1929–2004); her son J. Nicholas Wilson; The Metropolitan Museum of Art.

On June 2, 1841, D. Phyfe & Son issued a bill of lading to John L. Manning specifying a "French" and two "Grecian" bedsteads, one full size and the other a single (App. 1.9).[1] That this example is fashioned of the more expensive rosewood rather than mahogany, together with the price book description, suggests that it may indeed be the more costly "Grecian" version. Whether described as French or Grecian, this Gallic form, known also today as a sleigh bed, was, by 1850, proclaimed predominant by A. J. Downing: "The high four-post bedstead, with curtains, still common in England, is almost entirely laid aside in the United States for the French bedstead."[2]

Among those with an interest in the latest French Empire furniture designs, the "French bedstead" had emerged in New York by 1810 as an alternative to the common English-style high- and low-post bedstead. That same year the phrase appears in the New York cabinetmakers' book of prices, offering the first significant addition to the volume's roster of bedsteads since its inception in 1796.[3] By contrast to the customary British forms, which had long dominated America's Anglo society, the introduction of the French bedstead is attributed to the arrival of numbers of Frenchmen in the city, beginning with those fleeing the Revolution in 1789, followed by a wave in response to the slave insurrections in Saint-Domingue (now Haiti), and continuing with the reign of Napoleon I and the aftermath of the Napoleonic Wars.

One distinction between the Anglo and Gallic presentations was the bedstead's placement in the bedchamber. Ideally, the former was positioned in the center of the room, the headboard flush with the wall, which not only made it more prominent but also allowed for a greater circulation of air. By contrast, the French bedstead was placed lengthwise, its sides parallel to the wall or, alternatively, it was set within a specially designed alcove. Another divergence was their system for supporting bed curtains. Whereas the Anglo versions typically have flat testers from which the curtains are suspended, the French bedstead is distinguished by its use of a circular or semicircular canopy or crown either integral to the bed frame or suspended above from a hook in the ceiling, as was the case with the Manning bedstead. In 1816, Duncan Phyfe supplied James L. Brinckerhoff with a "Canopee Bedstead" with curving arms that spring from the tall back posts that supported the now-missing canopy (App. 2.3).

In the 1834 New York price book, the latest edition known, two models of the French bedstead are listed along with a new and closely related form, the "Grecian Bedstead." The differences between them, while difficult to discern, must nevertheless have been considerable judging from their base labor costs—the French beds at $4 and $8.50 apiece, as compared with their Grecian counterpart at $25. The price book does little to clarify these differences. It describes "French Bedstead, No. 2" and the "Grecian Bedstead" as having the same dimensions, "Six feet six inches long, three feet wide," and both are ornamented with "eagles' heads." Perhaps the distinction is

55

that the ends of the French bedsteads are more vertically oriented, with either turned or simple square posts with scrolled ends, while the Grecian option features ogee posts with scrolled ends and conforming veneered end panels like those on the present example.[4]

MKB

1. Bill of lading from D. Phyfe & Son to John L. Manning, June 2, 1841, Williams-Chesnut-Manning Papers, South Caroliniana Library, University of South Carolina, Columbia.
2. Downing 1850, pp. 415, 431.
3. The earliest edition of the New York cabinetmakers' price book (1796) records four types of bed frames, "cot bedstead," "Low Post Bedstead," "Field Bedstead," and "High Post Bedstead" (*The Journeymen Cabinet and Chairmakers' New-York Book of Prices* [New York, 1796], pp. 75–76).
4. New-York Society of Journeymen Cabinet Makers, *The New-York Book of Prices for Manufacturing Cabinet and Chair Work* (New York, 1834), pp. 120–26.

Plate 56

Cheval Glass, 1841

D. Phyfe & Son

Mahogany veneer, mahogany, looking-glass plate, brass; secondary wood: white pine
85 × 48 × 25 in. (215.9 × 121.9 × 63.5 cm)
Collection of Mr. and Mrs. Richard Kelly

Provenance: See Plate 55 through 1885 and 1889; by descent to Samuel Manning; [David Petrovsky]; (Northeast Auctions, Manchester, New Hampshire, April 3, 2005, lot 1226); the present owners.

Reference: Northeast Auctions, Manchester, New Hampshire, *Important New York Furniture and Decorative Arts: The Richard and Beverly Kelly Collection,* sale cat., April 3, 2005, lot 1226.

Period sources use the terms "screen" or "horse dressing glass" for monumental mirrors of this type, the word "horse" referring to the frame, constructed of a trestle base and two uprights between which the swinging glass is hung. Thomas Sheraton described the form as denoting "a kind of tall dressing-glass suspended between two pillars and claws [which could] be turned back or forward to suit the person who dresses at them." Somewhat later Rudolph Ackermann elaborated, noting that these "moving glasses are now generally introduced in the sleeping-apartments and dressing-rooms of our nobility and persons of distinction."[1]

In the United States, the production of looking glasses was largely within the domain of specialist frame makers rather than artisans employed in the cabinet trade. Because American craftsmen lacked the skills and facilities to produce silvered plate glass of the smoothness, clarity, and scale required, the framer relied on English and continental shops to grind and polish the surface and to apply the tin and mercury. Duncan Phyfe and his contemporaries made use of such imported mirrored glass in their furniture throughout the early nineteenth century. The 1847 Halliday & Jenkins' auction catalogue of the contents of the Phyfe warerooms cites a number of pieces that incorporated "French plate glass," including toilet, dressing, and pier tables, bureaus, sideboards and wardrobes, and "cheval glasses," a stylish French term for the more prosaic "horse dressing glass" described by Sheraton.[2]

The first references to the cheval glass in America occur in New York City. Perhaps the earliest of these is in the guise of a beautifully engraved paper label that the French émigré cabinetmaker Charles-Honoré Lannuier began to use about 1812. There the architectonic attributes of the form are fully evident in the columnar supports, the architrave topped by a pediment, and the tympanum framing a representation of the American eagle. Lannuier's influence may well account for the introduction of the "screen dressing glass" in the 1817 New York price book.[3]

Exactly when Duncan Phyfe first began to produce this imposing and expensive form is unknown, but it was probably sometime during the 1810s. This cheval glass is one of at least two "swing" glasses—referring to the way the mirrors pivot in their frames—that D. Phyfe & Son supplied to John L and Susan Hampton Manning in 1841 for Millford. They are the only examples of these glasses that can be securely documented to the Phyfe firm.[4] The Halliday & Jenkins auction catalogue lists four examples among the remaining stock, one finished in mahogany, the others fashioned of rosewood, the most magnificent being lot 323, "1 large rosewood splendid cheval Glass, 60in by 30in 7 feet high, OG cornice, back lined with purple silk."[5]

The finest furniture to emerge from the Phyfe shop in the 1830s and 1840s is characterized by the brilliant figured veneers that define the otherwise

56

understated aesthetic of the Grecian Plain style. Several components that make up the Manning cheval glass are shared with other furniture forms. The trestle base and stepped block feet with convex, or pulvinated, fronts, for example, are a configuration he employed for both pier and sofa tables (see Pls. 48 and 51), while the tapered, square columnar uprights and entablature are like those features on a mahogany wardrobe with a mirrored door with an "OG" (ogee) cornice of an identical profile (App. 2.8). Boldly architectonic, this cheval glass perfectly complemented the scale of the mansion's monumental Greek Revival interior architecture.

MKB

1. Sheraton (1803) 1970, vol. 1, pp. 202–3, 255–56; and Agius 1984, p. 178.
2. Halliday & Jenkins 1847, pp. 11, 12, 16.
3. Kenny, Bretter, and Leben 1998, pp. 81–82, 123. For other early New York examples, see Weidman 1984, p. 146, and Talbott 1995, p. 137.
4. Bill of lading from D. Phyfe & Son, to John L. Manning, June 2, 1841, Williams-Chesnut-Manning Papers, South Caroliniana Library, University of South Carolina, Columbia. The second cheval glass with a Manning history is now in a private collection.
5. Halliday & Jenkins 1847, lots 235, 263, 265, 323.

Detail, Plate 56

Plate 57

Nightstand, 1841

D. PHYFE & SON

Rosewood, mahogany veneer, brass, marble; secondary woods: mahogany, white pine, yellow poplar
Height, 31⅛ in. (79.1 cm); diam., 16⅜ in. (41.6 cm)
The Metropolitan Museum of Art, Purchase, Leo and Frances Bretter Gift, 2006 2006.401a, b

Provenance: See Plate 55.

Nightstands, or *nécessaires*, washstands, basin stands, and bidets are all forms used in American bedchambers and dressing rooms prior to the advent of the private bathroom that signals society's growing recognition of the importance of personal hygiene. Ideally the chamber pot would be kept close at hand, so underneath the bed was a logical and frequent accommodation. A more fastidious alternative entailed removing it from the open and storing this convenience away in a nightstand.[1] Thomas Webster, in his edifying *Encyclopaedia of Domestic Economy*, supplies a description of the nightstand, as well as an illustration: "These conveniences are frequently made in the form of pedestals, either round or square; sometimes with a marble top . . . which have a shelf in the middle."[2] Webster's entry and image relate closely to the design for a "Pillar Commode" that Robert Conner included in the slightly earlier *Cabinet Maker's Assistant*. Conner's illustration, far more informative than Webster's, shows the cupboard with its door ajar to reveal a chamber pot on the shelf, along with a basin and ewer stored directly below. Conner's term, "Pillar Commode," of course refers to its cylinder shape, which represents a segment of a classical column.[3]

Not surprisingly perhaps, the nightstand is a little-known and seldom discussed form in Duncan Phyfe's or any other early nineteenth-century American cabinetmaker's oeuvre. Halliday & Jenkins vended six of them at the dispersal of the Phyfe warehouse in 1847, and the appraisers of Phyfe's estate recorded a "Mahogany Night Stand . . . 1.00" in the "Middle Front Garret Room" at 193 Fulton Street. The Manning example is one of "2 night stands" cited in the June 2, 1841, bill of lading from D. Phyfe & Son.[4] In contrast to the nightstands recorded by Halliday & Jenkins and the estate appraisers, the Manning example is made of coopered pine boards veneered with rosewood and must therefore have been part of the Mannings' own bedroom suite, the most elaborate and expensive at Millford, where the surviving rosewood bedstead (Pl. 55), a basin stand (Pl. 58), and a large two-door wardrobe (App. 2.9) also once stood.   MKB

57

1. Webster 1845, p. 302, and Garrett 1990, pp. 88, 102, 135–36.
2. Webster 1845, pp. 302–3.
3. Conner 1842, p. 6.
4. McClelland 1939, p. 336; and bill of lading from D. Phyfe & Son to John L. Manning, June 2, 1841, Williams-Chesnut-Manning Papers, South Caroliniana Library, University of South Carolina, Columbia.

Plate 58

Basin Stand, 1841

D. Phyfe & Son

Rosewood veneer, mahogany; gilded brass, marble; secondary woods: yellow poplar, white pine, ash
34¾ x 38⅞ x 20½ in. (88.3 x 98.7 x 52.1 cm)
Collection of Richard Hampton Jenrette

Provenance: See Plate 55 through 1930; Mary Thompson Clark (d. 1923); her nephew Emory W. Clark (1868–1958); his son William R. Clark (1905–1983); his children, Emory W. Clark II, Carolyn Clark Fulcher, William Clark; the present owner.

This basin stand is very likely one of the four that were packed in crates and shipped to John L. Manning by D. Phyfe & Son on June 2, 1841. Listed among these pieces on the bill of lading (App. 1.9) were two "scroll Bason stands," an obvious reference to Phyfe's typical Grecian scroll legs, and the written proviso that the brass "Bason stand Railings" packed in Box 46 should be secured to the marble tops "by the nuts attached thereto."[1] The fact that the stand is veneered in rosewood as opposed to mahogany strongly indicates that it was used at Millford in the master bedchamber or in the adjacent private dressing room. Other extant rosewood bedroom furniture from Millford includes a Grecian bedstead (Pl. 55) that, sumptuously hung with curtains from a canopy, would have been the focal point of the room; a cylinder-shaped nightstand (Pl. 57); and a massive rosewood-veneered wardrobe with two plate-glass doors, square columns at the corners, and a deep cavetto frieze in the cornice, now in the collection of the Historic Columbia Foundation and on view at the Hampton-Preston House in Columbia, South Carolina (App. 2.9). Other rosewood furniture used in the master bedroom suite may have included one of the two "swing [glasses]" listed on the bill of lading, some taborets, a few side chairs, and a dressing table or bureau.

Because this piece of furniture was made to be shared, it might more accurately be described as a double basin stand. Listed in the 1847 auction sale catalogue of the contents of the D. Phyfe & Son furniture wareroom are several examples, including one described as a "mahogany Grecian double Basin Stand, scroll standards." The London furniture designer George Smith published a pattern for a double "wash hand table" (fig. 1, at left) in his *Cabinet-Maker & Upholsterer's Guide* (1826) that is very similar in design, proportion, and function to this stand by D. Phyfe & Son. With four scrolled "truss-shaped legs," the design is described by Smith as "wholly after the French taste." Like the Phyfe & Son basin stand, its top is marble, but the Smith version is slightly recessed within a narrow wooden frame as opposed to having added brass railings. Smith's design also provides information on the kinds of things that were necessary to complete one's daily ablutions in the early to mid-nineteenth century. In a separate plan he shows a neat arrangement of twin ceramic basins, water bottles, soap cups, tumblers, toothbrush trays, and tooth-powder boxes, while a handsome classically shaped water pitcher stands on the lower shelf. No doubt these items—all of the finest quality—would have been found arrayed on this richly veneered rosewood basin stand in the Mannings' own bedroom.   PMK

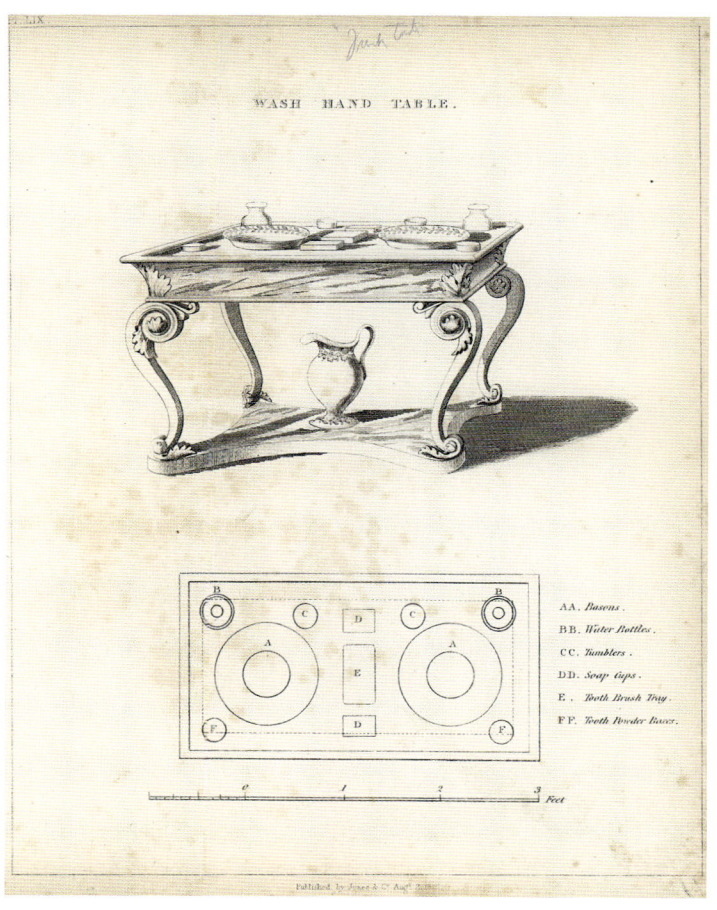

Figure 1. George Smith. Plate 59, *The Cabinet-Maker & Upholsterer's Guide* (1826). The American Wing, The Metropolitan Museum of Art

1. Bill of lading from D. Phyfe & Son to James L. Manning, June 2, 1841, Williams-Chesnut-Manning Papers, South Caroliniana Library, University of South Carolina, Columbia.

254 Duncan Phyfe

58

Plate 59

Ladies' Writing Fire Screen, 1841

D. Phyfe & Son

Mahogany veneer, mahogany, rosewood, marble; secondary woods: mahogany, white pine
50⅜ x 26 x 19⅜ in. (128.1 x 65.9 x 49.1 cm), closed
The Rick Patrick Trust

Provenance: Possibly Mary Cantey (Mrs. Wade Hampton I; 1780–1863); see Plate 55 through 1930; her daughter Ellen Williams Glover (Mrs. Cato D. Glover Jr.; 1899–1973); her daughter Sally Bland Glover and Charles Woolsey Johnson; (Sotheby's, New York, sale 7705, October 11, 2001, lot 233); The Rick Patrick Trust.

Reference: Sotheby's, New York, *Sotheby's Important Americana,* sale cat., October 11, 2001, lot 233.

Introduced during the late eighteenth century, the ladies' writing fire screen was an English innovation. One of the earliest visual and written references to it appears in *The Cabinet-Makers' London Book of Prices, and Designs of Cabinet Work* (1788), along with a companion form, the "Gentleman's Writing Fire Screen."[1] In his discussion of a related piece of furniture, Thomas Sheraton extols the virtues of the ladies' writing table, attributes that are equally applicable to the writing fire screen: "The convenience of this table is, that a lady, when writing at it, may both receive the benefit of the fire, and have her face screened from its scorching heat."[2]

One of the earliest known ladies' writing screens in New York, accented with line inlay and a complex marquetry patera, belonged to Ann Stevenson Van Cortlandt (1774–1821) of Van Cortlandt Manor in Croton-on-Hudson, New York. This considerably later example is the "Screen for Mrs. Hampton," as listed by D. Phyfe & Son on their June 2, 1841, bill of lading to John L. Manning.[3]

The writing fire screen resembles and functions as a fire screen. One side, however, is hinged to serve as a fall-front writing board that opens to reveal an interior configured in three horizontal tiers. The uppermost tier consists of a plain open shelf; the center tier—the most commodious—is designated for correspondence and other papers, which can be collated in two scalloped dividers; and the bottom tier comprises three small open boxes to house the various accoutrements necessary for writing. The boxes are described in the 1793 *Cabinet-Makers' London Book of Prices* as "a Fix'd case, fitted up for ink, sand, and wafers," and "a hollow in ditto for pens."[4] While reminiscent of related furniture forms with trestle bases, here in place of stepped blocks, simple curved ends are used to terminate the feet, and casters were applied so that the screen could easily be moved.

The evolution of the ladies' writing fire screen occurred concurrently with the development of the progressive academic curriculum for women, and one way to consider this advancement is to look at the furniture that was made specifically for women's educational and domestic activities. Duncan Phyfe's invoices and the Halliday & Jenkins 1847 auction catalogue include a number of forms clearly intended for use by the "fair sex," including a diminutive "Davenport Writing Desk," a "sewing chair," and what must have been a striking "ladies writing Screen . . . with marble top" fashioned entirely of zebra wood.

To give it a more feminine decorative aspect, the front (and back) of Mrs. Manning's writing screen was covered with silk that was pleated and fanned, possibly in a circular pattern, as evidenced by the layout lines that still can be seen on the subpanel.

MKB

1. Fastnedge 1962, p. 20, pl. 15.
2. Sheraton (1802) 1970, app., pp. 24–26, pl. 17, and p. 388.
3. Bill of lading from D. Phyfe & Son to John L. Manning, June 2, 1841, Williams-Chesnut-Manning Papers, South Caroliniana Library, University of South Carolina, Columbia.
4. *The Cabinet-Makers' London Book of Prices and Designs of Cabinet Work* (1793; reprinted, *Leeds Furniture History Society Journal,* 1982), pp. 82–83.

59

Plate 60

Cellaret, 1841

D. Phyfe & Son

Mahogany veneer; secondary woods: white pine, yellow poplar
22½ x 28 x 19 in. (57.2 x 71.1 x 48.3 cm)
Collection of Richard Hampton Jenrette

Provenance: See Plate 58.

Reference: T. G. Smith 1997, p. 738.

In 1794 the influential British designer George Hepplewhite noted that "Cellerets, called also *gardes de vin* . . . are of general use where sideboards are without drawers."[1] The sideboards without drawers are generally referred to as "sideboard tables." They were fine for serving or for the display of silver, glass, and porcelain, but they had no storage capacity to hold bottled spirits, deemed requisite for formal entertaining. Moreover, the sideboard table, in its configuration, could better accommodate a separate wine cooler or cellaret underneath. By 1810, while the sideboard table and cellaret continued to be understood as separate entities, as both were intended for the dining room, they came to be regarded as an ensemble and presented the option of being fashioned en suite. An early intimation of their pairing is suggested by their consecutive listing in the 1810 price book. This pairing continued through the 1840s, as evidenced by the "splendid rosewood sideboard Table, with very large French plate glass back, 2 drawers and 2 trays, and white marble top" and "splendid rosewood Cellant, cove top, and scroll standard to match," that Halliday & Jenkins offered at their dispersal of the Phyfe shop in April 1847.[2]

According to the 1841 bill of lading, D. Phyfe & Son supplied John L. Manning with a sideboard table and cellaret in the Grecian Plain style (App. 1.9), though today only the cellaret survives at Millford. In contrast to the cellaret that descended in Phyfe's own family (Pl. 24), the Manning example is larger, designed to accommodate six rather than four wine bottles. Its tapered coffer relates to a contour that Thomas Sheraton illustrated in 1803 in *The Cabinet Dictionary*. Corresponding to an engraving of two "wine cisterns," titled "Sarcophagus," he explains that the term "sarcophagus" is "a Greek word . . . denoting . . . *flesh eater*; but which we now shew . . . are in modern times appropriated to the use of *wine-drinkers*," adding, "such is the fate of many terms in the course of time by the various customs of different ages and countries."[3] More recently scholars have begun to reconsider this interpretation of form and function, considering the analogy drawn between this piece of furniture and the spirits it held. As Gerald Ward has pointed out, while it is possible to theorize about these associations and their significance, the cellaret is an object that by its very presence is evocative of the consumption of alcohol and, more important, the relationship of wine to the ritual passages of life and death.[4]

While the cellaret design derives from a range of historical sources, in fact it replicates a form that the ancients originated for the entombment of the dead. By the beginning of the eighteenth century, the sarcophagus was one of a number of

Alternate view, Plate 60

60

classical idioms being integrated into the lexicon of artistic expression. Appropriately, its earliest representations were realized, in the 1720s, in British funerary art. It was not, however, until the close of the century that they began to be translated to the decorative arts.[5]   MKB

1. Hepplewhite (1794) 1969, p. 7.
2. Halliday & Jenkins 1847, p. 15, lots 318, 319.
3. Sheraton (1803) 1970, vol. 2, pp. 300–302, pl. 66.
4. Ward 1988, pp. 442–44; see also Solny 1997–98 and Collins 2000.
5. Harold Mytum, author of *Mortuary Monuments and Burial Grounds of the Historic Period* (New York, 2004), has generously shared with me his insights into the introduction of this design in British mortuary art.

Plate 61

Window Seat, 1841

ATTRIBUTED TO D. PHYFE & SON

Rosewood veneer; secondary woods: white pine, yellow poplar, mahogany
16½ x 41⅞ x 17¼ (41.9 x 106.4 x 43.8 cm)
The Metropolitan Museum of Art, Gift of J. Nicholas Wilson, 2006 2006.400

Inscribed in grease pencil on inside back rail: "W. R. CLARK."

Provenance: See Plate 55.

Reference: T. G. Smith 1997, pp. 737, 739.

The set of four window seats specially designed for the double parlors at Millford occupied the paneled openings below the two windows that flanked the fireplaces in each of the resplendent rooms.[1] One is seen in situ, in the lower right foreground, in an early twentieth-century photograph of Millford (fig. 1, below). Window seats of unique design figure prominently in both the Manning and the Donaldson commissions (see Pl. 34), which suggests that these were generally specialty items produced strictly as bespoke work, although two "window seats" do appear in the 1847 auction catalogue of the contents of the D. Phyfe & Son shop.[2]

The window seats rest on casters and, when necessary, could be drawn away from the windows into the middle of the room for cleaning or possibly to be used as occasional seating along with the sets of chairs, taborets, and sofas and couches. However, unlike the sofas and couches, the back sides were left uncovered by even a secondary fabric, leaving the white pine backboards exposed. Conforming to the cyma-curved shape of the sides are thin, flat brackets attached to the front of the frame with four dowels. The pierced central demilune motif on the front rail appears also on the pair of ottomans made for the drawing room (see fig. 198) and relates to the plasterwork ceiling of Millford's domed circular staircase hall. The voids cut into the lobes reveal the figured damask silk behind them (reproduced from the original) and lend the effect of a garden trellis against a backdrop of flowers and vines. Alternatively, they can be interpreted as classical anthemia or, continuing in the vein of the pointed Gothic crest rails and banisters on the rosewood side chairs (Pl. 62), as half the tracery of a Gothic rose window.

In spite of their casters, the window seats, like the larger ottomans also used in the rooms, had fixed locations in the double parlors and imparted a

Figure 1. Drawing room at Millford Plantation. Photograph, early 20th century. Private collection

260   Duncan Phyfe

61

clear impression of architectonic presence and mass. With broad backs but no arms, the ottomans may have been placed in front of the folding mirrored doors that divided the double parlor when closed, or between the columnar screen when the mirrored folding doors were open, as shown in a modern photograph of these rooms (see fig. 196).[3] Because the ottomans also had casters, another option was to place them back-to-back, transforming them into a two-sided bench, called a *chancelier* in George Smith's *Guide* of 1828.[4]

MAT

1. None of the four window seats is listed in the D. Phyfe & Son bill of lading.
2. Halliday & Jenkins 1847, p. 3, lot 55. The reference to "1 pr window Seats scroll standards" is adjacent to lot 54 "1 mahogany taborette" and lot 56 "1 pr. Ottomans scroll standards," which suggests the variety of occasional seating furniture found in the Mannings' drawing room suite.
3. Loudon (1833, pp. 1060–61) suggested that ottomans "may be placed either against the walls of a room or in the open floor."
4. Smith's *chancelier* was intended to "occupy the central situation of spacious apartments . . . covered [in fabric to match] the curtains, sofas, and chairs in the room" (G. Smith 1828, p. 190).

Plate 62

Side Chair, 1841

ATTRIBUTED TO D. PHYFE & SON

Rosewood, rosewood veneer; secondary wood: ash
32⅛ x 17¼ x 20⅛ in. (81.6 x 43.8 x 51.1 cm)
Collection of Richard Hampton Jenrette

Provenance: See Plate 58 through 1958; his son Emory W. Clark II (b. 1938); [Francis D. McNairy]; the present owner.

Reference: T. G. Smith 1997, pp. 737, 739.

With the sculpted, narrow-waisted shape of the back, the rosewood side chairs from the Mannings' double parlor at Millford bear some resemblance to the Egyptian-influenced lotus-back banisters made by D. Phyfe & Sons in the late 1830s (see Pls. 49 and 50). Instead of the yoke-shaped crest rails on these chairs, however, the Millford chairs have a distinctive peaked crest and pointed silhouettes in the banisters that give them a decidedly Gothic aspect.[1] Although these side chairs were thought to be unique to Millford, a nearly identical set that descended in the family of Phyfe's nephew John Phyfe Jr. (1798–1890), a turner of hardwoods and ivory in New York, is also known.[2] The Millford chairs and some of the lotus-back models (Pl. 50) are rare in the use of solid rosewood for the frames. This is especially noteworthy in contrast to the upholstered French armchairs that D. Phyfe & Sons supplied to Manning for Millford (see fig. 118), where the mahogany frames were grain-painted to imitate the more expensive wood.

D. Phyfe & Son's design brilliantly incorporates a series of sharp Grecian ovolo molding profiles in the dramatic outline of the veneered banister and the turning pattern on the front legs, which, in their pointed shape, also allude to the Gothic style. As J. C. Loudon suggested of small, delicate drawing-room chairs of this type, "[T]heir appearance is light, and, their proportions being slender, they may be considered as not inelegant."[3] By the skillful use of richly figured rosewood in the sleek design that combines profiles drawn from both classical and Gothic design, D. Phyfe & Son created chairs that are a highly successful blend of these two styles.

MAT

1. The chair in Plate 62 is marked "III" on the inside of the rear seat rail. There are sixteen extant chairs from this set. Of the ten currently at Millford, the highest number is "XVI." The chairs are not listed in the D. Phyfe & Son bill of lading. Two chairs were once owned by Francis McNairy Antiques, Savannah, Georgia, and two are in a private collection in Columbia, South Carolina.
2. The chairs descended in the family of John Phyfe Jr.'s sister-in-law, Janette McNeish Ferguson (scholarship files, American Wing, Metropolitan Museum).
3. Loudon 1833, p. 1061.

62

Plate 63

Sofa, 1841

D. Phyfe & Son

Rosewood veneer, rosewood, rosewood grained mahogany; secondary woods: ash, white pine
37 x 87½ x 25 in. (94 x 222.3 x 63.5 cm)
Columbia Museum of Art, Columbia, South Carolina, Gift of Mr. and Mrs. W. R. Clark

Provenance: See Plate 58 through William R. Clark; 1964, Columbia Museum of Art.

The supreme pieces of seating furniture in the Millford double parlors are a pair of rosewood sofas.[1] Made en suite with the pair of couches (see fig. 197), they are distinguished by applied crossbanded rosewood strapwork that outlines their sinuous scrolled arms and backs and bracket feet.[2] Similar flat strapwork banding appears on the scrolled newel post of Millford's grand cantilevered circular staircase, as does the rounded teardrop inserted at the juncture of the sofa's scrolled ends and bracket feet. Couches, bedsteads, and case furniture made in Paris in the late Restauration style of the 1840s, including examples exported to the United States in this period, have similar flat banding. Three examples of this imported French furniture are the walnut bookcases ordered by Daniel Turnbull in 1845 for a new library wing at Rosedown Plantation in St. Francisville, Louisiana.[3]

As J. C. Loudon suggested, the great appeal of the serpentine frame of Grecian sofas and couches was founded in the "Greek cyma (wave), the most elegant and graceful of all curves; and . . . identical with [William] Hogarth's serpentine line of beauty."[4] The continuous line of the front seat rail and scrolled arms relates to earlier Grecian sofas by Phyfe, including the Brinkerhoff and Donaldson examples (Pl. 18 and fig. 165), but the breadth of the frame has expanded to suit the monumental scale of the Greek Revival interiors at Millford. A circular medallion centering the crest rail similar to that on the Manning sofa appears in a design in John Taylor's *Upholsterer's and Cabinet-maker's Pocket Assistant* (1825), where it represents the rising sun.[5]

MAT

1. One sofa is recorded on the D. Phyfe & Son's 1841 bill of lading. The second sofa, not mentioned in the bill of lading, is in a private collection in Aiken, Georgia, and was purchased from the Clark family prior to the sale of Millford to Richard H. Jenrette.
2. This decorative feature is also found on the feet of a mahogany couch attributed to Phyfe in the collection of Richard Kelly (Northeast Auctions, Manchester, N.H., *Important New York Furniture and Decorative Arts: The Richard and Beverly Kelly Collection*, sale cat., April 3, 2005, lot 1228).
3. T. G. Smith 2001, p. 773, and Word 1979, pp. 40–41.
4. Loudon 1833, p. 1059.
5. Reproduced in *Pictorial Dictionary* 1977, p. 301.

Plate 64

Occasional Table, 1841

ATTRIBUTED TO D. PHYFE & SON

Rosewood, rosewood veneer, rosewood-grained mahogany, marble; secondary woods: mahogany, white pine, yellow poplar
30⅞ x 42⅛ x 24⅛ in. (78.4 x 107 x 61.5 cm)
Mulberry Plantation, Camden, South Carolina

Provenance: See Plate 55 through 1930; her nephew David Rogerson Williams IV (1885–1969) and his wife, Martha Hill Williams (1893–1960); Mulberry Plantation.

Although this occasional table and its mate are not seen in the early twentieth-century photograph of the Millford double parlor (Pl. 61, fig. 1), they were in fact part of the same suite and descended in two different lines of the family along with other furniture from the set.[1] In addition to their family histories, certain design features on these tables clearly link them to the Millford suite. These include the strapwork banding that outlines the bottom edge of the apron and the trestle feet, which also appears on the sofas (Pl. 63) and couches. The scrolled table supports of solid mahogany are painted faux rosewood, another feature that relates them to the couches, sofas, and French armchairs. The rounded corners of the aprons match the rounded seat frames of the side chairs (Pl. 62). And the softly modeled lotus-leaf carving on the scrolls that support the top echo the ornamentation of the scrolled arm supports on the French armchairs (see fig. 118).

One of these occasional tables was used in each half of the double parlor. The English furniture designer George Smith referred to this form (see fig. 122) as an occasional table "intended . . . for the drawing room; in which case [it] should be executed wholly in rosewood."[2] Although occasional tables and sofa tables were discussed together with circular center tables in early nineteenth-century English pattern books, the latter form was far more popular among American consumers through the 1830s. By the 1840s, however, tastes were changing. When Duncan and James Phyfe closed their shop in 1847, they had six sofa tables in stock, including one "rich rosewood sofa Table, scroll standard elegantly carved, white marble top."[3] Eventually, by the 1850s, marble-top tables in the Old French styles of Louis XIV and Louis XV, more oblong or rectangular in form, became standard in American parlors. MAT

1. Neither this table nor its mate is listed in the D. Phyfe & Son bill of lading. The mate is in a private collection in Columbia, South Carolina.
2. G. Smith 1828, p. 195, pl. 118.
3. Halliday & Jenkins 1847, p. 10, lot 214.

Plate 65

Nesting Tables, 1841

D. PHYFE & SON

Rosewood, rosewood veneer
Largest: 29½ x 22 x 16 in. (74.9 x 55.9 x 40.6 cm); smallest: 27⅜ x 10⅛ x 12¼ in. (69.5 x 25.7 x 31.1 cm)
The Terian Collection of American Art

Provenance: See Plate 59 from 1863 through Sally Bland Glover and Charles Woolsey Johnson; (Sotheby's, New York, sale 7350, October 15, 1999, lot 70); Mr. and Mrs. Peter G. Terian; The Terian Collection of American Art.

References: Sotheby's, New York, *Important Americana*, sale cat., October 15, 1999, lot 70; T. G. Smith 1997, p. 739; Voorsanger and Howat 2000, pp. 297, 520, 590–91, no. 230.

Among the few pieces of Manning furniture mentioned on the bill of lading, where they are referred to as "Nest Tables," this set of six was still at Millford when the parlor was photographed in the early twentieth century (see Pl. 61, fig. 1, where they can be seen at left between the Jacobean chair and the candelabra). Such tables were more commonly sold in sets of four, hence the term "quartetto tables," which appears in the 1847 auction catalogue of D. Phyfe & Son's stock in trade.[1]

Nesting tables of this type were described in Thomas Sheraton's *Cabinet Dictionary* (1803) as a "kind of small worktable made to draw out of each other, and may be used separately, and again enclosed within each other when not wanted."[2] Such flexibility worked nicely with the large amount of seating furniture used in the Millford double parlor. Nesting tables were often associated with women. The early nineteenth-century English poet and critic Robert Southey observed: "You would take them for play things, from their slenderness and size, if you did not see how useful [ladies] find them for their work."[3] The interpretation of D. Phyfe & Son is quite similar to Sheraton's design, with rings turned into the solid rosewood supports in a simulation of bamboo. Sheraton's plate was also copied in China, where lacquered and gilded nesting tables were produced in large numbers for the Western market.[4] MAT

1. Halliday & Jenkins 1847, p. 4, lot 80. The largest of these nesting tables is illustrated in Voorsanger and Howat 2000 (p. 520, no. 230), shown with gilded decoration on the top which has since been removed.
2. Sheraton 1803, p. 293.
3. Quoted in Snodin and Styles 2001, p. 258.
4. Lee 1984, pp. 129, 156.

65

Plate 66

Box Sofa, 1840–47

NEW YORK

Mahogany, mahogany veneer; secondary woods: ash, yellow poplar
35 x 82¾ x 27¾ in. (89 x 210.2 x 70.5 cm)
Collection of Prof. Maan Z. Madina and Dr. Marilyn Jenkins-Madina

Provenance: [Place des Vosges, New York], 1998; the present owners.

In this handsome mahogany box sofa, Gothic detailing is melded seamlessly into a classical revival form made in the Phyfe shop from about 1820 until the late 1840s. The earliest box sofas thought to be by Phyfe use the design vocabulary of the enriched Grecian style (see fig. 89), and the one known documented example, dating from 1834 and in the Grecian Plain style (Pl. 43), has the Phyfe shop's signature scroll standards under the arms and cuffed, square feet. The crest rail on this sofa is like the one Phyfe used on a caned scroll-back sofa he made for William Bayard in 1807 (Pl. 4). The continuous use of the scrolled crest rail on sofas of various styles for nearly three decades speaks to Phyfe's conservative, incremental approach to change over time in his furniture designs.

This box sofa's superb proportions, restrained design, and superior materials and workmanship qualify it for serious consideration as a production of the Phyfe shop. The stacked front feet, with their blind lancet arches, step back like the base of a spire on a Gothic church. Like the support pillar on the Phyfe family checker stand of approximately the same date (Pl. 54), they are chamfered and veneered, even on the edges. Furthermore, the flat, chamfered cap on the top block of the front posts is faceted like that on the plinth of the checker stand. Some unseen structural details also link this Gothic box sofa to documented Phyfe examples. Key among them are the shaped wooden strips that provide the foundation for the crisp, squared upholstery edges. The front strip is easily removable, making it possible to replace the upholstery without damaging the frame. This wood-frame upholstering system—perhaps devised as a way for Phyfe to cut down on the expense of engaging an upholsterer to sew a true French edge—can be seen on the documented 1834 Phyfe box sofa shown in Plate 43.

According to family tradition, the documented 1834 box sofa was covered originally in horsehair, the fabric chosen to reupholster the present example as well. Haircloth was a fairly common upholstery material in the 1840s and is described as the covering on two Grecian sofas listed in the 1847 auction catalogue of the contents of the Phyfe & Son's warehouse. Other fabrics described in the catalogue for sofas include maroon and orange silk damask and dark purple and crimson plush. Round pillows are used at either end of this sofa, though it is also possible that square ones originally were used, both at the ends and across the back of the interior.   PMK

Detail, Plate 66

66

Plate 67

Sideboard 1840–47

ATTRIBUTED TO D. PHYFE & SON

51 x 54½ x 22½ in. (129.5 x 138.4 x 57.2 cm)
Rosewood veneer, rosewood-grained mahogany; secondary woods: mahogany, yellow poplar, white pine
Collection of Thomas Gordon Smith and Marika Wilson Smith

Provenance: (Nadeau's Auction Gallery, Windsor, Connecticut, January 1, 2003, lot 175); the present owners.

Reference: Nadeau's Auction Gallery, Windsor, Connecticut, *Important Annual New Year's Day Auction*, sale cat., January 1, 2003.

This trim, compact sideboard measuring only four-and-one-half feet wide is a prime example of D. Phyfe & Son's late Grecian Plain style case furniture. Its pedestal ends are small works of architecture in their own right, with sturdy socles defined by crossbanded veneers set on square cuffed feet, tall plate-glass doors with Gothic tracery, and finely proportioned cavetto cornices. The open center bay, which may originally have housed either a small matching rosewood cellaret or an open wine cooler, has a mirror-plate back and identical Gothic cusps and ogees cut into its fascia. The white-and-gray-veined marble top conforms to the shape of the façade and is original, as are the marble back and thin rosewood display shelf on top. The Grecian scroll standards at the front of the shelf are similar in design to the much larger ones found on pier and sideboard tables from the Phyfe shop, but in this application they are reversed and inverted.

By the 1840s, a new furniture form similar in design and scale to this sideboard and known as a chiffonier was gaining popularity in the sitting and drawing rooms of American homes. According to Thomas Webster, the author of *An Encyclopaedia of Domestic Economy* (1845), a chiffonier could "substitute for closets and a sideboard, and serve to hold wine, liquors, biscuits, or other refreshments; and on the top, and on a shelf supported by small pillows [pillars?] or brackets, are placed decanters,

Detail, Plate 67

67

glasses, or ornaments." He goes on to say that "in drawing-rooms they may be used instead of pier-tables."[1] Sideboards are often associated with dining-room use, but the fact that this example is relatively small in scale, has a top display shelf, and is veneered in rosewood, a wood most often reserved in this period for furniture used in the finest room in the house, strongly suggests that it may be precisely the kind of drawing-room chiffonier described by Webster.   PMK

1. Webster (1845, pp. 267–68) describes and illustrates three drawing-room chiffoniers, all with backs on the tops and a single long display shelf. One has plate-glass cupboard doors lined with fabric like this sideboard, and another has flanking pedestal cupboards and an open center bay.

Appendix I

Invoices and Accounts from Duncan Phyfe Relating to Furniture in This Volume

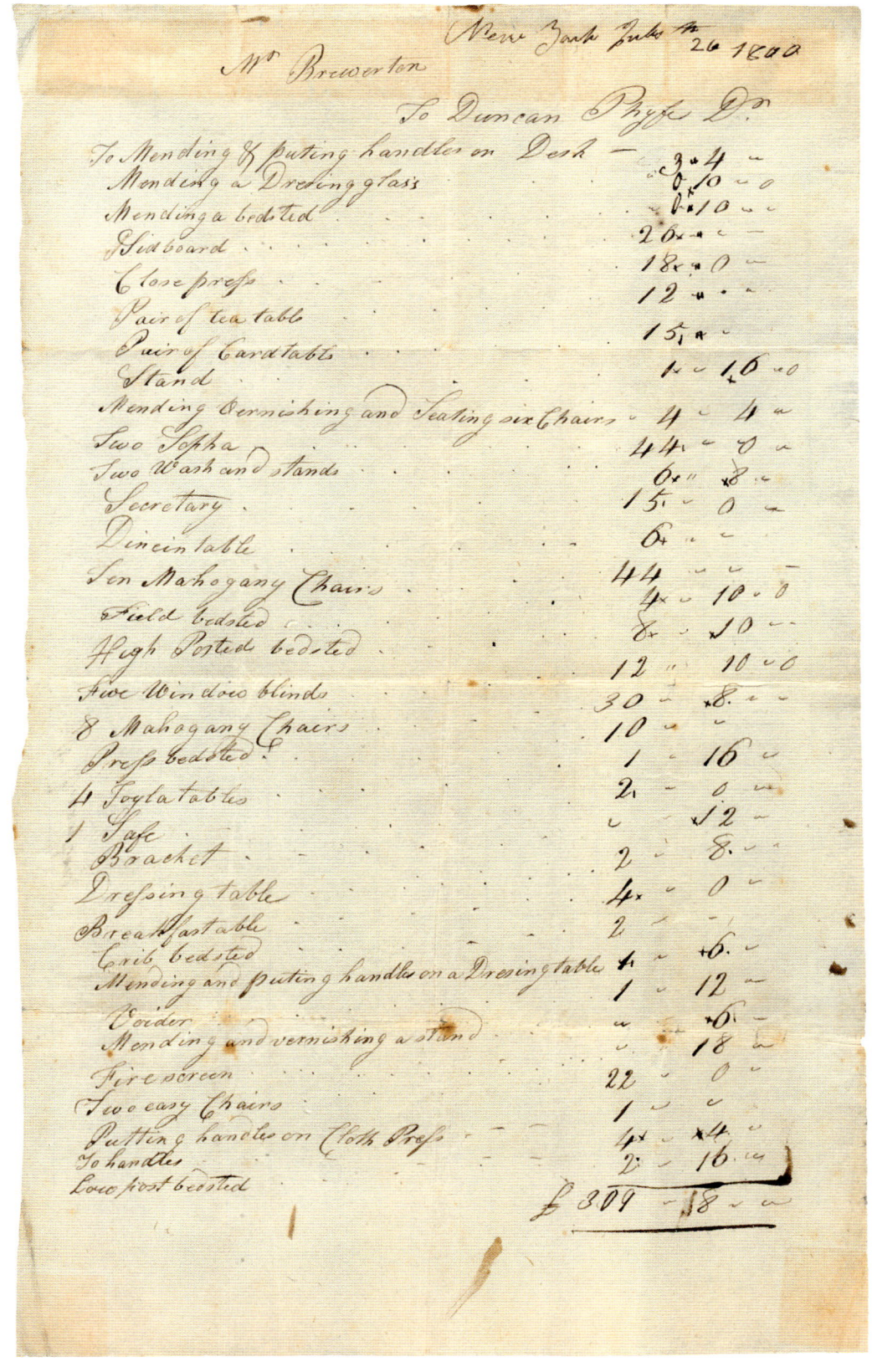

1.1. Invoice to a Mr. Brewerton, July 26, 1800. Carswell Rush Berlin

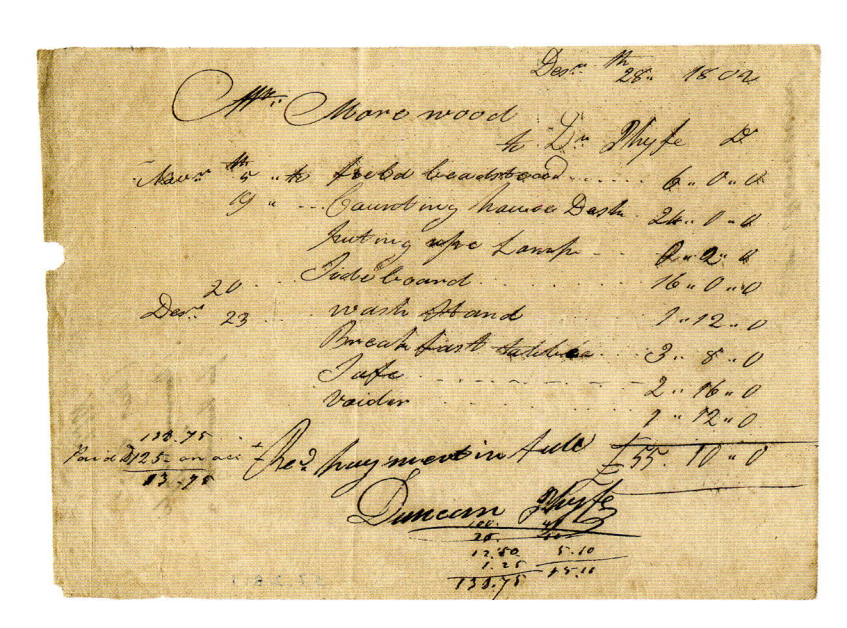

1.2. Receipted invoice to a Mr. Morewood, December 28, 1802. Museum of the City of New York, Gift of Henry L. Ferguson

1.3a. Invoice to Mr. William Bayard, November 21, 1807, Winterthur Museum, Winterthur, Delaware

1.3b. Receipted invoice to Mr. William [Bayard], November 21 1807. Bayard-Campbell-Pearsall Papers, Manuscripts and Archives Division, The New York Public Library, Astor, Lenox and Tilden Foundations

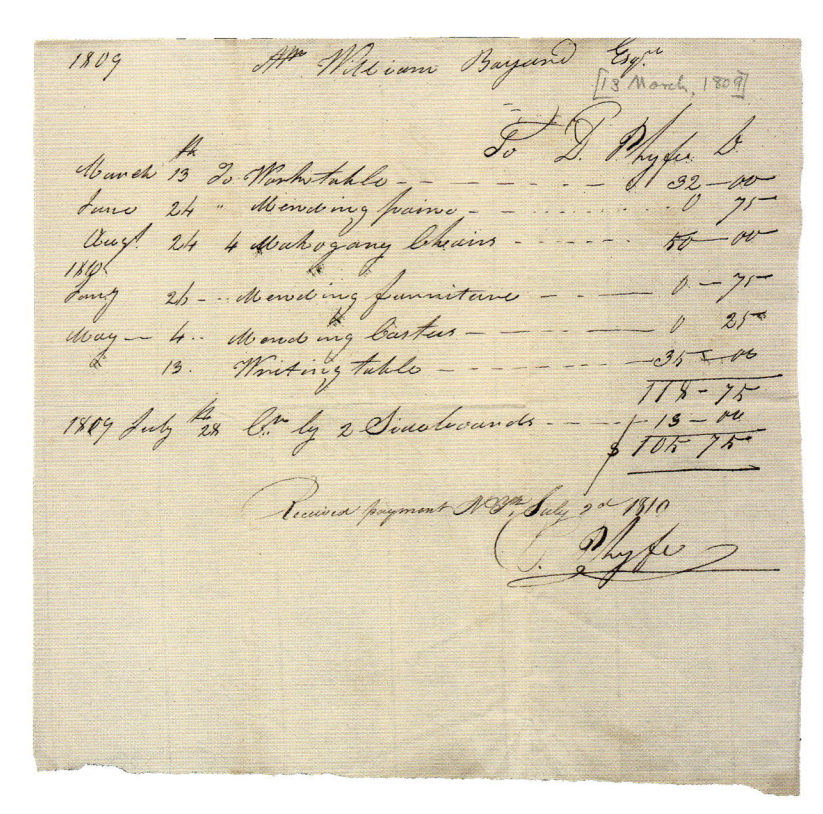

1.3c. Invoice to Mr. William Bayard, March 13, 1809–May 13, 1810 [receipted July 2, 1810]. Bayard-Campbell-Pearsall Papers, Manuscripts and Archives Division, The New York Public Library, Astor, Lenox and Tilden Foundations

274 *Duncan Phyfe*

Mr James Kellso   Bot of D. Phyfe

1812 Decemb 24	To Bed Rods	15 —
31	" Pair Foot Stools	13 —
1813 January 15	" Pair Bed Steps	35 —
February 9	" Piano Stool	25 —
	" Packing	1.25
25	" Urn Stand	5 —
April 7	" Set dining Tables	80 —
24	" Beaufet	28 —
May 10	" Work Table	52 —
		$244.25

Mr James Kellso   To D Phyfe

To Amount of Account Rendered	$244.25
1813 Oct 9 To Wardrobe	145 —
" Mending furniture	1.50
15 " Close Horse	2 —
	$392.75
By Dining Table	47 —
	$345.75

1.4. Two invoices to Mr. James Kelso, December 24, 1812–October 15, 1813. Collection of Mr. and Mrs. Jerome W. Blum

Mr James L Brinckerhoff   To D Phyfe Dr

1815 Sept 29	To Set Dining Tables	$180 —
—	" Removing & Varnishing 12 chairs	7.50
—	" Mending Chairs	" 75
—	" Removing & Varnishing Sofa	—
Oct 5	" Putting Up 3 Bedsteads	" 75
—	" Bed Cord	" 50
Nov 4	" Covering foot stool	1.50
1816 April 24	" Field Bedstead	15 —
—	" Putting Up one Do	" 50
30	" Pair Ward Robes	324 —
May 3	" Canapee Bedstead	200 —
6	" Mending Piano	10 —
—	" Night Table	28 —
7	" Tea Board	340 —
11	" Covering Piano Stool	3 —
16	" Pair Card Tables	135 —
—	" Tea Table	60 —
—	" Sofa	140 —
17	" Billiards	110 —
18	" 12 Mahogany Chairs Stuffed	264 —
—	" 8 Do Do Caned	176 —
27	" Easy Chair	60 —
—	" Making 2 Easy Chair covers & Binding	12 —
July 18	" 2 Bason Stands	55 —
1816 Oct 26	Recd Payment in full	$ 2125.50

D Phyfe

1.5. Receipted invoice to Mr. James L. Brinckerhoff, September 29, 1815–July 18, 1816 [receipted October 26, 1816]. Robert Troup Papers, Manuscripts and Archives Division, The New York Public Library, Astor, Lenox and Tilden Foundations

1.6. Invoice to Mr. [Charles Nicoll] Bancker, January 4, 1816. Winterthur Library, Joseph Downs Collection of Manuscripts and Printed Ephemera

1.7. Copy of an invoice to Messrs. H. & B. [for Robert Donaldson], August 21, 1822. Brooklyn Museum, Gift of Mrs. J. Amory Haskell

1.8. Receipted invoice to Mr. B[enjamin] Clark, August 16, 1834. Collection of Mr. and Mrs. Robert L. Hammett

278 *Duncan Phyfe*

Jas L. Manning Esqr.

Dr. Sir   New York June 2, 1841

We inclose you a list of the Boxes already shipped to the care of your agent in Charleston from which you will be able to know the contents of each Box, and they know the part of furniture which appertain to each other.

Please be particular to have the Boxes open'd from the Marked tops that it may not receive injury in removing it from the cases.

No. 1 Couch & Pills
2 do   3   do   } walnut
4 do
5 Sideboard Table
6 do & Cellaret
7 Sofa, 8. 4 Mahog arm chairs
9 4 Mahog arm chairs
10 2 Arm chairs & 4 small Mahy do
11 4 do   do   12 4   do   walnut
13 4 do   do   14 4 swing chairs
15 1 dinner wagon 16 2 scroll Bason stands
17 2 Large slabs   18 2 dinner wagons
19 Mahog Sideboard Table 20 swing Glass
21 Box Table leaves 22 corner Cupboard
23 Corner Cupboard 24 Wardrobe carcase
25 Box & Pillar of dining Table
26. Cornice, bases & columns of Wardrobe

[Recto]

27. Wardrobe door. 28. dining Table Top
29. Sideboard Top   30. 2 night stands
31. Swing Glass   32 Wardrobe carcase
33. Cornice Base & Columns do
34. Screen for Mrs. Hampton
35. Nest Tables   36. ends of French Bedstead
37, 38 & 39 Bedding. 40 Sides of do & knife boxes
41 End & laths of Grecian Bedstead.
42   do   of single   do
43 Sides castors & screws of French Bedstead
44 2 Bason Stands & 2 Corner Cupboard Tops
45 Hat Stand 2 Butlers trays
46 2 Round Stands & Bason stand Railings
47 2 Tops for round stands & 2 do for night stands.

You will please observe that the railing for bason stands is to be secured by the nuts attached thereto. Wee hope they will reach in good order and that they will be carefully opened. They have all been packed in the best manner.

The balance of the order will be shipped in from 3 to 4 weeks

Respt

Your Obd Servs—
D Phyfe & Son

[Verso]

1.9. Transcription of a letter and bill of lading to Jas [John] L. Manning, Esqr., June 2, 1841. Williams-Chestnut-Manning Family Papers, microfilm, South Caroliniana Library, University of South Carolina, Columbia

Appendix 2

Additional Documented Furniture

Furniture Relating to Invoices and Accounts from Duncan Phyfe

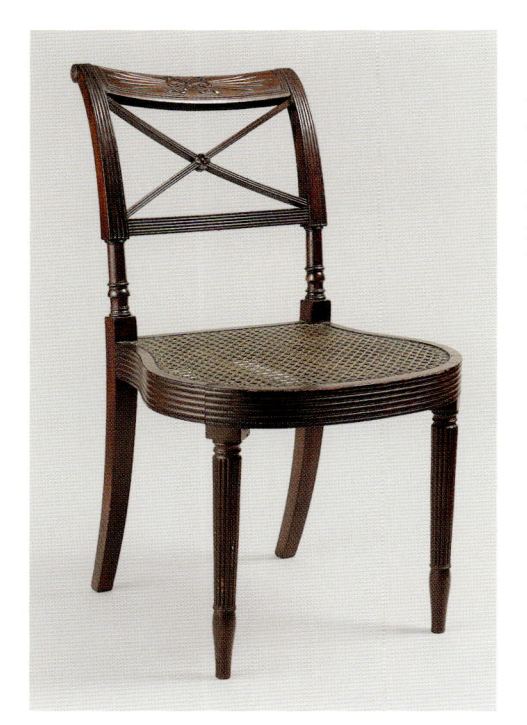

2.1 Side Chair, 1807.

Mahogany, 33 x 18¾ x 22¼ in. (83.8 x 47.6 x 56.5 cm). Collection of Mr. and Mrs. Roland W. Glidden

Notes: Listed on one of the two invoices dated November 21, 1807, to William Bayard (App. 1.3a or 1.3b).

2.2. French Press or Wardrobe, 1816

Mahogany, mahogany veneer, gilded gesso, *vert antique*, gilded brass
86 x 62 x 25¾ in. (218.4 x 157.5 x 65.4 cm)
Private collection

Notes: One of the "Pair [of] Ward Robes" listed on a receipted invoice dated October 26, 1816, to James L. Brinckerhoff (App. 1.5).

2.3. French Bedstead, 1816

Mahogany, mahogany veneer, gilded gesso, *vert antique*, gilded brass
66 x 80 x 57 in. (167.6 x 203.2 x 144.8 cm)
Private collection

Notes: Listed as a "Canapee Bedstead" on a receipted invoice dated September 29, 1815–July 18, 1816, to James L. Brinckerhoff (App. 1.5).
The original canopy and support arms are missing.

2.4. Basin Stand, 1816

Mahogany, gilded gesso, gilded brass, marble
32¼ x 15 in. (81.9 38.1 cm)
Present whereabouts unknown

Notes: One of "2 Bason Stands" listed on a receipted invoice dated September 29, 1815–July 18, 1816, to James L. Brinckerhoff (App. 1.5).

2.5. Taboret, 1841

Rosewood veneer, rosewood-grained mahogany
16 x 20¼ x 16 in. (40.6 x 51.4 x 40.6 cm)
Private collection, Pinewood, South Carolina

Notes: One of four taborets originally at Millford.

2.6. Corner Table, 1841

Rosewood veneer, rosewood-grained maple, marble
30⅝ x 20½ x 20½ in. (77.8 x 52.1 x 52.1 cm)
Collection of Richard Hampton Jenrette

Notes: One of four corner tables originally at Millford, three now in the collection of Richard Hampton Jenrette and one at the Historic Columbia Foundation, Hampton-Preston Mansion, Columbia, South Carolina.

2.7. Marble-top Stand, 1841

Mahogany veneer, mahogany, marble
26¾ x 27⅜ in. (67.9 x 69.5 cm)
Collection of Richard Hampton Jenrette

Notes: One of "2 Round Stands," the parts of which are listed in Boxes 46 and 47 on the bill of lading dated June 2, 1841, to John L. Manning (App. 1.9). Inscribed on underside of top: "No. 1 / Mr. J L Manning." The other stand is in the collection of the Historic Columbia Foundation, Columbia, South Carolina.

2.4

2.5

2.6

2.7

Appendix 2   281

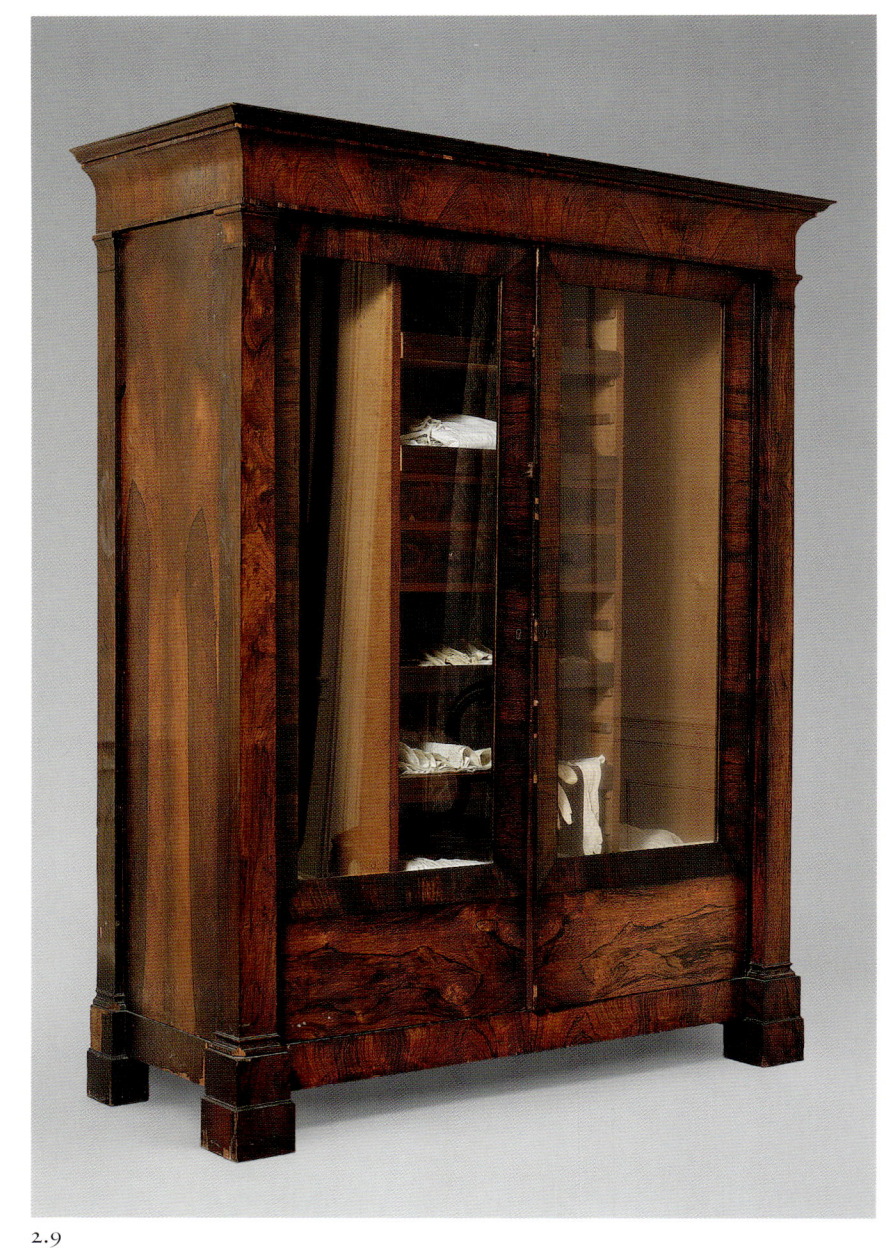

2.8

2.9

2.8. Wardrobe, 1841

Mahogany, mahogany veneer, looking-glass plate
94½ x 57¾ x 28 in. (240 x 146.7 x 71.1 cm)
Private collection, Pinewood, South Carolina

Notes: One of two wardrobes, the parts of which are listed in Boxes 24, 26, 32, and 33 on the bill of lading dated June 2, 1841, to John L. Manning (App. 1.9).

2.9. Wardrobe, 1841

Rosewood veneer, mahogany veneer, glass
86¼ x 66½ x 26¾ in. (219.1 x 168.9 x 67.9 cm)
Historic Columbia Foundation, Hampton-Preston Mansion, Columbia, South Carolina

Notes: One of two wardrobes, the parts of which are listed in Boxes 24, 26, 32, and 33 on the bill of lading dated June 2, 1841, to John L. Manning (App. 1.9). The original looking-glass plates have been replaced with clear glass.

2.10. Basin Stand, 1841

Mahogany, mahogany veneer, brass, marble
34¾ x 38⅞ x 20½ in. (88.3 x 98.7 x 52.1 cm)
Collection of Richard Hampton Jenrette

Notes: One of four "Bason Stands" listed in Boxes 16, 44, and 46 on the bill of lading dated June 2, 1841, to John L. Manning (App. 1.9).

2.10

2.11

2.11. French Bedstead, 1841

Mahogany veneer, mahogany
46 x 92 x 60 in. (116.8 x 233.7 x 152.4 cm)
Collection of Richard Hampton Jenrette

Notes: Listed in Boxes 36–40 on the bill of lading dated June 2, 1841, to John L. Manning (App. 1.9).

Appendix 2   283

Phyfe Family Furniture

2.12. Wardrobe, ca. 1820

Mahogany, mahogany veneer
88¾ x 48 x 22 in. (225.4 x 121.9 x 55.9 cm)
Descended in the family of Mary Phyfe Whitlock (1795–1870)
Present whereabouts unknown

2.13. Pembroke Table, ca. 1825

Mahogany, mahogany veneer
28¼ x 41½ x 49⅝ in. open (71.8 x 105.4 x 126.1 cm)
Descended in the family of Eliza Phyfe Vail (1801–1890)
Collection of Andrew Howell Gibbon

2.14. Chest of Drawers, ca. 1825

Mahogany, mahogany veneer
46¾ x 46⅜ x 23 in. (118.7 x 117.8 x 58.4 cm)
Descended in the family of Eliza Phyfe Vail (1801–1890)
Estate of Ronald S. Kane

Notes: The silver-plated drawer pulls are replacements.

284 *Duncan Phyfe*

2.15. Grecian Sofa, ca. 1825

Mahogany, mahogany veneer, brass
34 x 88 x 25 in. (86.4 x 223.5 x 68.5 cm)
Descended in the family of Eliza Phyfe Vail (1801–1890)
New York State Museum, Albany, Gift of the Wunsch Americana Foundation, 1983

2.16. Dressing Table with Mirror, ca. 1825

Mahogany, mahogany veneer, brass, looking-glass plate
58 x 37½ x 18¾ in. (147.3 x 95.3 x 47.6 cm)
Descended in the family of Eliza Phyfe Vail (1801–1890)
Collection of Glorianna H. Gibbon

2.17. Chiffonier or Occasional Table, ca. 1825

Mahogany, mahogany veneer, brass
30½ x 23 x 16¼ in. (77.5 x 58.4 x 41.3 cm)
Descended in the family of Eliza Phyfe Vail (1801–1890)
Collection of Glorianna H. Gibbon

Appendix 2

2.18. Wardrobe, ca. 1825

Mahogany, mahogany veneer, brass
88½ x 48 x 22 in. (224.8 x 121.9 x 55.9 cm)
Descended in the family of Eliza Phyfe Vail (1801–1890)
Present whereabouts unknown

2.19. Taboret, 1837–40

Mahogany veneer, mahogany
15⅝ x 21⅜ x 15½ in. (39.7 x 54.3 x 39.4 cm)
Descended in the family of Eliza Phyfe Vail (1801–1890)
Collection of Glorianna H. Gibbon

2.20. Crib, 1840–47

Mahogany veneer, mahogany
45 x 47½ x 22¼ in. (114.3 x 120.7 x 56.5 cm)
Descended in the family of James D. Phyfe (1814–1878)
The Metropolitan Museum of Art, Purchase, The Virginia and Leonard Marx Foundation Gift, 2010 2010.219

286 *Duncan Phyfe*

Furniture Labeled and Inscribed

2.21. Library Chair, 1811

Mahogany, maple, brass
41½ x 31⅛ x 37¼ in. (104.8 x 79.1 x 94.6 cm)
The White House, Washington, D.C., Gift of the Richard King Mellon Foundation, 1971

Notes: Inscribed on frame of chair back: "For Mr. Van Rensselaer Albany / Stuffed by L. Ackermann New York 1811 / L Ackermann Oct 18, 1811 Upholsterer / This frame made by D. Phyfe." The linen upholstery foundations are modern.

2.22. Card Table, 1820

Mahogany veneer, mahogany, gilded brass
31 x 36 x 18 in. (78.7 x 91.9 x 45.7 cm)
Present whereabouts unknown

Notes: Labeled in well, "D. Phyfe's / Cabinet Warehouse, / No. 170 Fulton-street, / New-York / N. B. Curled Hair Matrasses, Chair and / Sofa Cushions. / August, 1820." (see fig. 25).

2.23. Card Table, 1820

Mahogany, mahogany veneer
Dimensions unknown
Present location unknown

Notes: Labeled in well, "D. Phyfe's / Cabinet Warehouse, / No. 170 Fulton-street, / New-York / N. B. Curled Hair Matrasses, Chair and / Sofa Cushions. / August, 1820." (see fig. 25). When recorded in the Decorative Arts Photographic Collection, Winterthur Museum, in 1964, Paulette (Mrs. Alvin) Schwartzman, of Plainview, New York, then the owner of the table, stated that it was found "a great distance from New York."

Appendix 2   287

Bibliography

Abbott 1994
: James A. Abbott. *Classical to 19th Century America: The Influence of Berry Tracy on the Historic Interior*. Exh. brochure, Boscobel Restoration, Garrison, N.Y., August 10–November 10, 1994. Garrison, N.Y., 1994.

Ackermann 1809–28
: Rudolph Ackermann. *Repository of Arts, Literature, and Commerce, & C.* Published monthly. London, 1809–28.

Agius 1984
: Pauline Agius. *Ackermann's Regency Furniture & Interiors*. Introduction by Stephen Jones. Ramsbury, Marlborough, Wiltshire, 1984.

Alexander 1989
: Forsyth M. Alexander. "Cabinet Warehousing in the Southern Atlantic Ports, 1783–1820." *Journal of Early Southern Decorative Arts* 15, no. 2 (November 1989), pp. 1–42.

Anderson 1996
: Jean Bradley Anderson. *Carolinian on the Hudson: The Life of Robert Donaldson*. Raleigh, 1996.

Apicella 2007
: Mary Ann Apicella. *Scottish Cabinetmakers in Federal New York*. Hanover, N.H., 2007.

Armstrong 2001
: Tom Armstrong. *An American Odyssey: The Warner Collection of Fine and Decorative Arts, Gulf States Paper Corporation, Tuscaloosa, Alabama*. New York, 2001.

Avery 2002
: Kevin Avery. *American Drawings and Watercolors in the Metropolitan Museum of Art*. Vol. 1, *A Catalogue of Works by Artists Born before 1835*. New York, 2002.

Bancker 1869
: *A Collection of Rare and Valuable Books . . . Catalogue of the Entire Private Library of . . . C. N. Bancker . . . To Be Sold at Public Sale . . . Dec. 8, '69, and Following Days*. Philadelphia, 1869.

Banks 1972
: William Nathaniel Banks. "George Cooke, Painter of the American Scene." *The Magazine Antiques* 102, no. 3 (September 1972), pp. 448–54.

Barquist 1992
: David L. Barquist. *American Tables and Looking Glasses in the Mabel Brady Garvan and Other Collections at Yale University*. Essays by Elisabeth Donaghy Garrett and Gerald W. R. Ward. New Haven, 1992.

Barquist and Lasser 2003
: David L. Barquist and Ethan W. Lasser. *Curule: Ancient Design in American Federal Furniture*. Exh. cat., Yale University Art Gallery, New Haven, August 5, 2003–January 4, 2004. New Haven, 2003.

Barrett 1863–70
: Walter Barrett [Joseph Alfred Scoville]. *The Old Merchants of New York City*. 5 vols. New York, 1863–70.

Barter et al. 1998
: Judith Barter, Kimberly Rhodes, Seth A. Thayer, and Andrew Walker. *American Arts at The Art Institute of Chicago, from Colonial Times to World War I*. Chicago, 1998.

Bassett 1976
: Kendall H. Bassett. "The Apprenticeship of William Brown, Jr., to Duncan Phyfe." *Chronicle of the Early American Industries Association* 29, no. 4 (December 1976), p. 31.

Beach 1845
: Moses Beach. *The Wealth and Biography of the Wealthy Citizens of New York: Being an Alphabetical Arrangement of the Names of the Most Prominent Capitalists Whose Wealth Is Estimated at One Hundred Thousand Dollars and Upwards, with Sums Appended to Each Name, and Genealogical and Biographical Notices of the Principal Persons*. New York, 1845.

Bishop 1972
: Robert Bishop. *Centuries and Styles of the American Chair, 1640–1970*. New York, 1972.

Bivins 1989
: John Bivins. "A Catalog of Northern Furniture with Southern Provenances." *Journal of Early Southern Decorative Arts* 15, no. 2 (November 1989), pp. 43–91.

Blackmar 1989
: Elizabeth Blackmar. *Manhattan for Rent, 1785–1850*. Ithaca, N.Y., 1989.

de Bles 1929
: Arthur de Bles. *Genuine Antique Furniture*. New York, 1929.

Blum 1948
: Edith Victorson Blum. "Bot of D. Phyfe." *The Magazine Antiques* 54, no. 2 (July 1948), p. 109.

Blumberg 1966
: Arnold Blumberg. "The Strange Career of Joseph Binda." *South Carolina Historical Magazine* 67 (July 1966), pp. 155–66.

Boicourt 1951
: Jane Boicourt. "Duncan Phyfe." *The Magazine Antiques* 59, no. 6 (June 1951), pp. 473–75.

Bowie 1971
: Walter Worthington Bowie. *The Bowies and Their Kindred: A Genealogical and Biographical History*. Cottonport, La., 1971.

Boynton 1995
: Lindsay Boynton. *Gillow Furniture Designs, 1760–1800*. Royston, Hertfordshire, 1995.

Brown 1978
: Michael K. Brown. "Duncan Phyfe." Master's thesis, University of Delaware, Newark, 1978.

R. Brown 1822–35
: Richard Brown. *The Rudiments of Drawing Cabinet and Upholstery Furniture. . . .* 2 vols. London, 1822–35.

Bucher and Wheeler 1993
: Douglas G. Bucher and W. Richard Wheeler. *A Neat Plain Modern Stile: Philip Hooker and His Contemporaries, 1796–1836*. Clinton, N.Y., 1993.

Buck 1935
: Ralph Ogden Buck. "Duncan Phyfe Drop-Leaf Table." *Popular Mechanics Magazine* 64, no. 4 (October 1935), pp. 594–98.

Caldwell 1988
: Margaret B. Caldwell. "Classic Sport: Americana Collector Dick Button." *Art & Auction* 10 (January 1988), pp. 106–11.

Cameron 1965
: Viola Root Cameron, ed. *Emigrants from Scotland to America, 1774–1775*. Baltimore, 1965.

Carson 1979
: Marian S. Carson. "'The Duncan Phyfe Shops' by John Rubens Smith, Artist and Drawing Master." *American Art Journal* 11, no. 4 (October 1979), pp. 69–78.

Chadenet 2001
: Sylvie Chadenet, ed. *French Furniture: From Louis XIII to Art Deco*. Translated by John Goodman. Boston, 2001.

Chippendale 1762
: Thomas Chippendale. *The Gentleman and Cabinet-Maker's Director; Being a Large Collection of the Most Elegant and Useful Designs of Household Furniture, in the Most Fashionable Taste*. 3rd ed. London, 1762. First published 1754.

Colden 1825
: Cadwallader D. Colden. *Memoir, Prepared at the Request of a Committee of the Common Council of the City of New York and Presented to the Mayor of the City, at the Celebration of the Completion of the New York Canals*. New York, 1825.

Cole 1892
: George S. Cole. *A Complete Dictionary of Dry Goods*. Chicago, 1892.

Coleman 1992
: Feay Shellman Coleman. *Nostrums for Fashionable Entertainments: Dining in Georgia, 1800–1850*. Savannah, 1992.

Collard 1985
: Frances Collard. *Regency Furniture*. Woodbridge, Suffolk, 1985.

Collins 2000
: Jeffrey Collins. "*In Vino Vanitas*? Death and the Cellarette in Empire New York." In *American Artifacts: Essays in Material Culture*, edited by Jules David Prown and Kenneth Haltman, pp. 47–69. East Lansing, 2000.

Conger and Itsell 1991
: Clement E. Conger and Mary K. Itsell. *Treasures of State: Fine and Decorative Arts in the Diplomatic Reception Rooms of the U.S. Department of State*. Edited by Alexandra W. Rollins. New York, 1991.

Conner 1842
: Robert Conner. *Cabinet Maker's Assistant*. New York, 1842.

Cooper 1980
: Wendy A. Cooper. *In Praise of America: American Decorative Arts, 1650–1830. Fifty Years of Discovery since the 1929 Girl Scouts Loan Exhibition*. New York, 1980.

Cooper 1993
: Wendy A. Cooper. *Classical Taste in America, 1800–1840*. Exh. cat., Baltimore Museum of Art, June 27–September 26, 1993; Mint Museum, Charlotte, N.C., November 20, 1993–March 13, 1994; Museum of Fine Arts, Houston, May 1–July 24, 1994. Baltimore and New York, 1993.

Cooper 2002
: Wendy A. Cooper, with Tara L. Gleason and Katharine A. John. *An American Vision: Henry Francis du Pont's Winterthur Museum*. Washington, D.C., 2002.

Cornelius 1922a
: Charles Over Cornelius. "The Distinctiveness of Duncan Phyfe (1757–1854?)." *The Magazine Antiques* 2, no. 5 (November 1922), pp. 205–8.

Cornelius 1922b
: Charles Over Cornelius. *Furniture Masterpieces of Duncan Phyfe*. New York, 1922.

Cornelius 1922c
: Charles Over Cornelius. "New Light on Duncan Phyfe, Cabinetmaker." *Country Life* 42, no. 5 (September 1922), pp. 44–46.

D'Ambrosio 1999
: Anna Tobin D'Ambrosio, ed. *Masterpieces of American Furniture from the Munson-Williams-Proctor Institute*. Utica, N.Y., 1999.

Davidson and Stillinger 1985
: Marshall B. Davidson and Elizabeth Stillinger. *The American Wing in The Metropolitan Museum of Art*. New York, 1985.

Davis (1837) 1980
: Alexander Jackson Davis. *Rural Residences, etc.: Consisting of Designs, Original and Selected, for Cottages, Farmhouses, Villas, and Village Churches* (1837). New York, 1980.

Dietz and Watters 2009
: Ulysses S. Dietz and Sam Watters. *Dream House: The White House as an American Home*. New York, 2009.

Downing 1841
: Andrew Jackson Downing. *A Treatise on the Theory and Practice of Landscape Gardening*. New York, 1841.

Downing 1850
: Andrew Jackson Downing. *The Architecture of Country Houses; Including Designs for Cottages, Farmhouses, and Villas, with Remarks on Interiors, Furniture, and the Best Modes of Warming and Ventilating*. New York, 1850.

Downs 1941
: Joseph Downs. "Two Bequests and a Gift for The American Wing." *Bulletin of the Metropolitan Museum of Art* 36, no. 1, part 1 (January 1941), pp. 6–8.

Downs 1942
: Joseph Downs. "A Gift of New York Furniture." *Bulletin of The Metropolitan Museum of Art* 37, no. 5 (May 1942), pp. 136–38.

Downs 1943
: Joseph Downs. *The Greek Revival in the United States: A Special Loan Exhibition*. Exh. cat., The Metropolitan Museum of Art, New York, November 9, 1942–March 1, 1943. New York, 1943.

Downs and Ralston 1934
: Joseph Downs and Ruth Ralston. *A Loan Exhibition of New York State Furniture*. Exh. cat., The Metropolitan Museum of Art, New York, February 5–April 22, 1934. New York, 1934.

Downs Collection, Winterthur Library
: The Joseph Downs Collection of Manuscripts and Printed Ephemera, Winterthur Library, Henry Francis du Pont Winterthur Museum, Winterthur, Del.

Dyer 1915a
: Walter A. Dyer. "Duncan Phyfe Furniture." *House Beautiful* 37, no. 4 (March 1915), pp. 120–25.

Dyer 1915b
: Walter A. Dyer. *Early American Craftsmen*. New York, 1915.

Dyer 1921
: Walter A. Dyer. "Rare Old Furniture of Duncan Phyfe." *Country Life* 39 (January 1921), pp. 71–72.

Eberlein, McClure, and Holloway 1919
: Harold Donaldson Eberlein, Abbot McClure, and Edward Stratton Holloway. *The Practical Book of Interior Decoration*. Philadelphia, 1919.

Elmer 1872
Lucius Quintius Cincinnatus Elmer. *The Constitution and Government of the Province and State of New Jersey, with Biographical Sketches of the Governors from 1776 to 1845.* Newark, N.J., 1872.

Fastnedge 1962
Ralph Fastnedge, ed. *Shearer Furniture Designs, from the Cabinet-Makers' London Book of Prices, 1788.* London, 1962.

Fearon 1818
Henry Bradshaw Fearon. *Sketches of America: A Narrative of a Journey of Five Thousand Miles through the Eastern and Western States of America; Contained in Eight Reports Addressed to the Thirty-nine English Families by Whom the Author Was Deputed in June 1817, to Ascertain Whether Any, and What Part of the United States Would Be Suitable for Their Residence.* London, 1818.

Feld and Feld 2001
Elizabeth Feld and Stuart P. Feld. *Of the Newest Fashion: Masterpieces of American Neo-classical Decorative Arts.* Exh. cat., Hirschl & Adler Galleries, New York, November 24, 2001–February 2, 2002. New York, 2001.

Feld and Feld 2007
Elizabeth Feld and Stuart P. Feld. *For Work & For Play: A Selection Of American Neo-Classical Furniture.* Exh. cat., Hirschl & Adler Galleries, New York, January 10–February 10, 2007. New York, 2007.

Feld and Garrett 1991
Stuart P. Feld and Wendell Garrett. *Neo-Classicism in America: Inspiration and Innovation, 1810–1840.* Exh. cat., Hirschl & Adler Galleries, New York, April 27–June 7, 1991. New York, 1991.

Fennimore 1990
Donald L. Fennimore. "Egyptian Influence in Early Nineteenth Century American Furniture." *The Magazine Antiques* 137, no. 5 (May 1990), pp. 1190–201.

Flanigan 1986
J. Michael Flanigan. *American Furniture from the Kaufman Collection.* Exh. cat., National Gallery of Art, Washington, D.C., October 12, 1986–April 19, 1987. Washington, D.C., 1986.

Foot 1873
Samuel A. Foot. *Autobiography: Collateral Reminiscences, Arguments in Important Causes, Speeches, Addresses, Lectures, and Other Writings.* 2 vols. New York, 1873.

Franco 1973
Barbara Franco. "New York City Furniture Bought for Fountain Elms by James Watson Williams." *The Magazine Antiques* 130, no. 3 (September 1973), pp. 462–67.

Fraser 1883
William Fraser. *The Chiefs of Grant.* 3 vols. Edinburgh, 1883.

Frelinghuysen 1970
Elizabeth L. Frelinghuysen. "Collector's Notes: Lyell, Slover, Taylor, Phyfe et al." *The Magazine Antiques* 97, no. 1 (January 1970), pp. 119–20.

Garrett 1990
Elisabeth Donaghy Garrett. *At Home: The American Family, 1750–1870.* New York, 1990.

Garrett 2005
Elizabeth W. Garrett. "Entertainment of the Most Beautiful Kind: The House of William and Harriet Aiken, 1833–1860." Master's thesis, University of Delaware, Newark, 2005.

Gloag 1991
John Gloag. *A Complete Dictionary of Furniture.* Revised and updated by Clive Edwards. Woodstock, N.Y., 1991. First published 1952.

Gottesman 1938
Rita Susswein Gottesman. *The Arts and Crafts in New York, 1726–1776: Advertisements and News Items from New York City Newspapers.* New York, 1938.

Gottesman 1965
Rita Susswein Gottesman. *The Arts and Crafts in New York, 1800–1804: Advertisements and News Items from New York City Newspapers.* New York, 1965.

Gray 1994
Nina Gray. "Leon Marcotte: Cabinetmaker and Interior Decorator." In *American Furniture 1994*, edited by Luke Beckerdite, pp. 49–72. Milwaukee, 1994.

Greeley et al. 1872
Horace Greeley et al. *The Great Industries of the United States: Being an Historical Summary of the Origin, Growth, and Perfection of the Chief Industrial Arts of This Country.* Hartford and Chicago, 1872.

Groff 2003
John M. Groff. "'All That Makes a Man's Mind More Active': Jane and Reuben Haines at Wyck, 1812–1831." In *Quaker Aesthetics: Reflections on a Quaker Ethic in American Design and Consumption*, edited by Emma Jones Lapsansky and Anne A. Verplanck, pp. 90–121. Philadelphia, 2003.

Gross 1967
Katharine Wood Gross. "The Sources of Furniture Sold in Savannah, 1789–1815." Master's thesis, University of Delaware, Newark, 1967.

Hagen 1905
[Ernest F. Hagen.] "The Cost of Furniture a Century Ago." *House Beautiful* 17, no. 5 (April 1905), pp. 47–48.

Hagen [1907]
Ernest F. Hagen. "Duncan Phyfe Memorandum." Undated, but internal evidence indicates the manuscript was written in 1907. R. T. Haines Halsey Research Papers, Collection 56, 75x80.36, Joseph Downs Collection of Manuscripts and Printed Ephemera, Winterthur Library, Winterthur, Del. Reproduced in McClelland 1939, pp. 315–17.

Hagen 1908
Ernest F. Hagen. "Personal Experiences of an Old New York Cabinet Maker (1908)." Ernest F. Hagen Papers, 1881–1913, Collection 32, Joseph Downs Collection of Manuscripts and Printed Ephemera, Winterthur Library, Winterthur, Del.

Hall 1840
John Hall. *The Cabinet Makers' Assistant.* Baltimore, 1840.

Halliday & Jenkins 1847
Peremptory and Extensive Auction Sale of Splendid and Valuable Furniture . . . at the Furniture Ware Rooms of Messrs. Duncan Phyfe & Son, Nos. 192 & 194 Fulton Street, West of Broadway, Embracing Their Entire Stock, and of Their Own Well Known Manufacture, of Fashionable and Seasonable Furniture. Sale cat., Halliday & Jenkins, New York, April 16–17, 1847. New York, 1847.

Halsey and Cornelius 1922
Richard Townes Haines Halsey and Charles Over Cornelius. "An Exhibition of Furniture from the Workshop of Duncan Phyfe." *Bulletin of the Metropolitan Museum of Art* 17, no. 10 (October 1922), pp. 207–14.

Hamilton 1833
Thomas Hamilton. *Men and Manners in America.* 2 vols. London, 1833.

Hanyan 1996
Craig Hanyan. *De Witt Clinton and the Rise of the People's Men.* Montreal, 1996.

Hauserman 1968
Dianne D. Hauserman. "Alexander Roux and His 'Plain and Artistic Furniture.'" *The Magazine Antiques* 93, no. 2 (February 1968), pp. 210–17.

Hawley 1982
Henry Hawley. "An Empire Pier Table." *Bulletin of the Cleveland Museum of Art* 69 (December 1982), pp. 327–29.

Haygood and Thurlow 2007
Paul M. Haygood and Matthew A. Thurlow. "New York Furniture for the Stirlings of Wakefield, Saint Francisville, Louisiana." *The Magazine Antiques* 171, no. 5 (May 2007), pp. 126–35.

Heckscher 1997
Morrison H. Heckscher. "Duncan Phyfe, revisitus." *The Magazine Antiques* 151, no. 1 (January 1997), pp. 236–39.

Heckscher et al. 2001
Morrison H. Heckscher, H. Barbara Weinberg, and the curators of the American Wing. *A Walk through the American Wing.* New York, 2001.

Hepplewhite 1788
George Hepplewhite. *The Cabinet-Maker and Upholsterer's Guide; or, Repository of Designs for Every Article of Household Furniture, in the Newest and Most Approved Taste . . . by A. Hepplewhite and Co.* London, 1788.

Hepplewhite (1794) 1969
George Hepplewhite. *The Cabinet-Maker and Upholsterer's Guide.* Reprint of the 1794 3rd ed., with a new introduction by Joseph Aronson. New York, 1969.

Hewitt, Kane, and Ward 1982
Benjamin A. Hewitt, Patricia E. Kane, and Gerald W. R. Ward. *The Work of Many Hands: Card Tables in Federal America, 1790–1820.* Exh. cat., Yale University Art Gallery, New Haven, March 25–May 30, 1982. New Haven, 1982.

Hill 1967
John Henry Hill. "The Furniture Craftsmen in Baltimore, 1783–1823." Master's thesis, University of Delaware, Newark, 1967.

Hipkiss 1941
Edwin J. Hipkiss. *Eighteenth-Century American Arts: The M. and M. Karolik Collection of Paintings, Drawings, Engravings, Furniture, Silver, Needlework & Incidental Objects Gathered to Illustrate the Achievements of American Artists and Craftsmen of the Period from 1720 to 1820.* Cambridge, Mass., and Boston, 1941.

Hodges 1986
Graham Russell Hodges. *New York City Cartmen, 1667–1850.* New York, 1986.

Holloway 1922
Edward Stratton Holloway. *The Practical Book of Furnishing the Small House and Apartment.* Philadelphia, 1922.

Hope 1807
Thomas Hope. *Household Furniture and Interior Decoration, Executed from Designs by Thomas Hope.* London, 1807.

Hornor 1929
William M. Hornor Jr. "Two Early American Cabinetmakers Compared: Duncan Phyfe of New York and Henry Connelly of Philadelphia." *Country Life* 56, no. 5 (September 1929), pp. 47–48.

Hornor 1930
William M. Hornor Jr. "A New Estimation of Duncan Phyfe." *The Antiquarian* 14, no. 3 (March 1930), pp. 36–40, 96.

Howe et al. 1994
Katherine S. Howe, Alice Cooney Frelinghuysen, Catherine Hoover Voorsanger, Simon Jervis, Hans Ottomeyer, Marc Bascou, Ann Claggett Wood, and Sophia Riefstahl. *Herter Brothers: Furniture and Interiors for a Gilded Age.* Exh. cat., Museum of Fine Arts, Houston, August 21–October 23, 1994; High Museum of Art, Atlanta, December 13, 1994–February 12, 1995; The Metropolitan Museum of Art, New York, March 15–July 9, 1995. New York and Houston, 1994.

Hubbard 1875
Nathaniel Tuthill Hubbard. *Autobiography of N. T. Hubbard: With Personal Reminiscences of New York City from 1798 to 1875.* New York, 1875.

Hull 1906
Augustus Longstreet Hull. *Annals of Athens, Georgia: 1801–1901.* Athens, Ga., 1906.

Hunter 1918
George Leland Hunter. "The Period Styles: How to Mix without Messing Them." *Independent: Devoted to the Consideration of Politics, of Social and Economic Tendencies, of History, Literature, and the Arts* 93 (January 5, 1918), pp. 26–27.

Ingerman 1963
Elizabeth A. Ingerman. "Personal Experiences of an Old New York Cabinet-Maker." *The Magazine Antiques* 84, no. 5 (November 1963), pp. 576–80.

Jenrette 2000
Richard H. Jenrette. *Adventures with Old Houses.* Charleston, S.C., 2000.

E. Johnson 1993
Eugene J. Johnson, with photographs by Ralph Lieberman. *Style Follows Function: Architecture of Marcus T. Reynolds.* Albany, N.Y., 1993.

M. Johnson 1968
Marilynn A. Johnson. "John Hewitt, Cabinetmaker." *Winterthur Portfolio* 4 (1968), pp. 185–205.

Jones 1977
Edward V. Jones. "Two Creative Geniuses of Federal New York." *American Art Journal* 1, no. 1 (May 1977), pp. 5–14.

Joy 1977
Edward T. Joy. *English Furniture 1800–1851.* London, 1977.

Kenny 2000
Peter M. Kenny. "R. T. H. Halsey, Founder of the American Wing and Champion of Duncan Phyfe." *The Magazine Antiques* (January 2000), pp. 186–91.

Kenny 2003
Peter M. Kenny. "From New Bedford to New York to Rio and Back: The Life and Times of Elisha Blossom, Jr., Artisan of the New Republic. " In *American Furniture 2003*, edited by Luke Beckerdite, pp. 238–69. Milwaukee, 2003.

Kenny, Bretter, and Leben 1998
Peter M. Kenny, Frances F. Bretter, and Ulrich Leben. *Honoré Lannuier, Cabinetmaker from Paris: The Life and Work of a French Ébéniste in Federal New York.* Exh. cat., The Metropolitan Museum of Art, New York, March 17–June 14, 1998. New York, 1998.

Keno, Keno, and Freund 2000
Leigh Keno, Leslie Keno, and Joan Barzilay Freund. *Hidden Treasures: Searching for Masterpieces of American Furniture.* New York, 2000.

Kent and Levy 1909
Henry Watson Kent and Florence N. Levy. *The Hudson-Fulton Celebration . . . .* Vol. 2, *Catalogue of an Exhibition of American*

Paintings, Furniture, Silver, and Other Objects of Art, MDCXXV–MDCCCXXV. New York, 1909.

Keyes 1922a
Homer Eaton Keyes. "Cobwebs and Dust. Still Shrilling on Phyfe." *The Magazine Antiques* 2, no. 5 (November 1922), pp. 201–2.

Keyes 1922b
Homer Eaton Keyes. "Duncan Phyfe: Artist or Mechanic." *The Magazine Antiques* 2, no. 5 (November 1922), pp. 203–4.

C. King 1937
Caroline Howard King. *When I Lived in Salem, 1822–1866.* Brattleboro, Vt., 1937.

King 1829
Thomas King. *The Modern Style of Cabinet Work Exemplified in New Designs, Practically Arranged on 72 Plates Containing 227 Designs (Including Fragmental Parts).* London, 1829.

King (1829) 1995
Thomas King. *Neo-Classical Furniture Designs: A Reprint of Thomas King's "Modern Style of Cabinet Work Exemplified," 1829.* Introduction by Thomas Gordon Smith. New York, 1995.

King 1835–36
Thomas King. *The Cabinet Maker's Sketch Book of Plain and Useful Designs.* 2 vols. London, 1835–36.

Kirtley 2006
Alexandra Alevizatos Kirtley. "The Painted Furniture of Philadelphia: A Reappraisal." *The Magazine Antiques* 169, no. 5 (May 2006), pp. 134–45.

Kisluk-Grosheide, Koeppe, and Rieder 2006
Daniëlle O. Kisluk-Grosheide, Wolfram Koeppe, and William Rieder. *European Furniture in The Metropolitan Museum of Art: Highlights from the Collection.* New York and New Haven, 2006.

La Mésangère 1802–31
Pierre de La Mésangère. *Collection de meubles et objets de goût.* 4 vols. Paris, 1802–31.

Lee 1984
Jean Gordon Lee. *Philadelphians and the China Trade, 1784–1844.* Philadelphia, 1984.

Leslie 1840
Eliza Leslie. *The House Book; or, A Manual of Domestic Economy: For Town and Country . . . .* 3rd ed. Philadelphia, 1840.

Levy 1909
Florence N. Levy. "Phyfe Furniture in the Hudson-Fulton Exhibition at The Metropolitan Museum of Art." *Architectural Record* 26 (December 1909), pp. 455–61.

Lindsey 1991
Jack L. Lindsey. "An Early Latrobe Furniture Commission." *The Magazine Antiques* 139, no. 1 (January 1991), pp. 208–19.

Little 1931
Frances Little. *Early American Textiles.* New York, 1931.

Lockwood 1921
Luke Vincent Lockwood. *Colonial Furniture in America.* New, enl. ed. 2 vols. New York, 1921.

Loudon 1833
John Claudius Loudon. *An Encyclopædia of Cottage, Farm, and Villa Architecture and Furniture: Containing Numerous Designs for Dwellings, from the Cottage to the Villa . . . .* London, 1833. Reissued with revisions in 1835, 1836, 1839, 1842, 1846, 1850, 1857, 1863, and 1867.

Loudon 1839
John Claudius Loudon. *An Encyclopædia of Cottage, Farm, and Villa Architecture and Furniture: Containing Numerous Designs for Dwellings, from the Cottage to the Villa.* New ed. London, 1839.

Low 1976
Betty-Bright P. Low. "The Youth of 1812: More Excerpts from the Letters of Josephine du Pont and Margaret Manigault." *Winterthur Portfolio* 11 (1976), pp. 173–212.

Lyon 1872
Isaac S. Lyon. *Recollections of an Old Cartman.* Newark, N.J., 1872.

MacBean 1922–25
William M. MacBean. *Biographical Register of Saint Andrew's Society of the State of New York.* 2 vols. New York, 1922–25.

The Magazine Antiques, March 1943
Anonymous. "The Almanac: Phyfe Furniture at New York Museum." *The Magazine Antiques* 43, no. 3 (March 1943), p. 135.

Mallach 1966
Stanley Irwin Mallach. "Gothic Furniture Designs by Alexander Jackson Davis." Master's thesis, University of Delaware, Newark, 1966.

Marshall 1915
James Collier Marshall. "Duncan Phyfe, American Cabinet Maker." *Country Life in America* 27, no. 6 (April 1915), pp. 48–50.

McClelland 1939
Nancy V. McClelland. *Duncan Phyfe and the English Regency, 1795–1830.* New York, 1939.

McClure and Eberlein 1918
Abbot McClure and Harold Donaldson Eberlein. "In a Small Dining Room." *Independent: Devoted to the Consideration of Politics, of Social and Economic Tendencies, of History, Literature, and the Arts* 93 (February 2, 1918), p. 190.

McInnis and Leath 1996
Maurie D. McInnis and Robert A. Leath. "Beautiful Specimens, Elegant Patterns: New York Furniture for the Charleston Market, 1810–1840." In *American Furniture 1996,* edited by Luke Beckerdite, pp. 137–74. Milwaukee, 1996.

Milbert (1828–29) 1968
Jacques Milbert. *Picturesque Itinerary of the Hudson River and the Peripheral Parts of North America* (1828–29). Ridgewood, N.J., 1968.

Miller 1943
V. Isabelle Miller. "A New York Drawing Room of the Federal Period." *American Collector* 11 (January 1943), pp. 12–13, 19.

Miller 1956
V. Isabelle Miller. *Furniture by New York Cabinetmakers, 1650–1860.* Exh. cat., Museum of the City of New York, November 15, 1956–March 3, 1957. New York, 1956.

Mitchell 1995
William R. Mitchell Jr. *Edward Vason Jones, 1909–1980: Architect, Connoisseur, and Collector.* [Savannah], 1995.

Monkman 2000
Betty C. Monkman. *The White House: Its Historic Furnishings and First Families.* Washington, D.C., and New York, 2000.

C. Montgomery 1966
Charles F. Montgomery. *American Furniture, the Federal Period, in the Henry Francis du Pont Winterthur Museum.* New York, 1966.

F. Montgomery 1984
Florence Montgomery. *Textiles in America, 1650–1870.* New York, 1984.

Morley 1993
: John Morley. *Regency Design, 1790–1840: Gardens, Buildings, Interiors, Furniture.* New York, 1993.

Moses 1830
: Myer Moses. *Full Account of the Celebration of the Revolution in France in the City of New-York.* New York, 1830.

New York 1922
: "Furniture from the Workshop of Duncan Phyfe." Exhibition, The Metropolitan Museum of Art, New York, October 16–December 15, 1922. For the accompanying publication, see Cornelius 1922b.

New York 1929
: *Loan Exhibition of Eighteenth and Early Nineteenth Century Furniture & Glass: Examples of Lustre Ware, Lowestoft and Toile de Jouy Used in America during These Periods; Portraits by Stuart, Peale and Others.* Benefit exhibition for the National Council of Girl Scouts, American Galleries, New York, September 25th–October 9, 1929. New York, 1929.

New York 1963
: *American Art from American Collections: Decorative Arts, Paintings, and Prints of the Colonial and Federal Periods, from Private Collections.* Exhibition, The Metropolitan Museum of Art, New York, March 6–April 28, 1963. Catalogue by James Biddle. New York, 1963.

New York 1970
: *19th-Century America: An Exhibition in Celebration of the Hundredth Anniversary of the Metropolitan Museum of Art.* Vol. 1, *Furniture and Other Decorative Arts.* Exhibition, The Metropolitan Museum of Art, New York, April 16–September 7, 1970. Catalogue by Marilynn Johnson, Marvin D. Schwartz, and Suzanne Boorsch. New York, 1970.

New York 1993
: "Is It Phyfe?" Exhibition, Museum of the City of New York, March 10–December 19, 1993.

Ormsbee 1929
: Thomas Hamilton Ormsbee. "Phyfe né Fife." *The Magazine Antiques* 16, no. 6 (December 1929), pp. 496–99. Notes by Louis Guerineau Myers and Homer Eaton Keyes on pp. 498–99.

Ormsbee 1930
: Thomas H. Ormsbee. *Early American Furniture Makers: A Social and Biographical Study.* New York, 1930.

Ormsbee 1942
: Thomas Hamilton Ormsbee. "Autographed Duncan Phyfe Furniture." *American Collector* 11, no. 2 (March 1942), p. 5.

Otto 1965
: Celia Jackson Otto. *American Furniture of the Nineteenth Century.* New York, 1965.

Ottomeyer, Schröder, and Winters 2006
: Hans Ottomeyer, Klaus Albrecht Schröder, and Laurie Winters. *Biedermeier: The Invention of Simplicity.* Exh. cat., Milwaukee Art Museum, September 16, 2006–January 1, 2007; Albertina, Vienna, February 2–May 13, 2007; Deutsches Historisches Museum, Berlin, June 8–September 2, 2007; Musée du Louvre, Paris, October 15, 2007–January 15, 2008. Milwaukee, 2006.

Peck 1992
: Amelia Peck, ed. *Alexander Jackson Davis, American Architect, 1803–1892.* New York, 1992.

Peck 1996
: Amelia Peck. "The Richmond Room." In *Period Rooms in The Metropolitan Museum of Art,* pp. 219–23. New York, 1996.

Peck 2000
: Amelia Peck. "Robert de Forest and the Founding of The American Wing." *The Magazine Antiques* 157, no. 1 (January 2000), pp. 176–81.

Peirce 1976
: Donald C. Peirce. "American Painted Furniture at the Brooklyn Museum, 1675–1875." *The Magazine Antiques* 110, no. 6 (December 1976), pp. 1292–99.

Peirce 1979
: Donald C. Peirce. "New York Furniture at the Brooklyn Museum." *The Magazine Antiques* 115, no. 5 (May 1979), pp. 994–1003.

Percier and Fontaine 1812
: Charles Percier and Pierre-François-Léonard Fontaine. *Recueil de décorations intérieures; comprenant tout ce qui a rapport à l'ameublement, comme vases, trépieds, candélabres, cassolettes, lustres, girandoles, lampes, chandeliers, cheminées . . . .* Paris, 1812.

Pictorial Dictionary 1977
: *Pictorial Dictionary of British 19th Century Furniture Design: An Antique Collectors' Club Research Project.* Introduction by Edward Joy. Woodbridge, Suffolk, 1977.

Pintard 1940–41
: John Pintard. *Letters from John Pintard to His Daughter, Eliza Noel Pintard Davidson, 1816–1833.* 4 vols. New York, 1940–41.

Pollack 1998
: Jodi A. Pollack. "Three Generations of Meeks Craftsmen, 1797–1869: A History of Their Business and Furniture." Master's thesis, Parsons School of Design, New York, 1998.

Pradère 1989
: Alexandre Pradère. *French Furniture Makers: The Art of the Ébéniste from Louis XIV to the Revolution.* Translated by Perran Wood. Malibu, Calif., 1989.

Priddy 2004
: Sumpter Priddy. *American Fancy: Exuberance in the Arts, 1790–1840.* Milwaukee, 2004.

Quimby 1973
: Maureen O'Brien Quimby. "History in Houses: Eleutherian Mills in Greenville, Delaware." *The Magazine Antiques* 103, no. 3 (March 1973), pp. 550–60.

Rauschenberg and Bivins 2003
: Bradford L. Rauschenberg and John Bivins Jr. *The Furniture of Charleston, 1680–1820.* 3 vols. Winston-Salem, N.C., 2003.

Reynolds 1911
: Cuyler Reynolds, ed. *Hudson-Mohawk Genealogical and Family Memoirs.* 4 vols. New York, 1911.

Rini 2005
: Erik Rini. "Edward Holmes and Simeon Haines: Cabinetmakers in Empire New York City." *The Magazine Antiques* 167, no. 5 (May 2005), pp. 124–29.

H. Roberts 2001
: Hugh Roberts. *For the King's Pleasure: The Furnishing and Decoration of George IV's Apartments at Windsor Castle.* London, 2001.

Roberts (1827) 1977
: Robert Roberts. *The House Servant's Directory.* Reprint of 1827 ed., with a new foreword by Charles A. Hammond. Needham, Mass., 1977.

Rock 1984
: Howard B. Rock. *Artisans of the New Republic: The Tradesmen of New York City in the Age of Jefferson.* New York, 1984.

Rogers 1947
: Meyric R. Rogers. *American Interior Design: The Traditions and Development of Domestic Design from Colonial Times to the Present.* New York, 1947.

Rollins 1991
> Alexandra W. Rollins, ed. *Treasures of State: Fine and Decorative Arts in the Diplomatic Reception Rooms of the U.S. Department of State*. New York, 1991.

Rose 2001
> Anne C. Rose. *Beloved Strangers: Interfaith Families in Nineteenth-Century America*. Cambridge, Mass., 2001.

A. Sack 1993
> Albert Sack. *The New Fine Points of Furniture: Early American, Good, Better, Best, Superior, Masterpiece*. New York, 1993.

I. Sack 1969–92
> Israel Sack. *American Antiques from Israel Sack Collection*. 9 vols. Washington, 1969–92.

Schaffner 2010
> Cynthia Van Allen Schaffner. "Désiré Guilmard: *Le Garde-meuble, ancien et moderne*, 1839–1935: Introduction." Smithsonian Institution Libraries, Washington, D.C. www.sil.si.edu/DigitalCollections/Art-Design/garde-meuble/intro.htm. Accessed February 2010.

Scherer 1984
> John L. Scherer. *New York Furniture at the New York State Museum*. Alexandria, Va., 1984.

Scott 1981
> Kenneth Scott, comp. *Early New York Naturalizations: Abstracts of Naturalization Records from Federal, State, and Local Courts, 1792–1840*. Baltimore, 1981.

Sheraton 1793
> Thomas Sheraton. *Thomas Sheraton's Cabinet-Maker and Upholsterer's Drawing-Book*. 2 vols. London, 1793.

Sheraton (1802) 1970
> Thomas Sheraton. *The Cabinet-Maker and Upholsterer's Drawing-Book*. Reprint of the 1802 edition. Edited by Charles F. Montgomery and Wilfred P. Cole; new introduction by Lindsay O. J. Boynton. New York, 1970.

Sheraton 1803
> Thomas Sheraton. *The Cabinet Dictionary: Containing an Explanation of All the Terms Used in the Cabinet, Chair & Upholstery Branches, with Directions for Varnish-Making, Polishing, and Gilding; to Which Is Added a Supplementary Treatise on Geometrical Lines, Perspective, and Painting in General*. London, 1803.

Sheraton (1803) 1970
> Thomas Sheraton. *Thomas Sheraton's Cabinet Dictionary*. Reprint of the 1803 edition. Introduction by Wilfred P. Cole and Charles F. Montgomery. 2 vols. New York, 1970.

Sikes 1976
> Jane E. Sikes. *The Furniture Makers of Cincinnati, 1790 to 1849*. Cincinnati, 1976.

Singleton 1900
> Esther Singleton. *The Furniture of Our Forefathers*. New York, 1900.

Sloane 1987
> Jeanne Vibert Sloane. "A Duncan Phyfe Bill and the Furniture It Documents." *The Magazine Antiques* 131, no. 5 (May 1987), pp. 1106–13.

Small 1905
> Samuel Small Jr. *Genealogical Records of George Small, Philip Albright, Johann Daniel Dunckel, William Geddes Latimer, Thomas Bartow, John Reid, Daniel Benezet, Jean Crommelin, Joel Richardson*. Philadelphia, 1905.

G. Smith 1808
> George Smith. *A Collection of Designs for Household Furniture and Interior Decoration, in the Most Approved and Elegant Taste*. London, 1808.

G. Smith (1808) 1970
> George Smith. *George Smith's Collection of Designs for Household Furniture and Interior Decoration; with a New Index to the 158 Plates*. Reprint of the 1808 ed. Introduction by Constance V. Hershey; edited by Charles F. Montgomery and Benno M. Forman. New York, 1970.

G. Smith 1826
> George Smith. *The Cabinet-Maker and Upholsterer's Guide; Being a Complete Drawing Book, in Which Will Be Comprised Treatises on Geometry and Perspective as Applicable to the Above Branches of Mechanics*. London, 1826.

G. Smith 1828
> George Smith. *The Cabinet-Maker and Upholsterer's Guide*. London, 1828.

R. Smith 1958
> Robert C. Smith. "Late Classical Furniture in the United States, 1820–1850." *The Magazine Antiques* 74, no. 12 (December 1958), pp. 519–23.

R. Smith 1974
> Robert C. Smith. "The Furniture of Anthony G. Quervelle. Part IV, Some Case Pieces." *The Magazine Antiques* 105, no. 1 (January 1974), pp. 180–93.

T. G. Smith 1996
> Thomas Gordon Smith. *John Hall and the Grecian Style in America*. New York, 1996.

T. G. Smith 1997
> Thomas Gordon Smith. "Living with Antiques: Millford Plantation in South Carolina." *The Magazine Antiques* 151, no. 5 (May 1997), pp. 732–41.

T. G. Smith 2001
> Thomas Gordon Smith. "Quervelle Furniture at Rosedown in Louisiana." *The Magazine Antiques* 159, no. 5 (May 2001), pp. 770–79.

Snodin and Styles 2001
> Michael Snodin and John Styles. *Design & the Decorative Arts: Britain, 1500–1900*. London, 2001.

Solny 1997–98
> Susan Solny. "Some Unusual Stylistic Preferences in New York Cellaret Design, 1810–1834." *Studies in the Decorative Arts* 5, no. 1 (Fall–Winter 1997–98), pp. 83–183.

Still 1956
> Bayrd Still. *Mirror for Gotham: New York as Seen by Contemporaries from Dutch Days to the Present*. New York, 1956.

Stillinger 1980
> Elizabeth Stillinger. *The Antiquers: The Lives and Careers, the Deals, the Finds, the Collections of the Men and Women Who Were Responsible for the Changing Taste in American Antiques, 1850–1930*. New York, 1980.

Stillinger 1988
> Elizabeth Stillinger. "Ernest Hagen—Furniture Maker." *Maine Antique Digest*, November 1988, pp. 8D–16D.

Stokes 1915–28
> I. N. Phelps Stokes. *The Iconography of Manhattan Island, 1498–1909*. 6 vols. New York, 1915–28.

Stone 1825
> William L. Stone. "Narrative of the Festivities Observed in Honor of the Completion of the Grand Erie Canal Uniting the Waters of the Great Western Lakes with the Atlantic Ocean." In Colden 1825, pp. 289–408.

Storey 1934
Walter Rendell Storey. "New York's Heritage of Furniture Craft." *Parnassus* 6, no. 3 (March 1934), pp. 12, 39.

Strong 1952
George Templeton Strong. *The Diary of George Templeton Strong*. Edited by Allan Nevins and Milton Halsey. 4 vols. New York, 1952.

C. Stuart 1929
Charles Stuart. "Duncan Phyfe, Chairmaker." *The Antiquarian* 12 (July 1929), pp. 47–49, 74.

C. Stuart 1931
Charles Stuart. "Duncan Phyfe Furniture Inspires Modern Craftsmen." *Arts and Decoration* 35, no. 6 (October 1931), pp. 40–41.

S. Stuart 2008
Susan. E. Stuart. *Gillows of Lancaster and London, 1730–1840: Cabinetmakers and International Merchants: A Furniture and Business History*. 2 vols. Woodbridge, Suffolk, 2008.

Surowiecki 2007
James Surowiecki. "Financial Page: The Piracy Paradox." *The New Yorker*, September 24, 2007, p. 90.

Talbott 1995
Page Talbott. *Classical Savannah: Fine and Decorative Arts, 1800–1840*. Savannah, 1995.

Taylor 1825
John Taylor. *The Upholsterer's and Cabinet-Maker's Pocket Assistant*. London, 1825.

Thomas 1999
Frances Taliaferro Thomas. *Historic Dearing Street*. Athens, Ga., 1999.

Thornton 1993
Peter Thornton. *Authentic Décor: The Domestic Interior, 1620–1890*. London, 1993.

Thurlow 2006
Matthew A. Thurlow. "Aesthetics, Politics, and Power in Early-Nineteenth-Century Washington: Thomas Constantine & Co.'s Furniture for the United States Capitol, 1818–1819." In *American Furniture 2006*, edited by Luke Beckerdite, pp. 184–228. Milwaukee, 2006.

Tracy 1981
Berry B. Tracy. *The Federal Furniture and Decorative Arts at Boscobel*. New York, 1981.

Tracy and Gerdts 1963
Berry B. Tracy and William H. Gerdts. *Classical America, 1815–1845*. Newark, 1963.

Valentine 1929
U. Valentine. "Duncan Phyfe and the American Empire." *International Studio* 94 (November), pp. 42–44.

Venable 1998
Charles L. Venable. "Germanic Craftsmen and Furniture Design in Philadelphia, 1820–1850." In *American Furniture 1998*, pp. 41–80. Milwaukee, 1998.

Vincent 2008
Nicholas C. Vincent. "Philadelphia Pier Tables and Their Role in Cultures of Sociability and Competition." *American Furniture 2008*, edited by Luke Beckerdite, pp. 88–130. Milwaukee, 2008.

Voorsanger 2000
Catherine Hoover Voorsanger. "'Gorgeous Articles of Furniture': Cabinetmaking in the Empire City." In Voorsanger and Howat 2000, pp. 287–325.

Voorsanger and Howat 2000
Catherine Hoover Voorsanger and John K. Howat, eds. *Art and the Empire City: New York, 1825–1861*. Exh. cat., The Metropolitan Museum of Art, New York, September 19, 2000–January 7, 2001. New York, 2000.

Wall 1990
Joseph Frazier Wall. *Alfred I. du Pont: The Man and His Family*. New York, 1990.

Ward 1988
Gerald W. R. Ward. *American Case Furniture in the Mabel Brady Garvan and Other Collections at Yale University*. New Haven, 1988.

D. Warren 1998
David B. Warren, ed. *American Decorative Arts and Paintings in the Bayou Bend Collection*. Houston and Princeton, 1998.

P. Warren 1961
Phelps Warren. "Setting the Record Straight: Slover and Taylor, New York Cabinetmakers." *The Magazine Antiques* 80, no. 4 (October 1961), pp. 350–51.

Waters 1996
Deborah Dependahl Waters. "Is It Phyfe?" In *American Furniture 1996*, edited by Luke Beckerdite, pp. 63–80. Milwaukee, 1996.

Watkin and Hewat-Jaboor 2008
David Watkin and Philip Hewat-Jaboor, eds. *Thomas Hope: Regency Designer*. New Haven, 2008.

Waxman 1958
Lorraine Waxman. "French Influence on American Decorative Arts of the Early Nineteenth Century: The Work of Charles-Honoré Lannuier." Master's thesis, University of Delaware, Newark, 1958.

Webster 1845
Thomas Webster. *An Encyclopaedia of Domestic Economy*.... New York, 1845.

Weidman 1984
Gregory R. Weidman. *Furniture in Maryland, 1740–1940: The Collection of the Maryland Historical Society*. Baltimore, 1984.

Whitaker 1825
Henry Whitaker. *Designs of Cabinet and Upholstery Furniture in the Most Modern Style*. London, 1825.

Woodside 1986
Joan Woodside. "French Influence on American Furniture as Seen through the Engraved Designs of Pierre de La Mésangère's *Collection de meubles et objets de goût* Published from 1802 to 1835." 2 vols. Ph.D. diss., University of Chicago, 1986.

Word 1979
Ola Mae Word. *Reflections of Rosedown: A Rosedown Book*. [New Orleans], 1979.

Zimmerman 1999
Philip D. Zimmerman. "The American Sofa Table." *The Magazine Antiques* 155, no. 5 (May 1999), pp. 744–53.

Zimmerman 2005a
Philip D. Zimmerman. "The Architectural Furniture of Duncan Phyfe, 1830–1845." In *Important New York Furniture and Decorative Arts: The Richard and Beverly Kelly Collection*, pp. 12–19. Sale cat., Northeast Auctions, Manchester, N.H., April 3, 2005.

Zimmerman 2005b
Philip D. Zimmerman. "New York Card Tables, 1800–1825." In *American Furniture 2005*, edited by Luke Beckerdite, pp. 119–45. Milwaukee, 2005.

Index

Note: Page numbers in *italic* refer to illustrations and plates.

Abernethy and Kincardine parish, Scotland, 23, 24, 58n2
Ackerman, Lawrence, 35, 60n58, 66, 73, 111n4
Ackermann, Rudolph, *Repository of Arts . . .* , 79, 101, 108, 212, 218, 234, 250
Additional Revised Prices, 176
Aiken, William, 52, 62n157
Aiken-Rhett House, Charleston, S.C., 107, 113n83
Albany, N.Y., Fife family in, 23, 24, 26
Allen, Stephen, 57
Allison, Mary Cromwell, 134
Allison, Michael, 5, 35, 40, 42, 43, 52–53, 62n159, 112n40, 198
   card table, 74, 76, 176
   Pembroke table, 80, 81, 85
   pier table, 85, 86, 216, *216*
   sofa, 71, 73
American Advertising Directory, for Manufacturers and Dealers in American Goods, 50
American Art Association, N.Y., "Girl Scouts Loan Exhibition" (1929), *11*, 12, *13*, 240
American Institute Fairs, 50
American South
   New York cabinetmaking trade and, 3, 39
   Phyfe's reputation in, 29, 47
   trade with, 24, 29, 44, 49–50
   warehousemen in, 39, 40, 60n86
American Wing, Metropolitan Museum
   Joseph Downs as curator of, 14
   Gallery of the Early Republic, 8–9, *8*, *10*
   Greek Revival Parlor, 17, *18*
   Richmond Room, 17, 120
   Berry B. Tracy as curator of, 17–19
Anderson, Elbert, 35, 65
Anderson Galleries, N.Y., 11, 12
Andrew, Henry, 47
The Antiquarian, 14, 77, 118
Antique style. *See* Grecian style
Appleton, William, 46
Armstrong, William, *Aristocracy of New York*, 55
Association of Cabinet Makers, 51
Astor, John Jacob, 47, 97, 220
Aymar, Mr. and Mrs. John Q., 87–88, *89*

Baker, Calvin, 39, 42
Ball, John, 152n6
Baltimore, Md., 31
Bancker, Charles Nicoll, 29, 37, 120–22, 161, 188
   drawing of furniture, 37, 69, 120–21, *121*
   inventory of furniture, 67, 120, 153n17
   invoice from Duncan Phyfe (App. 1.6), 8, 10, 20n18, 120, 121, 188, 277
   Thomas Sully's portrait of, *121*
Bancker, Sarah Upshur Teackle, 120, 122
Barber, John F., 154n73
Baring, Alexander, first Baron Ashburton, 62n147
Baroque style, 90
Barquist, David, 188

basin stand, D. Phyfe & Son (Pl. 58), 95, 151, 253, 254, *255*
Baudouine, Charles A.
   French Restauration style and, 94
   Ernest F. Hagen and, 4
   label of, 54
   revival styles and, 105
   side chair, 108, *109*
   warehouse of, 53
Bauduy, Victorine du Pont, 36, 75, 77, 122–23, 124, 170
   Rembrandt Peale's portrait of, *122*
Bayard, Elizabeth Cornell, 115
Bayard, William, 12–13, 28, 37, 77, 78, 82, 111n28, 115–18, 120, 176, 178, 218, 268
   furniture (Pls. 1–5), 158, *159*, 160, *161*, *161*, *162*, *163*, *164*, *165*, 166, 185, 186, 192
   invoices from Phyfe (App. 1.3a–1.3c), 14, 71, 74, 111n4, 116–17, 118, 158, 162, 164, 274
   Gilbert Stuart's portrait of, 115, *116*
Beach, Moses, *Wealth and Biography of Wealthy Citizens of New York*, 54
Beaver Street, Lyell's business on, 34–35, 66
bedsteads
   French bedstead (App. 2.3), 248, 280
   French bedstead (App. 2.11), 283
   Grecian bedstead, D. Phyfe & Sons (Pl. 55), 151, 248, *249*, 250, 253, 254
   high-post bedstead (Pl. 42), 85, 224, *225*, 226
Belter, John Henry, 15
Benkard, Mrs. Harry Horton, 6
Biddle, James, 17
Biedermeier furniture, 136, 228, 244
Binda, Count Joseph, 146, 154n76, 154–55n79
Bland, Harry, 16–17
Blithewood, Dutchess County, N.Y., 133, *134*
Blossom, Elisha Jr., 34
Bonaparte, Joseph, 146
bookcases
   cylinder desk and bookcase, attrib. to Duncan Phyfe, 79, *79*, 198
   secretary bookcase, 39, 78–79, 124, *125*, 198
   secretary bookcase, attrib. to Duncan Phyfe (Pl. 33), 86, 90, 130, *132*, 198, 208, *209*, 210, 218
   writing table and bookcase (Pl. 25), 15, 86, 198, *199*, 200
Boscobel Restoration, 17, 19, 181
Boulle, André-Charles, 107, 212
Bourbon Restoration, 134, 234
Bowie, Thomas Lattimer, 15, 200n1
Bradley, Allan B. A., 6, 10–11, 12
Brewerton, George, invoice from Phyfe (App. 1.1), 28, 273
Brewster, Sir David, 222
Brinckerhoff, Charlotte Troup, 184–85
Brinckerhoff, James Lefferts, 19, 62n177, 184–85, 188, 193, 207
   furniture (Pls. 17–19), 184–86, *184*, *185*, *186*, *187*, 192, 196, 226, 264
   invoice from Phyfe (App. 1.5), 184, 185, 224, 276

Broad Street
   Joseph Meeks' building on, 42, 53
   view of, *43*
Broadway
   Samuel Foot's home on, 138
   furniture manufactories of, 3, 4, 53
   Hudson-Fulton Celebration procession on, *5*
Bronson, Mr. and Mrs. Frederick, 4, 9, 19n8
Bronson, Isabel Donaldson, 90, 130, *132*, 134, 154n47, 154n49, 210, 241
Brouwer, Jacob, 35, 60n89, 118, 152n6
Brouwer, John L., 63n177
Brown, William Jr., 46, *46*, 58n8, 61n116
Bruce, John, 28, 61n116
Bulkley, Erastus, 50
Bullock, George, 212
Burkhalter, Stephen, 62, 63n177
Burling, Samuel and William, 35
Burling, Thomas, 65
Butman, Asa, 45
Buttre, William, advertisement of, 41, 42

Campbell, Duncan Pearsall, 118, 216, 218
Campbell, Maria Bayard, 116, 118, 216, 218
canterburies
   attrib. to Duncan Phyfe (Pl. 36), 86, 130, 133, 212–13, *213*
   D. Phyfe & Sons, 35, 101, *103*
Caribbean, 3, 29, 39, 48–49
Carter, Robert, 65
Carter administration, 17
cellarets
   Duncan Phyfe (Pl. 24), 56–57, 78, 195–97, *195*, *197*, 213, 258
   D. Phyfe & Son (Pl. 60), 77, 95, 151, 174, 258–59, *258*, *259*
Census of Manufactures (1820), 40
chairs
   armchairs
     attrib. to Duncan Phyfe, 98, *100*, *141*, 142, 151, 262
     D. Phyfe & Sons or D. Phyfe & Son, 100, *103*
     D. Phyfe & Son, 97, 98, *109*, 147, 148, *149*, 151, *152*, 265
     August-Émile Ringuet-Leprince, 94, *105*
     Charles-Honoré Lannuier, 70–71, *72*, 85
     Hagen & Meier, 4, 9, *9*, 19n8
   curule chairs
     discussion of form, 69–71
     attrib. to Duncan Phyfe, 119, *119*, 178
     attrib. to Duncan Phyfe (Pl. 13), 69–70, 119, 168, 178, *179*, 180–81, 188, 192
     New York maker (Pl. 21), 178, 188, 190, *191*
   French chairs
     discussion of form, 96–99
     Duncan Phyfe, 97, 140, *141*
     attrib. to Duncan Phyfe (Pl. 46), 97, 138, 140, 228, 233–34, *234*
     D. Phyfe & Son, 97
   klismos chairs
     discussion of form, 69–71

296   *Duncan Phyfe*

Duncan Phyfe (Pls. 17, 20, 44), 37, 66, 66, 69, 81, 121, 136, 184, *184*, 185–86, 186n4, 188, *189*, 193, 228, 229
   New York maker (Pl. 22), 73, 192–93, *192*
library chairs
   Duncan Phyfe (App. 2.21), *287*
   attrib. to Duncan Phyfe, 74, *75*
lotus-back chairs
   attrib. to Duncan Phyfe or D. Phyfe & Sons (Pl. 50), 101, *104*, 108, 238–40, *239*
   D. Phyfe & Sons (Pl. 49), 101, *104*, 110, 144, 238–40, *238*, 240n1, 262
   D. Phyfe & Son, *108*
lyre-back chair, The Company of Master Craftsmen, 10, *10*
rocking chair, D. Phyfe & Son, 97, *99*
scroll-back chairs
   discussion of form, 69–71
   Duncan Phyfe (Pls. 1–3), 12, 69, 70–71, 73, 85, 90, 116, 158, *159*, *160*, *161*, 161n3, 164
side chairs
   Duncan Phyfe (App. 2.1), *280*
   attrib. to D. Phyfe & Son, 107–8, *108*, 239
   attrib. to D. Phyfe & Son (Pl. 62), 109–10, 151, 239, 260, 262, 262n1, 263, 265
   Charles A. Baudouine, 108, *109*
   English maker, 101, *105*
   New York maker, 66, *66*, 90, *90*, 108, *108*, 188, *190*
chaises gondoles. See French chairs
Chaloner, E. and W. Fleming, "Cutting and Trucking Mahogany in Honduras," *50*
Champlin, Seabury, 25
Charleston, S.C., 35, 36, 39, 40, 50, 174, 204
Charles X, 93, 234
Chatereau, P., 105
Chatham Street, Great Fire of 1811, 30
chest of drawers (App. 2.14), *284*
cheval glass, D. Phyfe & Son (Pl. 56), 151, 250, *251*, 252, *252*
Chinese style, 110
Chippendale, Thomas, 108
   The Gentleman and Cabinet-Maker's Director, 110, 198
Civil War, 151–52
Clark, Benjamin, 136
   invoice from Duncan Phyfe (App. 1.8), 93, 134, 227–28, 236, *278*
Clark, Deborah Morris Franklin, 134
Clinton, DeWitt, 30, 47, 58, 194
Clover, Peter, 45
Codazzi, Viviano (attrib.), *Roman Ruins*, 146
Colles, James, 11
The Company of Master Craftsmen, blueprint drawing of lyre-back side chair, 10, *10*
Connelly, Henry, 13
Conner, Robert, *Cabinet Maker's Assistant*, 253
consoles, 95
Constantine, John, 45
Constantine, Thomas, 43, 60n67
Consulat period, 69, 96, 111n17, 196, 210
Cooper, James Fenimore, 196
Cooper-Williams, Inc., 10
Cornelius, Charles Over, 6, 6–7, 13, 16, 19, 20n18, 68, 69, 111n16, 111n17, 112n41
   "The Distinctiveness of Duncan Phyfe," 8
   Furniture Masterpieces of Duncan Phyfe, 6–8, *7*, 16, 19
Corporation of the City of New York, 60n67
Country Life, 10, 13
Cowles, Alfred II, 136
Cowperthwaite, John K., 60n89

crib (App. 2.20), 244, 246, *286*
Cromwell, Pauline Bronson, 134
Cruger, Catharine, 123
Cruger, John, 28
Cummings, Thomas S., 146
Curran, James, 11
Curtis, Joel, 170n5
Curtiss, Glenn Hammond, 5
cylinder desk and bookcase, attrib. to Duncan Phyfe, 79, *79*, 198

Dacre, Henry, *Specie Claws*, 51, *52*
Dash, John B. Jr., 25
David, Jacques-Louis, *Madame Récamier*, 210
Davis, Alexander Jackson, 108, 109, *109*, 110, 129, 130, 133, 154n52, 154n53
   Blithewood, 134
Dearing, William and Eliza, 174
de Bles, Arthur, *Genuine Antique Furniture*, 13
Decatur, Susan Wheeler, 39
The Deepdene, Dorking, Surrey, 15
de Forest, Robert W., 5, 8, 20n13
Deming, Brazilia, 46, 50
Deming & Bulkley, 49–50, 89
   center table, 50, *51*
Democratic Party, 51
Democratic-Republican Party, 29–30
Devoe, John, 43
Dey Street, 26, 30, 31, 42, 58
d'Hancarville, Pierre, *Collection of Etruscan, Greek, and Roman Antiquities*, 69, 72, 228
Directoire period, 7, 69, 111n17
Dixey, John, 116
Dohrmann, Augustus L., 4
Dolan, John T., 35, 74, 164, 170n5
Donaldson, Robert, 17, 129–30, 133–34, 154n47, 208, 210–11, 264
   furniture (Pls. 32–36), 86, 87, 88, 89, 90, 99, 186, 198, 208, *209*, 210–13, *211*, *212*, *213*, 216, 260
   invoice from Phyfe (App. 1.7), 46, 130, 208, 236, *278*
   Charles Leslie's portrait of, *129*, 130
Donaldson, Samuel, 130
Donaldson, Susan Jane Gaston, 210–11
   George Cooke's portrait of, 130, *131*, 210
   harp of, 130, *131*, 211
Dorr, Henry, 181n1
Dove, William, 30, 35, 164
Downing, Andrew Jackson, 94, 129–30, 133, 154n55, 248
   The Architecture of Country Houses, 105–6
   Cottage Residences, 130
Downs, Joseph P., 14–15, 16
D. Phyfe & Son, 3, 32, 34, 46, 52–53, 59, 61n118, 61n119, 62n157
   armchair, 97, *98*, 109, 147, *148*, *149*, 151, *152*
   basin stand (Pl. 58), 95, 151, 253, 254, *255*
   cellaret (Pl. 60), 77, 95, 151, 258–59, *258*, *259*
   cheval glass (Pl. 56), 151, 250, *251*, 252, *252*
   couch, 100, *102*, 107, 148, *148*, *150*, 264
   dining table, 151, *152*
   drop-leaf table (Pl. 53), 58, 95, 99, 244, *245*
   ladies' writing fire screen (Pl. 59), 99, 256, *257*
   nesting tables (Pl. 65), 244, 266, *267*
   nightstand (Pl. 57), 151, 253, *253*, 254
   ottoman, 149, *150*, 260
   rocking chair, 97, *99*
   sideboard table, 147, *148*, 236
   sofa (Pl. 63), 107, 109, 148, 264, *264*, 265
   wardrobe (App. 2.8), 93, *93*, 232, 252, 253, 254, *282*
D. Phyfe & Sons, 51

canterbury, 35, 101, *103*
checker stand (Pl. 54), 98, 246, *246*, 247, 268
couch, 95, 107, 142, *143*, 144, 239
   Grecian bedstead (Pl. 55), 151, 248, *249*, 250, 253, 254
   lotus-back side chair (Pl. 49), 101, *104*, 110, 144, 238–40, 238, 240n1, 262
   pier table (Pl. 48), 136, 142, 144, 236, *237*, 239, 252
   taboret (App. 2.19), *286*
   trade card of, 33, 142, 239
   drawing of two chairs, attrib. to Duncan Phyfe, 37, 69, 120–21, *121*, 158, 161, 188
   dressing glass or toy bureau, D. Phyfe & Son or Duncan Phyfe (Pl. 52), 242, *243*
du Pont, Gabrielle Josephine de Pelleport, 122, 123, 170, 174
du Pont, Henry Francis, 11, 12–13, 15, 17, 174
du Pont, Pierre Samuel, 122, 153n23
du Pont, Victor Marie, 29, 36–37, 60n67, 75, 77, 122–23, 170, 174
Dyer, Walter A., 5, 7, 10, 19n9

East Indies, trade with, 115, 172
Edgewater, Barrytown, N.Y., 17, 129, 130, 133–34
Edwards & Baldwin, 36–37, 50, 136–37
   sofa, 37, *38*
Egerton, Abraham S., 43
Egyptian symbolism, 95, 101
E. I. du Pont de Nemours and Company, 122
Eleutherian Mills, Del., 123, *123*
Elizabethan style, 105
Ellis, Jesse, 128
Embargo Act of 1807, 29
English Regency style, 68–70, 74, 79, 82, 84, 100, 101, 118, 136, 146, 178, 185, 212, 240
Eoff, Garrett, 57
Erie Canal, 47, 48–49, *49*, 68
   commemorative medal, 47, *48*, 61n131
Erskine-Danforth Corporation, 10
Evans, George H., 62n150
export market
   oversupply and, 39
   Panic of 1819 and, 40
   Phyfe and, 29, 36, 37, 39–40, 44, 49

Fanewood, New Windsor-on-Hudson, 135, 136
Fearon, Henry Bradshaw, 112n50, 166
   Sketches of America, 49
Federalist Party, 29–30, 36
Few, Mary, 39–40, 124
Fife, Donald (father), 23, 58n6
Fife, Elizabeth Fraser, 58n4
Fife, Isabella (sister), 23
Fife, Isobel Grant (mother), 23, 26, 58n3, 58n5, 58n8
Fife, James (brother), 23, 30–31, 44, 59n38
Fife, John (brother), 23, 26, 28, 30, 34, 59n25
Fife, Mary (sister), 23
Fife, Robert (nephew), 28
Fife, William F. (nephew), 28
Fife family, 23, 58n5. See also Phyfe family
Fifth Avenue Auction Rooms, Inc., 11, 20n44
Fish, Nicholas, 47
Fisher, Robert, 31
Flaxman, John, *The Iliad of Homer*, 69
Fontaine, Pierre-François-Léonard, *Recueil de décorations intérieures*, 79, 82, 112n38
Foot, Jane Campbell, 138
Foot, Samuel Alfred, 18, 97, 137–38, 140, 228, 233, 234, *235*
   Ezra Ames portrait of, *138*

Index   297

footstool, attrib. to Duncan Phyfe (Pl. 14), 119, 178, 180–81, *180*
Ford administration, 17
Fox, George, 82, 134–136, 227–228
Franklin, Benjamin, 122
French chairs (*chaises gondoles*), 96–99, 97, 112n66
French Empire style, 7, 14, 79, 82, 85, 93, 118, 140, 214, 248
French Neoclassical style, 65
French Restauration style, 82, 93–99, 100, 108, 134, 138, 200, 264
French secretarys. See *secrétaires à abattant*
Friends of National Industry, 40
Fulton, Robert, 5, 30
Fulton Street
   Robert Kelly's workshop on, 44
   Phyfe's house on, 26, 30, 30, 40, 42, 54, 55–57, 55, 62n169, 62n172, 196, 246
   Phyfe's property on, 47, 54–55, 58, 62n177
Fulton Street, Phyfe cabinet warehouse on
   apprentices working in, 46, 61n116
   label and trade card used at, 31, 33
   map showing, 30, 41, 42
   Phyfe's purchase of, 47, 59n44
   Phyfe's sons working at, 32
   proximity of Robert Kelly's business to, 44
   renaming of street, 30
   sale and closing of, 3, 53
   showrooms of, 41, 53
   walkout of 1819, 45–46
   watercolor of, 6, 19, 40–42, *41*, 53, 60–61n95, *114*, 166

Galusha, Elijah, 15
Garvan, Francis P., 6, 12
Gaston, William, 130
Geib, John, 43, 61n100
General Society of Mechanics and Tradesmen of the City of New York, 24–25, 26, 35
George Anderson & Son, 39
George IV, 106
Georgian and Evening Advertiser, 40
Gibbons, William Jr., 29, 39
Gillespie & Walker, 84
Gillows & Co., 198, 240
Girard, Anthony, 36, 123
Goddard, John, 13
Gordon, Thomasin, 28
Gothic Revival style, 10, 18, 97, 105, 106, 108–10, 133, 151, 198, 239, 246, 262, 268, 270
Gracie, Archibald, 130
Grand Canal Celebration medal, 47, 48, 61n131
Grant, Duncan (grandfather), 58n2
Grant clan, 23, 58n3, 58n4
Great Fire of 1811, 30
Great Fire of 1835, 53
Grecian cross fronts, 69, 111n19
Grecian Plain style
   aesthetic of, 61n131, 68, 90, 93
   Alexander Downing on, 112n53
   Samuel Foot and, 18, 137–38, 140
   George and Maria Fox and, 134, 227, 228
   Ernest F. Hagen on, 65, 90
   Millford Plantation and, 100, 146, 151, 244
   Phyfe's interpretation of, 90, 93–101, 105–107, 109, 110, 111n12
   Lewis Stirling furniture and, 136–37
   Eliza Phyfe Vail and, 142, 144, 236
   Stephen Van Rensselaer IV and, 140, 142
Grecian style
   Michael Allison and, 73
   as archaeologically correct, 68, 158, 178, 182

   Deming & Bulkley and, 50
   Charles-Honoré Lannuier and, 70, 79, 81
   Phyfe's interpretation of, 3, 17, 52, 53, 65, 68–71, 73–79, 111n12, 116, 126, 174, 182, 186, 196, 210, 214, 218, 220, 264
Grecian style, ornamented, 79, 81, 84–90, 93, 100
Greek Revival architecture, 68, 93, 125, 134, 136, 142, 144, 264
Green-Wood Cemetery, Brooklyn, 56, 57–58
Griscom, Bronson and Sophie, 181
Guilmard, Désiré, *Le Garde-meuble, ancien et moderne*, 94, 107, *107*

Hagen, Ernest Ferdinand, 3–4, *4*, 9, 12, 20n31, 90. See also Hagen & Meier
   "Duncan Phyfe Memorandum," 4, 5, 6, 17, 65, 242
   "Personal Experiences of an Old New York Cabinet Maker," 3, 4
   sofa, 9, *9*
   study of Duncan Phyfe, 3, 4, 5, 10, 13, 19, 20n13, 59n43, 60n76, 60n95, 88, 90, 110, 205
Hagen, Frederick E., 4, 10, 19–20n9
Hagen, Henry A., 4, 10
Hagen & Meier, 4, 5, 19n5
   armchair, 4, 9, *9*, 19n8
Haines, Jane Bowne, 36, 37, 40, 81–82, 125–26
   Nathaniel Rogers's portrait of, *125*
Haines, Reuben III, 81–82, 125
Halliday & Jenkins, D. Phyfe and Son auction sale, 13, 15, 53, 94, 236, 250, 253, 256, 258
Halsey, Richard Townes Haines, 5–6, 8, 10, 12, 13
Hammond, James Henry, 3, 52
Hampton, Wade I, 144, 154n74
Haskell, Mrs. J. Amory, 12, 192
Havemeyer family, 4
Haviland, John, the Tombs, 95–96
Hay, Sir John, 50, 62n147
Hayden & Gregg & Co., 151, 155n86
Hayward, George, *View of City Hall . . .*, 28
Hearst, William Randolph, 11
Hepplewhite, George
   Cabinet-Maker and Upholster's Guide, 65, 111n17, 198
   on cellarets, 258
   Ernest F. Hagen on, 3
   influence on Phyfe, 7, 67, 74
   on sideboards, 195
Herculaneum, 119, 178
Herter Brothers, 4
Hewitt, John, 34, 35–36, 39, 43, 49, 50, 196
Heyer, William B., silver tea service, 36, *37*
Holmes & Haines, 89, 201, 216
Hooker, Philip, 140, 142
Hope, Thomas, 15, 16, 68, 210, 220
   Household Furniture and Interior Decoration, 79, 82, 84, 101, 158, 174, 178, 204–5
Hornor, William Mcpherson Jr., 13–14, 15, 16, 11n4, 118, 153n7
Horry, Harriott Pinckney, 36, 126, 128, 153n33
Houmas Plantation, La., 154n74
House Beautiful, 5, 10
House of History, Kinderhook, N.Y., 16, 21n67
Hudnut, Alexander M., 12, 20n46
Hudson-Fulton Celebration of 1909, 5, 11, 13
Huger, Sarah Elliott, 36, 37, 40, 43, 115, 126, 128–29, 182, 184

Imbert, Anthony, *Grand Canal Celebration*, 48–49
Ince, William, 108

Independent Republican Electors, 30
Inman, Henry, 146

Jackson, Andrew, 51
Jacob Frères, 111n16
James and George Phyfe, 34
James Phyfe, 34, *34*, 59n52
James Ruthven & Son, 34
Jarvis, John Wesley, 36
Jefferson, Thomas, 29–30, 122
Jennings, Walter B., 12
Jenny, Johan-Henrich, *View of Wall Street*, 27
Jenrette, Richard Hampton, 17, 133, 152
J. & J. W. Meeks, 53, 89
John Struthers & Son, 147, 155n84
Jones, Edward Vason, 17–19
Joseph Meeks & Sons
   broadside for, 91, 93, 97, 97, 108, 112n55, 234
   gilders and, 89
   pier table, 92, 93, 216
   success of, 46, 49
Journeymen Cabinet and Chair Makers of New-York, 45
J. & W. F. Phyfe, 34

Karr, Daniel, 47, 61n131
Kelly, Richard, 153n13
Kelly, Robert, 44, 61n111, 196
Kelso, James, 60n73, 77, 123–24, 170, 174
   invoices from Duncan Phyfe (App. 1.4), 76, 124, 275
Kennedy, Jacqueline, 17, 134
Kensington Company, 10
Kent, Henry W., 10–11
Keyes, Homer Eaton, 8, 20n17, 65, 66
King, Thomas
   Cabinet Maker's Sketch Book of Plain and Useful Designs, 100, 101, 103, 238
   Modern Designs for Household Furniture, 222, 224
   The Modern Style of Cabinet Work Exemplified, 100, 106, 107, 151
Kinloch, Mary I'on Lowndes, 128, 153n38
Kinnan, Alexander P., 42
Kip, Leonard, 49
Kittinger Company, 10
knife boxes, 35, 60n59
Knoblock, Edward, 15–16
Krieg, Ernest, 4

Lafayette, marquis de, 47
Lambert, John, 29
La Mésangère, Pierre de, *Collection de meubles et objets de goût*, 68, 79, 82, 82, 94, 95, 95, 98, 134, 178, 214, 234, 234
Lannuier, Charles-Honoré
   advertisements of, 208, 210
   armchair, 70, 72, 85, 161
   William Bayard as client of, 118, 140, 152n6
   James Brinckerhoff as client of, 185
   card table, 85, *85*, 118, 206
   City Hall of New York City and, 168
   financial struggles of, 47–48
   French Empire style and, 82, 84, 85
   Grecian style and, 70, 79, 81
   John Hewitt on, 35–36
   Parisian training of, 28
   Thomas Pearsall as client of, 119
   pier tables of, 216
   sculptural carved work of, 182
   Stephen Van Rensselaer IV as client of, 224
   White House and, 17
   worktables of, 203–4

La Rochefoucauld-Liancourt, duc de, 26
Late Regency style, 99–101, 105
Latrobe, Benjamin Henry, 158
Lefever, Minard, *The Beauties of Modern Architecture,* 147
Leon Marcotte & Company, 4
Le Roy, Bayard & McEvers, 28, 115
LeRoy and Bayard, 115
Lewis, Mrs. Henry Llewellyln Daingerfield Sr., 11
Livingston family, 16, 28, 112n66, 210
Livy, 220
London Cabinet-Makers' Union Book of Prices, 176
The London Chair-Makers' and Carvers' Book of Prices for Workmanship, 69, 70, 71, 73, 75, 111n17, 116, 162
Lorillard, Jacob, 51
Loring, David, 34, 59n54
Loudon, John Claudius, *Encyclopedia of Cottage, Farm, and Villa Architecture and Furniture,* 101, 103, 105, 238, 239, 262, 264
Louis-Philippe, 93, 94, 96, 100
Louis XIV style, 10, 52, 53, 94, 100, 105, 106–7, 148, 240, 266
Louis XV style, 10, 52, 94, 100, 105, 106, 107, 108, 108, 148, 151, 240, 266
Louzada, Isaac, 25, 58n14, 61n105
Love, C. Ruxton Jr., 18In1
Lyell, Fenwick, 34–35, 60n59, 66, 67

MacCulloch, George P., 28
The Magazine Antiques, 7–8, 19, 20n17, 65
Magee, Safety, 46
Mandeville, William, 30, 35, 47, 71, 111n28
Mangin, Joseph François, 26, 28
Manhattan Insurance Company, 42
Manning, John Laurence, 34, 37, 93, 137, 144–52, 236, 239. See also Millford Plantation
 bill of lading (App. 1.9), 279
 James DeVeaux portrait of, *145*, 146
Manning, Sally Bland Clarke, 147, 151
Manning, Susan Hampton, 144–52, 154n74
 James DeVeaux portrait of, *145*
Marcotte, Leon, 94
Marsh, Beverly, 46
Marshall, James Collier, 14
Marx, Samuel, 16
Matlake, John and Permilla, 63n178
Mayhew, John, 108
McClelland, Nancy Vincent, 14, 15, 16, 21n67, 68
 Duncan Phyfe and the English Regency, 1795–1830, 13, 15–17, *15,* 19, 21n66, 58n2, 58n5, 59n43, 115, 120, 134, 138, 153n34, 198, 200n1, 233, 238, 240, 242n2
McComb, John Jr., 26, 28, 115–16
McFarlan, Henry, 193
McIntire, Samuel, 17
McKearin, George S., 12
Mead, Staats M., 42
Meeks, John, 42, 44, 50, 52, 61n107
Meeks, Joseph, 42, 50, 54–55, 62n144
Meeks, Joseph W., 42, 44, 50, 52, 61n107, 152n6
Meier, J. Matthew. *See also* Hagen & Meier
 Ernest F. Hagen's partnership with, 4
Mercantile Advertiser, 46
The Metropolitan Museum of Art, New York
 American Wing, 8–9, *8,* 10, 13, 14, 17–19, 120
 "Furniture from the Workshop of Duncan Phyfe" exhib. (1922), 6–7, 10–11, 13, 14, 20n17, 68, 111n17, 136
 Hudson-Fulton Celebration exhibition (1909), 5, 6, 16, 20n13

"A Loan Exhibition of New York State Furniture" (1934), 14–15
"19th-Century America" exhib. (1970), 18
"Ninth Annual Exhibition of American Industrial Art" (1925), 10
 Van Rensselaer Hall, 142
Midwest, 3, 4, 47
Milbert, Jacques, 112n38
Miller, Decatur, 50
Millford Plantation, Sumter County, S.C., 144–51, *145*
Minturn, Sarah, 36, 126, 153n30
Mitchell S. Mitchell estate, Southbury, Connecticut, 32, *33,* 58, 244
Moffatt, Walter, 45
Monroe, James, 46–47, 57
Montgomery, Charles, 67, 111n17
Morel and Seddon, 234
Morewood, Edmund, invoice from Phyfe (App. 1.2), 28, 274
Morgan, Matthew, 53
Morgan & Saunders, 69
Morrell, George, 61n105
Morrell, Isaac W., 40, 44, 60n86, 60n89, 61n105, 63n177, 174
Morrell, Jacob P., 44, 61n105
Mulford, Mary, 112–13n70
Museum of the City of New York, "Is It Phyfe?" exhib. (1993), 19
Myers, Florence Guerineau, 12
Myers, Louis Guerineau, 6, 12, 65, 66, 174, 240–41

Nancy McClelland, Inc. *See* McClelland, Nancy Vincent
Napoleon I, 93, 248
Napoleon III, 94
Napoleonic Wars, 29, 248
National Advocate, 45
National Arts Club, 17
Nelson, Horatio, 69
Neoclassical style
 archaeologically correct interpretation of, 158
 card table design and, 164
 Robert Donaldson's Edgewater and, 133
 New York City Hall, 28
 Phyfe's interpretation of, 65–68, 77, 90, 110, 116
 revival styles and, 105
 sofa design and, 162
 White House and, 17
Newark Museum, "Classical America, 1815–1845" exhib. (1963), 17, 18
Newberry, George, 46, 61n119
Newbold, George, 59n44
The New Mirror, 53, 94, 106
New Orleans, 39, 50
The New-York Book of Prices for Manufacturing Cabinet and Chair Work, 70, 72, 73, 82, 83, 84, 112n54, 172, 183n5, 196–97, 205–6, 228, 241, 248
New York cabinetmaking trade
 American South and, 3, 39
 apprenticeships and, 24, 45–46, 61n116
 Baltimore and, 31
 bankruptcies of, 51
 community of craftsmen, 34–36
 competition in, 46, 49–53, 86, 112n50
 export market and, 39
 fine arts carting and, 26, 44
 large-scale manufacturing facilities of, 53
 Panic of 1819 and, 40, 51, 86
 Panic of 1837 and, 51
 Phyfe identified with, 12
 warehouse descriptions, 42

 War of 1812 and, 36, 60n67
 workmen of, 42–45
New York City. *See also* New York cabinetmaking trade; *and specific streets*
 city directories, 25–26, 30, 31, 44, 46, 52
 City Hall, 26, 28, *28,* 47, 68, 115, 116, 168
 as commercial center, 47, 49
 export trade and, 39, 47
 German immigration to, 4
 map of, 27
 Phyfe's apprenticeship in, 24
 population of, 47
 real estate values, 47
 views of, 27, 28
 War of 1812 celebration, 36
New-York Commercial Advertiser, 50, 53, 62n149, 94, 220, 235, 235n7
New-York Directory and Register for the Year 1789, 27
New-York Evening Post, 46, 47
New-York Gazette and General Advertiser, 31, 242
New York Harbor, 47
New-York Historical Society, 17, 204
New York Merchants Exchange Building, 220
The New-York Revised Prices for Manufacturing Cabinet and Chair Work, 13, 15, 44, 45
New-York Society of Cabinet-Makers, 45
New York State, land speculation in, 115
New York State Museum, Albany, Grecian sofa (App. 2.15), 285
New York Sun, 5, 19n8
New York Times, 5, 9, 23
Nichols, Isaac, 25
nightstand, D. Phyfe & Son (Pl. 57), 151, 253, *253,* 254
Nixon administration, 17
Non-Importation Act of 1806, 29
North River Bank, 49

Old French style, 100, 105, 106–8, 109, 148, 239–40, 266
Oneidacraft, 20
Ormsbee, Thomas Hamilton, 17, 58n6, 196
ottoman, D. Phyfe & Son, 149, *150,* 260

Palmer, William, 152n6
Panic of 1819, 40, 44, 45, 48, 51, 60n93, 86, 198
Panic of 1837, 3, 51
Parnassus, 14
Partition Street manufactory. *See also* Fulton Street cabinet warehouse
 appearance of, 42
 grand illumination for War of 1812, 36, 60n68
 labels used at, 31
 location of, 26, 27
 Phyfe's accumulation of property, 30, 59n35
 Phyfe's furniture from, 74, 168
 prominence of, 26, 28, 29
Paul, Dunbar, 40, 226
Payne, Mrs. Henry Wilmerding, interior view of home, 120, *121,* 180
P. B. Smith & Co., 46
Pearl Street, 35, 46
Pearsall, Frances Buchanan, 119
Pearsall, Thomas Cornell, 73, 74, 75, 79, 118–20, 153n13, 176, 178, 180–81, 181n1, 186, 192
 John Opie (attrib.) portrait of, 119, *119*
Percier, Charles, *Recueil de décorations intérieures,* 79, 82, 112n38
Perris, William, *Maps of the City of New York,* 30, 41, 42
Philadelphia, cabinetmaking in, 11, 13, 39
Phyfe, Ann Eliza Voorhis, 63n178

Index 299

Phyfe, Churchill B., 111n4
Phyfe, Duncan (1770–1854). *See also* Fife family
   American citizenship of, 28
   apprenticeship of, 24–25, 58n8
   attributions to, 13–14, 15, 18–19
   baptismal record of, 23, 58n2
   business records of, 16, 17, 28, 31, 32, 34, 35, 36, 43–44, 52, 59n44, 60n76
   as cabinetmaker, 26
   celebrity of, 3, 11, 14, 36, 37, 128
   in city directories, 30, 31
   clients of, 7, 16, 19, 20n18, 28, 36–37, 39, 60n57, 115, 123
   collectors, 8–13
   credit access of, 48
   customer relations of, 36–37, 39–40, 123, 124, 126, 184, 188
   death of, 23, 57, 58n1, 224
   documentation of pieces, 8, 12, 14, 15, 16, 19, 20n23, 61n121, 65, 198
   drawings of, 37, 60n76
   early career of, 23–26, 28–30
   estate of, 16–17, 30, 42, 49, 55, 58, 253
   exhibitions on, 6–7, 10–11, 13, 14, 20n17, 68, 111n17, 136
   export market and, 29, 36, 37, 39–40
   family of, 26, 30–34, 59n36
   family's immigration to United States, 23, 58n5
   fire department appointment of, 30
   Geib family and, 61n100
   Ernest Hagen's scholarship on, 3, 4, 5, 20n13
   Hudson-Fulton Celebration and, 5
   invoice to Charles Nicoll Bancker (App. 1.6), 8, 10, 20n18, 120, 121, 188, 277
   invoice to William Bayard (App. 1.3a–1.3c), 14, 71, 74, 111n4, 116–17, 118, 158, 162, 164, 274
   invoice to Mr. Brewerton (App. 1.1), 67, 273
   invoice to James L. Brinckerhoff (App. 1.5), 184, 185, 224, 276
   invoice to Benjamin Clark (App. 1.8), 93, 134, 227–28, 236, 278
   invoice to Robert Donaldson (App. 1.7), 46, 130, 208, 210, 236, 278
   invoice to James Kelso (App. 1.4), 76, 124, 275
   invoice to Mr. Morewood (App. 1.2), 67, 274
   as joiner, 25–26
   labels of, 30, 31, 40, 198, 200, 204, 206, 210, 218
   legacy of, 17–19, 57
   marketing Phyfe name, 46–47
   marriage of, 25, 36
   name modification, 26
   prices of furniture, 10, 12
   promissory notes, 58, 62–63n177
   property of, 30, 31, 42, 45, 47–49, 53–54, 58, 59n35
   proprietary independence of, 30
   reassessment of, 19
   reputation of, 29, 35, 36–37, 39, 43, 46–47, 48, 50, 52, 57, 90, 110, 115, 128, 146
   retirement of, 3, 42, 52, 53
   role as craftsman-mechanic, 54
   scholarship on, 3–8, 13–18, 19
   Scottish heritage of, 28
   signature of, 86, 87
   subcontracting of, 35, 67
   tool chest of, 17, 22, 246
   trade cards of, 30, 31
   will of, 5, 19–20n9, 31, 32, 62n173, 62n177
   workmen employed by, 39, 42–46, 75, 88–89, 123, 166, 182, 205
Phyfe, Duncan (1848–1919) (grandson), 16–17, 58
Phyfe, Duncan (b. 1818) (grandson), 32, 59n43, 60n95, 242
Phyfe, Edward D. (1808–1887) (son), 30, 31, 32, 56, 58, 63n178
Phyfe, George (1812–1857) (nephew), 34
Phyfe, Harry (grandson), 60n95, 63n178
Phyfe, Isaac M. (1796–1881) (nephew), 34
Phyfe, Isabella (ca. 1814–1841) (daughter), 30, 33–34
Phyfe, James (1800–1887) (nephew), 34, 59n52, 147
Phyfe, James Duncan (1814–1887) (son), 30, 31, 32, 32, 47, 49, 51–52, 57–58, 244, 246, 286
Phyfe, James G. (1797–1878), 98
Phyfe, John G. (1829–1907) (great-nephew), 59n52
Phyfe, John Jr. (1798–1872) (nephew), 34, 34, 61n131
Phyfe, Julia, 57, 58
Phyfe, Laughlin (ca. 1778–1869) (brother), 23, 30–31, 32, 58n5, 59n24, 59n39, 59n42
Phyfe, Michael (1794–1836) (son), 26, 30, 31–32, 42, 52, 62n154, 242
Phyfe, Rachel Louzada (ca. 1781–1851) (wife), 25, 30, 36, 57, 59n15, 224
Phyfe, Robert (1805–1890) (nephew), 34, 147
Phyfe, William (1803–1842) (nephew), 34
Phyfe, William (1813–1875) (son), 30, 31, 32, 58, 59n44, 61, 62n154
Phyfe, William H. P. (1855–1915) (grandson), 58
Phyfe, William M. (1810–1893) (nephew), 57
Phyfe & Brother, 34, 147, 151, 155n82
Phyfe & Company, 59n52
Phyfe family, 17, 30, 56, 57–58, 285–86
Phyfe & Jackson, 59n52
Pintard, John, 119
Pompeii, 119
Ponsot, George, 94, 112n59
Popular Mechanics Magazine, 10
Post, John J., 25, 35, 58n11, 66
Potter, Nathaniel, 144, 146, 154n75
Prime, Nathaniel, 180–81
Pugin, Augustus Welby Northmore, 108
Purdy, Emma (granddaughter), 242, 242n3

Queen Anne style, 10
Quick, Abraham, 40

Ralston, Ruth, 14–15, 16
Reade Street, Phyfe's property on, 47, 58, 58n14
Reed, Luman, 57, 98, 112–13n70
Regency Revival style, 15–16, 17
Reichardt, Charles Friedrich, 144, 154n75
Reifsnyder, Howard, 11, 12
Reisner, Jean-Henri, 232
Renaissance Revival style, 18, 94, 105
Republican Party, 51
revival styles of the 1840s, 105–10
Reynolds, Marcus T., 142
Richter Furniture Company, 10
Ringuet-Leprince, Auguste-Émile, 53, 94
   armchair, 94, 105, *105*
Robertson, Archibald, 61n131
Rococo Revival style, 65, 67, 101, 105, 106–8, 110
Rococo style, 18, 52, 53, 106, 110, 142, 151, 164
Rogers, Moses, 12, 115–16
Rogers, Susan Bayard, 117, 158
Roman sarcophagus, 73, *75*
Roosevelt family, 4
Rosedown Plantation, St. Francisville, La., 264
Roux, Alexander, 53, 94, 105
Rowland, Stanley J., drawings, 6, 7, 16
Ruthven, James, 34, 59n25, 164
R. & W. F. Phyfe, 34

Sack, Israel, 174
Saint Andrew's Society, 28, 59n25
Saint-Mémin, Charles Balthazar Julien Fevret de, [View of New York], 25
Salem, Mass., cabinetmaking trade in, 39
satinwood, 170, 170n2, 172, 176
Savannah, Ga., 29, 39, 39, 40, 44, 50
Savery, William, 13
Schinkel, Karl Friedrich, 154n75
Scott, Shapter & Morrell, 61n105
Scott, Walter, 124
Scott, William R., 15, 39
Scott & Morrell, 61n105
secrétaires à abattant
   attrib. to Duncan Phyfe, 230, 232, 232n1
   attrib. to Duncan Phyfe (Pl. 37), 90, 214, *215*, 230, 232
   attrib. to Duncan Phyfe, D. Phyfe & Sons, or D. Phyfe & Son (Pl. 45), 230, *230*, *231*, 232
   French maker, 94, *94*
secretary bookcases, 39, 78–79, 124, *125*, 198
   attrib. to Duncan Phyfe (Pl. 33), 86, 90, 130, *132*, 198, 208, 209, 210, 218
Sexton, Francis, 60n67
Seymour, John, 17
Seymour, Thomas, 17, 47–48
Shaefer, Robert, 44
Shaw, Joshua, *United States Directory . . . ,* 35
Shaw Furniture Company, 10
Shearer, John, 108
   The Cabinet-Makers' London Book of Prices, Designs of Cabinet Work, 77–78, *78*
Sheraton, Thomas
   The Cabinet Dictionary, 68, 73, 77, 162, 166, 190n4, 203, 213, 240, *240*, 258, 266
   Cabinet-Maker and Upholsterer's Drawing-Book, 65, 66, 111n17, 232
   on cheval glass, 250
   designs of, 185
   Gothic Revival style and, 108
   Grecian style and, 174, 178
   Ernest F. Hagen on, 3
   influence on Phyfe, 7, 67
   on knife cases, 60n59
   Neoclassical style and, 65
   on satinwood, 176
Sheraton style, 14, 65, 67
Shop and Warehouse of Duncan Phyfe . . . (unidentified artist), 6, 19, 40–42, *41*, 53, 60–61n95, 69, 114, 166
sideboards, 77–78, *78*, 118
   Duncan Phyfe (Pl. 24), 56–57, 78, 195–97, *195*, *197*, 213, 258
   attrib. to D. Phyfe & Son (Pl. 67), 110, 270–71, *270*, *271*
   John Shearer, 77–78, *79*
   New York City maker, 44, *44*
Skidmore, Thomas, 62n150
Sloane, Jeanne Vibert, 19
Sloane Coffin, William, 10, 20n35
Slott, Alexander, 205
Slover & Taylor, 35, 66, 67
Smedberg, Adolphus, 16
Smedberg, Mrs. Carl G., 16
Smedberg, Charles Gustavus, 16
Smith, Abigail Adams, 153n9
Smith, George
   The Cabinet-Maker and Upholsterer's Guide, 93, 99–100, *101*, 136, 154n58, 254, *254*, 261, 265
   Collection of Designs for Household Furniture and Interior Decoration, 79, 81, *81*, 99, 101, 108, 112n42, 113n71, 149, 210, *211*

on console supports, 227
Grecian style and, 174, 178, 210
on occasional tables, 265
on Old French style, 107
Smith, John Reubens, 61n95
Smith, Robert, 111n17, 207n1
Smith, Stephen, 153n9
snuffbox, possibly New York City, ca. 1810–15, 29
sofas
  box sofas
    attrib. to Duncan Phyfe, 82, 82, 228, 268
    Duncan Phyfe (Pl. 43), 82, 95, 136, 137, 227–29, 227, 228, 240n1, 268
    New York maker (Pl. 66), 110, 110, 268, 268, 269
  couches
    attrib. to Duncan Phyfe, 138, 139, 144, 155n89, 233–34
    D. Phyfe & Sons, 95, 107, 142, 143, 144, 239
    D. Phyfe & Son, 144, 147, 148, 100, 102, 107, 148, 150, 264
    Grecian couch or daybed, attrib. to Duncan Phyfe (Pl. 35), 73, 86, 88, 130, 208, 210, 212, 212
  Grecian sofas, 36–37, 81–82, 81, 125–26, 127
    Duncan Phyfe (App. 2.15), 82, 285
    Duncan Phyfe (Pl. 18), 64, 73, 81, 81, 184, 185, 185, 188, 264
    attrib. to Duncan Phyfe, 81, 82, 130, 131, 154n49, 212, 264
    attrib. to Duncan Phyfe (Pl. 15), 73, 119, 178, 180–81, 181, 192
    New York maker (Pl. 23), 73, 193–94, 193
  with lyre ends, 8–9, 8, 10
  scroll-back sofas
    Duncan Phyfe (Pl. 4), 71, 74, 82, 117, 158, 162, 163, 164, 268
    attrib. to Duncan Phyfe (Pl. 6), 71, 166, 167
  sofas
    attrib. to Duncan Phyfe, 66–67, 67
    D. Phyfe & Son (Pl. 63), 107, 109, 148, 264, 264, 265
    Edwards & Baldwin, 37, 38, 137
    Ernest F. Hagen, 9, 9
    Michael Allison, 71, 73, 74
Sonora Phonograph Company, 10
South America, 3, 39, 115
Southey, Robert, 266
Stackhouse, William, 45
stands
  basin stand (App. 2.10), 283
  basin stand (App. 2.4), 281
  checker stand, D. Phyfe & Son (Pl. 54), 98, 246, 246, 247, 268
  marble-top stand (App. 2.7), 281
State Street
  William Bayard's town house on, 28, 115–16, 158
  Robert Donaldson's house on, 130, 133, 154n47, 211
  Moses Rogers' house on, 115–16
  A. Weingartner, *View of State Street*, 115, 117
Steen, John, 45
Stirling, Lewis and Sarah Turnbull, 19, 37, 110, 136–37, 151, 226, 236
  P. R. Vallée potraits of, 137
Storey, Walter Rendell, 14
Stout, Mr. and Mrs. Andrew Varick, 12
Strickland, William, 125
Strong, George Templeton, 119
Stuart, Charles, 10
Stuyvesant family, 28

Sumter, Thomas Jr., 154n79
Super, Jacob, 125
Supplement to the London Chair-Makers' and Carvers' Book of Prices for Workmanship, 69, 71, 71, 73, 178, 190n4
Sypher & Company, 4

tables
  card tables, 79, 80, 81, 84, 185, 204, 207
    Duncan Phyfe (App. 2.22), 200, 201, 287
    Duncan Phyfe (App. 2.23), 200, 201, 287
    Duncan Phyfe (Pl. 5), 74, 78, 117, 120, 164, 165
    Duncan Phyfe (Pl. 26), 40, 85, 86, 87, 200–202, 201, 218, 224
    Duncan Phyfe (Pl. 27), 40, 85, 200–202, 202, 204, 206, 218, 226
    attrib. to Duncan Phyfe, 74, 84, 84, 85, 85, 118, 118, 164n2, 176, 183n4, 204, 204, 206
    attrib. to Duncan Phyfe (Pl. 12), 74, 79, 118, 119, 176, 177, 178
    attrib. to Duncan Phyfe (Pl. 29), 83, 84, 204–6, 205
    attrib. to Duncan Phyfe (Pl. 30), 206, 206
    attrib. to Duncan Phyfe (Pl. 31), 85, 183n4, 206–7, 207
    Michael Allison, 74, 76, 176
    Charles-Honoré Lannuier, 85, 85, 118, 206
    New York maker, 74, 76, 176
    New York maker (Pl. 11), 74, 176, 177, 178
  center tables, 135, 136, 154n58, 222, 236
    Duncan Phyfe (Pl. 32), 87, 88, 130, 132, 208, 208, 210, 218, 220, 236
    Duncan Phyfe (Pl. 41), 222, 222, 223, 224
    attrib. to Duncan Phyfe (Pl. 40), 87, 88, 88, 89, 186, 218, 220–21, 220, 221, 221n1
    Deming & Bulkley, 50, 51
    New York maker, 87–88, 88, 89, 89
  chiffonier or occasional table (App. 2.17), 166, 285
  corner table (App. 2.6), 151, 281
  dining tables, 135, 136, 154n58
    D. Phyfe & Son, 151, 152
  dressing table with mirror (App. 2.16), 285
  drop-leaf table, D. Phyfe & Son (Pl. 53), 58, 95, 99, 244, 245
  nesting tables, D. Phyfe & Son (Pl. 65), 244, 266, 267
  occasional table, attrib. to D. Phyfe & Son (Pl. 64), 100, 101, 107, 149, 151, 265–66, 265
  Pembroke tables
    Duncan Phyfe (App. 2.13), 174, 284
    Duncan Phyfe (Pl. 19), 62n177, 80, 81, 184, 186, 186, 187, 196, 226
    Michael Allison, 80, 81, 85
  pier tables, 37, 38, 92, 93, 95, 95, 134, 136, 236
    Duncan Phyfe (Pl. 16), 16, 82, 84, 126, 128, 128, 182–83, 182, 183, 196, 204
    attrib. to Duncan Phyfe, 82, 83, 129, 182, 182
    attrib. to Duncan Phyfe (Pl. 38), 85, 86, 216, 217, 218, 236
    attrib. to Duncan Phyfe (Pl. 39), 87, 89, 89, 216, 218, 218n1, 219
    deconstructed, attrib. to Duncan Phyfe, 95, 96
    D. Phyfe & Sons (Pl. 48), 136, 142, 144, 236, 237, 239, 252

    Joseph Meeks & Sons, 92, 93
    Michael Allison, 85, 86, 216, 216
  sideboards, 37, 136, 137, 151, 236
    D. Phyfe & Son, 147, 148, 236
  sofa tables, attrib. to D. Phyfe & Sons or D. Phyfe & Son (Pl. 51), 95, 96, 240–41, 241, 252
  worktables, 75, 79, 123–24, 124, 135, 136, 154n58, 168, 170, 174
    Duncan Phyfe (Pl. 7), 74–75, 168, 168n1, 169, 193
    Duncan Phyfe (Pl. 8), 75, 76, 77, 122, 122, 123, 124, 168, 170, 171, 172, 174, 203
    Duncan Phyfe (Pl. 10), 12, 15, 76–77, 77, 90, 174, 175, 179
    Duncan Phyfe (Pl. 28), 86, 198, 203–4, 203
    attrib. to Duncan Phyfe, 86–87, 133, 133
    attrib. to Duncan Phyfe (Pl. 9), 75, 76, 124, 170, 172, 172, 173, 203
    attrib. to D. Phyfe & Son, 98–99, 100
  writing table and bookcase (Pl. 25), 15, 40, 86, 198, 199, 200
taborets
  Duncan Phyfe (App. 2.5), 234, 281
  attrib. to Duncan Phyfe (Pl. 47), 95, 233, 234–35, 235
  D. Phyfe & Sons (App. 2.19), 286
Tatham, Charles Heathcote, 178
Taylor, Jacob, 35, 66
Taylor, John, *Upholsterer's and Cabinet-maker's Pocket Assistant*, 264
Taylor, J. S., 71, 111n28
Telfair, Mary, 39–40, 78–79, 124–25, 198
  Enrichetta Nardudcci's portrait of, 124
Thompson, Martin Euclid, 220
Thompson, Mary Clark, 152
Thorp, Andrew, 35, 166
Tiebout, Cornelius, New York City map, 27
Tiffany, Louis Comfort, 4
Tillou, Vincent, 25
Townsend, Howard, 161n3
Tracy, Berry B., 17–19, 170, 170n6
Trafalgar House, 69
Troup, Louisa, 4
Troup, Robert, 57, 184
Turcot, Peter, 185
Turnbull, John, 31, 59n25, 62n154
Turnier, Daniel, 25, 34, 35, 60n62, 176, 264

upholstery, in furniture trade, 35
Upjohn, Richard, 140, 142

Vail, Eliza Phyfe (1801–1890) (daughter), 30, 32–33, 33, 57, 58, 62n173, 99, 107, 137, 142, 143, 144, 224
  canterbury owned by, 35, 101, 103
  furniture descended in family of, 35, 100, 107, 111n4, 174, 224, 236, 238, 239, 242, 284, 285, 286
  Grecian sofa made for, 82, 285
  lotus-back side chair, D. Phyfe & Sons (Pl. 49), 101, 104, 110, 144, 238–40, 238, 240n1, 262
  pier table, D. Phyfe & Sons (Pl. 48), 136, 142, 144, 236, 237, 239, 252
  taboret, 234, 286
Vail, F. Percy (great-grandson), 17, 20n23, 242n2
Vail, William Jr., 32–33, 57, 58, 142, 143, 144, 224, 236
Vail & Reed, 32, 142
Valentine, D. T., *Manual of the Corporation of the City of New-York for 1859*, 115, 117

Valmere, New Market, N.J., 33, 142, 144, *144*
Van Boskerck, John, 40
Van Buren, Martin, 51
Van Cortlandt, Ann Stevenson, 256
Van Cortlandt family, 28
Vanderbeck, Isaac, 59n35, 59n44
Vanderpoel, James, 16
Van Deverter, Peter and Emily, 99
Van Rensselaer, Harriet Bayard, 118, 140, *140*, 142, 224
Van Rensselaer, Louisa, 142, 154n73
Van Rensselaer, Stephen III, 140
Van Rensselaer, Stephen IV, 97, 118, 140–42, *140*, 154n68, 224, 228, 234
Van Rensselaer, William Bayard, residence of, 142, *142*
Van Rensselaer Manor House, Albany, N.Y., 140, *141*, 142
Van Tassel, David, 46
Verplanck, Gulian Crommelin, 30, 51
Vesey Street
   Michael Allison's warehouse on, 42
   J. & J. W. Meeks on, 53
   Phyfe's property on, 47, 49
Vidal, Gore, 133
Voltaire, 122

Wakefield plantation, St. Francisville, La., 110, 136–37, 226
Walker, Robert, 35, 49
Wallace, Lila Acheson, 17
Wallace, Thomas, 35
Wall Street
   First Presbyterian Church on, 25, 27
   Thomas Pearsall firm on, 119
Waln, William, 158
Wardell, Charles, 49

wardrobes
   Duncan Phyfe (App. 2.2), *280*
   Duncan Phyfe (App. 2.9), *282*
   Duncan Phyfe (App. 2.12), *284*
   Duncan Phyfe (App. 2.18), *286*
   D. Phyfe & Son (App. 2.8), 93, *93*, 232, 252, 253, 254, *282*
War of 1812, 29–30, 36, 40, 84, 115, 126, 188, 193–94
Washington, George, 36
Washington Benevolent Society, 29, 46
Watts, Charles Jr., 48–49
Watts, Charles Sr., 34, 35, 48–49
Webster, Thomas, *Encyclopaedia of Domestic Economy*, 253, 270–71, 271n1
Webster-Ashburton Treaty, 62n147
Weeks, Mrs. Edward Carnes, 16
Wells, John, 16, 82, 84, 115, 126, 128–29, 153n34, 182, 196, 204
   John Frazee's bust of, *128*
Wells, Sabina Elliott Huger, 126, 128–29, 182
West, Grove B., 45
West, John E., 115
West Indies, 24, 29, 115, 123, 172, 176
Wheaton, Stephen, 128
Wheaton & Davis, 60n89
Whitehead, William, 65
White House, Washington, D.C.
   East Room, 47
   Green Room, *18*
   Jacqueline Kennedy and, 17
   library chair (App. 2.21), *287*
   pier table, 92, 93, 95, *95*, 134, 136, *236*
   side chair, by Charles A. Baudouine, 108, *109*
   window seats, 60n58
Whitlock, Duncan P. (b. 1821) (grandson), 57, 58
Whitlock, Margaret P. Ronaldson, 57

Whitlock, Mary Phyfe (1795–1870) (daughter), 30, 32, 33, 58, 61n105, 62n173, 99, 244, 244n2, 284
Whitlock, Sidney B., 32, 47, 61n105, 244n2
Whitlock, William Jr., 32, 61n105
Whitney, Stephen C., 186, 220
Whittredge, Euphemia Foot, 140, 233
   interior view of home, *234*
Whittredge, Worthington, 233
   Geneva House, 138, 140, *140*
   interior view of home, *234*
William and Mary style, 10
Wiminel, Peter, 45
window seats, 60n58
   Duncan Phyfe (Pl. 34), 86, *87*, 88, *88*, 89, 90, 99, 130, 208, 210, *211*, 211, 218, 224, 260
   attrib. to D. Phyfe & Son (Pl. 61), 149, 151, 260–61, *261*
Winterthur Museum, Phyfe Room, 12–13, *13*, 17, 116, 174
Wirt, William, 39
W. & J. Sloane, 10, 20n35
Wolcott, Oliver Jr., 60n67, 197
Woodruff, George, 14, 74, 164, 195
Woolley, Brittain L., 49
Workingmen's Party, 50–51, 62n150
Wright, Wilbur, 5
Wyck, Germantown, Pa., 36, 125, *127*

Yale University Art Gallery, 6
Young, Moses, 40, 74
Young, Stephen, 40, 74

Zeigler, Mary, 134, 136

Photograph Credits

Unless otherwise specified, all photographs were supplied by the owners of the works of art, who hold the copyright thereto, and are reproduced with permission. The Metropolitan Museum of Art has made every effort to obtain permissions for all copyright-protected images. For images that appear in this publication for which permission has not been received, please contact the Museum's Editorial Department. Photographs of works of art in the Metropolitan Museum's collection are by The Photograph Studio, The Metropolitan Museum of Art. Additional credits are as follows:

Gavin Ashworth: fig. 49
Courtesy of Carswell Rush Berlin: fig. 136
Brooklyn Museum: App. 1.7
Christie's Images Limited: fig. 41; App. 2.22
Cooper-Hewitt, National Design Museum, Smithsonian Institution/Art Resource: fig. 12
Barry Fikes: figs. 95, 182
Collection of Girl Scout National Historic Preservation Center, Lawrence X. Champeau: fig. 10

John Hall: fig. 162
Hirschl & Adler Galleries, Inc., New York: figs. 18, 137
Michael Hurley: fig. 156
Courtesy of Richard Hampton Jenrette: App. 2.11
James D. Julia Auctioneers: App. 2.12
Courtesy of Leigh Keno: App. 2.4
Library of Congress, Washington, D.C.: fig. 50
Sandy McCook, Inchtomach Scotland: fig. 15
The Metropolitan Museum of Art: Pls. 1, 2; Pl. 2, detail; Pl. 3; Pl. 3, detail; Pls. 4, 5, 7, 8, 10, 12, 16; Pl. 16, fig. 1; Pls. 17, 18, 19; Pl. 19, detail; Pl. 21; Pl. 21, fig. 1; Pls. 22, 23, 24; Pl. 24, detail; Pls. 25, 26, 27, 28; Pl. 29, fig. 1; Pls. 30, 31, 33, 34, 35, 36, 37, 38, 39, 40; Pl. 40, detail; Pl. 41; Pl. 41, detail; Pl. 42; Pl. 42, detail; Pl. 43; Pl. 43, detail; Pl. 44; Pl. 46, fig 1; Pls. 48, 49, 51, 52, 53, 54; Pl. 54, detail; Pl. 56; Pl. 56, detail; Pls. 58, 59, 60; Pl. 60, detail; Pl. 61, fig. 1; Pls. 62, 63, 64, 65, 66; Pl. 66, detail; Pl. 67; Pl.67, detail; figs. 2, 4, 5, 7, 9, 13, 21, 23, 24, 25, 27, 28, 29, 30, 31, 32, 35, 36, 37, 43, 54, 55, 57, 59, 71, 75, 77, 78, 81, 83, 84, 86, 87, 90, 92, 93, 94, 97, 99, 100, 101, 102, 103, 106, 110, 111, 112, 114, 115, 116, 118, 119, 123, 124, 125, 128, 129, 131, 140, 143, 144, 145, 151, 153, 158, 159, 160, 161, 164, 165, 166, 167, 168, 170–172, 173, 174, 178, 181, 184, 185, 186, 187, 188, 189, 190, 192, 193, 194, 195, 196, 197, 198, 199, 200; App. 1.1, 1.4, 2.1, 2.5, 2.6, 2.7, 2.8, 2.9, 2.10, 2.13, 2.14, 2.16, 2.17, 2.19, 2.21
Museum of Fine Arts, Boston, 2010: Pl. 11
John Reinhardt: App. 1.8
Sotheby's New York: App. 2.2, 2.3, 2.18
Courtesy of Elizabeth Stillinger: fig. 1
Telfair Museum of Art, Savannah, Georgia: fig. 155
Richard Walker: fig. 47
Tony Walsh, Cincinnati, Ohio: fig. 121
Katherine Wetzel: Pl. 45, fig. 1
Bruce White: fig. 141
Bruce White, © White House Historical Association: fig. 138
White House Historical Association: fig. 14
Winterthur Library, Winterthur, Delaware: fig. 11; App. 2.23

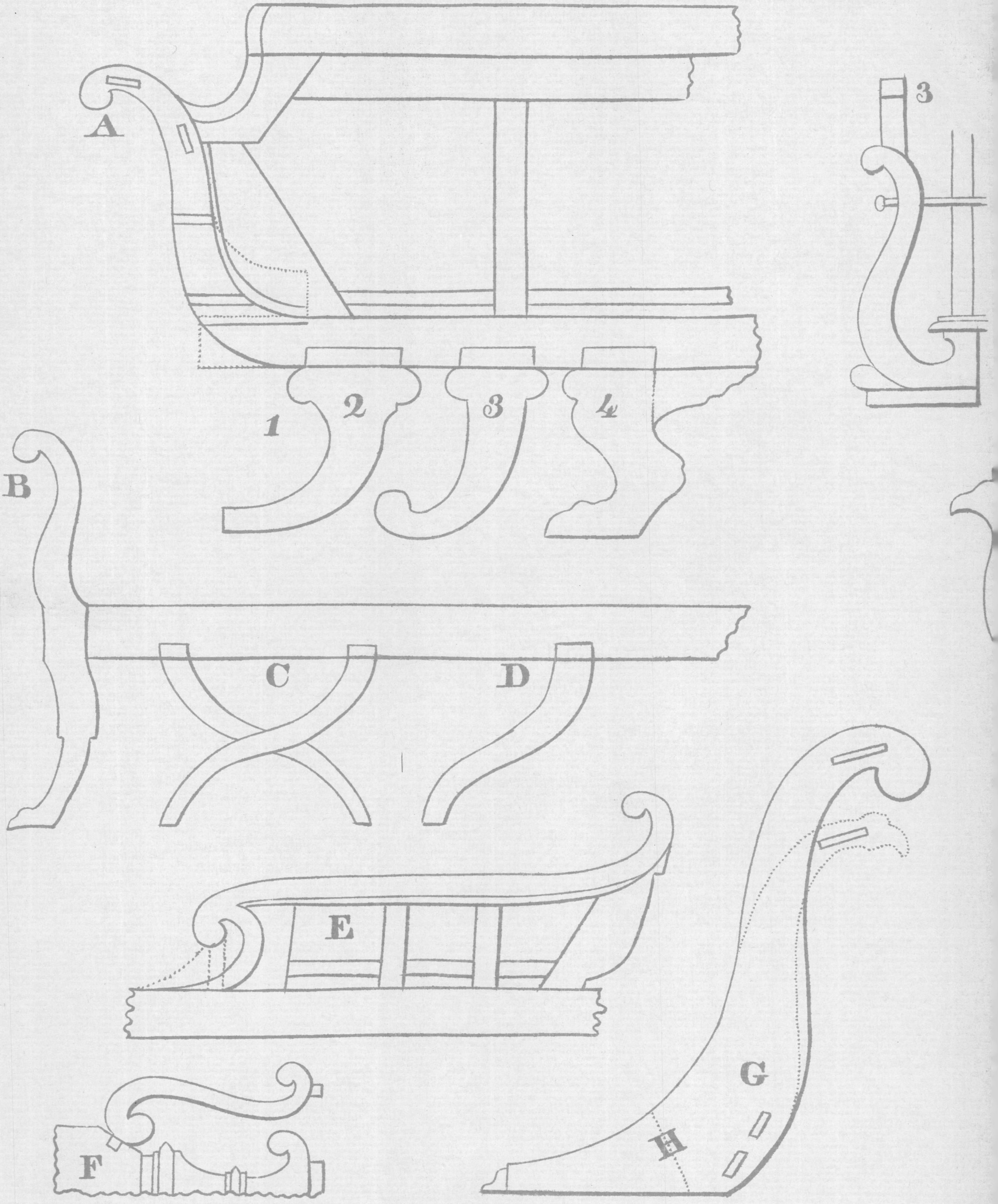
A
1
2
3
4
3
B
C
D
E
F
G
H